Career Choice in Management and Entrepreneurship

Career Choice in Management and Entrepreneurship

A Research Companion

Edited by

Mustafa F. Özbilgin

Professor of Human Resource Management, University of East Anglia, UK

Ayala Malach-Pines

Professor of Psychology and Head, Department of Business Administration, Ben-Gurion University of the Negev, Israel

Edward Elgar

Cheltenham, UK • Northampton, MA, USA

Published by
Edward Elgar Publishing Limited
Glensanda House
Montpellier Parade
Cheltenham
Glos GL50 1UA
UK

Edward Elgar Publishing, Inc.
William Pratt House
9 Dewey Court
Northampton
Massachusetts 01060
USA

A catalogue record for this book
is available from the British Library

Library of Congress Cataloguing in Publication Data

Career choice in management and entrepreneurship : a research companion /
edited by Mustafa F. Özbilgin, Ayala Malach-Pines
    p. cm.
    Includes bibliographical references and index.
    1. Career development. 2. Vocational guidance. 3. Management. 4.
    Entrepreneurship. 5. Master of business administration degree. I.
    Özbilgin, Mustafa. II. Malach-Pines, Ayala.

    HF5831.C2651435 2007
    658.0023—dc22

                                                          2007011684

ISBN 978 1 84542 844 0

Printed and bound in Great Britain by MPG Books Ltd, Bodmin, Cornwall

Contents

Contributors

Yehuda Baruch, University of East Anglia, UK
T. Alexandra Beauregard, London School of Economics, UK
Myrtle P. Bell, University of Texas at Arlington, USA
John Blenkinsopp, Teeside Business School, UK
Ronald J. Burke, York University, Canada
Nancy M. Carter, University of St Thomas, USA
Elizabeth Chell, University of Southampton, UK
Galit Chimo-Vugalter, Tel Aviv University, Israel
Laura A. Costanzo, University of Surrey, UK
Barbara P. Dexter, University of Derby, UK
Christoph Dörrenbächer, University of Groningen, The Netherlands
Dov Dvir, Ben-Gurion University, Israel
Cynthia Forson, Queen Mary, University of London, UK
William B. Gartner, Clemson University, USA
Mike Geppert, University of Surrey, UK
Patricia G. Greene, Babson College, USA
Shmulik Grimland, University of Haifa, Israel
Gözde İnal, Queen Mary, University of London, UK
Gilat Kaplan, Ben-Gurion University, Israel
Zahide Karakitapoğlu-Aygün, Bilkent University, Turkey
Mine Karataş-Özkan, University of Southampton, UK
Oshrit Kaspi-Baruch, Ben-Gurion University, Israel
Fatma Küskü, Istanbul Technical University, Turkey
Miri Lerner, The Academic College of Tel-Aviv–Jaffa, Israel
Ayala Malach-Pines, Ben-Gurion University, Israel
Tamar Milo, AMI Family Business Consulting, Israel
Eddy S.W. Ng, Trent University, Canada
Mustafa F. Özbilgin, University of East Anglia, UK
David Rae, University of Lincoln, UK
Paul W. Richardson, Monash University, Australia
Kadire Zeynep Sayım, Bilkent University, Turkey
Jennifer M. Sequeira, University of Southern Mississippi, USA
Kelly G. Shaver, College of Charleston, USA
Ruth Simpson, Brunel University, UK
Jane Sturges, King's College London, UK

Jawad Syed, University of Kent, UK
Cem Tanova, Eastern Mediterranean University, North Cyprus
Ahu Tatlı, Queen Mary, University of London, UK
Nicole M. Tysvaer, University of Michigan, USA
Vicky Tzoumpa, University of Surrey, UK
Agnes Utasi, University of Szeged, Hungary
Eran Vigoda-Gadot, University of Haifa, Israel
Helen M.G. Watt, Monash University, Australia
Dov Yanai, Genesis Consulting Group, Israel
Orenia Yaffe-Yanai, AMI Family Business Consulting, Israel
Jeongkoo Yoon, Ewha Women's University, South Korea

Introduction

Mustafa F. Özbilgin and Ayala Malach-Pines

The choice of a career is a complex and multifaceted process that includes all the spheres of a person's life (Hall, 1996). For one hundred years attempts have been made to classify the factors that influence this process. Most of these attempts include such factors as aptitudes, interests, resources, limitations, requirements and opportunities. Parsons (1909/1989, p. 5), for example, stated that 'in the wise choice of a vocation there are three broad factors: 1. A clear understanding of yourself, your aptitudes, abilities, interests, ambitions, resources, limitations and their causes. 2. Knowledge of the requirements and conditions of success, advantages and disadvantages, compensations, opportunities and prospects in different lines of work. 3. True reasoning on the relations of these groups of facts'. Parsons's work served as the cornerstone in the development of modern counseling theories that center on the person–environment fit (e.g. Edwards et al., 1998; Kristof, 1996; Swanson, 1996).

In the 1950s, Ginzberg (1951) classified the factors that influence career choices into: self, reality and key people, while Super (1953, 1957) classified them into: (1) Role factors – the self and the role; (2) Personality factors – intelligence, special abilities, preferences, values, approaches to work, 'personality' and general adaptability, and (3) Situational factors – social and economic status of the parents, religious background, home atmosphere, parents' approach, the general economic situation, a state of war or peace, and training opportunities. It is common today to view vocational choice as a process, the way Ginzberg did, and as an ongoing process that continues throughout the person's life, the way Super did. The modern perspective of 'life career development' is broad and holistic (Gysbers et al., 1998). It 'encompasses all spheres of activity and all corresponding facets of personal identity' (Hall, 1996, p. 7).

Despite their strengths, modern theories of vocational choice also have some serious weaknesses (Tang, 2003). One such weakness, which has been the focus of repeated criticism, is that they are not sophisticated enough in terms of their theoretical underpinnings and rarely extend to other countries outside the USA. It has been noted, for example, that they do not include the influence of contextual factors (such as educational and socioeconomic background, and the environment in which one grows up) (Tang, 2003). Growing globalization of the workforce increases the need to understand the cultural context of their work. The conclusion of nine analyses of modern career theories is that there is need for advance theory that is more contextual and multicultural (Savicas, 2003).

One response to this criticism has been the postmodern perspective. Postmodernism broadens career theories by focusing on plurality of perspectives, on the different social constructions of reality represented by different cultural perspectives and on the importance of the meaning individuals give to their experiences (Thorngren and Feit, 2001). Multiple points of view and cultural influences are central to postmodernism, a theoretical perspective that has already influenced our understanding of careers (e.g. Peavy, 1997; Richardson, 1993). The book sheds light on various antecedents, correlates and consequences of career choice in two very special professions – management and entrepreneurship – from different cultural, disciplinary and theoretical perspectives.

Managers and entrepreneurs are key players on the organizational stage, both described as enactments of archetypes, management as the activity of introducing order by coordinating the flow of things and people toward collective action; entrepreneurship as the making of new worlds (Czarniawaka and Wolff, 1991). Owing to their leading role, managers and entrepreneurs are often considered to have a major impact on the economy and social progress of nations. As such they are the focus of great interest. A large and steadily growing research literature attests to this interest. However, traditional studies of managers and entrepreneurs tend to be discipline specific (including, for example, the fields of psychology, sociology, economics, political science, or specific areas of management), with each discipline focusing on a different aspect of management, using different theoretical underpinnings and methodologies with little awareness of relevant data obtained in other disciplines. Little research has focused directly on the career choice of managers and entrepreneurs. This timely book addresses their career choice at the start of their careers as MBA (Master of Business Administration) students and in later stages of their careers. The focus on MBA students enables an exploration of a hotly contested issue regarding the value of an MBA education. The distinguished group of contributors examined whether it is possible to train managers and entrepreneurs and whether MBA study delivers its promised career outcomes in general and for groups across the fault lines of ethnicity and gender in particular.

The book is the most recent stage in a process that started in August 2003 in a Discussion Session held at the Academy of Management annual convention in Seattle, Oregon and led by Mustafa Özbilgin and Ayala Malach-Pines. It is hard to imagine a more typical Muslim name than Mustafa and a more typical Israeli name than Ayala, and a session led by Mustafa and Ayala raised some eyebrows as well as interest. It was titled 'Careers in the Middle East' and was the start of a great friendship and collaboration.

The next three-part stage included: an international symposium titled 'Work and non-work relationships, values and attitudes: A multi-cultural perspective', which was held in 2004 at the American Psychological Association convention; an international symposium titled 'Antecedents Correlates and Consequences of Career Choice in Management. A Multicultural and Interdisciplinary View', held in 2005 at the Academy of Management convention; and an international symposium titled 'An international interdisciplinary perspective on the antecedents, correlates and consequences of career choice in management', held in 2006 at the International Congress of Applied Psychology, in Athens, Greece. The participants in these symposia were an international, interdisciplinary group of scholars who joined forces with Ayala and Mustafa to create a new multifaceted vision of career choice in management and entrepreneurship in the twenty-first century. The scholars, both young and senior, come from China, Ghana, Greece, Hungary, India, Israel, Korea, North Cyprus, Turkey and the UK, and represent different disciplines, including: Business Management, Business Administration, Organizational Behavior, Public Administration, Political Science, Sociology, Clinical, Social and Organizational Psychology. They all share an interest in the multifaceted relationship between the antecedents of career choice in management and entrepreneurship (e.g. the environmental, sociological, familial and psychological influences propelling some people to become managers and entrepreneurs); the correlates of such career choices (e.g. MBA education and training) and a variety of outcome variables (e.g. national indicators of economic success and citizenship as well as personal indicators of job satisfaction). The cross-cultural interdisciplinary perspective enabled an examination of the role that culture plays in young people's path to become managers and entrepreneurs, including identification of certain groups (e.g. minorities and women) who do not always reach their full potential. The group jointly constructed a research instrument. The instrument addressed different aspects of career choice from different theoretical perspectives, and was translated by members of the group into different languages after much deliberation over the use of items that touched certain cultural sensitivities. All questions in the instrument were answered using similar scales. The three chapters in the first part of this volume are based on this cross-cultural study. However, some of the other chapters in the book were also written by members of the Career-Choice Research Network. The writers of these chapters address different aspects of career choice from different cultural and theoretical perspectives, focusing on different parts of the jointly collected data set. The participants in the cross-cultural study were all MBA students assumed to be similar in age, education, social and economic status, and career goals, and old enough to have some work experience. Most samples included a similar number of men and women. It should be noted that many of the respondents in the UK and Cyprus samples were foreign students, representing the situation in most MBA programs in these countries.

The combination of divergent cultures and an interdisciplinary perspective, using a jointly constructed research instrument, has generated a wealth of data. In the first part of the volume, each of the three chapters addresses a certain aspect of this multilayered view of career choice, discusses its specific theoretical underpinnings within the larger postmodern perspective, presents the relevant data gathered from the joint study, comments on the relevance of the data to the particular culture, and addresses the findings' theoretical and practical implications. Altogether, the three chapters offer a demonstration of both the promise and challenge involved in this type of cross-cultural interdisciplinary collaboration. The first chapter (Dexter et al.) describes the convergence and divergence of influences on career choice in management based on a comparative analysis of influences on career choices of MBA students in China, Ghana, Greece, Israel, Korea, North Cyprus, Turkey and the UK. This chapter provides the most comprehensive account of the collaborative study. It is followed by a chapter (Malach-Pines and Kaspi-Baruch) on the influence of culture and gender in the career choice of aspiring managers and entrepreneurs in Israel as compared to the UK, Turkey, North Cyprus and Hungary. In the third chapter, Agnes Utasi examines value preferences of management students in Hungary as compared to Cyprus, the UK and Israel, focusing on the influence of collectivistic attitudes and solidarity.

The second part of the book focuses on early influences on the career choice of managers and entrepreneurs, especially family influences. Within the plurality of perspectives offered in the book, this part can be viewed as representing the psychoanalytic perspective. This perspective contributes to life career development theories the dimension of unconscious career choices, based on the notion that 'the work that any person undertakes in almost any environment, excepting only the extremes of slavery and imprisonment, is to some extent determined by personal choice, made at several levels of consciousness' (Pruyser, 1980, p. 61). According to the psychoanalytic perspective, the unconscious determinants of a vocational choice reflect one's personal and familial history. People choose an occupation that enables them to replicate significant childhood experiences, gratify needs that were ungratified in their childhood and actualize occupational dreams passed on to them by their familial heritage (Bratcher, 1982; Kets de Vries, 1991, 1995; Obholzer and Roberts, 1997; Osipow and Fitzgerard, 1996; Pines and Yaffe-Yanai, 2001; Roe, 1956).

The family background and psychological make-up of managers and entrepreneurs have been the focus of extensive research. One branch of this research focused on the inner life and unconscious forces that compel people into their career choice and determine their behavior as managers and entrepreneurs (e.g. Kets de Vries, 1991, 1995, 1996; Pines, 2003; Pines et al., 2002; Zaleznik, 1991). This research, which was based on psychoanalytic work with managers, revealed, for example, that a high percentage of the fathers of successful managers were themselves successful managers and were distant fathers who did not have an intimate relationship with their sons. People who are unconsciously propelled to be managers have a reflexive longing to be in charge, in control, to be the father (Zaleznik, 1991). And a comparison between successful entrepreneurs and high-level managers demonstrated the managers' positive identification with their fathers as compared to the entrepreneurs' negative identification with theirs (Pines, 2003; Pines et al., 2002).

The second part starts with a more general perspective offered in Alexandra Beauregard's chapter (Chapter 4) on family influences on the career life cycle and Karakitapoğlu-Aygün and Sayım's chapter (Chapter 5) on the role of various relationships in the career choice of Turkish MBA students. The next two chapters are based on the psychoanalytic perspective. Gilat Kaplan's chapter (Chapter 6) describes the background and personality of serial high-tech entrepreneurs and managers in Israel, and Yaffe-Yanai et al. in their chapter (Chapter 7) focus on the family profiles of Israeli entrepreneurs and managers.

The third part of the book addresses the cultural determinants associated with the choice of a career in management and entrepreneurship (or, in one case, the choice to get out of a business career). An examination of the role of culture offers insights into the attributes of entrepreneurs and managers that vary, as compared to those that do not vary, with cultural contexts. McGrath et al. (1992), in their discussion of the question 'does culture endure or is it malleable?', suggest that entrepreneurs from different cultures share certain values that differentiate them from non-entrepreneurs. And, as noted by Chimo-Vugalter and Lerner in their chapter (Chapter 8), because different countries have distinct and sometimes contrasting cultures, there is a strong need for cross-cultural studies to increase our understanding of intercultural influences on entrepreneurs and managers.

In response to Leong and Brown's (1995) criticism of research on contextual variables in vocational psychology that has focused on establishing

either cultural validity (across different cultural groups) or cultural specificity (focus on a specific cultural group), the book in general, and the first
and third parts in particular, attempts to combine both perspectives by
comparing a focus on different countries with a focus on one particular
country.

The first two chapters in Part III represent cultural validity as both
present a comparison between two cultures (in the first, a comparison
between Israeli and Canadian MBAs; in the second a comparison between
Australian and American MBAs). The second two chapters represent
cultural specificity as both focus on one culture (in one, German-owned
subsidiaries in France; in the other Israeli high-tech entrepreneurs). More
specifically, in the first chapter (Chapter 8) Chimo-Vugalter and Lerner
focus on Canadian and Israeli MBA graduates as they compare and
contrast entrepreneurs and non-entrepreneurs. In the second chapter
(Chapter 9) Richardson et al. focus on Australian and American MBA
graduates as they address the question of what motivates them to change
to a teaching career. In the third chapter (Chapter 10) Dörrenbächer and
Geppert focus on German-owned subsidiaries in France as they address the
impact of foreign subsidiary managers' sociopolitical positioning (which
includes such things as national descent, professional background and personal career orientation) on their career choices and their subsequent
strategizing for subsidiary evolution. And in the fourth and last chapter in
this part (Chapter 11) Dvir and Malach-Pines focus on successful Israeli
high-tech entrepreneurs as they describe the cultural determinants of their
career choice.

The fourth part of the book contains three chapters that examine career
development and MBA education from multidisciplinary perspectives.
Studying careers from across disciplinary divides helps overcome two of
the common problems in the study of careers: overemphasis of macro-,
meso- or micro-perspectives (Özbilgin et al., 2005) and absence of sophistication in theorization of careers (Tang, 2003). The chapters in this
section bridge sociological, psychological, management and political perspectives, transcending their variable foci on levels of analysis and levels of
sophistication in their conceptualization of career choice and MBA education. Vigoda-Gadot and Grimland's chapter (Chapter 12) examines
career development and values change among MBA students from a
public administration perspective. Burke and Ng's chapter focuses on business students' views on jobs, careers and the job search process, bringing
forth the implications for universities and employers (Chapter 13).
Recognizing that career choice is studied in the process of education,
Baruch and Blenkinsopp argue that business education itself can be
framed as career choice (Chapter 14).

Whilst Part IV focused on career development and MBA education, Part V goes on to examine education, training and learning for managers and entrepreneurs. The homology of the debates on learning, entrepreneurship and management is a long-standing discussion on whether the two are innate or learned. Transcending these traditional arguments, Nooteboom (2000) has highlighted that whatever its origins and essence, learning in organizations and economies should be studied from multi-level and interdisciplinary perspectives. The chapters in this section serve to achieve this goal. Chell's chapter (Chapter 15) provides an assessment of the role of integrative capability in training and development of managers and entrepreneurs. In Chapter 16, Rae examines career making and learning for mid-career entrepreneurs. Costanzo and Tzoumpa (Chapter 17) provide an assessment of the engaging manager and the role of knowledge absorptive capacity from an organizational life-cycle perspective. The final chapter in the part is by Özbilgin and Tatlı (Chapter 18), who focus on career constraint in work placement and training experiences in the creative and cultural industries in London.

Career choice and diversity is studied in Parts VI and VII of this book. The interplay between career choice and diversity by ethnicity (Part VI) and gender (Part VII) are explored in depth. Whilst some authors have viewed career choice through very individualistic lenses, emphasizing the role of self in choice (Hakim, 1991), others have highlighted the influence of social context on choice (Gerson, 1986) and on self-assessment (Correll, 2001). An explicit focus on diversity by ethnicity and gender allows an understanding of social constructions of career choice by differently positioned groups and individuals. Part VI examines ethnic differences in experiences of career and career choice. The first chapter in the section is by Carter et al. (Chapter 19) and examines why and how nascent entrepreneurs make their career choices. Syed presents an exploration of career choices of skilled migrants and argues for a holistic perspective in Chapter 20. İnal and Karataş-Özkan offer a comparative study on career choice influences of Turkish Cypriot restaurateurs in North Cyprus and the UK (Chapter 21).

In the last part of the book (Part VII), three chapters examine the role of gender in career choice. Simpson and Sturges (Chapter 22) focus on gender and intrinsic and extrinsic benefits of MBA education. Two of the chapters examine the gender and ethnicity interplay, exploring issues of intersectionality: Sequeira and Bell examine the value of MBA education and its role in entrepreneurship for women and people of color in Chapter 23. Forson's chapter (Chapter 24) presents an assessment of intersectionality, context and choice in self-employed black women's careers.

DESCRIPTION OF CHAPTERS

Part I   Career Choice of MBA Students from Cross-National and Interdisciplinary Perspectives

In Chapter 1, Dexter et al. take a critical perspective on career choice, focusing on the significance of the context and relational dynamics of career choice and development by exploring the national, sectoral and cultural dynamics of career choice in each country under study. The findings of the cross-cultural survey study suggest that cross-national similarities are stronger than differences. Two different reasons are explanatory for these apparent similarities: the unifying impact of MBA internationally and the neoliberal influences in the form of elevating individual and agentic frames of thinking over social and structural frames of reference. In terms of future research and practice, three major concerns are identified: lack of awareness of path dependencies in the respondent population; lack of awareness of social conditions that shape choice; and lack of critical reasoning skills. The implications for career advisers are reported in the study.

In Chapter 2, Malach-Pines and Kaspi-Baruch address the influences of culture and gender on the career choice of MBA students aspiring to be managers and entrepreneurs. The study described aimed to shed light on various antecedents (e.g. the influence of key people) and correlates (e.g. the meaning of work) of the career choice of MBA students in Israel, the UK, Turkey, North Cyprus and Hungary. The study attempted to establish both cultural validity (across the five cultural groups), as well as cultural specificity (focus on a specific cultural group – Israel). Five hypotheses were examined: based on evolutionary and psychoanalytic theories, gender differences in variables related to career choice in management and entrepreneurship were expected to be more consistent and larger than the cross-cultural differences; based on social role theory, it was hypothesized that both gender and cross-cultural differences would be found; based on social construction theory, it was hypothesized that cross-cultural differences would be larger than gender differences. Findings showing consistently larger cross-cultural differences than gender differences did not support the evolutionary and psychoanalytic theories, partially supported social role theory, and strongly supported social construction theory. Based on existential theory, it was hypothesized that the meaning of work would be more important to Israeli students than it would be to students in other countries. This hypothesis was confirmed. Based on studies comparing entrepreneurs and managers, differences were expected between students aspiring to be entrepreneurs versus aspiring to be managers. This hypothesis was not confirmed, suggesting that an MBA may be more relevant to the career aspirations of students who want to be managers than those who want to be entrepreneurs.

In the third and last chapter of the section (Chapter 3), Utasi focuses on the values, especially those concerning collectivism and solidarity, of MBA students in Hungary as compared to North Cyprus, the UK, Israel and Turkey. The chapter describes various distinctive features of Hungarian society and offers a sociological analysis that addresses both the similarities and differences found between Hungarian students and students in the other countries. Utasi explains similarities found by the influence of globalization. The differences found are explained by the influence of socialization in general, and in the case of the Hungarian students by the influence of a value-ambivalent society that underwent four decades of socialism, with its destructive effect on traditional communities, and since 1989 has moved towards a neocapitalist market economy characterized by extreme individualism.

Part II Early Influences on the Career Choice of Entrepreneurs and Managers

The second part of the book focuses on family influences on the career choice of managers and entrepreneurs. It starts with Beauregard's discussion (Chapter 4) of the myriad ways in which one's family and personal life can affect one's career. A review of the literature demonstrates that career choice is influenced by people's values, attitudes and expectations concerning how work should be balanced with the rest of their life. Individuals are also susceptible to influence from their families of origin with regard to occupational choice and balancing work and family. Career advancement, decisions to change jobs or accept a geographical transfer are often affected by family commitments. The chapter identifies some of the implications of combining a career with a meaningful life outside work, for both organizations and individuals.

The second chapter (Chapter 5) explores the importance and functions of different relationships (e.g. mother, father, relatives, colleagues) in the career choice of Turkish MBA students. Understanding those relational influences is especially important in Turkey, which is characterized by a close network of ties of family and friends. The chapter also examines the links between individualistic and collectivistic value orientations and the influence of relationships on career choices. It reports the results of a study that show that fathers were rated as having the greatest influence, followed by lectures and mothers. Individualism was positively associated with being influenced by one's colleagues and managers. Furthermore, supporting the patriarchal nature of Turkish society, collectivism was closely associated with the involvement of fathers in the career decision-making process. To further clarify the role of relationships in career choices, interviews were conducted with 13 students. The data revealed that most of them made their decisions themselves. They referred to parents, relatives (uncles, aunts, siblings), senior managers, friends and lecturers, but did not identify any one particular individual as the most influential in their decisions. These results are discussed with reference to their theoretical and practical implications.

The third chapter in this part (Chapter 6), written within a psychoanalytic perspective by Kaplan, focuses on highly successful Israeli serial high-tech entrepreneurs and a comparison sample of high-ranking managers who were interviewed about their background and personality. The results of the comparison revealed that the entrepreneurs and managers share certain resemblance in traits and background: both tend to be highly educated (an MBA degree is common), with rich vocational experience, a complicated and highly demanding workplace, high degree of responsibility and autonomy, certain entrepreneurial qualities (that the CEOs share with the entrepreneurs). However, while most entrepreneurs were first-born (both objectively and psychologically), the majority of the executives were not (only 30 percent were). In addition, the early childhood experiences of executives seemed to be better than those of entrepreneurs, especially in terms of relationship with the father. The different childhood experiences facilitated the development of entrepreneurial traits such as unwillingness to accept authority, emotional instability and thinking out of the box. In addition, growing up in Israel involves two cultural themes: the struggle for existence and military service.

The fourth and last chapter (Chapter 7) was written by Yaffe-Yanai et al. based on their extensive experience in consultation and career development with owners and managers of enterprises. The chapter presents a psychological portrait of the typical entrepreneur, as compared to the typical manager, along with their 'passion quests' and distinct relations to their business. It suggests that they come from a different family dynamic, with different energy sources and motivations.

Entrepreneurs were often raised in relatively chaotic families in which the child was hardly visible. The fathers were often absent either physically or psychologically, and the mothers were often passionate dreamers, mostly of unfulfilled dreams. Managers, on the other hand, were usually raised by attentive parents, who had high expectations of them and, consequently, criticized them often. Their mothers were mostly well-functioning women. As for their typical dialogue, while entrepreneurs typically ask 'why' and strive to leave a legacy, managers ask 'how' and strive to be effective and to do a good job. Recommendations are made as to the nature of dialogue that may promote the consultation process with entrepreneurs and with managers.

Part III Entrepreneurs and Managers' Career Choice: Cultural Determinants

In the first chapter (Chapter 8) Chimo-Vugalter and Lerner compare the career paths of MBA graduates who became entrepreneurs with those of their MBA colleagues who did not, in Canada and in Israel. The focus on MBAs enabled an examination of a population with a relatively high propensity to undertake entrepreneurial careers. The chapter addresses the question: do demographic attributes, personality characteristics and family career patterns help distinguish MBA graduates who became entrepreneurs from MBAs who did not, in both the Israeli and the Canadian samples? And do cultural differences between Canada and Israel help distinguish the career paths taken by their respective MBA graduates?

Findings reported in the chapter show that the propensity to pursue an entrepreneurial career is higher for both Canadian and Israeli MBA graduates than it is for the general population. Furthermore, great cross-cultural similarity was found between the Canadian and Israeli MBA graduates in the propensity to pursue an entrepreneurial career. Multivariate examinations of the effect of career patterns, demographic factors and personality variables revealed that several of the variables included within these three clusters distinguish entrepreneurs from non-entrepreneurs in the Canadian and the Israeli samples.

In the second chapter (Chapter 9), Richardson et al. focus on individuals in Australia and the USA who previously pursued business-related careers, but were changing careers into primary and secondary school teaching. The authors first discuss the characteristics of those career switchers and then discuss their reasons for having chosen to leave a career in business and pursue instead a teaching career. It turns out that the career switchers perceived teaching as a career that is highly demanding, and one that provides for low return in terms of salary and social status. The fact that the career switchers were high on the intrinsic value of teaching suggests that teaching may afford different types of rewards that are not always inherent in business careers such as management or entrepreneurship.

Based on three case studies of German subsidiaries in France, the third chapter (Chapter 10) examines how foreign subsidiary managers' idiosyncratic actions as well as the political nature of headquarters–subsidiary relations influence subsidiary evolution. In line with a study on the impact of dominant actor groups on organizational control, the authors try to establish a link between the foreign subsidiary managers' nationalities, professional backgrounds and personal career orientations – referred to as the sociopolitical positioning of foreign subsidiary managers – their individual career choices and their follow-on strategizing with regard to the evolution of their subsidiaries. The chapter is based on an empirical study that focused on how subsidiary mandates (defined as temporary responsibilities either allocated by the headquarters or acquired by the individual subsidiary) are gained, developed or lost over time.

In the fourth and last chapter in this part (Chapter 11), Dvir and Malach-Pines describe the cultural determinants of the career choice of highly successful high-tech entrepreneurs in Israel. Israel has an unusually high number of high-tech entrepreneurs and companies, and is among the world leaders in high-tech start-ups. The success of Israeli high-tech entrepreneurs has raised curiosity worldwide, but very little academic research attention. The chapter examines two empirical studies that reveal interesting information about the determinants of the career choice of Israeli high-tech entrepreneurs. The studies reveal a certain common background (e.g. first-born, comes from a small family, is highly educated, has an advanced degree in a technical field, pursues a technical profession, served in the army in either a technical or a combat unit, was an officer and commanded people). In-depth interviews with these entrepreneurs reveal the powerful influence of the army service on their career development as well as the influence of Israeli culture.

Part IV   Multidisciplinary Perspectives on Career Development and MBA Education

The first chapter (Chapter 12) of this section is by Vigoda-Gadot and Grimland. The authors examine career development and values change in graduate studies from theoretical perspectives. The chapter deals with citizenry values and career development among graduate students in Business Administration (MBA) and in Public Administration (MPA) departments. The chapter focuses on a new type of protean career and on its contribution to forming citizenship values of various aspects (individual, collective, organizational and communal/national). MBA and MPA students are viewed as the potential future leaders in the business and public systems. The chapter explains how such values may be encouraged among them and what can be the expected benefits for businesses and for society. Because the modern type of career is values-driven, the mechanism that links values and career behavior will be explained. The mechanisms of COR (conservation of resources)/value priority and citizenship value levels of impact are proposed as a combined model that can explain and predict better than other models the behavior of the MBA/MPA population. Based on COR principles, people tend to choose behaviors (career) that are congruent with their principal values and work/behave accordingly. This manner of action takes place in the individual/organizational–communal or national level, and in the collective/organizational–communal or national layer. The chapter sets the ground for future empirical studies in this direction and offers some implications for such efforts.

The second chapter in this section addresses business students' views on jobs, careers and the job search process with specific implications for employers and universities. The chapter by Burke and Ng (Chapter 13) argues that university students continue to be a major source of hiring for skilled jobs such as managers. They are technologically aware and eager to learn, which makes them highly desirable in today's job markets. Business students were chosen because they are more likely to enter managerial and professional ranks, and will be highly sought after by organizations. Business schools have traditionally been a training ground for management education and a source of supply of managers to employers. The study on which the chapter is based explored the career aspirations and expectations, career choices and job search behaviors among a sample of 4851 university students enrolled in a business program. Specifically, it examined what attracts them to future opportunities, how they explore potential employers, and how they make career decisions. Findings show that cooperative students have more realistic expectations about their careers, and indicated knowledge of the specific industry, company, or career they were interested in, than non-cooperative students. The findings can provide an insight into the future of Canada's graduates and how well universities are supporting their careers.

In Chapter 14, Baruch and Blenkinsopp examine business education as a career choice. They argue that following the golden age of the MBA in the 1980s and 1990s, there has been diversification of business education, where alongside the 'traditional' MBA more specialized master's degrees are on offer, as well as a growing number of undergraduate degrees in business, management and related areas. While the MBA is still considered the flagship of business education, other alternatives are now on offer for prospective business students. In this chapter the authors discuss the value and relevance of business education as a career choice for individuals, and review the benefits versus possible pitfalls for managers and entrepreneurs in the global marketplace for these degrees.

Part V Education, Training and Learning for Managers and Entrepreneurs

In this first chapter (Chapter 15) of this part, Chell evaluates the role of integrative capability in training and development of managers and

entrepreneurs. Providing a critique of the nature of managers and entrepreneurs, Chell offers a discussion of situation-capability in respect of the
respective roles of managers and entrepreneurs. The chapter goes on to
argue that situation-capability alone as a skill to enable entrepreneurs and
managers to perform effectively is arguably necessary but not sufficient.
Therefore the key components and ingredients of the creation of new
knowledge and innovations are explored. Arguing for a context-sensitive
exploration of life courses and sense-making experiences of managers and
entrepreneurs, the chapter criticizes essentialist and biologically deterministic approaches to management and entrepreneurship. The chapter offers
a range of suggestions for program designs that are conducive to foster
training and development of managers and entrepreneurs.

Rae's chapter (Chapter 16) on career making and learning for mid-career
entrepreneurs explores the concept of mid-career entrepreneurship, with
particular reference to career making as a learning process. Rae explains
that mid-career entrepreneurs (MCEs) are those who, aged approximately
35–55, decide to start a business venture after a period of work as an
employee. Therefore mid-career entrepreneurship suggests a curious case
of a voluntary or enforced career change. The chapter examines 'career
making' for managers and entrepreneurs in mid-career from a learning perspective, explaining why such an emphasis on learning is important.

In Chapter 17, Costanzo and Tzoumpa provide a conceptual exploration
of the 'engaging manager' concept by drawing on the theory of the organizational life cycle, which allows for a reading of the growth phase of the
firm with its specific management requirements. The authors argue that the
'engaging' type of management style is particularly needed in the process of
growth, where the management is faced with survival challenges. In the
growth stage, firms need 'entrepreneurial management', which is realized by
the knowledge-absorptive capacity. The chapter goes on to demonstrate that
conceptualization of knowledge-absorptive capacity as a key capability of
the 'engaging manager' contributes to deepening our understanding of the
mechanisms that shape the engaging manager's five styles of thinking.

The final chapter of this part (Chapter 18) is by Özbilgin and Tatlı, who
argue that work placement may provide a significant path to employment
and entrepreneurial careers in creative and cultural industries. Drawing on
a field study of higher education institutions (HEIs), host organizations and
placement students in the London-based creative and cultural industries,
the authors demonstrate that work placement also presents constraints, particularly to those students who do not fit the subjective requirements set by
the host organizations. The process of work placement, from the outset of
allocation of work placement opportunities to management and evaluation
of the placement, is open to subjective bias. This subjectivity may limit the

choices of students from non-traditional backgrounds and may reduce the effectiveness of work placement in terms of enhancing personal and career development of students. Furthermore, the current arrangements of work placement fail to cater adequately for the students' needs to embark on careers in entrepreneurship, employment and management in the sector, starving them of essential experiences which could prepare them for successful future careers in the creative and cultural industries.

Part VI   Entrepreneurs, Managers, Career Choice and Diversity: Minority Issues

The career reasons of minority nascent entrepreneurs are examined in Chapter 19. Carter et al. explain that self-employment has often been considered an important option for demographic groups whose minority status might restrict their entry into the workforce. The social policy value of supporting minority entrepreneurship is recognized in federal and state contracting regulations that contain minority set-asides, and in the creation of inter-city business incubators by local economic development officials. Yet the success of these efforts may be limited by an incomplete understanding of the motivations of minority entrepreneurs. Using the only available nationally representative data set that contrasts individuals in the process of starting businesses (nascent entrepreneurs) with individuals in a comparison group, the authors compared the reasons that minority (Black and Hispanic) nascent entrepreneurs offer for starting new businesses to those of White nascent entrepreneurs and to career choice reasons offered by the comparison group. Six separate categories of career reasons were examined, and differences by career choice and race and ethnic status were identified.

In his conceptual chapter, Syed investigates career choices of skilled migrants from a holistic perspective (Chapter 20). Reflecting on Ho (2006), Syed explains that the conventional policy reliance on human-capital-based research tends to simplify much more complex cultural–environmental challenges faced by skilled migrants in the host economies. However, the proponents of human capital theory insist that skilled migration may be considered as capital mobility (Boeri, 2006), and that employment in the migrant economies is a transitional phenomenon because employment markets generally function as an integrative institution, seeking best-qualified and cheapest workers regardless of ethnic backgrounds (Nee et al., 1994). This chapter probes these lines of inquiry and endeavors to offer a holistic perspective of career choices of skilled migrants. The chapter argues that skilled migrants are a people living within a sociocultural and historical context, constituting much more than a factor of production flowing across international borders. Accordingly, there is a need to expand the research lens to incorporate economic as well as sociological and psychological aspects of migration.

The final chapter in this part (Chapter 21) is by İnal and Karataş-Özkan. It reports a study that seeks to generate comparative insights into the influences on career choices of Turkish Cypriot restaurateurs in North Cyprus and the UK. Drawing on the conceptual framework put forward, both career choices are examined. The study suggests three principal types of influences: family-related influences, economic influences, and self-related influences. These three influences form the basis of the formation of, and transformation between, different forms of capital that the participant Turkish Cypriot restaurateurs have developed in both North Cyprus and the UK.

Part VII   Entrepreneurs, Managers, Career Choice and Diversity: Gender Issues

In the first chapter in the last part of the book (Chapter 22), Simpson and Sturges study gender and intrinsic and extrinsic benefits of the MBA. The chapter reports findings from a qualitative research study conducted at a leading business school in Ontario, Canada. The research explores the argument that MBA has gendered benefits, as men are more likely to gain extrinsic benefits in terms of pay, status and marketability, whilst women are more likely to perceive that they gain intrinsic benefits. Findings of the study reported in this chapter suggest that, while both men and women gain intrinsic benefits from the MBA, they do so in different ways. The chapter goes on to explain these differences and the implications of such gender difference.

Sequeira and Bell assess the value of the MBA education and its role in entrepreneurship for women and people of color in Chapter 23. They explain that in the past two decades, many researchers have debated the value of the MBA degree, questioning its practicality and utility, and criticizing its ability to meet the needs of students. As students increase in diversity, with fewer Whites and men pursuing the MBA and more women and people of color doing so, it is important to investigate the utility of the MBA for these non-dominant group members. Thus this chapter considers the role that the MBA plays in career success for women and people of color and the extent to which the MBA prepares these groups for entrepreneurship. In so doing, it hopes to raise issues concerning whether women and people of color benefit from the MBA education and to emphasize the possible need for a different perspective when educating these groups and preparing them for business ownership.

In the very last chapter of the book Forson (Chapter 24) elaborates on intersectionality, context and 'choice', and examines the career choice influences of self-employed black women. It is well documented that career choice decisions of self-employed women are different from those of self-employed men. However, self-employed women are not a heterogeneous group and research on self-employed women has mainly focused on white women's career experiences. Although African and Caribbean women have high participation rates of paid employment, they are grossly underrepresented in self-employment compared to Black and Minority Ethnic (BME) men and other women generally. This chapter examines the influences on the self-employment decisions of African and Caribbean women business owners from two sectors of the London economy – the legal and hairdressing sectors – in order to contribute to an understanding of how migration, class, gender and ethnicity intersect in broader as well as more specific ways to affect the career choice decisions of black women. The chapter draws on literature on entrepreneurship as well as other sources to show how the women's self-employment career choice discourse has developed and outlines the qualitative, layered yet intersectional approach that the study takes to the examination of the influences on the decision to choose self-employment as a career.

The volume addresses a very important area of human experience – the world of work – from a perspective that aims to illuminate what is the same and what is different across cultures. In the global village of the twenty-first century it is crucial to expand one's vision to include other cultures and other theoretical perspectives beyond those offered by current vocational choice theories. The volume broadens these theories by focusing on the plurality of perspectives and the different social constructions of reality represented by different cultural perspectives.

REFERENCES

Boeri, T. (2006), 'Growth, labour markets and migration', paper presented at *Global Convergence Scenarios: Structural and Policy Issues*, OECD, Paris, 16 January.

Bratcher, W.E. (1982), 'The influence of the family on career selection: a family systems perspective', *The Personnel & Guidance Journal*, **61**: 87–91.

Correll, S. (2001), 'Gender and the career choice process: the role of biased self-assessments', *American Journal of Sociology*, **106**(6): 1691–730.

Czarniawaka, J.B. and Wolff, R. (1991), 'Leaders, managers, entrepreneurs on and off the organizational stage', *Organization Studies*, **12**: 529–46.

Edwards, J.R., Caplan, R.D. and Harrison, R.V. (1998), 'Person–environment fit theory: conceptual foundation, empirical evidence, and directions for future research', in C.L. Cooper (ed.), *Theories of Organizational Stress*, Oxford: Oxford University Press, pp. 28–67.

Gerson, K. (1986), *Hard Choices: How Women Decide about Work, Career and Motherhood*, Berkeley, CA: University of California Press.

Ginzberg, E. (1951), *Occupational Choice*, New York: Columbia University Press.

Gysbers, N.C., Heppner, M. and Johnson, J.A. (1998), *Career Counseling*, Boston, MA: Allyn & Bacon.

Hakim, C. (1991), 'Grateful slaves and self-made women: fact and fantasy in women's work orientations', *European Sociological Review*, 7(2): 101–21.

Hall, D.T. (1996), 'Long live the career', in D.T. Hall and associates (eds), *The Career is Dead – Long Live The Career*, San Francisco, CA: Jossey-Bass, pp. 1–14.

Ho, C. (2006), 'Migration as feminisation? Chinese women's experiences of work and family in Australia', *Journal of Ethnic and Migration Studies*, 23(3): 497–514.

Kets de Vries, M.F.R. (1991), 'On becoming a CEO', in M.F.R. Kets de Vries and Associates (eds), *Organizations of the Couch: Clinical Perspectives on Organizational Behavior and Change*, San-Francisco: Jossey-Bass, pp. 120–39.

Kets de Vries, M.F.R. (1995), *Life and Death in the Executive Fast Lane*, San Francisco, CA: Jossey-Bass.

Kets de Vries, M.F.R. (1996), 'The anatomy of the entrepreneur', *Human Relations*, 49: 853–83.

Kristof, A.L. (1996), 'Person–organization fit: an integrative review of its conceptualizations, measurement, and implications', *Personnel Psychology*, 49: 1–49.

Leong, F.T.I. and Brown, M.T. (1995), 'Theoretical issues in cross cultural career development: cultural validity and cultural specificity', in W.B. Walsh and S.H. Osipow (eds), *Handbook of Vocational Psychology*, 2nd edn, Hillsdale, NJ: Erlbaum, pp. 143–80.

McGrath, R.G., MacMillan, I.C., Yang, E.A.-Y. and Tsai, W. (1992), 'Does culture endure or is it malleable? Issues for entrepreneurial economic development', *Journal of Business Venturing*, 7: 441–58.

Nee, V., Sanders, J.M. and Sernau, S. (1994), 'Job transitions in an immigrant metropolis – ethnic boundaries and the mixed economy', *American Sociological Review*, 59(6): 849–72.

Nooteboom, B. (2000), *Learning and Innovation in Organizations and Economies*, Oxford: Oxford University Press.

Obholzer, A. and Roberts, V.Z. (1997), *The Unconscious at Work*, London and New York: Routledge.

Osipow, S.H. and Fitzgerald, L.F. (1996), *Theories of Career Development* (4th edn). Boston, MA: Allyn & Bacon.

Özbilgin, M., Küskü, F. and Erdoğmuş, N. (2005), 'Explaining influences on career "choice": the case of MBA students in comparative perspective', *International Journal of Human Resource Management*, 16(11): 2000.

Parsons, F. (1909/1989), *Choosing a Vocation*, Garrett Park, MD: Garrett Park Press.

Peavy, R.V. (1997), 'A constructive framework for career counseling', in T.L. Sexton and B.L. Griffin (eds), *Constructive Thinking in Counseling Practice, Research and Training*, New York: Teachers College Press, pp. 122–40.

Pines, A.M. (2003), 'Unconscious influences on career choice: entrepreneur vs. manager', *Australian Journal of Career Development*, 12(2): 7–18.

Pines, A.M., Sadeh, A., Dvir, D. and Yanai, Y.O. (2002), 'Entrepreneurs and managers: similar yet different', *International Journal of Organizational Analysis*, **10**(2): 172–90.

Pines, A.M. and Yaffe-Yanai, O. (2001), 'Unconscious determinants of career choice and burnout: theoretical model and counseling strategy', *Journal of Employment Counseling*, **38**: 170–84.

Pruyser, P.W. (1980), 'Work: curse or blessing?', *Bulletin of the Menninger Clinic*, **44**: 59–73.

Richardson, M.S. (1993), 'Work in people's lives: a location for counseling psychologists', *Journal of Counseling Psychology*, **40**: 425–33.

Roe, A. (1956), *Psychology of Occupations*, New York: Wiley.

Savicas, M.L. (2003), 'Advancing the career counseling profession: objectives and strategies for the next decade', *The Career Development Quarterly*, Alexandria, **52**: 87–96.

Super, D.E. (1953), 'A theory of vocational development', *American Psychologist*, **8**: 185–90.

Super, D.E. (1957), *The Psychology of Careers*, New York: Harper & Row.

Swanson, J. (1996), 'The theory is the practice: trait and factor/person–environment fit counseling', in M.L. Savickas and B.W. Walsh (eds), *Handbook of Career Counseling: Theory and Practice*, Palo Alto, CA: Davies-Black, pp. 93–108.

Tang, M. (2003), 'Career counseling in the future: constructing, collaborating, advocating', *The Career Development Quarterly*, Alexandria, **52**: 61–9.

Thorngren, J.M. and Feit, S.S. (2001), 'The career-o-gram: a postmodern career intervention', *The Career Development Quarterly*, Alexandria, **49**(4): 291–303.

Zaleznik, A. (1991), 'Leading and managing: understanding the difference', in M.F.R. Kets de Vries and associates (eds), *Organizations of the Couch*, San Francisco, CA: Jossey-Bass, pp. 97–119.

PART I

Career Choice of MBA Students from Cross-national and Interdisciplinary Perspectives

1. Convergence and divergence of influences on career choice: a comparative analysis of influences on career choices of MBA students in China, Ghana, Greece, Israel, Korea, North Cyprus, Turkey and the UK

Barbara P. Dexter, Cynthia Forson, Gözde İnal, Mine Karataş-Özkan, Fatma Küskü, Mustafa F. Özbilgin, Ayala Malach-Pines, Cem Tanova and Jeongkoo Yoon

INTRODUCTION

The international spread and proliferation of MBA programmes have attracted scholarly attention to the career choices of MBA students (Simmering and Wilcox, 1995) as well as to individual and organizational benefits of MBA programmes (Leeming and Baruch, 1998; Simpson, 2000). MBA programmes originated in the USA at the beginning of the last century and have spread internationally (Baruch and Peiperl, 2003).

The development of management education and MBA programmes is a part of this expansion, following the aforementioned international trend. However, the research to date has remained largely at a single level, either failing to recognize the situated and embodied nature of career choice across time and space or failing to recognize individual choice as relevant due to on over-emphasis on structural constraints. Exploring cross-national variation in multiple influences on career choice is the main purpose of this chapter. This chapter not only reveals convergence and divergence of influences of career choice across national borders, it also allows for a reading of individual choice in the context of individual and structural circumstances.

This chapter takes a critical perspective on career choice. It recognizes the significance of the context of career choice by exploring the unique national, sectoral and cultural dynamics of career choice in each country under study. It also examines the contested nature of career 'choice', reflecting on the argument that careers are the products of the interplay and interrelationships between structural constraints such as labour market conditions, education paths, family and social formations, legal and economic institutions and variable degrees of agency, which manifest themselves as different forms of capital, individual strategies and psychological dispositions (Özbilgin et al., 2005). The micro-level examines the micro-individual influences on career choice. The intermediate–organizational level is studied through an assessment of institutional contexts and relational constructs. Finally, the macro-level examines the structural considerations.

INFLUENCES ON CAREER CHOICE: A CONCEPTUAL FRAMEWORK

We contend that individual choice of career has three distinct attributes. It is (a) contextually situated (Shapero, 1971; Slater, 1980; Bourdieu, 1988; Barret et al., 1996; Bates, 1999; Borooah and Hart, 1999; Procter and Padfield, 1999; Clark and Drinkwater, 2000; Kyriacou and Coulthard, 2000; Simpson, 2000; Baruch, 2004; Wiseman, 2004); (b) relationally formed (Slater, 1980; Bourdieu, 1986; Hallissey et al., 2000); and (c) dynamically performed (Schein, 1978, 1985; Rhodes and Doering, 1983; Bourdieu, 1986, 1998; Hakim, 1991, 1996; Sturges et al., 2003; Baruch, 2004).

The contextual situatedness or embeddedness of career choice relates to an understanding of both the endogenous and exogenous influences on and attributes of education and employment systems that create path dependencies. Endogenous factors are educational and career structures that provide individuals with a fixed number of choices of career based on individual past performance, such as the results of certain educational, as well as recruitment and selection, tests. Exogenous influences are the influences of the social, economic, political and the general wider context in the country or the locality of the individual, leading to differentiated career paths. The endogenous and exogenous factors of contextual situatedness across the countries that we have studied in this project are markedly diverse.

Baruch and Peiperl (2003) have identified three streams of research pertaining to the possible effects of MBA studies: social identity, performance and competencies. Social identity theory (Turner, 1975; Tajfel, 1981) deals with the issues of social comparisons and social identity, both of which play an important role in the choice and pursuit of a career. Performance or managerial effectiveness is considered to be the second research stream, focusing on understanding whether and how graduate management education makes better managers (Dougherty et al., 1993; Finney, 1996; Shofield, 1996). Competencies are the third stream of research, looking at a combination of candidates' skills, abilities and qualities (McClelland, 1973; Boyatzis, 1983; Boyatzis and Renio, 1989).

Within career theory, it is generally recognized that 'career' is not a straightforward concept. Increasingly, 'career' is accepted as encompassing more than just work and job moves, as in Arnold's (1997, p. 16) definition of career as 'any sequence of employment-related positions, roles, activities and experiences' and Watts' (1996, p. 7) definition of 'individual lifelong progression in learning and work'. Most of this literature is on careers in general, rather than specifically on management careers, but the seminal work by Nicholson and West (1988) focused on management careers of middle and senior managers, and highlighted how career patterns had changed as the 1980s had progressed. These were mainly attributed to organizational changes, including restructurings and downsizing, practices that continued throughout the 1990s and into the twenty-first century. Other pertinent factors include: changes in employment patterns to include more outsourcing, part-time and short-term contracts (Arnold, 1997; Cappelli, 1999); more temporary and agency workers (Mallon and Duberley, 2000; Peters, 2000); including contract work for previous employers; a move from paternalism to independence (Bagshaw, 1997); an ethos of lifelong learning (Herriot et al., 1998; Watts, 1999) and a focus on employability (Kanter, 1989); more, smaller firms and an increase in self-employment (Watts, 1996); a move to more knowledge-based work, where people handle 'data, not things' (Drucker, 1992); privatization of previously public jobs (Handy, 1994); a reduced work ethic, alongside a debate on work–life balances (Schein, 1978; Handy, 1998) and a call for a more holistic, spiritual approach (Handy, 1998); a high number of people holding more than one job, especially part-time jobs (Arnold, 1997).

Choosing a career is viewed as a part of the developmental process that one follows by going through various cycles of opting among various career paths (Kniveton, 2004). Modern career models devised to embrace this new arena for careers reflect a plethora of metaphors, such as protean (Hall, 1976), portfolio (Handy, 1989) and boundaryless (DeFilippi and Arthur, 1994). Measures of success in careers have also changed. The literature suggests that there is a move away from the objective, external measures of success, with the emphasis on titles, money and status, to more internal, intrinsic measures, with the emphasis on fulfilment and work–life balance (Herriot, 1992; Arthur et al., 1999). However, a contrary view is offered by research in the UK and USA which showed that traditional upward mobility within their organizational hierarchy was still the key measure of success for many individuals (e.g. Cappelli, 1999; Mallon, 1999; Holbeche, 2000a, 2000b). Many MBA programmes are marketed on the basis of helping individuals with such career progression. The link between management development programmes and performance is a tenuous one and notoriously difficult to evidence (see Blackler and Kennedy, 2004; Dexter et al., 2006), but 'faith-based' decisions often prevail (CEML, 2002; Dexter et al., 2005).

Relationality is an important aspect of career choices. Our form of relationality takes four different forms: (1) relationality of the individual with him or herself, i.e. the inner dialogue in terms of career aspirations, motivations and ultimately choices; (2) relationality between the individual and his or her circumstances that are external to his or her institution of education and employment; (3) relationality between the individual and the organizational settings; and (4) relationality between the individual, his or her inner dialogue, and those circumstances of exogenous and endogenous nature. Whilst most studies of career choice have examined the subject either from the agentic perspective of the first form of relationality or through the lens of structural considerations of career opportunities and constraints, the final form of relationality, which considers relationality in the context of agentic and structural influences without reducing one to the other, is our preferred approach to relationality in this chapter.

The third aspect of career choice is dynamic performance. This aspect hosts the agentic perspective of careers which includes individual aspirations, likes, dislikes as well as choices that are unconstrained by external influences. Whilst this aspect of career choice assumes absence of contextual constraints, the situated context aspect focuses solely on the structural constraints, ignoring the agentic processes of choosing at the level of individual. The three-pronged approach adopted here allows for a reading of career choice as a phenomenon that resides in the individual and structural domain, as well as in the space between the two domains as a relational phenomenon.

METHODS

The study examined 21 different influences on career 'choice' (Özbilgin et al., 2005) in eight countries. These influences are identified through a literature review (Table 1.1). The statements in the career choice scale were tested in an earlier study with a different data set (Özbilgin et al., 2005). In order to identify differences between countries, multivariate and

Table 1.1   *Outlines three aspects of career choice with the respective items used in this study and their academic sources*

Influences on career choice	Source
Exogenous contextual situatedness	
Chance, luck and/or fate	Wiseman (2004); Baruch (2004)
Career choices are/were influenced by own sex	Simpson (2000); Procter and Padfield (1999); Slater (1980)
Career choices are/were influenced by own ethnicity	Slater (1980); Özbilgin (1998)
Career choices are/were influenced by own age	Slater (1980); Özbilgin (1998)
Career choices are/were influenced by own background	Slater (1980); Bourdieu (1998)
Endogenous contextual situatedness	
Ease of access to career of own choice	Shapero (1971); Bates (1999); Borooah and Hart (1999); Kyracou and Coulthart (2000); Clark and Drinkwater (2000); Barret et al. (1996); Slater (1980)
Lack of access to other career options	Shapero (1971); Bates (1999); Kyracou and Coulthart (2000); Clark and Drinkwater (2000); Slater (1980)
Quality of life associated with career of own choice	Hallissey et al. (2000); Baruch (2004)
Flexibility associated with career of own choice	Hallissey et al. (2000)
Autonomy associated with career of own choice	Hallissey et al. (2000)
Development opportunities associated with career of own choice	Hallissey et al. (2000); Schein (1985)
Promotion opportunities associated with career of own choice	Hallissey et al. (2000)
Training and education opportunities in career of own choice	Hallissey et al. (2000)
Superior financial rewards in career of own choice	Hallissey et al. (2000)
Relational formation	
Own acquaintances, friends and/or family	Slater (1980); Bourdieu (1986, 1998)
Own financial and economic conditions	Bourdieu (1986, 1998)
Love of career of own choice	Hallissey et al. (2000)

Table 1.1   (continued)

Influences on career choice	Source
Dynamic performance	
Own knowledge of labour and/or career market	Schein (1978, 1985); Baruch (2004); Bourdieu (1986, 1998)
Own education and training	Hakim (1991, 1996); Bourdieu (1986, 1998); Sturges et al. (2003); Rhodes and Doering (1983)
Own skills, competences and abilities	Baruch and Peiperl (2003); Schein (1978, 1985); Bourdieu (1986, 1998)
Free choice in making own career decisions	Slater (1980); Hakim (1991, 1996); Bourdieu (1998)

Source: Özbilgin et al. (2005).

univariate analyses are performed. The strength of the survey tool and the approach taken resides in the interdisciplinary and heterodox nature of the conceptual approach, paying particular attention to the intertwined nature of micro-, meso- and macro-level influences. The relational approach (Kyriakidou and Özbilgin, 2006) to careers that the chapter describes borrows elements from social constructionist, critical realist (Layder, 1993) and postmodernist approaches, as it recognizes career choice as an individual experience that is unique to each individual, with multilayered influences ranging from micro-psychological to macro-structural, and as an embodied phenomenon that has a socially, culturally and historically ascribed meaning.

RESULTS

The distributive characteristics of the project participants in different countries are diverse across both personal characteristics such as sex, age and marital status (see Table 1.2), as well as in terms of their organizational status and position (see Table 1.3). Absence of national statistics on MBA students and their distributive profiles frustrates any attempt at drawing conclusions regarding representativeness of our samples. Nevertheless, the demographic attributes of the survey participants may explain some of the national idiosyncrasies that emerge in the analysis of questionnaire responses.

Chinese, Ghanaian, Korean and Turkish respondents were predominantly male, and women constituted the majority of Israeli and Greek respondents.

Table 1.2   *General characteristics of Sample 1*

	China	Ghana	Greece	Israel	Korea	Turkey	Total
Sex							
Male[a]	79	22	39	39	123	69	371
	64.2	71	38.6	39	93.9	59.5	61.6
Female[a]	44	9	62	61	8	47	231
	35.8	29	61.4	61	6.1	40.5	38.4
Missing	3	0	1	1	0	0	5
Age							
Mean	28.92	35.52	27.36	32.85	41.20	23.46	31.28
Median	28	33	27	30	42	23	28
Mode	28	29[b]	25	25[b]	37[b]	23	25[b]
Std deviation	2.89	7.81	3.57	8.21	6.54	1.79	8.15
Min.	23	25	24	23	25	21	21
Max.	36	54	46	60	60	35	60
Marital status							
Single[a]	65	10	102	42	17	113	349
	51.6	32.3	100	43.3	13.2	97.4	58.1
Married[a]	60	21		44	110	2	237
	47.6	67.7		45.4	85.3	1.7	39.4
Separated[a]				1	1		2
				1	0.8		0.3
Divorced[a]				8	1	1	10
				8.2	0.8	0.9	1.7
Widowed[a]	1			2			3
	0.8			2.1			0.5
Missing	0	0	0	4	2	0	6
Total frequencies	126	31	102	101	131	116	607

Notes:
[a]   First row shows frequency; second row shows percentage within nationality.
[b]   Multiple modes exist. The smallest value is shown.

The predominance of women in the Israeli sample can be explained by the fact that management education has become the major gateway for Israeli women into a career in management, whereas military service provides this function for Israeli men. The predominance of men in the Korean sample can be explained by the mean age of the participant group. The mean age for the Korean respondents was 41. This is the oldest group across five countries. It is reasonable to expect male domination in older generation groups as increased female access to higher education and managerial ranks internationally has been a phenomenon of the last three decades. These data are

Table 1.3 General characteristics of Sample 2

	China	Ghana	Greece	Israel	Korea	Turkey	Total
Current job status							
No paid work	10	3	36			50	99
experience[a]	8	9.7	35.3			43.9	16.7
Experience of paid	37	7	38	14		32	128
work but now	29.6	22.6	37.3	14.7		28.1	21.6
I am unemployed[a]							
Currently doing paid	78	21	28	81	126	32	366
work[a]	62.4	67.7	27.5	85.3	100	28.1	61.7
Missing	1	0	0	6	5	2	14
Career goal							
Management[a]	23	11	22	47	25	36	164
	18.9	35.5	21.6	54.7	19.2	31.9	28.1
Own your own	30	14	21	4	24	41	134
business[a]	24.6	45.2	20.6	4.7	18.5	36.3	22.9
Entrepreneurship[a]	26	2	18	4	14	5	69
	21.3	6.5	17.6	4.7	10.8	4.4	11.8
Career advancement[a]	33	4	37	13	50	26	163
	27	12.9	36.3	15.1	38.5	23	27.9
Change[a]	8		4	1	8		21
	6.6		3.9	1.2	6.2		3.6
Other[a]	2			17	9	5	33
	1.6			19.8	6.9	4.4	5.7
Missing	4	0	0	15	1	3	23
Total	126	31	102	101	131	116	607

Note: [a] First row shows frequency; second row shows percentage within nationality.

also consistent with the rate of female managerial and administrative positions in Korea documented by the *Human Development Report* (UNDP, 2006). Turkey had the youngest cohort of respondents in the survey. This is in line with its young population. Turkey has the youngest population in comparison with other survey participants. Unsurprisingly, due to their youth, the Greek and the Turkish respondents were mostly single, whilst the Korean respondents were predominantly married and the Israeli respondents whose age was in the middle between Ghana and Turkey were about half single and about half married (see Table 1.2).

The current job status of the sample participants is also congruent with the age profiles of respondents. In comparison with Greek and Turkish respondents, the respondents from other countries were more likely to have employment experience and to be currently working. For example, all Israeli respondents had some paid work experience, and almost all (over 85 per cent) were currently doing paid work.

Whilst for the Chinese, Korean and Greek respondents the main career goal was advancement, for the Ghanaians and Turkish it was setting up their own business, for Israelis, managerial career was the main goal (a finding that corresponds with the higher rate of women in this sample, women who believe that an MBA will open career options in management for them; see Table 1.3). Setting up one's own business in Ghana, as in many other developing countries, is a primary career goal even among the well-qualified (Baryeh et al., 2000). This can be explained in terms of the general knowledge and experience of declining waged employment due to structural adjustments in the public sector and an insufficiently mature private sector (Killick, forthcoming) and low formal sector (public and private) wages (Xiao and Canagarajah, 2002), which are often inadequate to sustain those in paid employment.

Chinese, Ghanaians, Koreans and Israelis were predominantly white-collar professionals; Greek and Turkish respondents were mostly students. In terms of father's occupation, Chinese respondents' fathers were mainly blue-collar workers, Ghanaian, Israeli, Turkish and Greek respondents' fathers were of white-collar professions. Mothers' occupational status varied more extensively. For Turks, the main response was 'the other' category. This suggests that the occupational status list had a serious omission. For Chinese, Israeli, Greek and Ghanaian students, white-collar work was the main category for mother's occupational status. What seems most significant, however, is that in all groups the majority of mothers had paid work except for Koreans (see Table 1.4). For Korean students, the main mothers' occupational status was housewife.

The majority of the Ghanaian and Korean and half of the Chinese students were self-funding their MBA studies. While self-funding was the predominant source for Greek and Israeli students, they also drew on other sources. For Turkish students, parents were the key source of funding. This makes sense in context of their youth (see Table 1.5).

When compared to key influences on career choices of MBA students from Greece, Israel and Turkey (Özbilgin et al., 2005), China, Ghana and Korea appear divergent. The Ghanaians' endogenous contextual situatedness factors of development, and training and education opportunities, may be accounted for in the context of the low wages in their labour market where training and development opportunities may be the only substantial reward individuals have access to (Akyeampong and Stevens, 2002). Table 1.6 shows average scores for each statement.

Career choice of MBA students

Table 1.4   General characteristics of Sample 3

	China	Ghana	Greece	Israel	Korea	Turkey	Total
Occupational status							
White-collar/	66	17	28	49	66	35	261
professional[a]	55.5	56.7	27.7	53.3	50.8	33	45.2
Blue-collar/technical[a]	12	2			34		48
	10.1	6.7			26.2		8.3
Pink-collar/services[a]	6	2	1	20	20	2	51
	5	6.7	1	21.7	15.4	1.9	8.8
Student[a]	29	9	71	15		63	187
	24.4	30	70.3	16.3		59.4	32.4
Other[a]	6		1	8	10	6	31
	5		1	8.7	7.7	5.7	5.4
Missing	7	1	1	9	1	10	29
Father's occupational status							
White-collar/	32	14	55	45	34	47	227
professional[a]	27.8	45.2	55	52.3	26.2	40.9	39.3
Blue-collar/technical[a]	38	3	7	19	19	6	92
	33	9.7	7	22.1	14.6	5.2	15.9
Pink-collar/services[a]	5	4	27	13	3	3	55
	4.3	12.9	27	15.1	2.3	2.6	9.5
Student[a]	12	9	9	5	28	35	98
	10.4	29	9	5.8	21.5	30.4	17
Housework[a]	5	1		3	5	9	23
	4.3	3.2		3.5	3.8	7.8	4
Retiree[a]	1		2		5	1	9
	0.9		2		3.8	0.9	1.6
Other[a]	22			1	36	14	73
	19.1			1.2	27.7	12.2	12.7
Missing	11	0	2	15	1	1	30
Mother's occupational status							
White-collar/	38	11	46	29	4	44	172
professional[a]	31.1	35.5	45.1	34.9	3.1	40	29.8
Blue-collar/technical[a]	36		4	6	3	2	51
	29.5		3.9	7.2	2.3	1.8	8.8
Pink-collar/services[a]	9	2	22	22	5	9	69
	7.4	6.5	21.6	26.5	3.8	8.2	11.9
Student[a]	8	11	2	2	14	6	43
	6.6	35.5	2	2.4	10.8	5.5	7.4
Housework[a]	4	1	4	1	104	1	11
	3.3	3.2	3.9	1.2	80	0.9	1.9
Retiree[a]	1	1					2
	0.8	3.2					0.3

Table 1.4   (continued)

	China	Ghana	Greece	Israel	Korea	Turkey	Total
Other[a]	26	5	24	23		48	230
	21.3	16.1	23.5	27.7		43.6	39.8
Missing	4	0	0	18	1	6	29
Total	126	31	102	101	131	116	607

Note: [a] First row shows frequency; second row shows percentage within nationality.

Table 1.5   *General characteristics of Sample 4*

	China	Ghana	Greece	Israel	Korea	Turkey	Total
Funding for MBA study							
Self	61	20	45	39	91	15	271
	50	66.7	44.1	40.6	70.5	12.9	45.5
Parents	14	2	29	6		76	127
	11.5	6.7	28.4	6.3		65.5	21.3
Work	8	2		12	17	5	44
	6.6	6.7		12.5	13.2	4.3	7.4
Self and parents	28	1	28	14	2	12	85
	23	3.3	27.5	14.6	1.6	10.3	14.3
Self and work	10	4		14	18		46
	8.2	13.3		14.6	14		7.7
Other	1	1		11	1	8	22
	0.8	3.3		11.5	0.8	6.9	3.7
Missing	1	1		11	1	8	22
Total	126	31	102	101	131	116	607

Note: [a] First row shows frequency; second row shows percentage within nationality.

Table 1.7 shows the top and bottom five mean scores across all state-ments and six countries. It is interesting to note endogenous contextual situatedness, relational formation and dynamic performance. Exogenous contextual situatedness does not feature in the top five ranking any of the sample countries. On the contrary, exogenous contextual situatedness statements are a common feature of the bottom five means across all state-ments. In the case of China, Korea and Turkey, a few endogenous contextual situatedness statements appear in the bottom five means.

With the exception of China and Korea, superior financial rewards in choice of career does not feature as a significant influence on career choice.

Table 1.6   Average scores for each statement

	Mean[a]						Total
	China	Ghana	Greece	Israel	Korea	Turkey	
Contextual situatedness: exogenous							
Career choices are/ were influenced by own background	4.41	3.35	3.02	3.68	4.13	5.17	4.08
Chance, luck and/ or fate	4.07	2.65	2.95	3.83	4.43	4.45	3.92
Career choices are/ were influenced by own age	4.24	2.19	2.41	3.06	3.89	4.14	3.53
Career choices are/ were influenced by own sex	3.87	2.13	2.58	3.26	3.34	3.79	3.33
Career choices are/ were influenced by own ethnicity[b]	3.04	1.58	1.70	2.06	3.01	3.11	2.58
Contextual situatedness: endogenous							
Development opportunities associated with career of own choice	**5.66**	**6.13**	**5.21**	**6.24**	**5.76**	6.25	**5.83**
Promotion opportunities associated with career of own choice	**5.38**	5.74	**5.20**	**6.19**	5.39	6.26	5.67
Training and education opportunities in career of own choice	**5.45**	**6.10**	4.95	5.95	5.27	6.06	5.56
Quality of life associated with career of own choice	5.29	5.68	4.75	5.74	5.42	**6.29**	5.51
Superior financial rewards in career of own choice	**5.68**	5.42	4.66	5.67	**5.51**	5.77	5.47
Autonomy associated with career of own choice	4.61	5.03	4.69	5.69	5.43	5.61	5.19

Table 1.6   (continued)

	Mean[a]						Total
	China	Ghana	Greece	Israel	Korea	Turkey	
Flexibility associated with career of own choice	4.93	5.87	4.45	5.45	5.18	5.59	5.16
Ease of access to career of own choice	4.17	4.26	3.82	4.75	3.83	4.36	4.18
Lack of access to other career options	3.97	3.58	3.44	4.35	3.72	3.65	3.81
Relational formation							
Love of career of own choice	**5.38**	5.32	**4.99**	**5.99**	**5.88**	**6.38**	**5.71**
Own financial and economic condition	4.75	4.84	4.66	5.65	5.16	5.26	5.07
Own acquaintances, friends and/ or family	4.64	4.10	4.16	5.12	4.37	5.47	4.71
Dynamic performance							
Own skills, competences and abilities	5.63	**6.55**	**5.40**	**6.41**	**6.04**	**6.65**	**6.05**
Own education and training	5.33	**6.23**	**5.15**	**6.13**	**5.70**	**6.49**	**5.78**
Own knowledge of labour and/or career market	5.02	5.03	4.34	5.31	5.22	6.04	5.19
Free choice in making own career decisions	4.60	**6.39**	4.37	5.33	4.31	**6.29**	5.03

Notes:
[a]   All statements were measured by a 1–7 strongly disagree–strongly agree Likert scale and the mean indicates the selected frequency by each group for the acceptance of the statements (variables).
[b]   For Koreans, the term ethnicity in question number 18 was replaced with familial clan to take into account that Korea is a homogeneous ethnic society.

Across all six countries, it is interesting to note that a combination of individual love of career, skills, competencies and work-related opportunities are cited as important influences.

   What appears to be strongly evident across all countries is the fact that relational formation and dynamic performance factors, rather than exogenous or

Table 1.7   Top five and bottom five mean scores across all statements and six countries

	Top five		Bottom five	
	Items	Mean	Items	Mean
China	Superior financial rewards in career of own choice[c]	5.68	Career choices are/were influenced by own ethnicity[b]	3.04
	Development opportunities associated with career of own choice[c]	5.66	Career choices are/were influenced by own sex[b]	3.87
	Own skills, competences and abilities[a]	5.63	Lack of access to other career options[c]	3.97
	Training and education opportunities in career of own choice[c]	5.45	Chance, luck and/or fate[b]	4.07
	Love of career of own choice[d]	5.38	Ease of access to career of own choice[c]	4.17
Ghana	Own skills, competences and abilities[a]	6.55	Career choices are/were influenced by own ethnicity[b]	1.58
	Free choice in making own career decisions[a]	6.39	Career choices are/were influenced by own sex[b]	2.13
	Own education and training[a]	6.23	Career choices are/were influenced by own age[b]	2.19
	Development opportunities associated with career of own choice[c]	6.13	Chance, luck and/or fate[b]	2.65
	Training and education opportunities in career of own choice[c]	6.1	Career choices are/were influenced by own background[b]	3.35
Greece	Own skills, competences and abilities[a]	5.4	Career choices are/were influenced by own ethnicity[b]	1.7
	Development opportunities associated with career of own choice[c]	5.21	Career choices are/were influenced by own age[b]	2.41
	Promotion opportunities associated with career of own choice[c]	5.2	Career choices are/were influenced by own sex[b]	2.58
	Own education and training[a]	5.15	Chance, luck and/or fate[b]	2.95
	Love of career of own choice[d]	4.99	Career choices are/were influenced by own background[b]	3.02
Israel	Own skills, competences and abilities[a]	6.41	Career choices are/were influenced by own ethnicity[b]	3.11
	Development opportunities associated with career of own choice[c]	6.24	Career choices are/were influenced by own age[b]	4.14

Table 1.7   (continued)

	Top five		Bottom five	
	Items	Mean	Items	Mean
	Promotion opportunities associated with career of own choice[c]	6.19	Career choices are/were influenced by own sex[b]	3.79
	Own education and training[a]	6.13	Career choices are/were influenced by own background[b]	5.17
	Love of career of own choice[d]	5.99	Chance, luck and/or fate[b]	4.45
Korea	Own skills, competences and abilities[a]	6.04	Career choices are/were influenced by own ethnicity (familial clan)[b]	3.01
	Love of career of own choice[d]	5.88	Career choices are/were influenced by own sex[b]	3.34
	Development opportunities associated with career of own choice[c]	5.76	Lack of access to other career options[c]	3.72
	Own education and training[a]	5.7	Ease of access to career of own choice[c]	3.83
	Superior financial rewards in career of own choice[c]	5.51	Career choices are/were influenced by own age[b]	3.89
Turkey	Own skills, competences and abilities[a]	6.65	Career choices are/were influenced by own ethnicity[b]	2.58
	Own education and training[a]	6.49	Lack of access to other career options[c]	3.81
	Love of career of own choice[d]	6.38	Career choices are/were influenced by own sex[b]	3.33
	Quality of life associated with career of own choice[c]	6.29	Career choices are/were influenced by own age[b]	3.53
	Free choice in making own career decisions[a]	6.29	Ease of access to career of own choice[c]	4.18

Notes:
[a]   Exogenous contextual situatedness.
[b]   Endogenous contextual situatedness.
[c]   Relational formation.
[d]   Dynamic performance.

endogenous contextual situatedness factors, are reported to explain career choices of the respondents. This is congruent with the findings of earlier studies with a larger sample of respondents by Özbilgin et al. (2005), Küskü et al. (2007) and Tatlı et al. (2007), which highlighted that individuals are more likely to report individual-level rather than structural influences on their careers. In line with Özbilgin et al.'s findings, a study on Ghanaian female engineering students revealed that major motivating factors for the choice of engineering as a career were individual-level characteristics such as natural curiosity, mathematics and science ability, as well as family influence (Baryeh et al., 2000). Considering the relational context of career development, Kerka (2000) notes the importance of social relationships. Family influence is cited as an important dimension in a number of studies (Altman, 1997; Baryeh et al., 2000; Bloir, 1997; Ketterson and Blustein, 1997; Pines et al., 2002; Way and Rossmann, 1996; Young et al., 1997 as well as Kaplan, Chapter 6 and Yanai et al., Chapter 7, this volume). These studies report positive and negative aspects of family influence. Taking an ecological systems perspective, Way and Rossmann (1996) illustrate how career development is influenced by relationships with others and with the environment. Employment of effective learning strategies associated with proactive learning style is encouraged.

Gender, race and class are also noted as important micro- and meso-level dimensions, influencing career development (Kerka, 2000, 2003; Forson, Chapter 24, this volume). Moving from traditional person–environment fit theories towards a multifaceted approach in explaining career development processes, Flores et al. (2003) emphasize such factors as worldview, identity, values and context, which can be sufficiently explained through a comprehensive framework that takes into account the interrelated nature of micro-, meso- and macro-level aspects (e.g. Özbilgin et al., 2005).

The analysis of the data from a data set collected using the third-wave survey instrument has generated results that are worth reporting in this chapter, in relation to the career choices of MBA students in North Cyprus and the UK. Starting with the macro-aspects, there are five universities and 30 605 students (anticipated to reach 45 000 – that is, nearly one-quarter North Cyprus's population – when certain facilities are completed), 20 683 of whom are non-Cypriots, mainly from Turkey (18 398) (Hatay, 2005) and also from other countries. The growth in the number of non-Cypriots studying at North Cyprus's universities has brought a steady increase in the number of students in the island (Warner, 1999, p. 142). The five universities in North Cyprus offer MBA degrees. The high number of non-Cypriot students is also observed with the MBA students in the current study.

The UK has followed the USA in terms of the establishment of MBA programmes since the 1980s, when government interest in increasing global competitiveness brought management training to the fore. The Quality Assurance Agency (QAA) in the UK (QAA, 2006) describes studies in Business and Management as contributing towards 'the health and productivity of the U.K. and global economies', assisting 'organisations to be more competitive' by 'helping to improve the quality of management, leadership and business practice in organisations'. The end of the twentieth century witnessed the establishment of many business schools across Europe (Baruch and Peiperl, 2003). By 1999/2000, around 33 000 students in the UK were studying on a variety of MBA programmes, with around 12 000 MBA graduates in 2000 (QAA, 2006). There are now approximately 500 business schools across Europe, with an estimated 80 000 MBA graduates annually (Cameron, 2005). An increasing proportion of MBA students are international students, as recognition of the value of the training and the qualification gains momentum, especially in the ballooning Asian economy. The QAA welcomes this as 'particularly important for enriching the overall international learning experience' (QAA, 2006).

Table 1.8 shows sample characteristics in the UK and North Cyprus samples. There were some differences among the MBA students in North Cyprus and the UK. The mean age in North Cyprus was 26.11, with SD of 4.47, while the mean age in the UK was much higher and with a higher spread indicated, with a mean of 32.96 and SD of 8.18. The percentage of MBA students that regard their future work as a career in the UK sample was 69.89 per cent, whereas in North Cyprus it was 58.95 per cent.

Hofstede's research (1983) shows that Turkish and UK cultures are quite different on all of Hofstede's dimensions (see also Tanova, 2001). The Turkish culture is high on uncertainty avoidance and power distance dimensions, while the UK culture is low on these dimensions. Also, the UK culture is high on masculinity and individualism dimensions while the Turkish culture is low on these dimensions. As stated by Tanova (2003), Turkish Cypriots have close cultural and economic ties to Turkey. In Turkey, Turkish societal and organizational culture is a combination of 'Western' and 'Eastern' values (Aycan, 2001). This can also be applied to

Table 1.8   Sample characteristics – North Cyprus and UK

	North Cyprus %	UK %
Female	38.70	51.58
Full-time student – unemployed	39.42	31.96
Full-time student with a part-time job	24.04	3.09
Middle management	6.73	25.77
Single	81.08	48.42
My future work is . . .		
A job	22.11	19.35
A career	58.95	69.89
A calling	12.63	6.45
Other	5.26	3.23
A passion	1.05	1.08

Table 1.9   Survey items pertaining to 'collectivism' dimension

---

I feel proud if fellow students get a prize
Parents and children must stay together
Well-being of my fellow students is important to me
It is my duty to take care of my family
Pleasure is spending time with other people
Family members should stick together
I feel good when I cooperate with others
It is important to me to respect the decisions made by my group

---

North Cyprus. Collectivism was measured by eight items in this research. Table 1.9 illustrates these items.

The Cronbach's alphas were 0.62 and 0.66 for the UK and North Cyprus respectively. The cultural differences between UK and Turkish cultures were reflected in the collectivism scores of the respondents. The mean collectivism score for respondents from North Cyprus was 5.47, which is significantly higher than (t = 3.302, p < 0.001) the mean collectivism score for UK respondents, which was 5.12.

Possible effects of cultural differences were also indicated in the 'values toward charity' which were measured with five items. The Cronbach's alphas were 0.57 and 0.64 for the UK and North Cyprus respectively. The mean values toward charity scores were higher among respondents in North Cyprus (M = 4.51, SD = 1.12) compared to respondents in the UK (M = 3.88, SD = 0.98) t(207) = 4.27, p < 0.001.

We can see from Table 1.10 that in general the micro- and meso-influences have higher means in the respondents from North Cyprus. In both groups, among the micro-influences the skills, competencies and abilities are listed with the highest rank. However, among meso-influences, quality of life is the highest ranking in North Cyprus, whilst training and education opportunities followed by financial rewards are the highest ranking in the UK.

The only statistically significant result in comparing the individuals who may have influenced career choice was in the teacher/mentor (see Table 1.11). The teacher/mentor had more influence on the respondents from North Cyprus compared with the respondents from the UK. When we look at the ranks of the means, we see that teacher/mentor was the most influential in North Cyprus, followed by father; in the UK significant other/partner was the most influential, followed by manager. The 'father-influence' outranks the 'mother-influence' in both samples.

As a final element to report, Table 1.12 illustrates expectations from an MBA. In both the UK and North Cyprus, 'acquiring knowledge' and 'improving analytical skills and critical thinking' are the items with the

Table 1.10 Micro, meso and macro influences – North Cyprus and UK samples

	N		Mean		Std dev.		Rank		t-test	df	Sig.
	North Cyprus	UK	North Cyprus	UK	North Cyprus	UK	North Cyprus	UK			
Micro-influences											
My skills, competences and abilities	111	97	6.43	6.02	1.02	0.92	1st	1st	3.03	206	**0.003**
My education and training	112	97	6.42	5.53	0.78	1.28	2nd	2nd	6.20	207	**0.000**
I believe I have free choice in making my career decisions	111	97	6.05	5.24	1.28	1.40	3rd	3rd	4.40	206	**0.000**
My love of this career	111	97	6.00	5.14	1.37	1.36	4th	4th	4.51	206	**0.000**
My knowledge of labour and/or career market	110	97	5.79	4.54	1.10	1.51	5th	6th	6.87	205	**0.000**
My financial and economic conditions	109	97	5.44	4.76	1.49	1.47	6th	5th	3.27	204	**0.001**
Success stories of acquaintances, friends, family and others	112	97	5.10	4.29	1.46	1.58	7th	7th	3.85	207	**0.000**
Meso-influences											
Quality of life associated with this career	107	97	5.97	5.06	1.11	1.39	1st	4th	5.19	202	**0.000**
Promotion opportunities associated with this career	111	97	5.94	5.10	1.32	1.30	2nd	3rd	4.57	206	**0.000**

Table 1.10 (continued)

	N		Mean		Std dev.		Rank		t-test	df	Sig.
	North Cyprus	UK	North Cyprus	UK	North Cyprus	UK	North Cyprus	UK			
Training and education opportunities	111	97	5.94	5.28	1.22	1.22	3rd	1st	3.87	206	**0.000**
Financial rewards in this career	107	97	5.81	5.12	1.17	1.43	4th	2nd	3.79	202	**0.000**
Ease of access to this career	111	96	4.56	4.34	1.75	1.31	5th	5th	0.99	205	0.324
Lack of access to other career options	108	96	4.25	3.55	1.76	1.50	6th	6th	3.03	202	**0.003**
Macro-influence											
Chance, luck or circumstances	110	97	4.85	4.55	1.71	1.65			1.28	205	0.203

Table 1.11 Individuals who may have influenced career choice

	N		Mean		Std dev.		Rank		t-test for equality of means		
	North Cyprus	UK	North Cyprus	UK	North Cyprus	UK	North Cyprus	UK	t	df	Sig. (2-tailed)
Teacher/mentor	112	96	4.24	3.49	2.08	1.90	1	3	2.70	206	**0.007**
Father	111	97	3.86	3.45	2.12	1.87	2	4	1.47	206	0.142
Significant other/partner	79	97	3.68	4.03	2.16	1.87	3	1	−1.14	174	0.255
Manager	109	97	3.67	3.75	2.01	1.73	4	2	−0.32	204	0.753
Mother	112	97	3.55	3.36	2.07	1.85	5	6	0.71	207	0.482
Work colleagues	108	97	3.14	3.41	2.06	1.53	6	5	−1.07	203	0.286
Fellow students	110	96	3.11	2.79	1.96	1.71	7	8	1.23	204	0.221
Friends	110	97	3.04	3.20	2.00	1.63	8	7	−0.62	205	0.534
Another relative	111	97	2.73	2.57	1.87	1.68	9	9	0.66	206	0.512

Table 1.12   Expectations from an MBA – North Cyprus and UK samples

	N		Mean		Std dev.		Rank		t-test for equality of means		
	North Cyprus	UK	North Cyprus	UK	North Cyprus	UK	North Cyprus	UK	t	df	Sig.
Acquire knowledge	111	97	6.35	6.13	0.93	0.91	1	1	1.70	206	0.091
Improve analytical skills and critical thinking	111	97	6.30	6.07	1.04	0.98	2	2	1.60	206	0.112
Career advancement	111	96	6.19	5.74	1.14	1.12	3	5	2.86	205	**0.005**
Entrepreneurial competence	109	96	5.92	4.71	1.39	1.75	4	7	5.50	203	**0.000**
Enhanced value in the job market	110	97	5.91	5.96	1.40	1.14	5	3	−0.28	205	0.782
Managerial competence	110	97	5.79	5.89	1.63	1.04	6	4	−0.50	205	0.621
Social prestige	110	96	5.42	4.48	1.81	1.70	7	8	3.81	204	**0.000**
Salary gain	111	97	5.35	5.40	1.69	1.63	8	6	−0.22	206	0.826
Competence for setting up own business	111	95	5.22	4.18	1.92	2.00	9	9	3.79	204	**0.000**

highest means. The differences between the UK and North Cyprus were in career advancement, social prestige, entrepreneurial competence, and competence in setting up own businesses, which had higher means among respondents from North Cyprus.

CONCLUSIONS

The chapter provides an understanding of the cross-national divergence and convergence of influences on career choice in context, allowing for a reading of career 'choice' for the purposes of understanding the divergent, yet converging, nature of impacts on 'choice' and an understanding of the impact of contextual variations in these influences. In a study of eight countries as different as China, Ghana, Greece, Israel, Korea, North Cyprus, Turkey and the UK, it is reasonable to expect a high level of cross-national variation. However, our questionnaire study suggests that cross-national similarities were stronger than differences. It is difficult to offer a comprehensive explanation for this curious phenomenon. We considered two different reasons for the apparent similarities across career choices of MBA students from these countries.

The first reason can be argued as the 'MBA effects'. MBA study has a unifying impact internationally. It is an internationally recognized acronym and a higher education degree that attracts a broadly international body of students in higher education sectors of industrialized countries. The second explanatory factor is neoliberal influences. We can partly explain convergence of career choice influences with recourse to the neoliberal discourse, which has elevated individual and agentic frames of thinking over social and structural frames of reference when exploring issues of 'choice'.

Three major concerns include the following: lack of awareness of path dependencies in the respondent population; lack of awareness of social conditions that shape choice; and lack of critical reasoning skills. Considering the intertwined nature of micro-, meso- and macro-influences on career choices and development, it is important to raise awareness of the notion that early career aspirations may eventually get transformed by more realistic selections in parallel with a person's own capacities and realities of the labour market and resources available, in the current postmodern discourse and practice. This has implications for families, and for the education and training of career advisers. Raising awareness is an important step. The next step should be to develop and implement appropriate career counselling methods, by taking into account a fuller grasp of micro-, meso- and macro-influences, both nationally and globally.

REFERENCES

Akyeampong, K. and Stevens, D. (2002), 'Exploring the backgrounds and shaping of beginning student teachers in Ghana: toward greater contextualisation of teacher education', *International Journal of Educational Development*, **22**: 261–74.

Altman, J.H. (1997), 'Career development in the context of family experiences', in H.S. Farmer (ed.), *Diversity and Women's Career Development: From Adolescence to Adulthood*, Thousand Oaks, CA: Sage, pp. 229–42.

Arnold, J. (1997), *Managing Careers into the Twenty First Century*, London: Paul Chapman Publishing.

Arthur, M.B., Inkson, K. and Pringle, J.K. (1999), *The New Careers: Individual, Action and Economic Change*, London: Sage.

Aycan, Z. (2001), 'Human resource management in Turkey – Current issues and future challenges', *International Journal of Manpower*, **22**(3): 252–60.

Bagshaw, M. (1997), 'Employability – creating a contract of mutual investment', *Industrial and Commercial Training*, **29**(6): 187–9.

Barrett, G.A., Jones, T.P. and McEvory, D. (1996), 'Ethnic minority business: theoretical discourse in Britain and North America', *Urban Studies*, **33**(4–5): 783–809.

Baruch, Y. (2004), *Managing Careers: Theory and Practice*, Harlow, UK: Prentice-Hall.

Baruch, Y. and Peiperl, M. (2000), 'The impact of an MBA on graduate careers', *Human Resource Management Journal*, **10**(2): 69–90.

Baruch, Y. and Peiperl, M.A. (2003), 'An empirical assessment of Sonnenfeld's career systems typology', *International Journal of Human Resource Management*, **14**(7): 1266–82.

Baryeh, E.A., Obu, R.Y., Lamptey, D.L. and Baryeh, N.Y. (2000), 'Ghanaian women and the engineering profession', *The International Journal of Mechanical Engineering Education*, **28**(4): 334–46.

Bates, T. (1999), 'Exiting self-employment: an analysis of Asian immigrant-owned small businesses', *Small Business Economics*, **13**: 171–83.

Blackler, F. and Kennedy, A. (2004), 'The design and evaluation of a leadership development programme for experienced chief executives from the public sector', *Management Learning*, **35**(2): 181–203.

Bloir, K. (1997), 'Parenting that promotes resilient urban African American families: scholars describe the characteristics of their parents' parenting behaviors', paper presented at the Annual Conference of the National Council on Family Relations, Arlington, VA, November (ED 419 596).

Borooah, V.K. and Hart, M. (1999), 'Factors affecting self-employment among Indian and Black Caribbean men in Britain', *Small Business Economics*, **13**(2): 111–29.

Bourdieu, P. (1977), *Outline Theory of Practice*, Cambridge: Cambridge University Press.

Bourdieu, P. (1986), 'The forms of capital', in John G. Richardson (ed.), *Handbook of Theory and Research for the Sociology of Education*, New York: Greenwood Press, pp. 241–58.

Bourdieu, P. (1990), *The Logic of Practice*, Stanford, CA: Stanford University Press.

Bourdieu, P. (1998), *Practical Reason: On the Theory of Action*, Cambridge: Polity Press.

Bourdieu, P. and Wacquant, L. (1992), *An Invitation to Reflexive Sociology*, Cambridge: Polity Press.

Boyatzis, R.E. (1983), *The Competent Manager*, New York: Wiley.

Boyatzis, R.E. and Renio, A. (1989), 'Research article: the impact of a MBA programme on managerial abilities', *Journal of Management Development*, 8(5): 66–77.

Cameron, S. (2005), *The MBA. Handbook*, 5th edn, London: Prentice Hall.

Cappelli, P. (1999), *The New Deal at Work: Managing the Market-driven Workforce*, Boston, MA: Harvard Business School Press.

Clark, K. and Drinkwater, S. (2000), 'Pushed out or pulled in? Ethnic minority self-employment in England and Wales', *Labour Economics*, 7: 603–28.

Council for Excellence in Management and Leadership (2002), *Managers and Leaders: Raising Our Game. Report of the Council for Management and Leadership*, London: CEML.

DeFilippi, R.J. and Arthur, M.B. (1994), 'The boundaryless career: a competency based perspective', *Journal of Organizational Behavior*, 15: 307–24.

Dexter, B.P., Franco, G., Chamberlin, J.E. and Dexter, P.I. (2005), 'Helping Managers to become Leading Managers: evaluating the impact of leadership development at middle manager level in a city council organisation', paper presented at Studying Leadership: Future Agendas, The 4th International Conference on Leadership Research, University of Lancaster, UK, December.

Dexter, B.P., Franco, G., Chamberlin, J.E., Dexter, P.I., Hann, S. and Edwards, M. (2006), 'Turning managers into leading managers: the impact of leadership development at middle manager level in a city council organisation', in N. Kyriakidou (ed.), *International Reflections on Education and Business*, Athens: Atiner.

Dougherty, T., Dreher, G. and Whitely, W. (1993), 'The MBA as careerist: an analysis of early-career job change', *Journal of Management*, 19(3): 535.

Drucker, P.F. (1992), 'The new sociology of organizations', *Harvard Business Review*, Sept.–Oct.: 95–104.

Finney, M. (1996), 'Degrees that make a difference', *HR Magazine*, 41(11): 74–82.

Flores, L.Y., Spanierman, L.B. and Oabsi, B.M. (2003), 'Ethical and professional issues in career assessment with diverse racial and ethnic groups', *Journal of Career Assessment*, 11(1): 76–95.

Hakim, C. (1991), 'Grateful slaves and self-made women: fact and fantasy in women's work orientations', *European Sociological Review*, 7(2): 101–21.

Hakim, C. (1996), *Key Issues in Women's Work: Female Heterogeneity and Polarisation of Women's Employment*, London: Athlone Press.

Hall, D.T. (1976), *Careers in Organisations*, New York: Scott, Foresman & Company.

Hallissey, J., Hannigan, A. and Ray, N. (2000), 'Reasons for choosing dentistry as a career – a survey of dental students attending a dental school in Ireland during 1998–99', *European Journal of Dental Education*, 4: 77–81.

Handy, C. (1989), *The Age of Unreason*, London: Business Books.

Handy, C. (1994), *The Empty Raincoat: Making Sense of the Future*, London: Hutchinson.

Handy, C. (1998), *The Hungry Spirit*, London: Arrow Books.

Hatay, Mete (2005), 'Beyond numbers: an inquiry into the political integration of the Turkish "settlers" in Northern Cyprus', PRIO Report 4, PRIO Cyprus Centre.

Herriot, P. (1992), *The Career Management Challenge*, London: Sage.

Herriot, P., Hirsh, W. and Reilly, P. (1998), *Trust and Transition: Managing Today's Employment Relationship*, Chichester, UK: John Wiley & Sons.

Hofstede, G. (1983), 'The cultural relativity of organizational practices and theories', *Journal of International Business Studies*, **14**(2): 75–89.

Holbeche, L. (2000a), 'Work in progression', *People Management*, 8 June: 44–6.

Holbeche, L. (2000b), 'Jobs for this life', *Personnel Today*, 25 July: 24–5.

Kanter, R.M. (1989), *When Giants Learn to Dance: Mastering the Challenges of Strategy-management and Careers in the 1990s*, London: Routledge.

Kerka, S. (2000), 'Parenting and career development', ERIC Clearinghouse on Adult Career and Vocational Education, available at http://career.ucsd.edu/parents/PACD.stml.

Kerka, S. (2003), 'Career development of diverse populations', ERIC Clearinghouse on Adult Career and Vocational Education, available at www.ericdigests.org/2004/career.htm.

Ketterson, T.U. and Blustein, D.L. (1997), 'Attachment relationships and the career exploration process', *Career Development Quarterly*, **46**(2): 167–78.

Killick, T. (forthcoming), 'What drives change in Ghana? A political economy view of economic prospects', in E. Aryeetey and R. Kanbur (eds), *The Economy of Ghana: Analytical Perspectives on Stability, Growth and Poverty*, Oxford, James Currey.

Kniveton, B.H. (2004), 'The influences and motivations on which students base their choice of career', *Research in Education*, **72**, 47–57.

Kniveton, X. and Bromley, H. (2004), 'Influences and motivations on which students base their choice of career', *Research in Education*, November.

Küskü, F., Özbilgin, M. and Özkale, L. (2007), 'Against the tide: gendered prejudice and disadvantage in engineering study from a comparative perspective', *Gender, Work and Organization*, **14**(2): 109–29.

Kyriacou, C. and Coulthard, M. (2000), 'Undergraduates' views of teaching as a career choice', *Journal of Education for Teaching*, **20**(2): 117–26.

Kyriakidou, O. and Özbilgin, M. (2006), *Relational Perspectives in Organizational Studies: A Research Companion*, Cheltenham, UK and Northampton, MA, USA: Edward Elgar.

Layder, D. (1993), *New Strategies in Social Research*, Cambridge: Polity Press.

Leeming, A. and Baruch, Y. (1998), 'The MBA as a bridge over the troubled waters of discrimination', *Women in Management Review*, **13**(3): 95–104.

Mallon, M. (1999), 'Going portfolio: making sense of changing careers', *Career Development International*, **4**(7): 308–69.

Mallon, M. and Duberley, J. (2000), 'Managers and professionals in the contingent workforce', *Human Resource Management Journal*, **10**(1): 33–47.

McClelland, D. (1973), 'Testing for competence rather than intelligence', *American Psychologists*, **28**, 1–14.

Nicholson, N. and West, M. (1988), *Managerial Job Changes: Men and Women in Transition*, Cambridge: Cambridge University Press.

Özbilgin, M.F., Küskü, F. and Erdoğmuş, N. (2005), 'Explaining influences on career "choice": the case of MBA students', *International Journal of Human Resource Management*, **16**(11): 2000–2028.

Peters, T. (2000), *The Changing World of Work*, BBC radio 4 broadcast (20.30; 13 January).

Procter, I. and Padfield, M. (1999), 'Work orientations and women's work: a critique of Hakim's theory of the heterogeneity of women', *Gender, Work and Organization*, **6**(3): 152–62.

Pines, A.M., Sadeh, A., Dvir, D. and Yaffe-Yanai, O. (2002), 'Entrepreneurs and managers: similar yet different', *International Journal of Organizational Analysis*, **10**: 172–90.

Quality Assurance Agency (2006), *Masters Awards in Business and Management*, available at www.qaa.ac.uk/academicinfrastructure/benchmarks/masters/mba. pdf (accessed 28 September).

Rhodes, S.R. and Doering, M. (1983), 'An integrated model of career change', *Academy of Management Review*, **8**(4): 631–9.

Schein, E.H. (1978), *Career Dynamics: Matching Individual and Organisational Needs*, Reading, MA: Addison Wesley.

Schein, E.H. (1985), *Career Anchors: Discovering Your Real Values*, San Francisco, CA: University Associate Inc.

Schofield, P. (1996), 'The MBA: managers only, please', *Accountancy*, **117**(1233): 40–42.

Shapero, A. (1971), *An Action Programme for Entrepreneurship*, Cambridge, MA: MDRR Press.

Simmering, M. and Wilcox, I. (1995), 'Career exploration and identity formation in MBA students', *Journal of Education for Business*, **70**: 233–7.

Simpson, R. (2000), 'Winners and losers: who benefits most from the MBA?', *Management Learning*, **31**(2): 45–58.

Slater, M. (1980), *Career Patterns and the Occupational Image*, London: Aslib.

Sturges, J., Simpson, R. and Altman, Y. (2003), 'Capitalising on learning: an exploration of the MBA as a vehicle for developing career competencies', *International Journal of Training and Development*, **7**(1): 53–66.

Tajfel, H. (1981), *Human Groups and Social Categories: Studies in Social Psychology*, Cambridge: Cambridge University Press.

Tanova, C. (2001), 'Cross cultural variations in decision making: a study of cognitive styles of Turkish and British managers', Global HRM Conference: Comparative HRM-Learning from Diversity, ESADE, CRANET, Barcelona, Spain, 20–22 June.

Tanova, C. (2003), 'Firm size and recruitment: staffing practices in small and large organisations in North Cyprus', *Career Development International*, **8**(2): 107–14.

Tatlı, A., Özbilgin, M. and Küskü, F. (2007), 'Gendered occupational outcomes: the case of professional training and work in Turkey', in Jacquelynne Eccles and Helen Watt (eds), *Explaining Gendered Occupational Outcomes*, Ann Arbor, MI: American Psychological Association (APA) Press.

Turner, J. (1975), 'Social comparison and social identity: some prospects for inter-group behaviour', *European Journal of Social Psychology*, **5**(1): 5–34.

UNDP (2006), *Human Development Report 2006*, New York: Macmillan.

Warner, J. (1999), 'North Cyprus: tourism and challenge of non-recognition', *The Journal of Sustainable Tourism*, **7**(2): 128–45.

Watts, A.G. (1996), *Careerquake: Policy Supports for Self-managed Careers*, London: Demos.

Watts, A.G. (1999), 'Re-shaping career development for the 21st century', Occasional Paper, Centre for Guidance Studies, University of Derby.

Way, W.L. and Rossmann, M.M. (1996), *Learning to Work: How Parents Nurture the Transition from School to Work: Family Matters . . . In School to Work Transition*, Berkeley, CA: National Center for Research in Vocational Education.

Wiseman, R. (2004), *The Luck Factor: The Scientific Study of the Lucky Mind*, London: Arrow.

Xiao, Y. and Canagarajah, S. (2002), 'Efficiency of public expenditure distribution and beyond. A report on Ghana's 2000 public expenditure tracking survey in the sectors of primary health and education', Washington, report prepared for World Bank.

Young, R.A., Valach, L., Paseluikho, M.A., Dover, C., Matthes, G.E., Paproski, D.L. and Sankey, A.M. (1997), 'The joint action of parents and adolescents in conversation about career', *Career Development Quarterly*, **46**(1): 72–86.

2. Culture and gender in the career choice of aspiring managers and entrepreneurs

Ayala Malach-Pines and Oshrit Kaspi-Baruch

The choice of a career is a complex and multifaceted process that includes all the spheres of a person's life (Hall, 1996). Since the early 1900s, many attempts have been made to classify the factors that influence this process. Most of these efforts focused on such factors as aptitudes, interests, resources, limitations, requirements and opportunities (e.g. Parsons, 1909; Ginzberg, 1951; Super, 1953, 1957; Swanson, 1996). As a result, both traditional and modern vocational choice theories have been the focus of similar criticism: they do not address the myriad cultural contexts that influence people's career choice and shape its development (Fouad and Byars-Winston, 2005). While the importance of cultural variables is increasingly accepted and valued (Swanson and Gore, 2000), most modern vocational choice theories do not include the influence of such contextual factors as educational and socioeconomic background, and the environment in which the individual grows up (Tang, 2003). And cultural context was shown to make a difference in the way people make decisions and choose their work (Fouad and Byars-Winston, 2005). The meaning of work, the value placed on it, and the expectations about who should perform what type of work reflect the society in which work is organized (Carter and Cook, 1992). Work holds different meanings for different people as a function of their sociocultural experiences (Cheatham, 1990). Growing globalization of the workforce increases the need of career counselors to understand the cultural context of their work (Savicas, 2003).

In response to these and similar criticisms, the purpose of the study described in this chapter, advocating a culture-centered approach, was to shed light on various antecedents (e.g. the influence of key people and occupational home background) and correlates (e.g. the meaning of work and various work attitudes) of career choice of young men and women who are aspiring to two professions (management and entrepreneurship) from five cultural perspectives: Israel, the UK, Turkey, North Cyprus and Hungary.

Following Leong and Brown's (1995) criticism of research on contextual variables in vocational psychology, which has focused on establishing either cultural validity (across different cultural groups) or cultural specificity (focus on a specific cultural group), the current study attempted to combine both perspectives by comparing a focus on the five countries with a focus on one country – Israel.

Hofstede (1991) suggested four criteria for distinguishing among cultures: individualism versus collectivism (in a collectivistic culture the interest of the group prevails; in an individualistic culture, the interest of the individual prevails); power distance (the degree of inequality among people that is accepted in a particular culture); masculinity versus femininity (a masculine culture is characterized by assertiveness and competitiveness; a feminine culture is characterized by warmth and collaboration); and uncertainty avoidance (the degree to which people in a particular culture prefer structured over unstructured situations). According to Hofstede, Israelis are more individualistic than collectivistic, they are characterized by an extremely small power distance, are more feminine than masculine and are strong on uncertainty avoidance. The study that served as the basis for the current chapter examined the influence of these cultural characteristics on Israeli MBA students as compared to MBA students in the UK, Turkey, Cyprus and Hungary – countries that are very different from Israel on all four of Hofstede's (1991) criteria.

Life in Israel is stressful and fraught with uncertainties. Since Israel is a very small country (you can drive from north to south in eight hours and from west to east in two hours) with a small population (about seven million), there are few opportunities for occupational mobility. Men and women serve in the army and men bear the burden of military reserve service until they are 50. Aside from all this, Israel has a high percentage of Holocaust survivors and their offspring, and others who believe that the country was established on the ashes of the victims of the Holocaust. For them, the establishment and existence of Israel are a guarantee that the Holocaust will never happen again, because persecuted Jews now have a place that will open its gates to them. Israel is reminded frequently that there are still today those who would like it to be eliminated.

Since its establishment in 1948, Israel has been through five major wars. Even during periods of peace, soldiers are killed protecting its borders and civilians live with a constant threat of terrorist activity. People's bags are checked whenever they enter public places and periodically terrorists and bombs explode, causing death and injury.

It is important to note that the above description fits primarily those Israelis who were either born in Israel or came from Europe after the war who served in the army and lived in Israel during its first 50 years of existence, who helped to build it and identify with it. It fits less well Arab citizens and new immigrants who have arrived in Israel in recent years, especially those who came for economic rather than ideological reasons (Pines, 2004).

Interestingly, cross-cultural studies of burnout show that Israelis report relatively low levels of burnout (Etzion and Pines, 1986; Pines, 2004). An explanation that was offered, which fits existential theory (e.g. Becker, 1973), is that Israelis' lives have a greater sense of significance. People who confront regularly the death of young soldiers protecting their country's borders, who expect a terrorist bomb in every public place, are more acutely aware of death and consequently of the significance of their own lives. According to the existential perspective, people need to believe that their lives are meaningful, that the things they do are useful and important. Frankl (1976) wrote that 'the striving to find meaning in one's life is the primary motivational force in man' (p. 154). Becker (1973) argued, similarly, that people's need to believe that the things they do are meaningful is their way of coping with the angst caused by facing their mortality. In order to be able to deny death, people need to feel heroic, to know that their lives are meaningful, that they matter in the larger 'cosmic' scheme of things. Based on the existential perspective, it can be expected that the meaning of work will be more important to Israeli MBA students than it will be for students in other countries.

In addition to the role of culture, the current chapter examines the role of gender – a social phenomenon that refers to learned sex-related behaviors and attitudes of males and females – in the choice of careers in management and entrepreneurship. The examination of the role of gender in this context is important in light of three seemingly unrelated items: (a) the very small numbers of women in positions of top management and entrepreneurship; (b) the view of an MBA as a means for breaking through the glass ceiling into major management positions (Simpson et al., 2004); and (c) the growing numbers of publications noting women's relative advantage in management (e.g. Eagly and Johnson, 1990; Fisher, 1999; Helgesen, 1990). Four theories in psychology seem relevant to the role of gender in the context of career choice in management and entrepreneurship: evolutionary, psychoanalytic, social role and social construction theories.

According to *evolutionary* theory, during the thousands of years that modern man's ancestors traveled in small hunting and gathering bands, the sexes did different jobs and developed different skills (Buss, 1995; Buss and Schmitt, 1993; Darwin, 1871). As a result, modern-day men tend to place themselves in hierarchies whereas women tend to be more interested in cooperation, connections and networks. Based on the evolutionary perspective, men are 'innately' more interested in management roles than women.

According to feminist *psychoanalytic* theory, psychological gender differences, including men's competitive nature and preference for being at the top of pyramid-shaped organizations and women's preference for being at the heart of web-shaped organizations (Gilligan, 1982), are the result of different childhood experiences and different developmental tasks that boys and girls face in growing up (Chodorow, 1978). Based on psychoanalytic theory, as a result of their different childhoods, men are likely to be more interested in management roles than women.

Social role theory emphasizes social forces such as norms, stereotypes and gender role expectations (Basow, 1992; Eagly and Wood, 1999; Spence and Buckner, 2000; Wood and Eagly, 2002). Culture is defined as 'the collective programming of the mind which distinguishes the members of the group or category of people from another' (Hofstede, 1991, p. 5). Based on gender role theory, gender differences in management and entrepreneurship are a result of the different roles (Eagly and Wood, 1999; Wood and Eagly, 2002) and differences in real power that men and women have in organizations (Kanter, 1993). Based on social role theory, women are less interested in management roles than men because these are seen as masculine (Henning and Jardim, 1978).

According to *social construction theory*, reality is socially constructed (Bohan, 1997; Butler, 1990, 1993; DeLamater and Hyde, 1998; Gergen and Davis, 1997; Mednick, 1989). There is no one 'reality'. Different cultures have their unique understandings of the world. People tend to divide the world into opposites (we–them, men–women), and emphasize the differences between them while the similarity is often far greater than the difference (Tavris, 1992). Instead of emphasizing gender differences, social constructionists emphasize the subjective experience of individuals as well as cultural differences. Indeed, research has shown absence of cross-culturally consistent gender differences in the way men and women construe the meaning of values (Struch et al., 2002) and, regarding work-related attitudes, the results of a national study conducted in Israel showed no gender differences in values associated with entrepreneurship (Raz et al., 2006). Based on social construction theory, it can be expected that the cultural differences in variables associated with a career choice in management and entrepreneurship will be greater and more significant than gender differences. In the current study, these four theories were examined in the context of cultural and gender differences among MBA students, 'the workforce of the future', according to Burke and Ng (Chapter 13 in this volume), who are aspiring to become either managers or entrepreneurs in five countries – Israel, the UK, Turkey, Cyprus and Hungary. Based on evolutionary theory and psychoanalytic theory, gender differences in career aspiration are universal, and thus it can be expected that they will be larger and more consistent than the cross-cultural differences. Based on social role theory, it can be expected that there will be both gender and cross-cultural differences in the career aspirations of MBA students. Based on social construction theory, similarities between young men and women MBA students can be expected to be greater than the differences found between them, and gender differences will be smaller than the cross-cultural differences.

The context in which these cultural and gender differences will be examined in the current chapter, as noted before, is career choice in management and entrepreneurship. Managers and entrepreneurs were described as enactments of archetypes on the organizational stage, management as the activity of introducing order by coordinating the flow of things and people toward collective action, and entrepreneurship as the making of new worlds (Czarniawaka and Wolff, 1991). Significant scientific interest focused on these two leaders of the organizational stage (as examples of publications that focused on managers, see Kets de Vries, 1995; Lapierre, 1991; Maurer, 1999; Zaleznik, 1990, 1991; as examples of publications that focused on entrepreneurs, see Aldridge, 1997; Bonnett and Furnham, 1991; Brandstaetter, 1997; Cooper and Gimeno Gascón, 1992; Frese et al., 2000; Kets de Vries, 1996). Relatively little research compared the two.

Studies that compared managers and entrepreneurs showed different value orientation (Kecharanata and Baker, 1999), different mindsets (Reynierse, 1997) different business attitudes (Stimpson et al., 1993) and even different brain dominance (Buergin, 1999). A study that compared successful Israeli entrepreneurs and managers revealed a number of differences (e.g. entrepreneurs' greater love of challenge and managers' greater realism) as well as similarities (e.g. a similar need for control and a similar commitment) (Pines et al., 2002). Entrepreneurs also had a greater sense of significance in their work. The question why managers and entrepreneurs are who they are was answered within a psychoanalytic–existential framework that focuses on the managers' positive identification with their father and better relationship with both parents as compared to the entrepreneurs' negative identification with their father and greater identification with work. Based on this research, differences can be expected between aspiring entrepreneurs and managers in such things as the factors and people that influenced their career choice, the motivation for their career choice and the significance of work.

In summary, the following five hypotheses were examined in the study:

1. Based on evolutionary and psychoanalytic theories, it was hypothesized that gender differences in variables related to career choice in management and entrepreneurship would be more consistent and larger than the cross-cultural differences.

2. Based on social role theory, it was hypothesized that there would be both gender differences and cross-cultural differences in the variables related to these career choices.
3. Based on social construction theory, it was hypothesized that the cross-cultural differences would be larger than the gender differences.
4. Based on existential theory, it was hypothesized that the meaning of work would be more important to Israeli students than to students in other countries.
5. Based on studies comparing entrepreneurs and managers, it was hypothesized that differences would be found between students aspiring to be entrepreneurs and students aspiring to be managers.

METHOD

Participants

A total of 552 MBA students, assumed to be similar in age, education, socioeconomic status and career goals, comprised the subjects, 108 were Israelis (51 percent men and 49 percent women mean age 28), 108 Turks (50 percent men, 50 percent women, mean age 24), 104 from North Cyprus (61 percent men 39 percent women mean age 26), 95 from the UK (48 percent men, 52 percent women, mean age 33) and 137 from Hungary (49 percent men and 51 percent women, mean age 23).

Instrument

A self-report measure was especially assembled for the purpose of the study. It included seven parts: (1) a five-item measure of citizenship (e.g. giving money to charity) Cronbach's alpha = 0.63 (Vigoda, 2002); (2) a 16-item measure of individualistic versus collectivistic values (Triandis and Gelfand, 1998), Cronbach's alpha for the eight individualism items = 0.74, for the eight collectivism items = 0.62; (3) 14 factors that influenced one's career choice (Özbilgin et al., 2005); (4) the influence of various people on one's career choice (e.g. father, mother, friend, manager); (5) ten expectations from an MBA degree (e.g. acquire knowledge, career advancement); (6) seven work values (e.g. work's importance and significance) Cronbach's alpha = 0.86, nine-item protean view of career success (e.g. I navigate my own career according to my plans) versus four-item traditional view (career success means having job security within one organization) (Baruch, 2006), Cronbach's alpha for the protean items = 0.76, for the traditional items = 0.78; (7) biographical information (e.g. age, gender), occupational home background (father's and mother's occupations) and career goals (e.g. management, own one's own business, make money).

All questions were answered using seven-point scales ranging from 1 = not at all, never, etc. to 7 = very much so, all the time etc.).

Procedure

The instrument was translated from English into the various languages using back translation. The translated questionnaires were administered during class. Students were asked to volunteer for a cross-cultural study of career choice in management. They were assured that their responses would remain anonymous. Most students agreed to participate. Responding to the instrument took about 15–20 minutes.

RESULTS

In order to test the six key variables (meaning, collectivism/individualism, protean career/conventional career and citizenship) for cross-cultural and gender differences, a 5×2 multivariate analysis of variance (MANOVA) (country $\times$ gender) was performed. The analysis revealed a significant difference among the five countries: $F(24, 2144) = 9.52$, $p < 0.001$, $eta^2 = 0.10$. The means and standard deviation (SD) of the six measures in the five countries (in rank order according to the size of the means in the Israeli sample) as well as the results of a univariate analysis of variance (ANOVA) that was performed on each key measure separately are presented in Table 2.1.

Table 2.1   Means and standard deviations of the six measures in the five countries

Measures	Israel M (SD)	UK M (SD)	Turkey M (SD)	Cyprus M (SD)	Hungary M (SD)	F(4, 538)	Eta^2
Meaning	5.8 (0.9)	5.1 (0.8)	5.4 (1.1)	5.5 (1.2)	5.1 (0.9)	9.6***	0.05
Protean career	5.6 (0.6)	5.2 (0.7)	5.8 (0.7)	5.5 (0.8)	4.9 (0.8)	25.4***	0.07
Conventional career	5.7 (1.0)	5.1 (1.1)	5.6 (1.1)	5.5 (1.1)	5.1 (1.0)	9.4***	0.16
Collectivism	5.4 (0.7)	5.1 (0.7)	5.5 (0.6)	5.5 (0.8)	5.1 (0.8)	7.7***	0.17
Individualism	5.0 (0.8)	4.4 (0.8)	5.1 (0.8)	5.1 (1.0)	4.7 (0.8)	15.0***	0.10
Citizenship	4.5 (1.1)	3.9 (1.0)	4.4 (1.0)	4.5 (1.1)	3.5 (0.8)	27.1***	0.07

*** $p < 0.001$.

Table 2.1 reveals cross-cultural differences in all six variables, with large effect size for citizenship, medium effect size for individualism, and small effect size for all other measures. In order to identify the source of the differences, Scheffe paired comparison tests were performed. According to these tests, Israelis not only ranked highest for the meaning of work; they were among the countries that ranked highest for a protean view of career (the group included Israelis and Turks). They rated low on: individualism, collectivism and traditional view of career (the group included Israelis, Turks, Cypriots).

The 5×2 multivariate MANOVA also revealed significant differences between men and women $F(6, 533) = 4.97$, $p < 0.001$, $eta^2 = 0.05$. The small effect size suggests that gender explains only 5 percent of the difference found. The results of a univariate ANOVA that was performed on each measure separately for men and women revealed significant gender differences in only two variables: citizenship and work meaning; in both cases women's means were higher than men's means. For the meaning of work: $MW = 5.48$, $SD = 1.0$, $MM = 5.28$, $SD = 1.04$, $F(1, 538) = 7.28$, $p < 0.01$, $eta^2 = 0.01$. For citizenship: $MW = 4.24$, $SD = 1.08$, $MM = 3.99$, $SD = 1.0$, $F(1, 538) = 13,60$, $p < 0.001$, $eta^2 = 0.03$. No significant gender by culture interaction was found $F(24, 2144) = 1.15$, $p > 0.05$, which is to say that the differences between men and women are similar in the five countries.

A multivariate MANOVA (country $\times$ gender) was also performed on the ten expectations from an MBA degree the students had. The analysis revealed a significant effect for country: $F(40, 2108) = 8.89$, $p < 0.001$, $eta^2 = 0.14$ and for gender: $F(10, 524) = 4.27$, $p < 0.001$, $eta^2 = 0.08$, but no country $\times$ gender interaction effect: $F(40, 2108) = 1.25$, $p > 0.05$.

The means and standard deviations of the ten expectations in the five countries (rank ordered according to the means in the Israeli sample) as well as the results of a univariate ANOVA that was performed on each expectation separately are presented in Table 2.2.

As can be seen in Table 2.2, there were significant differences between the five countries in eight of the ten expectations the students were asked about, including: acquire knowledge, career advancement, enhanced value in the job market, improve my analytical skills and critical thinking, entrepreneurial competence, managerial competence, social prestige, and competence for setting up your own business. The only two expectations from an MBA degree that did not show a cross-cultural difference were career advancement and salary gain.

In order to identify the source of the differences among the countries in the ratings of the ten expectations, Scheffe paired comparison tests were performed. According to these tests, Israelis were among the countries that ranked highest in only two expectations: to acquire knowledge and

Table 2.2 *Means and standard deviations of the expectations from an MBA in the five countries*

Expectations	Israel M (SD)	UK M (SD)	Turkey M (SD)	Cyprus M (SD)	Hungary M (SD)	F country	Eta^2
Acquire knowledge	6.2 (0.9)	6.1 (0.9)	6.3 (1.0)	6.4 (0.9)	5.5 (1.4)	15.4***	0.10
Career advancement	6.2 (1.0)	5.7 (1.1)	6.4 (1.1)	6.2 (1.1)	5.5 (1.2)	14.4***	0.10
Value in job market	6.0 (1.1)	5.9 (1.2)	6.3 (1.2)	5.9 (1.4)	5.1 (1.4)	14.7***	0.10
Improve analytic skills	5.7 (1.3)	6.1 (1.0)	6.2 (1.0)	6.3 (1.1)	5.5 (1.3)	9.9***	0.07
Salary gain	5.5 (1.6)	5.4 (1.6)	5.8 (1.4)	5.3 (1.7)	5.3 (1.4)	1.5	0.01
Entrepren. competence	5.2 (1.5)	4.7 (1.8)	6.2 (1.1)	5.9 (1.4)	4.5 (1.6)	28.9***	0.18
Managerial competence	5.2 (1.7)	5.9 (1.0)	6.3 (1.0)	5.8 (1.6)	4.4 (1.6)	32.2***	0.19
Social prestige	4.9 (1.5)	4.5 (1.7)	5.5 (1.7)	5.4 (1.8)	5.3 (1.4)	10.5***	0.05
Career change	4.6 (1.7)	4.6 (1.8)	4.2 (2.1)	4.1 (2.2)	4.4 (1.7)	1.3	0.01
Set up own business	4.2 (2.0)	4.1 (2.0)	4.9 (2.0)	5.2 (2.0)	4.2 (1.8)	6.5***	0.05

*** $p < 0.000$.

enhanced value in the job market. They were among the countries that ranked lowest in the expectation of improving their analytic skills and for setting up their own business.

As noted earlier, the multivariate MANOVA also revealed a significant gender effect. Examination of the means and the F tests for gender (see Table 2.3) suggests that women rated as significantly more influential five expectations: to acquire knowledge (MW = 6.26, MM = 5.86), improve their analytical skills and critical thinking (MW = 6.06, MM = 5.78), enhance their value in the job market (MW = 5.97, MM = 5.66), managerial competence (MW = 5.52, MM = 5.32), and social prestige (MW = 5.26, MM = 5.01). There was no expectation that men rated higher than women.

An additional multivariate MANOVA (country × gender) was performed on the 14 factors that influenced the career choice of the students. The analysis revealed a significant effect for country: $F(56, 2028) = 8.56$, $p < 0.001$, eta$^2 = 0.19$ and for gender: $F(14, 504) = 3.87$, $p < 0.001$, eta$^2 = 0.10$, but no country × gender interaction effect $F(56, 2028) = 1.28$, $p > 0.05$.

Table 2.3 Means of men's and women's expectations from an MBA in the five countries

	Israel		UK		Turkey		Cyprus		Hungary		F gender	Eta^2
	M	W	M	W	M	W	M	W	M	W		
Acquire knowledge	6.0	6.4	6.0	6.3	6.0	6.6	6.2	6.6	5.3	5.7	23.8***	0.04
Career advancement	6.1	6.2	5.8	5.7	6.3	6.6	6.1	6.3	5.4	5.5	2.2	0.00
Value in job market	6.0	6.1	5.8	6.1	6.0	6.6	5.7	6.1	5.0	5.3	8.7*	0.02
Improve analytic skills	5.4	6.0	5.9	6.2	6.0	6.4	6.2	6.4	5.5	5.6	10.5**	0.02
Salary gain	5.6	5.4	5.6	5.3	5.8	5.8	5.2	5.5	5.2	5.4	0.0	0.00
Entrepren. competence	5.0	5.5	5.1	4.3	6.1	6.4	5.7	6.3	4.4	4.6	1.3	0.00
Managerial competence	4.9	5.5	5.7	6.0	6.2	6.4	5.7	5.9	4.3	4.4	4.4*	0.01
Social prestige	4.8	5.0	4.7	4.3	5.2	5.8	5.2	5.9	5.2	5.3	4.1*	0.01
Career change	4.5	4.7	4.7	4.6	4.3	4.1	4.0	4.3	4.5	4.3	0.0	0.00
Set up own business	4.5	4.0	4.7	3.6	5.2	4.7	5.0	5.5	4.2	4.3	3.2	0.01

* p<0.05; ** p<0.01; ***p<0.001.

The means and standard deviations of the 14 factors in the five countries (rank ordered according to the means in the Israeli sample), as well as the results of a univariate ANOVA that was performed on each factor separately, are presented in Table 2.4.

Table 2.4 reveals significant differences among the five cultures in all 14 of the factors that influenced the students' career choice: their skills and abilities, their education and training, promotion opportunities, the belief that they have free choice in making their career decision, their love of the career, financial rewards in the career, training and education opportunities in the career, their financial and economic conditions, their knowledge of the labor market, the quality of life associated with the career, success stories, chance, luck or circumstances, ease of access to this career and lack of access to other career options.

Table 2.4   Means and standard deviations of the factors that influenced career choice in the five countries

	Israel M (SD)	UK M (SD)	Turkey M (SD)	Cyprus M (SD)	Hungary M (SD)	F country	Eta^2
Skills and abilities	6.3 (0.8)	6.0 (0.9)	6.5 (0.7)	6.5 (0.9)	6.0 (1.2)	7.6***	0.10
Education and training	5.8 (1.3)	5.5 (1.3)	6.3 (0.8)	6.4 (0.8)	5.7 (1.2)	13.8***	0.10
Promotion opportunities	5.7 (1.1)	5.1 (1.3)	6.4 (0.9)	6.0 (1.4)	5.4 (1.2)	17.1***	0.12
Free choice	5.6 (1.1)	5.2 (1.4)	6.1 (1.1)	6.1 (1.3)	5.4 (1.4)	8.8***	0.06
Love of the career	5.6 (1.2)	5.1 (1.4)	6.4 (0.8)	6.1 (1.2)	5.0 (1.7)	24.9***	0.16
Financial rewards	5.4 (1.2)	5.1 (1.4)	6.3 (0.8)	5.9 (1.1)	5.6 (1.1)	15.8***	0.11
Training opportunities	5.2 (1.4)	5.2 (1.2)	6.0 (1.1)	6.0 (1.2)	5.2 (1.5)	11.8***	0.08
Financial conditions	5.0 (1.4)	4.7 (1.5)	5.5 (1.3)	5.5 (1.5)	4.1 (1.9)	17.1***	0.12
The job market	5.0 (1.5)	4.5 (1.5)	5.7 (1.1)	5.8 (1.1)	5.0 (1.4)	16.0***	0.11
Quality of life	4.9 (1.5)	5.1 (1.4)	6.4 (0.8)	6.0 (1.0)	5.5 (1.2)	26.9***	0.17
Success stories	4.5 (1.5)	4.3 (1.6)	4.9 (1.5)	5.1 (1.5)	4.4 (1.6)	5.1***	0.04
Chance, luck	4.1 (1.6)	4.6 (1.7)	5.0 (1.6)	4.8 (1.8)	3.0 (1.8)	27.7***	0.18
Ease of access	3.4 (1.5)	4.3 (1.5)	4.4 (1.4)	4.7 (1.7)	3.3 (1.4)	17.5***	0.12
Lack of other options	3.0 (1.6)	3.6 (2.0)	4.0 (1.6)	4.2 (1.7)	2.1 (1.0)	35.9***	0.22

*** p < 0.000.

In order to identify the source of the differences among the countries in the 14 factors, Scheffe paired comparison tests were performed. According to these tests Israelis were among the countries that ranked highest for rating only two factors as having influenced their career choice: their skills and abilities, and the belief that they had free choice in making their career decision. On the other hand Israelis were among the countries that rates lowest in: the influence of financial rewards, training opportunities, the quality of life offered by the career, knowledge of the job market and the ease of access into the career.

As noted earlier, the multivariate MANOVA also revealed a significant gender effect. Examination of the means for males and females and the F tests for gender (see Table 2.4) suggests that women rated as significantly more influential five factors: the training and education opportunities in the career (MW = 5.65, MM = 5.30), their own skills and abilities (MW = 6.36, MM = 6.12), their own education and training (MW = 6.04, MM = 5.80), the influence of luck, chance, or circumstances (MW = 4.34, MM = 4.07) and the lack of other options (MW = 3.41, MM = 3.19).

Another multivariate MANOVA (country × gender) was performed on the nine people who influenced the career choice of the students. The analysis revealed a significant effect for country: $F(36, 1748) = 7.15$, $p < 0.001$, $eta^2 = 0.13$ but no significant effect for gender: $F(9, 434) = 0.98$, $p = 0.46$, and no country × gender interaction effect $F(36, 1748) = 73$, $p = 0.088$.

The means and standard deviations of the influence of the nine people in the five countries (rank-ordered according to the means in the Israeli sample), as well as the results of a univariate ANOVA performed on each factor separately, are presented in Table 2.6.

The results reveal significant cross-cultural differences in the influence of father, mother, partner, manager, colleague and teacher/mentor. The largest difference was found in the influence of manager, colleague and teacher/mentor; the smallest significant difference was found in the influence of father. No differences were found in the influence of a relative, fellow student and friend. In order to identify the source of the differences, Scheffe paired comparison tests were performed. According to these tests Israelis ranked lowest in the influence of a teacher/mentor and were among the countries that ranked lowest in the influence of manager and partner.

A univariate ANOVA that was performed on each of the categories of people separately showed no significant gender differences.

When describing the goals the students had for their future, 32.8 percent wrote 'management', 20.3 percent 'own my own business' and 8.4 percent 'entrepreneurship'. The other 39 percent mentioned such goals as 'career advancement' (28.4 percent), 'make a lot of money' (6.3 percent) and 'career change' (3 percent).

Table 2.5   Means of men's and women's factors that influenced career choice in the five countries

	Israel		UK		Turkey		Cyprus		Hungary		F gender	Eta^2
	M	W	M	W	M	W	M	W	M	W		
Skills and abilities	6.2	6.4	5.9	6.1	6.3	6.6	6.4	6.6	5.9	6.2	9.2**	0.02
Education and training	5.7	6.0	5.6	5.4	6.0	6.6	6.3	6.6	5.6	5.8	7.4***	0.01
Promotion opportunities	5.9	5.5	5.3	5.0	6.1	6.6	5.9	6.1	5.4	5.5	0.0	0.00
Free choice	5.7	5.5	5.2	5.2	5.8	6.3	6.1	6.1	5.7	5.2	0.3	0.00
Love of the career	5.8	5.4	5.4	4.8	6.1	6.6	6.2	6.1	5.1	4.9	2.5	0.00
Financial rewards	5.6	5.3	5.4	4.8	6.2	6.3	5.9	6.0	5.5	5.7	1.1	0.00
Training opportunities	5.1	5.3	5.3	5.2	5.6	6.4	5.8	6.2	5.0	5.3	11.1**	0.02
Financial conditions	5.3	4.7	5.1	4.4	5.5	5.6	5.3	5.7	4.0	4.3	0.4	0.00
The labor market	4.9	5.0	4.9	4.1	5.4	6.0	5.8	5.8	5.1	4.8	0.2	0.00
Quality of life	5.0	4.9	5.1	5.0	6.2	6.6	6.0	6.1	5.5	5.5	0.3	0.00
Success stories	4.4	4.5	4.4	4.2	4.7	5.0	4.9	5.4	4.4	4.5	0.9	0.00
Chance, luck	3.9	4.3	4.5	4.7	5.0	5.1	4.4	5.4	3.0	3.0	5.4*	0.01
Ease of access	3.4	3.4	4.5	4.1	4.3	4.4	4.3	5.2	3.3	3.4	1.0	0.00
Lack of other options	2.8	3.3	3.7	3.4	3.9	4.2	3.7	4.9	2.2	2.1	5.3*	0.01

* $p < 0.05$; ** $p < 0.01$.

Table 2.6   Means and standard deviations of people who influenced career choice in the five countries

	Israel M (SD)	UK M (SD)	Turkey M (SD)	Cyprus M (SD)	Hungary M (SD)	F country	Eta^2
Father	3.7 (1.9)	3.5 (1.9)	3.6 (2.0)	4.0 (2.1)	4.4 (2.0)	3.41**	0.03
Mother	3.4 (1.8)	3.4 (1.9)	3.3 (1.8)	3.8 (2.1)	4.5 (1.9)	7.83***	0.07
Partner	3.3 (2.0)	4.0 (1.9)	2.5 (2.0)	3.6 (2.2)	3.3 (2.2)	4.96***	0.04
Friend	3.2 (1.8)	3.1 (1.6)	3.3 (1.7)	3.0 (1.9)	3.4 (1.8)	0.86	0.01
Fellow student	3.0 (1.8)	2.8 (1.7)	2.9 (1.5)	2.9 (1.5)	3.1 (1.7)	0.49	0.00
Manager	2.9 (1.9)	3.8 (1.7)	3.2 (2.0)	3.8 (2.1)	1.8 (1.5)	21.65***	0.16
Colleague	2.8 (1.7)	3.4 (1.5)	2.6 (1.8)	3.1 (2.1)	2.0 (1.5)	10.27***	0.09
Relative	2.7 (1.8)	2.6 (1.7)	2.1 (1.3)	2.5 (1.6)	2.3 (1.7)	1.50	0.01
Teacher/ mentor	2.5 (1.7)	3.5 (1.9)	3.0 (1.6)	4.4 (2.1)	3.4 (1.9)	10.20***	0.08

** $p < 0.01$; *** $p < 0.001$.

A comparison between the five countries in stated career goals revealed certain similarities (such as that making a lot of money was mentioned least frequently in all five countries). However, a Pearson chi^2 also revealed a significant cross-cultural difference (chi^2 (df12) = 62, $p < 0.001$). Thus, for Israeli (and to a lesser extent for the British) MBA students the goal that was mentioned most frequently was to be a manager (47 percent and 37 percent respectively). For the North Cyprus and Turkish students, the career goal mentioned most frequently was to be an entrepreneur and build one's own business (48 percent and 40 percent respectively). For the Hungarian students the most frequently mentioned career goal was career change or career advancement (46 percent).

Pearson chi^2 also revealed cross-cultural differences in mothers' occupations (chi^2 (df12) = 91.9, $p < 0.001$) and significant but somewhat smaller differences in fathers' occupations (chi^2 (df12) = 56.6, $p < 0.001$). Overall, the highest percentage of mothers were employees (40.5 percent) or unemployed (34.2 percent), and the lowest percentage were managers (11.7 percent) and entrepreneurs/business owners (13.6 percent). In comparison, the highest percentage of fathers were entrepreneurs or business owners (33.3 percent); only slightly fewer were employees (32.2 percent) or managers (26.7 percent). Very few fathers were unemployed (7.8 percent).

The students whose goal was to own a business and those whose goal was to become entrepreneurs were combined into one group that included

Table 2.7 *Aspiring entrepreneurs versus managers on the six measures: total sample*

	Aspiring entrepreneurs		Aspiring managers		F	p	Eta^2
	Mean	SD	Mean	SD			
Meaning	5.25	1.16	5.49	1.00	3.85	0.05*	0.01
Protean career	5.50	0.76	5.37	0.81	1.94	0.17	0.00
Conventional	5.56	0.97	5.25	1.18	6.60	0.01**	0.02
Collectivism	5.38	0.77	5.31	0.79	0.59	0.44	0.00
Individualism	4.96	0.89	4.84	0.92	1.40	0.24	0.00
Citizenship	4.17	1.13	4.24	1.04	0.33	0.57	0.00

* $p<0.05$; ** $p<0.01$.

about one-third of the sample (29 percent). This group, of aspiring entrepreneurs, was compared to the group of students (33 percent) who described themselves as aspiring to become managers.

A cross-cultural comparison revealed significant differences in the percentage of aspiring managers and entrepreneurs (Pearson chi^2 = 25.4 (df4), p = 000). Students in Israel and the UK had the highest percentage of aspiring managers (75 percent and 60 percent respectively), whereas students in Cyprus and Turkey had the highest percentage of those aspiring to become entrepreneurs or own their own business (65 percent and 54 percent respectively).

A comparison between the male and female students also revealed significant gender differences (Pearson chi^2 = 10.6 (df1), $p<0.001$). While a higher percentage of women aspired to become managers (W = 60 percent versus M = 40 percent), a higher percentage of men aspired to be entrepreneurs or own their own business (M = 88 percent versus W = 13 percent).

The results of the comparisons between the aspiring entrepreneurs and the aspiring managers that revealed significant differences are presented in Tables 2.7 and 2.8.

A multivariate MANOVA that compared aspiring entrepreneurs and aspiring managers on the six measures revealed a significant effect for career choice F(6, 311) = 4.40, $p<0.001$, eta^2 = 0.08. The means and standard deviations of the six measures as rated by aspiring managers and entrepreneurs as well as the results of a univariate ANOVA that was performed on each measure separately are presented in Table 2.7.

As can be seen in Table 2.7, there were significant differences between aspiring managers and aspiring entrepreneurs only on two measures: conventional career (aspiring entrepreneurs rated higher) and meaning of work (aspiring entrepreneurs rated lower).

A significant difference was also found for the Israeli sample $F(6, 56) = 3.23$, $p < 0.01$, eta$^2 = 0.26$. However, in the Israeli sample the significant differences were in the meaning of work (once again, aspiring managers rated higher) and in individualism (aspiring entrepreneurs rated higher).

A multivariate MANOVA comparing aspiring entrepreneurs and aspiring managers on the ten expectations from a career in management revealed again a significant effect for career choice $F(10, 304) = 8.89$, $p < 0.001$, eta$^2 = 0.23$. The means and standard deviations of the ten expectations as well as the results of a univariate ANOVA that was performed on each expectation separately are presented in Table 2.8.

According to Table 2.8, there were significant differences between aspiring managers and aspiring entrepreneurs only in three expectations: to acquire competence for setting up one's own business and entrepreneurial competence (aspiring entrepreneurs rated higher on both) and acquire managerial competence (aspiring managers rated higher).

When the same analysis was performed for the Israeli sample, the F test was again significant $F(10, 52) = 2.43$, $p = 0.019$, eta$^2 = 0.32$. The results of a univariate ANOVA performed on each expectation show only one significant difference between aspiring managers and aspiring entrepreneurs: the expectations to acquire competence for setting up one's own business (aspiring entrepreneurs rated higher).

Table 2.8   Aspiring entrepreneurs versus managers' expectations from an MBA: total sample

	Aspiring entrepreneurs		Aspiring managers		F	p	Eta^2
	Mean	SD	Mean	SD			
Set up own business	5.74	1.68	4.15	1.91	60.82	0.000***	0.16
Entrep. competence	5.77	1.52	5.36	1.45	5.86	0.016*	0.02
Managerial comp.	5.48	1.70	5.80	1.29	3.63	0.058*	0.01
Acquire knowledge	5.99	1.18	6.08	1.06	0.59	0.44	0.00
Career advance	5.97	1.28	5.98	1.15	0.00	0.95	0.00
Analytic skills	5.96	1.20	5.99	1.10	0.50	0.82	0.00
Value in market	5.76	1.39	5.81	1.32	0.10	0.76	0.00
Salary gain	5.46	1.50	5.47	1.54	0.00	0.96	0.00
Social prestige	5.10	1.80	5.13	1.55	0.36	0.85	0.00
Career change	4.46	2.70	4.22	1.92	1.10	0.30	0.00

* $p < 0.05$; *** $p < 0.001$.

However, a multivariate MANOVA comparing aspiring entrepreneurs and aspiring managers on the 14 factors that influenced their career choice did not reveal a significant effect for career choice for either the total sample $F(14, 282) = 1.55$, $p = 0.09$, or for the Israeli sample $F(14, 51) = 1.96$, $p = 0.065$. The results of a univariate ANOVA performed on each factor separately revealed significant differences only for the influence of success stories (4.9 versus 4.6) and for financial rewards (5.9 versus 5.6). Both influenced aspiring entrepreneurs more than aspiring managers (in both cases $p < 0.05$).

A multivariate MANOVA comparing aspiring entrepreneurs and aspiring managers on the nine people that influenced their career choice did not reveal a significant effect for career choice for either the total sample $F(9, 242) = 0.81$, $p = 0.61$, or for the Israeli sample $F(9, 54) = 1.52$, $p = 0.17$. However, it is noteworthy that for both aspiring entrepreneurs and aspiring managers, father was the most influential figure. In addition, for the Israeli sample, mother (3.7 versus 2.6, $p < 0.04$), a manager (3.3 versus 2.2, $p < 0.05$) and a fellow student (3.5 versus 2.3, $p < 0.01$) were rated as more influential by aspiring managers.

DISCUSSION

When the hypotheses stated at the onset of the study are examined in light of these findings, it seems that the first hypothesis, based on the evolutionary and psychoanalytic theories, that predicted gender differences in variables related to career choice in management and entrepreneurship of MBA students to be more consistent and larger than cross-cultural differences was not confirmed.

The second hypothesis, based on social role theory, that predicted both gender differences and cross-cultural differences, was partially supported. Gender differences and cross-cultural differences were found, but there were many more cross-cultural differences, and these differences were larger than the gender differences found.

The third hypothesis, based on social construction theory, that predicted that cross-cultural differences in variables related to career choice in management and entrepreneurship would be larger than gender differences, received the greatest support. As predicted by social construction theory, the findings seem to suggest that different cultures have unique understandings of the world of work. The career aspirations of MBA students and almost all the variables associated with this choice showed significant cross-cultural differences. Most importantly, there was a significant cross-country difference in the stated goals of the MBA students, this despite

certain similarities, such as that the goal of becoming a manager was mentioned by the largest percentage of students overall (33 percent) whereas
making a lot of money was mentioned by the smallest percentage. While
the former can be explained by the fact that the stated goal of an MBA is
management, the latter can be explained in the effect of social desirability.
However, there were significant differences in the percentage of students
who aspired to be managers (the highest percentages being Israelis and
British) or entrepreneurs and business owners (the highest percentages
being Cypriot and Turkish students).

When asked about the factors that influenced their career choice, MBA
students in all five countries rated highest their 'skills, competences and
abilities' and rated lowest 'lack of access to other career options'.
Nevertheless, there were significant differences in all 14 factors asked about.
The highest differences were found in the effect of 'chance, luck or circumstances' (rated highest by Turks and Cypriots and lowest by Hungarians
and Israelis) and 'the quality of life associated with this career' (rated
highest by Turks and lowest by Israelis).

MBA students in all five countries also showed significant differences in
such assumed correlates of career choice in management and entrepreneurship as traditional versus protean views of a career success, the sense
of meaning derived from work and citizenship (in the meaning derived
from work and citizenship Israelis rated highest and Hungarians rated
lowest; in the protean view of career success Turks and Israelis rated
highest and Hungarian rated lowest).

In terms of their expectations from an MBA, despite cross-cultural similarities (e.g. to acquire knowledge being rated highest or among the highest
expectations and setting up one's own business being rated lowest or among
the lowest), there were eight significant cross-cultural differences out of the
ten asked about (the highest being the expectations to acquire entrepreneurial and managerial competences).

When examining the influence of various people on their career choice,
while, as predicted by psychoanalytic theory (Pines et al., 2002), the father
was rated as the most influential person in all five countries, there were
significant differences in the ratings of six of the nine people asked. The
biggest differences were found in the ratings of a manager and a colleague
(in both cases rated highest in the UK and Cyprus and lowest in Hungary).
Cross-cultural differences were also found in fathers' and mothers' occupations in the five countries. Interestingly, the highest percentage of fathers
(over one-third – 33 percent) were entrepreneurs or business owners and
less than one-third (27 percent) were managers, only about one-tenth of the
mothers were managers (12 percent) or entrepreneurs and business owners
(14 percent). These findings support research on the background of entre-

preneurs and managers (e.g. Cromie et al., 1992; Cooper and Gimeno Gascón, 1992; Pines et al., 2002).

In comparison to the large cross-cultural differences, when gender differences were found, they were consistently smaller. For example, the cross-cultural difference in the choice of a career in management or entrepreneurship was larger than the gender difference, showing that while a higher percentage of women aspired to become managers, a higher percentage of men aspired to be entrepreneurs or own their own business.

Small yet significant gender differences were also found in citizenship and in the meaning of work. In both cases women's means were higher than men's. These findings can be explained by social role theory in the influence of social forces such as norms and gender role expectations (Basow, 1992; Eagly and Wood, 1999; Spence and Buckner, 2000; Wood and Eagly, 2002). They can also be explained by research on women's work motivation. For example, studies on women managers show them to be more invested emotionally in their work than men (Henning and Jardim, 1978), and research on women and men MBAs shows women to be more motivated and rewarded intrinsically and men more motivated and rewarded extrinsically by an MBA (Simpson and Sturges, Chapter 22, this volume). Similarly, Richardson et al. (Chapter 9, this volume) report gender difference in intrinsic motivation for changing from business-related careers into teaching.

An analysis of the ten expectations from an MBA revealed a significant gender effect (once again smaller than the effect for country). Women rated five of the expectations as significantly more influential than men did: to acquire knowledge, improve their analytical skills and critical thinking, enhance their value in the job market, improve their managerial competence, and social prestige. There were no expectations that men rated higher than women. These findings can be explained by women's reliance on education as the main path to management positions (Sommers-Hoff, 2000).

Analysis of the 14 factors that influenced their career choice also revealed a significant gender effect (again smaller than the effect for country). Women rated as significantly more influential on five factors: the training and education opportunities in the career, their own skills and abilities, their own education and training, the influence of luck, chance or circumstances, and the lack of other options. There were no factors that men rated higher than women. These findings can be explained again by women's greater belief in education as the path to management jobs, as well as their greater belief in luck and the reality of women's fewer career options when compared to men's.

Altogether, the findings related to gender provide strong support for social construction theory (in showing larger cross-cultural differences than gender differences), and some support for social role theory (in explaining some of the gender differences found, especially in the value placed on education) and no support for evolutionary and psychoanalytic theories (in showing women clearly interested in management).

Getting back to Leong and Brown's (1995) criticism of research in vocational psychology for establishing either cultural validity (across different cultural groups) or cultural specificity (with a focus on a specific cultural group), the current study can be viewed as demonstrating the advantage of combining both perspectives: a focus on the similarities and differences between the five countries and a focus on one culture – Israel.

Based on existential theory, the fourth hypothesis examined in the study was that Israelis would rate the meaning of work higher than students in other countries. This hypothesis was supported. Findings show that Israelis ranked highest for the meaning of work (work's importance and significance, the sense of success and satisfaction in it, the love for it and commitment to it) and Israel was among the countries that ranked highest for the protean view of career success (which included items such as 'I navigate my own career according to my plans and I take responsibility for my own development').

These findings can be explained by existential theory (Becker, 1973; Frankl, 1976) and by studies of burnout (Etzion and Pines, 1986; Pines, 2004) that suggest that because Israelis confront regularly the threat of death, they are more acutely aware of the significance of their life. The finding that Israelis rated highest, as factors that influenced their career choice, their skills and abilities and the belief that they had free choice in making their career decision can be explained by low power distance (Hofstede, 1991).

A cross-cultural comparison also showed significant differences in the percentage of aspiring managers versus entrepreneurs. Students in Israel had the highest percentage of aspiring managers whereas students in North Cyprus had the highest percentage of aspiring entrepreneurs.

The comparison between aspiring entrepreneurs and managers provided only partial support for the fifth hypothesis. While, as predicted, there were both similarities and differences between MBA students aspiring to be entrepreneurs and those aspiring to be managers, there were far fewer differences than similarities. The most meaningful differences, it seems, were found in the expectations from a MBA: the expectations to acquire competence for setting up one's own business, acquire entrepreneurial competence (aspiring entrepreneurs were higher in both) and acquire managerial competence (aspiring managers were higher). These findings can be viewed as validating the distinction made in the study between aspiring entrepreneurs and aspiring managers. Another important validation is the fact that Chimo-Vugalter and Lerner, who compared MBA graduates who became entrepreneurs with those who did not (Chapter 8 in this volume) report a similar percent (31.5 percent as compared to the 28.7 percent aspiring entrepreneurs in this study). They also report that this percentage is significantly higher – almost three times than the percentages of individuals who became entrepreneurs within the general population.

The most meaningful similarity found between aspiring entrepreneurs and managers was that, for both, father was the most influential figure in their career choice. Other than that, the differences found (e.g. that aspiring entrepreneurs rated lower the meaning of work) contradict the findings reported in other studies that compared successful entrepreneurs and managers (e.g. Pines et al., 2002) and may suggest that acquiring an MBA is not the typical educational path for aspiring entrepreneurs. Alternatively, as noted by Baruch and Blenkinsopp (Chapter 14 in this volume), business education may be the breeding ground for the next generation of entrepreneurs. In the Israeli sample, however, both mother and manager (an authority figure) were rated as more influential by aspiring managers than by aspiring entrepreneurs, findings that seem more in line with the well-adjusted picture of managers (see Pines et al., 2002; Kaplan, Chapter 6; Yanai et al., Chapter 7 in this volume).

Despite its obvious limitations (relatively small samples that despite all efforts were not as homogeneous as expected, using a self-report measure in a cross-sectional design), the findings have important theoretical and practical implications. Theoretically, they demonstrate the value of studies that combine cultural validity with cultural specificity and test several theoretical propositions (in this case, psychoanalytic theory, evolutionary theory, social role theory, social construction theory and existential theory). The practical implications point to the importance of culture- and gender-sensitive career counseling for young people who are considering careers in management and entrepreneurship.

Future studies will need to use larger samples, more countries, other methodology (including especially qualitative methods) and longitudinal research design (comparing pre- and post-MBA attitudes). Some of these studies are already in progress.

REFERENCES

Aldridge, J.H. (1997), 'An occupational personality profile of the male entrepreneur as assessed by the 16PF Fifth Edition', *Dissertation Abstracts International*, **58**(5B): 2728.

Baruch, Y. (2006), 'Career development in organizations and beyond: balancing traditional and contemporary viewpoints', *Human Resource Management Review*, **16**: 125–38.

Basow, S. (1992), *Gender Stereotypes and Roles*, Pacific Grove, CA: Brooks/Cole.

Becker, E. (1973), *The Denial of Death*, New York: Free Press.

Bohan, J.S. (1997), 'Regarding gender: essentialism, constructionism and feminist psychology', in M.M. Gergen and S.N. Davis (eds), *Toward a New Psychology of Gender*, New York: Routledge, pp. 31–47.

Bonnett, C. and Furnham, A. (1991), 'Who wants to be an entrepreneur? A study of adolescents interested in a Young Enterprise scheme', *Journal of Economic Psychology*, **12**: 465–78.

Brandstaetter, H. (1997), 'Becoming an entrepreneur: a question of personality structure?', *Journal of Economic Psychology*, **18**: 157–77.

Buergin, A.O. (1999), 'Differences between Swiss entrepreneurs and Swiss managers in brain dominance, achievement motivation, and locus of control', *Dissertation Abstracts International*, **59**(10A): 3877.

Buss, D.M. (1995), 'Psychological sex differences: origins through sexual selection', *American Psychologist*, **50**: 164–8.

Buss, D.M. and Schmitt, D.P. (1993), 'Sexual strategies theory: an evolutionary perspective on human mating', *Psychological Review*, **100**: 204–32.

Butler, J. (1990), *Gender Trouble: Feminism and the Subversion of Identity*, London: Routledge.

Butler, J. (1993), *Bodies that Matter*, London: Routledge.

Carter, R.T. and Cook, D.A. (1992), 'A culturally relevant perspective for understanding the career paths of visible racial/ethnic group people', in H.D. Lea and Z.B. Leibowitz (eds), *Adult Career Development: Concepts, Issues and Practices*, 2nd edn, Alexandria, VA: National Career Development Association, pp. 192–217.

Cheatham, H.E. (1990), 'Africentricity and career development of African Americans', *The Career Development Quarterly*, **38**: 334–46.

Chodorow, N. (1978), *The Reproduction of Mothering*, Berkeley, CA: University of California Press.

Cooper, A.C. and Gimeno Gascón, F.J. (1992), 'Entrepreneurs, processes of founding, and new firm performance', in D.L. Sexton and J.D. Kasarda (eds), *The State of the Art of Entrepreneurship*, Boston, MA: Kent Publishing, pp. 301–40.

Cromie, S., Callaghan, I. and Jansen, M. (1992), 'The entrepreneurial tendencies of managers: a research note', *British Journal of Management*, **3**: 1–5.

Czarniawaka, J.B. and Wolff, R. (1991), 'Leaders, managers, entrepreneurs on and off the organizational stage', *Organization Studies*, **12**: 529–46.

Darwin, C. (1871), *The Descent of Man and Selection in Relation to Sex*, New York: D. Appleton.

DeLamater, J.D. and Hyde, J.S. (1998), 'Essentialism vs. social constructionism in the study of human sexuality', *Journal of Sex Research*, **35**: 10–18.

Eagly, A.H. and Johnson, B. (1990), 'Gender and leadership style: a meta analysis', *Psychological Bulletin*, **108**: 233–56.

Eagly, A.H. and Wood, W. (1999), 'The origins of sex differences in human behavior: evolved dispositions versus social roles', *American Psychologist*, **54**: 408–23.

Etzion, D. and Pines, A.M. (1986), 'Sex and culture in burnout and coping among human service professionals', *Journal of Cross Cultural Psychology*, **17**: 191–209.

Fisher, H. (1999), *The First Sex: The Natural Talents of Women and How they are Changing the World*, New York: Random House.

Fouad, N.A. and Byars-Winston, A.M. (2005), 'Cultural context of career choice: meta analysis of race–ethnicity differences', *The Career Development Quarterly*, **53**: 223–33.

Frankl, V.E. (1976), *Man's Search for Meaning*, New York: Pocket Books.

Frese, M., Chell, E. and Klandt, H. (2000), 'Psychological approaches to entrepreneurship. Introduction', *European Journal of Work and Organizational Psychology*, **9**: 3–6.

Gergen, M.M. and Davis, S.N. (eds) (1997), *Toward a New Psychology of Gender*, New York: Routledge.

Gilligan, C. (1982), *In a Different Voice: Psychological Theory and Women's Development*, Cambridge, MA: Harvard University Press.

Ginzberg, E. (1951), *Occupational Choice*, New York: Columbia University Press.

Hall, D.T. (1996), 'Long live the career', in D.T. Hall and associates (eds), *The Career is Dead – Long Live The Career*, San Francisco, CA: Jossey-Bass, pp. 1–14.

Helgesen, S. (1990), *The Female Advantage: Women's Way of Leadership*, New York: Doubleday.

Henning, M. and Jardim, A. (1978), *The Managerial Woman*, New York: Pocket Books.

Hofstede, G. (1991), *Cultures and Organizations: Software of the Mind*, London: McGraw-Hill.

Kanter, M.R. (1993), *Men and Women of the Corporation*, New York: Basic Books.

Kecharanata, N. and Baker, H.G. (1999), 'Capturing entrepreneurial values', *Journal of Applied Social Psychology*, **29**: 820–33.

Kets de Vries, M.F.R. (1995), *Life and Death in the Executive Fast Lane*, San Francisco, CA: Jossey-Bass.

Kets de Vries, M.F.R. (1996), 'The anatomy of the entrepreneur', *Human Relations*, **49**: 853–83.

Lapierre, L. (1991), 'Exploring the dynamics of leadership', in M.F.R Kets de Vries et al. (eds), *Organizations of the Couch: Clinical Perspectives on Organizational Behavior and Change*, San Francisco, CA: Jossey-Bass, pp. 69–93.

Leong, F.T.I. and Brown, M.T. (1995), 'Theoretical issues in cross cultural career development: cultural validity and cultural specificity', in W.B. Walsh and S.H. Osipow (eds), *Handbook of Vocational Psychology*, 2nd edn, Hillsdale, NJ: Erlbaum, pp. 143–80.

Maurer, J. (1999), 'The proactive personality disposition and entrepreneurial behavior among small company presidents', *Journal of Small Business Management*, **37**: 28–36.

Mednick, M.T. (1989), 'On the politics of psychological constructs: stop the bandwagon, I want to get off', *American Psychologist*, **44**: 1118–23.

Özbilgin, M.F., Küskü, F. and Erdoğmuş, N. (2005), 'Explaining influences on career "choice": the case of MBA students', *International Journal of Human Resource Management*, **16**(11): 2000–28.

Parsons, F. (1909/1989), *Choosing a Vocation*, Garrett Park, MD: Garrett Park Press.

Pines, A.M. (2004), 'Why Israelis are less burned out', *European Journal of Psychology*, **9**: 1–9.

Pines, A.M., Sadeh, A., Dvir, D. and Yaffe-Yanai, O. (2002), 'Entrepreneurs and managers: similar yet different', *International Journal of Organizational Analysis*, **10**: 172–90.

Raz, A., Pines, A.M. and Schwartz, D. (2006), 'Venture culture and high-technology entrepreneurship', paper presented at the International Congress of Applied Psychology, Athens, Greece, July.

Reynierse, J.H. (1997), 'An MBTI model of entrepreneurism and bureaucracy: the psychological types of business entrepreneurs compared to business managers and executives', *Journal of Psychological Type*, **40**: 3–19.

Savicas, M.L. (2003), 'Advancing the career counseling profession: objectives and strategies for the next decade', *The Career Development Quarterly*, Alexandria, **52**: 87–96.

Simpson, R., Sturges, J., Woods, A. and Altman, Y. (2004), 'Career progress and career barriers: women MBA graduates in Canada and the UK', *Career Development International*, **9**: 459–77.

Sommers-Hoff, Christina (2000), *The War Against Boys*, New York: Simon & Schuster.

Spence, J.T. and Buckner, C.E. (2000), 'Instrumental and expressive traits, trait stereotypes and sexist attitudes: what do they signify?', *Psychology of Women Quarterly*, **24**: 44–62.

Stimpson, D.V., Narayanan, S. and Shanthakumar, D.K. (1993), 'Attitudinal characteristics of male and female entrepreneurs in the US and India', *Psychological Studies*, **38**: 64–8.

Struch, N., Schwartz, S.H. and Kloot, W.A. (2002), 'Meaning of basic values for women and men: a cross-cultural analysis', *Personality and Social Psychology Bulletin*, **28**: 16–28.

Super, D.E. (1953), 'A theory of vocational development', *American Psychologist*, **8**: 185–90.

Super, D.E. (1957), *The Psychology of Careers*, New York: Harper & Row.

Swanson, J. (1996), 'The theory is the practice: trait and factor/person–environment fit counseling', in M.L. Savickas and B.W. Walsh (eds), *Handbook of Career Counseling: Theory and Practice*, Palo Alto, CA: Davies-Black, pp. 93–108.

Swanson, J. and Gore, P. (2000), 'Advances in vocational psychology theory and research', in S.D. Brown and R.W. Lent (eds), *Handbook of Counseling Psychology*, 3rd edn, New York: Wiley, pp. 233–69.

Tang, M. (2003), 'Career counseling in the future: constructing, collaborating, advocating', *The Career Development Quarterly*, Alexandria, **52**: 61–9.

Tavris, C. (1992), *The Mismeasure of Women*, New York: Simon & Schuster.

Triandis, H.C. and Gelfand, M.J. (1998), 'Converging measurement of horizontal and vertical individualism–collectivism', *Journal of Personality and Social Psychology*, **74**: 118–28.

Vigoda, E. (2002), 'Administrative agents of democracy? A Structural Equation Modeling (SEM) of the relationship between public sector performance and citizenship involvement', *Journal of Public Administration Research and Theory*, **12**(2): 241–72.

Wood, W. and Eagly, A.H. (2002), 'A cross-cultural analysis of the behavior of women and men: implications for the origins of sex differences', *Psychological Bulletin*, **128**: 699–727.

Zaleznik, A. (1990), *Executive's Guide to Motivating People*, Chicago, IL: Bonus Books.

Zaleznik, A. (1991), 'Leading and managing: understanding the difference', in M.F.R. Kets de Vries et al. (eds), *Organizations of the Couch: Clinical Perspectives on Organizational Behavior and Change*, San Francisco, CA: Jossey-Bass, pp. 97–119.

3. Collectivistic attitudes and solidarity with a focus on Hungary: value preferences of management students in Cyprus, the UK, Israel, Turkey and Hungary

Agnes Utasi

The study described in this chapter focuses on the value preferences – especially values concerning collectivism and solidarity – of 567 management students in Cyprus, the UK, Israel, Turkey and Hungary. The focus of the sociological analysis offered in the chapter, and both the similarities and differences found using this analysis, is the Hungarian students. The similarities found are explained by the influence of globalization. The differences found are explained by the influence of socialization in value-mediatory communities in general, and in the case of the Hungarian students in the influence of a value-ambivalent society. Hungarian society underwent four decades of socialism with its destructive effect on traditional communities, and since 1989 has moved to a neocapitalist market economy and extreme individualism. Among the distinctive features of the Hungarian society, the chapter focuses on the value of solidarity.

PECULIARITIES OF THE HUNGARIAN SAMPLE

The sample was taken from MA management students in Israel, Turkey, the UK and Cyprus. In Hungary, two-level management training started only in the autumn of 2006; therefore, as opposed to the other countries, the distinction between the BA and MA levels was not possible. The Hungarian sample was chosen from the last two years' students of the five-year university program so as to guarantee the compatibility of the sample (total sample: N = 567). The subjects were selected among the students attending lectures on economics at two universities in Hungary (Budapest, Szeged). The girls proved more diligent in attending lectures; that is why the balance between the two sexes in the sample was ensured by weighting after data collection (total sample: N = 567, Hungarian sample: N = 138).

RESEARCH AIMS AND HYPOTHESES

Our analysis focused on the community attitude and solidarity values of the university students. According to our hypothesis, on the one hand, the value preferences of the students belonging to different national cultures show a partial generational similarity due to globalization. On the other hand, national–cultural particularities and the influence of socialization in value-mediatory communities are also included. Among the communities shaping value preferences, besides family and the school community, religion also exercises a significant influence. However, owing to the relatively small number of cases in the international sample, the cultural value-mediatory effect of different religions can be investigated only in the cases of students who defined themselves as Christian, Muslim, Jewish, atheist and 'not religious'. The great majority of the Hungarian sample describe themselves as 'Christian' or 'do not belong to any religion'. The present chapter focuses on the distinctive features of the Hungarian value preferences and their peculiarities, which differ from the cultural values of the other samples in the survey.

Besides the above-mentioned influences, the Hungarian students' values were also shaped by the anti-religious, secular ideology of the four decades of socialism and its destructive effect on traditional communities. After the political transformation of 1989, traditional communities were not reorganized, and up to the time of writing there has been little formation of civil communities; thus the integrative effect of communities is small in Hungary (Utasi, 2002). The value system of society changed markedly at the same time as socialism was replaced by the market economy in 1989. Private property and the market economy, in place of state ownership, developed very fast, and the size of state resources decreased in line with it, so that socialist social welfare was also radically reduced. Market economy competition was paralleled by extreme individualization, atomization of society, and a great increase in inequalities. Even socialism had begun to undermine traditional communities, and with the arrival of the neocapitalist market economy, the artificial, instrumentally or functionally motivated socialist communities of the socialist era also fell to pieces. The value system of Hungarian society has become ambivalent, and Hungarian university students are socialized in a society that mediates conflicting values.

CULTURAL DIFFERENCES IN THE UNIVERSITY STUDENTS' STATUS OF ORIGIN

International educational statistics show that a higher proportion of a given age group studies at university in more developed, wealthier societies than in poorer ones (Gazsó, 1976; Bourdieu, 1980; Boudon, 1973).

Consequently, in wealthier societies even the descendants of families of lower social status gain access to higher education in large numbers. Given that a smaller proportion of youth can attend universities in poorer societies, status reproduction among graduates is necessarily stronger there, and the ratio of students with high-status parents is apparently higher. It is also true that every society endeavors to increase its power partly by social mobility; thus it helps the outstandingly gifted children of low-status parents to gain access to universities by means of scholarships. Notwithstanding these kinds of effort, universities provide the opportunity to earn a degree and take up prestigious occupations mainly for the descendants of high-status, wealthy citizens in those societies that lack resources.

In the international sample, these differences are illustrated by the university students from societies with different levels of economic well-being and technical–social advancement. We examined the composition of the management students in each national sample with the help of a three-category variable of the father's occupation (employee; management/professional; entrepreneur/business owner); see Figure 3.1.

The children of the lowest-status group, the employees, have the greatest chance of being part of the management students' sample in the UK (40 percent) and Israel (31.7 percent). The corresponding figures are

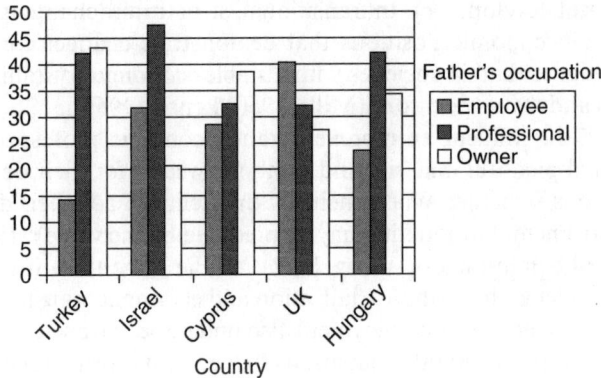

Figure 3.1   Distribution of the national sub-samples according to father's occupation (%) (management students, 2005/2006, N = 517)

significantly lower in Cyprus and Hungary (29 and 24 percent), and especially low in the Turkish sample (14 percent). It is evident from these facts
that in line with the growing economic well-being of societies, a growing
proportion of the descendants of lower-status families can gain access to
higher education.

International prestige research has also drawn attention to the fact that
the various university degrees and the status of the occupations that the
holders of a particular degree can pursue differ. As a result, it is reasonable
to assume that among university majors that prepare for more prestigious
occupations the ratio of status reproduction is higher, even in wealthier
countries, while there is a higher chance that young people who were socialized in lower-status families get into university majors that predestine them
for occupations with lower prestige (Treiman, 1977).

Our previous international research, carried out among university students (Pines et al., 2005), concluded that the prestige of high-tech entrepreneurs coincides with the level of developmental advance of the country
in question. This research also demonstrated that the prestige value of
lawyers – who had made wealth accumulation and 'money making' during
privatization lawful – and managers has been raised in Hungary, a country
that has just become a market economy and lacks resources. At the same
time, in the more affluent, technologically more developed Israel and the
USA, human values replaced material goods at the top of the value scale,
and together with this change, the medical profession had the highest prestige value (Utasi, 2002).

The sample of our present survey includes future management graduates. Based on the foregoing, we hypothesized that the prestige value of a
management degree differs in societies at diverse levels of well-being and
technological development. In transitional, structurally changing societies,
the value of economic positions that demonstrate a direct contact with
money is higher than in societies with a stable economy, crystallized social
structures and status positions (Mills, 1960; Lenski, 1966).

Most of the affluent entrepreneurs and economic professionals have
accumulated plentiful material and symbolic wealth for their descendants
in prosperous societies. When their children choose a career, direct economic instrumental rationality may be preceded by the value rationality of
professional commitment (Weber, 1982). At the same time, it is also true
that, in parallel with the industrialization and economic transformation of
societies, the structure of employment also undergoes a transformation: the
proportion of professional occupations that are not directly related to production is growing.

In our sample, the proportion of the descendants of self-employed and
entrepreneur parents studying economic-related topics in higher education

is lower (21–28 percent) in countries at a higher level of developmental advance, e.g. Israel and the UK, while in Turkey (43 percent), Cyprus (39 percent) and Hungary (34 percent) the corresponding rates are relatively higher. This trend suggests that in poorer countries it is so far more important for entrepreneur fathers, in possession of less financial capital, that the education of their children yields a profit, their investment is refunded, and the degree helps them to find a lucrative job in the economic sphere.

DIFFERENCES IN THE PRAXIS AND ATTITUDE OF SOCIAL SOLIDARITY AND CHARITY

Social solidarity that helps the weak, altruistic charity and/or reciprocity between members of society are the fundamental conditions of the functioning of primitive and agrarian societies (Durkheim, 1986; Parsons, 1951). In most cases, rapid industrialization forced open the limits of traditional mechanical solidarity, whilst, together with the process of individualization, welfare institutions were established in civilized societies that provide 'professional' help for the weak and the needy. The wealthier a society is, the more efficiently it is able to help those who are in need with institutional, organic solidarity (Durkheim, 1986). Moreover, when the economy prospers in a society, it offers more to those in need and it allocates more to the disadvantaged, but during recession, the level of organic solidarity remains low. However, there is no society so wealthy that it can dispense with mechanical solidarity and civil charity as part of the network of immediate social contacts. That is to say, interpersonal and civil community charity are indispensable means of social integration in both poor and wealthy societies (Fararo and Doreian, 1998; Pines et al., 2002).

Our previous research data suggest that the intensity of everyday solidarity towards others, towards strangers, is low in Hungary. This attitude is partly the consequence of the central redistribution of the socialist era and the social benefits of all-embracing state care. During the four decades of this social system, when wages were on a very low level, the 'patriarchal' party-state took care of those in need. Medical service was a universal right. The disabled and the old – if the family did not undertake to care for them – were placed in social welfare homes or chronic wards of hospitals. Each and every healthy man of active age was bound to work, so everyone received some income. Education was free of charge until the age of 18, and the number of young people who gained admission to free higher education was low and regulated. Begging and living on the street as a homeless person was forbidden. State care and wide-scale organic solidarity exempted the relatively wealthy from the moral law and ethical obligation of charity.

After the change of system, parallel with the rapid development of the market economy, keen competition and rivalry rose in Hungarian society. Inequality among the social strata had grown in great measure during a short period of time. Due to useful information received from personal relationships and to strokes of luck, some quickly rose to affluence during privatization. This group interprets its wealth solely as a personal merit, as the well-deserved reward for their capacity, and they blame those who lost their employment for laziness. These days, the wealthy rarely feel solidarity for those who lag behind. They seldom do charity work; rather they accumulate financial capital. Moreover, even social institutions are unable to provide the same aid as they used to during the socialist era. The marginalized can hardly rely on the charity of the few civil organizations in Hungary. According to the latest data, at the most every fourth adult is a member of a civil organization in Hungary, and only a small proportion of them take active part in the work of a charity organization (Utasi, 2004).

Sociological surveys also reveal that in Hungary almost everyone provides assistance if one of their close relatives is in need, especially the members of the nuclear family. However, charity for others, for strangers, only functions in the case of grave disasters, and it is limited to a short period of time. That is, traditional mechanical solidarity subsists after all, but the amplitude of the range of help has been almost exclusively reduced to the most intimate family circle (Utasi, 2002a).

The extent of the management students' charity is far lower in Hungary than in all the other countries of the sample. The level of charity was measured on a five-point scale in the survey: the subject (1) has given money to a beggar, (2) has donated goods or clothes through a charity organization, (3) has done voluntary work for a community, (4) has helped a student or other stranger by giving directions or guidance, and (5) has offered his/her seat on a bus or train to an old or disabled person who was standing. The first three indicators investigated the praxis of charity with material goods, while the remaining two referred to practices and attitudes of a moral nature (for more on this measure see Vigoda, 2002, and Vigoda and Grimland, Chapter 12 in this volume).

On the basis of the aggregated scale value of the first three questions, three-quarters of the students in the Hungarian sample never or very rarely practice material forms of charity. There are few civil organizations in Hungary, so the opportunities for practicing charity through such organizations are evidently rare. Israel and Cyprus take the lead in charity, where almost two-thirds of the students often do charity work. The mean of the index that measures the degree of giving assistance is the highest in Israel (11.5), and only slightly lower in Cyprus (11.2), but its standard deviation is the highest there. In the Hungarian sample, the mean of the charity index is only the half of the value measured in the leading countries (6.1). The standard deviation is the lowest here, too; in other words, charity is generally low, with the lowest measure among the Hungarian population.

Charitable attitudes and helpful conduct towards the weak are referred to by the scales that measure the degree of helping others with guidance and giving directions, and the occurrence of offering one's seat courteously. Answers to the latter two questions show significantly fewer differences between the national samples. Data demonstrate that supportive attitude and sympathetic courtesy are especially strong among the Turkish students, and almost as high in the Israeli and Cypriot sample. Compared to them, the attentiveness of the UK and Hungarian management students is only a little lower.

The graph of the aggregated five-factor charity index (SOLIDARITY), which covers the three kinds of charity practice and the two attitudes of courteous, helpful conduct, demonstrates the significant difference between the levels of charity in the countries studied (see Figure 3.2).

The observed levels of synthesized charity do not follow the differences in material well-being of the countries. For example, the Turkish do charity work more intensively that the English, although the economic conditions of the former are considerably worse. We hypothesize that the principal differentiating factor behind national differences in social solidarity and charity is not economic well-being, but the extent of macro-community integration and micro-community cohesion and the difference between

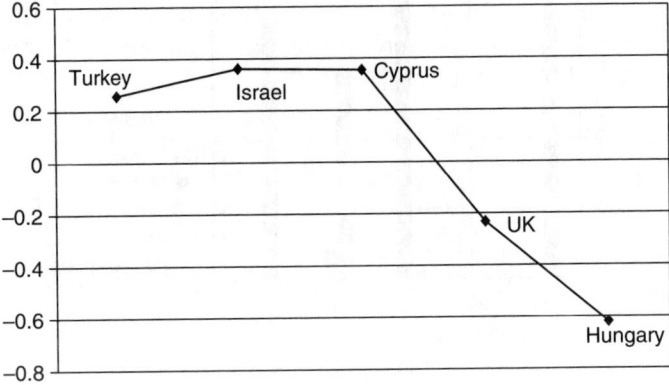

Figure 3.2   Trend of mean of the SOLIDARITY index (Z-score)
(management students, 2005/2006, N = 567)

value preferences. Thus the pursuit of the praxis of charitable values is a better indicator of the extent of integration in a certain society than the level of material well-being.

If we accept that the cultural values of a society have a stronger effect on charity than economic well-being, we may also assume that religion, as a mediator of cultural values, is also a differentiating factor of the extent of charity. The praxis of charity is the strongest among the followers of the Jewish and Muslim religions. In contrast, the solidarity of Christians, atheists and the non-religious is lower.

However, it is also known that the dominant religions are not the same in different countries of the sample. For example, the ratio of atheists and the non-religious is exceptionally high in Hungary (21.3 percent) and in the UK (32.4 percent), while their proportion is insignificant in the other three countries investigated. Christianity prevails in the UK and in the Hungarian sample, but Christians are rarely found in other countries of the sample (see Figure 3.3).

The very high ratio of atheists and non-religious people in the Hungarian sample is most likely related to the anti-religious ideology of the socialist era. Moreover, the demonstrated lack of solidarity among the Hungarian Christians is also connected to the socialist social transformation and the ambiguous modernization effects.

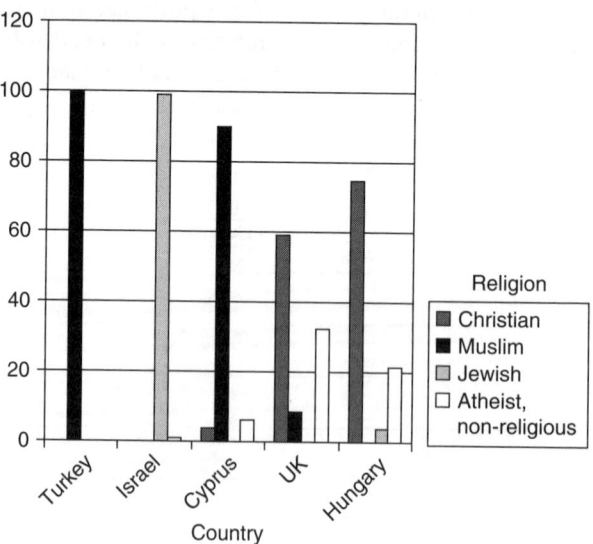

*Figure 3.3   Religious distribution of the national sub-samples (%)
(management students, 2005/2006, N = 567)*

If we examine the index of charity praxis along the religions, we find that the followers of the Jewish and Muslim religions are the most charitable. These two religions can essentially be found among the Israeli and Turkish students. Mostly Muslims live in Cyprus, too, and social solidarity and charity are also strong there.

Of course it remains to be seen why religions differ. After all, the praxis of affection and charity is accentuated in the value system of all world religions. Considering the weaker solidarity among the students in the UK and Hungary, we cannot conclude that Christianity bestows 'less' solidarity value to its believers than other religions. We consider the weakness of macro-community integration and ambiguous modernization in these two countries as owing to more decisive reasons. Due to strong secularization, the ratio of non-religious people is higher in these two countries of the sample than in the others. However, we also hypothesize a difference between Hungary and the UK with regard to the processes that led to secularization. Anglicanism used to be the established religion, and it expected considerable material support and tax from its members. Thus belonging to the Anglican Church carried prestige, and wealthy, high-status citizens were overrepresented in it. We detected this phenomenon in an international comparative survey (Utasi, 1989) as early as the 1980s: about one-third of the British are non-religious. This percentage was approximately ten times higher in the UK than in the 'socialist' Hungary of that time, where only 3.4 percent of the sample were non-religious in spite of the official anti-religious ideology (Utasi, 1989).

Consequently, secularization was primarily catalyzed by the general spread of rationalized values that accompanied modernization, by the radical separation of state and religion, and by the emergence of relatively strong civil communities in the UK. In Hungary, it resulted from the disintegration of traditional cultural communities and the reduction of community values, which went together with official anti-religious ideology and ambiguous modernization. However, providing help within the close family circle, that is traditional micro-social solidarity, has remained strong in both countries.

SIMILARITIES AND DIFFERENCES IN COLLECTIVE ATTITUDE AND INDIVIDUAL SELF-ASSERTION

In Hungary, macro-community integration and the pursuit of traditional cultural values were significantly reduced by the process of the development of the market economy after 1989. Hungarians were looking forward to the new system, but financial security, which had been available to everyone, but guaranteed only a low standard of living, vanished due to the change of economic structure. The inequality between the first and the tenth income deciles was doubled in a few years, from quadruple to octuple. Inequality between the strata was intensified in all fields (Andorka, 1995). Unemployment appeared. In the economy, intense individual competition loosened the ties with colleagues, neighbors and friends.

Instead of the one and only party of socialism, a multi-party political structure developed as the fundamental institution of democracy; the Russian army left the country, but civil society has not developed, and the democratic participation of citizens is insufficient. The feeling of security of the majority of society has been shattered: they feel defenseless, and they regard it as pointless to participate personally in the formation of democracy. Compared to the citizens of other countries, significantly fewer Hungarians feel that they are able to influence the measures of their government or participate in local decisions (Utasi, 2006).

Our research examined the scope of individuals' collective identity and attitude. It may include the whole society, thus helping macro-social integration; or only the close family, the immediate community; or individual lives with no concern for either macro- or micro-society, each following only his/her own interest. Our research differentiated these three dominant features of community attitude and mentality from the scale indicating values connected to life and attitudes towards others. We found different proportions of these types of community-integrated attitudes in each country investigated (see Table 3.1).

The attitude of self-dependence, avoiding relying on others if possible, is least frequent in the Hungarian sample. The attitude of independent decision making and autonomy at the workplace could not thrive during socialism in Hungarian society, which was used to the system of centrally controlled planning and the state of being employees, and which had to rely on state care. Work and even social–community life were mostly centrally controlled. This kind of functioning of the system was based on school education, which followed Prussian-like traditions and did not encourage the democratic expression of individual opinion. The centuries-long lack of national sovereignty also repressed the values of independence and self-reliance, because they were unattainable. Redistributive state care and lack of independence exercised an effect even on the simplest decisions of the individual, who carried neither the responsibility nor the burden of his/her essential life decisions. Thus state care chained the individual to him/herself and made them dependent on others.

Among university students, the lack of resources in society greatly affected the need for self-reliance. The relative poverty of families, the lack of a scholarship system that effectively helps the poor, juvenile unemployment and the

Table 3.1   *Agreement with items on attitude scales (grades 6–7)*
            (management students, 2005/2006, N = 567)

	Agree (%)				
	Turkey	Israel	Cyprus	UK	Hungary
I'd rather depend on myself than on others	67	71	68	49	41
It is important that I do my job better than others	81	71	66	34	35
If a fellow students gets a prize, I feel proud	66	71	63	28	30
Parents and children must stay together as much as possible	27	24	38	41	49
I rely on myself most of the time; I rarely rely on others	33	40	49	26	25
Winning is everything	14	20	24	8	6
The well-being of my fellow students is important to me	56	70	54	35	20
It is my duty to take care of my family, even if I have to make sacrifices	70	62	73	66	30
I often do 'my own thing'	34	32	36	24	45
Competition is the law of nature	59	47	56	28	55
To me, pleasure is spending time with other people	40	45	37	44	70
Family members should stick together, no matter the sacrifices required	81	31	70	27	59
My personal identity, independent of others, is very important to me	81	60	70	47	56
When another person does better than I do, I get tense and aroused	20	15	71	49	56
It is important to me to respect the decisions made by my group	60	65	63	55	42

lack of opportunities for working during their studies force young people into the role of children for a long period of time, and detain their need for self-dependence. As a result of these social conditions, fewer Hungarians expressed a need for self-dependence than in other countries of the sample. (The rates of those who chose grades 6–7 of the seven-grade scale were: Hungary, 41 percent; Turkey, 67 percent; Israel, 71 percent; Cyprus, 68 percent; the UK, 49.5 percent.)

The endeavor *to do one's job better than others* is also less characteristic of the management students of Hungary and the UK. In these two countries, at most every third student considers the outcome of their labor important (grades 6–7 on the scale). The Turkish are characterized by the strongest ambition for work: four-fifths of them and two-thirds of the Israeli and the Cypriots want to do their work better than others.

The grade on the attitude scale of *'winning is everything'* alludes to the rejection of keen competition and the need for success-oriented development. This attitude is the most rejected by the Hungarians: one-third of them reject the mentality of winning by any means. It is also true that at least one-fourth of the sample in each country and one-fifth in Israel reject the exorbitant ambition to win at any price. The preferred value of the competitive society of modernization is nowhere supported by the majority of the students (Beck, 2003).

However, it is also true that the majority of the subjects consider that *competition is the law of nature*, the Hungarians as well as the Turkish and the Cypriots. The British accept the least that competition is the natural law. They may follow the ancient principle that the goal of competition is not victory over others but over oneself (Aristotle, 1984). However, the value system and challenges of modern competitive societies are quite alien to the ancient ethical principle. In today's society, individual resources are necessarily unequal, so the result of a competition cannot be fair. Competitive societies are rarely able to appreciate the greatest individual investments. However, the majority of subjects regard competition as a natural part of life, accepting that it is not investment, but a good start, that is the key to success.

Feeling glad about the success of colleagues is the most widely accepted in cultures that emphasize community values the most: three-quarters of the Turkish and the Israeli sample and two-thirds of the Cypriots rated themselves on grades 6 or 7 of the scale. As opposed to these countries, negative rivalry among colleagues is stronger in the UK and Hungary. Only every fourth British and every third Hungarian indicated that they are able to feel glad about the success of their colleagues.

In Hungary, rivalry among colleagues intensified as a result of neocapitalism after the conversion to a market economy. Accompanying the change of the economic structure and privatization, workplaces that proved uneconomic were liquidated, and many employees were dismissed. The intense struggle for positions deepened the antagonism between colleagues, and broke the functionally cooperative collegial communities and instrumental friendships of the workplace. In addition, some colleagues who had similar capabilities and lived in similarly narrow circumstances during the socialist era luckily rose to affluence through legal, a-legal or illegal means. And the increasing wealth and status differences reduced rather than strengthened the ability to feel happy about the success of others.

In Hungary, entrance exams of students in their last academic year were also accompanied by intense competition. Only a low proportion of the age group of senior university students gained access to higher education, since the state-determined admission rates were low. Fellow students competed against each other: the success of one could mean the failure of the other. The ratio of university students among the young generation has recently doubled in Hungary. The previous rivalry among students will potentially decrease in their first or second school year.

A similar idea is investigated by the notion that the *well-being of fellow students is very important* to the respondent. Almost three-fourths of the Israeli and half of the Turkish and Cypriot sample agree with this statement. In contrast, in the UK sample only every third and in Hungary at most every fourth respondent regards the well-being of their fellow students as important.

The percentage of *self-assertive* management students is highest in the Hungarian sample. This attitude is probably reinforced by neocapitalism, which created extreme individualization and inequality. Solidarity that preserves social unity, the attitude of paying attention to the opinion and interest of others, together with charity as 'naïve mercy' (Weber, 1982), may be to an individual's disadvantage under the conditions of a market economy that generates extreme individualization. And as a consequence, the individual would fall behind in a competitive society. The strong individual desire for success is the preferred value in the Hungarian society lacking resources. At the same time, this value counteracts solidarity and a community attitude. Forty-five percent of the management students placed themselves on the two highest grades of the scale that measures the preference for individual advancement in all circumstances, whereas only one-third of the non-Hungarian students considered themselves self-assertive. In the UK, in addition, only one-fourth belonged to the respective group.

The strong self-assertive attitude, the desire for individual advancement and at the same time the urge to strive for security is stronger than individual self-realization and excellence. Based on the above, we can assume that the *time spent with others*, that is, *social life*, is most important for the Hungarian youth (70 percent). People from samples of other countries did not share this opinion (28 percent in the UK and 46 percent in Turkey). Moreover, time spent with others does not serve as a source of pleasure for almost four-fifths of the Cypriots.

In Hungarian society, the breaking of social ties and increased atomization are principally generated by individual efforts aimed at establishing financial security. Resulting from this tense struggle for consumption, financial security and individual advancement, the intimate social–community relations of the individual are reduced and the proportion of those having friends tends to decline under neocapitalism (Angelusz and Tardos, 1998; Utasi, 2002b). People were driven to form part of communities constructed in a formal and centralized manner by the former socialist framework; however, even emotionally motivated ties could work well within the boundaries of such a functional cooperation (Weber, 1987). The individual success orientation of today's society atomizes the individual and reduces what remains of the social ties, while the space and time for the establishment of new ties are not available.

The majority of those who think that *families should stay together as long as possible* are Hungarian. This assumption alludes to the preferred values of the traditional family; more precisely, it refers to the wish for the traditional union of the nuclear family. Every second Hungarian in the sample has a definite desire to achieve this. The British tend to view this question almost as important as Hungarians do (42 percent). Only one-third of the Cypriots and one-fourth of the Israelis and Turks thought that families should stay together. We found community solidarity very strong in the Israeli and Turkish societies; however, at the same time, individuals regard togetherness and the protection of the values of the close family as less indispensable. Moreover, about one-fifth of the Turks and Cypriots clearly reject this principle. However, the instrumental function of family ties serves as the basic condition of financial security and well-being of members of the family in Hungarian society. Moreover, among other traditional values, child-centeredness and the wish to protect the nuclear family maintained a prominently significant position. The praxis, however, does not accompany the family-centered attitude (Pongrácz and Spéder, 2003).

Another scale, according to which *family members should stay together regardless of the sacrifice required*, indicates only a partly similar attitude. Answers express concern for the functioning of the network of solidarity of the wider family. This principle involves mutual assistance within the family and altruism. This strong traditional solidarity is very common in Turkish families. On the one hand, 81 percent of the Turks, 71 percent of the Cypriots and 60 percent of the Hungarians think that solidarity between family members, regardless of the sacrifice required, is essential. On the other hand, only 31 percent of the Israelis and 27 percent of the British concur with this austere requirement.

The attitude requiring solidarity between family members is relatively strong in the Hungarian sample. The Hungarian management students accept the norm of supporting indigent family members, while they also regard individual advancement and self-assertive success as important. Resulting from the transformation to a market economy, the Hungarian pursuit of family values is largely ambivalent. The mechanical solidarity within the boundaries of the family remained strong; moreover, it became the only means for achieving social–community solidarity and charity.

Individuals expect their social environment to support their individual advancement and success goals by being integrated. However, Hungarians do not allow altruism to limit individuals in achieving their goals. The scale values responding to *it is my duty to take care of my family, even if I have to make sacrifices* demonstrate the above-mentioned fact. The value of individual, altruistic sacrifice for family members is least shared among the family-centered Hungarian youth, who prefer collective family integration: only 30 percent agree with making sacrifices for and altruism towards the family. Moreover, a great proportion (14 percent) categorically refuse to make individual sacrifices that serve family interests. Consequently, Hungarians accept solidarity tasks shared among members of the family, but only a few regard individual altruism as an obligation.

The opinion of the Hungarian students was probably formed by the prevailing attitude of the strongly child-centered Hungarian society. The young may have experienced, in time of hardship, the sacrifice expected from the older members of the family. Taking the burden off the shoulders of the young becomes a self-assertive attitude within the family. Diverging from Hungarians, 75 percent of the Cypriots, 70 percent of the Turks, 66 percent of the British and 62 percent of the Israelis believe that it is essential and compulsory to take care of their own family regardless of the circumstances.

TYPES OF COMMUNITY INTEGRATION AND SOLIDARITY

We analyzed the different attitudes and value preferences one by one, and some of the scales indicated significant differences among the countries. We searched for types of integration and the proportion and characteristics of certain types among the students of different countries by synthesizing the information content of particular scales. We differentiated three levels of social–community connectedness using cluster analysis (K-means cluster) based on the attitude variables:

1. Cluster 1: *Individual self-assertive*, focusing on individual advancement and success (20.5 percent overall, among Hungarians 38.3 percent);

2. Cluster 2: *Macro-community integration*, regarding the success and interest of the members of macro-society as equally important as those of their immediate environment (45.6 percent overall, among Hungarians 25 percent);
3. Cluster 3: *Micro-community integration*, considering the life and social contacts of the immediate community, especially the family, important (34 percent overall, among Hungarians 36.7 percent).

Of the three clusters, the attitude of the majority of the respondents was characterized by *macro-community integration* concerning the interests of the whole society. Furthermore, students from Turkey, Cyprus and Israel were most likely to share the attitude of *macro-community integration*. Their attitude was marked by connectedness to the surrounding community. Their micro-community attitude forms part of their macro-community attitude, in that they desire the immediate community to become integrated with the macro-community (see Figure 3.4).

In the international sample, the proportion of those who do not wish particularly to succeed in the modern, competitive macro-society is lower. At the same time, being together in a community is very important for them, which relates to the high quantity of time spent with the network of strong ties. Principally, they are integrated into the micro-community.

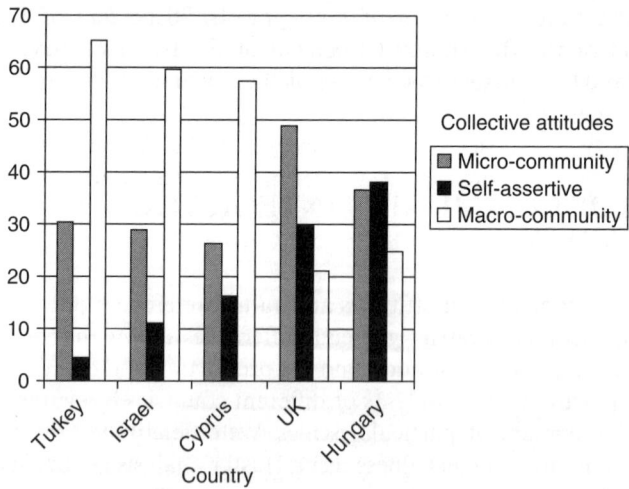

Figure 3.4 *Distribution of the national sub-samples according to collectivistic attitudes (%) (management students, 2005/2006, N = 567)*

According to these attitudes, the proportion of those who are most inte-grated into the community of relations of the family, relatives and friends is the highest in the samples of the UK and Hungary.

Self-assertive individuals are characterized by competition and success orientation. They wish to exceed others by relying on individual perform-ance. Their attitude is not at all community-oriented; even altruism towards their own family is rare. Self-assertive and individual success-oriented people are represented in high proportion in post-socialist Hungary. Hungarians frequently tend to break close ties in order to be successful in the fight, also competing with time, for security. Hungarian students are greatly influenced by individual success values. In Hungary, the rapid and forced individualization is a clear consequence of the extreme competition of the new market economy, the effect of the previously unfamiliar unem-ployment and the fear derived from insecurity.

If we examine the composition of the groups indicating different com-munity identities on the basis of the status of origin, we find that the highest ratio of the self-assertive is found among the descendants of entre-preneurs and among students whose fathers were employed in very low-status jobs. Undoubtedly, the self-assertive attitude of both groups is the result of social pressure. On the one hand, the emergence of the children of lower-status parents required individual effort that exceeded the average. On the other hand, the successors of entrepreneurs were socialized in such families where fathers were inspired by the market to make above-average individual efforts, more than in families of higher-education graduates or successful senior executives and managers. The children of profession-als and managers have the strongest community attitude involving the macro-community.

We investigated the levels of everyday praxis of solidarity characteristic of different types of community integration. Solidarity is found the least in the praxis of the self-assertive.

At the same time, there is no significant gap between the charity of those who show macro-community connectedness and the most powerful community integration, and those who follow a collective attitude indi-cating micro-community integration. The principal difference among the latter group lies in the fact that their praxis of solidarity is chiefly limited to the close ties, as their care activities are reduced to the bound-aries of the family, whereas the charity of the members with a macro-community integration attitude extends to a broader scale of society (see Figure 3.5).

When examining the charity of groups with community integration attitudes, we observed that solidarity of the individual self-assertive falls far behind that of those with a micro- or macro-community attitude.

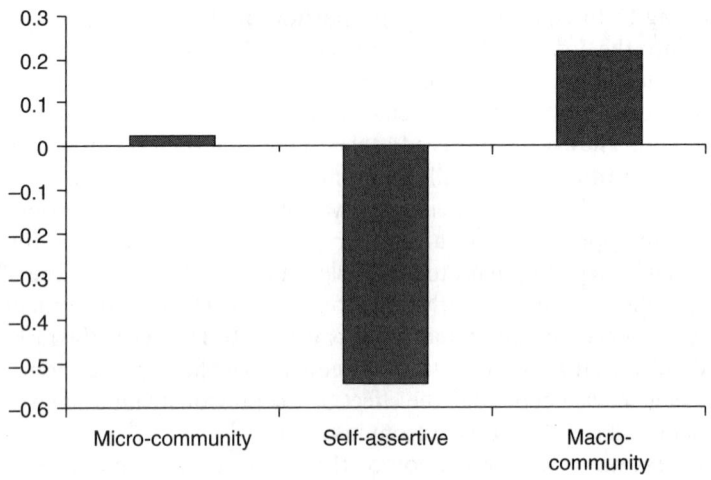

*Figure 3.5   Collectivistic attitudes and mean of SOLIDARITY index
(Z-score) (management students, 2005/2006, N = 567)*

COMMUNITY INTEGRATION TYPES TYPICAL OF THE GREAT RELIGIONS IN THE INTERNATIONAL SAMPLE

Muslims and Jews are characterized by a macro-community integration attitude. Among them, the number of individual success-oriented self-assertive is rather low; however, many of them live with micro-community attitudes.

The proportion of individual self-assertive who focus on personal advancement is the highest in the groups of Christians and those not related to any religion. Moreover, the non-religious and atheists tend to show less care for macro-community values and aims.

The dominant types of community integration are very well defined along the religions; however, one should not simplify this to the mere fact that a clear distinction may be made: there are religions that socialize towards community attitudes and there are others that promulgate contradictory values. We believe that the value-transmitting effect of religions may prevail under certain social, economic and political circumstances. It is clear that the majority of Christians, non-religious and atheists live in countries where the effects of secularization are the strongest.

Due to the above-mentioned reasons, the effect of religions that amplifies macro-community integration is weaker in the less secularized countries. Nevertheless, the micro-community attitude is quite strong in these countries.

REGRESSION MODEL OF THE DETERMINANTS OF CHARITY

The difference among cultures is very well defined in the survey on charity praxis and attitudes of students. None the less, the reason for the diverging levels of solidarity and charity, particularly the very low Hungarian charity level, remain to be discovered. Hence the reason for the regression analysis, which concludes the exploration of the dominant determinants of the field. The variable for solidarity is regarded as constant in the regression analysis. We investigated which of the three variables indicating objective conditions in the international sample: status of origin (1 = father is executive/manager/entrepreneur, 0 = employee); the effect of religious values (1 = religious attachment, 0 = atheist, not religious), and gender (1 = male, 0 = female) has the strongest effect on charity.

The final statistics of the linear regression demonstrate significant connection with all the variables involved. In other words, it indicates that among the explanatory β values the ties to any religion have the strongest effect ($\beta = 0.20$) in the sample; however, gender also plays a significant role ($\beta = -0.13$). In the latter case, the negative value suggests that females are more likely to contribute to charity than males. These two variables of the regression model explain around 30 percent of the solidarity index value. According to this, individuals with religious ties and females are more likely to be involved in caring activities. The status of origin and the often accompanying economic well-being did not show a significant relationship with the constant variable measuring charity; therefore it was omitted from the explanatory variables.

In our previous analysis, we gained knowledge regarding the lower level of Hungarian charity compared to other samples. At the same time, the proportion of those who have no ties to any religion is the highest in Hungary; however, according to the regression model of the international sample, the strongest determinant of charity is religion. Thus it was necessary to discover whether the strongest determinant is ties to a religion or derived from Hungary's specific social–economic circumstances.

The differentiating variable indicating national culture was included in the latest regression model. The constant remained the index measuring solidarity, while the explanatory variables were completed with the variable for national culture (1 = Hungarian, 0 = other). The assumption of national affiliation as the determinant in the Hungarian sample was verified by the final statistics of the analysis. This variable explained more the solidarity index than religion and gender in the first model (Country 1 $\beta = -0.351$).

The effect of gender was the same as in the first model, and furthermore, the negative value again indicates the female propensity for charity. We find religious ties among the explanatory variables; however, its value was lower. Furthermore, the positive value made it unambiguous that individuals with ties to any religion were more likely to express caring than the non-religious and atheists.

In the latest regression model, the status of origin is not a differentiating factor as it had no significant relation with the constant variable.

The findings proved that solidarity does not depend on social status or economic well-being; rather it results from value preferences and the effect of the community integration level. Students' solidarity, neither in the international nor in the Hungarian sample, depends on the economic status of the family in which they were socialized, and eventually, their caring activities are characterized by the value preferences that affected their collective attitudes.

SUMMARY AND CONCLUSIONS

Compared to the other countries, in the UK and Israel, children of the lowest-status group, employees, have the greatest chance of being management students. The corresponding figures are significantly lower in Cyprus and Hungary, and especially low in the Turkish sample. It is evident from these facts that in line with the growing economic well-being of societies, a growing proportion of the descendants of lower-status families can gain access to higher education.

At the same time, the proportion of the descendants of self-employed and entrepreneur parents with higher education is lower in countries with a higher level of technological advance such as Israel and the UK, while in Turkey, Cyprus and Hungary the corresponding rates are relatively higher. This trend suggests that in poorer countries it is more important for fathers who are self-employed, with lower financial capital, that the education of their children yields a profit, that their investment is refunded. An MBA degree is probably expected to help them to find a lucrative job in the economic sphere.

No such cross-cultural pattern is evident in the analysis of solidarity and civil charity that seem to be a part of the network of immediate social contacts. The reported levels of charity do not relate to the differences in economic well-being of the countries. The principal differentiating factor behind national differences in social solidarity and charity is not economic well-being, but the extent of macro-community integration and micro-community cohesion and the difference between value preferences.

The praxis of charity is promoted in the value system of all world religions. Considering the weaker solidarity among the students in the UK and Hungary, one cannot conclude that Christianity bestows 'less' solidarity value to its believers than other religions. The weakness of macro-community integration and ambiguous modernization in these two countries is probably due to other reasons: because of strong secularization, it is possible that the ratio of non-religious people is higher in these two countries than in the others.

Three dominant attitudes indicating values connected to life and attitudes towards others were differentiated. Different proportions of these types of attitudes were found in each country investigated. The attitude of the majority of the respondents was characterized by a macro-community integrational attitude that concerns the interests of the whole society. Students from Turkey, Cyprus and Israel were most likely to share the macro-community integrational attitude. Their attitude was marked by connectedness to the surrounding community. Their micro-community is perceived as forming a part of the macro-culture.

Those who are principally integrated into the micro-community are those who are most integrated into the community of relations of the family, relatives and friends. The highest on this dimension in the samples are the UK and Hungary.

Self-assertive individuals are characterized by competition and success orientation. Their attitude is not at all community-oriented; even altruism towards their own family is rare. Self-assertive and individual success-oriented people are represented in high proportions in post-socialist Hungary. In Hungary, the rapid and forced ambivalent individualization is a clear consequence of the excessive competition of the new market economy, the effect of the previously unfamiliar unemployment and the fear derived from insecurity. Solidarity is found the least in the praxis of the self-assertive.

Consequently, it seems that solidarity among university students does not depend on social status or economic well-being; rather it results from value preferences and the effect of community integration level. Students' solidarity, neither in the international nor in the Hungarian sample, depends on the economic status of the family in which they were socialized, and eventually, their caring activities are characterized by the value preferences that affected their collective attitudes.

REFERENCES

Andorka, R. (1995), 'A magyar társadalom: a múlt öröksége, a rendszerváltozás problémái és a lehetséges jövöbeli fejlödés 2005-ig, (Hungarian society: the heritage of the past, the problems of the change of regime, and the prospects of future development), Valóság, **38**(2): 60–91 and (3): 37–54.

Angelusz, R. and Tardos, R. (1998), 'A kapcsolathálózati eröforrások átren- dezödésének tendenciái a kilencvenes években' (Changing patterns of social network resources in the nineties), in T. Kolosi, I. Gy. Tóth and Gy Vukovich (eds), *Társadalmi Riport*, Budapest: TARKI, pp. 237–56.

Aristotle (1984), *Politika*, Budapest: Gondolat Kiadó.

Beck, U. (2003), *Risikogesellschaft. Auf dem Weg in eine andere Moderne*, Frankfurt: Suhrkamp.

Boudon, R. (1973), *L'inégalité des chances. La mobilité sociale dans les sociétés industrielles*, Paris: Collin.

Bourdieu, P. (1980), *Le capital social*, Actes de la Recherche en Sciences Sociales No. 31.

Durkheim, E. (1986), *A társadalmi munkamegosztásról* (*The Division of Labor in Society*), Budapest: Közgazdasági és Jogi Könyvkiadó.

Durkheim, E. (1987), *A társadalmi tények magyarázatához*, Budapest: Közgazdasági és Jogi Könyvkiadó.

Fararo, T.J. and Doreian, P. (1998), 'The theory of solidarity. An agenda of prob- lems', in P. Doreian and T. Fararo (eds), *The Problems of Solidarity*, Amsterdam: Gordon and Breach, pp. 1–33.

Gazsó, F. (1976), *Iskolarendszer és társadalmi mobilitás* (*Education System and Social Mobility*), Budapest: Kossuth Könyvkiadó.

Lenski, G. (1966), *Power and Privilege. A Theory of Social Stratification*, New York: McGraw-Hill.

Mills, C. (1960), *The Power Elite*, New York: Oxford University Press.

Parsons, T. (1951), *The Social System*, New York: Free Press.

Pines, A.M., Levy, H., Utasi, A. and Hill, T.L. (2005), 'Entrepreneurs as cultural heroes: a cross-cultural, interdisciplinary perspective', *Journal of Managerial Psychology*, **20**: 541–55.

Pines, A.M., Ben-Ari, A., Utasi, A. and Larson, D. (2002), 'A cross-cultural inves- tigation of social support and burnout', *European Psychologist*, **7**: 256–64.

Pongrácz, T. and Spéder, Zs. (2003), 'Párkapcsolatok az ezredfordulón' (Partnerships during the millennium), *Szociológiai Szemle*, 3.

Treiman, D.J. (1977), *Occupational Prestige in Comparative Perspective*, New York: Academic Press.

Utasi, A. (1989), *Emotional Crisis, Religions and Tension Easing Contacts* (in seven countries on three continents), Budapest, Institute for Social Sciences.

Utasi, A. (2002a), 'The human side of technical innovation and changes in the pres- tige of occupation', paper presented at the 25th International Congress of Applied Psychology, Singapore, 7–12 July.

Utasi, A. (2002b), *A bizalom hálója. Mikrotársadalmi kapcsolatok, szolidaritás* (*Micro-social Relationships and Solidarity: the Network of Trust Relationships*), Budapest: Új Mandátum.

Utasi, A. (2004), 'Subjective quality of life. Effect of trust and relationships in Hungarian society', paper presented at the 6th *International Conference of ISQOLS*, Philadelphia, 10–14 November.

Utasi, A. (2006), 'Társadalmi töke és bizalom' (Social capital and trust), *Kritika*, **35**(6): 6–9 and (7–8): 22–5.

Vigoda, E. (2002), 'Administrative agents of democracy? A Structural Equation Modeling (SEM) of the relationship between public sector performance and citizenship involvement', *Journal of Public Administration Research and Theory*, **12**(2): 241–72.

Weber, M. (1976), *Wirtschaft und Gesellschaft. Grundriss der vestehenden Sociologie*, Tübingen: Mohr.

Weber, M. (1982), *A protestáns etika és a kapitalizmus szelleme* (*The Protestant Ethic and the Spirit of Capitalism*), Budapest: Gondolat Kiadó.

PART II

Early Influences on the Career Choice of Entrepreneurs and Managers

4. Family influences on the career life cycle

T. Alexandra Beauregard

In an era when 49 per cent of UK workers report that balancing work and family responsibilities is an issue of significant concern to them (JP Morgan Fleming, 2003), the influence of family and personal life on career decisions is receiving increasing amounts of media attention. Today's business school graduates are 'looking for a workstyle to go with their lifestyle', claims the HR consultancy Hay Group (*The Economist*, 2006). 'Generation X and Generation Y workers, who are younger than 40, are more likely than boomers to say they put family before jobs', says an article in *USA Today* (Elias, 2004). 'Today's younger employees are working to live rather than living to work', states a newspaper manager in the journalism newsletter *Fusion* (Williamson, 2006).

These media sound bites are supported by ongoing research conducted by Schein (1978, 1993, 1996) on the construct of career anchors. An individual's career anchor can be described as his or her self-concept, incorporating perceived career-related abilities and talents, values, and motivations and needs (Schein, 1996). The five original career anchors consisted of technical/functional competence, managerial competence, security and stability, creativity, and autonomy and independence. More recently, however, the 'lifestyle' anchor has emerged as an offshoot of the 'security and stability' anchor, and is concerned not with economic stability like its predecessor, but with the stability of one's general life pattern. An employee identifying lifestyle as his or her career anchor values putting down roots in a given location, does not wish to be moved every few years for the sake of his or her career, and places a high priority on balance between work and the rest of life. In Schein's observations of MIT Sloan School of Management students over the past 30 years, a growing number have begun to identify lifestyle as their primary career anchor – as many as 50 per cent of executive students from the late 1980s onward (Schein, 1996).

This chapter examines the myriad ways in which one's family and personal life can affect an individual's career. A review of some of the key research literature reveals that career choice is influenced by an individual's values, attitudes and expectations concerning how work should be balanced with the rest of life. Individuals are also susceptible to influence from their families of origin with regard to occupational choice and prioritizing work over family, or vice versa. Career opportunities, in the form of prospects for advancement within an organization or more generally in one's chosen field, are affected by family commitments and the use of flexible working practices designed to assist employees balance their work and home responsibilities. The desire for a balanced lifestyle between work and family also affects decisions to change jobs or accept a geographical transfer, and can help to shape employees' intentions to leave an organization or an entire career. The chapter will conclude by identifying some of the major implications of employees' determination to combine career with a meaningful life outside of work, for both organizations and individuals.

CAREER CHOICE

Of the five career development stages identified by Greenhaus and Callanan (1994), occupational choice is perhaps one of those most influenced by family concerns, both present and anticipated. Preparation for work involves developing an occupational self-image, wherein an individual attempts to match his or her strengths and weaknesses, values and preferred lifestyle with the requirements and advantages of a range of occupations. Brown (2002) describes the process of choosing a career as one of estimating one's ability and values, estimating the skills and abilities required for success in a given occupation, and estimating the work values that will be satisfied by the various occupational alternatives available.

Impact of Work–Family Values on Career Choice

Values can be described as general evaluative standards that serve to influence an individual's behaviour so as to reach a desired end state (Rokeach, 1979). The availability of values-based information, specifying which values are likely to be reinforced in the workplace, has been shown to be influential in the career choice process (Judge and Bretz, 1992). As of late, research indicates that values among young workers may be shifting away from those of their predecessors; desired end states appear to reflect greater concern for a balanced lifestyle, involving flexible work schedules and respect for non-work activities, than for traditionally defined career success, involving high salaries, prestigious job titles, and intensive work hours. In a study of values among young people in four European countries, Lewis et al. (2002) found evidence that achieving work–life balance was of high importance to the participants. A study conducted in the USA found that young people were less likely to identify work as an important part of life than those of the same age a generation earlier (Smola and Sutton, 2002). Research by Smithson (1999) suggests that young people's occupational choices are influenced by the way in which they prioritize their work and family roles, and that they tend to place a high value on both work and family rather than on one or the other.

This generational shift in values may, however, be limited to Western nations. Research conducted in China suggests that the Chinese are less concerned than Westerners with choosing an occupation that allows sufficient time for non-work activities and interests (Shenkar and Ronen, 1987; Bu and McKeen, 2001). This may be attributable to Confucian tradition, which places duty above enjoyment and which sees work as a vital contribution towards the well-being of the family, and/or to the standard of living currently experienced by the mainland Chinese. Bu and McKeen (2001) suggest that having seen their predecessors lack the opportunity to excel due to economic and political restrictions, today's business students in China are determined to pursue career success and financial wealth even if it may be at the expense of their personal or family lives. This explanation is supported by research by Hui and Tan (1996), who report that university graduates in Taiwan, a more developed and prosperous society, expect their work life to adjust to their personal and family interests – echoing the changing generational values revealed in research on Western populations.

Impact of Family of Origin on Career Choice

Values and attitudes related to the balancing of work and family are influenced by a number of factors, including the family of origin and exposure to trends in the labour force. Over the last two or three decades, an increasing number of mothers have taken on paid employment (Duffield, 2002). This change in the employment pattern of women may exert an influence on the attitudes of young women in the process of considering the occupational choices available to them (Marks and Houston, 2002). Both young women and young men now appear to desire a more integrated approach to work and family, rather than the dominance of one area of life over the other. In developing the Career–Family Attitudes Measure (CFAM), Sanders et al. (1998) found that American high school students expressed a preference for integrating their choices regarding work and family, in contrast to making trade-offs between the two domains.

These work–family attitudes show evidence of being influenced by factors related to the family of origin. High school students who expressed positive attitudes towards a traditional family structure, with a homemaker mother and an employed father, were more likely to have grown up in such a family themselves (Sanders et al., 1998). This has clear implications for the continuing importance of work–family concerns in choosing a career; as increasing numbers of women participate in the labour market, a corresponding number of children will grow up with a different family structure on which to model their own values and attitudes concerning the combination of work and family roles likely to be afforded to them by a given occupation.

In addition to familial influence on an individual's preferences for combining work and family, research shows that the occupational choices made by parents can exert a direct influence on the career choices of their children. According to Brown (2002), family or group influence affect both the decision-making process and the career an individual chooses. Research by Corcoran and Courant (1987) demonstrated that the degree to which a mother's occupation and industry were stereotypically 'female' was positively related to the extent to which her daughter chose an occupation that was similarly sex-typed. This type of familial influence may be even stronger for individuals in collectivist cultures. In such cultures, respect for and obedience to one's parents is often a highly prioritized value (Lee, 1991), and the attitudes and values of family members may be the primary determinant of an individual's choice of career (Sue and Sue, 1990; Yagi and Oh, 1995).

Family influence on career choice may also manifest itself unconsciously. According to psychoanalytic theory, familial heritage plays a significant role in occupational choice. Individuals will tend to choose an occupation that enables them to satisfy needs that were unfulfilled in their childhood, and actualize dreams passed on to them by their family (Pines and Yanai, 2001). For example, in his psychoanalytic analysis of successful business leaders, Kets de Vries (1995) suggested that many successful managers embark upon their careers in order to compensate for the absence, either physical or psychological, of their fathers during childhood. 'The desire to be a manager expresses a desire to become one's own father. It means raising yourself again "the right way", with total control of your life' (Pines and Yanai, 2001, p. 172).

Impact of Work–Family Expectations on Career Choice

Young people's expectations regarding how they will combine work and family in the future also play a role in influencing career choice. Research by Okamato and England (1998, cited in Badgett and Folbre, 2003) suggests that young women take family responsibilities into account when choosing an occupation. Marks and Houston (2002) conducted a study of academically high-achieving girls aged 15 to 17 years, and found that their education and career plans were significantly influenced by perceived social pressure to give up work to care for their children. The more social pressure they perceived, the less certain they were about their plans to pursue educational qualifications and establish a career. According to Marks and Houston (2002), it is therefore more likely that these high-achieving girls will choose occupations in which they believe they can most easily combine work and family, and that these occupations will in all probability be in feminized professions such as nursing and teaching, which provide girls with examples of how this might be done in a way that male-dominated occupations such as science and technology do not. In this way, occupational sex segregation will be perpetuated.

Research conducted on the perceived attractiveness of individuals as dating or marriage partners provides further insight into the role of work and family expectations in determining career choice. In a survey of attitudes among undergraduate students majoring in science, most young men reported that women studying in male-dominated disciplines such as engineering, physics, chemistry and applied sciences were inherently unattractive (Seymour and Hewitt, 1997). In an experiment in which job type and job status were manipulated in dating profiles shown to participants, Badgett and Folbre (2003) found that men and women in occupations that do not conform to traditional gender stereotypes were rated as less attractive potential romantic partners. The prospect of incurring this type of penalty in the dating and/or marriage market, and by extension reducing one's chances of having a family of one's own, may well influence young people's career choices by deterring them from pursuing occupations perceived as non-traditional in terms of gender roles.

As we can see from these studies investigating young people's expectations of combining a career with finding a partner and having children, in addition to personal factors such as values, attitudes and demographics, the barriers, opportunities and support perceived to exist in one's environment affect the development of career interests (Tharenou, 2003). Here, too, work–family concerns play their part in determining occupational choice. In a study of Norwegian MBA graduates who had chosen either self-employment or a more traditional career as an employee within an organization, participants were asked to identify the main reason for choosing one career path over the other. Work load, incorporating family and leisure concerns, was cited by significantly more individuals who had chosen organizational employment rather than entrepreneurship, and was the second-most cited reason among this group behind job and financial security (Kolvereid, 1996). As a perceived barrier to work–life balance, the heavy work load expected from self-employment acted as a deterrent to those choosing traditional employment.

Anticipated support for future work–family issues also contributes to job pursuit intentions. In a study of MBA students and alumni, Honeycutt and Rosen (1997) hypothesized that individuals with salient family and work–life balance identities would be more inclined to find organizations offering flexible career paths attractive. They found instead that all participants were more attracted to firms that provided flexible career paths, regardless of identity salience. This suggests that the availability of work–life benefits acts as a proxy for organizational support, an idea supported by the findings of Casper and Buffardi (2004), whose research showed that work schedule flexibility and dependent care assistance offered by organizations had a positive relationship with job pursuit intentions. This link was fully mediated by anticipated organizational support. It appears that regardless of their current family commitments, job candidates are looking ahead to a future in which they anticipate barriers to work–life balance. Organizations that provide support for these anticipated problems will enjoy greater recruitment potential among this new generation of labour force entrants.

CAREER ADVANCEMENT

The second stage of Greenhaus and Callanan's (1994) career development model is concerned with entry into the organization chosen in the first stage. Here, too, work–life concerns come into play. In a longitudinal study of graduate trainees, Sturges and Guest (2004) found that achieving a balanced lifestyle is very important to the young workers both before they begin work, and once they have started at the organization. Once the participants had begun work, well over 80 per cent of them rated maintenance of a balanced lifestyle as being either important or extremely important.

The third stage of Greenhaus and Callanan's (1994) model involves career establishment and achievement. Traditionally a time of intense effort in an attempt to position oneself favourably on the hierarchical ladder, this stage may be undergoing changes in line with those observed in the occupational choice process. Loughlin and Barling (2001) observe that over the past two decades, many young workers have seen their parents undergo corporate restructuring and subsequent job loss after years of long hours, hard work and loyal service. As a result, the authors suggest, this new cohort of workers may be less inclined to make similar sacrifices in terms of leisure or family time for the sake of their jobs. Zemke et al. (2000) propose that young workers may be more interested in achieving work–life balance than in traditional work goals, such as advancing into positions of organizational leadership.

This interest notwithstanding, Sturges and Guest (2004) find that as graduates become embedded in their employing organization, the barriers to work–life balance pile up, primarily in the form of heavy demands on graduates' time and energy. In their interviews with graduate trainees, the authors concluded that while graduates are prepared to work long hours and maintain heavy workloads during the early stages of their career in order to advance within the organization, they see this very much as a short-term process. In the longer term, and once they begin to experience increased demands from their family responsibilities, they expect to work more reasonable hours and achieve a more balanced lifestyle. Should this not occur for whatever reason, they would consider leaving the organization – as they 'work to live, not live to work' (Sturges and Guest, 2004, p. 10).

At this third stage of Greenhaus and Callanan's (1994) model, in which an individual works to demonstrate competence, take on greater responsibility, and gain authority within the organization, access to opportunities for career development becomes very important. Access to these opportunities may be constrained in a number of ways related to family or non-work commitments. Career advancement can be affected by family structure, by the necessity of prioritizing one career over another in dual-earner partnerships, by a reduced ability to relocate for work purposes due to concern for uprooting one's spouse and/or children, and by the use of flexible working practices including family leave. Decisions regarding expatriate assignments are also heavily influenced by personal and family concerns.

Impact of Marriage on Career Advancement

There are three main theoretical perspectives on the role of marriage in determining career advancement. Human capital theory (Becker, 1975) holds that marriage is used as a proxy for stability and responsibility by organizations allocating wages and status. Men who are married, and especially those who have children, should therefore advance more than single men. Married women, in contrast, and especially those who have children, ought to take on less demanding jobs with lower pay in order to successfully combine employment with their household responsibilities (Becker, 1985). This would imply that single women, who have more time and energy for demanding jobs, are able to achieve greater career advancement than married women and/or those with children (Tharenou, 1999).

Second, there is the spousal support view (Kanter, 1977). This proposes that married men are able to invest more resources in their careers than single men because their wives, particularly those who are not employed themselves, provide their husbands with additional resources by managing the household and by contributing time and energy to the husbands' endeavours (Pfeffer and Ross, 1982). Married women, however, are more likely to provide resources for their husbands' careers rather than receive resources for their own careers from their husbands. According to this theory, therefore, married women will not be able to concentrate on their paid work to the same extent as single women, and will therefore experience less advancement in their careers (Tharenou, 1999).

Finally, conformance to social expectations theory (Landau and Arthur, 1992) posits that married men, as the primary earners in their families, need to advance further in their careers than single men, and that men with children need to advance even further. As women's primary role is to manage household and family responsibilities, it is not necessary for them to advance in their careers to the same degree as men.

Research findings appear to support the latter two perspectives to a greater extent than the propositions put forward by human capital theory. Valcour and Tolbert (2003) found that within dual-career couples, men's careers are given priority far more frequently than women's. Meanwhile, research by Kirchmeyer (2002) showed that having a spouse was associated with a higher income for male managers, and a lower income for female managers. The dominance of men's careers is in line with conformance to social expectations theory, and assists men's career success while helping to contribute to women's lower pay (Valcour and Tolbert, 2003).

Han and Moen (1998) found a negative relationship between marital stability and career advancement for women, a result consistent with both conformance to social expectations theory and spousal support theory. Also consistent with both these theories were the results of Schneer and Reitman (2002), who found that in a longitudinal study of MBA alumni, the highest earners were married men who had children, and the lowest earners were single, childless men. While these findings would also appear to support human capital theory, single women were found to achieve similar career progress as married women, rather than outperform them as implied by the precepts of human capital theory. A longitudinal study of managers and professionals conducted by Tharenou (1999) revealed that in the private sector, married fathers with stay-at-home wives enjoyed greater career advancement than married fathers in dual-earner partnerships, who in turn enjoyed greater career advancement than single men with no children. This too is consistent with spousal support theory, as the resources provided by wives to their husbands' careers diminish once the wives have their own careers requiring resources, and the single men receive no spousal support at all.

The implications of spousal support theory are that single women's careers should advance more than married women's, as the resources of single women can be devoted entirely to their own careers. Some of Tharenou's (1999) findings, however, appear to dispute this. Mothers in dual-earner partnerships enjoyed greater career advancement than single women, but less advancement than married women whose husbands were not employed. This suggests that husbands can also provide resources for their wives' careers, at least when their time and energies are not required for careers of their own.

It appears that, all other things being equal, having a spouse is preferable to being single in terms of career advancement. Whether this is due to the effects of spousal support, the benefits of conforming to social expectations, or to the greater perceived financial need of families compared to single individuals, married employees enjoy more progress within their occupations, with married men enjoying the greatest progress of all.

Impact of Children on Career Advancement

The gender difference observed in the effect of marriage on career advancement becomes even more pronounced when the impact of having children is examined. A survey conducted by *Opportunity Now* (2000, cited in Marks and Houston, 2002) revealed that 83 per cent of female respondents agreed that commitment to family responsibilities impedes women's career progress. The empirical literature would appear to bear out this conclusion. Stoner and Hartman (1990) found that the decision to have children, and the adjustments this decision required in terms of career strategies, was identified as detrimental to career progress by 80 per cent of the female managers, who believed their careers were damaged in some way by their household and family responsibilities. Valcour and Tolbert (2003) found that having children was associated with greater career progression within the same organization for men, but reduced career progression within the same organization for women. In a large-scale study of American public sector workers, having children was linked to greater career success for white men, but not for white women or for any ethnic minority staff (Daley, 1996). Research on mid-career managers by Kirchmeyer (2002) showed that having children was associated with increased income levels for men, but lower levels of pay for women.

These results can be explained by the propensity for women to take on the bulk of childcare and household responsibilities (Hundley, 2001; Sullivan and Lewis, 2001; Vanier Institute, 2000). Women are also more likely to perform intensive care activities for elderly relatives than are men (Mooney et al., 2002). So while men can enjoy the image of 'stable family man' while eschewing primary childcare responsibility, women – and ethnic minorities in Daley's (1996) research – are perceived by their employers as diverting their time and energy toward childcare, and of contributing less to the organization. Thus the presence of children assists men's career progress but obstructs that of employees whose priorities are assumed to lie elsewhere.

This theme of employer perceptions of women with children being less committed to the organization runs through the literature assessing the effects of children on career advancement. On the one hand, it is clear that the presence of children in the household requires some adjustment in terms of parents' work schedules, particularly if they have been accustomed to working long hours, socializing with clients after hours, and/or travelling for business purposes. In their interviews with managerial and professional women, Stoner and Hartman (1990) found that mothers of preschool-age children were unable to work the same number of hours and carry the same workload while devoting a sufficient amount of time and energy to their new family responsibilities. Other research has found that when dual-earner couples recognize the need for one partner to reduce their work hours and perhaps their career goals, women are disproportionately likely to be the ones to implement these cutbacks (Becker and Moen, 1999; Han and Moen, 2001).

On the other hand, there is also evidence that employers *assume* a reduction in organizational commitment or job effort when none may in fact exist. Among the female managers interviewed by Stoner and Hartman (1990), a number suggested that their decision to have children was interpreted by their employers as a signal regarding the prominence and priority of these women's careers. Many of the study participants reported that having children damaged their careers not because of actual conflict between work and family demands, but due to the assumptions made by management that such conflict would inevitably occur. Some women were excluded from after-hours meetings and other work functions because their employers assumed that they would be unable to attend due to family responsibilities. In organizations where long hours at work are the norm and are important for promotions, family commitments are seen as an obstacle to women's availability in the workplace. Having children is therefore perceived as an obstacle to women's career advancement.

Impact of Flexible Working Practices on Career Advancement

Issues related to time spent in the workplace crop up again in the literature chronicling the effects of using flexible working practices offered by organizations. In a survey conducted by Croner Consulting, 61 per cent of HR professionals reported a belief that employees are reluctant to use flexible working practices and other work–life benefits for fear of hindering their career prospects (*Management Services*, 2004). This reluctance may be justified in some cases. A study conducted in a Big Five accounting firm by Cohen and Single (2001) found that employees using flexible work arrangements were perceived as less likely to advance to partnership and more likely to leave the firm than employees not participating in flexible work arrangements. Teleworking has been linked to professional isolation, which in turn impedes professional development activities associated with career progress such as networking, informal learning and mentoring (Cooper and Kurland, 2002). Working reduced hours is frequently unavailable as an option for senior managerial and professional positions, and when it is available, part-time work is often stigmatized and part-time workers viewed as less committed to the organization and less suitable for promotion (Higgins et al., 2000; Raabe, 1996). As a result, employees have expressed concern that using flexible working arrangements will damage their prospects for career advancement (Houston and Waumsley, 2003; Lewis, 1997).

Women, due to their greater involvement in childcare and household responsibilities, make up the majority of those working reduced hours (Lundgren and Barnett, 2000) and are more likely to express interest in using other 'family-friendly' working practices (Butler et al., 2002). They are therefore more likely than men to reap any negative career consequences of using such practices. Men, however, may suffer unique penalties for making use of available practices. Individuals who behave in ways that are inconsistent with gendered social norms will often incur negative judgements from others (Mueller and Yoder, 1997). Hence men are frequently reluctant to participate in flexible working practices because they anticipate reprisal from their employers for deviating from the traditional sex-stereotyped view of men as 'breadwinners', a role emphasizing paid employment with long hours at work and little participation in family life (Powell, 1997). This reluctance may be justified. Allen and Russell (1999) found that men who took parental leave of absence were less likely to be recommended for organizational rewards than were men who did not take leave, while a laboratory experiment conducted by Butler and Skattebo (2000) demonstrated that men who reported missing work to care for a sick child were given lower performance ratings and lower recommendations for quarterly bonuses than were women reporting the same absences.

Time is an issue in these cases because time at the workplace is viewed by employers as a proxy for productivity, performance and organizational commitment (Bailyn, 1997). Raabe (1996) describes how organizational settings are rife with assumptions regarding the link between time at work and quantity and quality of output, and assumptions regarding the necessity for managers to work long hours in order to be constantly available for consultation, coordination and control. Senior managerial attitudes toward the promotion of those working fewer than standard full-time hours or those not visibly present in the workplace on a daily basis reflect these assumptions; those employees who do not devote the maximum amount of time possible to the organization are seen as less productive and less committed, and therefore less valuable (Lewis, 1997). As a result, individuals available to work long hours and be present in the workplace are better able to compete successfully for career development opportunities (Burke, 2001).

Impact of Family Leave on Career Advancement

In keeping with the idea that time away from the workplace has deleterious consequences for career progress, research indicates that taking family leave can result in career roadblocks (Waner et al., 2005). Judiesch and Lyness (1999) found that taking leave of any kind was associated with fewer subsequent promotions and smaller salary increases for managers, regardless of their performance ratings. As women are more likely to take family leave than men (Judiesch and Lyness, 1999; Kossek et al., 1999), these career roadblocks are predominantly faced by female employees. In Stoner and Hartman's (1990) research on professional and managerial women, respondents noted that maternity leave resulted in a loss of career momentum. Being away from the workplace removed these employees from the organizational focus, and raised questions among their managers regarding return dates, shifting priorities between work and family, and changes in commitment to the organization. According to Stoner and Hartman (1990), leaves of absence are inconsistent with managerial career progression, and those who take such leaves are apt to find that career opportunities occur less frequently.

   The effects of family leave on careers are far-reaching. Research by Jacobsen and Levin (1995) showed that women who had worked continuously for 20 years since their last employment interruption had still not caught up in terms of career progress with comparable women whose employment history was uninterrupted. It is perhaps knowledge of results such as this that deters some employees from taking the family leaves available to them. For instance, research by Finkel et al. (1994) found that over three-quarters of the female employees surveyed expected that taking maternity leave would have negative consequences for their careers, and only 30 per cent of those who gave birth took the full amount of leave provided by their employers. Similar concerns were identified in research reported by Hammonds (1997), Perlow (1995) and Schwartz (1995).

Impact of Family on Relocation Decisions

As we have seen, upward mobility within organizations can be challenging for individuals with family commitments. Equally, mobility between organizations can be difficult when career decisions are made with family circumstances taken into account. In dual-earner partnerships, it is common for men's careers to receive priority when decisions are made that may affect both spouses' careers (Pixley, 2000). Women may therefore be unable to relocate to advance their own careers due to the negative effects the move would have on their husbands' career progress. Reporting such results in their own research, Stoner and Hartman (1990) note that the female managers in their study were denied growth opportunities and promotions due to their lack of mobility. These women identified lack of mobility as the single greatest family obstruction to their career progress.

Feeling constrained in their ability to relocate, women reported choosing jobs based on family-friendliness rather than career impact (Stoner and Hartman, 1990). Positions that provided flexibility, additional time for family needs, or geographical proximity to children's schools or daycare were selected over those that would help career advancement. A reluctance to disrupt their children's social lives and schooling was also evident in women's explanations of their inability to relocate.

The priority assigned to husbands' careers over wives' also manifests itself in relocations that are beneficial to men's career progress, but disadvantageous for the career advancement of their spouses. If a man is offered a relocation opportunity that benefits his career, the decision is most often to take it, which results in disruption to the continuous employment of his wife with her organization (Valcour and Tolbert, 2003).

Impact of Family on Expatriation

The choice to accept expatriate assignments and the success of those assignments are heavily influenced by family considerations (Harvey, 1996). Research consistently identifies marriage, in the form of spousal attitudes and considerations regarding the impact of expatriation on the spouse's career, as the most frequent barrier to an individual's willingness to take on international work (Aryee et al., 1996; Brett and Stroh, 1995; Harvey, 1998). Punnett (1997) found that 80 per cent of employees who refused international positions cited family reasons, and the impact on their spouses' careers in particular, for doing so. Tharenou (2003) found that in addition to the presence of partners and their career considerations, more subjective family influences also affected individuals' receptivity to international assignments. Employees reported a reluctance to give up their current family life and social contacts for the purposes of working abroad, and these findings were also applicable to younger employees without children and/or partners.

Once again, we see gender differences in effect. Research by Linehan and Walsh (2000) indicates that more women than men perceive the necessity of choosing between family commitments and an international career. In their study, female international managers reported additional psychological strain and feelings of guilt when balancing an expatriate assignment with their responsibilities as a parent. The 'either–or' decision faced by these women is prompted by the perceived inflexibility of their organizations, their employers' assumptions regarding the primacy of women's role in child-rearing, and a male model of career success that does not take into account the effects of marriage, pregnancy, childcare and household work (Linehan and Walsh, 2000).

For those who do take on international assignments, factors related to family play a significant role in determining expatriates' satisfaction with those assignments and their overall success. Researchers have found that the success of expatriate assignments is strongly influenced by the adjustment of the expatriate's spouse and children to the foreign locale (Harvey, 1996). Failure to complete the assignment, which carries a penalty for career progression, is often attributed to family issues rather than work-related problems (Harvey, 1995).

Shaffer and Harrison (1998) found that the more family responsibilities an expatriate employee had, the more salient were family-related factors when the decision was being made as to whether or not to withdraw from the international assignment. Family responsibilities and the experience of the spouse during expatriation influenced expatriates' adjustment and non-work-related satisfaction, which in turn were associated with plans to search for other employment, general thoughts or consideration of quitting, and intentions to quit (Shaffer and Harrison, 1998).

The interplay between work and family can also exert a negative influence on expatriates' likelihood of successfully completing their assignments. The degree to which work demands interfere with family life, as well as the degree to which family responsibilities interfere with the fulfilment of work tasks, have been found to predict expatriate employees' assignment withdrawal cognitions (Shaffer et al., 2001). This sort of psychological withdrawal from work includes the intention to quit expatriate assignments before they are completed, and this intention to quit has widespread and negative implications for the expatriate employee's career (Black et al., 1992).

TURNOVER AND CAREER EXIT

The fourth stage of Greenhaus and Callanan's (1994) career model is entitled 'Mid-career', and is usually characterized by some sort of re-evaluation of career and life direction among workers. At this stage, employees who are dissatisfied with their career progress or current situation may consider withdrawing from their organization in favour of other pursuits. Leaving an organization often has profound implications for an individual's career. Either one takes up a new position elsewhere, which may or may not represent an improvement in career prospects, or one withdraws from the labour force altogether.

Decisions to forego one organization for another are frequently influenced by concerns with regard to work–life balance. Research consistently shows that organizations demonstrating support for their employees' personal lives and family commitments reap rewards in terms of increased attachment and reduced intentions to turnover. Sturges and Guest (2004) found a close, positive relationship between organizational support for non-work responsibilities and activities, and organizational commitment. Employees whose supervisors provide support for work–family issues report fewer intentions to leave the organization (Allen, 2001; Aryee et al., 1998), as do those who perceive a supportive organizational work–family culture, characterized by managerial support for work–life issues, fewer negative career consequences for using flexible working practices and other family-friendly programmes, and fewer organizational time demands placed on employees (Allen, 2001; Thompson et al., 1999). A supportive work–family culture has also been associated with female employees' plans to return to work more quickly after giving birth (Lyness et al., 1999), and employees who perceive organizational values that are supportive of work–life balance report greater satisfaction with their careers and less intention to quit (Burke et al., 2003).

For employees dealing with simultaneous work and family demands, flexible working practices or other family-friendly programmes can be very important in choosing whether to stay with or leave an employer. The availability of flexible work hours has been linked to organizational commitment and employee loyalty for those with caregiving responsibilities for children (Roehling et al., 2001; Scandura and Lankau, 1997). Research has also shown a positive relationship between the provision of voluntary reduced hours and employee retention (Williams et al., 2000), and between employee satisfaction with work schedule flexibility and intentions to leave the organization (Aryee et al., 1998). In a 1995 study by Grover and Crooker, four individual work–life practices – parental leave, childcare information and referral, flexible working hours, and financial assistance with childcare – were found to predict organizational attachment among employees, regardless of their family commitments. Similarly, Thompson et al. (1999) found a link between work–family benefit availability and turnover intentions, and women with school-aged children in Roehling et al.'s (2001) study reported higher levels of loyalty to the organization.

These associations between work–family support and turnover intentions can perhaps be explained by the concept of value congruence. Value congruence is said to occur when an individual employee and an organization share similar values (Meglino and Ravlin, 1998). Perrewe and Hochwarter (2001) suggest that value congruence would occur if an individual employee viewed participation in family activities as a crucial aspect of life, and these activities were supported by the employing organization. Such support could take the form of sympathetic and helpful supervisors, a culture that encourages work–life balance among employees, or the provision of work–life programmes such as flexible hours. In contrast, were an organization interested only in maximizing an employee's work outputs at the expense of the employee's personal life, and provided none of the above-mentioned supports, this would represent a lack of congruence. Research by Cable and Judge (1996) has linked value congruence to increased employee involvement and satisfaction with work, and fewer intentions to quit.

In some cases, problems balancing work with family commitments led to a decision to exit the labour force entirely. This tends to be a predominantly female phenomenon, although there is some evidence of increasing numbers of men opting out of successful careers in order to spend more time with their families (Cobb, 2006). In their study of female 'fast-track' managerial and professional employees who gave up their careers to stay home with their children, Stone and Lovejoy (2004) cited workplace inflexibility as a major factor prompting women to quit. Study participants spoke of the unavailability of reduced-hours options for high-level positions in their organizations, and reported that their choice was between working 40 hours or more per week or quitting. Among the women who had planned to continue working after having children, 40 per cent attempted to negotiate reduced work hours with their employer, but were denied.

Of those who were able to work part-time or make job-sharing arrangements, many women found that this reduction in work hours resulted in a 'career derailment' (Stone and Lovejoy, 2004, p. 69) that eventually influenced their decision to leave the workforce. Organizational restructuring also played a role in prompting women's decisions to leave; turnover of the managers to whom these employees reported disrupted the family-friendly work arrangements that had been negotiated, in turn leading to the turnover of the women themselves.

Family members also played their part in the decision-making process. Of the female managers and professionals who participated in Stone and Lovejoy's (2004) research, 72 per cent referred to the desire to spend more time with their children as a factor in their decision to quit. Three-quarters of these women left their jobs when their children were infants or toddlers. Spouses, too, played a role. Approximately two-thirds of the women in the study spoke of their husbands' key influence on the decision to quit. Often mentioned were the lack of assistance their husbands provided with parenting responsibilities, and their husbands' perception of the women's careers as secondary to their own, regardless of the status or income associated with those careers.

CAREER SATISFACTION AND SUBJECTIVE CAREER SUCCESS

Attitudes toward balancing a career with family commitments, as well as the actual experience of managing competing demands from work and from home, are likely to be a significant predictor of employees' satisfaction with their career outcomes (Sanders et al., 1998) and perceptions of career success. Career success can be assessed either objectively, by means of pay, promotion and status, or subjectively, by means of workers' reactions to their career experiences (Heslin, 2005; Hughes, 1958), and is thought to be associated with greater employee satisfaction, motivation and performance (Peluchette, 1993).

The intersection of attitudes and experiences in predicting satisfaction and perceived success can be explained by person–environment fit theory (French and Caplan, 1972), which posits that discrepancies between an individual's needs and preferences and the environment's ability to satisfy those needs and preferences will lead to stress and physical, psychological and behavioural strain. Based on this, Sanders et al. (1998) propose that if employees' expectations for the configuration of work life and family life are not met, the ensuing gap between their work–family attitudes and reality will produce dissatisfaction, strain and other negative repercussions. Correspondingly, if there is a good fit between work–family expectations and the actual intersection of work and family life, one would expect positive outcomes such as satisfaction and self-perceived success.

There is conflicting evidence for the effects of family commitments and work–life concerns on employees' career satisfaction and subjective perceptions of success. On the one hand, research has shown that women attempting to combine professional or managerial careers with family commitments report less job satisfaction, less job involvement, and less career satisfaction than women who chiefly emphasized their careers (Burke and McKeen, 1993). Kirchmeyer (2002) found that having children is associated with reduced perceptions of career success for female managers, and employees experiencing strong difficulties balancing competing work and home responsibilities have also reported lower levels of subjective career success (Peluchette, 1993).

On the other hand, Valcour and Tolbert (2003) found evidence that female employees with more children, and, presumably, a higher level of family demands, exhibit higher levels of perceived success in their work lives. The authors speculate that such a result may be due to the women's boundaryless career patterns that have allowed them to effectively integrate work and family demands. Other research has shown that managers in dual-earner partnerships report higher levels of satisfaction with their careers than managers in single-earner households (Schneer and Reitman, 1993). This increased level of satisfaction may be attributable to the ability of the dual-earners' career paths to permit these managers to fulfil the multiple roles of spouse, parent, and worker (Schneer and Reitman, 1993); commitment to multiple roles has been related to life satisfaction, self-esteem and self-acceptance among managerial women (Ruderman et al., 2002). 'Breadwinners', who focus to a greater extent on work while their non-employed spouses take care of family demands, may not feel a similar sense of fulfilment.

A study of female managers revealed several ways in which they considered family and household responsibilities to have influenced their careers in a positive way (Stoner and Hartman, 1990). The women spoke of honing skills at home that proved to be useful in the workplace: understanding and interacting with people, organizational skills and crisis management were identified as helping their performance on the job. A sense of fulfilment and contentment derived from family life was also thought to provide perspective on life, allowing the managers to put forth greater effort and enjoy higher levels of productivity at work. Some women spoke of family commitments as 'a change of pace that helps [me] to relax' (Stoner and Hartman, 1990, p. 9).

CONCLUSIONS

It is evident from this review of the literature that the influence of family members, and concerns for work–life balance, help to shape employee decision making and outcomes throughout the career life cycle. Some of the key implications for individuals pursuing a career and a family life, and for the organizations that hire them, are as follows.

Growing Significance of Work–Life Issues in Career-related Decision Making

Employees' concerns for balancing work and family are set to grow. Workers' values and expectations regarding the combination of work and family are modelled on those exhibited by their parents (Sanders et al., 1998), and dual-earner households are on the rise in both the UK and USA (Brannen et al., 1997; Cornell Employment and Families Careers Institute, 1999). As more and more young people whose parents were in dual-earner partnerships enter the workforce themselves, organizations will need to find ways to allow these young workers to meet their expectations of integrating a successful career with a meaningful family life. Students are being advised to familiarize themselves with family issues in the workplace, and to learn to thoroughly research employers' benefits packages before making decisions to apply for or accept a position (Waner et al., 2005). By so doing, it is to be hoped that a mismatch between young people's expectations of balancing work and home and the reality of doing so can be avoided, and person–environment fit can be achieved.

Importance of Organizational Family-friendliness for Recruitment and Retention

Job candidates take family considerations into account when searching for work, and employees do likewise when deciding whether or not to remain with their employers. It follows that organizations offering attractive benefits, flexible working practices and a supportive work–family culture will be in an advantageous position to both recruit and retain these workers. As developing countries become wealthier, this may soon become an issue for multinational firms that currently do not offer foreign workers the same benefits available to those working in the firm's home country. For instance, McKeen and Bu (1998) report that flexible working practices such as flextime, telework and part-time hours are generally absent in China, and that Western multinationals that provide these practices in North America do not usually make similar provisions available for their employees in China. The experience of Taiwan cited in Hui and Tan (1996) suggests that work–life issues will become more prominent in developing nations as the standard of living rises; multinational firms would therefore be advised to develop more family-friendly initiatives in these regions in preparation for this time.

Persistence of Gendered Parenting Roles and their Negative Effects on Women's Careers

As long as stereotyped views of mothers as primary caregivers for children and women as keepers of the household continue, women will struggle with progressing their careers alongside marriage and parenthood. By marginalizing those – predominantly women – who make use of flexible working practices or family leave, current societal attitudes toward the primacy of women's role in the home impede women who do not want to have to choose between having a family and pursuing a high-impact, successful career. These gendered assumptions about parenting roles also hinder men wishing to take a more active part in family life through participation in organizational work–life programmes. 'Organizations must not view balancing work and family as a woman's issue, but rather as a human issue' (Wentling, 1998, p. 21).

Effectiveness of Organizational Work–Life Programmes

As long as employees fear negative career consequences of using flexible working practices or family leave, these measures will have a limited impact on helping workers balance their jobs with their family responsibilities. Hence organizations are unlikely to enjoy any subsequent benefits attributed to the successful implementation of these practices (e.g. improved productivity, market performance and profit rates) (Meyer et al., 2001; Perry-Smith and Blum, 2000; Shepard et al., 1996). Instead, research demonstrates that loss of employee commitment and increased intentions to quit are probable repercussions of an organizational failure to foster a supportive environment in which employees can balance their work demands with their personal or family commitments (Aryee et al., 1998; Burke et al., 2003). The continued emphasis on time spent at work as a criterion of successful performance and suitability for promotion is a key factor in the failure of many work–life programmes to achieve their potential. Until organizations begin to shift toward measuring performance via outputs rather than inputs, work–life programmes will not live up to expectations, careers will continue to be stalled, and valuable workers will continue to be lost.

REFERENCES

Allen, T.D. (2001), 'Family-supportive work environments: the role of organizational perceptions', *Journal of Vocational Behavior*, **58**(3): 414–35.

Allen, T.D. and Russell, J.E. (1999), 'Parental leave of absence: some not so family-friendly implications', *Journal of Applied Social Psychology*, **29**: 166–91.

Aryee, S., Chay, Y. and Chew, J. (1996), 'An investigation of the willingness of managerial employees to accept an expatriate assignment', *Journal of Organizational Behavior*, **17**: 267–84.

Aryee, S., Luk, V. and Stone, R. (1998), 'Family-responsive variables and retention-relevant outcomes among employed parents', *Human Relations*, **51**(1): 73–87.

Badgett, M.V.L. and Folbre, N. (2003), 'Job gendering, occupational choice and the marriage market', *Industrial Relations*, **42**(2): 270–98.

Bailyn, L. (1997), 'The impact of corporate culture on work–family integration', in S. Parasuraman and J.H. Greenhaus (eds), *Integrating Work and Family: Challenges and Choices for a Changing World*, Westport, CT: Quorum Books, pp. 209–19.

Becker, G.S. (1975), *Human Capital*, Chicago, IL: University of Chicago Press.

Becker, G.S. (1985), 'Human capital, effort, and the sexual division of labor', *Journal of Labor Economics*, **3**: 533–58.

Becker, P.E. and Moen, P. (1999), 'Scaling back: dual-career couples' work–family strategies', *Journal of Marriage and the Family*, **61**(4): 995–1007.

Black, J.S., Gregersen, H.B. and Mendenhall, M.E. (1992), *Global Assignments*, San Francisco, CA: Jossey-Bass.

Bland, K.I. and Isaacs, G. (2002), 'Contemporary trends in student selection of medical specialties: the potential impact on general surgery', *Archives of Surgery*, **137**(3): 259–67.

Brannen, J., Moss, P., Owen, C. and Wale, C. (1997), *Mothers, Fathers, and Employment: Parents and the Labour Market 1984–1994*, Sheffield, UK: Department for Education and Employment.

Brett, J.M. and Stroh, L.K. (1995), 'Willingness to relocate internationally', *Human Resource Management*, **34**: 405–24.

Brown, D. (2002), 'The role of work and cultural values in occupational choice, satisfaction, and success: a theoretical statement', *Journal of Counseling and Development*, **80**: 48–56.

Bu, N. and McKeen, C.A. (2001), 'Work goals among male and female business students in Canada and China: the effects of culture and gender', *International Journal of Human Resource Management*, **12**(2): 166–83.

Burke, R.J. (2001), 'Workaholism in organizations: the role of organizational values', *Personnel Review*, **30**(6): 637–45.

Burke, R.J. and McKeen, C.A. (1993), 'Career priority patterns among managerial and professional women', *Applied Psychology: An International Review*, **42**: 341–52.

Burke, R.J., Oberklaid, F. and Burgess, Z. (2003), 'Organizational values, work experiences, and satisfactions among Australian psychologists', *International Journal of Organizational Analysis*, **11**(2): 123–35.

Butler, A. and Skattebo, A. (2000), 'What is acceptable for women may not be for men: the effect of family conflicts with work on job performance ratings', paper presented at the Annual Conference of the Society for Industrial and Organizational Psychology, New Orleans, Louisiana, April.

Butler, A., Smart, L., Gasser, M. and Li, A. (2002), 'Gender, outcome expectancies, and the use of family-friendly programs', paper presented at the Annual Conference of the Society for Industrial and Organizational Psychology, Toronto, Ontario, April.

Cable, D. and Judge, T. (1996), 'Person–organization fit, job choice decisions, and organizational entry', *Organizational Behavior and Human Decision Processes*, **67**: 294–311.

Casper, W.J. and Buffardi, L.C. (2004), 'Work–life benefits and job pursuit intentions: the role of anticipated organizational support', *Journal of Vocational Behavior*, **65**: 391–410.

Cobb, C. (2006), 'Real men don't climb the ladder', *Ottawa Citizen*, retrieved 10 February 2006, retrieved from www.canada.com/components/print.aspx?id= 8839102f-c0ff-4f51-afda-1ca437a.htm.

Cohen, J.R. and Single, L.E. (2001), 'An examination of the perceived impact of flexible work arrangements on professional opportunities in public accounting', *Journal of Business Ethics*, **32**: 317–28.

Cooper, C.D. and Kurland, N.B. (2002), 'Telecommuting, professional isolation, and employee development in public and private organizations', *Journal of Organizational Behavior*, **23**: 511–32.

Corcoran, M.E. and Courant, P.N. (1987), 'Sex-role socialization and occupational segregation: an exploratory investigation', *Journal of Post Keynesian Economics*, **9**: 330–46.

Cornell Employment and Families Careers Institute (1999), *Facts about the Demographics of Working Families*, Ithaca, NY: Cornell Employment and Families Careers Institute.

Daley, D.M. (1996), 'Paths of glory and the glass ceiling: differing patterns of career advancement among women and minority federal employees', *Public Administration Quarterly*, Summer: 143–62.

Duffield, M. (2002), 'Trends in female employment 2002', *Labour Market Trends*, **110**(11): 605–16.

The Economist (2006), 'Life beyond pay', 15 June, retrieved 24 July from www. economist.com/business/displayStory.cfm?story_id=7055931.

Elias, M. (2004), 'The family-first generation', *USA Today*, 12 December, retrieved 24 July 2006 from www.usatoday.com/printedition/life/20041213/bl_cover 13 .art.htm.

Finkel, S.K., Olswang, S. and She, N. (1994), 'Childbirth, tenure and promotion for women faculty', *Review of Higher Education*, **17**: 259–70.

French, J.R.P. Jr and Caplan, R.D. (1972), 'Organizational stress and individual strain', in A.J. Marrow (ed.), *The Failure of Success*, New York: Amacom, pp. 30–66.

Greenhaus, J.H. and Callanan, G.A. (1994), *Career Management*, London: Dryden Press.

Grover, S.L. and Crooker, K.J. (1995), 'Who appreciates family-responsive human resource policies: the impact of family-friendly policies on the organizational attachment of parents and non-parents', *Personnel Psychology*, **48**: 271–88.

Hammonds, K.H. (1997), 'Work and family: *Business Week*'s second survey of family-friendly corporate policies', *Business Week*, **96–99**: 102–4.

Han, S.-K. and Moen, P. (1998), *Interlocking Careers: Pathways through Work and Family for Men and Women*, IRRA 50th Annual Conference Proceedings, Madison, WI: Industrial Relations Research Association.

Han, S.-K. and Moen, P. (2001), 'Coupled careers: pathways through work and marriage in the United States', in H.-P. Blossfield and S. Drobnic (eds), *Careers of Couples in Contemporary Societies: From Male Breadwinner to Dual Earner Families*, Oxford: Oxford University Press, pp. 201–31.

Harvey, M. (1995), 'The impact of dual-career families on international relocations', *Human Resource Management Review*, **5**(3): 228–44.

Harvey, M. (1996), 'Addressing the dual-career expatriation dilemma', *Human Resource Planning*, **19**: 18–39.

Harvey, M. (1998), 'Dual-career couples during international relocation: the trailing spouse', *International Journal of Human Resource Management*, **9**: 309–31.

Heslin, P.A. (2005), 'Conceptualizing and evaluating career success', *Journal of Organizational Behavior*, **26**: 113–36.

Higgins, C., Duxbury, L. and Johnson, K.L. (2000), 'Part-time work for women: does it really help balance work and family?', *Human Resource Management*, **39**(1): 17–32.

Honeycutt, T.L. and Rosen, B. (1997), 'Family-friendly human resource policies, salary levels, and salient identity as predictors of organizational attraction', *Journal of Vocational Behavior*, **50**: 271–90.

Houston, D.M. and Waumsley, J.A. (2003), *Attitudes to Flexible Working and Family Life*, York: Joseph Rowntree Foundation Policy Press.

Hughes, E.C. (1958), *Men and their Work*, Glencoe, IL: Free Press.

Hui, C.H. and Tan, C.K. (1996), 'Employee motivation and attitudes in the Chinese workforce', in M.H. Bond (ed.), *The Handbook of Chinese Psychology*, Hong Kong: Oxford University Press, pp. 364–78.

Hundley, G. (2001), 'Domestic division of labor and self/organizationally employed differences in job attitudes and earnings', *Journal of Family and Economic Issues*, **22**(2): 121–39.

Jacobsen, J.P. and Levin, L.M. (1995), 'Effects of intermittent labor force attachment on women's earnings', *Monthly Labor Review*, **118**(9): 14–19.

JP Morgan Fleming (2003), *JP Morgan Fleming Quality of Life Survey*, London: JP Morgan Fleming Asset Management, August.

Judge, T.A. and Bretz, R.D. Jr (1992), 'Effects of work values on job choice decisions', *Journal of Applied Psychology*, **77**: 261–71.

Judiesch, M.K. and Lyness, K.S. (1999), 'Left behind? The impact of leaves of absence on managers' career success', *Academy of Management Journal*, **42**(6): 641–51.

Kanter, R.M. (1977), *Men and Women of the Corporation*, New York: Basic Books.

Kets de Vries, M.F.R. (1995), *Life and Death in the Executive Fast Lane*, San Francisco, CA: Jossey-Bass.

Kirchmeyer, C. (2002), 'Gender differences in managerial careers: yesterday, today, and tomorrow', *Journal of Business Ethics*, **37**: 5–24.

Kolvereid, L. (1996), 'Organizational employment versus self-employment: reasons for career choice intentions', *Entrepreneurship Theory and Practice*, Spring: 23–31.

Kossek, E.E., Barber, A.E. and Winters, D. (1999), 'Using flexible schedules in the managerial world: the power of peers', *Human Resource Management*, **38**(1): 33–46.

Landau, J. and Arthur, M.B. (1992), 'The relationship of marital status, spouse's career status, and gender to salary level', *Sex Roles*, **27**: 665–81.

Lee, K.C. (1991), 'The problem of the appropriateness of the Rokeach Values Survey in Korea', *International Journal of Psychology*, **26**: 299–310.

Lewis, S. (1997), ' "Family Friendly" employment policies: a route to changing organizational culture or playing about at the margins?', *Gender, Work and Organization*, **4**(1): 13–24.

Lewis, S., Smithson, J. and Kugelberg, C. (2002), 'Into work: job insecurity and changing psychological contracts', in J. Brannen, S. Lewis, A. Nilsen and J. Smithson
(eds), *Young Europeans, Work and Family*, London: Routledge, pp. 69–88.

Linehan, M. and Walsh, J.S. (2000), 'Work–family conflict and the senior female
international manager', *British Journal of Management*, **11**: 49–58.

Loughlin, C. and Barling, J. (2001), 'Young workers' work values, attitudes, and
behaviours', *Journal of Occupational and Organizational Psychology*, **74**: 543–58.

Lundgren, L. and Barnett, R.C. (2000), 'Reduced-hours careers in medicine: a strategy for the professional community and the family', *Community, Work and
Family*, **3**(1): 65–79.

Lyness, K.S., Thompson, C.A., Francesco, A.M. and Judiesch, M.K. (1999), 'Work
and pregnancy: individual and organizational factors influencing organizational
commitment, timing of maternity leave, and return to work', *Sex Roles*, **41**(7/8):
485–508.

Management Services (2004), 'Employees choosing work over perks', **48**(3): 3.

Marks, G. and Houston, D.M. (2002), 'The determinants of young women's intentions about education, career development and family life', *Journal of Education
and Work*, **15**(3): 321–36.

McKeen, C.A. and Bu, N. (1998), 'Career and life expectations of Chinese business
students: the effects of gender', *Women in Management Review*, **13**(5): 171–83.

Meglino, B. and Ravlin, E. (1998), 'Individual values in organizations: concepts,
controversies, and research', *Journal of Management*, **24**: 351–89.

Meyer, C.S., Mukerjee, S. and Sestero, A. (2001), 'Work–family benefits: which ones
maximize profits?', *Journal of Managerial Issues*, **13**(1): 28–44.

Mooney, A., Statham, J. and Simon, A. (2002), *The Pivot Generation: Informal Care
and Work after Fifty*, York: Joseph Rowntree Foundation Policy Press.

Mueller, K.A. and Yoder, J.D. (1997), 'Gendered norms for family size, employment, and occupation: Are there personal costs for violating them?', *Sex Roles*,
36: 207–20.

Peluchette, J.V. (1993), 'Subjective career success: the influence of individual
difference, family, and organizational variables', *Journal of Vocational Behavior*,
43: 198–208.

Perlow, L.A. (1997), *Finding Time: How Corporations, Individuals and Families can
Benefit from New Work Practices*, Ithaca, NY: Cornell University Press.

Perrewe, P.L. and Hochwarter, W.A. (2001), 'Can we really have it all? The attainment of work and family values', *Current Directions in Psychological Science*,
10(1): 29–33.

Perry-Smith, J.E. and Blum, T.C. (2000), 'Work–family human resource bundles
and perceived organizational performance', *Academy of Management Journal*,
43(6): 1107–17.

Pfeffer, J.P. and Ross, J. (1982), 'The effects of marriage and a working wife on occupational and wage attainment', *Administrative Science Quarterly*, **27**: 66–80.

Pines, A.M. and Yanai, O.Y. (2001), 'Unconscious determinants of career choice
and burnout: theoretical model and counselling strategy', *Journal of Employment
Counseling*, **38**: 170–84.

Pixley, J.E. (2000), 'Career hierarchy in dual-earner couples: implications for occupational attainment', Working Paper No. 00-14, Ithaca, NY: Bronfenbrenner
Life Course Center.

Powell, G.N. (1997), 'The sex difference in employee inclinations regarding
work–family programs: why does it exist, should we care, and what should be

done about it (if anything)?', in S. Parasuraman and J.H. Greenhaus (eds), *Integrating Work and Family: Challenges and Choices for a Changing World*, Westport, CT: Quorum Books, pp. 167–74.

Punnett, B.J. (1977), 'Towards effective management of expatriate spouses', *Journal of World Business*, 32(3): 243–57.

Raabe, P.H. (1996), 'Constructing pluralistic work and career arrangements', in S. Lewis and J. Lewis (eds), *The Work–Family Challenge: Rethinking Employment*, London: Sage, pp. 128–41.

Roehling, P.V., Roehling, M.V. and Moen, P. (2001), 'The relationship between work–life policies and practices and employee loyalty: a life course perspective', *Journal of Family and Economic Issues*, 22(2): 141–70.

Rokeach, M. (1979), 'From individual to institutional values: with special reference to the values of science', in M. Rokeach (ed.), *Understanding Human Values*, New York: Free Press, pp. 47–70.

Ruderman, M.N., Ohlott, P.J., Panzer, K. and King, S.N. (2002), 'Benefits of multiple roles for managerial women', *Academy of Management Journal*, 45(2): 369–86.

Sanders, M.M., Lengnick-Hall, M.L., Lengnick-Hall, C.A. and Steele-Clapp, L. (1998), 'Love and work: career–family attitudes of new entrants into the labor force', *Journal of Organizational Behavior*, 19: 603–19.

Scandura, T.A. and Lankau, M.J. (1997), 'Relationships of gender, family responsibility and flexible work hours to organizational commitment and job satisfaction', *Journal of Organizational Behavior*, 18: 377–91.

Schein, E.H. (1978), *Career Dynamics: Matching Individual and Organizational Needs*, Reading, MA: Addison-Wesley.

Schein, E.H. (1993), *Career Survival: Strategic Job/role Planning*, San Diego, CA: Pfeiffer, Inc.

Schein, E.H. (1996), 'Career anchors revisited: implications for career development in the 21st century', *Academy of Management Executive*, 10: 80–88.

Schneer, J.A. and Reitman, F. (1993), 'Effects of alternate family structures on managerial career paths', *Academy of Management Journal*, 36(4): 830–43.

Schneer, J.A. and Reitman, F. (2002), 'Managerial life without a wife: family structure and managerial career success', *Journal of Business Ethics*, 37: 25–38.

Schwartz, D.B. (1995), 'The impact of work–family policies on women's career development: Boom or bust?', *Women in Management Review*, 7: 31–45.

Seymour, E. and Hewitt, N.M. (1997), *Talking about Leaving: Why Undergraduates Leave the Sciences*, New York: Westview Press.

Shaffer, M.A. and Harrison, D.A. (1998), 'Expatriates' psychological withdrawal from international assignments: work, nonwork and family influences', *Personnel Psychology*, 51(1): 87–118.

Shaffer, M.A., Harrison, D.A., Gilley, K.M. and Luk, D.M. (2001), 'Struggling for balance amid turbulence on international assignments: work–family conflict, support and commitment', *Journal of Management*, 27: 99–121.

Shenkar, O. and Ronen, S. (1987), 'Structure and importance of work goals among managers in the People's Republic of China', *Academy of Management Journal*, 30(3): 564–76.

Shephard, E., Clifton, T. and Kruse, D. (1996), 'Flexible work hours and productivity: some evidence from the pharmaceutical industry', *Industrial Relations*, 35(1): 123–39.

Smithson, J. (1999), 'Equal choices, different futures: young adults talk about work and family expectations', *Psychology of Women Section Review*, 1: 43–57.

Smola, K.W. and Sutton, C. (2002), 'Generational differences: revisiting generational work values for the new millennium', *Journal of Organizational Behavior*, **23**: 363–82.

Stone, P. and Lovejoy, M. (2004), 'Fast-track women and the "choice" to stay home', *Annals of the American Academy*, **596**: 62–83.

Stoner, C.R. and Hartman, R.I. (1990), 'Family responsibilities and career progress: the good, the bad, and the ugly', *Business Horizons*, May–June: 7–14.

Sturges, J. and Guest, D. (2004), 'Working to live or living to work? Work/life balance early in the career', *Human Resource Management Journal*, **14**(4): 5–20.

Sullivan, C. and Lewis, S. (2001), 'Home-based telework, gender, and the synchronization of work and family: perspectives of teleworkers and their co-residents', *Gender, Work and Organization*, **8**(2): 124–45.

Sue, D.W. and Sue, D. (1990), *Counseling the Culturally Different*, 2nd edn, New York: Wiley.

Tharenou, P. (1999), 'Is there a link between family structures and women's and men's managerial career advancement?', *Journal of Organizational Behavior*, **20**: 837–63.

Tharenou, P. (2003), 'The initial development of receptivity to working abroad: self-initiated international work opportunities in young graduate employees', *Journal of Occupational and Organizational Psychology*, **76**: 489–515.

Thompson, C.A., Beauvais, L.L. and Lyness, K.S. (1999), 'When work–family benefits are not enough: the influence of work–family culture on benefit utilization, organizational attachment, and work–family conflict', *Journal of Vocational Behavior*, **54**: 392–415.

Valcour, P.M. and Tolbert, P.S. (2003), 'Gender, family and career in the era of boundarylessness: determinants and effects of intra- and inter-organizational mobility', *International Journal of Human Resource Management*, **14**(5): 768–87.

Vanier Institute of the Family (2000), *Profiling Canada's Families II*, Ottawa: Vanier Institute of the Family.

Waner, K.K., Winter, J.K. and Breshears, R.G. (2005), 'Family issues in the workplace: are students on track?', *Journal of Education for Business*, January/February: 145–8.

Wentling, R.M. (1998), 'Work and family issues: their impact on women's career development', *New Directions for Adult and Continuing Education*, **80**: 15–24.

Williams, M.L., Ford, L.R., Dohring, P.L., Lee, M.D. and MacDermid, S.M. (2000), 'Outcomes of reduced load work arrangements at managerial and professional levels: perspectives from multiple stakeholders', paper presented at the Annual Meetings of the Academy of Management, Toronto, ON, August.

Williamson, D. (2006), 'Young workers, new rhythms', *Fusion*, Summer, retrieved 24 July from www.naa.org/DiversityPages/Fusion-Newsletter/lead-story-summer 2006.aspx.

Yagi, D.T. and Oh, M.Y. (1995), 'Unemployment and family dynamics in meeting the needs of the Chinese elderly in the United States', *Gerontologist*, **25**: 472–6.

Zemke, R., Raines, C. and Filipeczak, B. (2000), *Generations at Work: Managing the Clash of Veterans, Boomers, Xers, and Nexters in Your Workplace*, Washington, DC: American Management Association.

5. Understanding the role of relationships in making career choices among Turkish MBA students

Zahide Karakitapoğlu-Aygün and Kadire Zeynep Sayım

INTRODUCTION

Relationships are central to human functioning. They serve as channels for social resources such as informational, emotional and instrumental support. However, the role of these relational influences in career progress is usually de-emphasized in the literature. Rather, work and relatedness have been perceived as two opposite and distinct modalities of human functioning. Accordingly, work is assumed to represent agency, individuality and separateness, whereas relatedness is assumed to imply dependency. Only in recent years has interest in understanding how relationships and careers are intertwined increased (Blustein, 2001; Blustein et al., 1997; Blustein et al., 2004; Flum, 2001; Schultheiss, 2003; Phillips et al., 2001; Schultheiss et al., 2001). This increased interest in relationships in the organizational research is a reflection of a general tendency away from individualistic explanations toward more relational and contextual ones in social sciences.

The recent research examining the interplay between work and relatedness points to the limitations of stereotypical individual autonomy at the workplace and argues that connectedness with others is essential. For example, based on an extensive literature, Baumeister and Leary (1995) concluded that relatedness is a basic need. Similarly, Bellah et al. (1985) illustrated that people find it difficult to imagine a good life as being lived alone. In their critique of American individualism, Bellah et al. (1985, p. 82) noted that 'for highly individuated Americans, there is something anomalous about the relation between parents and children, for the biologically normal dependence of children on adults is perceived as morally abnormal.' Hence, acknowledging the role of connectedness in human growth and development, in this investigation we broaden the current research by studying the influential role of significant relationships in the career domain. Most of the related research efforts in the area have focused exclusively on how relationships and networks are conducive to career mobility and advancement, overlooking the role of relationships in making career choices. There is, therefore, a need for research exploring what types of relationships matter, and how and why they are significant in making career choices. The present study specifically aims to explore the importance and functions of different relationships (mother, father, relatives, work colleagues, mentors etc.) in making career choices among Turkish MBA students.

CULTURE AND RELATIONAL INFLUENCES

Culture affects how people think and behave. National culture is embedded in everyday behavior. Accordingly, preferences for the role of social influences in making career choices may differ in individualistic and collectivistic settings. For example, in an individualistic environment where dependence on others is viewed in a negative light, one may value making career decisions independently and the involvement of others in this process is not welcomed. However, in a collectivistic environment where individuals are embedded in close networks, involvement of others may be quite valuable. We argue that understanding the influences of significant relationships on making career choices is especially important in Turkey since it has been considered as 'fundamentally collectivistic' in the literature (Hofstede, 1980). Individuals are strongly tied to family and kinship groups in Turkey. One's sources of self and identity basically refer to social and family networks. Social and familial relationships are regulated by social norms. Despite its fundamentally collectivistic nature, there have been some changes in Turkey in recent years toward individualism. Accordingly, individuals living in a rapidly changing society may be exposed to both individualistic and collectivistic value preferences and may adopt a 'bi-cultural pattern in which both are emphasized' (Freeman and Bordia, 2001, p. 118). Such tendencies were reported in self-definitions and values of urban and educated Turkish youth (Imamoğlu and Karakitapoğlu-Aygün, 1999, 2004; Karakitapoğlu-Aygün and Imamoğlu, 2002; Karakitapoğlu-Aygün, 2004).

Related research also argued that collectivism depends very much on which in-group (family, friends, co-workers etc.) is present (Triandis et al., 1990). For example, Göregenli (1997) found that when spouse, mother, sibling, friend, relatives, neighbor, co-worker, acquaintance and strangers have been presented as reference groups, Turkish people have been found to possess less collectivistic tendencies as the target group or person becomes more psychologically distant. Therefore it is important to understand the influences of significant relationships on career choices in Turkey, which is experiencing rapid socioeconomic changes. In line with the abovementioned research, which implies that individuals tend to report greater intimacy and harmony with in-groups including family and kin, the role of mothers, fathers, significant others/partners and relatives is expected to be greater than that of other non-kin groups. Moreover, since family collectivism is the most salient attribute of the Turkish culture, the roles of kin groups (i.e. mothers, fathers and relatives) were expected to be greater than those of other non-kin groups, including colleagues, managers and friends.

The present study further aims to examine the links between individualistic and collectivistic value orientations at the individual level and the influence of relationships in making career choices among Turkish MBA students. In recent years, culture-level constructs of individualism–collectivism (IC) have been criticized as oversimplifying a complex picture, ignoring within-culture variability and assuming an inherent opposition (Oyserman et al., 2002; Triandis et al., 1988). Accordingly, it has been claimed that those seemingly opposite tendencies may exist together in the same individual (idiocentrism and allocentrism at the individual level corresponding to culture-level IC) and same culture (Triandis et al., 1988). With these critiques in mind, we have tried to overcome those limitations in previous research by considering individual-level value orientations of IC. More specifically, we are interested in the questions 'Do individuals with more collectivistic value orientations tend to be influenced more by their relationships and vice versa?' and 'Which kind of relationships (family or friends, junior or senior work colleagues, mentors etc.) are more influential for individuals with a more collectivistic or individualistic orientation?'

These individual-level IC constructs emphasize separateness or uniqueness versus embeddedness in social relationships. Accordingly, a collectivistic person may be expected to value support from others in his/her career decision-making process, especially from family members and relatives. An individualistic person, on the other hand, might not value involvement of others in such an important issue for his/her personal life. However, recent developmental and social psychological research illustrates that these two constructs of IC or autonomy/independence-relatedness are complementary (Flum, 1994; Guisinger and Blatt, 1994; Imamoğlu, 2003). In other words, independence and autonomy may grow with relatedness and vice versa. Then, in the present study, one may expect both individualistic and collectivistic value orientations to have positive effects on the role of relationships in career decision making, with stronger effects for collectivism.

Furthermore, related research suggests that there is a positive relationship between collectivism and family relatedness; and individualism and peer relatedness (Benet-Martinez and Karakitapoğlu-Aygün, 2003; Kwan et al., 1997). The latter finding was explained by the fact that individualistic orientation leads people to have friends of their own choosing with whom they share interests and values. This research, although scant, implies that collectivistic tendencies are more associated with in-group members such as family, relatives etc., whereas individualistic tendencies seem to be associated with relationships involving friends and colleagues from school and work. Unfortunately, there is not much research investigating the differential role of peers, colleagues, mentors, managers etc. in career decision making. To fill this gap, juniors, peers, senior work colleagues, managers, lecturers, instructors and mentors were also included in the present study. In the light of the above-mentioned research, one may expect collectivism to have positive effects on the influences of family and kin (i.e. mothers, fathers, relatives or significant other) and individualism on the role of peers, work colleagues and managers. Perhaps individuals with a more individualistic orientation make their decisions themselves, signifying that they are the most important agent in making career choices. However, they may consciously and deliberately consult with their colleagues, managers, lecturers and instructors to get more information about their alternatives and to widen their options before making a vital decision for themselves. Then, individuals with more collectivistic orientations may be influenced by the opinions of their family and kin, whereas students with more individualistic orientations may be expected to consult with their peers, colleagues, managers from work, and lecturers and instructors from school.

GENDER AND RELATIONAL INFLUENCES

Another aim of the present study is to elucidate gender-related differences in the role of significant relationships in making career choices. The issue of gender has special significance in the context of career choice due to a long-standing controversy about the existence of gender difference in management and careers. Researchers differ in their opinions regarding the study of sex differences. For example, Baumeister (1988) advocates the abandonment of sex differences since they are no longer necessary or advisable. On the other hand, Eagly (1987), Rothblum (1988) and Lefkowitz (1994) propose the investigation of sex differences in organizational behavior to explore similarities as well as differences. As Eagly (1987, p. 756) puts it, 'null findings, if obtained consistently across studies, would help establish that women and men are similar in many respects'. We agree with these researchers and claim that sex differences or similarities in management and career choice are worth investigating. As Lefkowitz (1994, p. 341) suggests, 'even null findings are important information given the prevalence of gender stereotypes, and because the few robust differences that may be confirmed become even more noteworthy and interesting to explore'.

One line of gender research (e.g. Fisher, 1999) argues for significant differences among sexes in work attitudes, values and behaviors. For example, women have been found to emphasize relatedness and embed-dedness with others, opportunity for interaction with people, fair and con-siderate supervision, social approval and short-term career goals (Elizur, 1994; Lynn, 1993; Sagie et al., 1996). Men, on the other hand, were found to value independence, autonomy, money, competitiveness, rewards and long-term career goals. These differences between men and women appear to support the argument that women's reactions are different from those of men as a result of some biological factors or of differential sex-role social-ization (Chodorow, 1978; Fisher, 1999). According to this theorizing, today's gendered division of labor is explained by the differential interests of men and women. Men and women have particular predispositions or are being socialized differently and accept different gender roles. Therefore their career choices and work behavior reflect their orientations. Women tend to emphasize relatedness with others more than men do, implying stronger effects of relationships on women (Gilligan, 1982; O'Brien, 1996).

The other line of research, however, mostly representing a social per-spective, argues for lack of significant gender differences in management and careers. For example, Kanter (1977, 1993) argues that our attitudes and behaviors at work are determined by social structures in the workplace, but not personal dispositions. One of her arguments is that one's attitudes toward work and behaviors at the workplace have nothing to do with a person's sex, but with the person's position, job situations, and the tasks s/he does at the workplace. Women's weaker tendencies toward careers could then be explained by their being in subordinate positions in the organizations, not by their personality traits. Supporting Kanter's argu-ments, Lefkowitz (1994) found that gender-related differences in work pref-erences, values and attitudes were spurious effects of other variables such as job characteristics, age, tenure, income and occupational level. When these factors were controlled, genders tend to be similar in their preferences.

In the current chapter the issue of gender was examined at the beginning of the path towards a career in management among young men and women MBA students. By studying the possible gender effects in the role of rela-tionships in making career choices, the present study tries to increase under-standing of the theoretical controversy regarding the gender differences in careers and work life. With regard to gender issue in career choice, we adopted a discovery-oriented approach and derived no specific hypotheses. Rather, the aim was exploratory with regard to similarities or differences across genders in the Turkish context.

METHODOLOGY

The study consists of two parts. In the first, quantitative, part, the influence of relational agents in career choice and the links to individualistic–collectivistic value orientations were investigated as well as gender differences in the relational influences. In the second, qualitative, part, the roles that relationships play in shaping individuals' career choices were studied through in-depth semi-structured interviews.

Quantitative Study

Participants
A total of 116 (69 men, 47 women, with a mean age of 23.46) Turkish MBA students participated in the first part of the study. Students were drawn from three large well-known universities, two in Ankara and one in Istanbul. As shown in Table 5.1, almost half of the sample had no work experience and, consequently, mean length of service in current employment was low. In line with their current job condition, most of the students relied on their parents for MBA funding. Almost half of them reported starting their own business or entrepreneurship as their primary career goal, while the rest emphasized being a manager and advancement in their careers as major goals.

Measures and procedure
The Turkish and UK versions of the scales were checked through back translations. Native speakers of English and Turkish also checked the scales for wording, accuracy and clarity of items in both languages. Questionnaires were group-administered to students in class. The participants were assured that their responses would be anonymous and confidential.

Influences of relationships on career choice scale
Participants were asked to consider the listed individuals or groups in terms of their influence on their career choice. The relationships listed were: (1) mother; (2) father; (3) relatives; (4) friends; (5) junior work colleagues; (6) peer work colleagues; (7) senior colleagues; (8) senior managers;

Table 5.1   Sample characteristics (percentages in parentheses)

Variables	
No. of participants	116
Men	69 (59.5)
Women	47 (40.5)
Mean age	23.46
Mean years of high education	3.70
Mean years in current employment	2.04
Occupational status	
White-collar	35 (30.2)
Blue-collar	–
Pink-collar	2 (1.7)
Student	63 (54.3)
Other	6 (5.2)
Career goal	
Management	36 (31)
Own business	41 (35.3)
Entrepreneurship	5 (4.3)
Career advancement	26 (22.4)
Career change	–
Other	5 (4.3)
Funding for MBA study	
Self	15 (12.5)
Parents	76 (65.5)
Work	5 (4.3)
Self and parents	12 (10.3)
Self and work	–
Other	8 (6.9)
Current job condition	
No work experience	50 (43.1)
Unemployed	32 (27.6)
Doing paid work	32 (27.6)

(9) fellow students; (10) lecturers; (11) mentors; and (12) significant other/partner. The response scale was the 7-point Likert scale, where 1 indicated 'no influence at all' and 7 indicated 'great influence'.

Individualism–collectivism

Individualistic and collectivistic value orientations were also measured on a Likert scale, where 1 referred to 'strongly disagree' and 7 'strongly agree'. In this scale (Triandis and Gelfand, 1998), individualism was measured by six items, such as 'Winning is everything' and 'I'd rather depend on myself', whereas collectivism was measured by nine items, such as 'Parents and children must stay together as much as possible' and 'If a co-worker gets a prize, I feel proud'. Cronbach's alpha values were 0.70 for individualism and 0.64 for collectivism.

The Results of the Quantitative Study

To explore gender differences in types of relationships, t-tests were conducted. Moreover, in order to explore associations with individualistic and collectivistic value orientations, correlations between IC and relationship types were computed.

The importance of relationship types and gender differences

As shown in Table 5.2, fathers were rated as having the greatest influence on career choice of Turkish MBA students, followed by lecturers and mothers. Junior and peer work colleagues, on the other hand, were found to be least influential. Contrary to our expectations, relatives were reported to be among the group of agents who had relatively less influence on career choice of MBA students. Fellow students, friends, mentors and senior colleagues/managers were rated as having a moderate influence on career decision making. Moreover, gender-related analyses illustrated that there were no significant differences between genders in terms of the influence of relationship types. Rather, there were very weak trends for relatives, father and

Table 5.2   Gender differences in relationship types

	Men		Women		Entire sample		t
	M	SD	M	SD	M	SD	
Mother	3.35	1.89	3.80	1.89	3.53	1.89	−1.25
Father	3.77	1.94	4.16	2.00	3.92	1.96	−1.03
Relatives	2.43	1.63	2.02	1.35	2.27	1.54	1.40
Friends	3.26	1.89	2.91	1.79	3.12	1.85	0.98
Junior work colleagues	1.90	1.47	1.70	1.20	1.83	1.37	0.71
Peer work colleagues	2.03	1.63	2.05	1.56	2.04	1.60	−0.07
Senior colleagues	2.44	2.01	2.19	1.78	2.35	1.93	0.62
Senior managers	2.61	2.11	2.79	1.86	2.68	2.02	−0.44
Fellow students	3.48	1.74	3.41	1.91	3.45	1.80	0.20
Lecturers	3.54	1.97	3.75	1.97	3.62	1.97	−0.56
Mentors	2.84	2.03	3.02	2.02	2.91	2.02	−0.46
Significant other/partner	2.70	2.03	2.93	1.87	2.79	1.97	−0.62

mothers. Accordingly, women tended to be more influenced by their parents and men by their relatives, in comparison to the other gender.

Correlations between individual-level IC and relationship types

In terms of the correlations between relationship types and individualistic–collectivistic value orientations, our results revealed that individualism was a more important predictor of being influenced by one's significant relationships in Turkey (see Table 5.3). Interestingly, individualism was positively associated with being influenced by one's junior, peer and senior work colleagues, as well as the senior managers at the workplace. Collectivism, on the other hand, was only associated with the involvement of fathers in the career decision-making process, supporting the patriarchal nature of Turkish society.

Qualitative Study

In addition to quantitative data, qualitative data were gathered through interviews to deepen our understanding of the role that relationships play in shaping individuals' career decision-making process. To clarify the role of relationships in career choices, in-depth semi-structured interviews were conducted with 13 (8 men, 5 women) Turkish MBA students. Ten had engineering backgrounds, as is usually the case with Turkish MBA students, whilst the other three had social science degrees. Some of the interviewees were drawn from those who had already participated in the quantitative

Table 5.3   Correlations between type of relationships and individualistic–collectivistic values

	Turkey	
	Ind.	Col.
Father	0.08	**0.23***
Junior work colleagues	**0.23***	−0.00
Peer work colleagues	**0.22***	0.04
Senior colleagues	**0.35*****	0.17
Senior managers	**0.22***	0.14
Fellow students	0.06	0.07
Mentors	0.13	−0.07
Significant other/partner	0.12	0.06
Total influence of relationships	**0.20***	0.08

$p < 0.05$; ** $p < 0.01$; *** $p < 0.001$.

study. In the interviews, we asked them about the agents (e.g. 'We would like to elaborate on the people who have been influential in your career choice. Please rank the three most influential people (or groups of people) in your career choice decision-making process'), types of influences of these relations on the career choice (e.g. 'What kind of influences did this person have on your career choice?'; 'How did this person influence your career choice?') and the reasons of such influence (e.g. 'Why was it your mom/dad/uncle/etc. who had been most influential in your career choice?') to further elaborate the relations and their influences. After the first couple of interviews, it occurred to us that our participants actually made at least two career choices: first when they decided their area of study in their first degrees and second when they decided to do an MBA. Therefore we started to ask the same questions separately for their career choice decisions for their first degrees and then for their MBA degrees. The interviews were conducted in Turkish (the native language of both the interviewees and the interviewer), taped with the consent of the participants and transcribed verbatim. Transcriptions were coded for the agents and the relational dimension categories. Analyses of the transcriptions were done first within cases, and then across cases. The findings revealed, first, the influential agents, and second, the various relational influences they had on the career choices of Turkish MBA students. In the next section, we will discuss these findings within the framework of Schultheiss et al.'s (2001) relational influence dimensions by citing examples from the interviews.

Influential agents and relational dimensions

Our results showed that the three most influential relational agents reported included parents, close relatives (particularly uncles) and acquaintances (parents' friends and colleagues, distant relatives), high school teachers and university professors, friends, higher-level managers, and older siblings, not necessarily in this order.

Relational influence categories found were classified into those domains suggested by Schultheiss et al. (2001) as role model influences, emotional support, information support, esteem support and social integration. The results also revealed that the influential relations, their ranking and the type of influences can be different in the two different career choice stages, pointing to the importance of the timing of the decision.

Parents

In the majority of the cases, either both or one of the parents (particularly fathers) had been reported among the most influential people in the interviewees' initial career decision-making process in various relational dimensions. Parents, especially fathers, were first perceived as a positive role model when uninformed young students were trying to decide which profession to choose. The following account by Interviewee No. 1 illustrated this relational dimension, where the father acted as an admirable example that the interviewee had looked up to:

> My father is a mechanical engineer and so am I. He is a hardworking successful person; as a manager he had a good status in the society and in the smaller communities we lived in. He did not talk too much about the financial aspects of his profession at home, nothing more than what I had been able to observe, but within the family environment you kind of know. In any case, he had earned a decent living and provided a good living standard for our family; he was successful. So I thought I could be like this, I could own similar things. So I guess I saw him as a role model.

Our findings revealed that positive role model influences included those relational experiences where the participant felt the need for the approval and admiration of the influential person, for which Interviewee No. 12's account presented clear evidence:

> I am my daddy's girl. For me, he is in such a high place. I always take him as an ideal example. It is very important for me that my father is proud of me and that I honor him. He is my idol. Therefore his influence on me, on everything I do, is very great. He usually lets me be but it is very important for me to feel his presence in the background. I need to earn his approval and not disappoint him.

Mothers

In addition to fathers, mothers were also listed among the first or second most influential people in career choices. However, in only one case had a mother a positive role model influence in the initial career choice. As an engineering graduate from one of the best universities in Turkey, she had a profile of most role model fathers. She had worked at important government organizations and state-owned enterprises. Her prestigious university and continued relations with her university friends influenced Interviewee No. 3 in choosing to do an engineering degree at the same university. Additionally, Interviewee No. 1 took his mother as a positive role model when he wanted to make a career change from engineering and decided to do an MBA.

Mothers as the most influential people in career choice decisions were mostly found to play emotional and/or information support roles either on their own or together with fathers. As our participants' accounts indicated, mothers provided 'relational influences in terms of emotional support, closeness, encouragement and reducing stress and alleviating stress' (Schultheiss et al., 2001, p. 225). Interviewee No. 6, for instance, stated that his mother played a significant emotional support role when she encouraged him to make his own choice during the initial career decision-making process. She had defended the idea that the participant could select a different university from his father's preference for him. Interviewee No. 12 listed her mother as the second most influential person in her career decision-making process. This participant's mother played the more traditional Turkish mother role: first, as a mediator between the father and the daughter when the latter took an argumentative stance and wanted to make her own decisions; second, a caring role which signals the traditionally accepted approach towards women's employment or career in Turkey where the mother advised that her daughter should chose a 'woman's' job, which would not require too much hard work and effort. Interviewee No. 12 moreover indicated that:

> My mother is like my friend. She gives me advice like a friend. I consult her and she is my advisor. Her importance for me is more emotional. I trust her and believe that I should consider her suggestions seriously.

Some of the participants emphasized the significance of the emotional support dimension of their relations with both their parents in the career decision-making stage. Interviewee No. 10's account is a good example that shows the significance of an emotionally supportive relation with the parents:

> My parents have always encouraged me to do whatever I think would make me happy. It was the same when I decided to do an MBA. There were possibilities of going to the UK or to Istanbul. My father for instance suggested that I could go to Istanbul or to the States. But he never forced me to do anything. They always suggested alternatives. Then during the 1st semester I had experienced difficulties in adapting to the program here, basically because of my background in international relations as this is a very quantitative course and majority of the participants have engineering backgrounds. I had thought of leaving the program. My parents said I could leave it or ask for a suspension and then decide whether to go back or not. Such an understanding positive approach had helped a lot. I am influenced by people who have a positive approach. Also people in my life have a priority ranking: my mom, dad, friends, they are all very important for me. These people always showed their support to me.

In addition to emotional support, mothers took information support roles where they acted as a source of career information (Schultheiss et al., 2001). For Interviewee No. 7 his mother was a resource for direct career advice:

> I considered studying management among my other choices in the undergraduate level. But my mother told me that I could do an MBA on top of my engineering degree. So she influenced me to choose engineering instead of management.

Mothers typically offered career assistance by collecting information on specific courses, job opportunities and labor market conditions for their children, even if they were not the direct resource themselves. Interviewee No. 1's mother was reported to be very influential at the time of his career change decision from engineering to management when she pointed that he could get an MBA and provided information collected from her friends and their children studying for their MBAs and showed how they used it to make a career change, to help the participant to make his own career decision.

A distinctive dimension from those identified by Schultheiss et al. (2001) was reported by the Turkish participants in this study of their relations with their parents. It can be described as a combination of two dimensions by Schultheiss et al. (2001), namely, parent(s) acting as a source of conflict, and the importance of their specific personality characteristics (dominant and controlling) or ideas (ideology) held by them. However, in the Turkish context, the nature of the relationship was stronger than defined by Schultesiss et al. (2001) due to other important factors such as submissive attitude by children towards the authority of their parents. This dimension of the relationship to the parent(s), which is quite common in Turkey, we described as 'push influence'. In many ways, this might be considered not as a social 'support' relation, as it usually created pressure on the participants and influenced their career decision-making process negatively. An extreme example of such a relation was illustrated by Interviewee No. 11, who was strongly encouraged by her parents to choose a certain area, i.e. medicine, to study at university. She wanted to do media studies or law but when she could not convince her parents, she had chosen management as a 'proxy', although she did not know what management was exactly about. She thought it was a more prestigious field of study than media and was closer to her areas of interest than medicine. So she had chosen her profession after high school as a reaction to the pressure exerted upon her by her parents. This 'push influence' relation to her parents continued after her first degree, when they insisted that she should do an MBA. What her parents really hoped was that she would continue with an academic career, following their footsteps as well as other close relatives such as her uncle, 'at least in management'. The pressure exerted upon Interviewee No. 11 had resulted in a completely different career path for her, as she could not persuade her parents to let her make her own choice.

A similar account of 'push influence' was told by Interviewee No. 7, whose experience had not resulted in such a dramatic outcome:

Both my parents wanted me to study medicine very much. I did not want it at all but I thought I could be helpful to my family, had I become a doctor. My grandmother, my aunts, they all wanted me to go to medical school. I believed that it is a very prestigious profession as well. So I put it among my choices in the university placement exam. If I had been placed in the medical school, I would have studied there. My parents and relatives directly influenced me in my choice; and actually I could have ended up in the medical school.

This evidently common dimension among Turkish parents in their relations to their children at career decision-making stages was sometimes strongly resisted, as was told us by Interviewee No. 13. His father pushed him towards a more traditional choice of career, i.e. studying medicine to become a doctor:

You know, in the east [of Turkey] families want their children to study medicine. My father told me that I should definitely study medicine, as there is not any doctor in our family. But this pushy approach backfired on me and I resisted choosing to study medicine. I felt like he was forcing me and I insisted in my own decision.

Relatives and acquaintances

In addition to parents, trusted close relatives (particularly uncles) and more distant relatives and acquaintances (parents' friends and colleagues, neighbours, etc.) were reported among the most important relations in the career decision-making process. Their relations to the participants were influential in essentially two ways, first as a positive role model, and second as providers of information support. For Interviewee No. 3, his uncle had been very strongly influential as a positive role model, indicated in the following vignette:

My uncle had gone to Istanbul and studied and worked at the same time, earning his living. He has got such an incredible life now. He provides excellent education opportunities for his children. His current status in life is wonderful. When I considered his position, I thought to myself that I could be like that too. I don't know, somehow such strong characters influence me. I always think that they do the best and if I follow their footsteps I would do the best as well.

This uncle's experiences and accomplishments had influenced the participant so much that he had become the role model whom the participant aspired to resemble and made his career decision accordingly. Similarly, Interviewee No. 13's uncle was the most influential relation as a positive role model while making his career choice so that he followed his uncle's path:

My uncle studied and graduated from one of the best universities of Turkey. I come from Diyarbakir [one of the least developed towns, in the south-east of Turkey] and he was the first in our family who went to a big city and attended this particular university. He was the most popularly accepted person in my family. He had that very good image. He had this significant place in the family and his ideas were extremely valued by family members. He received an exceptional respect from all of us. He had painted me a picture where I should go to the same university. So I was attracted to the idea of going to this school.

For Interviewee No. 4, his uncle's success and respected position in the family were important factors that made the participant look up to him. He had also held an information support role, partly as a consequence of his admired position:

He is a very successful person in our family and someone I always trusted. He did not apply any pressure on me but he said that if he was going to make a choice now, he would have studied industrial engineering. He had also described the environment at his university as very attractive and told me that I would enjoy my four years of higher education period there. He also convinced me that I shall be able to find good job prospects after graduation and I could be promoted easily as a graduate of this particular school.

Many participants indicated that they had benefited from information support by distant relatives and acquaintances during their career decision-making process. The following account by Interviewee No. 13 can be given as a representative example of such an information support relation between the participant and various acquaintances:

Most Turkish students make uninformed choices at the time of the university placement exam. We don't know much about the professions, course contents, what kind of difficulties the courses or later the profession involve. These acquaintances who were in the academia provided me with such kind of information. They asked me about my interests and capabilities. They told me for instance engineering courses involve a great deal of mathematics and asked me whether I like maths that much or whether I feel I could be successful at it. They have experience and knowledge in career choice, they come across many different cases. Therefore I trust them.

One dimension that did not come up strongly in the accounts by the participants about their relations with parents was esteem support. It was, however, indicated in their relations with other relatives as well as school teachers and university professors. This dimension is described by Schultheiss et al. (2001, p. 226) as 'feeling pushed to perform up to one's potential, feeling another's confidence in their abilities, experiencing freedom regarding exploration and decision making, being encouraged to be responsible for one's decisions, and learning from one's mistakes'. The following account by Interviewee No. 3, for instance, demonstrates that she felt positively pushed by her close relatives to perform up to her fullest potential:

> I guess I have this image in the family as 'She can do this. She is good. She works hard.' They say, 'you like to study, you are apt to studying hard. You are an ambitious person, so you have to accomplish these at your age now.'

School teachers and university professors

School teachers and university professors were reported among the most influential people in the career decision-making process. Some of our participants indicated an esteem support relation with their high school teachers that had made them feel the latter's trust in their capability and potential, as evident in the following vignette by Interviewee No. 13:

> My high school teachers had steered me towards this university and engineering. This was basically because of the prestigious image of this university: no one from my high school had studied at this very well-known Turkish university before and they thought I could do it. They always told me that I was the one who could achieve such a success. And I would be very successful in the work life one day. And I really like to be praised, I am positively influenced by being praised. I am motivated when I know that people think about me as such.

Others were influenced by their professors' (especially in the MBA program) encouragement to perform up to their potential, as was mentioned by Interviewee No. 3:

> Some professors here at the MBA program had mentioned that I should have taken the top scores in the exams and asked me why I did not. I was motivated thinking that they had such an expectation from me, so I could do better.

For some participants, their relation with their university professors (at the undergraduate or postgraduate level) was a combination of positive role model and information support. Interviewee No. 2, for example, said that the positive, open environment at the department and opportunity for friendly conversations with the professors, their positive attitude towards students, knowledge and expertise in their fields and the examples they brought to the class had been very influential in his decision about how to continue his career after finishing the MBA. Interviewee No. 8 was also deeply influenced by the knowledge and experience of some of her instructors in the MBA program and decided to pursue her career in one specific branch of management. She felt that 'my career had found a path after I started this MBA programme. Previously it was all coincidence but now I think I am following a certain career path.'

Quite a few other participants indicated that the information support relation with their university professors was most important, as evident in the following quotation by Interviewee No. 6:

> I talked to my professors at my [engineering] department and here at the management department and decided to go for an MBA to be able to make a career change, from engineering to management.

Friends and co-workers

Another influential agent in the career decision-making process cited by the participants was their friends. Particularly at the initial career choice stage, relations with friends had a significant social integration dimension, which refers to 'having someone to talk things over with, sharing similar personality characteristics and interests, and sharing experiences (i.e. comfort and validation in universal experiences)' (Schultheiss et al., 2001, p. 225). This dimension was clearly illustrated by Interviewee No. 6 in the following:

> We had talked a lot among friends at school and the preparatory courses before the university placement exam. It was a very difficult period as many things were unknown to us. Perhaps we might have influenced each other with my close friends, as we all chose similar fields. This influence was not like 'let's go to the same university or department' and we ended up in various universities and departments. But it was more like talking things over and exchanging information.

Similar aspects of Interviewee No. 9's relation with his high school friends were emphasized in his account:

> When we were all preparing for the university placement exam, we discussed among ourselves what we should do. For instance, because we were all good in maths, we decided that our future professions should be in an engineering field. As female candidates, we did not prefer civil or mechanical engineering because of possible work environments. We thought computer engineering would suit us better. We were the same age, we had a similar thought process.

Relations with friends and co-workers at the same level were reported to have role model influences as well, particularly at the time of career change (from engineering to management by doing an MBA) decisions. Interviewee No. 4, for example, had made his decision to do an MBA primarily by looking at the examples of his working friends:

> I did not hear any encouraging, exciting information from my friends who had started working right after graduation: work was not exciting, they were not given much discretion or opportunities for creativity or initiative. Another older

friend had told me about the difficulties of combining work as an engineer in the production and married life with children. To have more alternatives such as working in the finance area, I decided to get an MBA.

The above account in fact was an example of a negative role influence, where the participant decided to do something not to be like the role models. There were positive role model influences as well, such as in the following account by Interviewee No. 8, who had decided to get an MBA degree by looking at the positive examples:

I had in fact always thought of doing an MBA. When I first graduated I actually collected information about an MBA program at this university. But then I started working and attended another masters program in engineering, but not an MBA. Then at this workplace, my co-workers were pursuing MBAs so I took example of them.

Higher-level managers

The other group of influential agents in career decision reportedly included higher-level managers at the workplaces. In addition to parents and close relatives, these people had also evidently been influential as someone the participants admired deeply for their current status and wealth, and took as their 'hero'. These relations had sometimes worked as career counselors, by giving advice on how to proceed with their careers in certain sectors. For Interviewee No. 2, for instance, one top-level manager at his workplace had been extremely influential in deciding to do an MBA to change his career, as explained in the following excerpt from the interview:

This person is also a family friend and he had been very supportive and influential in my career development. He has now a substantial amount of wealth and status as the partner of an American law company while he used to work in a garage 10 years ago. He is a self-made man, who had worked while studying. He is fluent in English, you know, which is very important to work in a multinational company. He had suggested that I should do an MBA and I should go to [the name of the university]. He had shown me the way, he is the one who had opened me the doors. I am financially and emotionally indebted to him. If he was not in my life, I would not be sitting in front of you today.

Similarly, Interviewee No. 9 had decided to follow a managerial career by following the example of one top-level manager at his workplace:

When I worked at an IT company as a trainee, the general manager told me that he had an electronic engineering degree and then got an MBA from this school and now he has become the general manager. So I thought to myself I could walk the same road.

One final illustration of higher-level managers as the most influential 'relations' in career decisions comes from Interviewee No. 11, who had decided to do an MBA, first, by following the example of good role models in the profession, and second, by complying with her current organization's promotion policies and better career prospects:

> All the managers in this multinational bank have at least one masters degree. My managers told me that they would consider my career planning after I get my masters degree. So I started this program to extend my career alternatives, in the banking sector or another sector. Moreover I met visionary, really smart and very social high-level managers. They impressed me a lot about choosing banking in the first place. I am not yet completely sure about pursuing a career in banking but these top-level managers I met in this organization had influenced me by their status in the society.

Success stories

We have two interesting findings in the qualitative part of this study. First, even if they cannot really be considered as 'relations', some well-known entrepreneurs and business people had an influence on some of the interviewees in their career decision making by having success stories to tell. The following quotation by Interviewee No. 2 demonstrates such an influence:

> Large companies' bosses that I follow from the media or Internet have been very influential on my decision in doing an MBA. I read the life stories of big names, such as Bill Gates or Ted Turner. I am influenced by these people's successes, not by the success of the corner store owner, you know. And I want to be like them.

Interviewee No. 6, as an ambitious person at the beginning of his career, explained why he had been positively influenced by the success stories of such people:

> I read success stories of well-known international entrepreneurs, such as how Henry Ford made it or the person who had established Xerox made it. Their independent minds, earning a lot of money and different way of looking at things, had all influenced me.

Such a 'relation' that can be influential in career decision making was not considered by us when developing the questionnaire; therefore it was not listed among the relationship types to be ranked by the participants according to the significance of their influence. It was, however, mentioned by a few interviewees when talking about the career decision-making process and how they took note of such stories. Therefore this may be an important relation to be considered in future research.

'Myself'

The second interesting finding was also about a 'relation' that was not considered by us among the most significant people in career decision making. A number of participants listed 'themselves' explicitly among the three most influential persons in making their career choices. As a very confident and ambitious person, Interviewee No. 2 told us the following:

> I was not influenced too much by any one, except by this high-level manager who had been very important by showing me the direction. I have been involved in acting for a long time and it is not very common to change from acting to business. But it all happened entirely by my own decision. When I came here for the [MBA] interview, I could not speak almost any English, my exam scores were not high, I did not even have a GMAT score. But I sat in front of the panel and said 'I am going to do this. I have to do this. I will do this and I am going to do it well.' So they took me in. I rank 'myself' in the first place as I think everyone should rank himself/herself as the most significant person to do something like an MBA. At the end of the day, if you don't want to do something, you don't do it, no one can influence you to.

Interviewee No. 6 also ranked himself among the most influential people in both his initial career choice and later for his career development decision. The following demonstrates how he had used his own discretion in choosing his future careers:

> At the time of my initial career choice I had followed the developments in the IT sector closely from the Internet. I was interested in computing and collected information about this field. So I made my own decision. After I graduated as an electronic engineer, I went to the States, and worked and studied at the same time. At that time, I realized that I did not want to do an academic career because it was not the right career path that would take me to the point that I wanted to reach. It was during that time, while reading on marketing for instance I realized that I had a very technical approach to issues. I searched about how I could develop my career and that was how I decided that I needed to do an MBA. So I decided on my own to go for an MBA. I told my parents after I made my decision and they did not have any influence. They just asked whether I had considered it thoroughly.

These participants were concerned about taking control of their careers themselves, although they asked for information or were given advice by some relations. Interviewee No. 9 explained how he had decided about his career himself, while he was also influenced by his friends and some relatives and acquaintances:

> I felt that I had to make a change because I was afraid that my life would continue like this, writing codes in front of a computer. In order to extend my career alternatives while using my engineering background I decided to do an MBA.

My parents and some acquaintances suggested that I should work for some time first and then decide. They were concerned that my engineering education would have been wasted. But I made my mind to do an MBA. So it was my own decision and taking initiative. My family members do not understand me, they do not know much about engineering or management. They have a different perspective of career and jobs.

Interviewee No. 13's account about how and why he ranked himself as the third most influential person in making his career decisions clearly shows some common personality characteristic of the participants:

At the end of the day, I made my own decision. I don't like to make my decisions according to other's thoughts. Plus I like to be different from the crowd and be the best in my area. I had thought about going abroad, be different and accomplish big successes. Therefore my own decision making was most important. OK, it was my uncle who told me about this university and get me thinking about studying there. Hence I ranked him as the most influential person in my initial career decision making. But I would not have studied there, had I not decided to. For instance, if I had wanted to study medicine, I would have accomplished that as well.

The above quotations taken from the interview transcriptions showed how the participants explicitly claimed their own significance in career decision making. One last participant, Interviewee No. 5, did not so overtly make a point by listing herself as one of the most influential people in this process. But it was understood from her interview that she had made her own decisions both at the initial and later career choice stages without being influenced too much by any of her social relations. Information support and some emotional support had been all that she had taken from 'others', including her parents and other close relatives.

In sum, from this qualitative study it is evident that a number of agents play various relational roles in the career decision-making process. In terms of agents and relational dimensions involved, decision making in career choice is argued to be a multidimensional and multi-level complicated process. Table 5.4 summarizes the findings of our qualitative research in terms of these agents and the relational dimensions of their influence.

DISCUSSION

In this study, we explored the relatively uninvestigated domain of relational influences on the career choice of MBA students. We have a number of significant findings reached by using a combined qualitative and quantitative research approach. In this section we discuss these findings within the research framework presented earlier.

Table 5.4   Influential agents and relational dimensions in career decision-making process

	Role model influence	Emotional support	Information support	Esteem support	Social integration
Fathers	+	+	+		
Mothers		+	+		
Relatives and acquaintances	+		+	+	
School teachers and university professors			+	+	
Friends and colleagues					+
Higher-level managers	+				

Emerging Themes in the Interviews

One interesting theme emerging in the interviews was the timing of the career decision. In other words, the respondents made a distinction between their initial career choices at the undergraduate level and later career choices at the graduate level. The results suggested differences in the importance and functions/roles of relationship types depending on the timing of the career decision. Accordingly, fathers (parents), relatives and teachers acted as influential agents for the initial career decisions. In terms of the roles/functions of these relationship types, the results revealed that these people provided information and emotional support, acted as positive role models, and played more directive and leading roles for the early career choices.

For the later career choices at the graduate level regarding pursuing an MBA degree, the respondents usually referred to individualistic and independent decision making and appeared as confident, ambitious and hardworking students with high aspirations. Having finished their undergraduate studies, they realized that they did not actually want to work as engineers in these particular areas. So they consciously made a decision to change career or widen their options. However, this finding does not necessarily deny the importance of others in career decision making. Rather than solely relying on the influence of others in various relational dimensions, MBA students asked for specific suggestions and direction while making important decisions. Possibly in this way they enhanced their feelings of self-efficacy (Lent et al., 1994).

At this later career choice stage, the types of relational agents were more or less similar to those reported for initial choices, with the addition of university professors, acquaintances, co-workers and higher-level managers. However, there were differences in the roles/functions of those relationship types. In these later career choices, the influence of those agents took on more of a supportive role as opposed to the directive and leading role in the initial career choices. Those information sources helped MBA students understand their options and, consequently, make a more informed choice. Self-driven, ambitious, more experienced and educated individuals made more conscious decisions, reporting themselves as the most important influential agent in making the career (change) decision. Interestingly, people at the graduate level were influenced by famous success stories of well-known entrepreneurs. That is, they decided to pursue more ambitious careers 'by being different from the crowd' and by using their abilities and potential to improve themselves further through their MBA.

These results suggest that career choice is a complex phenomenon. The type (leading or supportive) and the extent of influence exerted by others differ depending on the time of the decision (i.e. initial and later career path choices) and type of relationship. Individualistic decision making can be more valid in later career choices for particular people (i.e. highly educated, ambitious, self-driven people with probably a more individualistic value orientation). Individualistic decision making does not necessarily mean exclusion of others in career choice. Rather, it seems to include asking for the opinions of trusted people, where the ultimate decision was made independently.

Another important theme that emerged in the participants' reports of the most influential people in their career choice was trust, which encapsulated two elements. The interviewees trusted those people who presumably knew them well (i.e. parents, close relatives, friends and teachers). Second, they trusted those they deemed to have expert knowledge of career opportunities, the labor market and advantageous entry routes to these through the education system. Trusted people acted as most influential regarding in particular the initial career choices, i.e. undergraduate degrees.

Consistent with previous research, our findings also confirmed the importance of social support (Blustein, 2001; Lent et al., 1994; Phillips et al., 2001; Schultheiss et al., 2001; Schultheiss et al., 2002) and role modeling (Schultheiss et al., 2001) in career choice. The nature of support that emerged in the interviews, such as emotional, informational and esteem support, is consistent with the theoretical functions of support in well-being. In other words, the role of support reported in this investigation is related to enhancing one's ability to deal effectively with stressful situations such as those encountered in career decision making. The present study also contributes to the literature on conceptualizations of work by expanding the understanding of how individuals learn about and prepare for their careers. The results suggest that MBA students learn about the world of work from the important people surrounding them. They turn to those people for advice and support. Consequently, those relational agents act as role models, and sources of support and career information for the MBA students.

Not many students reported a 'push influence', especially by their parents who created some pressure on the participants, which negatively influenced their career decision-making process. This finding suggested that incompatible values and expectations of parents and their children may result in conflict, stress, resistance and negative experiences about the involvement of parents. However, the number of respondents who reported such negative experiences was quite small and the majority in general seemed to feel supported and assisted.

Influential Agents and Relational Dimensions

In terms of who these influential agents are, the results of the quantitative and qualitative studies revealed mostly parallel conclusions. One such result was that parents were rated as having the greatest influence on career choice of Turkish MBA students. This finding is in line with other research, which emphasizes the role of family influence and parental acceptance in collectivistic settings (Leong, 1991; Singarevelu et al., 2005). For example, Tang et al. (1999) illustrate that parental acceptance, not personal interest, determines Asian Americans' career choices. Among the family members, parents, particularly fathers, seem to play the most important role in the career choice of Turkish MBA students. This finding is also consistent with other research from collectivistic contexts where decision making is influenced by family values expressed mostly by the father (McWhirter et al., 1998; Singarevelu et al., 2005). It can also be explained by the paternalistic features of Turkish culture where support, care and protection characterize the relationships (Aycan, 2001). In such a context, the involvement of fathers in career decision making of their children is not surprising. The results of the qualitative study support these conclusions by illustrating that fathers emerge as the source of information and emotional support for their children. They were also taken as role models, influencing the participants by their status, high-level positions and financial conditions. Although parents were by far the most often cited influential relations, mothers were rarely regarded as role models; their influence was usually limited to emotional and information support.

Another parallel finding of the quantitative and qualitative studies was the influence of school teachers and university professors in the career choice of Turkish MBA students. The qualitative investigation revealed that they had evidently influenced the participants by their knowledge of and experience in specific areas to choose certain fields and universities. The significance of the information support dimension of the relation with these agents was primarily due to poorly informed students at their initial career choice stage. As there is no careers advice service in Turkey, high school instructors acted as such, but within their very limited knowledge of both the students and education routes that lead to career opportunities. Suggestions were made mostly according to the most popular, that is prestigious, areas of study and students' levels of attainment. Such positive encouragement and reinforcement of students' potential could increase students' career aspirations and outcomes.

One dissimilar finding across two studies was related to the influences of relatives in career choice. The quantitative study indicated that relatives were rated as having the least influence on career choice of Turkish MBA students, which was surprising given the family-oriented collectivism in Turkey. Yet the results of our qualitative study revealed that well-trusted relatives and acquaintances who achieved a successful career would emerge as sources of expert knowledge about career opportunities and act as role models, having been the first and/or most successful person in the family, especially uncles as sources of expertise and knowledge drawing on their field (i.e. engineering). These inconsistent findings across the two studies emphasize the importance of using both qualitative and quantitative methods in career choice research in order to better delineate the roles and functions of relationships in career decision making.

Gender Differences in Relational Influences

Regarding gender differences in the influence of relationships in making career choices, no significant effects were observed for any of the relationship types. This interesting finding is supportive of the social perspective in the literature, which argues for the lack of significant gender differences in management and careers (Erez et al., 1989; Kanter, 1977, 1993; Lefkowitz, 1994). Accordingly, our women and men respondents reported similar relational influences, which challenges women's relationality (Chodorow, 1978; Gilligan, 1982). Therefore one can conclude that the extent of gender differences in work values and attitudes tends to decrease as more and more women become a part of the individualistic work realm. One should also keep in mind that our sample consisted of MBA students who came from upper socioeconomic backgrounds. With increased educational attainment and socioeconomic status, Turkish women are becoming more independent and autonomous in terms of values and self-definitions (İmamoğlu and Karakitapoğlu-Aygün, 2004; Karakitapoğlu-Aygün, 2004) and more successful in their careers (Aycan, 2004). Therefore, among such an educated and career-oriented group, gender is less likely to play a significant role in the career decision-making process. The lack of gender differences is also supportive of the idea that in a sociocultural environment where establishing and maintaining relationships with others is a main concern, as in Turkey, women and men may equally conceptualize themselves in relational terms (Karakitapoğlu-Aygün, 2004).

IC and Relationship Types

Finally, IC-related analyses revealed that collectivism was not as important as expected in predicting the influence of significant others in career decision making. As mentioned before, literature on career development emphasizes the influence of collectivist values on career choice behaviors (Leong, 1991; Schultheiss, 2003; Tang et al., 1999). Accordingly, collectivism was associated with strong influence and guidance from others regarding career choice. In the current quantitative investigation that link was only present for fathers, but not for any of the other significant relationship types. This positive association between collectivism and involvement of fathers in career decision making may be perceived as a consequence of the paternalistic characteristics of Turkish culture. However, the lack of significant correlations between collectivism and the influence of other relationship types, especially the other kin members, including mothers and relatives, is interesting. One explanation for this finding may be the changing nature of values in Turkey (Imamoğlu and Karakitapoğlu-Aygün, 1999, 2004). As mentioned before, Turkey has been undergoing a rapid change towards more individualism in recent years. This changing pattern of values was possibly reflected in the career choices of MBA students. In such times of transition, 'fulfilling one's own desires and expectations has become as important as (if not more than) fulfilling other's wishes and expectations' (Aycan and Fikret-Paşa, 2003, p. 139). The lack of significant associations between collectivism and the influence of significant others can also be explained by the small sample size and the nature of quantitative investigation. Future qualitative research is needed to further elaborate on the differences among relationship types of MBA students who have individualistic or collectivistic value orientations.

The second IC-related finding was that individualism was positively associated with being influenced by one's junior, peer and senior colleagues, and managers. This finding was in line with our expectations. As mentioned before, students with a more individualistic orientation may rate themselves as the most important agents in their career decisions. They may also be more proactive in gathering occupational information, experiences, advice and opinions to increase confidence in their ability to make their own decisions. As they emphasize self-development and personal choice, they may be trying to maximize the benefits of their social networks. As will be recalled, one of the aims of the quantitative study was to answer the question 'Which kind of relationships are more influential for individuals with a more collectivistic or individualistic orientation?' The answer to this question on the basis of our quantitative study would be that fathers seem to be more influential for people with a collectivistic orientation, whereas colleagues from work are more so for people with an individualistic orientation. However, the answer to this question should be further studied through qualitative studies, as our interview results suggested that the majority of our respondents reported some kind of influence from their parents although they were independent decision makers.

Implications

Although the present study investigated one culture, used a homogeneous sample and collected qualitative and quantitative data with a limited number of respondents, the results have some implications for career theory and practice. Traditional Western career choice theories emphasized independent thought and judgment in career choice. Accordingly, consulting with others has been conceptualized as an obstacle to successful career decisions. Our findings, however, provided general support for the valuable use of others in career decision making. By delineating the link between individual-level IC orientations and the influence of relationships in career choice, the present study also shed light on the differential role of relationships for individuals with different value orientations. In short, the results of the present investigation suggest that while considering career choice, sociocultural factors should be taken into consideration. In a fundamentally collectivistic context, getting relational support may provide an informative view of the real-life context, as well as the ability to cope with the ambiguities associated with career decision making. In such an environment, relational support may not imply conformity, dependency or anomaly (Bellah et al., 1985), but rather a healthy functioning. Therefore career choice seems to be a more complex and intricate issue that should be studied from multiple perspectives (e.g. individual, relational, sociocultural) than most conceptualizations of career choice literature suggest.

Our findings also have some implications for career choice counselors. First, it might be important for counselors to consider how and to what extent their clients are influenced by their particular relationships in career decision making. Second, and perhaps more important, our study has a cultural approach. Counselors can make use of our findings while dealing with clients from various ethnic and cultural backgrounds. They can moreover consider individual-level value orientations of clients in terms of IC, and the implications of such value orientations on types and functions of significant relationships. In our study, for instance, although decision makers were independent and active in their career choice, they nevertheless appreciated support and help from significant others. Therefore counselors may pay attention to the fact that significant relationships and their involvement may be quite valuable in the decision-making process of their clients. Finally, it should be noted that since there are no professional career advice services in Turkey, parents, relatives and instructors seem to act as such. The role of the relationships might have been found to be different if such professional services had been in place. More professional advice services would result in better-informed decision making in career choice.

REFERENCES

Aycan, Z. (2001), 'Human resource management in Turkey: current issues and future challenges', *International Journal of Manpower*, **22**(3): 252–60.

Aycan, Z. (2004), 'Key success factors for women in management in Turkey', *Applied Psychology: An International Review*, **53**(3): 453–77.

Aycan, Z. and Fikret-Paşa, S. (2003), 'Career choices, job selection criteria, and leadership preferences in a transitional nation: the case of Turkey', *Journal of Career Development*, **30**(2): 129–44.

Baumeister, R.F. (1988), 'Should we stop studying sex differences altogether?', *American Psychologist*, **43**: 1092–5.

Baumeister, R.F. and Leary, M.R. (1995), 'The need to belong: desire for interpersonal attachments as a fundamental human motivation', *Psychological Bulletin*, **117**(3): 497–529.

Bellah, R.N., Madsen, R., Sullivan, W.M., Swidler, A. and Tipton, S.M. (1985), *Habits of the Heart: Individualism and Commitment in American Life*, New York: Harper & Row.

Benet-Martinez, V. and Karakitapoğlu-Aygün, Z. (2003), 'The interplay of cultural syndromes, and personality in predicting life-satisfaction: comparing Asian- and European-Americans', *Journal of Cross-Cultural Psychology*, **34**: 38–60.

Blustein, D.L. (2001), 'The interface of work and relationships: critical knowledge for 21st century psychology', *The Counseling Psychologist*, **29**: 179–92.

Blustein, D.L., Phillips, S.D., Jobin-Davis, K., Finkelberg, S.L. and Roarke, A.E. (1997), 'A theory-building investigation of the school-to-work transition', *The Counseling Psychologist*, **25**: 364–402.

Blustein, D.L., Schultheiss, D.E.P. and Flum, H. (2004), 'Toward a relational perspective of the psychology of careers and working: a social constructionist analysis', *Journal of Vocational Behavior*, **64**: 423–40.

Chodorow, N. (1978), *The Reproduction of Mothering: Psychoanalysis and the Sociology of Gender*, Berkeley, CA: University of California Press.

Eagly, A.H. (1987), 'Reporting sex differences', *American Psychologist*, **42**: 756–7.

Elizur, D. (1994), 'Gender and work values: a comparative analysis', *Journal of Social Psychology*, **134**: 201–12.

Erez, M., Borochov, O. and Mannheim, B. (1989), 'Work values of youth: effects of sex or sex role typing?', *Journal of Vocational Behavior*, **34**: 350–66.

Fisher, H. (1999), *The First Sex: The Natural Talents of Women and How They are Changing the World*, New York: Random House.

Flum, H. (1994), 'The evolutive style of identity formation', *Journal of Youth and Adolescence*, **23**: 489–98.

Flum, H. (2001), 'Relational dimensions in career development', *Journal of Vocational Behavior*, **59**: 1–16.

Freeman, M.A. and Bordia, P. (2001), 'Assessing alternative models of individualism and collectivism: a confirmatory factor analysis', *European Journal of Personality*, **15**: 105–21.

Gilligan, C. (1982), *In a Different Voice: Psychological Theory and Women's Development*, Cambridge, MA: Harvard University Press.

Göregenli, M. (1997), 'Individualist and collectivist tendencies in a Turkish sample', *Journal of Cross-Cultural Psychology*, **28**: 787–93.

Guisinger, S. and Blatt, S.J. (1994), 'Individuality and relatedness: evolution of a fundamental dialectic', *American Psychologist*, **49**: 104–11.

Hansen, J.I. (1988), 'Changing interests of women: myth or reality?', *Applied Psychology: An International Review*, **37**: 133–50.

Hofstede, G. (1980), *Culture's Consequences: International Differences in Work-related Values*, Beverly Hills, CA: Sage.

Imamoğlu, E.O. (2003), 'Individuation and relatedness: not opposing but distinct and complementary', *Genetic, Social and General Psychology Monographs*, **129**(4): 367–402.

Imamoğlu, E.O. and Karakitapoğlu-Aygün, Z. (1999), '1970lerden 1990lara değerler: Üniversite düzeyinde zaman, kuşak ve cinsiyet farklılıkları' ('Value preferences from the 1970s to the 1990s: cohort, generation and gender differences at a Turkish university'), *Türk Psikoloji Dergisi (Turkish Journal of Psychology)*, **14**(44): 1–22.

Imamoğlu, E.O. and Karakitapoğlu-Aygün, Z. (2004), 'Self-construals and values across different cultural and socio-economic contexts', *Genetic, General and Social Psychology Monographs*, **130**(4): 277–306.

Kanter, R.M. (1977), *Men and Women of the Corporation*, New York: Business Books.

Kanter, R.M. (1993), *Men and Women of the Corporation*, New York: Business Books.

Karakitapoğlu-Aygün, Z. (2004), 'Self, identity, and emotional well-being among Turkish university students', *Journal of Psychology*, **138**: 457–78.

Karakitapoğlu-Aygün, Z. and Imamoğlu, E.O. (2002), 'Value domains of Turkish adults and university students', *Journal of Social Psychology*, **142**: 333–51.

Kwan, V.S.Y., Bond, M.H. and Singelis, T.M. (1997), 'Pan-cultural explanations for life-satisfaction: adding relationship harmony to self-esteem', *Journal of Personality and Social Psychology*, **73**: 1038–51.

Lefkowitz, J. (1994), 'Sex-related differences in job attitudes and dispositional variables: now you see them, . . .', *Academy of Management Journal*, **37**(2): 323–49.

Lent, R.W., Brown, S.D. and Hackett, G. (1994), 'Toward a unifying social cognitive theory of career and academic interest, choice and performance', *Journal of Vocational Behavior*, **45**: 79–122.

Leong, F.T.L. (1991), 'Career development attributes and occupational values of Asian American and White American college students', *Career Development Quarterly*, **39**: 221–30.

Lynn, R. (1993), 'Sex differences in competitiveness and valuation of money in twenty countries', *Journal of Social Psychology*, **133**: 507–11.

McWhirter, E.H., Hackett, G. and Bandalos, D.L. (1998), 'A causal model of the educational plans and career expectations of Mexican American high school girls', *Journal of Counseling Psychology*, **45**: 166–81.

O'Brien, K.M. (1996), 'The influence of psychological separation and parental attachment on the career development of adolescent women', *Journal of Vocational Behavior*, **48**: 257–74.

Oyserman, D., Coon, H.M. and Kemmelmeier, M. (2002), 'Rethinking individualism and collectivism: evaluation of theoretical assumptions and meta-analyses', *Psychological Bulletin*, **128**: 3–72.

Phillips, S.D., Christopher-Sisk, E. and Gravino, K.L. (2001), 'Making career decisions in a relational context', *The Counseling Psychologist*, **29**: 193–213.

Rothblum, E.D. (1988), 'More on reporting sex differences', *American Psychologist*, **43**: 1095.

Sagie, A., Elizur, D. and Koslowsky, M. (1996), 'Work values: a theoretical overview and a model of their effects', *Journal of Organizational Behavior*, **17**: 503–14.

Schultheiss, D.E.P. (2003), 'A relational approach to career counseling: theoretical integration and practical application', *Journal of Counseling and Development*, **81**: 301–10.

Schultheiss, D.E.P., Kress, H.M., Manzi, A.J. and Glasscock, J.M.J. (2001), 'Relational influences in career development: a qualitative inquiry', *The Counseling Psychologist*, **29**: 216–39.

Schultheiss, D.E.P., Palma, T.V., Predragovich, K.S. and Glasscock, M.J. (2002), 'Relational influences on career paths: siblings in context', *Journal of Counseling Psychology*, **49**: 302–10.

Singaravelu, H.D., White, L.J. and Bringaze, T.B. (2005), 'Factors influencing international students' career choice: a comparative study', *Journal of Career Development*, **32**(1): 46–59.

Tang, M., Fouad, N. and Smith, P. (1999), 'Asian American's career choices: a path model to examine factors influencing their career choices', *Journal of Vocational Behavior*, **54**: 142–57.

Triandis, H.C. and Gelfand, M.J. (1998), 'Converging measurement of horizontal and vertical individualism and collectivism', *Journal of Personality and Social Psychology*, **74**: 118–28.

Triandis, H.C., Bontempo, R., Villareal, M.J., Asai, M. and Lucca, N. (1988), 'Individualism and collectivism: cross-cultural perspectives on self-in-group relationships', *Journal of Personality and Social Psychology*, **54**: 323–38.

Triandis, H.C., McCusker, C. and Hui, C.H. (1990), 'Multimethod probes of individualism and collectivism', *Journal of Personality and Social Psychology*, **59**: 1006–20.

6. Serial high-tech entrepreneurs and managers in Israel: background and personality

Gilat Kaplan

Only recently (mid-2006) a large high-tech company in Israel was purchased by a very well-known investor. Warren Buffett bought 'Ishkar', an Israeli high-tech company, for four billion dollars. This large acquisition is merely one representative of the worldwide interest in the Israeli high-tech industry, which is considered to be second only to Silicon Valley (De Fontenay and Carmel, 2004). This phenomenon enhances curiosity and interest in the locomotives of that industry – high-tech entrepreneurs and managers.

In this chapter the spotlight focuses on highly successful serial high-tech entrepreneurs and a comparison sample of high-ranking managers (executives) who were interviewed about their background and personality. The interviews were conducted and analyzed within the framework of psychoanalytic theory. The purpose of this chapter is to reveal the factors and motivations that influenced high-tech entrepreneurs and managers to choose the career they have chosen.

Psychoanalytic theory regards itself as the art of human relationships at every level and phase (Hatav, 2003). Freud regarded it as a form of treatment but also as a new branch of science (Mitchell and Black, 1995). Psychoanalysis is a theory that uses its tools and concepts to deepen the understanding of other fields such as social sciences, art, literature and even politics (Hatav, 2003). The basic assumptions of psychoanalysis are that early childhood experiences with the parents create the basic structure of the psyche and a person's developing unique personality (Freud, 1913, 1914, 1915, 1920, 1923a, 1924). The basic structure contains anxieties and defenses against them, quality of interpersonal relationships, and cohesiveness of identity. All of these are unconscious. A person may be aware only of his wishes and impulses but not of their origin (Freud, 1923a).

The present chapter is based on the assumption that childhood experiences of serial entrepreneurs as a group have similar elements that influenced their motivation to become entrepreneurs. Managers, on the other hand,

share childhood experiences that are somewhat different from those of entrepreneurs that influenced their motivation to become managers.

BECOMING A HIGH-TECH ENTREPRENEUR

Serial high-tech entrepreneurs are defined as entrepreneurs who tend to
create enterprises one after the other in the high-tech arena. After founding a firm, they tend to focus on it, but when it reaches a certain phase or
magnitude, instead of continuing to manage it, they transfer the management to another manager and move to the next enterprise (MacGarth,
1996; Scott and Rosa, 1996). The current research focused on entrepreneurs
who succeeded with at least one enterprise and continued to found another.

A high-tech industry is one that develops and uses novel and advanced
technology in a variety of fields such as computers, electronics, ICT, and
other industries such as medical, biotech, military and agricultural. The
extent of the usage of new technologies may vary from mostly existing technologies to technologies that did not exist before. As a result, novelty is
common in its social and political environment (De Fontenay and Carmel,
2004; Shenhar et al. (forthcoming).

Schumpeter (1965) argued that entrepreneurs are unique individuals who
emerge in new situations. Most people are looking for stability and security
whereas entrepreneurs are driven by different motivations: their psychological needs are to feel appreciated, worthy, meaningful and acknowledged.
Their needs are actualized via an urge to build their kingdom, their willingness to fight for it and for its victory, and to gain superiority by working hard
and making big sacrifices.

What distinguishes them from others is their ability to anticipate and
visualize the future, their tendency towards innovation (which scares most
people) and their ability to implement it (Schumpeter, 1965). Drucker
(1985) added that creativity, in the sense of innovation, is the core characteristic of entrepreneurs: entrepreneurs always look for a change, respond
to it and use it as an opportunity.

According to Schumpeter (1965), the role of entrepreneurs is to change
society. They can carry this out because entrepreneurs act according to
their instincts and vision. They are relatively free of the constraints
imposed by tradition, values or relationships. They do not fear ambiguity
and they have the ability to create a world – to transform their will into a
firm. These patterns can be acted out only by a certain, unique person who
has evolved with a particular psychological background.

Kets de Vries, a psychoanalyst and a professor of business administration, conducted a psychoanalysis of an entrepreneur, thereby revealing and

describing his inner world. De Vries concluded that entrepreneurs (despite their abilities and remarkable achievements) tend to feel insecure in close relationships, suffer from unstable self-esteem and use manic defenses (denial, split, idealization–devaluation, hyperactivity) against those painful feelings (Kets de Vries, 1996). De Vries regarded the entrepreneur's suffering as related to his childhood and his relationships mainly with his father and his mother. The father was perceived as missing (his patient's father was sick and then died), the patient's mother was perceived as dominant and controlling. The entrepreneur felt unseen, unappreciated; he longed for the protective and loving touch that he remembered from his father's treatment of him.

Kets de Vries's case study was reinforced by academic literature relying on research and clinical work with entrepreneurs. Scholars who used a psychoanalytic framework for understanding the entrepreneur's inner world revealed certain early childhood experiences which seem connected to the underlying motivation to become an entrepreneur (Dvir and Pines, Chapter 11 in this volume; Kets de Vries, 1996; Pines, 2003; Pines et al., 2002). They concluded that salient characteristics of the entrepreneur's inner world in early childhood were that most were first-born in their family of origin, they did not identify with their fathers, and their mothers were experienced as controlling/domineering and unsupportive.

According to psychoanalytic theory the absence of the father might be connected to less conformism and difficulties of accepting authority and reality. In this chapter it is argued that certain people, such as entrepreneurs, might transform the lack of a father figure into creativity and thinking out of the box.

In the current research four hypotheses were questioned regarding those characteristics of the entrepreneur's family of origin. High-ranking high-tech executives were chosen as a comparison group due to the similarities of the two populations:

1. Based on scholars (Hisrich and Brush, 1986) it was hypothesized that more entrepreneurs would be first-born in their family of origin than executives.
2. Based on scholars (Kets de Vries, 1996) it was hypothesized that more entrepreneurs would perceive their fathers as missing than executives.
3. Based on scholars (Kets de Vries, 1996) it was hypothesized that more entrepreneurs would perceive their mothers as less supportive than executives.
4. Based on scholars (Drucker, 1985) it was hypothesized that more entrepreneurs would describe themselves as creative and with the ability to think out of the box than executives.

METHOD

Subjects

Forty-two serial high-tech entrepreneurs including 39 men (93 percent) and three women (7 percent). Average age was 48.6 years (SD 6.87). Among them 83 percent were married.

Thirty-eight high-ranking executives (mainly CEOs) in high technology included 32 men (84 percent) and 6 women (16 percent). Average age was 45.6 years (SD 5.98). Among them 97 percent were married.

Instrument

The research was carried out via a semi-structured, in-depth psycho-analytic interview based on a half-structured questionnaire including questions regarding: order of birth, family background, early childhood memories and free associations, questions regarding traits and character-istics. The questionnaire was partly based on a questionnaire taken from the research done by Pines et al. (2002). Cronbach's alpha for the person-ality traits = 0.86.

In the current research Cronbach's alpha for identifying with the father = 0.88, and Cronbach's alpha for identifying with the mother = 0.89.

Procedure

Eighty participants: 42 entrepreneurs and 38 executives were interviewed by an in-depth interview following a half-structured questionnaire. The interview was conducted by the researcher, a senior clinical psychologist, in the interviewee's office or the researcher's office according to convenience. The interview started after assurance of privacy and a quiet place. The interview lasted one hour to two hours. Discretion and anonymity were assured.

RESULTS

The four hypotheses of the research were tested by: t-tests for independent samples for testing the hypothesis regarding the 'unsupportive mother' and the hypothesis regarding 'creativity' and 'thinking out of the box', Chi-square analyses for independence for testing the significance of differences between entrepreneurs and managers regarding 'order of birth' and 'the missing father'.

In addition, the qualitative data gathered by the interviewees via the half-structured in-depth interview were analyzed and explained by psychoanalytic theory.

All four hypotheses were confirmed.

Hypothesis 1: Birth order – 71 percent of the serial high-tech entrepreneurs were first in the order of birth while only 39.5 percent of the high-tech executives were first in the order of birth ($\chi^2 = 8.28$, $p > 0.5$).

Hypothesis 2: The missing father – 59.5 percent of the serial high-tech entrepreneurs reported (without been asked) that they perceived their father as missing, while only 24 percent of the high-tech executives did so ($\chi^2 = 10.49$, $p > 0.01$).

Hypothesis 3: Unsupportive mother – on a 7-point scale (from 1 = not at all to 7 = very much), the mean grade that serial high-tech entrepreneurs reported their mother as supportive was 3.29, while high-tech executives reported as 4.78, $t = 3.18$, $p > 0.01$.

Hypothesis 4: Creativity and thinking out of the box – on a 7-point scale (from 1 = not at all to 7 = very much), the mean grade that serial high-tech entrepreneurs perceived their creativity was 6.08, while high-tech executives perceived as 5.53, $t = 2.20$, $p > 0.05$. On a 7 point scale (from 1 = not at all to 7 = very much), the mean grade that serial high technology entrepreneurs perceived their ability of thinking out of the box as 6.22 while high technology executives perceived as 5.57, $t = 3.25$, $p > 0.01$.

DISCUSSION

All four hypotheses of the research were confirmed, suggesting that highly successful serial high-tech entrepreneurs and senior high-tech executives in Israel do differ in terms of early childhood experiences even though they share a remarkable resemblance.

The basis for the hypotheses is that the entrepreneurs' childhood featured a unique relationship with their parents. As a result, certain common characteristics were revealed in the entrepreneurs' inner world:

1. Entrepreneurs tend to be first in the order of birth in their family of origin. Being the first has psychological consequences which will be elaborated shortly.
2. Entrepreneurs tend to experience their fathers as missing. The missing figure of the father in the internal world may lead to a fragmented or

impaired father figure, a father figure with whom the entrepreneurs find it hard to identify.

3. Entrepreneurs tend to experience their mother as not supportive. However, they stress the fact that the household was organized and controlled by the mothers, who tried to push them to gain the highest possible marks at school, expected much of them and were willing to make sacrifices for that purpose. The entrepreneurs' abilities and competences, on the other hand, may indicate that in early infancy, mothers who were 'good enough' made the 'entrepreneurs-to-be' feel that they trusted them and believed in their abilities and competences.

4. As a result of the early relationships with their parents, the 'entrepreneurs-to-be' remained with an unfulfilled need to have an idealized father figure and therefore did not establish stable self-esteem. Their self-esteem varies from omnipotence to a painful feeling of emptiness and failure. Both feelings may push them to be high achievers.

5. The lack of a supportive mother may lead the entrepreneurs to seek in a close relationship a 'perfect mirror' or a 'twin soul'. For instance, they need their wives to be totally supportive and understanding and to dedicate themselves to their fulfillment. That kind of relationship with others is called by the one of the psychoanalytic schools 'relations of part object'. The person is not regarded as a whole person; he is regarded according to his function or meaning to the perceiving individual.

THE FATHER FIGURE

The relationship with their father that most serial high-tech entrepreneurs experienced in their childhood was either of a loving father who was a weak person, or a critical, neglectful father, who failed to give the child a sense of security, or a missing father, who was not at home and not available to the child.

The father role in classic psychoanalytic theory (Freud, 1930) is to be an agent of socialization – to help the child overcome his impulses and drives and to adjust to the social order, rules and law. For that purpose the father should be perceived as strong and present. The way the father figure is experienced and internalized is critical in an extremely important phase in the child's emotional development – the Oedipal phase. In this phase (between ages 3 and 5) the child is experiencing a genital sensitivity and interest which are directed toward the mother. At the same time the child realizes that the mother is the father's sexual partner and that they share something in which he cannot participate. Moreover, the child fears that his father will punish him for his unacceptable wishes and could castrate him. As a result, if everything goes well, the child represses his sexual wishes toward the mother, and to avoid being punished by father, he resolves identifying with his father. A child who fails to resolve the Oedipal complex will not be able to accept fully the reality principle, and his emotional stability will be impaired.

Having an impaired father figure interferes with the child evolving toward accepting rules and authority, accepting his abilities and disabilities, and respecting tradition and order.

This current chapter confirmed the hypothesis that the entrepreneur's father figure was impaired, meaning that the child – the entrepreneur-to-be – enters the Oedipal phase and finds that no big father restricts him. His father is weak or absent. It is possible that the entrepreneur-to-be could feel an Oedipal triumph, which means that he could be with his mother in a dyad without real threats from his father. On one hand the entrepreneur-to-be might feel omnipotent, all-powerful, beyond the restriction of the father who symbolizes reality. As a result the entrepreneur-to-be might develop the ability to think creatively and out of the box without being restricted by rules that narrow the world he experiences as all-possible. The entrepreneur, therefore, may reject authority and restricting frameworks. He becomes capable of thinking without previous assumptions – thinking out of the box, being creative and original.

On the other hand, there is a huge price tag. Without someone to identify with, you are all alone in a scary world. You do not belong. You are not protected. Those painful feelings are mostly unconscious. The psychological defenses against them are manic defenses: denial, split, idealization versus devaluation and hyperactivity that prevent the entrepreneurs from feeling the void in themselves.

RELATION TO OTHERS

The entrepreneur's relations with others tend to be partial and restricted. It is possible that the entrepreneur's mother has been experienced as a background, an environmental mother – a figure with no face that is expected to satisfy his needs. The same wishes are directed toward his wife. She is perceived as a twin soul, a woman who would do anything for him – even die for him, as one entrepreneur stated. The wife is a 'part object' not a person in her own right.

To sum up, the research revealed that entrepreneurs tend to be first born in the order of birth, they tend to have experienced an absent father who is experienced as an impaired father figure, their mothers were experienced as unsupportive, and their salient traits are: creativity and thinking out of the box. Based on psychoanalytic theory it is assumed that entrepreneurs' early experiences (mainly during the Oedipal phase) might facilitate the development of entrepreneurial traits such as creativity and thinking out of the box, along with unconscious unstable self-esteem, loneliness and tendency to hyperactivity.

Becoming a high-tech entrepreneur usually needs high formal education, very high drive for achievement and being dominant and responsible. He may have obtained these traits by being the first born and the subject of great parental expectations. Being the first born means having a competition with his siblings along with the anxiety that his place could be taken (the way a first born feels when another sibling is born).

BIRTH ORDER

Yanai et al. (Chapter 7 in this volume) suggested that their work as organizational consultants with entrepreneurs led them to conclude that most entrepreneurs are not first-born. Based on the research described in this chapter as well as other studies of Israeli high-tech entrepreneurs (e.g. Dvir and Pines, Chapter 11 in this volume; Pines et al., 2004), high-tech entrepreneurs are mostly first-born.

The difference between the two diverse conclusions touches a most controversial topic in the research on entrepreneurs: the different definitions and typology of entrepreneurs and the problematic of generalizations from one group of entrepreneurs to another. Entrepreneurs are a homogeneous group in terms of the atmosphere they have grown in and their family dynamic, but they may differ in other characteristics. For instance, regarding socioeconomic background, high-tech entrepreneurs tend to grow up in a middle-class family, in comparison to low-tech entrepreneurs and small business owners who often grow up in lower-class families. It is possibly that the same distinction applies to birth order.

Current research revealed that most serial high-tech entrepreneurs are first born. Moreover, those who were not first born described themselves as 'the child that the parents were counting on' – a state of mind that could be called 'being first born psychologically'. Sulloway (1996) claimed that first-born are more achievement driven, mostly in an intellectually arena, and more intelligent. They are competitive, and responsible in comparison to their siblings. Those traits may develop in an atmosphere of being first, responding to the expectations that parents express for achievement, and being a 'big, responsible boy or girl', especially when other siblings are born. A high-tech entrepreneur, who usually needs high formal education, is a very high achiever and is dominant and responsible, may have gained those traits by being first-born and experiencing great expectations and competition with his siblings along with the anxiety that his place would be taken (the way a first-born feels when another sibling is born).

A Case Study: Mr A – a Successful Serial High-tech Entrepreneur

Mr A is a successful serial high-tech entrepreneur. He has established four firms and has been managing the current one for the last year and a half. Mr A is married to his girlfriend from high school and has three children. He is 49 years old, and has a master's degree in engineering. Mr A looks a little older than his age, has a soft expression and gentle gestures, but one could sense that he has something strong and as hard as steel inside.

In his family of origin, Mr A is first-born and has a brother and a sister. Asking Mr A about memories regarding his childhood revealed a gloomy picture, especially regarding his relationship with his father:

> I don't remember my home with colors . . . the only thing I do remember about my home and childhood is in dark colors . . . I don't remember much, once I think about it, only that I was very independent and I wanted to leave home. The reason was probably my dad . . . I think I became independent because my dad didn't give me any support at all, no foundation to what I am. I was suppressed . . . my father used to say about everything I did or built: 'See it's no good . . . it's going to be broken anyhow . . . it is not going to work.'

Mr A said: 'My father was a survivor from the Holocaust. That made him scared, frightened from life, trying to be like a wallpaper . . . not to be seen. He was the opposite of entrepreneur, always frightened, always looking for security and stability.'

He also mentioned one occasion on which his father had insulted him: 'When will you find a decent job with a payroll? Are you still doing that monkey business?'

Mr A – Conclusions

The theme of the father's need for security appears to be a common past experience that entrepreneurs share. Many of them say that their fathers were the opposite of entrepreneurs, were weak and some of them hurt their sons' feelings with criticism and pessimism. The children's wish to identify with those fathers was denied and the child felt he was stronger than his father and wanted to be independent and leave his father's home.

The theme of a father who is a survivor of the Holocaust was common to some of the eldest entrepreneurs. Some spoke about their 'broken' fathers and made connections to their wish to become unlike their fathers. The theme of having the Holocaust in the back of their minds urged them to become entrepreneurs in the high-tech arena. They said: 'We as a country cannot afford to lose, we are so successful in technology because we have no choice . . . we must succeed, otherwise the road would bring us back to Hitler.' The Holocaust is a common and unforgettable experience because of the constant threat to the existence of Israel. Almost all of the entrepreneurs compared their experience in high technology to the experience of living in Israel. As one entrepreneur phrased it: 'We must rely on high-technology and be the best we can . . . besides, we are used to it – we live in a constant struggle for survival and high-tech is a constant struggle for survival.'

Living in a country with a constant threat to its existence made service in the army obligatory. Many entrepreneurs declare that military service served as an incubator for high-tech entrepreneurs. Military service demands huge responsibility from the soldiers, exposure to novel and sophisticated technologies and novel problem-solving techniques, the opportunity to participate in large projects, to create and improvise. It enables soldiers to lead others, to work in a team and to work very hard. Few entrepreneurs mentioned that Israel is a start-up in itself, an unsecured country, with constant changes, a country that is young and fragile. Almost all of the entrepreneurs agreed that growing up in Israel influenced their ability to be high-tech entrepreneurs.

BECOMING A HIGH-TECH SENIOR MANAGER

In recent research high-tech senior executives were compared to high-tech entrepreneurs, and it was discovered that those two types of figures in the high-tech arena share certain traits and background. Similarly to entrepreneurs, senior executives tend to be highly educated (MBA degree is common), with rich vocational experience, having a complicated and highly demanding position, a high degree of responsibility and autonomy, and the highest positions (CEO etc.), executives have certain entrepreneurial qualities (Kaplan, 2006).

Nevertheless, the early childhood experiences of senior executives seem to be different from those of entrepreneurs. The executives are characterized by the following childhood experiences in the family of origin and psychological motivations and characteristics:

1. The majority of the executives are not first-born (only 30 percent are).
2. The executives tend to have better perceived relationships with the father (than entrepreneurs), and they tend to identify with him.

3. The childhood of the executives is experienced as good. Their mothers are experienced as more supportive.
4. Executives tend to live by rules and tradition and not to rebel. Creativity is not their most salient characteristic.

Becoming a senior executive (especially CEO) assumes that the person feels that he or she wants to be at the top of the pyramid, to be perceived as the first in their group, and, in short, to be seen and noticed and to control others. Some scholars (Maccoby, 2003; Kets de Vries, 1993) connect managing and leadership with narcissistic personality, a personality that needs to be at the center at all times in order to maintain psychic balance. In this chapter the challenge is to connect the wishes to become an executive in high technology with the finding about those people's childhood experiences.

Similar to high-tech entrepreneurs, some of the high-tech senior executives said that in their childhood (and sometimes in their adolescence) their father was missing. Others said that he was around but was busy. It means that for some of the executives the father was not at home while the other executives experienced him as partially available to them. However, executives and entrepreneurs had a differently perceived missing father. For most entrepreneurs, the inner image of the father is fragile, fragmental or symbolized by a black hole (Mr A said that his experience at home was of black color), while most executives experienced their father's figure (even though missing) as strong and existing, and worth identifying with.

According to classical psychoanalytic theory, the father's most important effect on the psychic life of the child occurs in the Oedipal phase. If the child enters this phase feeling that his father is strong and powerful, he will be able to accept the authority of reality and law: the law that says that Mommy belongs to Daddy, and wishing to have her for himself is forbidden. The resolution of this phase is by identifying with the father and becoming strong and powerful like him (in order to have a woman like his, one day). However, experiencing a missing father or an unavailable one leaves a wound in a child's heart. A child needs to be loved, protected and taken care of by his father, and the absence or the lack of that attention is painful. A possible hypothesis is that the child solves the enigma 'Why is my father not with me?' by answering to himself (unconsciously) 'I am not important enough.'

The central topic that engages people with narcissistic features relates to their self-esteem and self-value. It is possible that the child will continue identifying with his father and thereby become a conforming and adjusted member of society. That enables him to belong to a group of people, but he would require a special place that will make sure the executive-to-be is seen and feels important. Some executives are very competitive people. Perhaps another solution to the father's absence and unavailability is the child's attempts to compensate for his loneliness by competition. That means that the executive-to-be develops a wish to be greater than the deserting father, perhaps in order to get his attention. Competition and repressed feelings of longing for the father can be experienced (without heavy denial, like entrepreneurs) mainly in a warm, secure environment. Most executives declare that they had good enough mothers and a good enough upbringing which enabled them to adjust and to belong.

Unlike entrepreneurs, executives have an inner sense of hierarchy, law and reality. Their main wish is to be seen, to be important and to be acknowledged as those who make people behave according to their wishes.

BIRTH ORDER

One of the findings of the current research is that most executives are not first in the order of birth in their family of origin. In fact, only a third are. Entrepreneurs, and especially successful and serial ones, 'need' to be first-born. By their conscious wish to select the lifestyle of a pioneer, they need every childhood experience in leading and every aptitude in order to create a new reality and to build a new world. First-born have plenty of opportunity to exercise leadership, responsibility and meeting very high expectations from their parents.

Executives, on the other hand, need less past expertise. They want to become the first in a row or the king of their kingdom, but the kingdom is already created by the entrepreneurs. They enter a company, a firm, or an organization that already exists. Their wish is to be seen and to manage others (a wish most entrepreneurs do not have – they usually do not like to manage others). Narcissistic features, what characterize executives, do not have an automatic correlation with birth order but are strongly correlated with narcissistic vulnerability caused by the perceived absence of an adoring and an attentive father.

Case Study: Mr B – High-tech Executive

Mr B is a successful manager; he is the CEO of a promising high-tech company established four years ago. Mr B is 43 years old, married with two children. He is tall and pleasant looking, characterized by a sense of humor, and he can be charming. On a closer inspection one could sense his anxiety around people, especially in a close contact.

Mr B has a MBA degree and a bachelor's degree in engineering.

He was born and grew up in a distant little town characterized by middle and working-class people. In his family of origin he was second in the order of birth, but was considered to be the smartest. When asked about childhood memories he recalled an unpleasant feeling of being an outsider in the family. He said: 'No one really understood me . . . I was considered to be a strange bird . . . They thought I was smart but did not understand what I want and why. I felt strange.'

He had a warm relationship with his mother even though deep inside he did not appreciate her because he thought she was a warm and a caring person but not smart enough and not a person to learn from. His father was a busy man, mainly in social activities; he had a central role and a major social position in their community and he was always busy doing important things.

Mr B was a very good scholar. He got good grades and was invited as a gifted child to join a boarding school which specialized in teaching gifted children from a low socioeconomic background. His family was a traditional one with a religious lifestyle. Mr B felt since adolescence that their lifestyle did not suit him but he tried not to make his parents angry and gave his preferences a low profile. His wisdom and curiosity were channeled to scientific issues. He read a lot and had dreams about a better future elsewhere. During military service he met his future wife and they got married. He left home and went to study engineering mainly because he was interested in technology, hoped to meet people like him and to be in an environment in which he would feel comfortable.

Mr B is considered to be a very much appreciated CEO, and the company he manages is flourishing. During the interview with him he connected his career with the loneliness he felt in his childhood even though he felt he was raised fairly. He has ambivalent feelings toward his father. On one hand he was proud of his position in the community and the important things he was doing; on the other hand he did not feel a real connection between them. He felt an outsider in his own family, fantasizing that if he had had a warmer, more loving father, he would have felt much better in the world and more secure about the place he holds and about how much he is loved and accepted by people.

SUMMARY

This chapter deals with a comparison of two very closely related figures in high-tech industry: high-tech entrepreneurs and high-tech executives. The research described discovered that even though serial high-tech entrepreneurs and high-tech executives share some common features, their childhood experiences, particularly order of birth and relationships with their fathers and mothers, are different.

The specific early childhood experiences the entrepreneurs reported might effect the entrepreneurs' vocational motivations and some of their vocation-related traits: creativity and thinking out of the box.

Entrepreneurs tend to experience an absent and weak father with whom it was hard to identify. During their psychosexual development in the Oedipal phase the entrepreneur-to-be feels that the father cannot restrict him. This might trigger evolving traits such as omnipotence, lack of perceived restrictions, creativity and thinking out of the box.

An unsupportive perceived mother and being first born in the family of origin facilitate the developing personality of a pioneer: creative, omnipotent, a leader with an urge to create a world, to invent and make things happen.

Executives tend to have an absent but respected father. The child could respect such a father and fear him, and by that, accept the rules and order that the father represents. With such a father the child could identify and compete. The wish to be better and exceed the father may result in the wish to be the best and first, and to manage others within the organization.

REFERENCES

De Fontenay, C. and Carmel, E. (2004), 'Israel's Silicon Wadi: the forces behind cluster formation', in T. Bresnahan and A. Gambardella (eds), *Building High-Tech Clusters: Silicon Valley and Beyond*, Cambridge: Cambridge University Press, pp. 40–77.

Drucker, P. (1985), *Innovation and Entrepreneurship*, London: Heinemann.

Freud, S. (1913), 'Totem and taboo', in J. Starchey (ed.), *The Standard Edition of the Complete Psychological Work of Sigmund Freud*, Vol. 13, London: Hogarth Press, pp. 1–161.

Freud, S. (1914), 'On the history of the psychoanalytic movement', in J. Starchey (ed.), *The Standard Edition of the Complete Psychological Work of Sigmund Freud*, Vol. 14, London: Hogarth Press, pp. 3–66.

Freud, S. (1915), 'Instincts and their vicissitudes', in J. Starchey (ed.), *The Standard Edition of the Complete Psychological Work of Sigmund Freud*, Vol. 14, London: Hogarth Press, pp. 109–40.

Freud, S. (1920), 'Beyond the pleasure principle', in J. Starchey (ed.), *The Standard Edition of the Complete Psychological Work of Sigmund Freud*, Vol. 18, London: Hogarth Press, pp. 3–64.

Freud, S. (1923a), 'The ego and the id', in J. Starchey (ed.), *The Standard Edition of the Complete Psychological Work of Sigmund Freud*, Vol. 19, London: Hogarth Press, pp. 3–66.

Freud, S. (1923b), 'The infintile genital organisation', in J. Starchey (ed.), *Standard Edition of the Complete Psychological Work of Sigmund Freud*, Vol. 19, London: Hogarth Press, pp. 141–5.

Freud, S. (1924), 'The dissolution of the Oedipal complex', in J. Starchey (ed.), *The Standard Edition of the Complete Psychological Work of Sigmund Freud*, Vol. 19, London: Hogarth Press, pp. 173–9.

Freud, S. (1925), 'Some psychical consequences of the anatomic distinction between the sexes', in J. Starchey (ed.), *The Standard Edition of the Complete Psychological Work of Sigmund Freud*, Vol. 19, London: Hogarth Press, pp. 243–58.

Freud, S. (1930), 'Civilization and its discontent', in J. Starchey (ed.), *The Standard Edition of the Complete Psychological Work of Sigmund Freud*, Vol. 21, London: Hogarth Press, pp. 59–145.

Hatav, J. (2003), 'Introduction – psychoanalysis now', in J. Hatav (ed.), *Psychoanalysis: Theory and Practice*, Dyonon: Tel Aviv University, pp. 19–29 (in Hebrew).

Hisrich, R.D. and Brush, C. (1986), 'Characteristics of the minority entrepreneur', *Journal of Small Business Management*, **24**(4): 1–8.

Kaplan, G. (2006), *Background and Personality Variables of Serial High-technology Entrepreneurs in Israel*, PhD dissertation, Beer Sheva: Ben Gurion University.

Kets de Vries, M.F.R. (1993), *Leaders, Fools and Imposters*, San Francisco, CA: Jossey-Bass.

Kets de Vries, M.F.R. (1996), 'The anatomy of the entrepreneur: clinical observations', *Human Relations*, **49**(7): 853–79.

Maccoby, M. (2003), *The Productive Narcissist: The Promise and Peril of Visionary Leadership*, New York: Broadway Books.

MacGarth, R.G. (1996), 'Options and the entrepreneur: towards a strategic theory of entrepreneurial wealth creation', *Academy of Management Proceedings, Entrepreneurship Division*, pp. 101–5.

Mitchell, S.A. and Black, M.J. (1995), *Freud and Beyond*, New York: Basic Books.

Pines, A.M. (2003), 'Unconscious influence on career choice: entrepreneur vs. manager', *Australian Journal of Career Development*, **12**(2): 7–18.

Pines, A.M., Dvir, D. and Sadeh, A. (2004), 'The making of Israeli high-technology entrepreneurs: an exploratory study', *The Journal of Entrepreneurship*, **13**: 30–52.

Pines, A.M., Sadeh, A., Dvir, D. and Yanai, O. (2002), 'Entrepreneurs and managers: similar yet different', *The International Journal of Organizational Analysis*, **10**: 172–90.

Schumpeter, J.A. (1965), 'Economic theory and entrepreneurial history', in E.C.J. Aiken (ed.), *Exploration in Enterprise*, Cambridge, MA: Harvard University Press, pp. 45–64.

Scott, M. and Rosa, P. (1996), 'Opinion: has a firm level analysis reached its limits? Time for rethink', *International Small Business Journal*, **14**: 81–9.

Shenar, A., Dvir, D., Milosevic, D., Mulenburg, J., Patanakul, P., Reilly, R., Ryan, M., Sage, A., Sauser, B., Srivannaboon, S., Stefanovic, J. and Thamhain, H. (forthcoming), 'Toward a NASA-specific project management framework', revised and resubmitted for *Engineering Management Journal*.

Sulloway, F.J. (1996), *Born to Rebel: Birth Order, Family Dynamics and Creative Lives*, New York: Pantheon Books.

7. Entrepreneurs and managers: a family portrait – family dynamics, language and modes of effective dialogue

Orenia Yaffe-Yanai, Dov Yanai and Tamar Milo

For almost three decades, we helped enterprises make placement and promotion decisions. We also provided career counseling to thousands of individuals at various career stages and in a wide range of vocational spheres. These processes are similar in that one is asked to understand the job requirements, diagnose the individual's personality, and determine the degree of match between a cluster of job requirements and the individual make-up of skills and personality traits. Whether our client was a public enterprise, a family-owned business, a top-level executive or a young university graduate, the key to a successful placement was the same – finding the best fit between the job requirements (in terms of skills, company culture, industry environment) and the individual's personality (in terms of energy sources, family dynamics, the role of the individual within his family, childhood wounds and longings).

Another source of insights into the complex interrelationships among vocations, personality and family dynamics was our extensive work with individuals, couples and families on their vision, their calling and their career quests. Our work with family-owned businesses over the last decade has given us insight into the conflict-laden interaction between entrepreneurs and managers within the enterprise, as well as some keys to successful conflict resolution dialogues between them.

We gradually learned that through the study of family background and family dynamics, we could better identify, understand and consult our clients. Such processes are carried out together with our clients and imply the unfolding, exploring and understanding of their psychological make-up, motivation, passion, sources of strength, fears and multigenerational family legacies. In doing so we are defining and identifying our clients' unique 'language' and 'vocabulary', and learn to converse in their language. This enables us to be more effective in our dialogue with them, and in solving communication break-downs between them and their various partners (family members and fellow workers) and, above all, with themselves.

In our experience, family dynamics reveals people's basic emotional pain, which drives their personal quests and motivation, and leads to the roads along which they develop the legacies of past generations.

Together with our clients we have learned that identifying the sources of passion is one of the major consulting tools. To quote Bill Gates: 'Your potential is our passion.' Passion is the source of meaning for one's very being and doing. When people's barriers or obstacles are identified and then removed or bypassed, the passion flows towards self-fulfillment of one's calling.

Uncovering family dynamics teaches about the sources of energies, motivations and the meaning of lifelong passion quests. It also unravels traps and expected difficulties. Awareness and understanding of one's inner story is the beginning of change, as the Jewish thinking expresses so beautifully: 'Everything is foreseen yet freedom of choice is given . . . .' (Rabbi Akiva, *Sayings of Our Fathers*, 3, 39). In other words, being aware of the script that one is playing is the prerequisite for altering it.

After years of involvement in career choices, placement decisions and conflict resolution within organizations and family businesses, we learned how to:

(a) look for a match between personality and job requirements;
(b) understand the origins and the developmental factors that make an entrepreneur as compared to those that make a manager; and
(c) uncover the language spoken by each group, in order to promote an effective dialogue between them and within the consultation process.

This chapter presents some of our observations and insights with regard to these three types of roles, and the people who fulfill them, in the context of the family-owned enterprise.

It is easy to tell an entrepreneur or a manager when you see one. You just need to know what you are looking for, in other words, what each of them should look like or convey. The first of those features is the passion that fuels them.

THE PASSION

Entrepreneurs are hardly ever satisfied. Their hunger constantly nourishes their passion. Watching an entrepreneur, one is reminded of Lacan's view that passion originates from a deficiency that cannot be fulfilled. Therefore it can never be satisfied (Lacan, 1977). Whoever has worked with successful entrepreneurs has felt their burning eyes and the passion inside them. Listening to Bill Gates saying in a lecture that 'we have to do something about Google because if we don't . . .', one realizes that for him it feels like a matter of life and death, in spite of Microsoft's might and leadership position. Similarly, a successful client entrepreneur put it even more bluntly. He said that 'his passion was "wild". . .' and that he 'could not tame it', admitting that actually he did not want to tame it – he liked the temper and the feel of the burning urge to strive for the unimaginable!

Entrepreneurs crave to create a new world out of chaos. This new world should always be bigger, greater and stronger, and leave a greater impact on the universe. For successful entrepreneurs only the sky is the limit and, at times, not even that. Managers' passion is different. It is modified. It is controlled and well tamed – more sublimated. Managers want to introduce order into the chaos. They aim at the execution of measurable goals in an existing universe. They lead people to reach clever and effective solutions. They are always critical of their achievements and constantly look for better and more effective solutions, only to discover that there are even better ones ahead. Managers want to achieve remarkable results but such that are within the world's laws and order. Indeed, they devote themselves to making order, taking control and motivate people to run an existing growing world.

HANDLING ONE'S PASSION

Passion is not easy to sustain and manage. Some of our clients said that they were terrified to discover their passion, 'because if I discover it, how would I contain it?' We have come to realize that this worry does not apply to the entrepreneur, since for him the more passion, the better. He immerses himself in his passion and, in doing so, may lose other interests in life: family, body, or news. He might die burning with passion. Often entrepreneurs are enslaved by their creations. We could call them passion-haunted individuals. Consequently they are extremely competitive, strive for unexpected results, and courageously look for non-conventional, creative methods and strategies. They are dedicated to the fulfillment of their vision, in spite of everything.

Managers, on the other hand, tend to invest their energy in building an internal personality 'infrastructure' in order to contain and lead an intense passion. They do not allow themselves to be lost in it. Managers are careful, conservative and anxious to be creative within the rules. They are worried as to the effects their actions may have on the people who surround them and on their organizations; they look for collaboration, affiliation and teamwork. They take seriously their responsibility for others and for their own well-being.

RELATIONSHIP TO THE BUSINESS

Entrepreneurs do not usually have a strong sense of ownership (nor did their parents toward their own child). They do not accept their material assets as a given, but rather as something they should constantly fight for. Their attitude toward what they officially own may seem paranoid, as they are constantly afraid that it will be taken away from them. This, however, does not mean that their relationship to their assets is meek – the opposite is true. Entrepreneurs feel that the business 'is me'. It is the extension of the self, with no barriers between them. As one entrepreneur, the founder of a large family-owned business, once told us: 'the business is the painting that I have created. I will not allow anyone, including my children, to scrabble on my painting.' Like so many other entrepreneurs, he felt that he was on his own and could (or should) do whatever he felt was right.

Managers, on the other hand, feel that what they run and manage is theirs, even when legally that is not the case. They have acquired a sense of ownership early in their childhood, when their accomplishments were appreciated and their belongings were recognized as being theirs. This laid the foundation for an underlying object relation that can be paraphrased as: 'this is mine' versus 'this is me' of the entrepreneur. The manager feels that the business is his and collaborates with his surroundings in order to protect and promote it. In so doing he takes into account facts, rules, possibilities, risks and consequences.

Adizes (2004), the world-famous management expert, gives us an interesting insight into the difference between entrepreneurs and managers when he says that managers put out fires that have been so brilliantly set by entrepreneurs. In other words, a business in a state of order and control is an achievement for the manager, while for the entrepreneur it is an unbearably dull and boring state of affairs. The latter is constantly on the look for new opportunities and new alternatives which require immediate action. The inner chaos that resides inside the entrepreneur is what causes unrest and worry for the manager, making the collaboration and dialogue between them very challenging indeed.

MANAGERS, ENTREPRENEURS AND THE FAMILY-OWNED BUSINESS

Nowhere is the confusion between the roles of entrepreneurs and managers as common as in family-owned businesses. It is the source of conflict between owners and non-family managers and often also between founders and successors. A few common examples may clarify this statement. The entrepreneur–founder of a business brings his recently graduated son into the business. He dreams of having his son close to him, carrying out his spoken and unspoken wishes and overseeing the business he has built. The allure of the title, status and power, combined with a deep sense of commitment to the family business, make the son accept the position. However, he quickly finds out that his father strangles any initiative he proposes and expects him to be the administrative–conservative manager that the founder himself had never been.

In another common situation two cousins are appointed jointly to run the family-owned business. While one of them is continuously looking for expansion and for new products and markets, the other is terrified by the level of risk caused by these initiatives and strives to minimize financial exposure and stabilize the control systems in the company. Mutual accusations are quick to follow, with the other family members serving as live loud-speakers of the conflicting voices.

In a third example, the owner of a thriving family-owned business decides to hire an external CEO. He chooses an experienced manager who would, it is hoped, introduce management practices into the enterprise. But the clashes between the two begin after a very short honeymoon period. The CEO's attempt to determine lines of command clashes with the owner's habit of cutting through the line of command directly to the employees. Decision-making policies and expense approval procedures introduced by the CEO are continuously overruled by the owner. Worse yet, the owner comes up with new business initiatives and new tasks daily, making yesterday's plans and priorities obsolete. He has little patience to review plans and progress, thus leaving the CEO with little or no feedback. Frustration and disappointment grow on both sides, until one of them decides to give up.

Successful entrepreneurs who are the founders of the family business find themselves in the role of managers as the business grows. They are usually poor at introducing structure, order and hierarchy and long, therefore, for someone who could do it for them. However, when the long-awaited manager enters the enterprise and attempts to establish structure and regulations, the 'battle' begins. It is as if a foreign organism has infiltrated the organization, causing all the 'antibodies' of the immune system to act up.

It can be a 'life-or-death' war, as a professional non-family manager once told us. We met him at a Family-Owned Businesses convention and listened to his fascinating experiences in four different family businesses. He told us how his employers would hire him in order to install structure, control systems and rules in the business, yet he would find himself on the verge of being fired once he had carried out their wishes. He talked about them crossing hierarchy lines, approving expenditures without telling anyone, firing mid-level managers without consulting their direct superiors and signing new, previously unconsidered deals concurrently with other large investments. Since he knew that he would be on a collision course with his employers sooner or later, he made it his policy to keep a distance from them. He would decline any invitation to their homes, would not accept shares in their company, and would take only cash compensation. It was also his policy to change jobs once every four to six years. Listening to his story, we wondered about his motivation and about the underlying need that was seeking gratification through this unusual career. 'What's in it for you?' we dared ask. The manager answered instantaneously: 'It's about killing my father every day, only to get in the next morning, and kill him again.' Indeed, the roots of the differences, and consequently the conflicts between entrepreneurs and managers, lie in the family environment they grew up in.

THE FAMILY SYSTEM

Our multiple observations have taught us that entrepreneurs often come from chaotic families, where structure, role definition and emotional stability are poor, if not altogether absent. They come from families where order and laws or hierarchies hardly exist. Their family is by and large poorly functioning as a family, and the child has not been *seen*, neither by the father nor by the mother. In our experience, the actual physical or emotional absence of the father of the entrepreneur-to-be is very prominent. Emotionally, this child is an 'orphan'. Thus, in his adult life, he will constantly re-create fatherless situations. He will have a hard time functioning in a hierarchical organization, unless he himself is at the top of the hierarchy. In that case he will probably tend to cut across hierarchy lines and ignore rules and policies, always creating new rules instead. In extreme cases, the entrepreneur will act not only as if he were fatherless, but also as if he had no God. At times he may experience himself as God.

Being left alone as children, entrepreneurs have had to create the rules upon which to act and be responsible for their enforcement. They were free to choose, create and do. Freedom was the other side of their painful experience of emotionally undernourished childhood. It remains a source of pain, as well as of courage, to break the rules and create new ones and to interpret reality in a new way, discovering previously unrecognized business opportunities.

The chaotic situation at home created another opportunity for this child – that of living in the future. The present feels too lonely and painful. He can hardly bear being in the present and has to create an inner story that relates to a future which is envisioned by him alone (Kets de Vries, 1989; Lapierre, 1991). So the practice of 'playing' in the future, and experiencing it as an almost actual reality, is something that is so often found in entrepreneurs' attitudes and arguments. They build their playground in the future, which is where they feel comfortable playing. When they were children, time schedules were not clearly set by their parents. They were not supervised by a parental figure and therefore had to create their own performance criteria, which could often be extremely and capriciously demanding.

Not surprisingly, the inner child of the entrepreneur-to-be is extremely imaginative. This child is alive when dealing with future dreams and possibilities, and easily forgets that these are only future plans. As adults, most of us like to plan and dream, but the entrepreneur needs to constantly play the game and 'live' in his or her dreams, where everything is possible. Since their childhood experience has been that they had little to lose, they are less afraid of failure or loss as grown-ups. They perceive their families as having been poor and unhappy anyway, so they can take risks. In fact, they often do not consider their courageous actions as risks at all.

Managers, on the other hand, come mostly from fairly stable families. Their attentive parents watch over them, usually know what they do and set expectations for them. Criticism, which is the counterpart of expectations, is abundant as well. This combination of care, supervision, expectations and feedback makes their mistakes particularly painful. Their inner experience is that they have a lot to lose and, therefore, it is better to be cautious and avoid risks.

MOTHERS OF ENTREPRENEURS AND MOTHERS OF MANAGERS

Another parameter along which entrepreneurs and managers differ remarkably is the role their mothers assume in their lives. The entrepreneur's mother, who hardly 'sees' her child, is often self-centered. She is also a passionate and powerful dreamer, usually of unfulfilled dreams. She has ambitions for her child but rarely does anything about them. Her unrealized dreams are often passed on to her child as a painful longing and a powerful source of inspiration. If dreams are the name of the game for mother and child, there is also wishful thinking that if a dream (this time the child's dream) becomes a reality, he will be seen by his mother for who he really is. This longing becomes the inner source of endless motivation for the child. It explains why, even as a very successful adult, the entrepreneur has the persistent, emotional experience of not being seen and continues to fuel an endless ambition for achievements, awards and recognition.

The situation is very different for managers who come from functional families that are well structured, hierarchical, and where rules and orders are set and enforced. Managers had a present father figure. He was often a manger himself who was involved, along with the mother, in 'teaching' managerial skills to his chosen child. While he took an active role in the child's education in collaboration with the mother, the ambition was nevertheless hers. The manager's parent, often the father for the female manager and the mother for the male manager, is constantly and explicitly dissatisfied with his or her results. In their family of origin there was a constant demand for a better outcome. It was never good enough. This is one of the hidden connections between the manager and the entrepreneur, who is never satisfied with his manager, causing the manager to want to be better.

Mothers of managers are well connected to reality and often are good teachers to their chosen child, the manager-to-be. She is often an effective mother who provides a managerial role model for her chosen offspring, who becomes her 'deputy'. She supervises him and generously rewards and criticizes him. She is not a frustrated person but a realistic one who is well and even pragmatically connected to reality. She has good common sense and intuition, and is often ambitious for her child and takes responsibility and invests energy in the child's upbringing. This is why it is so natural for the manager to bring up young managers and to teach them how to grow and improve.

BIRTH ORDER

Our observations, by and large, substantiate Sulloway's study (1997) in which he concluded that first-born children identified with authority figures, whereas younger ones rebel against authority. In the traditional family businesses of the 'old economy' most of the entrepreneurs we encountered were not first-born children. Many of them, however, assumed the role of a first-born. It seems that even in poorly functioning families, first-born children receive closer attention from their parents. Before any sibling comes along, first-born children are exposed mostly to adult conversations, which instill in them a conventional way of thinking, together with some rules and regulations that were established by the adults and which they try to abide by, in order to gain parental recognition and to avoid painful criticism. Second-born or youngest children of poorly functioning families are not as bound to the adult world conventions, giving them the freedom to make up their own rules and create their fantasized world.

Psychologically, however, entrepreneurs-to-be often assume responsibility for their siblings and feel that they have to be their care takers or saviors. One of our clients was the second of four children in a family where both parents had been abused in their childhood. The father was often absent from the house and the mother worked hard to provide for the family. The oldest brother won parental approval by being a good student and a well-behaved child. His way of coping with the dysfunctional home environment was to mentally record the children's experiences and memories. When we met the siblings as adults, it became apparent that the oldest brother had retained detailed memories of their childhood, while the others had erased most of them from their conscious memory. Not surprisingly, he became a successful accountant. The second brother, on the other hand, assumed full responsibility for his younger sister since he was eight years old. He took her to school, fed her, took her with him to the playground and protected her from the neighborhood kids. Even as a young adult he could not let go of the deep sense of responsibility toward his sister, who was by now perfectly capable of taking care of herself. As a child he entertained dreams of becoming rich and providing for his entire family. We met him as an energetic entrepreneur who had original business ideas and seemed to be on his way to financial success.

The founder of a large service company was the fourth child in a family of new immigrants, born after three girls. His father died suddenly when he was 14 years old. In his late twenties, he and his wife quit their jobs, took out their compensations and made the initial investment needed to start the company. He proved to be a shrewd businessman and a talented entrepreneur, and the business prospered. In the process he assumed the role of leader and savior of the entire family, helping his sisters financially and providing employment for nephews and nieces in need. Psychologically, he had become the first-born son. The phenomenon of 'birthright stealing', known to us from the story of Jacob and Esau in the Book of Genesis, could be one explanation for Kaplan's (Chapter 6 in this volume) finding that entrepreneurs in high-tech companies in Israel were mostly first-born, 'either physically or psychologically'.

It should be noted that while our observations were in line with previous studies (Kets de Vries, 1996), they were mostly based on family-held companies, which could be generally classified as 'old economy'. Other studies, such as Kaplan's (Chapter 6 in this volume), Hisrich and Brush's (1986) and Pines et al.'s (2002), conducted in high-tech enterprises, found that the majority of entrepreneurs in those new-economy ventures were first born. It is possible that the explanation for the opposite findings lies in the unique attributes of new-economy ventures. For one, high-tech ventures are technology based. Their leaders must be familiar with state-of-the-art developments in their field and should base their innovations on sound scientific and technological grounds. It requires a logical, step-by-step mode of thinking, which is always well connected to reality, even when it goes one step beyond the existing present. It takes a person who abides by the rules and who is concerned with efficacy, efficiency and form to become an innovator in the new economy. In other words, individuals who are capable of starting a new high-tech venture should have many of the typical manager's characteristics: they live in reality and they want and need to be well connected to it. They are less concerned with leaving an impact on the world. Rather, they are interested in facts: how much, how and with whom. Order, law and regulations are the realm within which they operate and which they strive to improve. They have to consider facts and means. They take the current situation to its next step, rather than argue with it.

Second, the type of ownership in high-tech companies also differs from that in most traditional industries. The rapid growth of high-tech companies is supported by investments from venture-capital funds and other financial institutions. Ownership is thus shared with partners who run the partnership as executives would. Successful high-tech entrepreneurs should, therefore, have managerial discipline and willingness to submit their own dreams to the decisions of the board of directors.

Additional investigation of the issue of birth order among entrepreneurs in various types of industry could give us a deeper insight into the family portrait of entrepreneurs and managers.

TWO CASE STUDIES

The founder of a large, successful enterprise was the youngest of three brothers. His mother was a courageous dreamer who left their homeland when he was five years old, taking the children with her. His elder brother assumed the role of the father, but this youngest son became his mother's emotional 'partner' and dream-mate. His uprooted childhood was rough. Excelling in boxing was his way of compensating for the inferiority he felt. His physical strength enabled him to protect his brothers in unfavorable situations, making him the family leader. His childhood dreams and his longing for a father figure nourished the drive and the vision to make an impact and become big and successful. He described himself by saying: 'I was born an entrepreneur. I tried desperately to become a manager, but was not very successful at it. Then came the biggest challenge – that of becoming an owner.' Indeed, management was foreign and challenging for him. He had no sense of hierarchy and could easily confuse his managers by cutting through hierarchical lines, or giving conflicting instructions. The consultation process helped him to limit himself to the 'why' issues, delegating those of 'what' and 'how' to his managers. When his own children grew up and started to enter the business, he became aware of their sense of ownership toward the products and the production plants, which they had and he lacked. Seeing them helped him understand his role as an owner and to realize that he should not intervene in managerial issues, even when his instinct was to do so, whether or not he knew what to do. Learning how to be a father to his children, his managers and to his life creation – the business – was his greatest and most rewarding challenge.

The hired CEO of a family-owned business, with whom we have worked, was the eldest of three, the son of a father who was a mid-level manager and a very organized home-maker. Both parents were dedicated. The father used to take him to the desert, teaching him to drive at a relatively young age, thus developing his courage. The mother set high expectations of him, delegated to him some of the responsibilities for his younger siblings, and provided him with feedback. Her expectations and criticism channeled his ambition and shaded any personal dream or passion with guilt. As a CEO he was highly devoted to the entrepreneurial founder, who admired his ambition, his systematic mode of operation and his endless motivation for work. His employees could always rely on him and trusted his judgment. In the consultation process, we focused on the inner permission to have his own dreams, to think 'out of the box' and, consequently, to allow the managers around him to grow as well.

THE RELATIONSHIP BETWEEN ENTREPRENEURS AND MANAGERS

Knowing the family background of entrepreneurs can help us understand why they so often view themselves as terrific managers, while in fact they may have very poor managerial skills. The family system in which they grew failed to teach them about hierarchy, authority, control or stability. Often at times they took care of their siblings, assuming the role of the family 'savior', and tended to be protective and over-controlling. Yet in the absence of a role model, many of them never learned to provide a systematic structure, to set manageable expectations from others and to provide feedback – the key factors of proper management. They often lack managerial aptitudes and confuse management with ownership, thinking that because they own the business, they are managing it. The truth of the matter is that often they lack both the sense of ownership and of management. When the enterprise grows and prospers, the entrepreneur begins to feel that he badly needs a 'deputy', in other words, a manager. Moses, the biblical entrepreneur, needed Aaron, just as Don Quixote, the literary entrepreneur, needed Sancho Panza. This loyal and effective managerial figure may be discredited and fiercely criticized. But the bottom line is that the entrepreneur depends on his manager, just as the latter depends on his 'boss's' criticism, for feedback.

CONDUCTING CONSULTATIONS WITH ENTREPRENEURS AND MANAGERS

Entrepreneurs are motivated by their compelling vision. They strive to 'create a world' and to leave a landmark behind them. Their concern is with the purpose and reason for what they do. Adizes (2004), in his description of Entrepreneurs (E) points out that their language contains mainly the question 'Why?' – 'Why should I do . . .?' or 'Why shouldn't I do . . .?' In their determination to fulfill their passion and to 'create a world', they are concerned with the aim or vision for doing (why) and with whether their act would make a difference, rather than with the correct manner in which to make it happen (what, how and when). In studying the biographies of great innovators, statesmen and business tycoons, one often marvels at their relative disregard for public criticism, as well as for warnings of difficulties and hurdles. It is as if they were 'immune' to outside criticism and reality checks, being propelled by the internal energy of their vision and passion. Such behavior is better understood when family background is taken into consideration, often revealing the absence of authority figures, or a systematic family structure and properly set expectations and feedback.

To capture the entrepreneur's attention, the consultant should speak the 'right' language, focusing on the vision, the reason for it and the impact it might have. In order to be effective in the consultation process, the consultant must assume a role that is familiar and comfortable for the entrepreneur. Knowing that many entrepreneurs were 'fatherless children', it is recommended that the consultant act as a partner, team member or confidant, rather than as a 'super-parent' or 'guru'. Entrepreneurs have not been taught the language of subordinates, which includes listening and receiving criticism, and therefore communicate poorly with authority figures. Moreover, being engrossed in their vision, their messages to the organization may be unclear and even confusing. A consultant who can apply a variety of communication styles can be valuable in clarifying the entrepreneur's vision, explaining it to the organization and exploring – with the manager – the 'how', 'what', 'when' and 'who' aspects of the vision.

It is exactly these last four types of question that are the key ingredients of the manager's language. As sons and daughters of properly functioning families, managers operate within a set of expectations and objectives. Their ambition is not only to reach the objectives set for them, but to do so efficiently, correctly and profitably, and to be credited for it. Managers draw satisfaction from a good plan that is properly executed. They are interested in employee satisfaction, are concerned with their image as managers and strive to prevent criticism. As children, they have seen their parents evaluating plans, weighing up pros and cons and changing course of action accordingly. Consequently, consultants who work with managers find them in general receptive to their criticism and advice, and cooperative in revising vision statements. They are usually willing to invest in sharing their vision with the entire organization, in order to set the stage for effective execution.

RECOMMENDATIONS

What are the practical implications of these differences in language and communication for the work of the consultant? First, the dialogue with a manager revolves around issues of feasibility (if), execution (how, when, where, who), performance (how much) and criticism (how else). In this dialogue, the consultant is expected to assume a parental role and act as an authority figure, a mentor and sometimes even a guru. He can expect to be listened to with reverence and discipline, even when his advice may not be practiced. Consulting an entrepreneur requires an altogether different terminology and inter-relating, a partner or an echo. Discussing the 'why' and 'why not' aspects of a vision requires creativity and optimism, and a long-term orientation on the part of the consultant. Skepticism may be particularly detrimental. The role of the consultant is that of a sibling with complementary skills whose contribution is valued but not considered essential – entrepreneurs do not usually favor becoming dependent on their consultants.

Some consultants can flexibly switch from one role to the other and adapt the suitable terminology for each client, thus working effectively with the founder and the manager of an enterprise. In other cases, it is recommended to use a team of two consultants, who can jointly provide the full necessary repertoire of role and communication patterns.

Second, consultants are often called to mediate between founders and managers, and tend to do so by arranging a family-like, three-party meeting to discuss the issues at stake. However, in light of their family background, many entrepreneurs are unaccustomed to family assemblies and may feel uncomfortable in this type of setting. A separate meeting with each client, with the consultant serving as messenger, is often more effective. Alternatively, we have had successes in solving conflicts between founders and managers in the presence of two consultants – one for each client. Working as a team, the consultants can provide the full range of styles and maintain the trust of both clients throughout the conflict solving process.

Last, but not least, the consultant could enhance the entrepreneur's leadership by magnifying his role as the source of inspiration, but minimizing the expectation for him to act as a teacher. This differentiation between inspiration and teaching is particularly important in the family-owned business setting, where offspring expect their father to be their business mentor. The disappointment often results in anger and animosity between the generations. Consultants, who are cognizant of the psychological portrait of both groups, should manage expectations and promote the establishment of appropriate settings for the founder's leadership. We have worked with founders who learned to exert their influence and leadership through their contribution in the board of directors, their speeches at company meetings and their impressive presentations to their managers. At the same time, they entrusted their external board members with the task of preparing the next generation for ownership and management. They were at their best communicating optimistically and enthusiastically their passion and their dreams, to the benefit of the entire organization.

REFERENCES

Adizes, I. (2004), 'Management/mismanagement styles: how to identify a style and what to do about it', in *Leadership Trilogy*, Vol. 2, Santa Barbara, CA: Adizes Institute Publishing.

Hisrich, R.D. and Brush, C. (1986), 'Characteristics of the minority entrepreneur', *Journal of Small Business Management*, **24**: 1–8.

Kaplan, G. (2006), *Background and Personality Variables of Serial High-technology Entrepreneurs in Israel*, PhD dissertation, Beer Sheva: Ben Gurion University.

Kets de Vries, M.F.R. (1989), *Prisoners of Leadership*, New York: Wiley.

Kets de Vries, M.F.R. (1996), 'The anatomy of the entrepreneur', *Human Relations*, **49**: 853–83.

Lacan, J. (1977), *Ecrits: A Selection* (A. Sheridan, trans.), New York and London: W.W. Norton.

Lapierre, L. (1991), 'Exploring the dynamics of leadership', in M.F.R. Kets de Vries et al. (eds), *Organizations on the Couch: Clinical Perspectives on Organizational Behavior and Change*, San Francisco, CA: Jossey-Bass, pp. 69–93.

Pines, A.M., Sadeh, A., Dvir, D. and Yanai, Y.O. (2002), 'Entrepreneurs and managers: similar yet different', *International Journal of Organizational Analysis*, **10**(2): 172–90.

Pines, A.M. and Yanai, O. (2000), 'Unconscious influences on the choice of a career: implications for organizational consultation', *Journal of Health and Human Services Administration*, **21**: 502–11.

Sulloway, F.J. (1997), *Born to Rebel*, New York: Vintage Books.

PART III

Entrepreneurs and Managers' Career Choice: Cultural Determinants

8. Contrasting entrepreneurs and non-entrepreneurs among Canadian and Israeli MBAs

Galit Chimo-Vugalter and Miri Lerner

INTRODUCTION

Some researchers claim that successful entrepreneurs have qualities beyond being merely capable executives and that 'the entrepreneurial event' takes shape through the interaction of both personal and environmental factors (Malecki, 1997). According to this view, specific personal traits, such as the willingness to take risks, help determine the success or failure of entrepreneurs (Sexton and Bowman, 1985). Other scholars suggest that one's upbringing and education level are the most critical factors in shaping entrepreneurs; whether one had an entrepreneurial parent or parents seems particularly significant (Malecki, 1997; Roberts, 1991). Roberts (1991) suggests that family background, goal orientation, personality, motivation, education, age and work experience are the personal factors that most influence entrepreneurial activity.

Although there are many studies that identify the characteristics of entrepreneurs, few have explored the explicit influence of an MBA education on entrepreneurial performance. One exception is Robinnet (1985), who shows that universities and research institutions have been fruitful environments for entrepreneurship development and that MBA curricula, especially entrepreneurship courses, majors and programs, help entrepreneurs initiate and succeed at business ventures (see also McMullan et al., 1985). Robinnet argues that MBA programs provide students with role models to foster their incipient interest in entrepreneurship and the practical skills to turn their ideas into businesses. According to the human capital approach developed by Mincer (1974), education level is an indicator of cognitive skills, abilities, productivity, stability and accommodation to new roles. And, as noted by Baruch and Blenkinsopp (Chapter 14 in this volume), human capital theory suggests that the labor market rewards, either directly or indirectly, the investments that individuals make in themselves. There is clear evidence to suggest that such investments can result in increased opportunities and actual career progress.

Although the role of education in fostering entrepreneurship has been debated, theoretical and statistical evidence has been produced that formal education in general, and management education in particular, has a positive impact on entrepreneurship (Bird, 1993). Many studies show that entrepreneurs have higher educational levels than the average population (Brockhaus and Horowitz, 1986; Robinson and Sexton, 1994). Nonetheless, the research findings are not conclusive on this issue.

An examination of the role of culture in entrepreneurship might offer some insight into whether the attributes of entrepreneurs vary with cultural contexts. McGrath et al. (1992b) suggest that entrepreneurs from different cultures share certain values that differentiate them from non-entrepreneurs. Since rates of entrepreneurial activity vary across cultures, it may be that some values are associated with increased entrepreneurship, regardless of the home culture (McGrath et al., 1992a). In this context, McGrath et al. (1992a, p. 132) claim that 'entrepreneurs are more like each other than they are different and more different from everyone than they are from each other ... The entrepreneurs have a persistent and characteristic value orientation, irrespective of the values of their base culture'. Most studies comparing entrepreneurs with non-entrepreneurs have been conducted in the USA. But because different countries have distinct and sometimes contrasting cultures, internationalization has created a strong need for cross-cultural studies to increase our understanding of intercultural entrepreneurship (e.g. Adler et al., 1986; Busenitz and Lau, 1997).

The research described in this chapter attempts to fill the gaps in the literature by comparing the career paths of MBA graduates who became entrepreneurs with their MBA colleagues who did not in two relatively homogeneous samples – one in Canada, the other in Israel. The focus on MBAs enabled an examination of a population with a relatively high propensity to undertake entrepreneurial careers. The research compares Canadian MBA graduates of the University of British Columbia with Israeli MBA graduates of Tel Aviv University. In both samples graduates who became entrepreneurs were compared with fellow graduates who did not become entrepreneurs. The career patterns of the respondents and their family members, demographic data (background variables) and personality characteristics (self-reported) were surveyed and analyzed. Conducting a cross-cultural comparison among Canadian and Israeli samples regarding entrepreneurship enabled a test of the relevance of US-based theories of entrepreneurship in other contexts.

Two primary research questions were addressed in the study: (a) Do demographic attributes, personality characteristics and family career patterns help distinguish MBA graduates who became entrepreneurs from MBAs who did not, in both the Israeli and the Canadian samples? and (b) Do cultural differences between Canada and Israel help distinguish the career paths taken by their respective MBA graduates?

The chapter is organized as follows. First, the conceptual framework used to compare the samples is presented and the hypotheses generated from that framework. This is followed by a discussion of the methods used to test the hypotheses and the data analyses used to test them. Lastly, the results are presented, their implications discussed, and some conclusions offered.

LITERATURE REVIEW

The conceptual framework used in the present research draws on the demographic approach (Bird, 1989, 1993; Katz and Brockhaus, 1993), social learning theory (Scherer et al., 1990; Bandura, 1977, 1986), and the personality approach to entrepreneurship (Sexton and Bowman, 1986; McClelland, 1961; McClelland and Winter, 1969; Shaver and Scott, 1991; Shaver et al., 1996). The demographic approach, which focuses on the importance of demographic variables in understanding entrepreneurial career, is integrated with social learning theory, which focuses on career pattern selection. These two approaches are combined with the personality approach, which considers that individual characteristics are the most important predictors of the decision to become an entrepreneur. Each of these approaches is described more fully below.

It is now widely recognized that entrepreneurial activity varies across cultures and that entrepreneurship is influenced by cultural values (Peterson, 1988; Sundbo, 1991). The conceptual framework developed in the present research thus considers cultural theories to be important (Hofstede, 1980, 1991; Triandis, 1980, 1990), particularly those that focus on cross-cultural aspects of entrepreneurship (McGrath et al., 1992a; McGrath et al., 1992b; Busenitz and Lau, 1997).

Figure 8.1 presents an overview of the general framework used in the study to explore the factors that influence the decision to pursue an entrepreneurial career.

Social Learning Theory and Entrepreneurial Career Preference

An individual's career selection process usually spans several decades and is the outcome of numerous environmental, socio-psychological and personality influences. Numerous descriptive studies, aimed at isolating the reasons why an individual pursues an entrepreneurial career, have identified

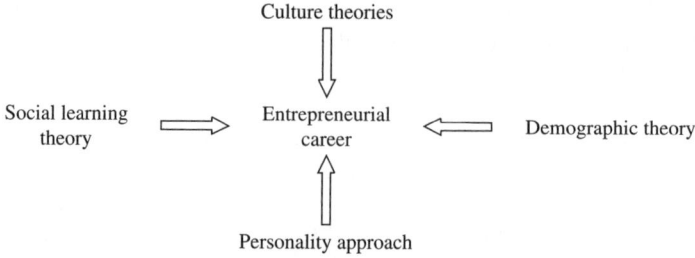

Figure 8.1   Conceptual framework of the study

the presence of a parent who, at some time during the child's life, also pursued an entrepreneurial career (e.g. Hisrich and Brush, 1985; Gartner, 1985). Some researchers (e.g. Ronstadt, 1985; Scherer et al., 1989, 1990) have suggested that parents influence children's entrepreneurial career choice through a process of role modeling, which occurs when social behavior is informally observed and then adopted by a learner. The individual learns by example rather than by direct experience (Bandura, 1977). Observational learning can thus either encourage or discourage a person from entering a career field similar to the one observed (Mitchell and Krumboltz, 1984). This observational learning process and subsequent cognitive evaluations may lead to an alteration in career preference through altering an individual's (1) educational and vocational aspirations, (2) expectations about the possibility of entering the career field in question, or (3) evaluation of the personal skills and abilities required to perform in that career or occupation (Mitchell and Krumboltz, 1984). Hence social learning theory appears to be a viable conceptual framework for explaining entrepreneurial career selection.

The Demographic Approach

The dynamic nature, relevance and importance of demographic variables (e.g. gender, age, education and financial status) in explaining entrepreneurial careers have often been studied (Bird, 1993; Carsrud et al., 1993). Experiences such as those that might appear on a résumé contribute to the development of drives, skills, abilities and competencies important to entrepreneurship, as well as to the values and incentives that energize the entrepreneurial idea. Another line of research, which relates to the demographic approach, focuses on the participation of the family in business ventures (Upton and Heck, 1997; Wortman, 1994). Bird (1993) claims that it is the choice of the entrepreneurial path that distinguishes entrepreneurs from managers and from the general population. In other words, entrepreneurs are more like other entrepreneurs than they are like their peers in the 'general population'.

The Personal Approach

Research with a psychological/personality focus has continuously sought to identify universal traits that differentiate entrepreneurs from non-entrepreneurs (McClelland and Winter, 1969; Brockhaus and Horowitz, 1986; Sexton and Bowman, 1985). The question of whether there are any statistically significant differences in attributes, attitudes and traits of entrepreneurs as compared to non-entrepreneurs has been frequently addressed (Sexton and Bowman, 1985; Begley and Boyd, 1986; Bellu, 1988; Dubini and MacMillan, 1988; Smeltz, 1990; Amit and Muller, 1995; Erez and Edelding, 1991). Building on McClelland's (1961) and McClelland and Winter's (1969) research, which focused on the psychological attributes of entrepreneurs, Brockhaus and Horowitz (1986) pointed to four key characteristics of the successful entrepreneur: the need for achievement, propensity for risk taking, a locus of control and the ability to tolerate ambiguity. The desire to be 'one's own boss' is an important motive that inspires both men and women to take the social, psychological, financial and personal risks involved in initiating a new venture.

McClelland (1961) and McClelland and Winter (1969) claim that entrepreneurial behavior is mainly characterized by the willingness to take risks. Successful entrepreneurs, living in a world of high levels of risk and ambiguity, actually manage risks carefully (Bird, 1989). They take on challenging but achievable assignments, and they prefer immediate and accurate feedback regarding the consequences of their activities. Entrepreneurs consider their steps and evaluate risks based on information that may not be accessible and available to others. While other studies showed mixed results, McGrath et al. (1992a), in their comparative study of entrepreneurs and non-entrepreneurs in eight countries, supported earlier work that suggests that entrepreneurs can tolerate risk and ambiguity.

The Cultural Aspect

Researchers seeking to explain the genesis of entrepreneurship have broadened the scope of inquiry to incorporate cultural beliefs and values (Peterson, 1988; Alange and Scheinberg, 1988; Abramson et al., 1993). Not all societies foster entrepreneurial activity with equal effectiveness (Birch, 1987; Shapero, 1985; Birley, 1987). Shapero and Sokol (1982) claimed that rates of business formation vary from society to society because different cultures have different beliefs about the desirability and feasibility of beginning a new enterprise.

A major factor in determining the relative level of entrepreneurship across societies, and in different periods within the same society, is 'legitimization'. To the extent that entrepreneurship is legitimate within a society, the demand for it is higher; the supply of it is higher, and more resources are allocated to the entrepreneurial function (Etzioni, 1987). Entrepreneurship may be regarded as the prime activity of society, as an activity acceptable but of secondary importance, or as an activity suitable only for a minority of the population. All else being equal, the higher the legitimization of entrepreneurship within a society, the more the educational system (including the family and on-the-job programs) dedicates itself to educating and training entrepreneurs (Etzioni, 1987). Legitimization also has an effect on individual preferences and influences the number of young people who choose business careers over public service. It also influences how rapidly universities expand the facilities of their business schools.

The most widely cited work on the role of culture is that of Hofstede (1980, 1983, 1984, 1991), suggesting that shared values endure over time and are fairly consistent within cultures because they have been institutionalized. Hofstede defines culture as 'the collective programming of the mind which distinguishes the member of one human group from another' (1984, p. 21). These mental programs refer to prescribed ways of doing things or ways of acting. They are transferred through genetic linkage and/or are learned by individuals through their cultural system, particularly during childhood and early development. At the core of mental programs are culture and values, which are 'a broad tendency to prefer certain states of affairs over others' (ibid., p. 18).

Based upon the above approaches, a number of hypotheses were proposed regarding the relationships among demographic variables, career patterns, personality attributes and the choice of an entrepreneurial career. Figure 8.2 presents the research model with its various variables, which are assumed to correlate with the choice of entrepreneurial path.

The Research Contexts: Canada and Israel

The study was conducted simultaneously in Canada and in Israel, two developed countries that are well known for their advanced research and development initiatives. Before we discuss the research methods, we highlight a few noteworthy and relevant characteristics of the two study countries. While the population of Canada is about 32 million, the population of Israel is about 7 million; the geographical area and population of Israel

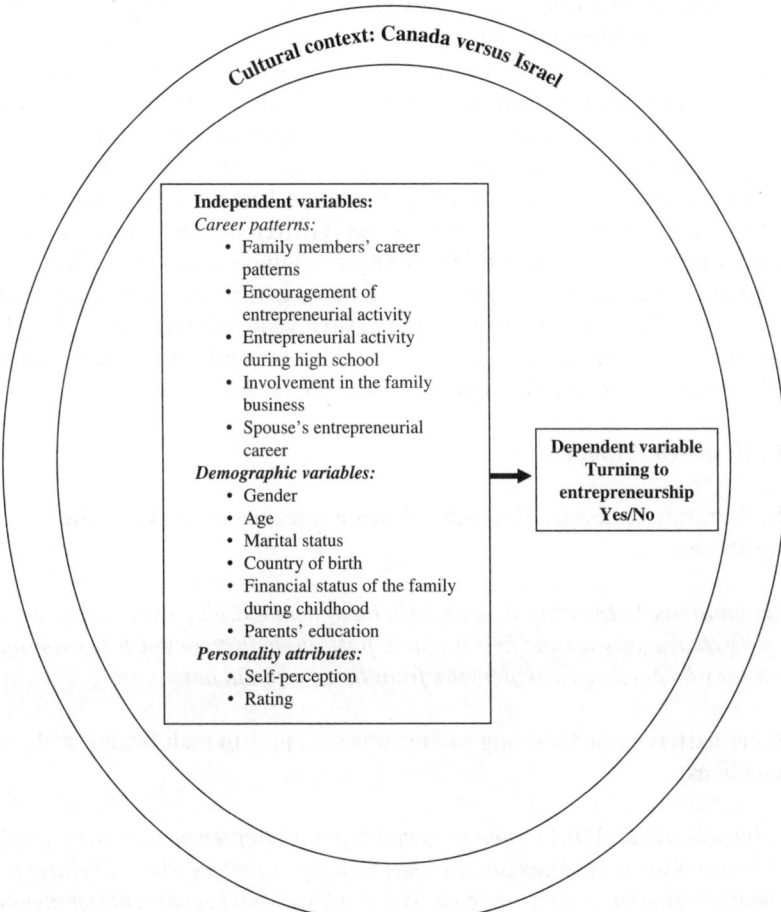

Figure 8.2   The research model

make it a 'small' country, especially relative to Canada. Both Canada and Israel are countries with a large immigrant population. Canada in general, and British Columbia in particular (from which the Canadian sample was drawn), has a large number of immigrants who became citizens. Over half of the Jewish population of Israel was born outside the country and the majority of the other half are sons and daughters of immigrants.

Israel is a country characterized by a large public sector. In 1997, 85 percent of its general labor force was employed by the public sector. In 1997, 16.4 percent of the male workforce and 5.1 percent of the female workforce was self-employed or an employer (*Israel Year Book*, 1998).

Canada, on the other hand, is well known as a country with a long tradition of public and cultural support for business formation. Small business incubators provide facilities and special services for entrepreneurs, some of which are university-based or sponsored by the government, non-profit economic development groups, or municipal agencies (Brandt, 1991). The percentage of the workforce that was self-employed in 1996 was 15.7 percent for males and 8.8 percent for females (*Canada Year Book*, 1997).

The *Global Entrepreneurship Monitor* (GEM), a cross-national study, shows that total entrepreneurial activity in Canada is usually higher than in Israel expressed as a percentage of new-venture start-ups (Reynolds et al., 2001; Acs et al., 2004). The study also revealed that in terms of high-tech start-ups reflected by venture capital investments as a percentage of GDP, Israel was rated the highest among the GEM countries.

The Research Hypotheses

The literature review leads to the following three hypotheses and their sub-hypotheses:

Hypothesis 1: In both Israel and Canada, demographic variables, person-ality characteristics and family career patterns help distinguish MBA grad-uates who became entrepreneurs from those who did not.

Career patterns (the following sub-hypotheses apply to both Israelis and Canadians)

Hypothesis 1a: MBA graduates who became entrepreneurs are more likely to have parents, siblings and extended family members who had entrepre-neurial experience than are those MBAs who did not become entrepreneurs.

Hypothesis 1b: MBAs who became entrepreneurs have the following char-acteristics: (1) they were encouraged more to engage in entrepreneurial activities during their childhood, and (2) they participated more in entre-preneurial activities during adolescence (e.g. they worked during high school) than the MBA graduates who did not become entrepreneurs.

Hypothesis 1c: MBAs who became entrepreneurs were more involved in their family businesses than were the MBA graduates who did not become entrepreneurs.

Hypothesis 1d: MBAs who became entrepreneurs are more likely to have entrepreneurial spouses than are MBAs who did not become entrepreneurs.

Demographic variables

Hypothesis 1e: Men are better represented than women in the group of MBAs who became entrepreneurs relative to the group of MBA graduates who did not.

Hypothesis 1f: MBAs who became entrepreneurs are older and more likely to be married than the MBA graduates who did not become entrepreneurs.

Hypothesis 1g: Among the MBA graduates who consider themselves immigrants, a higher percentage became entrepreneurs than graduates who do not consider themselves immigrants.

Hypothesis 1h: Relative to MBAs who did not become entrepreneurs, MBAs who pursued entrepreneurial careers come from families of heterogeneous financial status and experienced ups and down in the financial stability of the family during childhood.

Hypothesis 1i: The parents of the MBAs who became entrepreneurs have higher levels of education than do the parents of MBA graduates who did not become entrepreneurs.

Personality characteristics

Hypothesis 1j: Personality attributes (e.g. willingness to take risks, vision, creativity and innovativeness, and ability to handle ambiguity) distinguish MBAs who became entrepreneurs from those who did not.

Hypothesis 2: Relative to their Israeli counterparts, Canadian MBA graduates have a higher propensity to pursue entrepreneurial careers. (This hypothesis derived from the fact that, unlike Israel, Canada has a long tradition of support for entrepreneurship.)

Hypothesis 3: The propensity to pursue an entrepreneurial career is higher for Canadian and Israeli MBA graduates than it is for non-MBAs in the general population of their respective countries.

METHOD

Samples

The Israeli sample consisted of MBAs from Tel Aviv University who graduated in the years 1974/5, 1979/80, 1984/5, 1989/90 and 1991/2. The

Canadian sample consisted of MBAs from the University of British Columbia who graduated in the years 1974, 1979, 1984 and 1989. The data were collected in 1994–95. Because of the small size of the Israeli sample, the Israeli data were augmented with data collected in 1996.

Survey Procedures

A survey was conducted by mailing a questionnaire (presented in Amit and Muller, 1996) to MBAs drawn from lists of graduates of the faculties of management of the two universities. The survey was designed to extract information about the respondents' business/entrepreneurial experience, educational backgrounds, demographic information and personal attributes. For the Israeli respondents, the questionnaire was translated from English into Hebrew.

To test the hypotheses, in each of the two sub-samples MBAs who became entrepreneurs were compared to MBAs who did not by means of chi-square analyses (χ^2) and t-tests. The characteristics the two sub-samples were also compared. Finally, logistic regression analyses were performed to examine which variables distinguish between the MBAs who became entrepreneurs and those who did not in the Canadian and Israeli sub-samples and in the whole research population.

The Entrepreneurial Variable: Dependent Variable

Respondents were asked if during their professional career they had ever contributed to the formation of a new venture in any of the following ways: (1) as founder, (2) as a member of the founding team, (3) as a key employee, (4) in some other capacity. For the purposes of the study, an entrepreneur was defined as an individual who was either a founder or a member of the founding team of a new venture; 'key employees' and 'others' were considered non-entrepreneurs. The survey also asked whether the respondent's mother, father, siblings, other relatives of the family and/or spouse had been entrepreneurs (as just defined).

The Independent Variables

Career patterns of the respondents and their families
Parents were considered entrepreneurs if either the mother or the father or both had had an entrepreneurial career. The encouragement a respondent received during childhood to pursue an entrepreneurial career was measured using an ordinal 5-point scale ranging from 1 to 5, where 1 represented having been encouraged and 5 represented having been discouraged.

Subsequently the responses 1 and 2 were combined into one category representing having been encouraged and the responses of 3, 4 and 5 into one category representing having been discouraged.

Working during high school was measured by the question: 'Did you work at any part time/temporary job during high school?' Respondents were asked to answer 'yes' or 'no'. Overall involvement in entrepreneurial activity was measured by the question: 'Were you ever involved in the family business?' Respondents were asked to answer 'yes' or 'no'.

Involvement of the extended family in a family business as owners or managers was measured by the question: 'Is there a business in which your extended family is involved as owners/managers?' Respondents were asked to answer 'yes' or 'no'.

Spouses' entrepreneurial career was measured by the question: 'Has your spouse started or participated in the formation of a business?' Respondents were asked to answer 'yes' or 'no'.

Demographic variables
The financial status of the family during childhood was measured using an ordinal 5-point scale ranging from rich (1) to poor (5). The categories were combined to make three categories. Ups and downs in the financial stability of the family during childhood were measured on an ordinal 3-point scale ranging from many (1) to none at all (3). The categories were collapsed into two categories.

Immigrant status was measured by the question: 'Were you an immigrant?' Respondents were asked to answer 'yes' or 'no'. The education level of the respondents' parents was measured on an ordinal 3-point scale ranging from elementary (1) to college graduate or other post-high school (3). The categories were combined to make two categories: one category included the responses 'elementary' and 'high school or above'; the second category included the responses 'college, graduate, or other post high school'. The survey also contained questions on the respondent's gender, age, marital status, number of children and type of residence.

Personal attributes
Respondents were asked to rank 13 attributes according to how important they believed they were in creating and managing an entrepreneurial business. They were also asked to identify the five attributes most characteristic of themselves (see the list of attributes in Tables 8.5 and 8.5a).

Cultural variables
Cultural affiliation was measured by being an Israeli or a Canadian MBA.

Table 8.1   Sample description

Variable	Canadians % (N=160)	Israelis % (N=166)	Significance
Gender			
Male	78.7	83.6	
Female	21.3	16.4	$\chi^2=1.27$
Age			
25–34	48.1	21.1	$\chi^2=201$***
35–44	46.9	48.8	
45–54	5.0	25.3	
55+	–	4.8	
Country of origin			
Non-immigrants	52.5	79.4	$\chi^2=16.3$***
Immigrants	47.5	16.3	
Marital status			
Married	71.9	89.6	$\chi^2=26.24$***

*** $p \leq 0.001$.

Sample description
The composition of the Canadian and Israeli samples is shown in Table 8.1. The table shows significant differences between the Canadian and the Israeli MBA samples according to the respondents' demographic background. Both samples were composed mostly of males, although there were fewer females in the Israeli sample. The Israeli respondents were significantly older than their Canadian counterparts and the percentage of the married respondents was significantly higher in the Israeli sample; the percentage of immigrants in the Israeli sample was significantly lower than in the Canadian sample.

RESULTS

About one-third of the two samples, 36.3 percent of the Canadian MBAs and 31.5 percent of the Israeli MBAs, became entrepreneurs (see Table 8.2).

As the table clearly shows, the percentages of entrepreneurs in both samples were significantly higher – almost three times – than the percentages of the individuals who became entrepreneurs within the general population in their countries in the respective years. These data strongly support the hypothesis that the propensity to pursue an entrepreneurial career is higher for Canadian and Israeli MBA graduates than it is for the general population of their respective countries (Hypothesis 3).

Table 8.2 *Percentages of entrepreneurs among the Canadian MBAs versus among Canadian workforce and among Israeli MBAs versus Israeli workforce by gender*

	Canada				Israel			
	MBAs	Sample	Workforce population		MBAs	Sample	Workforce population	
	%	N	%	N (in thousands)	%	N	%	N (in thousands)
Males	44.3	99	15.7	7 768.5	35.5	138	16.4	1 155.4
Females	6.1	56	8.8	6 549.0	11.1	21	5.1	884.8
Total	36.3	166	12.6	14 317.5	31.5	160	11.5	2 040.2

Sources: *Canada Year Book* (1997); *Israel Year Book* (1998), pp. 12–27.

Although the percentage of entrepreneurs among the Canadian MBAs was a bit higher than among their Israeli counterparts, the differences are not significant. This finding leads to the rejection of Hypothesis 2, which posited that Canadian MBAs would have a higher tendency to pursue entrepreneurial careers than their Israeli counterparts.

Table 8.3 compares the career patterns of entrepreneurs and non-entrepreneurs among Israeli and Canadian MBAs and their family members.

The right-hand column of Table 8.3 shows that the Canadian MBAs were raised in more entrepreneurial families than were their Israeli counterparts. Almost half of the Canadian respondents stated that they were encouraged to pursue entrepreneurial activities during their adolescence; only about one-quarter of the Israelis were so encouraged (48.8 percent versus 26.2 percent; $p < 0.001$). Most of the Canadian respondents stated that they worked during high school, while less than half of the Israelis stated that they did so (83.1 percent versus 44 percent; $p < 0.001$). Almost 40 percent of the Canadian respondents were involved in their family business, compared to only 19.4 percent of the Israeli respondents ($p < 0.001$). Forty-two percent of the Canadian respondents' siblings had entrepreneurial careers; only 19.1 percent of the Israeli respondents' siblings did so ($p < 0.001$).

Half of both the Canadians and the Israeli MBAs had parents with entrepreneurial career patterns; 60 percent of the Canadian entrepreneurs versus 46 percent of the non-entrepreneurs had parents in business ($p < 0.06$) and members of the extended family in business ($p < 0.001$). These findings support Hypothesis 1a for the Canadian MBAs, and not for the Israeli MBAs.

Table 8.3 *A comparison of career patterns of entrepreneurs versus non-entrepreneurs among Israeli and Canadian MBAs and their family members (%)*

Career-pattern variables	Canadians			Israelis			Canadians	Israelis	
	Non-entrepreneurs	Entrepreneurs	χ^2	Non-entrepreneurs	Entrepreneurs	χ^2	Total	Total	χ^2
Respondent	63.7	36.3	–	68.0	32.0	–	36.3 (58)	31.5 (53)	0.68
Mother in business	13.9	24.6	2.86~	11.7	22.4	3.04~	17.7	15.1	0.38
Father in business	43.1	56.1	2.47	44.5	51.0	0.58	47.8	46.6	0.047
Parents in business	46.1	60.3	3.01~	46.0	50.9	0.35	50.9	49.1	0.43
Siblings in business	38.2	46.5	4.62	23.1	20.4	0.14	41.2	19.1	17.3**
Extended family in business	41.2	60.3	5.44**	46.0	51.0	0.35	48.1	47.6	0.010
Encouragement of entrepreneurial activity	39.2	65.5	12.55**	25.0	28.8	0.27	48.8	26.2	23.9***
Working during high school	84.3	81.0	0.28	42.5	47.2	0.32	83.1	44.0	53.7***
Involvement in the family business	31.4	51.7	6.45**	17.1	24.0	1.02	38.8	19.4	14.3***
Spouse's entrepreneurial career	18.8	28.3	1.66	18.6	14.6	0.37	22.6	17.3	1.21

~ $p < 0.06$; * $p \leq 0.05$; ** $p \leq 0.01$; *** $p \leq 0.001$.

Interestingly, the number of times that the respondent's father started or participated in the formation of a business (according to the respondent) was significantly correlated with the respondent's entrepreneurial career for both Israelis and Canadians ($r = 0.36$** and $r = 0.22$** respectively). These findings support the social learning theory of entrepreneurship discussed earlier and emphasize the importance of role modeling for entrepreneurs.

A comparison of the Canadian entrepreneurs and non-entrepreneurs along the dimensions 'encouragement of entrepreneurial activities' and 'involvement of the respondents and the extended family in business as owners/managers' showed that the two groups are significantly different. Sixty-six percent of the entrepreneurs versus 39.2 percent of the non-entrepreneurs responded that they were encouraged to pursue entre-preneurial activities during their childhood ($p < 0.001$). Furthermore, 52 percent of the entrepreneurs versus only 31.4 percent of the non-entrepreneurs were involved in their family businesses ($p < 0.001$). These findings support Hypotheses 1b and 1c for the Canadian respondents. No significant differences were found between Canadian entrepreneurs and non-entrepreneurs in the level of participation in entrepreneurial activities during their adolescence; nor were any differences found in their siblings' entrepreneurial career patterns.

Contrary to the results for the Canadian respondents, all the hypotheses regarding career patterns of the Israeli respondents and their families were rejected (H1a,b,c). In other words, Israeli MBA entrepreneurs and non-entrepreneurs were not significantly different in any of the above variables, with the exception of the mother's entrepreneurial career (22.4 percent of the entrepreneurs versus 11.7 percent of the non-entrepreneurs had mothers in business; $p < 0.08$). Hypothesis 1(d), regarding the spouse's entrepreneurial career pattern, was rejected for both the Canadian and the Israeli samples.

An examination of the demographic data in Table 8.4 revealed that the gender and age composition of the entrepreneurs and the non-entrepreneurs was significantly different for both the Canadian and the Israeli sample. For the Canadian sample, 96 percent of the MBA graduates who became entrepreneurs were males while only 68.7 percent of the non-entrepreneurs were males ($p < 0.001$). Similarly, for the Israeli sample, 94.2 percent of the MBAs who became entrepreneurs were males while only 78.8 percent of the non-entrepreneurs were males ($p < 0.01$). H1(e) regarding gender was thus supported.

Table 8.4 revealed that almost 90 percent of the Israeli entrepreneurs were at least 35 years old, while 74.3 percent of the non-entrepreneurs were that age ($p < 0.03$). In contrast, only 10 percent of the Canadian entrepreneurs and only 2 percent of the non-entrepreneurs were at least 35 years old

Table 8.4   A comparison of demographic variables of entrepreneurs versus non-entrepreneurs among Israeli and Canadian MBAs (%)

Demographic variables	Canadians			Israelis			Canadians	Israelis	
	Non-entrepreneurs	Entrepreneurs	χ^2	Non-entrepreneurs	Entrepreneurs	χ^2	Total	Total	χ^2
Gender – % males	68.7	96.4	16.4***	78.8	94.2	5.74**	78.7	83.6	1.27
Age – % 35 years old and over	2.0	10.3	10.0**	74.3	88.7	4.46*	5.0	70.1	20.1***
Marital status – % married	63.8	79.3	2.49	89.4	90.0	0.14	71.9	89.6	16.3***
Immigrants	47.1	48.3	0.02	21.2	19.2	0.08	47.5	20.6	26.24***
Financial status of the family during childhood – % average income	49.0	43.1	0.58	55.4	57.7	0.11	46.9	56.1	3.5
Ups and downs in the financial stability of the family	44.1	40.4	0.21	73.2	63.5	1.61	7.5	3.0	10.97**
Mother's education – % academic education	41.4	45.6	0.26	20.7	35.3	3.92*	42.9	25.3	11.0***
Father's education – % academic education	60.0	49.9	3.03	33.3	45.1	2.22	54.8	37.0	10.1**

* $p \leq 0.05$; ** $p \leq 0.01$; *** $p \leq 0.001$.

(p<0.006). Hypothesis 1(f) regarding age was thus supported in both the Israeli and Canadian samples. However, the hypothesis regarding marital status was rejected for both samples. Hypothesis 1(g) regarding the higher rates of immigrants among the entrepreneurs, and Hypothesis 1(h) regarding past financial status, were both rejected for both the Israeli and Canadian samples. Among the Israeli sample, 35.3 percent of the entrepreneurs but only 20.7 percent of the non-entrepreneurs reported that their mothers had a high level of education (p<0.04). This finding supported Hypothesis 1(i) regarding higher parental education level only for the Israeli sample.

In summary, the above results indicate that among the demographic variables considered, MBA graduates who became entrepreneurs differ from their non-entrepreneurial counterparts only in age and gender (and in higher mother education level for the Israeli sample).

Personal Attributes

Hypothesis 1(j) posed that personality attributes (e.g. 'willingness to take risks', 'vision, creativity and innovativeness' and 'ability to handle ambiguity') distinguish MBAs who became entrepreneurs from those who did not. This hypothesis was examined by considering both the self-reported attributes and the attributes respondents considered most important in creating and managing an entrepreneurial business (see Tables 8.5 and 8.6).

Table 8.5 compared the self-reported attributes of MBAs who became entrepreneurs with those reported by MBAs who did not become entrepreneurs for both the Israeli and the Canadian sub-groups. Table 8.6 compared the attributes that entrepreneurs and non-entrepreneurs in both samples considered most important in creating an entrepreneurial business.

The five most frequently mentioned attributes were the same among the Israeli and Canadian respondents (both entrepreneurs and non-entrepreneurs): personal integrity, ability to organize, ability to adapt to new situations, ability to communicate, and ability to handle sustained periods of intense effort. However, these five attributes were ranked differently by the four sub-groups.

Entrepreneurs and non-entrepreneurs also had similar lists of the attributes considered most important for entrepreneurial success (although in different orders): the ability to organize, vision, creativity and innovativeness, the ability to adapt to new situations, and willingness to take risks. The choice of the same top four characteristics may reflect a perception of successful entrepreneurs that is beyond culture.

A deeper comparison of the Israeli and Canadian lists of self-reported attributes revealed that Canadian and Israeli MBAs had different self-perceptions. Of the 13 characteristics given, six self-reported attributes

Table 8.5 A comparison of self-reported attributes of entrepreneurs versus non-entrepreneurs among Israeli and Canadian MBAs (%)

Personal attributes	Canadians			Israelis			Canadians	Israelis	χ^2
	Entrepreneur (n = 53)	Non-entrepr. (n = 102)	χ^2	Entrepreneur (n = 53)	Non-entrepr. (n = 113)	χ^2	Total (n = 160)	Total (n = 166)	
Adapt to new situations, and act rapidly	41.3	45.1	0.45	49.0	48.6	-0.05	55.6	65.7	11.55***
Ability to build and lead a team	41.3	34.3	-0.89	35.8	45.1	1.14	39.3	37.9	0.27
Ability to communicate	60.3	68.6	1.06	45.2	44.2	-0.12	38.7	17.5	76.03***
Ability to handle ambiguity	18.9	21.5	0.39	18.8	28.3	1.37	8.7	25.3	76.94***
Handle sustained periods of intense effort	48.2	51.9	0.45	43.4	41.6	-2.2	40.0	33.1	6.28*
Working relationships with buyers, suppliers	12.0	21.5	1.6	30.2	33.6	0.44	9.4	14.5	8.18**
Ability to negotiate	29.3	25.5	-0.51	22.6	34.5	1.62	25.0	22.3	1.32
Ability to organize, control, focus, execute	72.4	84.3	1.72~	56.6	65.5	1.1	78.1	61.45	42.93***
Experience and familiarity with the industry	25.8	26.4	0.08	26.4	21.2	-0.74	32.5	31.9	0.49
Luck	12.0	2.9	-1.97*	1.9	5.3	1.02	22.5	31.9	14.81***
Personal integrity	46.5	60.7	1.75~	70.0	67.2	-0.33	16.2	10.8	8.3*
Vision, creativity and innovativeness	39.6	38.2	-0.18	43.4	38.0	-0.65	63.7	77.1	27.57***
Willingness to take risks	32.7	17.6	-2.08*	37.7	21.2	-2.13*	69.4	68.0	0.25

~ $p < 0.06$; * $p \leq 0.05$; ** $p \leq 0.01$; *** $p \leq 0.001$.

Table 8.6   A comparison of attributes considered most important in creating and managing a business among Israeli and Canadian MBA entrepreneurs versus non-entrepreneurs (%)

Personal attributes	Canadians			Israelis			Canadians	Israelis	
	Entrepreneur (n = 53)	Non-entrepr. (n = 102)	χ^2	Entrepreneur (n = 53)	Non-entrepr. (n = 113)	χ^2	Total (n = 160)	Total (n = 166)	χ^2
Adapt to new situations, and act rapidly	51.7	57.8	0.75	69.8	63.7	-0.77	43.8	48.8	0.83
Ability to build and lead a team	48.3	34.3	-1.7~	41.5	36.2	-0.64	36.9	42.2	0.95
Ability to communicate	50.0	32.3	-2.2**	18.8	16.8	-0.32	65.6	44.6	12.15**
Ability to handle ambiguity	6.9	9.8	0.62	3.9	21.2	1.76*	20.6	25.3	4.04*
Handle sustained periods of intense effort	36.2	42.1	0.74	24.5	37.1	1.68~	50.6	42.2	3.92*
Working relationships with buyers, suppliers	8.6	9.8	0.25	17.0	13.2	-0.63	18.1	32.5	37.84***
Ability to negotiate	27.6	23.5	-0.57	28.3	19.4	-1.27	26.9	30.7	0.58
Ability to organize, control, focus, execute	75.8	79.4	0.52	54.7	64.6	1.22	80.0	62.6	49.40***
Experience and familiarity with the industry	27.6	35.3	1.00	39.6	28.3	-1.46	26.3	22.9	0.49
Luck	22.4	22.5	0.02	30.1	32.7	0.33	6.3	4.2	0.68
Personal integrity	22.4	12.75	-1.5	17.0	8.0	-1.55	55.6	68.0	17.62***
Vision, creativity and innovativeness	0.0	71.5	2.7**	64.1	83.2	2.77**	38.8	39.8	0.03
Willingness to take risks	70.7	68.6	-0.27	60.4	71.7	1.41	23.1	26.5	0.49

~ p < 0.06; * p ≤ 0.05; ** p ≤ 0.01; *** p ≤ 0.001.

were significantly different. Canadians described the ability to communicate, the ability to handle sustained periods of intense effort, and the ability to organize as characteristics of themselves more frequently than did the Israelis. By contrast, the Israelis considered themselves able to handle ambiguity and able to maintain good working relationships more frequently than did the Canadians.

A comparison of the Israeli and the Canadian responses concerning the attributes considered most important for entrepreneurial success (Table 8.6) shows that nine out of the 13 attributes were significantly different for the two groups. The Canadian respondents ranked the ability to communicate, the ability to handle sustained periods of intense effort, the ability to organize, and personal integrity significantly higher than did the Israelis. On the other hand, the Israelis ranked vision, creativity and innovativeness, ability to adapt to new situations, luck, ability to handle ambiguity, and ability to maintain good working relationships significantly higher than did the Canadians.

Some interesting cross-cultural differences were found in the personal-attribute profiles of the Canadians and the Israelis, regardless of the pursuit of entrepreneurial career. The ability to handle ambiguity and the ability to maintain good working relationships were two salient attributes that the Israeli respondents ranked higher than did their Canadian counterparts.

A comparison of entrepreneurs and non-entrepreneurs (without distinguishing the samples by nationality) showed that the self-reported attribute of 'willingness to take risks' significantly distinguished entrepreneurs from non-entrepreneurs. For the Israeli sample, this self-reported attribute was the only attribute that distinguished entrepreneurs from non-entrepreneurs. These findings are consistent with the literature discussed above. However, Hypothesis 1(j) was supported only with regard to the attribute 'willingness to take risks'.

Multivariate Examination

The analysis thus far has considered the differences regarding individual variables between MBAs who became entrepreneurs and those who did not. Multivariate examinations were also conducted by means of logistic regression analysis in order to classify subjects as those MBAs who became entrepreneurs and other MBAs who did not, according to the three clusters of predictor variables in each of the Canadian and Israeli samples.

The logistic regression analyses included nine variables originating from the three clusters considered thus far, which were found as significantly differentiated between entrepreneurs and non-entrepreneurs in the former examinations. The demographic variables included gender, age, mother's education, economic status during childhood, and whether there were ups and downs in the family's financial status during the respondent's childhood. The career-pattern variables included encouragement of entrepreneurship, involvement in family business, having entrepreneurial parents, and a willingness to take risks as a personal attribute.

Table 8.7 presents the findings of three logistic regression models: a model for the Canadian sub-sample, another for the Israeli sub-sample and the third for the whole research sample (in which another variable of the dichotomous cultural affiliation was also included). Each of the regression models contrasts the log odds of becoming an entrepreneur against the odds of not becoming an entrepreneur among the MBAs.

The results show that all three models effectively and significantly classify the MBAs as entrepreneurs or non-entrepreneurs. The logistic regression analysis of the Canadian sub-sample shows that gender (i.e. being male) and age (being older) are the variables that most successfully distinguish MBAs who became entrepreneurs from their fellow graduates who did not. The analysis of the Israeli sub-sample reveals that a willingness to take risks, gender, and having a mother with a high level of education are the variables that most clearly distinguish MBAs who became entrepreneurs from their fellow graduates who did not.

Interestingly, when the whole sample (Canadians and Israelis) is considered, cultural affiliation does not distinguish between the MBAs who became entrepreneurs and their counterparts who did not. The variables that most clearly distinguish MBA graduates who became entrepreneurs from their non-entrepreneurial counterparts are gender, a willingness to take risks, the encouragement of entrepreneurial activities during childhood, having a mother with high education and involvement in the family business.

Gender appears as a discriminating variable in both samples; thus gender was controlled. The results of the logistic regression models of each of the two male sub-samples and that of the whole male research populations are presented in Table 8.8 (the small number of women in the two samples did not justify performing such analyses separately for female MBAs).

Among the Canadian male MBAs, the main discriminating variable was involvement in a family business. This finding suggests that for the Canadian MBAs, the odds of becoming an entrepreneur are much higher if they are males who were involved in family businesses.

For the Israeli MBAs, the odds of becoming an entrepreneur are higher if they are males, and are willing to take risks. The variable of having a mother with higher education does not maintain its significance after controlling for gender.

Table 8.7   Logistic regression analyses of demographic, career patterns and personality variables associated with becoming entrepreneurs among Israeli and Canadian MBAs and the total research population (estimated standard errors in parentheses)

	Total research population		Canadian sample		Israeli sample	
	B (S.E.)	Exp (B)	B (S.E.)	Exp (B)	B (S.E.)	Exp (B)
Demographic variables						
Gender	1.93*** (0.51)	6.91	2.22** (0.78)	9.17	1.73*** (0.29)	5.64
Age	0.51* (0.22)	1.66	1.11** (0.38)	3.02	0.22 (0.29)	1.25
Mother's education	0.81** (0.31)	2.25	0.72 (0.31)	2.06	0.99* (0.45)	2.70
Financial status of the family during childhood	0.18 (0.20)	1.19	0.22 (0.29)	1.25	0.17 (0.28)	1.19
Ups and downs in the financial stability	0.30 (0.25)	1.35	0.08 (0.34)	1.08	0.63 (0.41)	1.90
Career patterns						
Parents' entrepreneurial career	0.21 (0.30)	1.23	0.61 (0.45)	1.84	−0.14 (0.42)	0.87
Family encouragement of entrepreneurial activities	−0.44* (0.23)	0.64	−0.43 (0.31)	0.65	−0.51 (0.39)	0.60
Involvement in family business	0.74* (0.34)	1.35	0.73 (0.46)	2.10	0.65 (0.52)	1.93
Personal attributes						
Willingness to take risk	0.77** (0.30)	1.85	0.40 (0.47)	1.50	0.96* (0.42)	2.62
Culture						
Cultural affiliation (Canadian/ Israeli)	0.62 (0.44)	1.86	–	–	–	–
Model χ^2	54.23***		38.55***		23.15**	

* $p < 0.05$; ** $p < 0.01$; *** $p < 0.001$.

Table 8.8   *Logistic regression analyses of demographic, career patterns and personality variables associated with becoming entrepreneurs among Israeli and Canadian male MBAs and the total male research population (estimated standard errors in parentheses)*

	Total male research population		Canadian male sample		Israeli male sample	
	B (S.E.)	Exp (B)	B (S.E.)	Exp (B)	B (S.E.)	Exp (B)
Demographic variables						
Age	0.47*	1.60	1.10	3.00	0.14	1.15
Mother's education	0.66*	1.94	0.55	1.73	0.79	2.20
Financial status of the family during childhood	0.12	1.12	0.18	1.19	0.12	1.12
Ups and downs in the financial stability	0.32	1.37	0.17	1.18	0.52	1.69
Career patterns						
Family encouragement of entrepreneurial activities	−0.57*	0.56	−0.58~	0.56	−0.67	0.51
Parents' entrepreneurial career	0.05	1.05	0.42	1.52	−0.28	0.75
Involvement in family business	0.79*	2.20	0.97*	2.63	0.56	1.74
Personal attributes						
Willingness to take risk	0.82**	2.29	0.43	1.54	1.05**	2.87
Culture						
Cultural affiliation (Canadian/ Israeli)	0.58	1.79	–	–	–	–
Model χ^2	27.59***		18.91**		14.37*	

~ $p < 0.06$; * $p < 0.05$; ** $p < 0.01$; *** $p < 0.001$.

When whole male sample (Canadians and Israelis) is considered, cultural affiliation does not distinguish between the male MBAs who became entrepreneurs and their counterparts who did not. However, for the whole male MBA research sample, the odds of becoming an entrepreneur are higher if they are older, have a mother with higher education, had been encouraged to engage in entrepreneurial activities during their childhood and are willing to take risks.

DISCUSSION AND CONCLUSION

The study addressed the following research questions: Do demographic variables, personality characteristics, and family career patterns distinguish MBA graduates who became entrepreneurs from MBAs who did not become entrepreneurs? Are there differences between Canadian and Israeli MBA graduates regarding their propensity to become entrepreneurs? Furthermore, do these two apparently homogeneous samples share an 'MBA university culture?' And does the entrepreneurial personality profile, which developed in the Western cultural context, apply across diverse cultural boundaries, such as in the cultural contexts of Canada and Israel?

Consistent with the study's expectations, the propensity to pursue an entrepreneurial career is higher for Canadian and Israeli MBA graduates than it is for the general population of their respective countries. This finding clearly suggests that the propensity to become an entrepreneur and the realization of entrepreneurial aspirations are higher among those who chose and graduated from MBA programs. Moreover, the finding may suggest that the proliferation of graduate management programs, including entrepreneurship programs in the two countries, reflects a growth in entrepreneurial aspirations and contributes to their realization.

Contrary to the study's expectations, Canadian MBAs did not have a significantly higher tendency to pursue entrepreneurial careers than did their Israeli counterparts. Thirty-two percent of the Israeli sub-sample and 36.3 percent of the Canadian sub-sample pursued entrepreneurial careers. This cross-cultural similarity is surprising in light of the finding regarding the gap in the exposure to a family business environment among the two samples.

A comparison of the Israeli and Canadian sub-samples shows that more of the Canadian MBAs were raised in entrepreneurial families that encouraged them to participate in entrepreneurial activities during high school. Moreover, the percentage of Canadian MBAs who were involved in family businesses is double that of Israeli MBAs. The findings also show that the Canadian MBA graduates who became entrepreneurs were more likely to have parents and extended family members who had entrepreneurial experience than were those MBAs who did not become entrepreneurs. By contrast, among the Israeli MBAs, no such significant differences were found.

The findings corroborate previous studies that highlight the importance of parents and other family members as entrepreneurial role models (Scherer et al., 1989, 1990; Gartner, 1985; Bird, 1993; Brockhouse and Horwitz, 1986; Hisrich and Brush, 1985). The social learning theory (Bandura, 1977, 1986) explains the advantage of growing up in an entrepreneurial environment for pursuing an entrepreneurial career. It emphasizes the process of socialization, which is started in childhood, through which the individual internalizes motivations and relevant values, and acquires knowledge, skills and capital.

In light of the above findings and social learning theory, one could have expected that the rate of those pursuing entrepreneurial careers among the Canadians MBAs would have been higher than that of their Israeli counterparts. This expectation was refuted. Although Canadians had family environments more conducive to choosing an entrepreneurial career, the percentage of Canadian MBAs who became entrepreneurs was not significantly higher than the percentage of Israelis.

An explanation of this finding may be that a cross-cultural resemblance deriving from the two cultural sets of norms and values overrides the impact of the encouragement of entrepreneurship within the Canadian family context. The economic, social and cultural values embedded in the Israeli environment that contribute to the promotion of entrepreneurship are clearly reflected in the formation in Israel of many technological start-ups that are supported by institutional incubators as well as by private, local and international venture capital. These environmental processes may also explain the attractiveness of choosing an entrepreneurial career path to individuals who are exposed to them, such as MBA graduates.

These findings support the hypothesis that one's cultural milieu influences one's propensity to become an entrepreneur. This finding is especially salient since the educational level of both the Canadian and the Israeli respondents was controlled for. In fact, education is often considered a factor that enables and fosters entrepreneurial initiatives (Bygrave, 1994; Amit and Muller, 1995). These findings suggest that an entrepreneurial propensity is multidimensional.

Having an immigrant origin is another widely explored factor with a potential effect on the choice of an entrepreneurial career. However, the hypothesis regarding the higher rates of immigrants among entrepreneurs versus non-entrepreneurs was rejected in both MBA samples.

There is an ongoing debate about whether entrepreneurs are 'different' from non-entrepreneurs (Gartner, 1985; McGrath et al., 1992a). In a cultural context, the relevant question is whether or not the values of the base culture differentiate entrepreneurs from non-entrepreneurs in the same way across different countries. Multivariate examinations of the effect of career patterns, demographic factors and personality variables on becoming entrepreneurs revealed that several of the variables included within these three clusters distinguish entrepreneurs from non-entrepreneurs for the Canadian and the Israeli MBAs.

The results reveal that for both the Israeli and Canadian sub-samples, the self-reported attribute of 'a willingness to take risks' significantly distinguished entrepreneurs from non-entrepreneurs. This finding corroborates previous research results (McClelland, 1961; McClelland and Winter, 1969; Zimmerer and Scarborough, 1996). Among the Israeli sub-sample, this self-reported attribute was the only personal attribute that distinguished entrepreneurs from non-entrepreneurs in the logistic regression. Moreover, the findings show that after controlling for gender, which appeared as a discriminating variable in both samples, the willingness to take risks remained the only significant discriminating variable for the male Israeli MBAs. Among the Canadian male MBAs, the main discriminating variable was involvement in a family business. These findings support the assertion that entrepreneurs are distinct in certain dimensions from their non-entrepreneurial counterparts, regardless of culture.

Limitations of the Study

While the homogeneity of the research population of the two samples of MBAs enabled the examination of the research questions while controlling for education, this homogeneity also limited the ability to generalize the research findings. One limitation is rooted in the fact that using a sample of MBAs from one Canadian university does not exactly represent all Canadian MBAs, and data from one Israeli university do not represent all Israeli MBAs. Furthermore, the small sample sizes and the fact that both samples consisted mostly of men limit the ability to extrapolate to the general population. Another constraint is rooted in the fact that the study did not include venture-performance data, and it did not reveal whether MBAs who became entrepreneurs are better performers than those without an MBA education.

Future Research

Further research should conduct cross-cultural comparisons among MBA graduates from different countries for a broader understanding of the influence of culture on entrepreneurial career preferences. It might also be useful to explore entrepreneurial career preferences among graduates from other faculties in order to more fully analyze the value of education on entrepreneurship. It is further suggested that the performance of the ventures of MBA graduates who became entrepreneurs be compared with that of the ventures of entrepreneurs without an MBA.

Implications

The present research revealed the contribution of higher management education to the propensity to pursue an entrepreneurial career in two countries, showing that the tendency towards entrepreneurship among both Canadian and Israeli MBAs is higher than that in the general population of their countries. McGrath et al. (1992a) suggested that a comparison of entrepreneurial and managerial values might provide additional insights into the interrelations between social culture, wealth creation and cultural beliefs. The comparative study of entrepreneurs and non-entrepreneurs focusing on two homogeneous samples of MBAs from two cultural backgrounds provides some insight into the interrelations between education, other demographic variables, social culture and entrepreneurial careers.

REFERENCES

Abramson, N.R., Lane, H.W., Nagai, T. and Takagi, H. (1993), 'A comparison of Canadian and Japanese cognitive styles: implications for management interaction', *Journal of International Business Studies*, **24**(3): 575–87.

Acs, Z.J., Arenius, P., Hay, M. and Minniti, M. (2004), *Global Entrepreneurship Monitor – 2004 Executive Report*, Wellesley, MA: Babson College and London Business School.

Adler, N.J., Doctor, R. and Redding, S.G. (1986), 'From the Atlantic to the Pacific century: cross-cultural management reviewed', *Journal of Management*, **12**(2): 295–318.

Alange, S. and Scheinberg, S. (1988), 'Swedish entrepreneurship in a cross-cultural perspectives', paper presented at the Eighth Annual Babson College Entrepreneurship Research Conference, Wellesley, MA, May.

Amit, R. and Muller, E. (1995). '"Push" and "pull" entrepreneurship', *Small Business and Entrepreneurship*, **12**: 124–35.

Amit, R. and Muller, E. (1996), 'A comparison of entrepreneurs and non-entrepreneurs: attributes and attitudes', *Executive* (January): 18–23, 37–42. (In Hebrew.)

Bandura, A. (1977), *Social Learning Theory*, Englewood Cliffs, NJ: Prentice-Hall.

Bandura, A. (1986), *Social Foundations of Thoughts and Action: A Social Cognitive Theory*, Englewood Cliffs, NJ: Prentice-Hall.

Begley, T.M. and Boyd, D.P. (1986), 'Psychological characteristics associated with entrepreneurial performance', in R. Ronstadt et al. (eds), *Frontiers of Entrepreneurship Research*, Wellesley, MA: Babson College, pp. 146–65.

Bellu, R.R. (1988), 'Entrepreneurs and managers: are they different?', in B.A. Kirchhoff et al. (eds), *Frontiers of Entrepreneurship Research*, Wellesley, MA: Babson College, pp. 16–30.

Birch, J.G. (1987), 'Profiling the entrepreneur', *Business Horizons*, **29**(5): 13–16.

Bird, B.J. (1993), 'Demographic approaches to entrepreneurship: the role of experience and background', in J.A. Katz and R.H. Brockhaus (eds), *Advances in Entrepreneurship, Firm Emergence and Growth*, London: JAI Press, pp. 11–48.

Bird, B.J. (1989), *Entrepreneurial Behavior*, Glenview, IL: Scott Foresman.

Birley, S. (1987), 'New ventures and employment growth', *Journal of Business Venturing*, **1**(1): 107–17.

Brandt, E. (1991), 'Incubators: a safe haven for new businesses', *Journal of Property Management*, **56**(1): 52–9.

Brockhaus, R.H. and Horowitz, P. (1986), 'The psychology of the entrepreneur', in C. Kent, D.L. Sexton and R.W. Smilor (eds), *The Art and Science of Entrepreneurship*, New York: Ballinger.

Busenitz, L.W. and Lau, C.M. (1997), 'A cross-cultural cognitive model of new venture creation', *Entrepreneurship Theory and Practice*, **20**(4): 25–39.

Bygrave, W.D. (1994), *The Portable MBA in Entrepreneurship*, New York: Wiley.

Canada Year Book (1997), 'Labor force by class of worker, 1996 Census'.

Carsrud, A.L., Galio, C.M. and Kernochan, R. (1993), 'Demographics in entrepreneurship research', in J.A. Katz and R.H. Brockhaus (eds), *Advances in Entrepreneurship, Firm Emergence and Growth*, Vol. 1, London: JAI Press, pp. 49–81.

Dubini, P. and MacMillan, I.C. (1988), 'Entrepreneurial prerequisite in venture capital backed projects', in B.A. Kirchhoff et al. (eds), *Frontiers of Entrepreneurship Research*, Wellesley, MA: Babson College, pp. 46–58.

Erez, M. and Edelding, R. (1991), *The Profile of the Israeli Entrepreneur: Biographical Attributes, Motives and Cognitive Causes*, Tel-Aviv: Golda Meir Institute of Social and Labor Research, Tel-Aviv University (in Hebrew).

Etzioni, A. (1987), 'Entrepreneurship, adaptation and legitimization: a macro-behavioral perspective', *Journal of Economic Behavior and Organization*, **8**: 175–89.

Gartner, W.B. (1985), 'A conceptual framework for describing the phenomenon of new venture creating', *Academy of Management Review*, **10**(4): 696–706.

Hisrich, R.D. and Brush, C.G. (1985), 'Women and minority entrepreneurs: a comparative analysis', in E.B. Hornaday et al. (eds), *Frontiers of Entrepreneurship Research*, Wellesley, MA: Babson College, pp. 566–86.

Hofstede, G. (1980), *Culture's Consequences: International Differences in Work Related Values*, Beverly Hills, CA: Sage.

Hofstede, G. (1983), 'The cultural relativity of organizational practices and theories', *Journal of International Business Studies*, **14**: 75–89.

Hofstede, G. (1984), 'The cultural relativity of the quality of life concept', *Academy of Management Review*, **9**: 389–98.

Hofstede, G. (1991), *Cultures and Organizations: Software and Mind*, London: McGraw-Hill.

Israel Year Book (1998), Vol. 49, Jerusalem: The Israeli Statistical Bureau.

Katz, J.A. and Brockhaus, R.H. (1993), *Advances in Entrepreneurship, Firm Emergence and Growth*, Vol. 1, London: JAI Press.

MacMillan, I.C., Siegel, R. and Subba Narshima, P.N. (1985), 'Criteria used by venture capitalists to evaluate new venture proposals', *Journal of Business Venturing*, **1**: 119–28.

Malecki, E.J. (1997), 'Entrepreneurs, networks, and economic development', in J.A. Katz and R.H. Brockhaus (eds), *Advances in Entrepreneurship, Firm Emergence and Growth*, London: JAI Press, pp. 57–118.

McClelland, D.C. (1961), *The Achieving Society*, New York: Van Nostrand Reinhold.

McClelland, D.C. and Winter, D.G. (1969), *Motivating Economic Achievement*, New York: Free Press.

McGrath, R.G. and MacMillan, I.C. (1992), 'More like each other than anyone else? a cross-cultural study of entrepreneurial perceptions', *Journal of Business Venturing*, 7(5): 419–29.

McGrath, R.G., MacMillan, I.C. and Scheinberg, S. (1992a), 'Elitists, risk-takers and rugged individualists? An exploratory analysis of cultural differences between entrepreneurs and non-entrepreneurs', *Journal of Business Venturing*, 7: 115–35.

McGrath, R.G., MacMillan, I.C., Yang, E.A.-Y. and Tsai, W. (1992b), 'Does culture endure or is it malleable? Issues for entrepreneurial economic development', *Journal of Business Venturing*, 7: 441–58.

McMullan, E., Long, W. and Wilson, A. (1985), 'MBA concentration on entrepreneurship', *Journal of Small Business and Entrepreneurship*: 18–22.

Mincer, J. (1974), *Schooling, Experience and Earnings*, New York: Columbia University Press.

Mitchell, L.K. and Krumboltz, J.D. (1984), 'Social learning approach to career decision making: Krumboltz's theory', in D. Brown and L. Brooks (eds), *Career Choice and Development*, San Francisco, CA: Jossey-Bass.

Peterson, R.A. (1988), 'Understanding and encouraging entrepreneurship internationally', *Journal of Small Business Management*, 26(2): 1–7.

Reynolds, P.D., Camp, S.M., Bygrave, W.D., Autio, E. and Hay, M. (2001), *Global Entrepreneurship Monitor: 2001 Executive Report*, Kauffman Center for Entrepreneurial Leadership at the Ewing Marion Kauffman Foundation.

Roberts, E.B. (1991), *Entrepreneurs in High Technology*, New York: Oxford University Press.

Robinnet, S. (1985), 'What school can teach entrepreneurs', *Inc.*, 50–58.

Robinson, P.B. and Sexton, E.A. (1994), 'The effect of education and experience on self-employment success', *Journal of Business Venturing*, 9(2): 141–56.

Ronstadt, R. (1985), 'The educated entrepreneurs: a new era of entrepreneurial education is beginning', *American Journal of Small Business*, 9: 7–23.

Scherer, R.F., Adams, J.S. and Wiebe, F.A. (1989), 'Role model performance effects on development of entrepreneurial career preference', *Entrepreneurship Theory and Practice*, 14(3): 53–71.

Scherer, R.F., Adams, J.S. and Wiebe, F.A. (1990), 'Developing entrepreneurial behaviors: a social learning theory perspective', *Journal of Organizational Change Management*, 2: 16–27.

Sexton, D.L. and Bowman, N. (1985), 'The entrepreneur: a capable executive and more', *Journal of Business Venturing*, 1(1): 129–40.

Sexton, D.L. and Bowman, N. (1986), 'Validation of personality index: comparative psychological characteristics analysis of female entrepreneurship, managers: Entrepreneurship students and business students', in R. Ronstadt et al. (eds), *Frontiers of Entrepreneurship Research*, Wellesley, MA: Babson College, pp. 40–57.

Shapero, A. (1985), 'Why entrepreneurship? A worldwide perspective', *Journal of Small Business Management*, 23(4): 105.

Shapero, A. and Sokol, L. (1982), 'The social dimensions of entrepreneurship', in C.A. Kent, D.L. Sexton and K.H. Vesper (eds), *Encyclopedia of Entrepreneurship*, Englewood Cliffs, NJ: Prentice-Hall, pp. 72–88.

Shaver, K.G. and Scott, L.R. (1991), 'Person, process, choice: the psychology of new venture creation', *Entrepreneurhip Theory and Practice*, **16**(Winter): 23–45.

Shaver, K.G., Gartner, W.B., Gatewood, E.J. and Vos, L.H. (1996), 'Psychological factors in success at getting into business', *Frontiers of Entrepreneurship Research*, Wellesley, MA: Babson College, pp. 77–90.

Smeltz, W.J. (1990), 'Empirical comparison of personality attributes between traditionally motivated entrepreneurs and ethically motivated entrepreneurs', in N.C. Churchill et al. (eds), *Frontiers of Entrepreneurship Research*, Wellesley, MA: Babson College, pp. 1–16.

Sundbo, J. (1991), 'Strategic paradigms as a frame of explanation of innovations: a theoretical synthesis', *Entrepreneurship and Regional Development*, **3**: 159–73.

Triandis, H.C. (1980), *Values, Attitudes and Interpersonal Behavior*, Lincoln, NE: University of Nebraska Press.

Triandis, H.C. (1990), *Individualism and Collectivism*, Boulder, CO: Westview Press.

Upton, N.B. and Heck, R.K.Z. (1997), 'The family business: dimension of entrepreneurship', in D.L. Sexton and R.W. Smilor (eds), *Entrepreneurship 2000*, Chicago, IL: Upstart, pp. 243–66.

Wortman, M.S. Jr (1994), 'Theoretical foundations for family-owned business: a conceptual and research-based paradigm', *Family Business Review*, **7**(1): 3–27.

Zimmerer, T.W. and Scarborough, N.M. (1996), *Entrepreneurship and New Venture Formation*, Englewood Chiffs, NJ: Prentice-Hall.

9. What motivates people from business-related careers to change to teaching?

Paul W. Richardson, Helen M.G. Watt and Nicole M. Tysvaer

INTRODUCTION

It is commonplace to observe that people who switch from one career to another do so for a variety of reasons. These may relate to remuneration, job security, the need to develop and challenge oneself, a desire to develop new skills and abilities, a quest for new experiences, to address a set of personal goals, or various combinations of these and other less well-articulated reasons. At its base, in any career change is some level of recognition that the current occupation is not a good fit for the individual. The process may involve a 'push' out of the present career, necessitating the search for new options. It may alternatively entail a 'pull' into another career and consequently away from the career currently being pursued. When a change to teaching requires further education, loss of income for at least a year, and is accompanied by a decline in occupational prestige, which is often the case when people leave business-related careers, then we might ask why people would choose such a course of action.

The motivations, aspirations and profiles of career switchers to teaching have been the subject of sporadic research interest across different countries over the last two decades (Serow and Forrest, 1994; Mayotte, 2003; Priyadharshini and Robinson-Pant, 2003; Richardson and Watt, 2005). These researchers have all suggested that for people who choose to move to teaching, the rewards of salary and career prestige are not a high priority. Their decision to seek a career change is based more on a desire to fulfil other goals and motivations, although researchers have not always sought to relate these to robust theoretical models concerning goals or motivation. Our 'FIT-Choice' (Factors Influencing Teaching Choice) programme of research is an exception in that it is founded on the comprehensive 'expectancy-value' motivational framework of Eccles and her colleagues

(Eccles (Parsons) et al., 1983; Wigfield and Eccles, 2000). Although the Eccles et al. 'expectancy-value' model was initially designed to explain adolescents' – especially girls' – participation in mathematics-related activities, it has since been applied to participation in mathematics-related and other types of careers (e.g. Watt, 2006; Watt, in press), and we have developed this framework within the specific context of teaching as a career choice (see Richardson and Watt, 2006; Watt and Richardson, 2007).

For a society that explicitly evaluates career success on measures of salary and the corollary of career prestige, a considered decision to forego both in favour of, for instance, personal satisfaction, the rewards from making a social contribution, and a desire to keep learning, is often evaluated harshly by previous work colleagues and society at large. Over the last three decades there have been many changes in the nature of careers and career structures, but even one and a half decades ago in the context of the US, it could be observed that 'leaving the business world for teaching' was in the minds of many an 'implausible choice' (Crow et al., 1990, p. 197). Since that time little has changed in terms of social attitudes and values, reward structures and occupational prestige. Even though in surveys across different countries, the work and contributions of teachers are valued by parents and the community more generally (OECD, 2005), their rewards in terms of both salary and perceived occupational prestige are modest when compared with business-related careers, making teaching an intriguing career change for people from those professions.

The Present Study

Our study focuses on 90 individuals who previously pursued business-related careers, and who are now changing careers into primary and secondary school teaching. These people have prior qualifications ranging from undergraduate degrees through to Master's in Business Administration (MBA); as well as career experience in fields that include banking, human resources and marketing. They form a subset of our larger sample of commencing pre-service teacher education candidates across three Australian (N = 758) and two US universities (N = 121), studying in the 'graduate entry' mode. This mode provides an accelerated preparation programme typically entailing one to two years of teacher education that is available in a number of countries including Australia and the US. It is not uncommon for people in these programmes, which are open to candidates with relevant prior university qualifications, also to have experience in previous careers.

Table 9.1   Participants who pursued careers prior to teaching within and across cohorts

		Full sample N	Students with prior careers		Prior business professionals		
			n	% of full cohort	n	% of prior careers	% of full cohort
University	USyd	190	65	34.2	19	29.2	10.0
	Monash	280	121	43.2	32	26.4	11.4
	UWS	288	102	35.4	26	25.5	9.0
	UM	86	40	46.5	8	20.0	9.3
	EMU	35	15	42.9	5	33.3	14.3
Country subtotals	Australia	758	288	38.0	77	26.7	10.2
	USA	121	55	45.5	13	23.6	10.7
Grand totals	Total	879	343	39.0	90	26.2	10.2

Notes: USyd = University of Sydney; UWS = University of Western Sydney; UM = University of Michigan; EMU = Eastern Michigan University.

Of our entire sample of commencing Australian and US graduate-entry pre-service teacher education candidates (N = 879), 342 (38.9 per cent) had previously pursued another career, and 258 (29.4 per cent) had seriously considered an alternative career to teaching. Of those who had pursued previous careers, 90 (26.3 per cent) had been engaged in business-related careers (10.2 per cent of the full sample); and of those who had seriously considered a different career, 42 (16.3 per cent) had been business-related (4.8 per cent of the full sample; see Table 9.1).

In this chapter, we first examine the characteristics of people who switched to teaching from business-related careers, and then examine their reasons for having chosen teaching as a career. All information was collected via self-report surveys administered to participants during their first semester of teacher education, through 2002 and 2003 across five universities in Australia and the US. We explore participants' demographic background characteristics, enrolment details, professional histories, degree qualifications, motivations for choosing a career in teaching, perceptions about the profession, satisfaction with their choice of teaching as a career, and comparative satisfaction with their prior business-related careers.

WHO CHOOSES TO SWITCH FROM BUSINESS-RELATED CAREERS TO TEACHING?

Demographic Background Characteristics

Two-thirds of the graduate teacher education students with prior business credentials were female – a proportion reflective of the pre-service teacher education population in general, in which candidates are predominantly women. More individuals from business-related career backgrounds undertook secondary pre-service teacher education (62.5 per cent) than primary/elementary; and the men were more likely than the women to choose secondary teacher education ($\chi^2(1) = 3.90$, p = 0.048). More than three-quarters of the men (76.7 per cent) chose secondary teaching, while similar proportions of women chose each of secondary (55.2 per cent) and primary teaching.

The youngest business career switcher was 22 years old on commencing teacher education and the eldest 55, with the average age being 32 years. On average, females tended to be slightly younger (M = 30.76 years, SD = 7.91) than males (M = 33.97 years, SD = 8.78, F(1,86) = 3.020, p < 0.10). The boxplots in Figure 9.1 show the distributions of ages for males and females in the sample. Although the age range was greater for women than for men, several of the older females were outliers, denoted by circles in the female boxplot. If we consider only the interquartile ranges represented by the solid rectangles in Figure 9.1, which discount the highest and lowest 25 per cent in each group, the age ranges for the middle 50 per cent of men were more dispersed than those for women.

As an indication of family economic background, participants nominated their parents' combined income from the period during which participants had attended high school. The average parent annual income was in the $60 001–$90 000 range, and the mode was $30 001–$60 000. A small percentage (12.2 per cent) identified low parental incomes of less than $30 000 per year, and a near equal percentage (13.2 per cent) identified high parental incomes of more than $120 000 annually. Figure 9.2 displays the percentage of students in each parental income category, which did not differ across gender groups.

The vast majority of participants spoke English as their primary language at home (87.8 per cent). The second most common home language was Chinese (5.6 per cent). These proportions reflect those for the 'FIT-Choice' full Australian sample (see Richardson and Watt, 2006). Most US students had parents born in the US (88.5 per cent of those 13 individuals), compared with 46.2 per cent of Australian parents born domestically. Small numbers in the US sample imply that we should not over-interpret

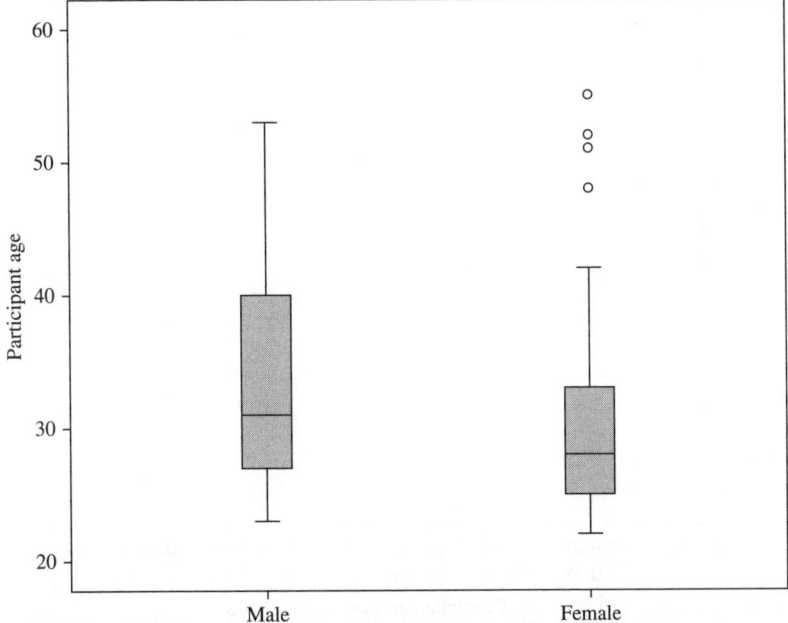

Note: The box length is the interquartile range and the solid bar represents the median value. 'o' denotes outliers with values between 1.5 and 3 box lengths from the upper or lower edge of the box.

Figure 9.1   Age profiles for men and women entering teaching from business-related careers

these differences in proportions. For the Australian cohort, parents' birth places included several countries in Europe, as well as Asia and the Middle East.

Professional Histories

Participants switching out of business-related careers into teaching came from 25 different career backgrounds. The most frequent were marketing, accounting, business management, finance, human resources and retail sales. We grouped prior careers according to their status relative to teaching, as identified by the US Department of Labor *O*NET* employment classification system (US Department of Labor Employment and Training Administration, 1998). *O*NET* classifications rank careers on a scale ranging from 1 to 5, based on required educational preparation and average salaries (see Richardson and Watt, 2006). Teaching is classified as a '4' on

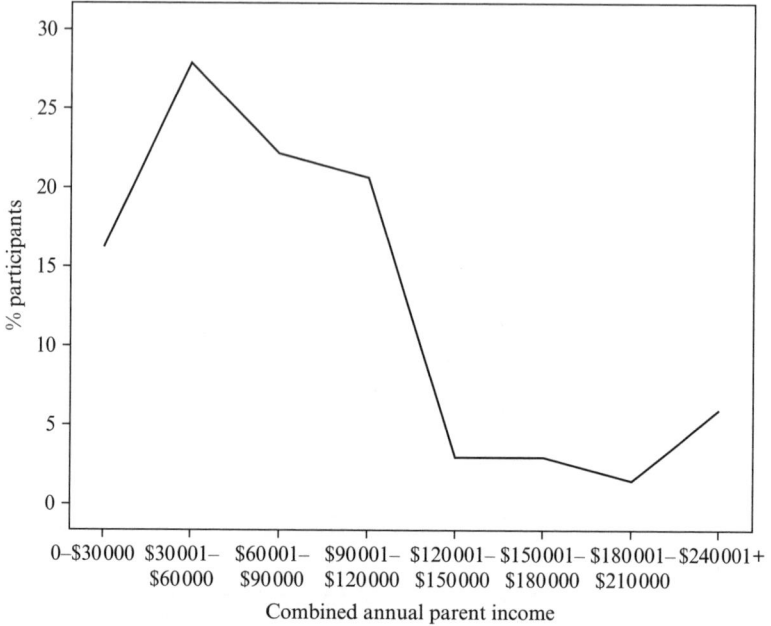

Figure 9.2   Parental income backgrounds for career switchers from business-related careers

the 5-point scale. The vast majority of prior business-related positions (68.9 per cent) also ranked a '4' on the *O*NET* classification, suggesting lateral career moves for those switching into teaching with respect to career status. Approximately 19 per cent of the survey participants came from prior business careers that ranked higher than teaching (e.g. business management, business consulting and information technology consulting), and 12 per cent from careers that ranked lower (e.g. retail sales, bookkeeping and hospitality management). Figure 9.3 illustrates the types of business positions held by the incoming graduate students, indicating which were higher, similar and lower occupational statuses relative to teaching.

Degree Qualification Backgrounds

Former business professionals typically entered pre-service graduate teacher education with an undergraduate degree (68.5 per cent), followed by 12.4 per cent with undergraduate Honours degrees, and 19.1 per cent a postgraduate degree. Women and men had similar prior levels of qualification $(\chi^2(2) = 2.72, p = 0.26)$. Undergraduate degree credentials

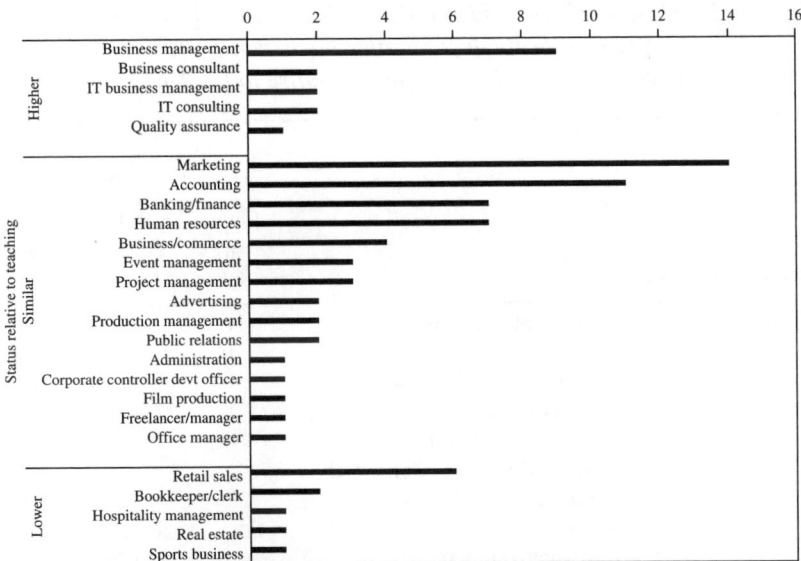

Figure 9.3   Numbers of people switching from business-related careers of higher, similar and lower status than teaching

covered a wide range of disciplines, including fine arts, music, psychology, computer science and sociology. Twenty-six of the respondents who had undergraduate degrees (42.6 per cent) held their qualifications in business-related fields such as economics, public relations, marketing and business management. Of those who held an undergraduate Honours degree, four (36 per cent) were in business-related fields; while eight (47.1 per cent) of the participants with postgraduate qualifications held business-related degrees including MBA, Law, and Master of Science in Accounting. Table 9.2 shows the numbers of people holding undergraduate, undergraduate Honours and postgraduate degree qualifications that were business-related or not, broken down by their prior career status relative to teaching.

The timing of when business career switchers had obtained their earlier degree qualifications varied substantially, from 1972 through 2004. Although the range was greater for women (1972–2002) than for men (1983–2004), the mean difference was not statistically significant ($F(1,84) = 1.18$, $p = 0.28$). There was a strong correlation between age and prior qualification year for women ($r = -0.80$, $p < 0.001$), meaning that the older the woman, the earlier her qualification year. In contrast, there was a far weaker relationship for men ($r = -0.32$, $p < 0.10$; see Figure 9.4), meaning that timing of prior qualification was not strongly related to men's ages.

Table 9.2 *Undergraduate, undergraduate Honours, and postgraduate degree qualifications for business switchers from careers of lower, similar and higher status relative to teaching*

		Career status relative to teaching		
		Lower n	Similar n	Higher n
Undergraduate degrees				
Business-related	BA Communications	1	2	–
	B Commerce	1	5	1
	B Commerce (Marketing)	1	–	1
	BA (Economics)	1	–	–
	BA (Public Relations)	–	1	–
	B Applied Science (Consumer Science)	–	1	–
	B Economics	–	1	–
	B Music/Commerce	–	1	–
	B Arts/B Business Management	–	2	–
	B Business	–	4	–
	B Business Admin.	–	–	1
	B Economics	–	–	1
	B Technology Management (Manuf.)	–	–	1
Other	B Science	1	2	–
	B Arts	1	9	2
	B Arts (Fine Arts)	1	–	1
	B Theology	1	–	–
	Visual Art	1	–	–
	BA (Psychology and Sociology)	–	1	–
	B Agricultural Science	–	1	–
	B Applied Science (Human Movement)	–	1	–
	B Applied Science (Statistics)	–	1	–
	B Mathematics	–	1	–
	B Mechanical Engineering	–	1	–
	B Social Science	–	1	–
	BA (Psychology)	–	2	–
	B Applied Science	–	2	–
	BA (Art theory)	–	–	1
	Sociology	–	–	1
Undergraduate Honours degrees				
Business-related	B Marketing	–	1	–
	Economics & Communications	–	1	–

Table 9.2   (continued)

		Career status relative to teaching		
		Lower n	Similar n	Higher n
	Aviation Management	–	–	1
	B Business Admin. Summa Cum Laude	–	–	1
Other	Music	1	–	–
	BA (Sociology)	–	1	–
	B Arts	–	1	–
	B Computer Science	–	1	–
	B Science	–	1	–
	Psychology	–	1	–
	Law	–	–	1
Postgraduate degrees				
Business-related	MBA	–	1	1
	Grad. Certificate of Business	–	1	–
	Grad. Dip. Accounting	–	1	–
	M Commerce	–	1	–
	M Science (Accounting)	–	1	–
	Public Relations	–	1	–
	Business	–	–	1
	Grad. Certificate in IT Management	–	–	1
Other	B Arts (Honours)	1	–	–
	B Applied Science	–	1	–
	Grad. Dip. Librarianship	–	1	–
	Grad. Certificate	–	1	–
	M Arts	–	1	–
	M Science (Computer & Info. Sci.)	–	1	–

It may be that these women were more likely to complete their university qualifications closer to high school completion than men if they entered university sooner or directly following high school completion. Alternatively, perhaps women tend to stay in business-related fields for longer than men before switching out – because we did not ask the number of years that participants had worked in their prior career, we are unable to evaluate this speculation. It could also be that women are more likely to drop out from and later retrain and re-enter the workforce, due to factors such as child-rearing and family commitments.

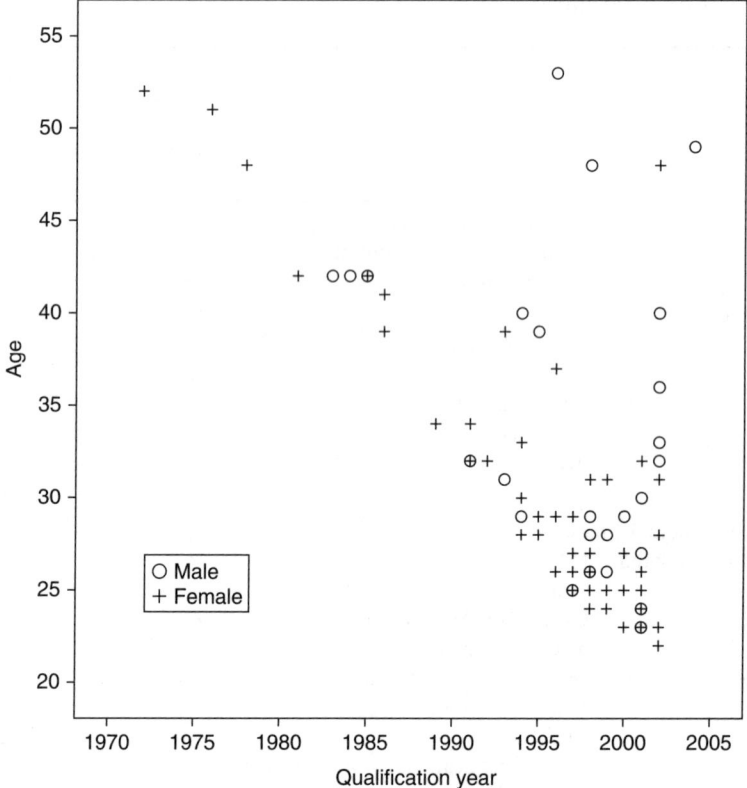

Figure 9.4   *Scatterplot of men's and women's ages on entering*
teacher education against year of prior qualification
(r = −0.32 p < 0.10 for men; r = −0.80 p<0.001
for women)

There was no statistically significant difference between the proportions of men and women who had children (13 (43 per cent) of men, 22 (37 per cent) of women, $\chi^2(1) = 0.37$, p = 0.54), although this does not necessarily imply that these men and women would have had similar family responsibilities, since mothers traditionally still carry a greater involvement in child rearing, and as a consequence are subject to more disrupted career paths than men. Not surprisingly, people who had children were older than those who did not (F(1,84) = 49.24, p<0.001, M = 38.26, SD = 8.46 for those having children, M = 27.81, SD = 5.06 for those without). This was similarly the case for both men and women, with no statistically significant interaction effect of gender and having children on age.

WHAT MOTIVATES PEOPLE TO SWITCH FROM BUSINESS-RELATED CAREERS INTO TEACHING?

Why Make a Career Change?

To begin, we explored through participants' open-ended responses the reasons this group of career switchers gave for wanting a teaching career. As we might expect, embedded within participants' responses were also their most salient reasons why they had left their previous careers in a business-related field. For some, the need for change rested on dissatisfaction with various aspects of the working life they had experienced in the 'corporate world'. This was often driven by the need to achieve a better balance between work and other aspects of life, and, importantly, to be engaged in a career they perceived as meaningful, fulfilling, satisfying, challenging and rewarding. These perceptions often figured in the reasons why individuals had rejected their careers in business; and conversely what they perceived a career in teaching would provide. The desire to work in a people-friendly environment, and to feel that the work one was engaged in was making a difference by contributing to the community, also lay at the base of the reasons why people had given up a business-related career.

Some of these individuals were in their mid-twenties and could only have spent a few short years in the corporate environment following their graduation from university, while others who were in their forties and older had invested much more time. Intriguingly, their reasons for seeking a career switch into teaching were often very similar. For instance, a 42-year-old male said that 'after 16 years in the corporate sector I felt that I wasn't making a difference', while a 26-year-old male insisted that he wanted 'to do something meaningful/rewarding in my life'. Despite differences in the number of years invested in the corporate world, the reasons for choosing teaching and for leaving corporate life behind could be very similar. This was also true of the female participants. One 24-year-old woman observed: 'I have worked in the corporate world and while there were financial rewards it was ultimately unsatisfying. I am hoping teaching will be a much more (emotionally) rewarding profession and I love kids!!' Another 31-year-old woman stated that she 'worked a corporate job for eight years. Want a people friendly job more suited for a family (kids).'

The lack of career satisfaction that accrued from a career in the corporate sector was explicitly nominated by males and females alike who were switching to teaching – a 27-year-old male said he was 'unsatisfied with job as a marketing analyst' and complained that the 'hours were too long with lots of work going unnoticed', and a woman of 37 wanted to use her 'professional knowledge in a meaningful way in a career that provides flexibility of conditions'. The desire for a more meaningful and satisfying career was mentioned in various guises, with participants using words such as 'reward-ing', 'satisfying', 'challenging', 'diverse' and 'interesting' to describe their perceptions of a career in teaching. These switchers into teaching wanted to know they were contributing something positive to society, which their previous experiences in business-related careers hadn't provided, and that their labour would make a difference by influencing the lives of children and young people. Such sentiments were to be found in comments includ-ing: 'I believe teaching is an under-valued career essential to the direction of society and pushes me to continue learning as well' (29-year-old male), and 'I want a career which contributes to a just society and has satisfaction regardless of remuneration' (25-year-old female).

Not surprisingly, the refrain of liking and wanting to work with children and adolescents to help them understand themselves and their place in the world was an important reason for seeking a change to teaching. For people who will teach in primary and secondary school contexts, the desire to have a career that allows them to make a difference by helping shape the future for young people is perhaps a fundamental requirement. Those who do not like or even dislike children would be ill advised to take on teaching, even in the short term. Table 9.3 brings together some of the voices of male

Table 9.3   Sample reasons for switching to teaching

Primary	Secondary
Second career. To help children and be part of the solution to education challenges. (Male, 49)	I am very interested in this career because I love to assist kids. (Male, 53)
I have worked with kids for the past 8 years. I find it very rewarding and hopeful to the future. (Female, 48)	I enjoy spending time with teenagers. I feel that I can provide positive support and encouragement in their learning endeavours. (Female, 51)
I love children and interested [*sic.*] in child development/education. Also I want skills to teach my own children because I don't trust the system alone. (Female, 31)	Enjoy working with teenagers. Always had an interest in teaching. (Female, 33)
Brought up in educational family always involved with organizing school age children on programs and always loved being with children – feel like it's been a 'calling'. (Female, 28)	I wanted to help kids learn skills and knowledge for later life because this is hard to do when everything else that is important to them in life is going on. (Female, 26)

and female prospective primary and secondary teachers of varying ages for whom the desire to work with children and adolescents was strongly registered.

The comments made by these prospective teachers indicated their perception of the intrinsic value of teaching together with a belief in their inherent ability to make a difference in the lives of young people by working with them in shaping their futures. For people who have experienced careers in business-related fields it is intriguing that they had such strongly held beliefs in relation to working with children and adolescents. In seeking a career change into teaching, they may be fulfilling a need that has remained somewhat dormant while they pursued other career options. For these people, teaching represents the realization of an 'ideal' career fit that provides for meaningful and socially valuable work, and affords the individual opportunities for further learning and professional development.

Quantitative Comparisons of Motivations and Perceptions Related to Teaching

Motivations for choosing teaching as a career were measured using our 'FIT-Choice' scale (see Richardson and Watt, 2006; Watt and Richardson, 2007). The motivations assessed by this measure include intrinsic values, personal utility values (job security, time for family, job transferability), social utility values (the desire to shape the future of children/adolescents, enhance social equity, make a social contribution, work with children/ adolescents), self-perceptions of individuals' own teaching abilities, the extent to which teaching had been a 'fallback' career choice, social influences, and prior positive teaching and learning experiences. Each factor was measured by multiple items with response options ranging from 1 (not at all important) through 7 (extremely important). The 'FIT-Choice' scale has been validated in Australian (Watt and Richardson, 2007) and international settings (see Watt et al., in preparation), and provides a sound framework with which to investigate teaching motivations and perceptions. Measuring the extent to which each of multiple possible motivations led individuals to choose a teaching career allows us to interpret which motivations were the strongest for business career switchers. Participants also rated the extent of their agreement with a number of propositions about the teaching profession, relating to the extent to which they perceived teaching as high in task demand (expert career, high demand) and task return (social status, salary). They rated the amount of social dissuasion they had experienced from teaching as a career choice, their career choice satisfaction for each of their previous business-related careers, and their current choice of teaching as a career.

Why choose teaching?

The highest-rated motivations for choosing teaching included perceived teaching abilities, the intrinsic value of teaching, the desire to make a social contribution, shape the future, and to work with children/adolescents (see Figure 9.5). The lowest-rated motivation was choosing teaching as a 'fallback' career, followed by social influences of others' encouragement. Motivations that were rated in between included the desire to enhance social equity, having had positive prior teaching and learning experiences, job security, job transferability, and time for family. Figure 9.5 presents mean ratings for each motivation, separately for males and females.

Few systematic differences were evident between the teaching motivations for men and women changing out of business-related careers. The only statistically significant difference occurred for intrinsic value ($F(1,80) = 7.089$, $p = 0.009$), where women rated their liking and interest for teaching as having been more influential in their career decision. There was a trend for women's perceptions of their perceived teaching abilities to have influenced their choice of teaching more than men ($F(1,80) = 2.999$, $p = 0.087$), as well as their desire to work with children/adolescents ($F(1,80) = 3.131$, $p = 0.081$).

These gender differences in motivations for having chosen teaching as a career held true regardless of whether participants were undertaking

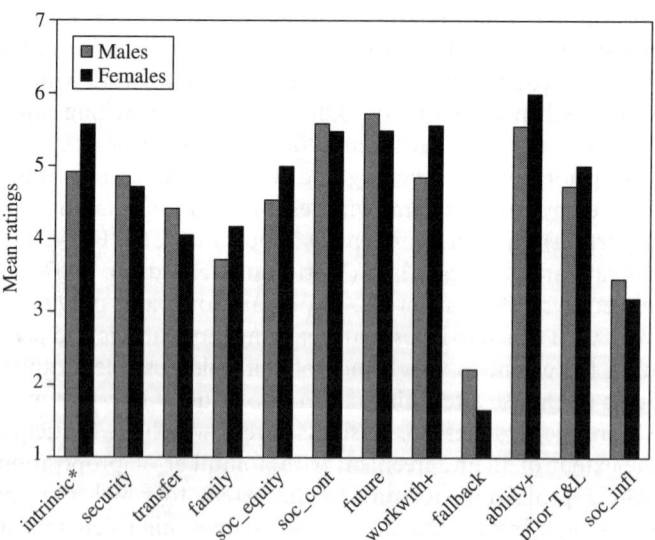

* $p < 0.05$, + $p < 0.10$.

Figure 9.5   Gendered motivations for choosing teaching as a career

primary or secondary teacher education. The one exception was for the desire to enhance social equity, where gender differences were in opposite directions among secondary versus primary pre-service teachers $(F(1,80) = 4.847, p = 0.031)$. This interaction effect was due to a trend for females undertaking secondary teacher education to rate it lower than males $(F(1,53) = 2.893, p < 0.10)$, while there was no statistically significant gender difference among men and women in primary education (see Figure 9.6). There was one main effect of primary versus secondary pre-service teacher education for job transferability $(F(1,80) = 4.112, p = 0.046;$ primary $M = 3.76, SD = 1.67;$ secondary $M = 4.43, SD = 1.51)$, where secondary pre-service teachers regardless of their gender were more likely to have been influenced by the character of teaching as a 'transferable' job – allowing them to travel or choose where they wished to live. In the Australian context it is possible to transfer between the various states of the country without having to take further examinations, although the various states and territories are now requiring professional registration before employment as a teacher is possible. Australian graduates continue to be highly sought after to fill positions overseas, perhaps fuelling the perception of teaching as a 'transferable' career. This situation is not the case in the US or in many European countries (OECD, 2005).

Perceptions about the profession
Participants generally perceived teaching as a career that is high in demand – and low in return. They rated teaching as a highly demanding career, bringing with it a heavy workload, high emotional demand, and

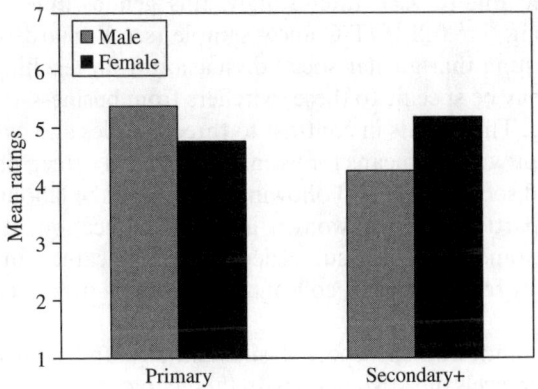

+ $p < 0.10.$

Figure 9.6   Gender by level interaction on the desire to enhance social equity

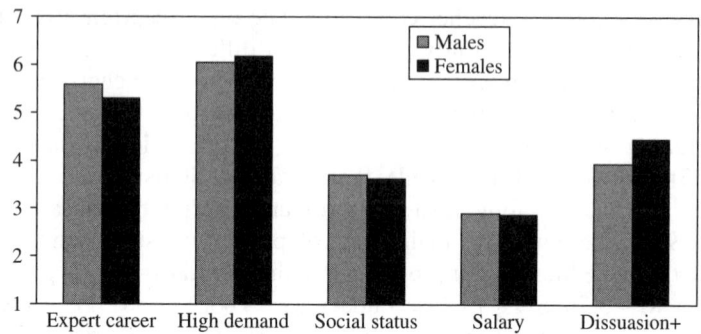

+ p<0.10.

Figure 9.7   Gendered perceptions about teaching as a career

generally requiring hard work. They also rated teaching as a highly expert career, in terms of requiring high levels of specialized and technical knowledge, while at the same time they perceived it – even on entry to teacher education – as relatively low in social status, and paying a low salary.

Few systematic differences were evident between males and females in their perceptions about teaching, and no differences occurred between primary and secondary pre-service teachers. The one gender difference held true irrespective of whether individuals were in primary or secondary teacher education, where women tended to have had more experiences of people trying to dissuade them from a teaching career ($F(1,84) = 3.379$, $p = 0.070$; see Figure 9.7). Interestingly, this gender difference was not evident among our full 'FIT-Choice' sample (see Richardson and Watt, 2006), suggesting that greater social dissuasion from teaching as a career for women may be specific to these switchers from business-related careers into teaching. This stands in contrast to three decades ago, when teaching and nursing provided a means for women to secure a career, financial independence and social mobility. Following changes in the labour market and the greater participation of women in higher education, it would now appear that women who have succeeded in entering careers in business are discouraged by friends, family, colleagues and others from seeking a career in teaching.

Both men and women reported substantially and statistically significantly higher levels of satisfaction with their choice of teaching as a career than with their previous business-related career ($F(1,83) = 43.676$, $p < 0.001$; see Figure 9.8). There was also a significant interaction effect of gender and career ($F(1,83) = 5.371$, $p = 0.023$), where females reported

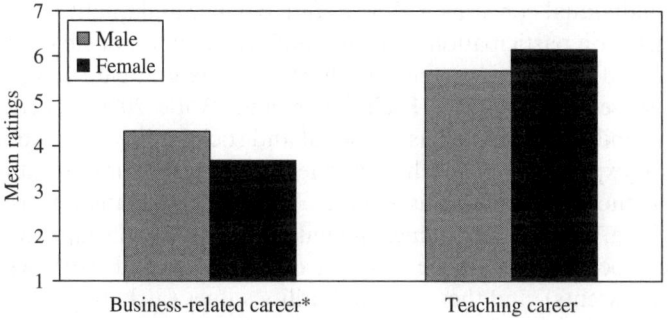

* p<0.05.

Figure 9.8   *Males' and females' satisfaction with previous business-related careers and satisfaction with the choice of teaching as a career*

lower satisfaction with their prior business-related careers than men $(F(1,83) = 4.118, p = 0.046)$. However, both men and women were equally highly satisfied with their current choice of a teaching career.

DISCUSSION

A substantial proportion of people switching their careers into teaching came from business-related fields and held business-related degree credentials. Career switchers into teaching from these career backgrounds have attracted increasing research interest, with the common intuition that these individuals would be unlikely to be attracted to a career in teaching, which seems an 'implausible choice' (Crow et al., 1990). Although business career switchers were young on average, there was a large age range, implying that business professionals made the switch out of those careers and into teaching at different points in time and after having spent differing amounts of time in their prior business careers. Notably, most business switchers were making lateral career moves into teaching in terms of their career status. Fewer came from previous business-related occupations which were of higher or lower career status. Lateral career moves would suggest that the perception of teaching as lower in occupational prestige needs to be tempered. It also provokes the question of whether those who switch out of business careers into teaching are those who failed to succeed in their previous career – either in objective terms (e.g. status or salary), or in terms of their own personal needs and ambitions (see Pines, 2002). Failure to succeed might also be interpreted as careers in business failing to meet deeper individual concerns with work/life balance and quality of working life focused on participation in meaningful, socially responsible work.

Similar to findings across entire cohorts of undergraduate and graduate-entry pre-service teachers (Richardson and Watt, 2006), participants' teaching ability-related beliefs, personal and social utility values and positive prior experiences of teaching and learning were all important motivations for choosing teaching as a career. Values included the intrinsic value of teaching, social utility values (including the desire to shape the future, enhance social equity, make a social contribution and work with children/adolescents), and then personal utility values (including job security, time for family and job transferability). Teaching was not typically considered a 'fallback' career for business career switchers into teaching. Nor was encouragement from others a strong factor in individuals' choice of teaching as a career. In fact, participants reported relatively strong experiences of social dissuasion from teaching – more so for women.

Participants perceived teaching as a highly demanding career, and one that provided for low return in terms of salary and social status. Simultaneously they reported high levels of satisfaction with their choice of teaching as a career. The fact that these pre-service teachers rated highly the intrinsic value of teaching suggests that a teaching career may afford different types of rewards that are not always inherent in other occupations. For example, teaching may provide a domain where individuals feel they can readily derive a sense of existential significance from their work (Pines, 2002). Because perceptions were assessed near the beginning of participants' first year of teacher education, clearly they had chosen teaching as a career despite perceptions of teaching as high in demand and low in return, and despite experiences of others attempting to dissuade them from their choice. Satisfaction with the choice of teaching as a career was significantly and substantially higher than satisfaction with previous business-related careers, for both men and women.

The gender differences that were evident in motivations and perceptions related to teaching resonate with findings from prior research. Women were more motivated than men by interest, the desire to work with children/adolescents, and their perceived teaching abilities. They also reported lower levels of satisfaction with their prior business-related careers than the men. In Chapter 2 of this volume, Malach-Pines and Kaspi-Baruch's study of MBA students found that women reported higher levels of citizenship (such as giving money to charity) as well as the meaning of work in terms of its importance and significance. In that study, women also rated their perceived abilities to have influenced their career choice more than men. These findings are consistent with ours: women in both studies were more motivated by intrinsic, social and altruistic career dimensions, and perceptions of their own abilities, in their career decision. In other research, Eccles and her colleagues have long argued and demonstrated that adolescents' and young adults' ability beliefs and intrinsic and importance/utility values are highly influential in their career choices (e.g. Eccles (Parsons) et al., 1983; Eccles (Parsons), 1984; Eccles, 1984; Eccles et al., 1984; Ethington, 1991; Meece et al., 1990). Further, it has been found that perceptions regarding usefulness are more salient for girls' and women's career choices, at least in the domain of mathematics (Watt, in press; Watt, 2006).

Women had experienced more social dissuasion from teaching as a career, regardless of whether they were undertaking primary or secondary school teacher education. Similar proportions of women were undertaking primary and secondary teacher education, while a greater proportion of men had selected secondary teacher education – consistent with proportions in the teaching workforce more generally. Of course, our gender comparisons are only within the sample of individuals who switched out of business-related careers into teaching, and substantial gender differences probably exist among the population of business professionals who do not enter or consider a career in teaching. Malach-Pines and Kaspi-Baruch (Chapter 2, this volume) identified women MBA candidates as holding higher expectations than men regarding their qualification in relation to acquiring knowledge, improving analytical skills, enhancing their job market value, competence and social prestige. Such higher levels of expectation may be presumed to be less easily met than the more modest expectations of men, and may even produce higher levels of career burnout for women business professionals (see Pines, 2002).

It is particularly interesting that business career switchers accounted for a sizeable proportion of career switchers into teaching across the full sample, implying that teaching is an attractive career alternative for business professionals. The fact that these individuals' motivations for entering teaching reflect those from across our full pre-service teacher sample shows that business professionals are attracted into teaching for the same types of reasons as are other individuals. Future studies could fruitfully sample business professionals to directly explore their career satisfaction, considered career alternatives, motivations for entering the business world, and perceptions regarding the intrinsic, altruistic and extrinsic rewards their career provides. Just how many business professionals *do* leave their careers for careers such as teaching due to a perceived lack of social meaning and contribution? It also remains to be seen whether the somewhat idealized perceptions of teaching as a career as registered by our participants will be reshaped in schooling contexts and education systems where the nature and substance of teachers' work is being remade (OECD, 2005) as an outcome of a pervasive educational reform agenda.

AUTHORS' NOTE

Watt and Richardson contributed equally to the chapter. The research was funded by an ARC Discovery Grant awarded to Paul W. Richardson and Helen M.G. Watt (equal co-chief investigators), and Jacquelynne S. Eccles (partner investigator); and by a Monash University Faculty of Education Small Grant awarded to Watt and Richardson. We would like to thank Dr Ray Debus from the University of Sydney and Professor Jacquelynne Eccles from the University of Michigan for valuable discussions about our ideas.

REFERENCES

Crow, G.M., Levine, L. and Nager, N. (1990), 'No more business as usual: career changers who become teachers', *American Journal of Education*, **98**: 197–223.

Eccles, J.S. (1984), 'Sex differences in achievement patterns', in T. Sonderegger (ed.), *Nebraska Symposium on Motivation*, Vol. 32, Lincoln, NE: University of Nebraska Press, pp. 97–132.

Eccles, J.S., Midgley, C. and Adler, T. (1984), 'Grade-related changes in the school environment: effects on achievement motivation', in J.G. Nicholls (ed.), *Advances in Motivation and Achievement: The Development of Achievement Motivation*, Vol. 3, Greenwich, CT: JAI Press, pp. 283–331.

Eccles (Parsons), J.S. (1984), 'Sex differences in mathematics participation', in M.W. Steinkamp and M.L. Maehr (eds), *Advances in Motivation and Achievement*, Vol. 2: Women in science, Greenwich, CT: JAI Press, pp. 93–137.

Eccles (Parsons), J., Adler, T.F., Futterman, R., Goff, S.B., Kaczala, C.M., Meece, J.L. et al. (1983), 'Expectancies, values, and academic behaviors', in J.T. Spence (ed.), *Achievement and Achievement Motivation*, San Francisco, CA: W.H. Freeman, pp. 75–146.

Ethington, C.A. (1991), 'A test of a model of achievement behaviors', *American Educational Research Journal*, **28**: 155–72.

Mayotte, G.A. (2003), 'Stepping stones to success: previously developed career competencies and their benefits to career switchers transitioning to teaching', *Teaching and Teacher Education*, **19**(7): 681–95.

Meece, J.L., Wigfield, A. and Eccles, J.S. (1990), 'Predictors of math anxiety and its consequences for young adolescents' course enrollment intentions and performances in mathematics', *Journal of Educational Psychology*, **82**: 60–70.

OECD (2005), *Teachers Matter: Attracting, Developing and Retaining Effective Teachers*, Paris, OECD.

Pines, A.M (2002), 'Teacher burnout: a psychodynamic existential perspective', *Teachers and Teaching: Theory and Practice*, **8**: 121–40.

Priyadharshini, E. and Robinson-Pant, A. (2003), 'The attraction of teaching: an investigation into why people change careers to teach', *Journal of Education for Teaching: International Research and Pedagogy*, **29**(2): 95–112.

Richardson, P.W. and Watt, H.M.G. (2005), ' "I've decided to become a teacher": influences on career change', *Teaching and Teacher Education*, **21**(5): 475–89.

Richardson, P.W. and Watt, H.M.G. (2006), 'Who chooses teaching and why? Profiling characteristics and motivations across three Australian universities', *The Asia-Pacific Journal of Teacher Education*, **34**(1): 27–56.

Serow, R.C. and Forrest, K.D. (1994), 'Motives and circumstances: occupational-change experiences of prospective late-entry teachers', *Teaching and Teacher Education*, **10**(5): 555–63.

US Department of Labor Employment and Training Administration (1998), *O*NET: The Occupational Information Network*, Washington, DC: US Government Printing Office.

Watt, H.M.G. (2006), 'The role of motivation in gendered educational and occupational trajectories related to math', in H.M.G. Watt and J.S. Eccles (eds), 'Understanding women's choice of mathematics and science related careers: longitudinal studies from four countries', *Educational Research and Evaluation*, **12**(4): 305–22.

Watt, H.M.G. (in press), 'What motivates males and females to pursue sex-stereotyped careers?', in H.M.G. Watt and J.S. Eccles (eds), *Explaining Gendered Occupational Outcomes: Examining Individual and Social Explanations Through School and Beyond*, Washington, DC: APA Books.

Watt, H.M.G. and Richardson, P.W. (2007), 'Motivational factors influencing teaching as a career choice: development and validation of the "FIT-Choice" scale', *The Journal of Experimental Education*, **75**(3): 167–202.

Watt, H.M.G., Richardson, P.W., Klusmann, U., Kunter, M., Beyer, B. and Trautwein, U. (in preparation), 'Motivations for choosing teaching as a career: an international comparison using the "FIT-Choice" scale'.

Wigfield, A. and Eccles, J.S. (2000), 'Expectancy-value theory of achievement motivation', *Contemporary Educational Psychology*, **25**: 68–81.

10. The impact of foreign subsidiary managers' sociopolitical positioning on career choices and their subsequent strategizing: evidence from German-owned subsidiaries in France

Christoph Dörrenbächer and Mike Geppert

INTRODUCTION

Subsidiaries, like multinational corporations (MNCs) as a whole, have a history. Founded or created in a historical situation for a specific end, they develop over time, reflecting multifaceted changes in their internal and external environment. Based on the conceptualization of MNCs as intraorganizational networks (Hedlund, 1986; Ghoshal and Bartlett, 1990), it is especially since the 1990s that subsidiary related research has gained a growing academic interest. This research concentrates on four topics: (1) role specialization of subsidiaries; (2) subsidiaries' internal and external network relations; (3) headquarters–subsidiary relations; and (4) subsidiary role development, or, in other words, subsidiary evolution (Birkinshaw, 2001).

The evolution of subsidiaries over time is mainly seen as a function of subsidiary capabilities, headquarters' strategic intentions and location-specific advantages of the country the subsidiary is located in (for an overview see Dörrenbächer and Gammelgaard, 2006). However, relatively little has been said about micro-political processes and key actors' interests and strategies underlying subsidiary evolution, despite constant claims that MNCs should be understood as political systems, where different groups as well as individual actors try to secure options, realize interests and achieve success (Westney and Zaheer, 2001; Fischer, 2005; Bélanger and Edwards, 2006).

Based on three case studies of German subsidiaries in France, this chapter explores how foreign subsidiary managers' idiosyncratic actions as well as the political nature of headquarters–subsidiary relations influence subsidiary evolution. In line with Fligstein's (1990) study on the impact of dominant actor groups on organizational control, we try to establish a link between foreign subsidiary managers' nationality, personal career orientations, and professional backgrounds – here referred to as their sociopolitical positioning – their individual career choices and their subsequent strategizing with regard to the evolution of their subsidiaries. Empirically we will focus on how subsidiary mandates are gained, developed or lost over time, with mandates being defined as temporary responsibilities either allocated by the headquarters or acquired by the individual subsidiary (Birkinshaw, 1996).

The chapter starts with a short discussion of the literature on subsidiary evolution. The basic aim of this section is to demonstrate that micro-political aspects, including career issues, have so far been neglected in this literature. Next, our key factors: (1) actors' nationality, (2) actors' career orientations and (3) actors' professional backgrounds will be operationalized and put into the perspective of the wider organizational and institutional environment. Following some notes regarding methodology, the cases are presented. Their aim is threefold. First, the cases studies try to shed some light on the rationales behind the career choices taken by the individual foreign subsidiary managers. Second, the case studies explore to what extent the foreign subsidiary managers' subsequent idiosyncratic actions with regard to subsidiary evolution are defined by their sociopolitical positioning. Third, the case studies look at what happens to foreign subsidiary managers' strategies in the headquarters–subsidiary interactions on subsidiary evolution. The concluding section presents a cross-case analysis and highlights some areas for further career-related research on managers of foreign-owned subsidiaries.

SUBSIDIARY EVOLUTION AND FOREIGN SUBSIDIARY MANAGERS' SOCIOPOLITICAL POSITIONING

For quite a long time organization studies, like the international business and management literature, saw MNCs as hierarchical entities where headquarters (HQ) and their managers had absolute power. It was not until research looked at corporations from different home countries, or from different societal backgrounds, that this picture changed. Thus research done by Stopford and Wells (1972) on US multinationals and Franko (1976) on European multinationals showed that European MNCs decentralized decision making much more strongly than US MNCs. One of the first authors who translated these empirical findings into a more theoretical concept was Gunnar Hedlund. In his famous 1986 article 'The hypermodern MNC – a heterarchy?', he stressed that heterarchical MNCs – unlike hierarchical ones – have many centres, and that subsidiaries are given a strategic role, not only for their own subsidiary but for the multinational as a whole (Hedlund, 1986). What followed were rather similar concepts, such as the MNC as an integrated network (Bartlett and Ghoshal, 1989), or the MNC as a 'transnationally differentiated network', a term coined by Nohria and Ghoshal (1997) about ten years later. In all of these concepts, the role of the HQ was put into perspective and power structures within the multinational were seen as more diverse, context-related and relationship-based. Given this turn in the perception of MNCs, it is not surprising that in the 1990s research started to put a stronger emphasis on subsidiaries and their respective managers. A subsidiary can be defined as a discrete value-adding activity of an MNC outside its home country (Birkenshaw, 2001). This general definition implies that subsidiaries can vary a great deal with regard to the scope and the scale of their operations, the environment of their location, as well as with regard to their strategic importance for the MNC. Depending on these differences, foreign subsidiary managers exert more or less influence within the MNC, with subsidiary evolution, i.e. the gain of new or the development of existing mandates, being one of the basic mechanisms for foreign subsidiary managers to enhance their reputation, power and influence within the MNC.

Following the basic premises of the micro-political approach, actors are neither the executive organs of given structures, nor fully autonomous. They are bound by rules, restrictions and resources. However, such structural ties do not foreclose systematic and individual variations in strategies and behaviour. Systematic variations occur due to different functional or hierarchical backgrounds in organizations, different educational and professional backgrounds (Pfeffer, 1993; Fligstein, 1990), as well as in the case of MNCs different sub-unit, national and cultural backgrounds, with all these factors influencing the translation, interpretation and integration of external conditions into actor behaviour. Individual variations in actor strategies occur due to the fact that the organizational behaviour of actors always takes into account the individual interests of the actor (Küpper and Felsch, 2000). Very often these interests are selfish, relating to autonomy, power and career ambitions in organizations. However, individual interests might also be shaped by altruistic ideas and beliefs (Ortmann, 1988), personal identity construction (Weick, 1995) or group dynamics (Lee and Lawrence, 1985). In short: the interactions of key actors in organizations are to some extent institutionally and structurally constrained, but there is always room for interpretation and manoeuvre (Crozier and Friedberg, 1980).

These general considerations also apply to key actors in MNCs such as foreign subsidiary managers, the focus of this chapter. Focusing on foreign subsidiary managers' career choice and their subsequent strategizing on subsidiary evolution, it is proposed here that these processes are strongly influenced by the interplay of some actor-related sociopolitical factors such as nationality, career orientation and professional background with some MNC internal and external institutional features. This proposition is in line with a more specific argument made by Özbilgin et al. (2005) on career choice, stating that individual decisions regarding a specific occupation or organization are based on a complex interplay of micro-level factors such as individual agency, dispositions and different forms of social capital available, meso-level factors such as professional backgrounds or *habitus* and macro-level factors such as contextual circumstances in and beyond the organization in question.

Foreign Subsidiary Managers' Sociopolitical Positioning: Nationality, Career Orientation and Professional Background

Following a well-established categorization, foreign subsidiary managers are either parent country nationals (PCN or expatriates), host country nationals (HCNs or inpatriates), or third country nationals (TCNs) (Harzing, 1999). These different types of staff are ascribed different orientations. Usually PCNs are seen as strongly following a transnational orientation due to their familiarity with the MNC's overall goals, policies and practices. Very often they are seen as most efficient in exercising HQ control over the subsidiary. However, this transnational orientation is only with PCNs that do not go native, e.g. by marrying a local partner, converting to the locally dominant religion, or taking up permanent local residence, as Loveridge (2006) stresses. HCNs or inpatriates on the other hand are seen as basically having a local orientation, due to their socialization in the host country and their familiarity with the social, political and economic environment of that country (Harvey et al., 1999). However, following Petersen et al. (1996, 2000), a strong local orientation is only present in HCNs that do not have international career options. Whether such options exist basically relates to the career schemes of the MNC and the skills of the HCN. Third country nationals or TCNs are often ascribed a generically more balanced orientation between the local and the transnational. However, following Harzing (1999), their number is very small compared to PCNs and HCNs. Finally there is a growing number of foreign subsidiary managers who do not fit any of the categories discussed above, due to their binational, bilingual and/or bicultural biography. However, to what degree these 'hybrids' do follow a local or a transnational career orientation and how this relates to their biography is still an open question.

Next to nationality, the individual career aspirations of foreign subsidiary managers have an important impact on career choices and their subsequent strategizing. Classic career development models postulate that the career aspirations of a individual manager depend on her/his career stage, with the early career years aiming at becoming established, the mid-career years defined as a phase of career advancement and maintenance, and the late career years as adjustment to retirement (Hall and Nougaim, 1968). Newer research has shown that these concepts, which strongly correlate career aspirations with age, are too rigid to cover the blurring of standard biographies. Thus Hall (2002) proposes a more open framework, relating the career aspirations of an individual to his/her perception of whether she or he is established or not. Whether or not a subsidiary manager of an MNC is satisfied with his/her present career stage or not depends on various individual factors such as age, family situation, health, self-assessment of talents etc. These individual characteristics, however, have to be related to organizational features, such as MNC-specific career schemes and staffing policies, appraisal and compensation policies as well as support systems (Peltonen, 1992; Stahl et al., 2002). Furthermore, situational features associated with specific career steps have to be taken into account, most prominently issues of geographic mobility (Mayrhofer, 1996), anticipated work conditions (work atmosphere, burden of work etc.), and changes in tasks and responsibilities. Changes in tasks and responsibility in particular are ascribed a great impact. Following Schein (1978/1990), career anchors inside the person (defined by self-perceived talents and abilities, by self-perceived motives and needs as well as by self-perceived attitudes and values) function as driving and constraining forces on career decisions and choices (ibid., p. 164). Based on these premises, Moss Kanter (1989) distinguishes between a bureaucratic, a professional and an entrepreneurial career orientation, with the bureaucratic orientation being defined by the logic of advancement in a given organization, the professional orientation based on the logic of increasing knowledge and reputation, and the entrepreneurial orientation based on the logic of increasing autonomy and innovation.

MNC-internal and -external Institutional Impacts

The foreign subsidiary manager's sociopolitical positioning influencing his/her career choice, as well as the way s/he implements this choice, has to be seen in relation to MNC-internal and MNC-external factors. Some relevant MNC-internal factors have already been mentioned such as career schemes, staffing and compensation policies. Apart from these factors, which specifically relate to International Human Resource Management (IHRM) issues, there are also some more general MNC-internal (or organizational) settings that might have an influence on foreign subsidiary managers' career choice and subsequent orientation with regard to mandate development practices. Based on Penrose's (1959) pioneering work, many authors have maintained that the capabilities available to a subsidiary, encompassing, e.g. managerial expertise (Rugman and Douglas, 1986), product portfolios (Hood et al., 1994), specialized technologies (Egelhoff et al., 1998) and internal R&D processes (Pearce, 1999; Florida, 1997; Taggert, 1998), have an influence on the opportunities of subsidiaries and their managers to successfully develop their mandates. Another important factor is the host country's institutional settings (Becker-Ritterspach, 2006). While these factors describe the resources on which subsidiary managers' behaviour is based (or limited), HQ assignment is another important source for mandate development practices (Egelhoff et al., 1998). Whether or not the HQ is willing to allocate knowledge, resources and strategic responsibilities to a subsidiary might depend on other subsidiaries' success or failure (Delany, 1998). Altered market conditions (Prahalad and Doz, 1987; Birkinshaw and Hood, 1998) or changes in the political and institutional environment (Djelic and Quack, 2003) might also have an impact on the reallocation of resources in the MNC. Changes in the institutional environment in particular are considered to have a strong impact.

Thus the increasing internationalization of capital markets is triggering massive corporate restructurings (e.g. Useem, 1996). These changes were understood to be especially strong in MNCs from coordinated market economies such as Germany (Vitols, 2004; Jürgens et al., 2000) or Finland (Tainio et al., 2001). Here management control is increasingly challenged by stock market control, favouring short-term results over long-term stability and financial goals over technical ones. However, there are still notable discrepancies according to size, industry and the legal form of an MNC as to what extent this logic of financialization (or shareholder value) applies, as Dörrenbächer (2004) has shown for German MNCs. At the same time this new logic faces support and opposition inside the MNC, not only along the dichotomy of capital and labour, but also among key actors in the MNC along national, structural, functional and hierarchical divides.

RESEARCH DESIGN AND CONTEXT

The mini-case studies presented here are taken from an ongoing research project on entrepreneurship and subsidiary evolution in German MNCs.

This project tries to map and explain actor rationales in processes of mandate development and upgrading in French affiliates. The research design is exploratory and mainly based on qualitative interviews conducted in French subsidiaries, covering different industries, HQ policies and subsidiary management nationalities. The three mini-case studies are selected from a first round of interviews in French subsidiaries of German MNCs. Based on intensive preparatory work, semi-structured interviews, lasting between two and three hours, were conducted with key subsidiary managers. The interviews were taped, transcribed and triangulated with the analysis of various documents. Given the exploratory nature of this chapter, the mini-cases presented are initial interpretations of company cases, based on a limited number of interviews. Thus the basic purpose of the mini-case studies is to illustrate how career choices and strategies of subsidiary managers with regard to mandate development are construed by selective and reflexive integration of individual traits and interests, different social practices within the MNC as well as institutional and socioeconomic patterns relevant to the MNC and the subsidiary.

All mini-case studies were drawn from German MNCs that are currently undergoing great changes, more or less 'alienating' these firms from the traditions of the so-called 'German model', which is usually characterized by highly regulated labour relations, patient capital (the idea rests on the implicit promise of German banks to help firms even when they are in trouble) and a general orientation of the management towards technical aims (e.g. Katzenstein, 1980; Albert, 1991; Streeck, 1997). The fact that the case studies are rooted in institutionalizing rather than in institutionalized arenas (see e.g. Djelic and Quack, 2003) means that there are both a high level of management turnover and a marked openness to bottom-up incentives of mandate development and subsidiary evolution, with the latter especially feasible for managers of French subsidiaries that operate in a quite developed economic, technological and institutional environment (e.g. Albert, 1991; Whitley, 2001; Kleiner, 2004).

THREE MINI-CASE STUDIES

Case 1: This young, ambitious Franco-German manager with considerable international job experience, a hierarchical career orientation and a financial professional background used his insider knowledge of innovative changes at a local competitor as well as his subsidiary's mandate to promote structural reforms in the overall MNC. He thereby advanced the financialization of the MNC and qualified himself for a career at the HQ.

To initiate organizational reforms at the overall MNC level and thus to qualify for a top management career within the HQ was one of the basic aims of the young and ambitious chief executive officer (CEO) of the French regional company of a large German service firm. Born in Germany and raised in France, the 38-year-old manager who studied in Germany clearly follows a hierarchical career orientation. Following a trainee programme at a large German bank and a short assignment as financial adviser of an engineering firm, he has worked at the German service MNC for about ten years. So far, all his assignments at the German MNC have been abroad, with the first seven years spent in Asia. When the German MNC decided to sell its Asian subsidiaries, he decided to stay with the MNC. He was appointed chief financial officer of one of the MNC's French subsidiaries in 2002, and he became CEO of the French regional office in 2003.

The CEO does not consider this to be his last career step. His personal statements and the way he uses his subsidiary's mandate to interfere in strategizing processes at the HQ level indicate his high career ambitions. In addition to relationship management and corporate governance of the different subsidiaries operating in France, the relatively small French regional office is responsible for developing the MNC's corporate strategy for Western Europe, encompassing tasks such as M&A, lobbying and business intelligence. It is therefore dependent on the much larger strategic development department in Germany. However, the most important proposal for mandate development brought forward by the French CEO was not focused on further international expansion, but on the restructuring of the business organization in Germany, where more than 90 per cent of the business activity takes place.

The French CEO's basic ideas for quite far-reaching structural reforms of the MNC's overall organization were inspired by recent organizational developments of a major French competitor. Based on new technologies, the French competitor turned its product-oriented organization into a customer-specific organization, unleashing a strong potential for rationalization (e.g. two full-fledged divisions had been condensed into one). Guided by his HQ-oriented career orientation and his professional experience as financial adviser, the French CEO carefully 'benchmarked' the organizational changes of the competitor. Based on a wide array of contacts with the competitor's top management and basic local stakeholders such as trade unions, client organizations or regulation authorities, the CEO and his staff were able to prepare a solid analysis of the organizational change at the French competitor and to draft a proposal and a detailed feasibility study for a similar change at the German MNC.

This proposal, especially its rationalization effects, was basically in line with the overall strategy of the management board, which was under strong pressure to increase shareholder value due to falling share prices. However, there was strong opposition to this change, especially in the two divisions affected. Thus, before the board of management was officially approached with the proposal, a large coalition of internal and external supporters was formed. This task was taken over by the strategic development department of the HQ, since both the political weight of the regional company in France, as well as the personal reputation of its CEO, appeared to be too weak to successfully form a coalition. Coalition building appeared to be rather undetermined, according to the French CEO, since 'even if you try hard to find out, you never know exactly what impact, personal relationships and reputation a person has'. In this case, a coalition of about 20 people was formed, including almost all managing directors below the board of directors, some consultants and influential investment bankers. The coalition turned out to be powerful enough to persuade the board of directors to implement the proposal.

So far, there have been no direct career rewards for the French CEO, who kept on lobbying for 'his' proposal after the strategic development department had formally taken over the task. However, his reputation at HQ and especially among the board of directors has definitely increased.

Case 2: A German expatriate manager close to retirement, with some international experience and a strong engineering background, successfully meets the challenging requirements of a new HQ-assigned mandate basically by drawing on subsidiary and MNC-related practice material bundles. However, his intentions to upgrade the mandate and, accordingly, to maintain/improve his reputation and personal achievements failed due to a strict shareholder value orientation of the HQ.

Technical and organizational challenges were this 57-year-old manager's basic rationale for becoming the CEO of a newly founded French subsidiary of a Bavarian automotive supplier. Despite his considerable experience in similar positions in different national and foreign subsidiaries of the German conglomerate to which the Bavarian automotive supplier belongs, it ultimately proved difficult to fulfil the requirements of this HQ-assigned mandate. Integrated into one of the most innovative car production networks worldwide, the French subsidiary was supposed to ramp up a blueprint to use new material in mass car production. Immediately after production started, it became clear that basic process innovations were needed to meet the quality criteria set by the car's end producer. A painful trial-and-error process was required to cope with these problems. Thus mandate development in this case was aimed first to meet the challenging technological requirements in order to develop the assigned mandate.

Accordingly, the French CEO negotiated with the HQ on additional financial resources. However, his requests for such financial investments were either ignored by the divisional HQ in Bavaria or rejected with phrases such as: 'Don't bother us; it's your job to fix the problems there.' This refusal of HQ power holders to support this difficult but at the same time very promising project of the subsidiary was mainly due to a dramatic shift in the overall orientation of the conglomerate and the automotive supply division. Once a technologically driven company, the conglomerate ran into deep trouble due to some unlucky speculations and irregularities. As a result a new CEO was appointed by the major shareholders. Since this new CEO was a turnover specialist, the MNC's former innovation orientation was replaced by an orientation towards shareholder value and short-term results. Controlling and accounting functions were strongly upgraded all over the conglomerate; as a result, the automotive supply division was no longer seen as the core business. This caused upheavals at the divisional HQ. Many managers left, and more emphasis was put on financial control.

The French CEO was dealing rather proactively with the constraints of missing HQ resources in order to improve productivity and quality standards. As a university-trained materials scientist who initially worked for 13 years in the R&D department of a large German chemical company, the subsidiary manager started by addressing detailed technical problems. His professional experiences as researcher, based on, e.g., lifelong learning attitudes, strong analysing and designing skills, were indeed very helpful to meet the new challenges of mandate development. However, managerial strategizing went beyond personal experiences and knowledge. Thus, by using local core competences and the rather small financial resources, he initiated a mandate enhancement by establishing a small local R&D unit. Even when the local labour market did not provide the qualifications needed, his reputation, build up in the 30 years of his professional career, enabled him to attract newly qualified personnel and motivate his own staff to support his political strategies. The success of this mandate development initiative was supported by establishing a stable and low-conflict atmosphere within the subsidiary, e.g. by paying financial incentives, fixing a stable core team of 250 employees and following a generally consensus-oriented management style when dealing with the works council and individual workers.

The first two to three years were mainly dedicated to troubleshooting. Many of the initial technical and organizational problems were solved and performance improved. However, as the subsidiary manager put it, 'In those years, I served my time in hell.' Nevertheless, the manager considered his achievements as 'very fruitful', despite initial problems. The efforts to meet the performance goals associated with the mandate formed the basis for the attempts to enhance the mandate later on.

The main strategy to enhance the mandate of the subsidiary was to further explore the potential of the technological achievements gained so far and their use on a larger scale. As the CEO was almost at the end of his career, it seems to be more a question of reputation, personal satisfaction and maybe also economic care for the overall division of the MNC than individual career ambitions that the subsidiary manager was getting actively engaged in mandate development games at the HQ level. However, he failed to further explore and fully exploit the potential of the French subsidiary. While he was successful in placing some of his specialists in other subsidiaries as well as in the central R&D lab of the automotive division, he did not get HQ approval for a crucial investment proposal for a significant upgrading of the subsidiary's capabilities. The HQ was interpreting such long-term commitments as insufficient to realize short-term profits, or as the French CEO put it, 'The HQ is not interested in measures that bring cash in 3 years, he wants to see cash in 1.5 years'. That indicates an increasing influence of financial control mechanisms in this company, undermining longer-term oriented strategies based on established engineering skills and technological innovation.

Case 3: A locally oriented, middle-aged inpatriate of a subsidiary providing marketing and maintenance services for a German supplier of agricultural machinery enhances the mandate of his subsidiary step by step. He develops a rather entrepreneurial career orientation in order to develop local market opportunities by facilitating internal practices and resources as well as his close personal relationships to HQ to promote his subsidiary. This strategy is supported by the still quite long-term, trust-based orientation of the family-owned German MNC.

After receiving a degree in mechanical engineering, this French manager started his career with a one-year internship at the HQ of the family-owned German MNC. Having returned to France, he worked in a company that imported the products of the German MNC. Within a few years, his relationship with the HQ of the German MNC stabilized due to day-to-day business contacts. When serious managerial problems occurred at the French importer, the German MNC took over the French importer in 1987 and appointed its former intern as CEO of the newly acquired sales and maintenance subsidiary.

At first, the new CEO concentrated on building up state-of-the-art practices in his subsidiary to better fulfil the tasks assigned by HQ (basically, market screening, market communication, distribution, and product adaptation). The subsidiary was then relocated from a larger city centre close to Paris to a more rural area, as proposed by the new CEO. The aim of this relocation was to create more space for a planned increase in business activity. However, the 1992 agricultural reform that caused tremendous cutbacks in demand for agricultural machinery stopped the subsidiary's growth. The company's turnover collapsed in the following years, which led to a massive reduction of staff, from about 70 to 35.

Backed on site by one of the sons of the owner family (now one of the managing directors of the MNC), the French CEO started looking for new business opportunities in France. As a result he succeeded in outcompeting the French service subsidiary of another German MNC that produces a complementary range of agricultural machinery. The French service subsidiary of the other German MNC was closed down and the task was taken on by the French CEO and his subsidiary. In this takeover process, the French CEO could demonstrate a well-functioning sales and maintenance organization. The HQ gave credibility and support to the negotiations with the other German supplier.

After taking on this new task, the French subsidiary almost doubled in size, gaining critical mass for new entrepreneurial activities. This time, the stagnation of the German market as well as the dominant position of the German MNC on its home market led to shift strategizing processes towards increasing the company presence within the French market. Although the French CEO and HQ had reached a general consensus that the French market should increase in importance within the MNC, the HQ appeared unwilling to support this local strategy. The French CEO lobbied for this move and started to change internal practices at his subsidiary to better exploit the French market. Thus he decided to hire German-speaking product managers for every important product to improve the adaptation of products and services as well the development of new products for the local market. These measures were quite successful, and they expanded the French subsidiary's competencies in product development. Moreover, they led to the introduction of a similar product manager structure at HQ.

Another example of how the French CEO advanced the mandate of his subsidiary by micro-political strategizing at the HQ level was his 'market communication' project, improving the company's standing in the local French market. Initially, HQ was not enthusiastic about the French CEO's idea to develop a product catalogue that includes information on all MNC products for the French market. Up to now information on MNC products was given on separate product information sheets. However, the increased reputation of the French CEO, his close personal relationship with one of the owner–managers (the manager who once was expatriated for a year to the French subsidiary), together with organizational cultural patterns which support the development of high-trust relationships, enabled him to succeed in his local catalogue project. Finally, the new catalogue turned out to be a great success, and HQ decided to adopt the idea and to integrate the separate product information sheets into a catalogue for the German market to achieve comparable sales gains.

Despite his increasing reputation and influence in strategizing processes within the HQ, the French CEO was never interested in a career at HQ for several reasons. One reason was that the family-run MNC offered only a few top management positions to non-family members. Furthermore, the French CEO could easily satisfy his entrepreneurial orientation by the many challenging tasks he encountered in developing the French subsidiary's mandate. The French CEO recently gained HQ's approval to move the subsidiary again to a more spacious location, which was seen as the foundation for future growth and subsidiary upgrading.

DISCUSSION AND CONCLUSION

Our illustrative presentation of the mini-case studies has shown that the socio-political positioning of foreign subsidiary managers – i.e their nationality, career orientations and professional backgrounds – matters when analysing career choices and the subsequent strategizing of these actors with regard to mandate development processes. Of course these processes were also influenced by institutional structures of the MNC itself, and certain home and host country institutional features.

The interplay of these factors is particularly evident looking at the career choices the protagonists of our case studies made. Following Hall (1976), career choice is not a single event at the beginning of a working career but a choice that takes place at several different times throughout an individual's working life. This is very obvious in all three cases described. Thus the young and ambitious manager of the large German service firm in Case 1 had to reconsider his initial choice to enter the German service firm when this firm decided to sell its Asian subsidiaries where he was expatriated to initially. The manager in the second case was already close to retirement when he took the decision to become the head of the French subsidiary. Career choices during his work life not only covered several choices regarding organizations and organizational sub-units, but an occupational choice too, since he started his career as a researcher in a laboratory of a large chemical company and it was only in his mid-career that he turned to general management. Recurring career choices are less obvious in the third case described. However, as stressed by the manager in the interview, the initial choice was confirmed several times over the years: he stayed in his position, since severe challenges this particular subsidiary faced from time to time strongly correlated with his outspoken entrepreneurial career orientation.

Looking at the rationale underlying the career choices touched upon in our three mini-case studies, it becomes very obvious that instrumental desires of progress in the organizational hierarchy only play a role in the first case. Here the move from a peripheral Asian subsidiary to the French subsidiary was also a step closer to the headquarters in Germany, with increased options for further advancement. In the two other cases progress within the hierarchy of the organization was not at all a motive in the career choice in question. In the case of the manager close to retirement (Case 2), the personal and technological challenge associated with the new job in the French subsidiary was the most important individual factor in the choice, while in the remaining case the local manager had reached the highest position in the local subsidiary rather early on, and never considered a career in the German headquarters, which is closely related to the strong decision-making autonomy he has in the French subsidiary compared to a position at headquarters. These findings on the micro-level of the self, which clearly reflect a hierarchical (Case 1), a professional (Case 2) and an entrepreneurial (Case 3) career orientation as defined by the framework of Moss Kanter (1989), seem to support traditional career stage models. These models differentiate between early career years where establishment and advancement in the hierarchy play a predominant role, and mid-career years, in which an increased awareness of the scare time left leads to more concern about maintaining what has already been achieved (e.g. autonomy in the third case) and producing something lasting and worthwhile (e.g. a new process technology in the second case) (Hall, 1976, 2002).

As well as the impact of career stage and general career orientation, the mini-case studies also demonstrated the impact of various more institutionalized meso- and macro-level factors on career choices and the subsequent strategizing of key foreign subsidiary managers. In the first two cases described, the impact of educational background is obvious. Having a strong financial background, the young and ambitious manager of the German service firm in Case 1 was especially attracted by the mandate of the French subsidiary to provide business intelligence, a mandate he interpreted strongly according to his educational background by drafting a large-scale cost-saving programme. In the second case, scientific curiosity built up during long years of education including a master's degree and a PhD in materials science played a important role in the decision of the manager close to retirement to take on the technological challenge associated with the new position as CEO of the French subsidiary.

While nationality only played a strong role in the third case, where the local ties of the French manager more or less excluded a career in the German headquarters, contextual circumstances in and beyond the MNC were important factors influencing or stabilizing all three career choices and the subsequent strategizing of the actors with regard to subsidiary evolution. In the first case it was the headquarters decision to sell its Asian subsidiaries and an acute lack of internationally minded and talented people to offer our young and ambitious manager the vacant job as CEO of the French operations. Once installed in France, this manager capitalized host country resources by taking the overall restructuring of a French competitor as a template for a similar restructuring proposal that he addressed to the headquarters. In the second case an overall change in internal corporate governance towards stronger financial control marginalized the division to which the imminently retiring manager was affiliated. This strongly influenced his decision to move to the French subsidiary. The strict financial orientation of the headquarters also influenced the way that this manager later on tackled the problems associated with the new job. He basically drew on his personal as well as on locally available resources. In the third case, the family ownership of the MNC implied limited career opportunities for non-family members and did not support a career in the headquarters. Moreover, changes in the external market as well as frequent opportunities for further expansion satisfied the strong entrepreneurial spirit of the French CEO and kept him in his position over quite a long period of time.

In summary, and in more general terms, a close relationship between local subsidiary manager's career choices and their subsequent strategizing is obvious. Both processes are strongly guided by the long-term orientating influence of the sociopolitical positioning of these actors as well as their embeddedness in a specific organizational and national home and host country environment. However, the case studies also revealed that the level of decision-making power associated with the position of a foreign subsidiary manager allows for a certain flexibility in how the career choice is enacted later on. How this room for manoeuvre is used in different organizational settings, with regard to different issues as well as by different types of foreign subsidiary managers, is an interesting area for more detailed further research.

REFERENCES

Albert, M. (1991), *Capitalisme contre Capitalisme*, Paris: Seuil.
Bartlett, C.A. and Ghoshal, S. (1989), *Managing Across Borders. The Transnational Solution*, Boston, MA: Harvard Business School Press.
Bartlett, C.A. and Ghoshal, S. (1997), 'The transnational organization', in D.S. Pugh (ed.), *Organization Theory: Selected Readings*, London: Penguin, pp. 64–82.
Becker-Ritterspach, F. (2006), *The Hybridisation of Local MNE Production Systems. The Case of Subsidiaries in India*, Groningen: SOM.

Bélanger, J. and Edwards, Paul (2006), 'Towards a political economy framework: TNCs as national and global players', in A. Ferner, J. Quintanilla and C. Sánchez-Runde (eds), *Multinationals, Institutions and the Construction of Transnational Practices. Convergence and Diversity in the Global Economy*, Basingstoke, UK: Palgrave Macmillan, pp. 24–51.

Birkinshaw, J. (1996), 'How multinational subsidiary mandates are gained and lost', *Journal of International Business Studies*, **27**(3): 467–95.

Birkinshaw, J. (2001), 'Strategy and management in MNE subsidiaries', in A.A. Rugman and T.L. Brewer (eds), *The Oxford Handbook of International Business*, Oxford: Oxford University Press, pp. 380–401.

Birkinshaw, J. and Hood, N. (1998), 'Multinational subsidiary evolution: capabilities and charter change in foreign-owned companies', *Academy of Management Review*, **23**(4): 773–95.

Crozier, M. and Friedberg, E. (1979), *Macht und Organisation. Die Zwänge kollektiven Handelns*, Königstein: Athenäum.

Crozier, M. and Friedberg, E. (1980), *Actors and Systems. The Politics of Collective Action*, Chicago, IL: University of Chicago Press.

Delany, E. (1998), 'Strategic development of multinational subsidiaries in Ireland', in J. Birkinshaw and N. Hood (eds), *Multinational Corporate Evolution and Subsidiary Development*, Basingstoke, UK: Macmillan Press, pp. 239–67.

Djelic, M.-L. and Quack, S. (2003), 'Conclusion: globalization as a double process of institutional change and institution building', in M.-L. Djelic and S. Quack (eds), *Globalization and Institutions. Redefining the Rules of the Economic Game*, Cheltenham, UK and Northampton, MA, USA: Edward Elgar, pp. 302–33.

Dörrenbächer, C. (2004), 'Fleeing or exporting the German model? The internationalization of German multinationals in the 1990s', *Competition and Change*, **8**(4): 443–56.

Dörrenbächer, C. and Gammelgaard, J. (2006), 'Subsidiary role development: the effect of micro-political headquarters–subsidiary negotiations on the product, market, and value-added scope of foreign owned subsidiaries', *Journal of International Management*, **12**: 266–83.

Egelhoff, W.G., Gorman, L. and McCormick, S. (1998), 'Using technology as a path to subsidiary development', in J. Birkinshaw and N. Hood (eds), *Multinational Corporate Evolution and Subsidiary Development*, Basingstoke, UK: Macmillan Press, pp. 213–38.

Fischer, F. (2005), 'Revisiting organizational politics: the postempiricist challenge', *Policy and Society*, June: 1–23.

Fligstein, N. (1990), *The Transformation of Corporate Control*, Cambridge, MA: Harvard University Press.

Florida, R. (1997), 'The globalization of R&D: results of a survey of foreign-affiliated R&D laboratories in the USA', *Research Policy*, **26**: 85–103.

Franko, L.G. (1976), *The European Multinationals*, Greenwich, CT: Greylock Press.

Ghoshal, S. and Bartlett, C. (1990), 'The multinational corporation as a differentiated organizational network', *Academy of Management Review*, **15**(4): 603–25.

Hall, D.T. (1976), *Careers in Organizations*, Glenview, IL: Scott, Foresman & Co.

Hall, D.T. (2002), *Careers In and Out of Organizations*, Thousand Oaks, CA: Sage.

Hall, D.T. and Nougain, K. (1968), 'An examination of Maslow's need hierarchy in an organizational setting', *Organizational Behavior and Human Performance*, **3**: 12–35.

Harvey, M.G., Novicevic, M.M. and Speier, C. (1999), 'Inpatriate managers: how to increase the probability of success', *Human Resource Management Review*, **9**(1): 151–81.

Harzing, A.-W. (1999), *Managing the Multinationals. An International Study of Control Mechanisms*, Cheltenham, UK and Northampton, MA, USA: Edward Elgar.

Hedlund, G. (1986), 'The hypermodern MNC – a heterarchy?', *Human Resource Management*, **25**(1): 9–35.

Hood, N., Young, S. and Lal, D. (1994), 'Strategic evolution within Japanese manufacturing plants in Europe: UK evidence', *International Business Review*, **3**(2): 97–122.

Jürgens, U., Naumann, K. and Kupp, J. (2000), 'Shareholder value in an adverse environment: the German case', *Economy and Society*, **29**(1): 54–79.

Katzenstein, P.J. (1980), 'Problem or model? West Germany in the 1980s', *World Politics*, **32**: 577–98.

Kleiner, T. (2004), 'Building up an asset management industry: Anglo-Saxon logic in France', in M.-L. Djelic and S. Quack (eds), *Globalization and Institutions. Redefining the Rules of the Economic Game*, Cheltenham, UK and Northampton, MA, USA: Edward Elgar, pp. 57–82.

Küpper, W. and Felsch, A. (2000), *Organisation, Macht und Ökonomie. Mikropolitik und die Konstitution organisationaler Handlungssysteme*, Wiesbaden: Westdeutscher Verlag.

Lee, R. and Lawrence, R. (1985), *Organizational Behaviour. Politics at Work*, London: Hutchinson.

Loveridge, R. (2006), 'Embedding the multinational enterprise: the micro-processes of institutionalisation in developing economies', in M. Geppert and M. Mayer (eds), *Global, National and Local Practices in Multinational Companies*, Basingstoke, UK: Palgrave Macmillan, pp. 189–219.

Mayrhofer, W. (1996), *Mobilität und Steuerung in international tätigen Unternehmen. Eine theoretische Analyse*, Stuttgart: Schäffer-Poeschel.

Moss Kanter, R. (1989), 'Careers and wealth of nations: a macro-perspective on the structure and implications of career forms', in M.B. Arthur et al. (eds), *Handbook of Career Theory*, Cambridge: Cambridge University Press, pp. 506–21.

Nohria, N. and Ghoshal, S. (1997), *The Differentiated Network. Organizing Multinational Corporations for Value Creation*, San Francisco, CA: Jossey-Bass.

Ortmann, G. (1988), 'Macht, spiel, konsens', in W. Küpper and G. Ortmann (eds), *Mikropolitik. Rationalität, Macht und Spiele in Organisationen*, Opladen: Westdeutscher Verlag, pp. 13–26.

Özbilgin, M., Küskü, F. and Erdoğmuş, N. (2005), 'Explaining influences on career "choice": the case of MBA students in comparative perspective', *International Journal of Human Resource Management*, **16**(11): 2000–2028.

Pearce, R. (1999), 'The evolution of technology in multinational enterprises: the role of creative subsidiaries', *International Business Review*, **8**: 125–48.

Peltonen, T. (1992), 'Managerial careers in multinational organisations: towards a typology', CIBR Working Paper Series 2/1992, Helsinki: HSE Press.

Penrose, E. (1959), *The Theory of the Growth of the Firm*, Oxford: Oxford University Press.

Peterson, R.B., Napier, N. and Shim, W.S. (1996), 'Expatriate management: the differential role of national multinational corporation ownership', *The International Executive*, **38**: 543–62.

Peterson, R.B., Napier, N. and Shim, W.S. (2000), 'Expatriate management: a comparison of MNCs across four parent countries', *Thunderbird International Business Review*, **42**: 145–66.

Pfeffer, J. (1993), 'Organizational demography', *Research in Organizational Behaviour*, **5**: 299–357.

Prahalad, C.K. and Doz, Y. (1987), *The Multinational Mission: Balancing Local Demands and Global Vision*, New York: Free Press.

Rugman, A. and Douglas, S. (1986), 'The strategic management of multinationals and world product mandating', in H. Etemad and L.S. Dulude (eds), *Managing the Multinational Subsidiary: Response to Environmental Changes and to Host Nation R&D Policies*, Beckenham, UK: Croom Helm, pp. 90–101.

Schein, E.H. (1978/1990), *Career Anchors* (revised), San Diego, CA: University Associates.

Stahl, G.K., Miller, E.L. and Tung, R.L. (2002), 'Toward the boundaryless career: a closer look at the expatriate career concept and the perceived implications of an international assignment', *Journal of World Business*, **37**: 216–27.

Stopford, J.M. and Wells, L.T. (1972), *Managing the Multinational Enterprise. Organization of the Firm and Ownership of Subsidiaries*, New York: Basic Books.

Streeck, W. (1997), 'German capitalism: does it exist? Can it survive?', in C. Crouch and W. Streeck (eds), *Political Economy of Modern Capitalism*, London: Sage, pp. 33–54.

Taggert, J.H. (1998), 'Strategy shifts in MNC subsidiaries', *Strategic Management Journal*, **19**: 663–81.

Tainio, R., Huolman, M. and Pulkkinen, M. (2001), 'The internationalization of capital markets: how international institutional investors are restructuring Finnish companies', in G. Morgan, P.H. Kristensen and R. Whitley (eds), *The Multinational Firm. Organizing Across Institutional and National Divides*, Oxford: Oxford University Press, pp. 153–71.

Useem, M. (1996), *Investor Capitalism*, New York: Basic Books.

Vitols, S. (2004), 'Continuity and change: making sense of the German model', *Competition and Change*, **8**(4): 331–8.

Weick, K.E. (1995), *Sensemaking in Organizations*, Thousand Oaks, CA: Sage.

Westney, E.D. and Zaheer, S. (2001), 'The multinational enterprise as an organization', in A.A. Rugman and T.L. Brewer (eds), *The Oxford Handbook of International Business*, Oxford: Oxford University Press, pp. 349–79.

Whitley, R. (2001), 'How and why are international firms different? The consequences of cross-border managerial coordination for firm characteristics and behaviour', in G. Morgan, P.H. Kristensen and R. Whitley (eds), *The Multinational Firm. Organizing Across Institutional and National Divides*, Oxford: Oxford University Press, pp. 27–68.

11. Determinants of career choice of Israeli high-technology entrepreneurs

Dov Dvir and Ayala Malach-Pines

Israel has an unusually high number of high-technology entrepreneurs and companies, and is among the world leaders in high-tech start-ups. About 4000 high-tech companies make Israel the largest concentration of high-tech companies in the world outside of California – of which 1500 are start-ups. On the cutting edge of technological development in software, telecommunications, biotechnology and information technology, Israeli high-tech and start-up companies are known for their creativity, innovation and ingenuity. The vast majority of marketing and sales activities of Israeli high-tech companies take place outside of Israel.

According to the National Science Foundation, there is no single preferred method for identifying high-technology industries. Such industries depend on science and technology innovation that leads to new or improved products and services. They generally have a substantial economic impact, fueled both by large research and development (R&D) spending, and a higher than industry average sales growth. If an industry's proportion of R&D employment is equal to at least the average proportion of R&D employment in all industries, it can be considered high-tech. The professional occupations most indicative of high R&D activity, thus of high-tech, are engineers, physical and life scientists; computer scientists; and health professional specialties. Engineering and science technicians are also employed in significant proportions in high-tech companies.

For many years, following the establishment of the State, Israel's most important industries were agriculture, light industry and labor-intensive production. A small country with limited natural resources, Israel has capitalized on its highly skilled, educated and innovative workforce. The results reveal a knowledge-based, technologically advanced market economy with first-class high-tech capabilities in the telecommunications, IT, electronics, and life sciences industries (Israel Embassy, 2005).

Israel today is made up of a population of some 7 million people with a GDP of $123.7 billion (2005). It has the world's highest number of engineers in its workforce – twice as high as the USA and Japan. The percentage of engineering students out of the whole student population was 11.9 percent in 1998 and the percentage of natural sciences and mathematics students during the same period was 14.8 percent.

Israel also has one of the most educated workforces in the world, with 20 percent of Israelis aged 25–64 holding academic degrees. Many high-tech professionals spend several years in the military in highly sophisticated technical units, where they gain invaluable experience using advanced military-generated technologies that are Israel's specialty.

Israel invests heavily in R&D. The percentage of high-tech production in the overall GDP is the highest in the world. Ninety percent of venture capital investments are channeled to start-up companies, resulting in the largest number of start-up companies in the world in proportion to its population. These start-ups contribute to about 35 percent of the growth in the information communication technology (ICT) and software fields in Israel – the main contributors to the high-tech industry. Venture capital investment, which finances approximately 50 percent of Israel's high-tech industry, is the highest in the world in relation to its GDP (Israel Embassy, 2005).

Israeli civilian high-tech exports rose by nearly 10 percent in 2005, to $16.6 billion. They represent nearly half of Israel's industrial exports, the highest percentage anywhere in the world. When defense exports are added, the figure rises to nearly $20 billion. Initial estimates are for the high-tech industry to grow again by at least 10 percent in 2006. Much growth is expected to come from the hundreds of start-ups established in recent years. More than 200 new ventures joined the ranks in 2005 alone. Many are founded by entrepreneurs looking to replicate earlier successes. The Israel Venture Association estimates that the country now has more than 2000 start-ups in various stages of development (Sandler, 2005).

Some start-ups established in the early to mid-1990s have developed into local giants, employing thousands. Among the major global leaders are companies such as Check Point Software Technologies in Internet security, Comverse Technology in telecommunications services, NICE Systems in the field of digital recording platforms, and medical-device maker Syneron Medical. Others have been gobbled up by industry giants such as Cisco Systems, which has spent more than $1 billion on buying Israeli start-ups in recent years.

The success of Israeli high-tech industry and Israeli entrepreneurs has raised curiosity worldwide, but very little academic research attention. The current chapter explores, based on two empirical studies conducted in recent years, the antecedents to the career choice of Israeli entrepreneurs.

These in-depth, exploratory investigations focused on the background and self-description of successful Israeli high-tech entrepreneurs, with the aim of identifying elements in their background – both personal and professional – that may account for their career choice.

ON THE PERSONALITY AND FAMILY BACKGROUND OF ENTREPRENEURS

Studies on the background of entrepreneurs suggest that they tend to be first-born (Hisrich and Brush, 1986; Pines et al., 2004), from ethnic and religious minority groups (Kasdan, 1965) with substantial formal education (Cooper, 1986; Pines et al., 2004), with a father who was self-employed (e.g. Cromie et al., 1992) and an involved parent or family that supported early start-up activities (Dyer and Handler, 1994; Carroll and Mosakowski, 1987; Malecki, 1997; Roberts, 1991).

As noted by Chimo-Vugalter and Lerner (Chapter 8 in this volume), some researchers believe that successful entrepreneurs have unique qualities and specific traits that determine their success. The majority of studies on the psychology of entrepreneurs are based on this belief. These studies document the distinct personality traits that tend to characterize successful entrepreneurs. The traits that are mentioned most often in these studies include: risk taking, need for control, internal locus of control, autonomy, distrust, independence, assertiveness, initiative, creativity, achievement motivation, confidence, optimism, imagination, persistence in problem solving, single mindedness, leadership, decisiveness, competitiveness and desire for applause (e.g. Bonnett and Furnham, 1991; Boyd and Vozikis, 1994; Brandstaetter, 1997; Busenitz, 1999; Cromie, 2000; Fraboni and Saltstone, 1990; Frese, 2000; Johnson, 1990; Koh, 1996; Kuratko and Hodgetts, 1995; Lynn, 1969; McClelland, 1987; Sexton and Bowman, 1985; Solomon and Winslow, 1988; Timmons, 1989; Winslow and Solomon, 1989).

However, findings regarding the psychology of entrepreneurs have not always been consistent (van Gelderen, 2000; Shaver, 1995; Watson et al., 1995). Some of these inconsistencies may be explained by findings of studies that identified different personality types capable of achieving entrepreneurial success (Cooper, 1973; Miner, 1997, 2000; Schrage, 1965). Other explanations were offered by writers who argued that entrepreneurship is a complex human trait that can be found in many people to different degrees and is not unique to entrepreneurs (van Gelderen, 2000; Shaver, 1995). A third explanation is based on the observation that 'the entrepreneurial event' is determined by the interaction of both personal and environmental factors (Malecki, 1997).

Nevertheless, the greatest critics of research on the psychology of entre-preneurship argue that the entrepreneurial personality is nothing but a myth (Shaver, 1995) and that the trait approach has failed in the case of entrepreneurs (Gartner, 1988).

One way to respond to this criticism without abandoning the trait approach to entrepreneurship is to focus on a specific group of entrepre-neurs and use a control group. This was done in a study that focused on successful Israeli entrepreneurs in the high-tech industry who were com-pared to high-ranking managers in the same industry (Pines et al., 2002). Findings of the study revealed a number of similarities (similar levels of energy, self-confidence, commitment and need for control), as well as differences, between the managers and the entrepreneurs. At the heart of these differences seemed to be a cluster of traits characterizing entre-preneurs, and significantly less so managers, all suggesting a greater identification with work and a willingness to take great risk to make dreams come true. The most notable of these traits included love of challenges, greater risk taking, initiative, independence and creativity. Managers, on the other hand, rated themselves higher in realism.

It could be argued that the traits in which entrepreneurs rated themselves higher than did managers have a high social desirability and reflect the entre-preneurs' big ego more than 'real' differences in personality. The fact that the self-ratings of managers and of the control group of self-proclaimed entrepreneurs (managers who perceive themselves as entrepreneurs, but have done nothing to pursue such a career) were significantly lower seems to suggest that this was not the case. These traits are most likely a part, if not of the entrepreneurs' personality, then of their persona.

The answer to the question why the entrepreneurs were who they were focused on their negative identification with father and greater identification with work as compared to the managers' positive identification with father and better relationship with both parents.

Psychoanalytic work with entrepreneurs (e.g. Kets de Vries, 1996; Pines, 2002, 2003; Yaffe-Yanai et al., Chapter 7 in this volume) focuses on their childhood and on the unconscious forces that determine their career choice. It portrays the childhood of entrepreneurs as often involving deprivation and turmoil, with such themes as 'escape from poverty' and 'the parent who went away' dominating their life stories. The father is portrayed as absent, remote, unpredictable and rejecting; the mother as strong, controlling, keeping the family together and assuming part of the father's traditional role. These early experiences of rejection, parental inconsistencies and control are assumed to result in considerable controlled rage, hostility, guilt and suspiciousness of people in positions of authority (Kets de Vries, 1976, 1977, 1980, 1985, 1996).

This clinical picture received tentative support in work with Israeli high-tech entrepreneurs (Pines, 2002, 2003) and in the results of two recent studies in which successful Israeli entrepreneurs were compared to high-ranking managers in high-tech industry (Pines et al., 2002; and Kaplan, Chapter 6 in this volume). The results, which showed a much better relationship between managers and their parents than between entrepreneurs and their parents, can be interpreted (as suggested by Yaffe-Yanai et al., Chapter 7 and by Kaplan, Chapter 6) as meaning that entrepreneurs tend to be, or perceive themselves as being, psychological orphans.

While both entrepreneurs and managers may have a 'father issue', the issue they have varies considerably. For the entrepreneurs, the father is a negative identification figure, whereas for the managers, the father is a positive identification figure. While both may experience an absence of a father in their childhood, for the managers the father is someone they identify with and want to get approval from (which may help to explain their desire to succeed within an organizational setting). For the entrepreneurs the father is someone they do not identify with and may even be motivated to prove wrong (which may account for their desire to break free of existing frameworks and build new ones).

In addition to family dynamics, upbringing and education are most critical factors in shaping entrepreneurs (Chimo-Vugalter and Lerner, Chapter 8 in this volume; Malecki, 1997; Roberts, 1991). A follow-up study of the Pines et al. (2002) comparison between high-tech entrepreneurs and managers focused on a unique and presumed homogeneous group of successful Israeli high-tech entrepreneurs (Pines et al., 2004). The goal of this follow-up study was to identify elements in the personal and professional background of these entrepreneurs that seem relevant to their career as entrepreneurs in general and to being Israeli entrepreneurs in the field of high technology in particular. The study involved in-depth interviews with a group of successful high-tech entrepreneurs.

Findings revealed that the vast majority of the entrepreneurs interviewed were men, over half were first-born and the vast majority came from small families (two to three children). One of the entrepreneurs explained the significance of being first-born to his entrepreneurial career: 'As the firstborn you are not afraid of adults. You are a pathfinder. No one teaches you about the world; you learn the world and represent it. It's the challenge that builds the personality of the entrepreneur, the strong ambition.'

All the entrepreneurs interviewed described themselves as actively involved in the management of their company. They had, on average, three previous places of work.

The entrepreneurs were relatively old (their average age was 45) and highly educated (their average education was 18 years), 80 percent had an academic degree (about 30 percent had a doctorate, 30 percent had an MSc. and 20 percent had a BSc.). The majority (over 60 percent) had technical education (industrial engineering, electronics, computers). Their specific field of education was typically related to their profession. Approximately half of the men served in the army in technical units; the other half were in combat units. The majority (almost two-thirds) were officers and commanded people.

ON THE INFLUENCE OF THE MILITARY SERVICE

The most poignant finding that emerged from the interview material was the influence of the army service on the career development of these high-tech entrepreneurs. Here are some examples.

The first example is of an entrepreneur who was a major in the most revered commando unit of the Israeli army, first as a fighter, then as a team commander and finally as a platoon commander. He had no doubt about the contribution of the military service to his entrepreneurial career:

> First of all, you learn to believe in yourself, because you passed very difficult tests, you passed difficult struggles, you passed things that seemed at first glance to be impossible – and you managed to pass them. So first is the self-confidence that enables you to approach new things. There are very few things that you tell your-self 'I can't do this.' On the contrary, at times it takes you time to learn what you can't do. Self-confidence is closely tied to entrepreneurship. In order to be an entrepreneur you need self-confidence, and confidence in whatever you are about to do, confidence that you are going to succeed. There are many failures along the way, and you need to be sure that despite those failures you are going to succeed! Despite the disappointments, despite things that don't line up in a straight row . . .
>
> Secondly, no one tells you what to do. You have to invent yourself every day. This too seems related to the creative abilities that are required in the army. When you are alone in the field, it's just you and God. No one will tell you what to do and where to go. In the army, you constantly struggle with creative problem solving. Not for the first time, of course, but there it is for real. In life it's a game. There it is real. If you make a mistake, you die. This builds your self-confidence.
>
> But the attitude of society towards the army also has an influence. My commando unit is considered an elite unit. Everyone treats you as if you are good, so you have to be good. People who served in combat or commando units have an advantage. It's not enough, but it's very helpful. Many entrepreneurs I know come from a similar background. Combat units, officers.

A second example is of an entrepreneur who served in an intelligence unit. He too described the army experience as very relevant to his entrepreneurial career:

> The service in the army offered me a lot of independence in terms of my thinking. There were situations in which I chose to develop a certain project as part of my

work, and I could follow it from beginning to end. I had a great deal of independence. This may be related to my career as an entrepreneur. It is also possible that the same reason that made me become an entrepreneur also made me take responsibility in the army, because you could also do the job without being independent. I think that the issue of independence is critical. After all, most of the high-tech entrepreneurs tend to be very young. I think that this very early experience with a great deal of responsibility, no matter what you do in the army, you can be a team commander or a platoon commander, you are responsible for the lives of 20–30 people, and you are only a child yourself. I think that this experience of a great personal responsibility can motivate people to think big, rather than think small.

I think that the personal responsibility is something that can give a man the feeling that he can carry out a project. This by itself doesn't develop in you entrepreneurship, unless you have entrepreneurship in your head. The experience of having the sole responsibility for a project will help you not to give up and not to give in, but rather say 'I can do it.'

A third example is of an entrepreneur who was a company commander during his army service, and who believed that it had a significant influence on his life:

It was a very significant part of my life and it influenced my character in terms of coping with stressful situations, in terms of the path I chose later, in terms of who I am, in terms of the way I look at the world . . . I felt very mature at age 21. The tasks I received influenced what I do today. The army not only shaped my character, but opened windows of opportunity for me. My entire life is a continuation of the army. At age 21, you are given responsibility for people . . . I don't see any other place in the world in which a youth of 21 gets such a responsibility for people's lives. Think about it. You put a lot on the shoulders of a youth of 21. I carried a lot of staff that it took me years to become aware of. You are in situations in which you see friends killed, it's not easy.

An entrepreneur has to have a vision, an individual vision, and a creative vision. The army puts order into things. But the army can also mislead. People who climb high and fast in the army because of their skills may miss the mark. Take a captain, who is 22 and commands a company, you are equivalent to a senior manager at age 45–50 in terms of your ability to do things, your power. You reach so high, so fast, that later on you are going to find it difficult in civilian life. It's difficult to put yourself in the right proportion.

On the other hand, the army teaches you skills. You get the tools, tools for managing things. At age 21–22, you can accomplish such things as taking a project and completing it, bringing it all the way to the end. The problem is that in civilian life the tools are different. In the army you don't have economic problems; you don't have to bring the financial issues into consideration. The army confronts you with the kind of effort and challenges that once you struggle with, everything you do afterwards seems trivial in comparison. You go for broke, and many times this is why you succeed, because you've been trained to do it; it was enforced into your consciousness.

When asked why Israel has a high percentage of entrepreneurs, he says:

It's a combination of things. First is the drive to succeed. People don't want to live without purpose. And there is social influence. The Israeli society has great influence. What others are doing influences us more than it influences people in other countries. The influence definitely exists, but not to the same extent. People are always looking at each other. And they are competitive with each other. Competitiveness is a characteristic of the Israeli society, but it is also a characteristic of the entrepreneur. I think that part of the entrepreneurial drive is competitiveness. In the army you compete in everything, every unit has its unit pride. In order to ask a person to reach his limits, you need to give him a reason; unit pride is part of the reason.

Another entrepreneur who refused to be an officer and served as a technical person during his army service described similar experiences and concluded that his career as entrepreneur had a great deal to do with his army experience:

The army is a rigid framework that rewards people who think like entrepreneurs. I remember how when I first arrived at my base, a friend called 'Danny' took me on a tour and showed me the tricks of how to 'beat the system'. He later became a Chief Executive Officer (CEO) of a large communications company . . . I like starting new things, creating something from nothing. I don't like coming to an existing place and burning out as an employer. Starting from scratch is much more interesting.

I want to work on my own terms and maximize what I can do with my time. After being drafted I was stationed in a well-known technical unit. My reputation preceded me so they knew I was good. Someone who understood me asked me to work with him. He promised I'd get the conditions I want, and I did. I really enjoyed my work with him, but I also got into trouble because I didn't fit the army structure. In the army there is hierarchy and they don't like individualists, at least not in the place I was. It annoyed people that someone does things differently. The fact that I could contribute in two hours what someone else contributes in a whole day didn't matter.

For young people who have technical education, who are involved, are independent thinkers and enjoy challenges and risk taking, the army provides opportunities for taking responsibility, for taking risks, for following entrepreneurial projects from start to finish, for competition and for team work. Indeed, serving in an elite technology-based unit, responsible for building innovative high-tech instruments, seems important to the professional and personal development of many Israeli high-tech entrepreneurs and their network of like-minded friends with whom they later go on to build joint ventures. An example is NICE Systems, one of the leading companies in the area of audio and video storage devices. The firm was established by a group of eight people who served together in the same unit, working on the development of a sophisticated electronic warfare system. They all left the military at the same time and decided to start a new venture together. Interestingly, the head of the project they worked on in the army became the general manager of that firm. Some of the other better-known companies that were established and managed by people who served in the Israeli intelligence corps include Israeli high-tech companies such as Check Point, Comverse, Electronics for Imaging (EFI), Alvarion, ECI, AudioCodes and MetaLink.

All these entrepreneurs had experience as project managers during their military service. A recent study that focused on the relationship between project managers and the projects they manage (Dvir et al., 2006) showed that managers who are high in perceiving (who tend to be flexible rather than pre-planned and prefer unpredicted events to programmed events) and who are high in intuition (who prefer the innovative to the practical and work on development rather than on production) prefer high-tech projects as compared to low-tech projects. In contrast, managers who have an avoidant attachment style (characterized by avoidance and withdrawal in times of stress) tend to avoid managing high-tech projects and prefer less innovative projects.

Besides their family dynamic and experience in the army, there is yet another influence on the career trajectory of successful Israeli high-tech entrepreneurs. Researchers seeking to explain the antecedents of entrepreneurship have focused in their studies on cultural beliefs and values, based on the assumption that rates of entrepreneurship vary from society to society because different cultures have different beliefs about the desirability and feasibility of starting a new enterprise (e.g. Peterson, 1988; Shapero and Sokol, 1982). Is there something about the Israeli culture that encourages high-tech entrepreneurship?

ON THE INFLUENCE OF THE ISRAELI CULTURE

One of the best-known Israeli characteristics is lack of respect for authority and status (the Hebrew word *hutzpa* is a well-known trade mark). A similar characteristic is the preference for direct talk (*dugri*) over what are considered by Israelis 'phony niceties'.

Israel's characteristic lack of respect for authority is viewed as the result of a democratic and egalitarian nuclear family in which children are central and parental control relatively permissive (Davids, 1983; Mikulincer et al., 1993; Peres and Katz, 1990). Cross-cultural research showing that Israelis are characterized by an extremely small power distance (Hofstede, 1991) also fits this pattern. Other cultural values encourage Israelis to face challenges, confront problems, and use active and direct coping strategies (Brodai, 1998; Pines and Aronson, 1988). All these are important values for entrepreneurs.

When trying to describe what makes an entrepreneur, one of the entrepreneurs interviewed in the Pines et al. (2004) study said:

> First of all is total loyalty to your authentic self and a burning desire to actualize it. The second thing is having dreams. The third is willingness to take risks, readiness to pay the price and take the responsibility for mistakes. The fourth, a critical one for an entrepreneur, is sticking to the goal, and persistence. The fifth, a reservoir of alternative strategies in case things don't work as planned. The sixth is the ability to recuperate quickly.

The GEM (*Global Entrepreneurship Monitor*) findings suggest that Israeli social norms stress individualism, materialism and independence. In tandem, acceptance of entrepreneurship as a driving force in the personal lives and in market development is gaining strength. The entrepreneur has become Israel's newest cultural hero and role model, a figure to be respected and emulated by large parts of the younger generation (Lerner and Avrahami, 1999).

A recent cross-cultural study of high-tech entrepreneurs as cultural heroes showed similar results (Pines et al., 2005). In the study, MBA students in Israel, the USA and Hungary were asked to compare high-tech entrepreneurs to other professionals (physicians, teachers, managers, social workers, scientists, journalists and lawyers) in terms of their perceived social status and value to society. The students were also asked to rate themselves on the traits that were identified in previous research as characterizing successful high-tech entrepreneurs, and to respond to questions that measure risk-taking tendencies.

Results of the study suggest that Israeli MBA students perceive entrepreneurs as significantly more important than do Hungarian and US students. Israeli students also seem to identify with high-tech entrepreneurs to a greater extent. Their self-descriptions were higher on five of six entrepreneurial traits that showed significant cross-cultural difference, including commitment, persistence, independence, love of challenge and initiative. The Israeli students also described themselves as significantly more likely to leave a secure job that guarantees a modest income to join a start-up company than the Hungarian and the US students.

SUMMARY

It seems that the career choice of Israeli high-tech entrepreneurs is influenced by a combination of certain personality traits, family dynamics, educational background, a unique army experience, and a culture that values entrepreneurial traits. While these personal traits, family dynamics and educational background are not unique to Israeli high-tech entrepreneurs, the kind of army experience described earlier in combination with the Israeli cultural values are very unusual and seem to indicate a good person–environment fit (e.g. Spokane et al., 2000). Military service, which in many cases requires the ability to cope with stressful challenges, independent thinking and tremendous responsibility, and provides opportunities for accomplishing projects from beginning to end, seems to fit both the Israeli character and high-tech entrepreneurship.

Many of the high-tech start-ups were initiated by entrepreneurs who had the opportunity to serve as technical personnel in elite intelligence, communication and software development units or special combat units. The proportion of such start-ups out of the total number of start-ups instituted in recent years in Israel is much larger than their proportion in the population.

The fact that Israel has one of the most educated workforces in the world, together with the traits that collectively portray Israelis (love of challenges, risk taking, initiative and independence), also affects the choices many technically educated and gifted Israelis make to be a high-tech entrepreneur. The studies on which this chapter is based are all exploratory in nature; nevertheless they generate some fascinating research questions, such as: Do Israeli high-tech entrepreneurs reflect psychological phenomena or sociological phenomena? Could the military service as officers and the high academic education be reflective of high social status by birth, as is the case in other countries? Does the experience as high-tech project managers drive people to look for a career that will be at least as challenging as what they have experienced? These are some of the questions that need to be addressed in future research.

Despite the limitations of these studies – small samples and ex-post design – they shed light on both personal and professional aspects that may account for the career choice and success of a unique group of Israeli high-tech entrepreneurs. The studies broaden the subject population of research on entrepreneurs, most of which was done in Europe and North America, to the case of Israeli high-tech entrepreneurs whose success has aroused great curiosity but very little academic research attention.

However, in order to understand the interesting phenomenon of Israel's rapid development of entrepreneurship and what the Israeli story can tell other countries that are trying to create an entrepreneurial boom, future research will need to replicate the findings of the current exploratory studies with a large representative sample of Israeli high-tech entrepreneurs. Future research should also compare successful entrepreneurs to less successful or failed entrepreneurs, and one-time entrepreneurs to serial entrepreneurs, as well as to the base population. The last should be done in order to address the research tradition on entrepreneurship that argues that entrepreneurs do not differ from the base population in terms of their personality, and that you cannot predict on the basis of personality traits who is likely to choose to be an entrepreneur and who is not (see Chimo-Vugalter and Lerner, Chapter 8 in this volume).

In summary, our exploratory studies make a modest contribution to the existing literature on entrepreneurs by identifying some of the elements in the making of successful Israeli entrepreneurs, including unique elements in their background and upbringing in a young and small country that struggles with many social, economic and defense problems, but nevertheless finds enough energy and resources to generate a flourishing high-tech industry.

REFERENCES

Bonnett, C. and Furnham, A. (1991), 'Who wants to be an entrepreneur? A study of adolescents interested in a Young Enterprise scheme', *Journal of Economic Psychology*, **12**: 465–78.

Boyd, N.G. and Vozikis, G.S. (1994), 'The influence of self-efficacy on the development of entrepreneurial intentions and actions', *Entrepreneurship Theory and Practice*, **19**: 25–38.

Brandstaetter, H. (1997), 'Becoming an entrepreneur: a question of personality structure?', *Journal of Economic Psychology*, **18**: 157–77.

Brodai, A. (1998), 'Similarities and differences in preferred coping styles in the eyes of Israeli adolescents from different cultures', *The Educational Counselor*, **7**: 37–75.

Busenitz, L.W. (1999), 'Entrepreneurial risk and strategic decision making: it's a matter of perspective', *Journal of Applied Behavioral Science*, **35**: 325–40.

Carroll, G.R. and Mosakowski, E. (1987), 'The career dynamics of self-employment', *Administrative Science Quarterly*, **32**: 570–89.

Cooper, A.C. (1973), 'Technical entrepreneurship: what do we know?', *Research and Development in Management*, **3**: 59–64.

Cooper, A.C. (1986), 'Entrepreneurship and high technology', in D.L. Sexton and R.W. Smilor (eds), *The Art and Science of Entrepreneurship*, Cambridge, MA: Ballinger, pp. 153–68.

Cromie, S. (2000), 'Enterprising behaviour of ordinary people', *European Journal of Work and Organizational Psychology*, **9**: 7–30.

Cromie, S., Callaghan, I. and Jansen, M. (1992), 'The entrepreneurial tendencies of managers: a research note', *British Journal of Management*, **3**: 1–5.

Davids, L. (1983), 'What's happening in the Israeli family? Recent demographic trends', *Israel Social Science Research*, **1**: 34–40.

Dvir, D., Sadeh, A. and Pines, A.M. (2006), 'Projects and project managers: the relationship between project managers' personality, project types and projects success', *Project Management Journal*, **37**(5): 36–48.

Dyer, W.G. and Handler, W. (1994), 'Entrepreneurship and family business: exploring the connection', *Entrepreneurship Theory and Practice*, **19**: 71–83.

Fraboni, M. and Saltstone, R. (1990), 'First and second generation entrepreneur typologies: dimensions of personality', *Journal of Social Behavior and Personality*, **5**: 105–13.

Frese, M. (2000), 'Psychological approaches to entrepreneurship', *European Journal of Work and Organisational Psychology*, **9**(1), 128.

Gartner, W.B. (1988), ' "Who is an entrepreneur?" Is the wrong question', *American Small Business Journal*, **12**: 11–31.

Hisrich, R.D. and Brush, C. (1986), 'Characteristics of the minority entrepreneur', *Journal of Small Business Management*, **24**: 1–8.

Hofstede, G. (1991), *Cultures and Organizations: Software of the Mind*, London: McGraw-Hill.

Israel Embassy (2005), *Facts and Figures, Israel: Economic Features*, www.israelemb. org/economics/ff.htm.

Johnson, B.R. (1990), 'Towards a multidimensional model of entrepreneurship: the case of achievement motivation and the entrepreneur', *Entrepreneurship Theory and Practice*, **14**: 39–54.

Kasdan, L. (1965), 'Family structure, migration and the entrepreneur', *Comparative Study of Society*, **7**(4): 345–57.

Kets de Vries, M.F.R. (1976), 'What makes entrepreneurs entrepreneurial?', *Business and Society Review*, **17**: 18–23.

Kets de Vries, M.F.R. (1977), 'The entrepreneurial personality: a person at the cross-roads', *Journal of Management Studies*, **14**: 34–58.

Kets de Vries, M.F.R. (1980), 'Stress and the entrepreneur', in C.L. Cooper and R. Payne (eds), *Current Concerns in Occupational Stress*, New York: John Wiley and Sons.

Kets de Vries, M.F.R. (1985), 'The dark side of entrepreneurship', *Harvard Business Review*, **85**: 160–68.

Kets de Vries, M.F.R. (1996), 'The anatomy of the entrepreneur', *Human Relations*, **49**: 853–83.

Koh, H.C. (1996), 'Testing hypotheses of entrepreneurial characteristics', *Journal of Managerial Psychology*, **11**: 12–25.

Kuratko, D.F. and Hodgetts, R.M. (1995), *Entrepreneurship*, Fort Worth, TX: Dryden Press.

Lerner, M. and Avrahami, Y. (1999), 'Israel executive report. Research on entrepreneurship and economic growth', Special Report, *Global Entrepreneurship Monitor*.

Lynn, R. (1969), 'Personality characteristics of a group of entrepreneurs', *Occupational Psychology*, **43**: 151–2.

Malecki, E.J. (1997), 'Entrepreneurs, networks, and economic development', in J.A. Katz and R.H. Brockhaus (eds), *Advances in Entrepreneurship, Firm Emergence and Growth*, London: JAI Press, pp. 57–118.

McCelland, D.C. (1987), 'Characteristics of successful entrepreneurs', *Journal of Creative Behavior*, **21**: 219–33.

Mikulincer, M., Weller, A. and Florian, V. (1993), 'Sense of closeness to parents and family rulers: a study of Arab and Jewish youth in Israel', *International Journal of Psychology*, **28**: 323–35.

Miner, J. (1997), *The Psychological Typology of Successful Entrepreneurs*, Westport, CT: Quorum Books/Greenwood Publishing Group.

Miner, J. (2000), 'Testing the psychological typology entrepreneurship using business founders', *Journal of Applied Behavioral Science*, **36**: 43–69.

Peres, Y. and Katz, R. (1990), 'The family in Israel: change and continuity', in R. Bar Yosef and L. Shamgar-Hendelman (eds), *Families in Israel*, Jerusalem: Academon (in Hebrew), pp. 115–24.

Peterson, R.A. (1988), 'Understanding and encouraging entrepreneurship internationally', *Journal of Small Business Management*, **26**: 1–7.

Pines, A.M. (2002), 'The female entrepreneur: burnout treated using a psychodynamic existential approach', *Clinical Case Studies*, **1**: 171–81.

Pines, A.M. (2003), 'Unconscious influences on career choice: entrepreneur vs. manager', *Australian Journal of Career Development*, **12**: 7–18.

Pines, A.M. and Aronson, E. (1988), *Career Burnout: Causes and Cures*, New York: Free Press.

Pines, A.M., Dvir, D. and Sadeh, A. (2004), 'The making of Israeli high-technology entrepreneurs: an exploratory study', *The Journal of Entrepreneurship*, **13**: 30–52.

Pines, A.M., Sadeh, A., Dvir, D. and Yanai, O. (2002), 'Entrepreneurs and managers: similar yet different', *The International Journal of Organizational Analysis*, **10**: 172–90.

Pines, A.M., Levy, H., Utasi, A. and Hill, T.L. (2005), 'Entrepreneurs as cultural heroes: a cross-cultural, interdisciplinary perspective', *Journal of Managerial Psychology*, **20**: 541–55.

Roberts, E.B. (1991), *Entrepreneurs in High Technology*, New York: Oxford University Press.

Sandler, N. (2005), 'Israel's reborn tech boom', *BusinessWeek online*, 20 December.

Schrage, H. (1965), 'The R and D entrepreneur: profile of success', *Harvard Business Review*, **43**: 56–69.

Sexton, D.L. and Bowman, N. (1985), 'The entrepreneur: a capable executive and more', *Journal of Business Venturing*, **1**: 129–40.

Shapero, A. and Sokol, L. (1982), 'The social dimensions of entrepreneurship', in C.A. Kent, D.L. Sexton and K.H. Vesper (eds), *Encyclopedia of Entrepreneurship*, Englewood Cliffs, NJ: Prentice-Hall, pp. 72–88.

Shaver, K. (1995), 'The entrepreneurial personality myth', *Business and Economic Review*, **41**: 20–23.

Solomon, G.T. and Winslow, E.K. (1988), 'Toward a descriptive profile of the entrepreneur', *Journal of Creative Behavior*, **22**: 162–71.

Spokane, A.R., Meir, E.I. and Catalano, M. (2000), 'Person–environment congruence and Holland's theory: a review and reconsideration', *Journal of Vocational Behavior*, **57**: 137–87.

Timmons, S.A. (1989), *The Entrepreneurial Mind*, Andover, MA: Crick House Publishing.

van Gelderen, M.W. (2000), 'Enterprising behavior of ordinary people', *European Journal of Work and Organisational Psychology*, **9**: 81–8.

Watson, W., Ponthieu, L. and Doster, J. (1995), 'Business owner–managers' descriptions of entrepreneurship: a content analysis', *Journal of Constructivist Psychology*, **8**: 33–51.

Winslow, E.K. and Solomon, G.T. (1989), 'Further development of a descriptive profile of entrepreneurs', *Journal of Creative Behavior*, **23**: 149–61.

PART IV

Multidisciplinary Perspectives on Career
Development and MBA Education

12. Career development and values change among MBA students: a theoretical perspective and practical avenues

Eran Vigoda-Gadot and Shmulik Grimland

INTRODUCTION

Recent decades have witnessed a growing interest in political and citizenship values as related to modernized states and societies (e.g. Almond and Verba, 1963; Barber, 1984; Brady et al., 1995; Cohen and Vigoda, 1998, 2000). These have received little, if any, attention in career management literature (e.g. Altman and Post, 1996; Derr, 1986; Hall, 1996b; Super, 1986; Niles and Goodnough, 1996; Greenhaus, 1987; Gutteridge et al., 1993) and, as far as could be found, no study has dealt with the citizenship values of future-leading cadre in management, business or administration. As this group is expected to have a profound effect on a nation's economic and social development as well as general well-being, it is important to look at the citizenship values of those in a position to become leaders, eventually, in their respective countries.

Contemporary organizations face an increasingly broad role in the postmodern society that is based in large part on an effective blend of values and business strategies (Hofstede, 1991; Holland, 1985). Corporate responsibility that fosters a value-positive orientation contributes to superior performance through better risk management, improved organizational functioning, increased shareholder confidence and enhanced public standing. Thus, today, corporate accountability is as vital to the bottom line as an effective business model. This is why students of management (i.e. MBAs) or students of public administration (i.e. MPAs) are urged to assume a broad stakeholder model of the firm or the public agency, one that consists of ethics, culture, environmental standards, product safety and community investment values (Paine, 2003). This is the very group for which citizenship values matter the most.

Since corporations, MBAs and MPAs are global phenomena, we suggest a theoretical framework that tries to explain how citizenry values can be nurtured among this group of future influential individuals. We also argue that citizenship behavior improves organizational functioning by creating social capital as well as increasing efficiency and enhancing productivity (Bolino et al., 2002). There is also an empirical indication that citizenship behavior is related to overall organizational effectiveness (Koys, 2001; Podsakoff et al., 2000). Moreover, on the communal or national level, citizenship behavior is related to political involvement and participation, community attachment and connectedness (Battisoni and Hudson, 1997; Verba et al., 1995) that are all positive aspects of human conduct in the society. This chapter is, therefore, an attempt to portray directions in the future study of values among tomorrow's leaders in business management and public administration. The original idea was stimulated by an ongoing multinational study and longitudinal data collection from several countries across the globe. The theoretical framework focuses on several variables that represent the individual's good-citizenship values and political perceptions (e.g. organizational citizenship behavior – OCB, altruism, charity, perceptions towards democracy, and political efficacy) that are dominant in today's discourse of modern nations.

The chapter opens with a general discussion of career development in modern societies. It then tries to correlate the theory of career development with values change and especially with the evolution of good-citizenship values as suggested in a model proposed by Vigoda and Golembiewski (2001). It is suggested that improving the citizenship values of graduate MBA and MPA students, who choose a career in business or in government administration, may have a major impact on a country's economic development, modernity, and social as well as political standing in the international arena. Following Perry and Katula (2001), this is done by developing: life skills, such as the ability to formulate solutions to social problems, awareness of the world, and ability to work cooperatively (Aguirre International, 1999; Astin and Sax, 1998); higher ability to formulate solutions to social problems (Eyler et al., 1997); civic engagement (Brehm and Rahn, 1997); sense of community (Chavis and Wandersman, 1990); social responsibility, such as compassion for the disenfranchised of society (Fenzel and Leary, 1997); and citizen efficacy and social conscience (Marks, 1994). It is further suggested that this knowledge is viable for future research in the field that may better link career management with social and political values of the individual and the state.

TOWARDS MODERN CAREERS: THE PROTEAN APPROACH AND THE MEANING OF VALUES

One characteristic of modern careers is frequent job change, either caused by dynamic market economics or initiated by the individual (Hall and Chandler, 2005; Peiperl and Baruch, 1997). The single lifelong employment relationship with one employer tends to be rarer, with people tending to have a multiple career in different organizations and areas (Arthur et al., 2005; DeFillipi and Arthur, 1994). In order to succeed in different stages of their career, people need to plan their career carefully, utilize their investment in education and the experience gained from their earlier career stages.

The study of careers has benefited from a number of theoretical perspectives. Some sociologists view the career as an issue that is related to social functioning (Barley, 1989; Featherman and Hauser, 1978), whereas psychologists tend to consider the career as a profession and a means of self-development and enrichment (Holland, 1985; Shepard, 1984). Much emphasis has been placed on the compatibility between the personality of the worker and his/her profession, while seeing the benefit for both the individual and the organization. Contemporary frameworks see the career as a multidisciplinary issue. It comprises aspects from psychology, sociology, anthropology, economics and political science. Issues such as status and rank; wealth, property and earning capacity; social reputation, prestige and influence; knowledge and skills; friendship and network connections; health and well-being; culture and career; labor markets and economic conditions are discussed in career research. In modern times, the career has evolved from a classical concept of employment or profession to have a much wider meaning.

One of the leading career research perspectives nowadays is the notion of protean career, where the person, not the organization, is in charge of career development. The protean career is characterized by greater mobility, a more holistic life perspective and developmental progression (Hall, 1996a; Briscoe et al., 2006). The career is driven by personal values and the main success criteria are subjective (Hall, 2004; Baruch and Blenkinsopp, Chapter 14 in this volume). This follows from today's changeable employment conditions, which have altered what employees can expect and what they want from the employment relationship (Arthur et al., 2005). Downsizing processes and high competition in the local and global economy have changed people beliefs. Now they know that even if they work well, they could lose their job (Hall and Moss, 1998). In response to this uncertainty, employees have developed career tactics in which the career is viewed as the development of self (Arthur et al., 2005; Hall and Chandler,

Table 12.1   From traditional career to protean career, and the centrality of values

Issue	Protean career	Traditional career
Who is in charge?	Person	Organization
Degree of mobility	High	Lower
Success criteria	Psychological success	Position level – salary
Key attitudes	Work satisfaction – professional commitment	Organizational commitment
Core values	Freedom – growth – calling (find meaning in work) – adaptability – self-fulfillment – altruism – civic virtues (at organizational, communal and national levels)	Advancement – loyalty – obedience

2005). People who are protean-type careerists are continual learners, always open to new possibilities, viewing their career as a series of learning cycles (Hall and Mirvis, 1996). In order to proceed successfully with a protean career, people need to acquire two 'metacompetencies': adaptability and self awareness (Hall, 2004). This requirement follows from the fact that the world changes so fast that assessing people and developing a fixed set of competencies looks less relevant to successful performance. It is more effective to develop greater adaptability and self-awareness for the employees, which will equip them to learn from their experiences and develop new skills on their own (Briscoe and Hall, 1997). Hall (2004) claims that in order to advance successfully, it is important to develop both metacompetancies. A person with high adaptability and low self-awareness is not following his or her path, but someone else's. An individual with high self-awareness and low adaptability is one who avoids taking action. A person who is low in adaptability and self-awareness is in a state of rigidity, only following orders (Hall, 2004).

Following Hall (2004) and Hall and Chandler (2005), Table 12.1 sums up the main differences between the traditional and the protean career, while emphasizing the centrality of citizenship values.

Following this key aspect, the current chapter tries to show how the mechanism of values–career acts and demonstrates it using MBA/MPA students at the beginning of their career path.

THE RELATIONSHIP BETWEEN MODERN CAREERS AND VALUES: THEORETICAL PERSPECTIVES

The conceptual framework of this work is based on two sources, COR (conservation of resources) and values priority relevance. The COR framework encloses several stress theories and tackles stress and strain relationships (Hobfoll, 1989; Wright and Hobfoll, 2004). Lazarus and Folkman (1984, p. 19) defined stress as 'a particular relationship between the person and the environment that is appraised by the person as taxing or exceeding his or her resources and endangering his or her well being'. Implicit in this definition is that stress is not the result of an imbalance between objective demands and response capabilities, but the perception of such an imbalance. The COR framework suggests that stress is most likely to be experienced when there is an actual loss of resources, there is a perceived threat of resource loss, a situation in which individual resources are perceived to be inadequate to meet work demands, or when the anticipated returns are not obtained on investment of resources (Hobfoll, 1989, 2001). COR theory assumes that there are four prime resource categories – (a) object resources (e.g. home); (b) condition resources (e.g. socioeconomic status); (c) personal resources (e.g. self-esteem or values); (d) energy resources (e.g. time) – that are valued by the individual and serve as means for the attainment of goals (Freund and Riediger, 2001). During stressful situations the individual has to offset one resource loss with other resources. After initial loss, fewer resources are available for stress resistance, and the person is less resilient and more vulnerable to stressors (Hobfoll, 1989). Hobfoll and Shirom (2000) proposed four conclusions from COR theory: (a) individuals must bring in resources in order to prevent the loss of resources; (b) individuals with a greater pool of resources are less susceptible to resource loss and are more capable of resource gain; (c) those individuals who do not have access to strong resource pools are more likely to experience increased resource loss; (d) strong resource pools lead to greater likelihood that the individual will seek opportunities to risk resources for increased resource gain. Therefore resources are exhaustible commodities; once spent they are not available for other tasks or goals. In the context of career development, the COR perspective enables individuals to concentrate their energies and resources in the most promising direction relevant to their career development. Inasmuch as a protean career is value driven and core values are the engine that moves an individual's work life, one can expect values such as calling or self-fulfillment, in domains beyond the organizational setting (communal or national), to affect career development. Typical for this behavior will be working in a non-profit organization, where a combination of some earning and doing well for others gives meaning and fulfills individuals' inner drives (values).

The second framework is personal values and priority of values. Value is defined as 'an enduring belief that a specific mode or end-state of existence is personally or socially preferable to an opposite mode of conduct or end state of existence' (Rokeach, 1973, p. 5). Examples of values (which are also culture dependent) are social recognition, inner harmony, meaning in life and sense of belonging (Sagiv and Schwartz, 2000). Values are considered to be a dominant force in people's lives (Rokeach, 1973). In the words of Rokeach (1973, p. 3), 'the consequences of human values will be manifested in virtually all phenomena'. As Sagiv and Schwartz (2000) note, values are desirable goals, varying in importance, that serve as guiding principles in people's lives. Values have been shown to be consistent from one situation to another (Sexton and Bowman-Upton, 1991) and affect individuals' occupational choice and vocational behavior (Brief et al., 1979; Walker et al., 1982). Moreover, values have been found to be predictive of career fit, and individuals are looking for careers that are congruent with their value systems (Beutell and Brenner, 1986; Brenner et al., 1988). The value priority view implies that individuals are motivated by their important personal values and act accordingly (Sagiv and Schwartz, 2000). Thus, action taken in pursuit of each type of value may conflict or be compatible with the pursuit of other values. According to Sagiv and Schwartz (2000), some values, such as achievement, tradition and security, are correlated to subjective well-being. Thus, values and career choice, as well as career development, may be mutually related. Values may lead to career choice in the early stages of vocational search, but career choice and development may also affect one's values during the training process, especially during the crucial stages of education and professional schooling. A potential outcome of the career–values association may be that MBA/MPA students (who are quite advanced in their professional lives and who were exposed to additional social domains during their studies) can re-prioritize their values and follow a career with a new set of drivers (values) such as citizenship values.

Values Priority Approach

As seen previously, the new type of career is driven by individual values, and success is measured psychologically, where satisfaction and well-being are the faces of this success (Hall, 2004; Heslin, 2005; Hall and Chandler, 2005). Two lines of research will now be demonstrated connecting values priority: well-being and job-related values (Sagiv and Schwartz, 2000; Gooderham et al., 2004).

Sagiv and Schwartz (2000) investigated the relationship between value priorities and both cognitive and affective aspects of subjective well-being. They have shown that there are two ways in which individuals' differences are related to subjective well-being. In the first, individuals' subjective well-being might depend upon their profile of value priorities. People for whom particular values are highly important may have a more positive sense of well-being than persons guided by a different set of values. Thus subjective well-being may be associated with emphasizing specific values (e.g. compassion) rather than others (e.g. security). The second way suggests that realizing any of one's values increases personal well-being. In other words, people's sense of well-being may be unrelated to their value profile, depending instead upon how successful they are in satisfying whatever values are important to them. Sagiv and Schwarz's research was based on Schwartz's (1992) theory of universals in the content and structure of basic values. Schwartz (1992) developed ten motivationally distinct types of values from universal requirements of human existence. The critical content aspect that distinguishes among the different values is the type of motivational goals they express. An example of motivational value is 'Achievement: personal success through demonstrating competence according to social standards' (Sagiv and Schwartz, 2000, p. 179).

Sagiv and Schwartz's sample was based on students (in psychology and business administration) and adults in Israel and Germany. Their main results were that achievement, self-direction, stimulation, tradition, conformity and security values were correlated with affective well-being. An additional result that came out of their research was that congruity between people's values and their environment promotes well-being regardless of the particular values to which people attribute importance. People are likely to experience a positive sense of well-being when they emphasize the same value that prevails in their environment.

An additional perspective of interest is the relationship between job-related values and students, in the context of the present chapter especially those in business/political administration and in relation to gender. Business students have traditionally held materialistic job-related values (Cavanagh, 1984). Unfortunately, there doesn't seem to be any research related to public administration graduates. Following Gooderham et al. (2000), materialistic job values are: high annual salary, good physical working conditions and rapid career progress; non-materialistic job values are: interesting work tasks, good social relations, development of personal qualifications, variation in work tasks, agreement between job requirement and one's own abilities, high degree of job autonomy, job security and flexible work hours. It is interesting to note that the taxonomy of these job values follows the modern distinction between the traditional and the protean career.

Traditionally, studies (in the American culture) found gender differences related to job values: young women were more concerned with the well-being of others, they were less likely than young men to accept materialism and competition, and were more likely than young men to emphasize the importance of finding meaning in life (Beutel and Marini, 1995). Similar results were found in a Scandinavian sample (Nilsen, 1992). Nowadays, there is a shift in gender differences related to job values. Research in American and Scandinavian samples shows that gender-based differences in job-related values are decreasing (Marini et al., 1996; Gooderham et al., 2004). Based on a Norwegian sample, there is a small difference between male and female students, where female students are more likely than male students to favor non-materialistic job values (Gooderham et al., 2004).

FOSTERING GOOD-CITIZENSHIP VALUES IN GRADUATE STUDIES: SOCIAL, POLITICAL AND EDUCATIONAL IMPLICATIONS

Based on the theoretical framework suggested thus far, it is possible to explain how job values are changing in recent years and in what context this change should be analyzed. Following Gooderham et al. (2004), changing values can be explained by motivation theory. Motivation theory implies that there are two main work motives: the first is instrumental or existential and the second relates to expressive outcomes (i.e. Maslow, 1954; Herzberg, 1966; Alderfer, 1969). Instrumental motives are income and rapid career progress, whereas expressive motives are the possibility of personal growth and self-actualization. These two modes are not exclusive; they can reside concurrently in the same individual (Alderfer, 1969). Moreover, motivation profiles are not static. Baethge (1992) argues that Western society is becoming more and more individualistic as a consequence of modernization processes strengthened by the welfare state. Baehtge (1992) also suggests that changes involving education and work lifestyle have a high impact on value orientation of young German adults. Gooderham et al. (2004) studied a Norwegian sample and found that personal development is a major motivational force among students of both genders, they also found that men are significantly more materialistic than women, but the difference is not very great.

Maccoby (1988) claims that the changes in work motivation have their origin in changes in the social norms that started in the 1960s in the USA. The young generations were shaped by an increase in the standard of living, by new political movements that attacked bureaucracy as an organizational model, by higher emphasis on individuals' rights, by new technology and growing participation of women in the labor force. Processes such as global competition, liberalized trade regimes, and developments in information and communication technologies have delayered and flattened bureaucratic industrial hierarchies all in order to achieve flexibility and survivability (Gooderham et al., 2004; Maccoby, 1988). As Maccoby (1988, p. 20) argues, 'As organizations flatten out, there will be less opportunity for promotion. The traditional incentives of hierarchy, money, status and power will be in short supply.' Applying the COR principle here will imply that people will now shift to values that are more easily obtained, namely less materialistic and more growth oriented – a typical protean career tenet. With the changes in the public and private sectors and the emergence of a new sector, the non-profit one, where good-citizenship values are leading non-profit organizations, MBA/MPA students can expand their umbrella of values and develop a career oriented toward 'calling' and self-fulfillment as good-citizenship values (e.g. altruism or charity).

On what level should the new work values change be analyzed? Following Vigoda and Golembiewski's (2001) line of thought (which was applied originally to citizenship behavior), it is suggested to research the changes in values at the individual and the collective level. The individual level comprises the altruism and voluntarism of persons in the national, communal and organizational setting. The collective level includes organized or semi-organized behaviors represented by interest groups, volunteers' associations, volunteers' programs and non-profit organizations. The individual level refers to personal actions and reactions taken by the individual; these actions are spontaneous actions of unorganized persons who do altruistic actions aimed at enhancing the prosperity and development of their environment. Individuals may show compassion for others by contributing time, money and other resources to help the unable and provide assistance for others whenever the situation requires it without seeking any personal advantage or compensation (Vigoda and Golembiewski, 2001). The collective level comprises semi-organized and fully organized actions initiated by groups of individuals. This type of activity emerges when a group shares mutual interests and all members are willing to be actively involved in collective efforts. Typical groups are neighborhood associations, *ad hoc* groups that seek limited ecological goals, volunteer programs inside organizations and even altruistic support groups offering help to those in need from others that have experienced similar needs (e.g. supporting families in distress, etc.).

The collective level of analysis also includes highly organized and fully institutional collective endeavors. The best representative of this category is the not-for-profit sector (Vigoda and Golembiewski, 2001). The values level of analysis can also be sharpened by applying the two-dimensional

*Table 12.2   Good-citizenship behavior and value-oriented career
development of MBA/MPA students*

	Organizational	Communal & National
Individual	Micro-citizenship → employees' performance	Macro-citizenship → personal welfare
	Enriching MBA/MPA students with values of helping other individuals (i.e. OCB-I)	**Enriching MBA/MPA students with values of helping individuals in the community (i.e. altruism, charity)**
Collective	Midi-citizenship → organizational performance	Meta-citizenship → social welfare
	Enriching MBA/MPA students with values of helping the organizational community (i.e. OCB-O)	**Enriching MBA/MPA students with values of helping the state and the society (i.e. perceptions towards democracy, political efficacy)**

construct proposed by Vigoda and Golembiewski (2001) to the multidimensional concept of citizenship behavior and the public service system. In the context of values impact analysis, it will be two-axes research, one to include the individual and collective level, and the second to include the setting level, i.e. the organizational and communal/national level (see Table 12.2). By carrying out simultaneous research in both domains, a better understanding of values and priority of values impact may be achieved. First we will explain the different domains of the analysis and later on how MBA/MPA schools can reveal these values to different student populations.

The first domain of analysis is the area of the individual and organizational level. This domain is highly relevant to the MBA and MPA students, because most of them are working and studying concurrently, especially the executive MBA/MPA students. Employees may present a high level of participation in workplace activities and greater willingness to support others even when not asked or ordered. These are what Organ (1988) calls 'good organizational citizens'. Organ (1988) originally proposed five types of organizational citizenship behavior (OCB): conscientiousness, sportsmanship, courtesy, altruism and civic virtues. Conscientiousness refers to the extent to which an individual is punctual, high in attendance and goes beyond normal requirements and expectations. Sportsmanship refers to the extent to which an individual does not complain unnecessarily or makes a big deal out of small issues. Courtesy ascribes behaviors that prevent problems from occurring to others by doing things such as giving advance notice and passing along information. Altruism refers to behaviors that help others with existing job-related problems. Civic virtue refers to the extent to which one contributes to political issues in an organization in a responsible manner. Later on, an additional distinction was proposed, OCBs directed at other individuals (OCB-I) and OCBs not directed at any specific employee but that benefit the organization (OCB-O) (Williams and Anderson, 1991). Organ (1997) suggested that OCB-I should include the dimensions of altruism and courtesy, while OCB-O relates to conscientiousness. Recent work by Coleman and Borman (2000) suggests that OCB-O may include civic virtue as well. The good-citizen employee differs from other individuals in the organization who show lower levels of citizenship behavior or absolutely no positive behaviors. Positive behavior in an organizational setting has been shown to have a direct and significant impact on employees' performance (Vigoda, 2000). Using organizational citizenship behavior measures can probably distinguish different types of employees in the organization and very likely improve the explanatory power and predictability of organizational-behavior models (Vigoda and Golembiewski, 2001). Enriching organizations with employees who are better organizational citizens may have an educational spillover effect on the public, improve the image of organizations and make the contact with citizens more fruitful and efficient both economically and socially.

The second domain of analysis is the collective and organizational level, and refers to actions taken inside the organization based on the collective voice groups of individuals, rather then individual actions. This activity is fashioned by groups for the sake of other groups or for the sake of the organization as a whole. The group's activities focus on better attainment of wider objectives and goals in the workplace, not only on personal targets or interests. Methods such as quality circles, team-building strategies and management by objectives emphasize the general encouragement of work groups to become more actively entrepreneurial at various stages of production (Hirschman, 1970). Groups are more powerful than detached individuals and set more challenging goals, which are later translated into a massive improvement in goods and services (Vigoda and Golembiewski, 2001). Collective action also enhances communitarianism and a sense of cooperation that can spill over into extra-organizational environments (Sobel, 1993). In this way organizations can serve as habitats for the growth of citizenship awareness and the development of sensitivity toward others, in organizations or social groups (Vigoda and Golembiewski, 2001).

The third domain of analysis is individuals' activity on the national and communal level. In this domain, people act for the sake of others in the wider society. They are ready to express their altruistic tendencies and willingness to help other citizens in the national or communal arena. People's spontaneous actions are aimed at enhancing the prosperity and development of the environment in general, by means that increase the welfare of their fellow citizens. People may help others by showing tenderness, kindness or generosity. They can contribute time or money to the disabled and provide assistance for children in need, elders, minorities or other less able groups. They seek no personal advantage or compensation. People in the intimate workplace may learn how to use their personal resources more effectively and then transfer them into the wider society (Peterson, 1990). An additional characteristic of this domain is that people engaged here act one-on-one or one-on-group, avoiding any relationship with organized groups of volunteer associations (Vigoda and Golombiewski, 2001).

The last domain is the collective and national/communal level. Here people act in a way that arises from altruistic dispositions, conscientiousness and extensive acceptability of constructive citizenship duties and responsibilities. Typical actions involve participation in associations and non-profit organizations, while more and more organized citizens are taking action when the state is unable or unwilling to do so (Vigoda and Golembiewski, 2001).

To sum up the mechanisms relating protean career–values–citizenship values and the domains of analysis, the following can be asserted: with the change in labor markets, globally and locally, new types of career have emerged which are value driven; consequently, citizenships values have a higher impact on individuals' driving forces (e.g. careers). Because the domains of life–work activities are so intertwined and the congruency impact of values and the environment looks so complicated, an analysis that blends together individual/collective and organizational/communal and national activities probably provides a better understanding of people's behaviors.

In order for the above-mentioned activities (based on inner values) to be revealed to MBA/MPA students, the following activities are proposed; some of them are already implemented in the Israeli academic environment: to broaden the sample entering MBA/MPA studies to sectors such as natural sciences, humanities, behavioral sciences or education; to include case studies in non-profit organizations; to encourage participation in studies in other fields, such as environment, health, law or social work, and to require mandatory activity in non-profit organizations as a part of the course. These activities will expose students to others, and may influence and shift their values towards good-citizenship behavior, which may enable a richer self-fulfilling career.

SUMMARY AND IMPLICATIONS

With the emergence of new types of careers, especially the protean one, which is value-driven, relating values and career development may prove a good explanatory framework. This is a highly relevant issue, mainly due to the fact that values and careers are dominant forces in the lives of individuals and societies, especially in the present dynamic and turbulent times. By relating career development and values among MBA/MPA students, a prominent future group, a better understanding can be achieved of their future behaviors in different settings – organizational, communal and national. The proposed theoretical model of good-citizenship values, which relates individual/collective values to different settings, can map better the impact of the association career–values–well-being. This better understanding may help to improve organizational performance, and communal and national welfare. An additional advantage of the multidimensional good-citizenship values model is that it enables us to examine value changes in more complex environments and consequently predict social behaviors (related to career) of MBA/MPA degrees holders and others in a more realistic way. For example, it can include an emerging sector beyond the public and private sectors such as the non-profit sector, which is service oriented, measured by performance indicators different from those of the private or public sector, and is conducted by a different organizational culture.

Values and career development are complex issues, and the full relationship between them has potential for additional research. In order to understand better the complicated relationship between values (with emphasis on citizenship values) and successful career development, the following investigations are proposed: the relationship between values and different concurrent environments, especially in different settings such as organizational, communal and national; to get a better understanding of both direct and mediated/moderated relationships between values and outcomes, such as career or performance (in the organizational or societal environment); the impact of value changes on career development and success in different cultural settings, European and Asian; the values and careers of MPA students and graduate populations, mainly in different communal and national environments; comparing additional populations such as engineering, law, natural sciences and humanities; career and values in the non-profit sector; and the impact of gender and different types of marital associations on the triangular mechanism of career–values–citizenship values.

REFERENCES

Aguirre International (1999), *Making a Difference: Impact of AmeriCorps State/national Direct on Members and Communities 1994–1995 and 1995–1996*, Washington, DC: Corporation for National Service.

Alderfer, I.O. (1969), 'An empirical test of a new theory of human needs', *Organizational Behavior and Human Performance*, **4**: 142–75.

Almond, G.A. and Verba, S. (1963), *The Civic Culture: Political Attitudes and Democracy in Five Nations: An Analytic Study*, Boston, MA: Little Brown.

Altman, B.W. and Post, J.E. (1996), 'Beyond the "social contract"', in Douglas T. Hall and Associates (eds), *The Career is Dead – Long Live the Career*, San Francisco, CA: Jossey-Bass, pp. 46–71.

Arthur, M.B., Khapova, S.N. and Wilderom, C.P.M. (2005), 'Career success in a boundaryless career world', *Journal of Organizational Behavior*, **26**: 177–202.

Astin, A.W. and Sax, L.J. (1998), 'How undergraduates are affected by service participation', *Journal of Collage Student Development*, **39**: 251–63.

Baethge, M. (1992), 'Changes in work and education as constituting factors of social identity. Theoretical and political implications', in T. Halvorsen and O.J. Olsen (eds), *Det kvalifsete samfunn?*, Oslo: Ad Notam Gyldental, pp. 22–35.

Barber, B. (1984), *Strong Democracy: Participatory Politics for a New Age*, Berkeley, CA: University of California Press.

Barley, S.R. (1989), 'Careers, identities and institutions: the legacy of Chicago School of sociology', in M.B. Arthur, D.T. Hall and B.S. Lawrence (eds), *Handbook of Career Theory*, Cambridge: Cambridge University Press, pp. 41–66.

Battisoni, R.M. and Hudson, W.E. (1997), *Experiencing Citizenship: Concepts and Models for Service-learning in Political Science*, Washington, DC: American Association for Higher Education.

Beutel, A.M. and Marini, M.M. (1995), 'Gender and values', *American Sociological Review*, **60**: 436–48.

Beutell, N.J. and Brenner, O.C. (1986), 'Sex differences in work values', *Journal of Vocational Behavior*, **28**: 29–41.

Bolino, M.C., Turnley, W.H. and Bloodgood, J.M. (2002), 'Citizenship behavior and creation of social capital in organizations', *Academy of Management Review*, **27**: 505–22.

Brady, H.E., Verba, S. and Schlozman, K.L. (1995), 'Beyond SES: a resource model of political participation', *American Political Science Review*, **89**: 271–94.

Brehm, J. and Rahn, W. (1997), 'Individual-level evidence of causes and consequences of social capital', *American Journal of Political Science*, **41**: 999–1023.

Brenner, O.C., Blazinni, A.P. and Greenhaus, J.H. (1988), 'An examination of race and sex differences in managerial work values', *Journal of Vocational Behavior*, **32**: 336–44.

Brief, A.P., Van Sell, M. and Aldag, R.J. (1979), 'Vocational decision making among women: implications for organizational behavior', *Academy of Management Review*, **4**: 521–30.

Briscoe, J.P. and Hall, D.T. (1997), 'Grooming and picking leaders: using competency frameworks: do they work? An alternative approach and new guidelines for practice', *Organizational Dynamics*, Autumn: 37–51.

Briscoe, J.P., Hall, D.T. and Frautchy DeMuth, R.L. (2006), 'Protean and boundaryless careers: an empirical exploration', *Journal of Vocational Behavior*, **69**: 30–47.

Cavanagh, G.F. (1984), *American Business Values*, 2nd edn, Englewood Cliffs, NJ: Prentice-Hall.

Chavis, D.M. and Wandersman, A. (1990), 'Sense of community in the urban environment: a catalyst for participation and community development', *American Journal of Community Psychology*, **18**: 55–81.

Cohen, A. and Vigoda, E. (1998), 'The growth value of good citizenship: an examination of the relationship between civic behavior and involvement in the job', *Applied Psychology: An International Review*, **47**: 559–70.

Cohen, A. and Vigoda, E. (2000), 'Do good citizens make good organizational citizens? An empirical examination of the effects of citizenship behaviors and orientations on organizational citizenship behavior', *Administration and Society*, **32**: 596–624.

Coleman, V.I. and Borman, W.C. (2000), 'Investigating the underlying structure of the citizenship performance domain', *Human Resource Management Review*, **10**: 25–44.

DeFillipi, R.J. and Arthur, M.B. (1994), 'The boundaryless career: a competency-based perspective', *Journal of Organizational Behavior*, **15**: 307–24.

Derr, C.B. (1986), *Managing the New Careerists*, London: Jossey-Bass.

Eyler, J., Giles, D., Root, S. and Price, J. (1997), 'Service learning and the development of expert citizens', paper presented at the annual meeting of American Educational Research Association, Chicago, IL, March.

Featherman, D.L. and Hauser, R.M. (1978), *Opportunity and Change*, New York: Academic Press.

Fenzel, M.L. and Leary, T. (1997), 'Evaluating outcomes of service learning courses at parochial schools', paper presented at the annual meeting of American Educational Research Association, Chicago, IL, March.

Freund, A.M. and Riediger, M. (2001), 'What I have and what I do: the role of resource loss and gain throughout life', *Applied Psychology: An International Review*, **50**: 370–80.

Gooderham, P., Nordhaug, O., Ringdal, K. and Birkelund, G.E. (2004), 'Job values among future business leaders: the impact of gender and social background', *Scandinavian Journal of Management*, **20**: 277–95.

Greenhaus, J.H. (1987), *Career Management*, New York: CBS College Publishing.

Gutteridge, T.G., Leibowitz, Z.B. and Shore, J.E. (1993), *Organizational Career Development: Benchmarks for Building a World-Class Workforce*, San Francisco, CA: Jossey-Bass.

Hall, D.T. (1996a), 'Protean careers of the 21st century', *Academy of Management Executive*, **10**: 8–16.

Hall, D.T. (1996b), *The Career is Dead – Long Live the Career*, San Francisco, CA: Jossey-Bass.

Hall, D.T. (2004), 'The protean career: a quarter-century journey', *Journal of Vocational Behavior*, **65**: 1–3.

Hall, D.T. and Chandler, D.E. (2005), 'Psychological success: when the career is calling', *Journal of Vocational Behavior*, **26**: 155–76.

Hall, D.T. and Mirvis, P.H. (1996), 'The new protean career: Psychological success and the path with a hearth', in D.T. Hall and Associates, *The Career is Dead – Long Live the Career: A Relational Approach to Careers*, San Francisco, CA: Jossey-Bass, pp. 15–45.

Hall, D.T. and Moss, J.E. (1998), 'The new protean career contract: helping organizations and employees adapt', *Organizational Dynamics*, **26**: 22–38.

Herzberg, F. (1966), *Work and the Nature of Man*, Cleveland, OH: Work Publishing.

Heslin, P. (2005), 'Conceptualizing and evaluating career success', *Journal of Organizational Behavior*, **26**: 113–36.

Hirschman, A.O. (1970), *Exit, Voice and Loyalty*, Cambridge, MA: Harvard University Press.

Hobfoll, S.E. (1989), 'Conservation of resources: a new attempt at conceptualizing stress', *American Psychologist*, **44**: 513–24.

Hobfoll, S.E. (2001), 'The influence of culture, community, and the nested-self in the stress process: advancing conservation of resources theory', *Applied Psychology: An International Review*, **50**: 337–421.

Hobfoll, S.E. and Shirom, A. (2000), 'Conservation of resource theory: application to stress and management in workplace', in R.T. Golombiewski (ed.), *Handbook of Organization Behavior*, New York: Dekker, pp. 57–81.

Hofstede, G. (1991), *Cultures and Organizations: Software of the Mind*, London: McGraw-Hill.

Holland, J.L. (1985), *Making Vocational Choices: A Theory of Personality and Work Environments*, Englewood Cliffs, NJ: Prentice-Hall.

Koys, D.J. (2001), 'The effects of employee satisfaction, organizational citizenship behavior, and turnover on organizational effectiveness: a unit level, longitudinal study', *Personnel Psychology*, **54**: 101–14.

Lazarus, R.S. and Folkman, S. (1984), *Stress, Appraisal and Coping*, New York: Spinger.

Maccoby, M. (1988), *Why Work? Leading the New Generation*, New York: Simon and Schuster.

Marini, M., Pi-Ling Fan, M., Finley, E. and Beutel, A.M. (1996), 'Gender and job values', *Sociology of Education*, **69**: 49–65.

Marks, H.M. (1994), 'The effect of participation in school-sponsored community service programs on students' attitudes toward social responsibility', unpublished doctoral dissertation, University of Michigan.

Maslow, A.H. (1954), *Motivation and Personality*, New York: Harper & Row.

Niles, S.G. and Goodnough, G.E. (1996), 'Life-role salience: a review of recent research', *The Career Development Quarterly*, **45** (September): 65–85.

Nilsen, A. (1992), *Women Ways of Caring. A Life-course Approach to the Occupational Careers of Three Cohorts of Engineers and Teachers*, Bergen: Department of Sociology, University of Bergen.

Organ, D.W. (1988), *OCB: The Good Soldier Syndrome*, Lexington, MA: Lexington Books.

Organ, D.W. (1997), 'Organizational citizenship behavior: it's construct clean-up time', *Human Performance*, **10**: 85–97.

Paine, L.S. (2003), *Value Shift: Why Companies Must Merge Social and Financial Imperatives to Achieve Superior Performance*, New York: McGraw-Hill.

Peiperl, M.A. and Baruch, Y. (1997), 'Back to square zero: The post-corporate career', *Organizational Dynamics*, **25**: 7–22.

Perry, L.L. and Katula, M.C. (2001), 'Does service affect citizenship?', *Administration and Society*, **33**: 330–65.

Peterson, S.A. (1990), *Political Behavior*, Thousand Oaks, CA: Sage.

Podsakoff, P.M., MacKenzie, S.B., Paine, J.B. and Bachrach, D.G. (2000), 'Organizational citizenship behaviors: a critical review of the theoretical and empirical literature and suggestions for future research', *Journal of Management*, **26**: 513–63.

Rokeach, M. (1973), *The Nature of Human Values*, New York: Free Press.

Sagiv, L. and Schwartz, S.H. (2000), 'Values priorities and subjective well being: direct relations and congruity effects', *European Journal of Social Psychology*, **30**: 177–98.

Schwartz, S.H. (1992), 'Universals in content and structure of values: theoretical advances and empirical tests in 20 countries', in M.P. Zanna (ed.), *Advances* in *Experimental Social Psychology*, Vol. 25, New York: Academic Press, pp. 1–65.

Sexton, D. and Bowman-Upton, N. (1991), *Entrepreneurship: Creativity and Growth*, New York: Macmillan.

Shepard, H.A. (1984), 'On the realization of human potential: a path with heart', in M.B. Arthur, L. Bailyn, D.J. Levinson and H.A. Shepard (eds), *Working with Careers*, New York: Columbia University Press, pp. 25–46.

Sobel, R. (1993), 'From occupational involvement to political participation: an explanatory analysis', *Political Behavior*, **15**: 339–53.

Super, D.E. (1986), 'Life career roles: self-realization in work and leisure', in Douglas T. Hall and Associates (eds), *Career Development in Organizations*, San Francisco, CA: Jossey-Bass, pp. 95–119.

Verba, S., Sclozman, K.L. and Brady, H.E. (1995), *Voice and Equality: Civic Voluntarism in American Politics*, Cambridge, MA: Harvard University Press.

Vigoda, E. (2000), 'Internal politics in public administration systems: an empirical examination of its relationship with job congruence, organizational citizenship behavior and in-role performances', *Public Personnel Management*, **29**: 185–210.

Vigoda, E. and Golembiewski, R.T. (2001), 'Citizenship behavior and the spirit of new managerialism: a theoretical framework and challenge for governance', *American Review of Public Administration*, **31**: 273–95.

Walker, J.E., Tausky, C. and Oliver, D. (1982), 'Men and women at work: values within occupational groups', *Journal of Vocational Behavior*, **21**: 17–36.

Williams, L.J. and Anderson, S.E. (1991), 'Job satisfaction and organizational commitment as predictors of organizational citizenship and in role behaviors', *Journal of Management*, **17**: 601–17.

Wright, T.A. and Hobfoll, S.E. (2004), 'Commitment, psychological well being, and job performance: an examination of conservation of resources (COR) theory and job burnout', *Journal of Business and Management*, **9**: 389–406.

13. Business students' views on jobs, careers and the job search process: implications for universities and employers

Ronald J. Burke and Eddy S.W. Ng

INTRODUCTION

It is estimated that, by 2010, Canada could lack 1.5 million skilled workers (Corporate Leadership Council, 2003). As the demand for skills continues to rise, the competition for skilled workers will intensify, leading to a war for talent. University students continue to be a major source of hiring for skilled jobs such as managers, professionals and technical workers (Rynes et al., 1997). They are technologically savvy, which makes them highly desirable in today's job markets (Burke and Ng, 2006; Ware, 2005). University students are also eager to learn, and are more easily socialized into an organization's norms and culture, compared to experienced hires (Loughlin and Barling, 2001; Ruiz-Quintanilla and Claes, 1996; Van Vianen, 2000). These factors in combination make students a target of competition for the workforce of the future.

There is already an abundance of literature that has focused on applicant attraction strategies and organizational recruitment practices (e.g. Barber et al., 1994; Barber et al., 1999; Heneman and Berkley, 1999; Rynes and Barber, 1990; Rynes et al., 1997) to help organizations compete for talent. What is missing is an understanding of how job applicants seek out information, investigate, and decide among alternative job opportunities (Cable and Turban, 2001). This knowledge, of university students in particular, is especially important because they represent the workforce of the future, and also because they have work values and expectations different from previous generations (Loughlin and Barling, 2001; Smola and Sutton, 2002). It should be noted that it is the students who will be selecting which organizations they want to work for, based on the kinds of working conditions, opportunities and flexibility employers can offer.

In this study, we explore the career aspirations and expectations among a sample of 4851 university students enrolled in a business program. Specifically, we examined what attracts them to future opportunities, how they explore potential employers, and how they make career decisions. It is expected that the findings can provide an insight into the future of Canada's graduates, the expectations that are demanded of future employers, and how well universities are supporting their careers.

Business schools have traditionally been a training ground for management education and a source of supply of managers to employers. In recent years, however, the role of business schools has been increasingly questioned (Starkey and Tempest, 2005). There are suggestions that business education does not correlate with career success (Pfeffer and Fong, 2002). With rising tuition fees, business schools are increasingly pressured to live up to their promises to students by attempting to deliver great career results (Pfeffer and Fong, 2004). Student satisfaction with academic support services (e.g. career services) is low (EBI, 2004), while employers are complaining that students are more interested in achieving their career goals than learning and personal development (Pfeffer and Fong, 2004). The question of whether students have realistic career expectations also needs to be answered (Waryszak, 1999). Students, employers and academics are all calling for more business programs to incorporate a clinical or cooperative education component to make management education relevant to jobs and organizations (Bergman, 1978; Pfeffer and Fong, 2002; Thiel and Hartley, 1997).

In this study, we seek to explore students' expectations, career choices, and job search behaviors. We also examine the role of campus career services in shaping students' career expectations and how cooperative education influences some of the students' expectations and aspirations. Cooperative education allows students to acquire essential skills by being exposed to the reality of the world of work beyond the boundaries of the campus, thus enhancing their self-confidence and career directions (see Garavan and Murphy, 2001).

THEORETICAL FRAMEWORK

Recruitment Literature

Research on recruitment has received a great deal of attention over the past 30 years (Breaugh and Starke, 2000). However, much of the recruitment literature has focused on recruitment efforts and applicant attraction strategies (e.g. Barber et al., 1994; Barber et al., 1999; Heneman and Berkley, 1999; Rynes and Barber, 1990; Rynes et al., 1997). Most of this research targeted one of three areas: (1) recruitment sources (e.g. do different sources of recruitment result in different outcomes?); (2) recruiters (e.g. do recruiter impressions make a difference in applicant attraction?); and (3) realistic job previews (e.g. does providing accurate job information result in higher satisfaction post hire?) (see Rynes, 1991 for a review). We extend previous research by also examining the characteristics of the applicant pool, and how they are influenced by organizational-level variables. It is believed that investigating the applicant pool characteristics (e.g. size, quality of applicants) is important because it is a measure of a firm's recruitment success (Turban and Cable, 2003).

We begin by 'going inside the heads of potential applicants' to understand what job or organizational characteristics are important to students, how they seek out information about potential employers, and how they make career decisions. The goal of this research is to help organizations understand the attitudes and behaviors of their targeted applicants so they can decide on what type of recruitment efforts will provide the greatest return (i.e. generate the most applicants). We draw upon Cable and Turban's (2001) 'employer knowledge framework' to help explain the students' expectations and how they make career choices. Cable and Turban (2001, p. 115) defined employer knowledge as 'beliefs that a job seeker holds about a potential employer'. This knowledge is important because it determines how job applicants pursue and process information about an organization, what they expect from the organization as employees, and whether they accept jobs with the organization.

According to Cable and Turban, applicants broadly evaluate a firm based on the physical attributes of the employer, e.g. firm size, geographical location (employer information); attributes about the jobs being offered by the firm, e.g. pay levels, benefits, advancement opportunities (job information); and the types of individuals who would be potential co-workers (people information). Because applicants often do not have complete information about a firm, these three categories of organizational information provide an insight into the firm (i.e. what type of organization is it?). In theory, different people are attracted to different attributes of a firm (e.g. good pay and benefits, good people to work with). The individual difference hypothesis (Rynes, 1991) also suggests that different firms reach out to applicant groups with different characteristics (e.g. expectation, ability, motivation). Consistent with the employer knowledge framework and the individual difference hypothesis, we argue that different job and organizational attributes will appeal to applicants with different characteristics.

The employer knowledge framework also suggests that employer familiarity (i.e. awareness) and reputation play an important role in a firm's perceived attractiveness as a potential employer (Collins and Stevens, 2002;

Lievens et al., 2005). According to marketing literature (e.g. Aaker, 1991), awareness demonstrates an individual's cognition or knowledge about an organization's existence. A high level of employer familiarity or awareness is desirable because an applicant can recall the name of an employer (when prompted with a salient fact about the firm), and associate information they receive down the road with that employer. Employer reputation concerns the public evaluation of an organization. It conveys popular beliefs about a firm, which applicants may find attractive and desire to associate themselves with (e.g. a trendy or prestigious firm to work for) (Turban and Cable, 2003). Previous research has found that applicants rated socially responsible firms more attractively as potential employers (e.g. Gatewood et al., 1993; Highhouse et al., 1999; Turban and Greening, 1996).

Finally, the realistic information hypothesis (Breaugh and Starke, 2000; Rynes, 1991) proposes than an individual may possess more realistic information concerning a job or an organization as a result of having been exposed to the reality of work. We argue that cooperative students, who have some work experience, have more accurate information of what a job entails, have insight into their own capabilities (e.g. knowledge, skills) and desires (e.g. what they want from a position or an employer).

METHODS

This research is part of a broader research project commissioned by a consortium of large Canadian companies interested in better understanding the views of university students on jobs, organizations, careers and perceptions of their organization. The original data were collected from 20 771 respondents in Canada in 2004 using an Internet-based survey. Respondents enrolled in business programs were selected for this study, because of our interest in management education. The students' majors included accounting (n = 592), actuarial science (n = 163), computer science and information technology (n = 1405), business or commerce (n = 2594), and human resources (n = 157). The business students (n = 4851) represented 23 percent of the original data set.

Table 13.1 shows the demographic characteristics of the sample. Most of the respondents were studying full time (91 percent), pursuing an undergraduate degree (86 percent), in a university program (80 percent), studying in Ontario (54 percent), graduating in the year of the study or a year later (61 percent), in their third or fourth year of study (44 percent), and 22 years old or younger (61 percent). Males were slightly more numerous than females (51 percent). Respondents also resided in each of the ten Canadian provinces and three territories. Respondents from British Columbia,

Table 13.1   Demographic characteristics of sample

	N	%	Total
Status			
Full-time	4388	90.8	
Part-time	445	9.2	
Province or territory			
British Columbia	853	17.6	
Alberta	663	12.5	
Saskatchewan	67	1.4	
Manitoba	18	0.4	
Ontario	2635	54.5	
Quebec	447	9.2	
New Brunswick	114	2.4	
Nova Scotia	84	1.7	
Prince Edward Island	4	0.1	
Newfoundland/Labrador	8	0.2	
Yukon	1	0.0	
North West Territories	0	0.0	
Nunavut	0	0.0	
Type of post-secondary school			
University	3843	75.6	
College or institute of technology	875	18.1	
University college	62	2.1	
CEGEP[a]	4	0.1	
Other	5	0.1	
Level of degree			
Bachelor's	3390	86.5	
Master's	436	11.1	
PhD	12	0.3	
Other	79	1.6	
Grades			
A+ (90–100%)	365	7.5	
A (80–89)	1141	23.6	
B+ (78–79)	1126	23.3	
B (74–77)	1107	22.9	
B− (70–73)	655	13.5	
C (60–69)	426	8.8	
D (50–59)	20	0.4	
F (<50)	1	0.0	
Current year of study			
1	906	18.7	
2	1127	23.3	
3	1135	23.5	

Table 13.1   (continued)

	N	%	Total
4	994	20.5	
5	201	11.2	
6	315	6.5	
7	160	3.3	
Year of graduation			
2004	1564	32.3	
2005	1392	28.8	
2006	984	20.3	
2007	585	12.1	
2008	199	4.1	
2009	31	0.6	
2010	84	1.7	
Age			
19 or younger	717	14.9	
20–22	2229	46.4	
23–25	1028	21.4	
26–28	338	7.0	
29–30	152	3.2	
Over 30	378	7.0	
Gender			
Female	2340	48.9	
Male	2444	51.1	
Options (of those measured)			
Aboriginal	45	2.0	0.9
Disabilities	69	3.0	1.4
Visible minority	1237	42.0	25.5
Work status			
Part-time	1652	34.6	
Full-time	637	13.3	
Neither	2487	52.1	
Hours worked			
0–5		14.7	
6–10		18.8	
11–15		16.3	
16–20		100	
21–25		7.4	
26–30		4.7	
31 or more		22.1	

Note: [a] Collège d'enseignement général et professionnel.

Alberta and Ontario were overrepresented in the sample; students in the other provinces and territories were underrepresented. Thus while the sample was large, the respondents were not a random or representative sample of students in Canadian universities.

Measures

Job and organizational attributes

Respondents were asked to assess the importance of 14 items pertaining to their desired job and organizational attributes, using a 5-point scale (1 = not at all important, 5 = essential). The mean ratings of the 14 items are presented in Table 13.2.

These 14 items were factor-analyzed using the principal components varimax rotation procedure. Four factors emerged accounting for 58 percent of the common variance and all had eigenvalues greater than 1.0. The four factors were 'People' (e.g. good people to work with) – two items ($\alpha = 0.85$); 'Reputation' (e.g. commitment to social responsibility) – five items ($\alpha = 0.68$); 'Work' (e.g. challenging work) – four items ($\alpha = 0.64$); and 'Benefits' (e.g. job security) – three items ($\alpha = 0.57$). These four measures were all significantly and positively intercorrelated ($p < 0.001$), and correspond to Cable and Turban's people, job and employer dimensions of the employer knowledge framework.

Table 13.2   Desired job characteristics

	X	SD	N
Opportunities for advancement	4.6	0.72	4832
Good training opportunities, developing new skills	4.3	0.81	4823
Good people to work with	4.3	0.83	4834
Good people to report to	4.2	0.84	4826
Challenging work	4.0	0.89	4825
Good initial salary	4.0	0.88	4839
Work–life balance	3.9	0.98	4829
Job security	3.9	0.96	4828
Opportunities to have a personal impact	3.8	0.98	4827
Good health and benefits plan	3.7	1.04	4830
Organization is a leader in its field	3.5	1.00	4821
Commitment to diversity	3.4	1.22	4826
Commitment to social responsibility	3.3	1.08	4823
Opportunity to travel	3.0	1.22	4832

Notes: X = Mean; SD = Standard Deviation; N = Number.

Employer kowledge

The students were also asked to respond to 14 items that assess their knowledge about organizations (i.e. familiarity, according to Cable and Turban, 2001) and the organizations' recruitment practices (e.g. companies need to spend more time meeting and talking to students on campus; it is often best for the person supervising me to conduct the interview). The mean ratings for each of the items are presented in Table 13.3.

Table 13.3   Employer knowledge

	X	SD	N
1. Most big companies offer more or less the same in terms of employment experiences.	2.8	1.02	4781
2. I would not consider working for a company that I had not heard about before.	2.3	1.01	4779
3. If I like a company's products/services I will be much more interested in working for them.	4.1	0.82	4778
4. Companies and organizations need to spend more time meeting and talking with students on campus.	4.0	0.84	4768
5. Company-sponsored speakers on campus are a good way of promoting a company as a good place to work.	4.0	0.85	4773
6. I often read brochures, annual reports, and editorials on organizations where I might be interested in working.	3.3	1.07	4769
7. A hiring firm should hold after-school functions like receptions and information sessions.	3.9	0.82	4772
8. It is best to have the person who will supervise me conduct the job interview.	3.9	0.91	4770
9. An organization that offers international opportunities interests me.	4.0	1.06	4767
10. Career fairs are highly useful in helping decide what organization I want to work for.	3.4	1.04	4771
11. I expect to use the Internet for my job search.	4.2	0.87	4758
12. I expect my campus career services office to find me a job.	2.9	1.19	4762
13. Companies should participate in career fairs even if they don't have any jobs currently available.	3.3	1.11	4771
14. I like the branded giveaways (e.g. pens, etc.) that companies sometimes hand out at career fairs.	3.6	1.04	4772

Notes: X = Mean; SD = Standard Deviation; N = Number.

Respondents also rated how good each of 30 of Canada's largest and best-known employers (almost all private sector firms) would be as a place to start their careers. Ratings were made on a 10-point scale (1 = poor, 10 = excellent). The reliability of this measure was 0.98. The mean across all 30 items was 4.8, indicating that all potential employers were generally seen as only moderately good places to start their careers. Responses ranged in every case from 1 to 10. Respondents were also asked if they had any knowledge of the industries, careers and companies they wished to work for, and how long they expected to stay with their first employer.

Job search process
We focused on campus career services as they are a primary source of information for university students seeking employment (Pritchard et al., 2004). Respondents indicated if they had used their career services, and if so, how effective their services were in providing help with in six areas (e.g. understanding their interests and skills, establishing career goals, developing a job search strategy). Respondents also indicated how import-ant it was for them to receive help, and their satisfaction with each of the six areas. Finally, respondents were asked to indicate the factors that influenced their career planning. The scores are shown in Table 13.4.

RESULTS

Multiple regression analyses were undertaken to examine the relationships between the applicants' characteristics and their desired job and organiza-tional attributes, employer knowledge, and job search behavior. The appli-cants' characteristics considered in this study were age, gender, whether respondent was in a cooperative study program, whether respondent was a full-time or part-time student, whether respondent was currently working as well as going to college or university, year in their program, and the expected year of graduation.

Job and Organizational Attributes

Women, cooperative students and full-time students rated 'People' (e.g. good people to work with) higher (βs = -0.11, -0.03 and 0.04, respec-tively). Women, students with lower grades, in their earlier year of study, and non-cooperative students also rated 'Reputation' (e.g. commitment to social responsibility) higher (βs = -0.17, 0.05, -0.05 and 0.64, respec-tively). Students having higher grades, women and cooperative students rated 'Work' (e.g. challenging work) higher (βs = -0.10, -0.07 and -0.04,

Table 13.4   Job search process (career services)

	X	SD	N
If you used campus career services, how effective were they in helping you with . . .?			
Understanding my interests and skills	2.9	0.75	2690
Establishing career goals	2.8	0.72	2633
Résumé writing and interview skills	3.7	0.87	3012
Developing a job search strategy	0.31	0.83	2885
Identifying job opportunities	3.3	0.79	3184
Connecting directly with employers	3.2	0.74	3006
Importance of help with . . .			
Understanding my interests and skills	4.0	1.03	4772
Establishing career goals	4.0	0.99	4771
Résumé writing and career skills	4.4	0.84	4763
Developing a job search strategy	4.2	0.86	4764
Identifying job opportunities	4.5	0.73	4758
Connecting directly with employers	4.5	0.73	4761
Satisfaction with career services			
Career counsellor	3.2	0.79	2025
Career/job fairs	3.0	0.76	2709
Job search workshops (e.g. résumé writing, interviewing, etc.)	3.4	0.82	2649
Employment information sessions	3.4	0.84	2476
Job listings	3.6	0.87	3316
Resource materials (print, video, online)	3.2	0.75	2464
Career services website	3.5	0.83	3132
Résumé Ássistance	3.6	0.79	2721

Notes: X = Mean; SD = Standard Deviation; N = Number.

respectively). Finally, women, students studying full time, students with lower grades, in their earlier years of study, and non-cooperative students rated 'Benefits' (e.g. job security) more highly (βs = −0.14, −0.06, 0.06, −0.05 and 0.04, respectively).

In general, students found the most desirable job and organizational attributes were 'opportunities for advancement', 'good training opportunities and skill development', 'good people to work with', 'good people to report to', 'challenging work' and 'a good initial salary' (all with means greater than 4.0). From an employer's perspective, these are fortunately under a firm's control and are likely to contribute to both employee retention and firm performance. However, firms will have difficulty meeting expressed needs for advancement, as not everyone can be promoted. As a result, firms will need to develop realistic expectations during the recruiting process, or seek out students with more realistic expectations (e.g. cooperative students).

Employer Knowledge

First, respondents had uncertain views on whether big companies offered similar employment experiences. In other words, larger firms appeared to be unable to distinguish themselves and the employment experience they can offer to students. Students were also more interested in working for firms whose products or services they like, and less willing to work for firms they know little about, suggesting the importance of employer familiarity (Cable and Turban, 2001). The respondents also believed that organizations should spend more time meeting with students on campus, sponsoring speakers, and holding company information sessions. However, the students also found written material (provided by organizations) to be less helpful, had low expectations that their campus career offices would get them a job, and expected to use the Internet in their job searches. This suggests a shift away from traditional recruitment mediums (i.e. career services, company brochures) to more sophisticated channels such as the Internet.

A majority of the respondents indicated knowledge of their preferred industry (77 percent), although fewer knew their specific careers (60 percent), and still fewer indicated knowledge of specific companies (21 percent). The most preferred industry (two choices could be made) were financial services (36 percent), IT (32 percent), advertising (27 percent) and management consulting (25 percent). Most students indicated a preference for large companies (65 percent), followed by medium-sized companies (55 percent), government/public service (36 percent), and running their own businesses (32 percent).

Men, cooperative students and those nearing graduation indicated greater knowledge of a particular industry in which they wanted to work ($\beta s = -0.07$, 0.06 and 0.04, respectively). Students in later years of study, having a higher GPA (grade point average), nearing graduation and in cooperative programs indicated greater knowledge of a specific company that they would work for ($\beta s = -0.09$, 0.07, 0.08 and 0.06, respectively). Older students, those nearing graduation, cooperative students and students with higher GPAs also indicated greater knowledge of their preferred careers ($\beta s = -0.15$, 0.05, 0.04 and 0.03, respectively).

Students in their earlier years of study, non-cooperative students, older students and students having higher grades rated the 30 companies as better places to start their career ($\beta s = 0.08$, 0.05, 0.04 and 0.03, respectively). It should be noted that almost one-third of the sample did not provide responses to these 30 items (firms). These students did not have enough information on these specific companies on which to base their responses in any meaningful way. These figures ranged from a low of 10 percent for one employer to a high of over 50 percent for another.

Finally, respondents indicated how long they would like to stay with their first employer. Seventeen percent indicated less than 2 years; 38 percent indicated 3–5 years, 8.5 percent indicated 6–10 years; 14 percent indicated more than 10 years; and 23 percent indicated that they did not know. Less than half of the respondents (41 percent) indicated a preference for finding an organization for their whole career; 30 percent indicated a preference for working for more than one organization, and 29 percent did not know their preferences.

Job Search Process

Only about one-third (30 percent) of the respondents reported using their campus career services regularly (six or more times). The most common reasons for not using them included not being aware of services offered (8 percent), doubting services would be helpful (6 percent), not needing career help (6 percent), believing services were not oriented to them (4 percent) and inconvenience (4 percent). Students who used their campus career services rated them at 3.1 (3 = Good). Only a small number of users (4 percent) had no opinion.

Non-cooperative students, students in later years of study, full-time students, older students, women and students with higher GPAs made greater use of their career services during the past year (βs = -0.16, 0.08, -0.06, 0.06, -0.04 and -0.03, respectively). Students with higher grades, non-cooperative students, students in their earlier years of study and older students rated help from career services more highly (βs = 0.11, 0.04, 0.04 and 0.04, respectively). Students using their career services rated them more highly if they were cooperative students and graduating in later years (βs = -0.06 and 0.05, respectively). Students in earlier years of study, and younger students who had not used their career services, rated them lower (βs = -0.12, -0.07 and 0.08, respectively).

Students with higher GPAs, cooperative students and men also indicated more confidence in their job search following use of their university career services (βs = -0.14, -0.07, -0.06 and 0.04, respectively). A majority of business students also indicated they would be willing to accept less than their ideal job in order to start their careers (79 percent); only 2 percent would not do so.

Finally, respondents were asked about the factors that influenced their career planning. They indicated online employment resources (39 percent), parents (36 percent), friends (34 percent), professors (28 percent), printed resource material (28 percent) and campus career center staff (22 percent) to be important influences when making their career choices.

Cooperative Students

Students involved in cooperative education (n = 1870) were also compared with students not involved in such programs (n = 2785). Because of the large sample sizes, most differences reached statistical significance (p<0.05). Students in cooperative programs were younger, had higher grades, were more likely to be full time, were in later years of study and included more men; cooperative and non-cooperative students expected to graduate at the same time.

Students in cooperative programs rated 'People' and 'Work' more highly than non-cooperative students, while non-cooperative students rated 'Reputation' and 'Benefits' more highly than cooperative students. Cooperative students also used their campus career services more frequently during the past year, rated their services more highly, and had more confidence in their job search based on using these services. Cooperative students also indicated greater knowledge of specific companies they wanted to work for, the industries, and specific careers, than did non-cooperative students. Cooperative students also rated the 30 companies lower as good places to start their careers than did non-cooperative students.

DISCUSSION

It is predicted that there will be a shortage of skills in the next decade. Employers will be engaged in a war for talent and are targeting university students to fill their managerial and professional positions. In light of this, employers will need to connect with university students to understand their work values and expectations. This study examines the views of university students on jobs, careers and their job search process among a large sample of Canadian university students enrolled in a business program. Business students were chosen because they are more likely to enter managerial and professional ranks, and will be highly sought after by organizations. The following comments are offered in summary.

First, the cooperative students in this study appeared to have more realistic expectations about their careers, and indicated knowledge of specific industry, company, or career they were interested in, than non-cooperative students. Cooperative students also expressed more confidence in their job search, and used their campus career services more frequently. This suggests that cooperative students have a greater 'self-insight' (Breaugh, 1992) of their own abilities, desires, expectations and self-confidence than their non-cooperative counterparts. Thus, if employers are concerned with positive post-hire outcomes (e.g. job satisfaction, retention) among new recruits, then they should seek to participate in cooperative education programs, to help influence the expectations of university students. Second, cooperative students were also more concerned with the 'People' and 'Work' dimensions of a firm, and less on a firm's 'Reputation' and 'Benefits'. Cooperative students were also less likely than non-cooperative students to rate the top 30 companies as good places to start their career. This suggests that cooperative students, having been exposed to the realities of work, placed a different emphasis on the desired job and organizational attributes than non-cooperative students, and did not necessarily find firms with a great reputation (the top 30 firms) to be more attractive. Consequently, employers must use different strategies to appeal to cooperative students, as image and reputation alone were not sufficient to appeal to this group of students.

Students with high abilities (GPA) also reported similar preferences to those of cooperative students. They also expressed greater confidence in their job search, and indicated more knowledge of the industry and careers they were interested in than those with lower grades, suggesting a high degree of self-insight. Students with higher grades also rated 'Work' as an important attribute, while those with lower grades indicated a firm's 'Reputation' and 'Benefits' as being important. However, students with higher grades used career services more often, and rated the top 30 firms as good places to start, signaling that they do not have as much information about employers as cooperative students have, on which to base their career decisions.

There also appears to be a shift in the job search process (toward computers and the Internet) among university students in general. Consistent with the EBI (2004) findings, students have low expectations of their campus career services, were less satisfied with them, and consequently use them less frequently. Students also indicated a preference for more employer presence on campus (e.g. sponsoring speakers, information sessions, career fairs). Thus universities are well advised to revamp the services currently being offered, to both students and prospective employers, and to examine the role of career services in light of the Internet age.

In this research, we explored the career aspirations and expectations of university students, and extended previous literature on recruitment by examining the applicant pool characteristics and organizational-level variables. Although there is an abundance of research on applicant attraction strategies, it appears that the values, expectations and job search process among university students have shifted. Both universities and employers have an important role to play in fostering more realistic expectations among students, who will be the workforce of the future. In this regard, we believe that universities and employers will benefit significantly from cooperative education. Cooperative education can highlight some of the realities of jobs and careers in contemporary organizations. Employers should also be concerned with their image and reputation among university students. Although cooperative students rated reputable employers lower than non-cooperative students, those with higher abilities (i.e. grades) appear to have little information about prospective employers. Thus there is tremendous value for employers to invest their time and efforts on campus to increase their familiarity and reputation among the student population.

In closing, a few limitations should be noted to put the findings in perspective. First, the sample is dominated by students from three provinces and may have limited generalizability. In addition, the size of the sample is large, and thus many relationships and differences were significant. Third, this sample, being more highly educated, may not be representative of all Canadian youth aged 18 to 30, but represents an important segment of the Canadian workforce.

AUTHORS' NOTE

Preparation of this manuscript was supported in part by the Business Administration Program, Trent University, and the Schulich School of Business, York University. Lisa Fiksenbaum participated in the data analysis. We thank D-Code Consulting for making the data available to us.

REFERENCES

Aaker, D.A. (1991), *Managing Brand Equity: Capitalizing on the Value of a Brand Name*, New York: Free Press.

Barber, A.E., Daly, C.L., Giannantonio, C.M. and Phillips, J.M. (1994), 'Job search activities: an examination of changes over time', *Personnel Psychology*, **47**(4): 739–66.

Barber, A.E., Wesson, M.J., Roberson, Q.M. and Taylor, M.S. (1999), 'A tale of two job markets: organizational size and its effects on hiring practices and job search behavior', *Personnel Psychology*, **52**(4): 841–67.

Bergman, B. (1978), 'Employer evaluations in cooperative education programs', *Human Resource Management*, **17**(3): 31–2.

Breaugh, J.A. (1992), *Recruitment: Science and Practice*, Boston, MA: PWS-Kent.

Breaugh, J.A. and Starke, M. (2000), 'Research on employee recruitment: so many studies, so many remaining questions', *Journal of Management*, **26**(3): 405–34.

Burke, R.J. and Ng, E.S.W. (2006), 'The changing nature of work and organizations: implications for human resource management', *Human Resource Management Review*, **16**: 86–94.

Cable, D.M. and Turban, D.B. (2001), 'Establishing the dimensions, sources and value of job seekers' employer knowledge during recruitment', in G.E. Ferris (ed.), *Research in Personnel and Human Resource Management*, New York: Elsevier Science.

Collins, C.J. and Stevens, C.K. (2002), 'The relationship between early recruitment-related activities and the application decisions of new labor-market entrants: a brand equity approach to recruitment', *Journal of Applied Psychology*, **87**(6): 1121–33.

Corporate Leadership Council (2003), *State of the Canadian Workforce*, Washington, DC: Corporate Executive Board.

Education Benchmarking, Inc. (2004), 'Student satisfaction with career services' (feature article on management education), Internet site: www.webebi.com/research, retrieved 15 June 2005.

Garavan, T.N. and Murphy, C. (2001), 'The co-operative education process and organizational socialization: a qualitative study of student perceptions of its effectiveness', *Education and Training*, **43**(6): 281–302.

Gatewood, R.D., Gowan, M.A. and Lautenschlager, G.J. (1993), 'Corporate image, recruitment image, and initial job choice decisions', *Academy of Management Journal*, **36**(2): 414–27.

Heneman, H.G. III and Berkley, R.A. (1999), 'Applicant attraction practices and outcomes among small businesses', *Journal of Small Business Management*, **37**(1): 53–74.

Highhouse, S., Zickar, M.J., Thorsteinson, T.J., Stierwalt, S.L. and Slaughter, J.E. (1999), 'Assessing company employment image: an example in the fast food industry', *Personnel Psychology*, **52**: 151–72.

Lievens, F., Van Hoye, G. and Schreurs, B. (2005), 'Examining the relationship between employer knowledge dimensions and organizational attractiveness: an application in a military context', *Journal of Occupational and Organizational Psychology*, **78**: 553–72.

Loughlin, C. and Barling, J. (2001), 'Young workers' work values, attitudes, and behaviours', *Journal of Occupational and Organizational Psychology*, **74**: 543–58.

Pfeffer, J. and Fong, C.T. (2002), 'The end of business schools? Less success than meets the eye', *Academy of Management Learning and Education*, **1**(1): 78–95.

Pfeffer, J. and Fong, C.T. (2004), 'The business school "business": some lessons from the US experience', *Journal of Management Studies*, **41**(8): 1501–20.

Pritchard, R.E., Potter, G.C., Damminger, J. and Wriggins, B. (2004), 'Implementing a course-embedded resume and professional employment action plan preparation program for college of business juniors', *Journal of Education for Business*, **79**(6): 348–53.

Ruiz-Quintanilla, S.A. and Claes, R. (1996), 'Determinants of underemployment of young adults: a multi-country study', *Industrial & Labor Relations Review*, **49**(3): 424–38.

Rynes, S.L. (1991), 'Recruitment, job choice, and post hire consequences', in M.D. Dunnette (ed.), *Handbook of Industrial and Organizational Psychology*, 2nd edn, Palo Alto, CA: Consulting Psychologists Press, pp. 399–444.

Rynes, S.L. and Barber, A.E. (1990), 'Applicant attraction strategies: an organizational perspective', *Academy of Management Journal*, **15**(2): 286–310.

Rynes, S.L., Orlitzky, M.O. and Bretz, R.D. Jr (1997), 'Experienced hiring versus college recruiting: practices and emerging trends', *Personnel Psychology*, **50**(2): 309–39.

Smola, K.W. and Sutton, C.D. (2002), 'Generational differences: revisiting generational work values for the new millennium', *Journal of Organizational Behavior*, **23**: 363–82.

Starkey, K. and Tempest, S. (2005), 'The future of the business school: knowledge challenges and opportunities', *Human Relations*, **58**(1): 61–82.

Thiel, G.R. and Hartley, N.T. (1997), 'Cooperative education: a natural synergy between business and academia', *S. A. M. Advanced Management Journal*, **62**(3): 19–24.

Turban, D.B. and Cable, D.M. (2003), 'Firm reputation and applicant pool characteristics', *Journal of Organizational Behavior*, **24**: 733–51.

Turban, D.B. and Greening, D.W. (1996), 'Corporate social performance and organizational attractiveness to prospective employees', *Academy of Management Journal*, **40**(3): 658–72.

Van Vianen, A.E.M. (2000), 'Person–organization fit: the match between newcomers' and recruiters' preferences for organizational cultures', *Personnel Psychology*, **53**(1): 113–49.

Ware, J. (2005), 'The changing nature of work: technology. The future of work blog', (online) Internet site: www.thefutureofwork.net/blog/archives/000322.html, accessed 15 September.

Waryszak, R.Z. (1999), 'Students' expectations from their cooperative education placements in the industry: an international perspective', *Education and Training*, **41**(1): 33–40.

14. Business education as a career choice

Yehuda Baruch and John Blenkinsopp

INTRODUCTION

The highly competitive nature of current labor markets leads people to strive to gain skills, competencies and qualifications that will make them better leaders and managers – in academic terms, they seek to develop their human capital (Becker, 1964). Human capital theory (Becker, 1964) suggests the labor market rewards, either directly or indirectly, the investments that individuals make in themselves. Further, it is claimed that such investments can result in increased opportunities (Becker et al., 1990) and actual career progress, for both mid-level managers and top executives (Baruch et al., 2005; Judge et al., 1995). There is clear evidence to suggest that investments in human capital may be translated into economic wealth (Baruch and Peiperl, 2000; Baruch et al., 2005; Becker et al., 1990).

People seek to make an investment that will yield the best return. Societies, via labor markets, value and reward certain occupations over others, and managerial positions are among the more desired ones. One way to reach managerial roles or to progress faster on managerial ladders is by studying business and management. Gaining a first degree or second degree is the typical route for this, and the Master in Business Administration (MBA) remains the flagship of business education. Whether the MBA remains the 'right tool for the job' for business and management is widely debated – there has been significant criticism of the entire MBA concept and its contribution, with prominent scholars questioning its value and relevance (Bennis and O'Toole, 2005; Gabriel, 2005; Grey, 2004; Kretovics, 1999; Mintzberg, 2004; Pfeffer and Fong, 2002; Porter and McKibbin, 1998).

In this chapter we examine the antecedents and possible outcomes of business education[1] as a major career choice that can be taken at an early career stage (first degree) or at a later stage (e.g. the MBA). We analyze the decision in terms of both tangible and intangible benefits for graduates and for their employers. The heterogeneity of business education is mirrored in the variety of expectations which individuals bring to this important career choice, and these will be explored. We develop a contingency perspective on the value of business education, with a view to understanding its added value for graduates and their future career, and identify individual and organizational factors that affect the value of the degree. We shall compare the prospective benefits and value with the potential pitfalls and costs. Despite the hype, we argue that business education continues to have much to offer individuals in career terms, and map out a number of avenues for further research in this important area.

THE GROWTH OF BUSINESS EDUCATION

The MBA is the best-known and most widely accredited developmental-based learning program in business education, and it continues to be the flagship qualification in this field (Carnall, 1992; Clegg and Ross-Smith, 2003; Kieser, 2004; Tiratsoo, 2004). Starting in the USA at the beginning of the twentieth century, the MBA spread in the second half of that century, with new business schools emerging in the UK in the 1970s, later joined by other European institutions, and in the 1990s by institutions in the Far East. Following the worldwide trend of spreading the MBA, other options such as specialized Masters and undergraduate degrees in business became prominent in universities around the globe. As we demonstrate here, this growth stems from the value of these degrees and their relevance to the business community. Business education continues to spread, and in many universities is fast becoming the largest program area. Many students opt for these programs in order to embark on a managerial career; others may chose it as possible preparation for an entrepreneurial career;[2] some will do so at an early stage, studying business as their first degree. Many still opt to take an MBA, which continues to have strong appeal – in the USA alone there are over 120 000 graduates each year (Altschuler, 2005), and over 10 000 in the UK. Whilst MBA graduates have traditionally sought employment with blue-chip companies, that is not necessarily the case today. Many small and medium-sized firms have joined the race to improve their managerial ranks through recruiting MBAs (McLarty, 2000). Even not-for-profit organizations, local and federal government agencies increasingly send their fast-track and general mangers on these programs (GMAC, 2005).

Business education is very heterogeneous. There is considerable variation even within the MBA itself: full-time versus part-time, executive versus conventional (Alsop, 2005; Heimovics et al., 1996), US-oriented versus European-oriented; case-study versus textbook based; face-to-face versus online delivery (Arbaugh, 2005). Even more variety exists in specialized

Masters programs, covering everything from art management to e-business, international HRM to sports marketing. Finally, there are numerous first degrees in business, with a major divide between business management (with its many variations of focus) and accounting/finance/economics-focused degrees. For simplicity, within the present chapter we will focus on the MBA. As the flagship program, it has been the focus of considerable research over the years, research which we believe can usefully be applied to more specialized Masters programs in business. We view undergraduate business education as qualitatively different, however, and this will be discussed later.

BUSINESS EDUCATION AS A CAREER CHOICE

Studying for a business degree requires a substantial investment in terms of time, money and dedication. A typical full-time MBA program lasts for two years, though one year is common in Europe, where MBA students are generally required to have work experience before enrolling on a program. The financial investment involved is considerable, in particular for study at a prestigious business school. A two-year program at Harvard Business School or Sloan School of Management would cost over $50 000 per year, and in Europe INSEAD and London Business School have fees similar to those of leading US business schools. Tuition fees are lower for MBAs at less prestigious institutions, and the costs of Masters programs are usually lower still. Nevertheless, even the lowest fees amount to a substantial financial investment, particularly when loss of earnings is factored in to the equation. Part-time studies eliminate the loss of earnings, but fees are often similar to those of full-time programs, albeit spread over a longer timescale. One of our MBA students commented, 'After a house, this MBA is the most expensive thing I'll ever buy!'

Against this background, we can see that a decision to enroll on a program represents a major financial undertaking and whilst a range of factors will influence this decision, the perceived impact on future career prospects will be a significant consideration. Business education is seen as instrumental in facilitating individuals moving into the managerial ranks, in accelerating promotional prospects for those already in management, and enabling those embarking on a managerial career move, either internal or external to the present employer, to make more effective transitions. In the future, having a degree in business may become a prerequisite for entering the managerial ranks – with no formal professional qualifications for being a 'manager', this is the closest alternative and can be seen as a proxy for such a qualification. Acquiring an MBA increases employability and is seen as looking good on the CV of those on the lookout for a managerial career (Kane, 1993). Note however that if it is gained in early career, this may make graduates overqualified for the low-level positions that may be a necessary step in career progression.

The marketing of MBA programs often emphasizes career success, and in a sense looks beyond the program itself to a future in which the graduate applies the knowledge gained, network built, and skills developed to make headway in the world of business. Yet the student's motivation may be at least as much about learning – s/he wants to learn, develop, improve. We might therefore suggest that MBAs are being marketed on the assumption of an organizational career mindset, yet many students are approaching business education with a mindset of the protean career, where the individual is in charge of his/her own career (Hall, 1996).

CAREER PROMISE OF BUSINESS EDUCATION

According to Useem and Karabel (1986), universities and other educational institutions bestow three distinct types of human capital upon their graduates: 'scholastic capital' (the amount of knowledge acquired), 'social capital' (personal contacts, network ties) and 'cultural capital' (the value society places on symbols of prestige). To these, Baruch et al. (2005) have added 'inner value capital' and 'market value capital' (see Coleman, 1988).

Looking at 'scholastic capital', business education programs provide a valuable range of knowledge necessary for managers to become more effective and efficient. Business education provides a considerable base of advanced knowledge, skills and competencies. While some programs have unique features (e.g. a special focus such as e-business or finance), there is considerable common ground within the curriculum of programs such as the MBA. As a result, the graduate gains essential knowledge required for effective performance in managerial roles.

Acquiring the wide range of management-related competencies induces 'inner value capital', which means that graduates gain a higher sense of self-esteem, self-efficacy and confidence (Baruch et al., 2005). Boyatzis and Renio's (1989) pioneering study showed the positive impact of MBA on competencies. Self-efficacy is a well-validated antecedent of performance (Bandura, 1977, 1997) and there is strong evidence that the MBA indeed improves the self-efficacy of MBA graduates (Baruch and Peiperl, 2000; Baruch and Leeming, 2001). Graduates often improve their sense of value, professionalism and competence, all of which contribute to their ability to manage effectively (Boyatzis and Renio, 1989).

Business education is also ideal for acquiring 'social capital', which is manifested in networking and in generating a web of personal contacts. Intra- and extra-organizational networks increase the human capital contribution to organizational success (Nohria and Eccles, 1992). The cohort of a specific class, even the full alumni of the university, serve as a foundation stone for networking, and being part of the network is a great asset for individual members (Higgins, 2005).

'Cultural capital' is apparent in the value that people within a society place on symbols of status (Tajfel, 1981). A degree in business, especially when gained from a top-ranked business school, adds to individual prestige. Although it was a relatively new entrant to the list of high-status professions, professional management gained considerably in prestige during the twentieth century. The MBA, by serving as its most esteemed accredited certificate, was instrumental in the accelerated rise in the perceived worthiness of being a manager by profession.

Lastly, the 'market value capital', which comes from all of the above, can be manifested in the improved remuneration that business education contributes to its graduates. A considerable number of databases indicate that, for example, MBA graduates can aspire to significant improvement in their level of earnings (*Business Week*, 1996; Merritt and Chambers, 2004; Rapert et al., 2004), although evidence suggests that the financial value of the MBA has declined (MacErlean, 1993). This follows the basic economic rule of supply and demand, with ever-rising numbers of graduates entering the market each year. Nevertheless, even taking into account the full cost of studying (including loss of earnings), the return on investment is still positive: data from recent years continue to indicate that an MBA helps to improve income (*Business Week*, 2005), and this is not restricted to graduates of top business schools (Baruch et al., 2005).

Focusing on personal development, the MBA has been found to be an exceptionally positive learning exercise, comprising several aspects such as intellectual stimuli and knowledge gains (Ainsworth and Morley, 1995; Baruch and Peiperl, 2000; Dougherty et al., 1993; Woolgrove, 2005). MBA graduates gain higher levels of self-esteem and self-efficacy in handling managerial processes. This is expected to lead on to better job performance, since having an MBA enhances self-confidence, self-esteem and self-efficacy, and all are proven antecedents of both performance and career success (Bandura, 1977, 1997; Gist and Mitchell, 1992; Branden, 1998). A further benefit of MBA studies, especially when undertaken at a reputable institution, is the prospect of creating and maintaining a valuable network (Higgins, 2005).

We noted earlier the considerable criticism of the MBA (e.g. Pfeffer and Fong, 2002; Porter and McKibbin, 1998), and there is much substance to this, certainly inasmuch as it relates to the issue of whether the pedagogical approach taken prepares managers for their future roles (see also Mintzberg, 2004). Pfeffer and Fong (2002) extend the criticism to a questioning of the general added value of the MBA, but they offer no strong evidence to support their critique.

Business education can also be a significant factor in reducing various forms of discrimination. This has been attributed to the qualification serving as a professional one. A manager with a business degree is perceived more as a professional manager, and less as a woman or a person of ethnic minority. Thus the professionalization of management also contributes to tackling discrimination (Baruch and Leeming, 2001; Montgomery and Powell, 2003; Simpson, 2000; Simpson et al., 2005), which is of benefit to the individual and wider society. Note however that in the face of continuing evidence of a pay gap related to gender and ethnicity, we might suggest the effect is compensatory, not a complete solution – business education may provide women and ethnic minorities with an added value to their résumé which partly counterbalances the effects of discrimination.

In this discussion we have shown how business education can generally be seen to offer added value for individuals. The gains are not restricted to the contribution to the human capital of graduates. They are also to do with professionalism, image and career prospects. However, its worth to the individual will partly be determined by the way it answers the specific needs for which the graduate embarked on the program. For some the major aim is to improve their salary, for others it could be promotability, and for yet others it may be the enabling of career change. The measurement of the impact of business education is not simple, even when taking financial returns as the yardstick (Bowles et al., 2001).

DOES BUSINESS EDUCATION LIVE UP TO ITS CAREER PROMISE

We have already noted the considerable financial investment involved in business education, but the time required for completion is also a considerable investment – the actual time invested is much higher than the classroom instruction time, as students are required to conduct assignments, read, and prepare for sessions and exams. Full-time students leave the labor market for a year or two, and whilst part-time students remain in the workplace, the tendency for them to make space for their studies by 'taking the foot off the accelerator' in terms of their jobs can have major implications. The former means significant losses of earnings. The latter is intangible, and thus not easy to evaluate. Studying part time means the emphasis and devotion that could be placed on work and family must now be shared with the demands of study, thus reducing resources invested in each domain. Ironically, then, this can have a negative impact on career prospects, even though the studies are pursued with career considerations in mind. For entrepreneurs, this would mean a delay in starting their business, which must be weighed against the added value in terms of the knowledge and skills gained to be able to run the business more effectively after graduating.

Studying for any degree, especially part time, can take its toll in the form of additional stress on family life as students juggle the demands of the managerial role and studentship obligations, as well as between work and family (Greenhaus and Beutell, 1985; Yang et al., 2000). Sometimes it is possible to apply work-related experience to both purposes (for example writing assignments on real business issues). Shadowing assignments are another example of work-related experience gained as part of studies. All these strategies for managing part-time study will be essential if the conflicts between work, home and study are not to take their toll on the student.

The question is – do the benefits outweigh the costs – in other words, is the MBA worth it? As demonstrated above, business education has many attractions, but also a possible negative impact. Baruch (1995) suggested that career decisions could be understood in terms of a push–pull model, based on Lewin's field theory. Certain forces would pull the individual towards a particular course of action; other forces would push him or her away from it. For the decision to study for an MBA, pull factors might include a felt need to develop managerial competence, a desire to increase earning potential, strong support from an employer, input from careers guidance, and job insecurity (including redundancy). Push factors might include cost, work pressures, difficult personal circumstances and low self-efficacy. On the latter point, it is notable that the MBA's continuing strong brand and the image of what 'an MBA' (i.e. a manager with this qualification) looks like can lead to individuals over-estimating the difficulty involved in undertaking an MBA program (push factor) and the cachet and market value of obtaining it (pull factor).

For many, business education is indeed a good, useful path, and the benefits spread from the individual to the organizational and national levels. However, it is not necessarily the answer for all. Who would be unlikely to benefit from business education? It may seem rather obvious to suggest that it is best suited for those pursuing a career in business, but the prestige of the qualification means it is sometimes encouraged for individuals whose occupational interests lie elsewhere. Where people are happy and content with their professional roles (Assouline and Meir, 1987), business education will not be appealing and might even be considered a waste of time and effort.

At the other end of the scale there are the top executives, who are already at the highest echelons. Studying for an MBA will not enrich their managerial experience in the way it will do for younger and junior/mid-level managers (Hunt and Baruch, 2003). The investment required for MBA studies may not lead to a worthwhile return, as they will lose time and reduce job commitment, which is essential in top positions. They may however still benefit from 'executive' MBA programs, set up for and directed to the needs of top business executives, enabling them to share views and ideas with their counterparts in similar positions in other organizations.

Professionals in specific sectors form another group for whom business education would not produce a significant added value: for medical doctors, lawyers, even accountants, the benefits of gaining an MBA or a specialized Masters degree in business are questionable. Specialist managers in fields such as HR and marketing may obtain significant benefit from undertaking a Masters degree in their specialist field rather than the more generalist MBA (Baruch et al., 2005).

We argue that although the claimed benefits of business education are plausible, they may not live up to the somewhat hyped expectations, at least in terms of return on investment. The MBA seems to substantially increase managerial competencies and enhance the self-esteem of graduates. However, unless the degree is taken at a top business school, graduates should not expect direct or immediate financial compensation, or even recovery of their investment in the studies. As discussed earlier, it was typically found that these graduates earned more than their counterparts, but when the investment involved is entered into the equation, many programs may not pass muster. That is not to say there are not tangible benefits; rather that the widespread and simplistic belief that 'an MBA will add $XXXX to your salary' may be misleading. Nevertheless, the MBA does on the whole improve employability, i.e. the ability to get a job. Once the graduate is engaged in the job, the direction and pace of advancement is more up to the person, though possessing an MBA may provide a halo effect which enhances the graduate's perceived promotability.

A TYPOLOGY FOR BUSINESS EDUCATION AS A CAREER CHOICE

Gunz (1989) suggests that managerial careers develop through the interaction of individual and organizational career logics. We might apply a similar notion to examining whether business education represents a beneficial career choice. To do so, we propose three career orientations among those whose roles can be broadly classified as managerial – technocrats, general managers and entrepreneurs (see Table 14.1).

Technocrats see themselves primarily in terms of their profession (e.g. engineering, finance). In organizations with dual-ladder careers systems, technocrats are likely to avoid the move into a 'pure' management role, so business education is relevant to technocrats only inasmuch as they pursue the managerial career route. Even these 'technocratic managers' may continue to construe themselves in terms of their profession, and business education would therefore be a beneficial career choice only if they intended to remain in an organization that places value on such qualifications – any external moves would be based on their technical expertise.

For general managers, management *is* their profession and business education is an obvious career choice. There are however some exceptions to the rule. For managers pursuing careers within a single organization, the benefits of business education will be closely tied to the stance taken towards qualifications by the company – where career progression is based on experience and performance, the costs of undertaking business education would be worthwhile only if they led to substantial improvements in the manager's performance. In organizations where business education *is* valued, there will still be individuals who have reached their present position without qualifications, on the basis of their experience and track record. However, as we noted, there is a trend towards viewing qualifications in business as an entry requirement, so fewer and fewer

Table 14.1   *Career orientation and the benefits of business education*

	Business education a beneficial career choice?	
	Yes	No
Technocrats	If management forms a significant component of the role *and* organization values business education	Where individual remains on technical career route
General managers	In most situations	If organization places no value of business education; if individual has progressed to senior level without it
Entrepreneurs	If company growth leads to business management as the entrepreneur's primary role	If entrepreneur's primary business input is professional or technical expertise

'unqualified' people will get the opportunity to enter the managerial ranks.

For entrepreneurs, the benefits of business education will be closely tied to the nature of their major input to the business. In small firms, where the owner's technical or professional expertise is the major source of competitive advantage, business education may be of limited benefit. However, as the company grows, the entrepreneur may find that his or her contribution is now more about running the business (as an organization), and the competencies provided by business education may make a significant contribution to overall performance.

For all three types, we must factor in the labor market. We have mentioned the influence of the internal labor market on technocrats and general managers, but clearly managers also need to be aware of developing a CV which would also be attractive in the external labor market. We have referred to business education as an investment, in this instance it might be thought of as insurance – the MBA as a lifejacket, it is hopefully never needed, but worn just in case!

SOCIAL BENEFITS OF BUSINESS EDUCATION – THE CASE OF ENTREPRENEURSHIP

The idea that business education can have positive benefits for wider society is consistent with the prevailing view that well-managed organizations will provide a healthier economy, provide jobs, deliver better public services etc. We will illustrate this view with a discussion of the relatively recent emphasis on entrepreneurship in the curriculum.

Many individuals seeking a career in business may plan to achieve their ambitions through starting a business of their own. The role of education in entrepreneurship has been a matter of considerable interest to governments who are attracted by the notion that business education might be the breeding ground for the next generation of entrepreneurs. At the same time, entrepreneurial careers are seen as offering a possible route to a business career for individuals and groups who may experience discrimination in more traditional career routes.

The logic of this approach is difficult to fault, but there are obvious weaknesses in the educational provision. As a field of study, business is often criticized for being overly oriented towards large companies and public organizations, and the knowledge and skills developed by business students lean heavily towards the running of existing organizations. Ironically, opportunities for successful business start-up may actually be more widely available to students in departments outside of the business school (especially engineering, IT and the natural sciences) who have knowledge and skills that are more directly marketable, i.e. can be sold to customers rather than to employers (Baruch et al., 2006). It may be that the contribution of business education to entrepreneurship will come from making it available to non-business students, and from the downstream benefits to entrepreneurs of having well-educated staff capable of running their business.

LOOKING AHEAD – THE GROWTH OF UNDERGRADUATE BUSINESS EDUCATION

The growth of undergraduate business education may have a significant impact on the role of MBA and Masters programs. A growing proportion of managers have studied business administration for their first degree (Ainsworth and Morley, 1995; Baruch et al., 2005). For them the scholastic capital gain will be marginal, because after in-depth study of managerial theories and practice for three years, they will be better acquainted with the material taught than a typical MBA student. They may join simply to refresh their memory and for the other human capital benefits of networking and learning experience. Business schools will have to develop special programs to fit the needs of business graduates.

Viewing business education through the lens of career, it should be noted that the considerations in choosing a first degree are somewhat different. In many countries the first degree is subsidized or free, and the choice here is whether to opt for business education or a non-vocational degree (perhaps having in mind the option of future Masters-level study in business). If business education is chosen, this may not represent an active career choice. In the UK, for example, the growth of undergraduate business education seems to reflect a degree of anxiety about student debt and future employment, rather than a positive choice of a business career. Business education becomes a safe option, offering the attractions of student life with the reassurance that you're working towards a qualification which has value on the labor market.

DIRECTIONS FOR FUTURE RESEARCH

This chapter has been based on the premise that the decision to pursue business education can be viewed as a career choice. It implicitly portrays business students as future-oriented (Gunz, 1989) career planners weighing up the pros and cons of a major life decision. Indeed, it seems almost unthinkable that anyone would invest that much effort, time and money without such careful deliberation. Yet anyone who has ever taught within a business school will know this is not a wholly accurate portrayal – there are many students who have a well-honed career plan, but there are also many for whom their plan could be captured in the phrase 'I'll get my MBA and then I'll see what's out there'. Feldman and Whitcomb (2005) suggest that young people are taking longer to 'launch' their careers, and an important avenue for research would be to explore whether the choice of business education is a continuation of the period of extended career exploration and indecision. Blenkinsopp and Scurry (2007) note that the growing numbers of what they term GRINGOs (graduates in non-graduate occupations) may develop a 'just a job' narrative to account for their failure to develop their careers – for such individuals a return to education, to study for an MBA or a Masters, may be a choice made in the hope it will help them finally 'launch' their careers. Taken together, these trends suggest that business education can be viewed as a career choice in three different ways – part of a definite plan, as a stage in an ongoing exploration, or as a hopeful gambit aimed at sparking a career into life. We noted earlier that the value of business education to the individual could best be assessed in terms of whether it answers the perceived needs of the individual. Understanding these three different orientations to business education as a career choice will provide a firmer basis for evaluating its success.

International variations in the role and value of business education need to be explored further. Labor market segments vary in the emphasis they place on qualifications, with some having a highly credentialist orientation such that level of education defines quite precisely the level of entry and even in some cases the level to which one can progress. Malach-Pines and Kaspi-Baruch (Chapter 2 in this volume) suggest there are also important cultural differences in orientation to career, and therefore in the purpose for which individuals might undertake business education.

In this chapter we have not touched on the role of organizations and business firms in creating the demand for business education. Organizations utilize their resources and assets to obtain and retain competitive advantage, and the all-too-true cliché that 'our people are our most valuable assets' needs to be reflected in investment in the right people (Pfeffer, 1998). Organizations depend on people and their management. The intangible assets, embedded in people, form the primary organizational capability for corporate growth and wealth creation (Mayo, 2001; Pfeffer, 1998; Quinn, 1996; Teece, 1997). Within the context of business education, the question remains: what is the added value bestowed upon graduates' competence by business education? Does it improve the quality of managerial talent? If so, what are the implications for employers and the wider community?

CONCLUSIONS

There is a clear need to discuss and examine the role and effectiveness of the MBA degree. Although subjected to much recent criticism from within the system (Mintzberg, 2004; Pfeffer and Fong, 2002), the MBA is still the flagship of management education (Carnall, 1992). In this chapter we have presented a comprehensive analysis of the value of business education to individuals and pointed out the benefits as well as possible pitfalls.

There is clear evidence that gaining a business degree improves human capital, which encompasses scholastic capital, social capital and cultural capital (Boyatzis and Renio, 1989; Useem and Karabel, 1986), inner value capital and market value capital (Baruch et al., 2005). The quality of the school attended, in terms of research, teaching, resources and reputation (to name but the most prominent factors), would influence the added value gained for its graduates, and can be expected to contribute to their future career success, be it internal or external (Ng et al., 2005).

In the 1960s, Townsend (1970) predicted the demise of business schools within 20 years. He failed to recognize the actual need and the added value that business education provides for individuals, organizations and societies. With the right sensitivity to the needs of the stakeholders (graduates, employers and the wider society), we believe that the MBA will maintain its role and positive reputation, despite the above-mentioned criticism.

NOTES

1. For ease of reference, we will use the term 'business education' to refer to the full spectrum of business, finance and management education.
2. The term is used here and throughout in its everyday sense, meaning a career based on self-employment or business start-up, rather than Kanter's (1989) broader idea of an entrepreneurial career as 'one in which growth occurs through the creation of new value or new organizational capacity'.

REFERENCES

Ainsworth, M. and Morley, C. (1995), 'The value of management education: views of graduates on the benefits of doing an MBA', *Higher Education*, **30**(2): 175–87.
Alsop, R. (2005), 'Exec MBA programs saturate some markets', *College Journal*, from the *Wall Street Journal*, www.collegejournal.com/mbacenter/mbatrack/20041213-alsop.html.
Altschuler, C.L. (2005), 'What will an MBA get you?', *Chicago Tribune*, 18 September.

Arbaugh, J.B. (2005), 'Is there an optimal design for online MBA courses?', *Academy of Management Learning and Education*, **4**(2): 135–48.

Assouline, M. and Meir, E.I. (1987), 'Meta-analysis of the relationships between congruence and well-being measures', *Journal of Vocational Behavior*, **31**(3): 319–32.

Bandura, A. (1977), *Social Learning Theory*, Englewood Cliffs, NJ: Prentice-Hall.

Bandura, A. (1997), *Self Efficacy*, New York: W.H. Freeman.

Baruch, Y. (1995), 'Business globalization – the human resource management aspect', *Human Systems Management*, **14**(4): 313–26.

Baruch, Y. (2004), *Managing Careers: Theory and Practice*, Harlow, UK: FT–Prentice Hall/Pearson.

Baruch, Y., Bell, M. and Gray, D. (2005), 'Generalist and specialist graduate business degrees: tangible and intangible value', *Journal of Vocational Behavior*, **67**(1): 51–68.

Baruch, Y., Blenkinsopp, J., Dane, M., Evans, T., Fuller, T., Hanage, R. and Jackson, C. (2006), *Advising Entrepreneurial Students: Information and Guidance for Careers Advisers*, Birmingham, UK: National Council for Graduate Entrepreneurship.

Baruch, Y. and Leeming, A. (2001), 'The added value of MBA studies – graduates' perceptions', *Personnel Review*, **30**(5): 589–601.

Baruch, Y. and Peiperl, M.A. (2000), 'The impact of an MBA on graduates' career', *Human Resource Management Journal*, **10**(2): 69–90.

Becker, G. (1964), *Human Capital*, New York: Columbia University Press.

Becker, G.S., Murphy, K.M. and Tamura, R. (1990), 'Human capital, fertility, and economic growth', *Journal of Political Economy*, **98**(5), part 2: S12–S37.

Bennis, W.G. and O'Toole, J. (2005), 'How business schools lost their way', *Harvard Business Review*, **83**(5): 96–104.

Blenkinsopp, J. and Scurry, T. (2007), 'Hey GRINGO: the HR challenge of graduates in non-graduate occupations', *Personnel Review*, **36**(4): 623–37.

Bowles, S., Gintis, H. and Osborne, M. (2001), 'The determinants of earnings: a behavioral approach', *Journal of Economic Literature*, **39**(4): 1137–76.

Boyatzis, R.E. and Renio, A. (1989), 'Research article: the impact of an MBA on managerial abilities', *Journal of Management Development*, **8**(5): 66–77.

Branden, N. (1998), *Self-Esteem at Work: How Confident People Make Powerful Companies*, San Francisco, CA: Jossey-Bass.

Business Week (1996, 2005), www.businessweek.com/archives/1996/b3498174.arc.htm.

Carnall, C.A. (1992), *MBA Futures: Managing MBAs in the 1990s*, Basingstoke, UK: Macmillan.

Clegg, S.R. and Ross-Smith, A. (2003), 'Revising the boundaries: management education and learning in a post-positivist world', *Academy of Management Learning and Education*, **2**(1): 85–98.

Coleman, J. (1988), 'Social capital in the creation of human capital', *American Journal of Sociology*, **95**: S95–S120.

Dougherty, T.W., Dreher, G.F. and Whitely, W. (1993), 'The MBA as careerist: an analysis of early-career job change', *Journal of Management*, **19**(3): 535–48.

Feldman, D.C. and Whitcomb, K.M. (2005), 'The effects of framing vocational choices on young adults' sets of career options', *Career Development International*, **10**(1): 7–25.

Gabriel, Y. (2005), 'MBA and the education of leaders: the new playing fields of Eton?', *Leadership*, **1**(2): 147–63.

GMAC® (2005), *Corporate Recruiters Survey*, Washington, DC: GMAC.

Gist, M.E. and Mitchell, T.R. (1992), 'Self-efficacy: a theoretical analysis of its determinants and malleability', *Academy of Management Review*, **17**(2): 183–211.

Greenhaus, J.H. and Beutell, N.J. (1985), 'Sources of conflict between work and family roles', *Academy of Management Review*, **10**: 76–88.

Grey, C. (2004), 'Reviving business schools: the contribution of critical management education', *Academy of Management Learning and Education*, **3**(2): 178–86.

Gunz, H. (1989), 'The dual meaning of managerial careers: organizational and individual levels of analysis', *Journal of Management Studies*, **26**(3): 225–49.

Hall, D.T. (1996), *The Career is Dead – Long Live the Career*, San Francisco, CA: Jossey-Bass.

Heimovics, D., Taylor, M. and Stilwell, R. (1996), 'Assessing and developing a new strategic direction for the executive MBA', *Journal of Management Education*, **20**(4): 462–78.

Higgins, M. (2005), *Career Imprints: Creating Leaders Across an Industry*, San Francisco, CA: Jossey-Bass.

Hunt, J. and Baruch, Y. (2003), 'Developing top managers: the impact of interpersonal skills training', *Journal of Management Development*, **22**(8): 729–52.

Judge, T.A., Cable, D.M., Boudreau, J.W. and Bretz, R.D. (1995), 'An empirical investigation of the determinants of executive career success', *Personnel Psychology*, 485–519.

Kane, K.F. (1993), 'MBAs: a recruiter's-eye view', *Business Horizons*, **36**(1): 65–71.

Kanter, R.M. (1989), 'Careers and the wealth of nations: a macro-perspective on the structure and implications of careers', in M.B. Arthur, D.T. Hall and B. Lawrence (eds), *A Handbook of Career Theory*, Cambridge: Cambridge University Press, pp. 506–21.

Kieser, A. (2004), 'The Americanization of academic management education in Germany', *Journal of Management Inquiry*, **13**(2): 90–98.

Kretovics, M. (1999), 'Assessing the MBA: what do our students learn?', *Journal of Management Development*, **18**(2): 125–36.

MacErlean, N. (1993), 'Master classes', *Accountancy*, **111**(1195): 29–34.

Mayo, A. (2001), *The Human Value of the Enterprise*, Yarmouth, ME: Nicholas Brealey.

McLarty, R. (2000), 'Evaluating graduate skills in SMEs: the value chain impact', *Journal of Management Development*, **19**: 615–28.

Merritt, J. and Chambers, E. (2004), 'The best business schools', *Business Week*, 11 October.

Mintzberg, H. (2004), *Managers not MBAs: A Hard Look at the Soft Practice of Managing and Management Development*, San Francisco, CA: Berrett-Koehler.

Montgomery, M. and Powell, I. (2003), 'Does an advanced degree reduce the gender wage gap? Evidence from MBAs', *Industrial Relations*, **42**(3): 396–418.

Ng, T.W.H., Eby, L.T., Sorensen, K.L. and Feldman, D.C. (2005), 'Predictors of objective and subjective career success: a meta-analysis', *Personnel Psychology*, **58**: 367–409.

Nohria, N. and Eccles, R.G. (1992), 'Face-to-face: making network organizations work', in N. Nohria and R.G. Eccles (eds), *Networks and Organizations*, Boston, MA: Harvard Business School Press, pp. 288–308.

Pfeffer, J. (1998), *The Human Equation*, Boston, MA: Harvard Business School Press.

Pfeffer, J. and Fong, C.T. (2002), 'The end of business schools? Less success than meets the eye', *Academy of Management Learning & Education*, **1**(1): 78–95.

Porter, L.W. and McKibbin, L.E. (1998), *Management Education and Development: Drift or Thrust into the 21st Century*, New York: McGraw-Hill.

Quinn, J.B. (1996), 'Managing professional intellect: making the most of the best', *Harvard Business Review*, **74**(2): 71–80.

Rapert, M.L., Smith, S., Velliquette, A. and Garreston, J.A. (2004), 'The meaning of quality: expectations of students in pursuit of an MBA', *Journal of Education for Business*, **80**(1): 17–24.

Simpson, R. (2000), 'Winners and losers: who benefits most from the MBA?', *Management Learning*, **31**: 331–51.

Simpson, R., Sturges, J., Woods, A. and Altman, Y. (2005), 'Gender, age, and the MBA: an analysis of extrinsic and intrinsic career benefits', *Journal of Management Education*, **29**: 218–47.

Tajfel, H. (1981), *Human Groups and Social Categories*, Cambridge: Cambridge University Press.

Teece, D.J. (1997), 'Capturing value from knowledge assets: the new economy, markets for know-how, and intangible assets', *California Management Review*, **40**(3): 55–79.

Tiratsoo, N. (2004), 'The "Americanization" of management education in Britain', *Journal of Management Inquiry*, **13**(2): 118–27.

Townsend, R. (1970), *Up the Organization*, London: Coronet Books.

Useem, M. and Karabel, J. (1986), 'Pathways to top corporate management', *American Sociological Review*, **51**: 184–200.

Woolgrove, M. (2005), 'Valuing an MBA: what benefits have Massey MBA graduates received from their degree?', unpublished MBA thesis, Massey University, New Zealand.

PART V

Education, Training and Learning for
Managers and Entrepreneurs

15. The training and development of managers and entrepreneurs: the role of integrative capability

Elizabeth Chell

INTRODUCTION

The theme of this chapter is the training and education of future managers and entrepreneurs. Do our extant education programmes (such as the MBA) meet the needs of future managers and entrepreneurs? If not, how should their education best be achieved? Should such programmes be developed to meet government and industry agenda to produce people with capability, and, if so, what does this mean? Whilst there is an economic context that is driving this agenda, there are also deeper questions about the psycho-social basis of managers' and entrepreneurs' learning and development needs that, arguably, once understood, should assist in the design of more effective programmes of teaching and learning. Thus the objective of this chapter is to consider the basis of those particular learning and development needs and their implications. But, in scoping these issues in a holistic way, some mention, however brief, should be made of the political and economic backdrop, as well as the position being taken in respect of the nature of entrepreneurship and innovation.

Successive governments on a world stage have positioned their country on issues of productivity and competitiveness (Chell and Allman, 2003). Some, including the UK, found their country's performance wanting; this is for the now familiar reasons of regenerating and transforming relatively old and stagnant industries to produce a new economy or because the particular economy is being generated from a relatively new and low base. The issues at the economic level may differ, but the requirements for human capital that is talented, skilled and capable is beyond question. Thus, to meet this requirement, there has been a demand for a labour force that is multifarious: diverse to meet the evident skills gaps and talented to help generate new industry, but above all capable in management and innovative in entrepreneurialism. How do we, and indeed how should we, produce people with high management and innovative capability?[1] Furthermore, can we generate people through our education and training system that excel in management and are also recognized as effective entrepreneurs? Or is this asking too much either of our systems or of people?

Before addressing such issues, there are cross-cutting themes of environment and culture that create national and regional variations in the conditions that influence entrepreneurial processes and outcomes to be borne in mind (Delmar and Davidsson, 2000; Minniti et al., 2005; Wennekers, 2002). Innovative activity (such as new firm formation, firm and employment growth) is more prevalent in resource rich environments (Kodithuwakku and Rosa, 2002; Shane, 2003, p. 147). Moreover, variation occurs at industry level; for example, the greater the industry concentration in a particular sector, the more difficult nascent entrepreneurship and innovation in that sector (Shane, 2003). Conversely, the greater industry fragmentation, the greater the prevalence of small operators, and the more likely 'structural holes', differential distribution of knowledge across a sector, and opportunities, will emerge (Burt, 1992; Aldrych, 1999).

However, whilst the prevailing national, regional, environmental and industry conditions affect entrepreneurial outcomes and performance, the process of entrepreneurship and innovation has some generic features. Innovation requires the ability to *create* something novel that is valued, and as such allows the entrepreneur to reap a profit. Creativity is thus crucial to opportunity identification. However, it is the centrality of capabilities such as this that leads some to argue that entrepreneurship cannot be taught. In this chapter, therefore, the exposition of such an issue is fundamental.

Pursuing the argument further, there is a lay view that entrepreneurship is about 'being the right person, in the right place at the right time'. Being the 'right person', however, does not necessarily equate to being born with a particular trait or set of traits. Rather, it may be construed that, due to the individual's level of knowledge and understanding, s/he is more likely to have that unique insight that is the innovation.[2] Furthermore, innovative capability requires practical intelligence, creativity and wisdom (Sternberg, 1985, 2003). 'Practical intelligence', in the context of innovation, involves information-processing ability, absorptive capacity, verbal ability, practical problem-solving capability and is context specific (Glynn, 1996). It has also been dubbed to be 'streetwise' (ibid., p. 1100). 'Creativity' involves idea-generation, envisioning and the ability to reconstruct what Shane (2003) terms 'the means–end framework'. 'Creative intelligence' contrasts with 'analytic intelligence' (Sternberg, 1985). Wisdom is that ability to generate insights; it involves sound judgement, and also counterfactual thinking – the ability to test an idea to destruction (Gaglio and Katz, 2001; Gaglio, 2004). Further, enabling conditions at the level of individual and team include: intrinsic motivation (e.g. enjoyment), cognitive playfulness (playing with ideas) and innovative intentions (Glynn, 1996; Bird, 1988). Moreover, situational factors that mediate or moderate entrepreneurial performance include the absence of constraints, adequate resources and support.

Such constraints and enablers are reflected in national and regional differences (Chell, 2001; Shane, 2003). Moreover, national cultural variation shapes the ways of being and doing of a people and as such influences how activities such as entrepreneurship and innovation are resourced and supported. Culture encompasses the organization of society, the expression of power and the treatment of men and women (Hofstede, 1991). Gender differences in various spheres may thus emerge within societies that treat men and women differently. Of relevance to entrepreneurship would be, for example, restriction on access to education, to knowledge and information. Similar effects may arise from impoverished societies where similar restrictions would create disadvantaged communities. Education is often used as a proxy in quantitative studies for 'human capital' (Arenius and Minniti, 2005); however, it may not equate to practical intelligence identified above. Institutional frameworks and rules govern and constrain how people can operate (Foucault, 1979). The political economy may vary from capitalism – a market economy that, in general, provides suitable conditions for entrepreneurship to flourish – to, say, a centralized planned economy that inhibits and constrains innovation (Schumpeter, 1963; Wennekers et al., 2002; Pittaway, 2005). Hence, it is important to bear in mind such macro- and meso-contextual issues; however, this chapter concerns the identification and development of capabilities at the micro-level, specifically at the so-called 'individual–opportunity nexus' (Shane, 2003, p. 9).

Such challenges within a politico-economic context raise concerns about the extant education and training systems; in this chapter we shall focus on the tertiary system, while recognizing that what happens at prior levels is likely to be fundamental for later developments. Focusing at the tertiary level brings into focus the role of institutions of higher education, and in particular of business schools within the sector. More recently, it has raised the issue of the role and integration of knowledge and technology transfer within universities. By painting this background, we can position the MBA and other potential post-experience programmes, and we can look critically at their design for delivering education and training of managers and entrepreneurs.

At the level of the business school,[3] there are questions of how theory and practice are integrated in the classroom, whether the aim is to produce generic management capability, and how the business school is positioned in relation to knowledge and technology transfer capability within the institution. Kurt Lewin half a century ago argued that 'there is nothing as practical as a good theory'; however, business schools have been criticized for their inability to integrate academic rigour with application. Others argue that the MBA as a qualification is merely used as a stepping stone in the career ladder of the aspiring manager, but has lost its cutting edge and its utility in producing personnel with effective management capabilities. Yet others argue that experience is the only effective test bed for developing and honing managerial capability. This is especially apposite when considering the case of the entrepreneur; indeed the old chestnut 'entrepreneurs are born and not made' continues to resonate within both a lay and an academic context.

This chapter begins with a critique of the nature of managers and entrepreneurs, and follows with a discussion of situation capability in respect of their respective roles. Situation capability alone as a skill to enable entrepreneurs and managers to perform effectively is arguably necessary but not sufficient; we therefore explore the role of imagination and intuition in the creation of new knowledge and innovations. We then argue that such capabilities are not inborn despite the neurological configuration of the brain and a person's genetic make-up. Rather, managers and entrepreneurs shape the path of their businesses by taking meaningful steps within their life space. The socio-political milieu in the business and economic world has set a context of global competitiveness that shapes both managers' and entrepreneurs' goals; we thus consider what this may mean for the development of capability to innovate and pursue opportunities. Finally, we pose the dilemma for education and training of managers and entrepreneurs in developing their innovative capability, and we make some positive suggestions for post-experience programme design.

MANAGERS AND ENTREPRENEURS: THE ISSUE OF ESSENTIALISM

What is a manager? Who is an entrepreneur? These questions have peppered the academic literature and the power-point presentations of teachers of management and entrepreneurship over the past several decades. But what is the key issue here? There are a number of interrelated issues: first, the tendency to create inventories of characteristics; second, the inconsistency or lack of agreement between different authors' lists; third, questions concerning the derivation of the characteristics; and fourth, the essentialist nature of the approach.

Both Stewart (1982) and Mintzberg (1973) focused on the role or job of management: how managers typically spend their time. Mintzberg, typical of this approach, has produced a list of ten managerial roles. However, whether we would agree with this list is not of itself important; what is clear is that all these characteristics are process roles. The job of a manager is thus to elicit a performance outcome by working with, and through, other people. To function effectively, what does the manager need to know; what skills and abilities should he or she exhibit? The position that we have provisionally adopted could be developed further by differentiating between focus on tasks versus focus on situations. Task knowledge is likely to be specific, drawing on abilities and skills that are relevant to executing the specific, narrowly defined job task. Task knowledge is likely to be technical – pertinent to the job performance to the best of the incumbent's ability. Situation capability relates to process knowledge. It requires the development of competences in understanding the problematic nature of a situation that has arisen in a broad sense and being able, with relevant others, (the team, for example) to arrive at various potential/feasible solutions. Whilst task knowledge is technical, acquired and applied when required to execute the task, situation capability develops experientially and heuristically. This preliminary analysis suggests that the necessary elements of a manager's skills' set are: problem-solving capability, team leadership and situational analysis.

The question of 'who is an entrepreneur?' has been shown to be particularly controversial (Gartner, 1989; Meredith et al., 1982; Chell et al., 1991). Definitions have varied from the idea that the entrepreneur performs an economic function, though the role has depended on the school of thought (Hébert and Link, 1988). Interestingly, whilst economists have identified process-related skills such as the ability to make judgemental decisions (Casson, 1982), other economists have highlighted certain personality characteristics, for example, Shackle – imagination – and Kirzner – alertness to opportunities. Further, one should not overlook research that has singled out attributes that also have been said to typify the entrepreneur as a risk taker, as someone who strives to achieve and/or someone who is self-efficacious and independent (Brockhaus, 1982; McClelland, 1961; Chen et al., 1998). This essentialist approach has led many to assume that entrepreneurs are born not made, and that it is not possible to teach entrepreneurship. Furthermore, the views that entrepreneurs are 'born' with a trait set that is identifiable through psychometric testing, and moreover, that there is something 'essential' about the nature of entrepreneurs, have been challenged (Chell, 1985; Gartner, 1989; Ogbor, 2000). Rather it has been argued the 'entrepreneur' is socially constructed (Bouchikhi, 1993; Chell, 2000; Ogbor, 2000). The approach that suggests one can construct lists of entrepreneurial attributes (for example, Timmons, 1985; Gibb, 1993; Bird, 2002) has been heavily criticized (Bouchikhi, 1993). Bouchikhi suggests that entrepreneurial behaviour emerges from the situation (see also Chell, 2000), although such a social constructivist approach requires further elucidation (see Chell, 2007a, 2008). Theoretically, it is argued that behaviour is limited by social context and situations that are rule-governed, but it is not determined by it, due to the ability to remember past situations and imagine future possibilities (Martin and Sugarman, 1996; Chell, 2007a). The entrepreneur can thus move forward developing his or her novel ideas by a process of counterfactual thinking (Gaglio, 2004).

Returning to the role-related approach enables us to ask what the entrepreneur is attempting to do and how. Economic entrepreneurs pursue opportunities with a view to accumulating capital and creating wealth, whereas social entrepreneurs aim to create social value. This pared-down definition also enables us to apply the distinction between task knowledge and situation capability. We suggest that an entrepreneur, like a manager, primarily needs the latter rather than technical knowledge; s/he can deploy other people in the organization to implement his or her decisions and draw on their technical skills.[4]

THE ROLE OF MANAGERS AND ENTREPRENEURS: SITUATION CAPABILITY

Situation capability is defined as 'integrative abilities that enable the person to address complex sets of problems that typify particular situations'. Such a person has the capacity to 'efficiently identify a problem and coordinate an appropriate response' (Connell et al., p. 127).

> Alex is the CEO of a company that designs electronic devices. His role in the company is primarily to identify (by following current events, tracking economic indicators and forecasts, ordering and digesting market research and so forth) and coordinate a response to high-level situations (for example, threats or opportunities) that may be significant for the company for better or for worse. (Ibid., p. 128)

Ability is specific and may of itself be developed, but there is a fundamental categorical difference between ability, such as solving mathematical equations, and the ability to draw on and synthesize different pieces of intelligence. The manager (CEO) and entrepreneur are comparable in that they develop and utilize integrative skills rather than narrowly defined, content-specific domain knowledge and modular ability. The abilities that a person brings to a situation, when applied, become realized competences that occur after learning and experience in a specific domain (Connell et al., 2003, p. 144). This results in an observable performance that is identified through the application of specified criteria.

The situation at time *t* is the state of the world as perceived with a problem that requires a solution. If the problem is to provide a mathematical solution, then the task is to transform the current state (no maths solution) to the required state (maths solution) and a new situation. Note that there may be different ways of arriving at the solution. If, however, the problem is to provide a business solution to a competitive situation that the firm is in, then there are a number of issues or problems that should be solved simultaneously, such as: what does my marketing director believe to be the right strategy?; can we increase our production of widgets?; is it possible to produce the next generation of widgets by Christmas? The role of the entrepreneur, owner–manager or chief executive officer is to take delivery of the solutions to the elements of the situation and provide an integrated solution to transform the situation the firm is in (of perceived competitive threat) to a new situation: threat reduced; crisis over. Whether the incumbent has achieved the goal or has resolved the situation is a matter of judgement by peers; in other words, it is socially construed.

Our education system has tended to be geared towards developing *specific* capabilities in individuals and is less able to produce individuals with planning and synthesizing capabilities. The objective of programmes such as the MBA and entrepreneurial programmes such as the MBV (Master of Business Venturing) or Master of Enterprise (MEnt), arguably, should address synthesizing capabilities. One issue, however, is the extent or level of base domain knowledge that is a prerequisite for effective integrative capability. This we argue should be at the threshold of appreciation and understanding rather than application by the manager or entrepreneur. There is also an issue in respect of creativity and imagination: are they fundamental to the ability to integrate knowledge across domains?

THE ROLE OF IMAGINATION AND INTUITION

Both senior managers and entrepreneurs who leading their companies have in common the need to operate strategically, projecting their minds forward and thus thinking in 'future space'. In so doing, entrepreneurs could be said to back their imagination (Shackle, 1979). The manner in which this is done is, arguably, intuitive (Allinson et al., 2000; Sadler-Smith and Shefy, 2004), although there are different ways of knowing (Nonaka and Takeuchi, 1995). Thus, as Hamel and Prahalad (2002) ask: 'what skills and capabilities must we begin to build now if we are to occupy the industry high ground in the future?' The convention has been to assume rational analysis; however, fast-moving situations, and high levels of ambiguity and uncertainty, limit the effectiveness of this approach; interpretive management, which is an open-ended process, is, arguably, more effective in these circumstances (Lester et al., 2002, p. 34): 'interpretation no less than invention is a highly creative process. To encourage creativity . . . the manager . . . needs to act less like an engineer and more like the leader of a jazz combo'.

Thus, to be globally competitive, companies are urged to be innovative, creative and effective at decision making. To think in these ways requires a relaxed environment, with reduced time pressure – a condition that may not obtain in a prevailing climate that is harsh and unrelenting. However, to force the pace of problem resolution and decision making may appear efficient, but is not necessarily effective. Time pressure produces focus on a narrow range of potential solutions and a need to select one of them, whereas to obtain a creative solution requires the expansion of the problem space and a consideration of a wide range of potential solutions (Claxton, 2001; Kaufmann, 2002). Also, enabling conditions such as intrinsic motivation (satisfaction), cognitive playfulness and serious innovative intentions are important (Glynn, 1996). Furthermore, whilst a radical innovation may be the approach that would lift a company out of its stagnant position, the more modest adaptation of existing know-how may be more acceptable, keeping personnel in their comfort zones (Ekvall, 2002), but less competitive.

The alternative, innovative and highly creative approach should start with problem solving, where idea generation is crucial and the deferment of judgement essential to avoid premature closure on a solution (Kaufmann, 2002, p. 53). However, the forces that drive creative thinking are largely unconscious and intuitive, and draw on cognitive capabilities in the imagination. Such latent ability is a part of the functioning of the brain and thus common to all; it does *not necessarily* lead to the best outcomes (Sadler-Smith and Shefy, 2004). What it does do is enable individuals to draw on all their faculties and to consider a wider range of possible solutions to complex problems.

Several authors, however, argue that creative and intuitive problem solving is a function of domain-specific knowledge that has accumulated over a lengthy period of time (up to ten years) and that this is essential for them to exhibit expert performance (Chase and Simon, 1973; Kaufmann, 2002, p. 51). The instances of domain-specific knowledge, though, include chess grand masters, composers, mathematicians and painters:

> The point is that a higher level of organised, domain-specific knowledge gives the expert access to more powerful problem-solving methods. Thus, high-level cognitive abilities should not be seen as existing apart from knowledge. Rather, powerful cognitive operations seem only to materialise in a system of well-organised, extensive knowledge. (Kaufmann, 2002, pp. 51–2)

There are two problems with this argument: one is that there appears to be confusion between creativity and expert performance; and second, the accumulation of domain-specific knowledge may be a different process to the ability to arrive at a creative solution that draws on knowledge from different domains. Accumulating patterns of chess moves such that one can eventually exhibit an expert performance that renders one a world champion may not (and intuitively does not seem to) be the same process as thinking 'outside the box' to produce solutions that to others appear at first blush counter-intuitive (e.g. dispensing money through a hole in the wall).

Intuition has its place in management decision making (Sadler-Smith and Shefy, 2004). First, to distinguish it from rationality and conscious thought processes, intuition includes two components: intuitive intelligence or the ability to arrive at a solution without conscious thoughts, and intuitive feelings in which the subconscious process of problem solving is accompanied by unconscious feelings that the individual may not be able to articulate or name. Intuition should be distinguished from tacit knowledge even though the subconscious element is shared.

Nonaka and Takeuchi (1995) take our understanding of knowledge to a different level. Knowledge, they argue, is related to human action and includes intention, social action and production of meaning. Knowledge is either tacit (subjective) or explicit (objective, or we would prefer to use the term 'public'). The problem is often to convert tacit to explicit knowledge, during which process learning occurs. The business problem that a company may be facing is how to develop a competitive advantage; the organizational problem is how to extract knowledge from a range of personnel with widely different capabilities, including technical know-how, located in different departments. The management problem is how does a manager extract innovative solutions to issues of product development when knowledge is so widely distributed (and in some cases the paths of relevant people do not cross)? Nonaka and Takeuchi provide a solution to these issues. Bringing people together in small groups to discuss the problem, initially to extract tacit knowledge with a view not only to make that knowledge public, but through its newness thereby to create new concepts, ideas and ways of experiencing reality, which becomes a potential source of innovation. Each member of the group may have domain-specific knowledge, but by sharing, new knowledge is created and a process of integration and synthesis occurs. If the manager or group leader is able to cultivate a relaxed atmosphere, lacking pressure, then s/he is also likely to draw on individuals' tacit knowledge. Evaluation of potential solutions may be deferred until this process is judged to be complete. Nonaka and Takeuchi describe the steps of the 'knowledge spiral' as follows: (a) socialization whereby personnel come together and build 'a field of interaction'; (b) externalization, triggered by meaningful dialogue in which metaphor and analogy are used to help flush out tacit knowledge and understanding; (c) methods for combining extant explicit with new explicit knowledge, for example by networking, newly created knowledge and existing knowledge from different parts of the organization are crystallized into something new; (d) 'learning by doing', i.e. implementation that triggers the internalization of new knowledge.

The skills and capabilities that are required of leaders of this process include: sympathetic understanding, respect for each person's ideas, ability to conceptualize, play back and summarize what has been said, ability to play 'devil's advocate' in order to stimulate debate and tease out counterfactual thoughts, and the ability to champion new ideas. None of these skills concerns domain-specific or technical knowledge; we return to our earlier question: should that be a given in a manager or entrepreneur?

DeFillipi and Arthur (1998) argue that there are two kinds of knowledge inherent in organizations that should be drawn upon to arrive at effective strategic decisions: they are human (knowing their trade) and social (knowing each other) capital, and they are interdependent. Relationships between creative individuals and staff with a business perspective require constant dialogue in order to drive an enterprise along. Hence, the role of facilitative group leadership should not be seen solely as that of a manager, but an entrepreneurially led venture, arguably, should also adopt this approach. Successful entrepreneurs do not necessarily have the technical knowledge of the industry sector their business is in, but they are able to extract implicit knowledge and know-how to good effect. Some well-known examples illustrate this: the entrepreneur Simon Woodruffe, who founded Yo Sushi!, had a background in the music industry, not the hospitality industry; Anita Roddick had a background in art and teaching, not in the production of cosmetics when she founded The Body Shop; Henri Strzelecki – a Polish postwar immigrant – founded Henri-Lloyd in partnership with Angus Lloyd in 1964, neither of whom had the technical knowledge to produce foul-weather clothing nor hands-on business management experience (see Chell et al., 1991 for this and other examples). The key to understanding what happens in companies that appear to extract knowledge for purposes of innovation and development is the concept of 'relationships'. These relationships are developed within the company; they are separate and distinct from external relationships developed through networking (Chell and Baines, 2000). So, is this ability to form and manage relationships a personality trait or a competence that can be learned and developed?

THE SOCIAL CONSTRUCTION OF CAPABILITY

We take as a given that human beings possess certain neurological assemblages in the brain that permit the development of various abilities; this brain structure is particular to the human species and is not inclusive of all possible abilities – some of which are peculiar to other animal species, for example, echolocation, scenting and so forth. However, the brain structure is the necessary requirement from which the person, given various external conditions, can acquire expertise (in a particular ability) and competence that is the perceived performance. The conditions are a part of the person's life space from which they make sense of everyday occurrences (Berger and Luckmann, 1966; Weick, 1995). Powell and Royce (1978), in a fascinating paper, identified six basic neurological systems in the human species that are integrated to produce personality, self-image, worldview, lifestyle and in general 'paths to being'. What we take from this paper is the view that the development path includes personal development objectives and a 'search for meaning in life' that individuals pursue during the life course. These are shaped as a consequence of negotiation of personal circumstances, coloured by a developing worldview, self-image and life/value systems. We take this as being germinal to the education of adults in business and other walks of life.

In making their way in the world, the individual acquires concepts – a set of labels that enables the identification of objects, situations and behaviours. These labels are acquired through discourse (Gergen, 1999). Through the faculty of memory the individual is able to remember and build their personal repertoire of labels. The nature and meaning of an object, situation or specific behaviour is negotiated during discourse, and their meaning may be contested – potentially could always be contested. The development of one's understanding of life events, occurrences and behaviour occurs through a process of discussion and emerges as a consequence of this social interaction in the context of the person's life space, worldview and perceived self-image. However, we should go beyond this statement to identify the role that relationships play in fashioning what may be thought, what actions are taken and what scope that person has.

In contrast to the Powell and Royce position, which focuses on development of the individual and more specifically *individually* driven development of meaning, social constructionism identifies as primary the *social generation* of meaning. Social intercourse generates a sense of 'facticity' as we identify patterns of behaviour that people label using 'typificatory schema' (Berger and Luckmann, 1967). The 'form of life' that a person is engaged in shapes behaviour, and indicates what is appropriate, or not, within the 'rules of the game' (Wittgenstein, 1978). Public knowledge also gives a sense of 'facticity'; for example, disciplinary regimes enable us to classify, describe and explain and give a sense of social ordering. Within such, there are conventions – socially derived rules – that dictate what may be known, what may be considered to be true within that regime (Foucault, 1979; Gergen, 1999). Disciplinary regimes may also be considered to form elite communities of knowledge or practice that are indicative of expertise, but also of the power of the cognoscenti over the lay individual or group (Deetz, 1996). A person may wish to challenge or contest such knowledge, and it is perhaps in that position in which we may place the innovator or entrepreneur. This is the entrepreneur *qua* 'rule-breaker', the Schumpeterian individual who engages in 'creative destruction' (Schumpeter, 1934). Moreover, what counts as skill or competence is socially construed within a particular domain or life space, given meaning by the exercise of judgement, criteria for assessing effective performance.

INNOVATION AND CHANGE: THE PART PLAYED BY A MANAGER AND AN ENTREPRENEUR

A person's worldview shapes the extent to which they consider that there is a need, on the one hand, for stability and routine responses to problems or, on the other hand, innovation and change. Kanter (1983, 1989 and 1995) has argued cogently that, in the current business and economic world, global competitiveness has necessitated the development of innovative (if not intrapreneurial) managerial behaviour. The latter she characterizes as the ability to be able to connect, to collaborate and to create synergies. Hence, she emphasized the importance of coordinated action and relationship building. This is more than process management, but includes both integrative capability and social nous to facilitate relationship building at both local and global levels.

Schumpeter provides a theoretical background to the role of the entrepreneur as a proactive, dynamic force whose role in economic development was essentially disruptive (frame breaking). The entrepreneur is someone who would perforce break the rules governing economic equilibrium by introducing an innovation that produced dramatic change. Economic development is thus a process defined by the carrying out of new combinations of factors of production, resulting from the creation of a new product or alteration in its quality or qualities; the development of a new method of production, perhaps enabling the entrepreneur to reduce the cost of the unit; opening a new market; capturing a new source of supply that reduces the cost of production; or is so innovative that it results in a reorganization of the industry (Schumpeter, 1934,

p. 78). This kind of innovation assumes a depth of knowledge of an industry – we would suggest tacit knowledge – creativity, novelty and high activity. It is the ability to act as a catalyst, to think 'outside the box', to exhibit both counterfactual capability and the ability to synthesize disparate ideas that create something truly new (Baron, 1998; Chell et al., 1991; Gaglio, 2004).

Schumpeter argued that only at that point of creative destruction was the individual an entrepreneur; otherwise he or she was a capitalist or business man or woman. This would explain in part why many entrepreneurs are described as 'serial' or 'habitual' entrepreneurs. Once the innovative idea has been accepted, it is important to be able to translate the vision and make it a reality; this implementation process is fundamentally a task for management (Chell, 2001, pp. 181–2; Chell and Tracey, 2005). Entrepreneurs may thus relinquish responsibility for execution and implementation of their vision to a key subordinate or subordinates.

But what is the link (if any) between such innovative behaviour and creativity? In the mid-twentieth century the white line that was painted along the centre of a road to separate two lanes of traffic was fitted with a series of in-set frames comprising a soft white rubberized cushion, with a pair of glass, reflective 'cat's eyes' that picked up the light from car headlights in the dark of night and indicated to oncoming traffic the boundary of their lane. It was an innovation – Cat's Eyes® – that saved lives and made its inventor, Percy Shaw, rich. The story is that he was driving home one night along an unlit road and caught sight of a cat, in the middle of the road, whose eyes shone out of the darkness at him and which gave him the idea. It was the ability to take one idea from one context and, through an act of imagination, envision it in a different context that is the innovation. The question is: could anyone do it?

It has been argued that the link between the creativity and training is somewhat tenuous, because high levels of training do not necessarily yield commensurate exhibitions of creativity (Simonton, 2003, pp. 224–5). Further, some creative people opt out of the learning/education process before they attain complete domain mastery. 'Unlike experts who strive to master everything known so far, creators wish to venture into the unknown, to ask new questions rather than learn old answers' (ibid., p. 225). This is why, as argued above, there is a difference between creativity and expert performance.

But is there simply one route to innovation and entrepreneurship? Kirzner (1973), for example, developing a different economic theoretical position to that of Schumpeter, argues that in practice information is imperfectly distributed and that some individuals are better placed to take advantage of this fact. Thus any one individual may at any one time have access to information that others cannot access; this may be due to his or her greater industry knowledge and ability to identify pertinent information, or synthesize information to enable him or her to arrive at a different conclusion from the other. This conclusion suggests that there is an opportunity to be exploited. Gaglio and Katz (2001) argue that opportunity identification is the most distinctive and fundamental of entrepreneurial behaviours. If this is so, how it is defined and elaborated, as a set of behaviours, practical skills and/or knowledge, is also crucial to know. They adopt a Kirznerian approach; that is, they suggest that entrepreneurs that exploit opportunities are in a position where information is differentially distributed such that they and they alone can recognize an opportunity. This suggests that entrepreneurs, sensitized by their understanding of the particular industry, technology and/or market context, are able to identify and interpret the opportunity. Others without that prior knowledge or experience would not be in a position to recognize the opportunity (Shane, 2000). From this sensing that something has changed, the entrepreneur seeks to understand how the change will affect the industry, the market and/or society, and realizes that there is a need to break the status quo; this results in innovative opportunities (Gaglio, 2004, p. 536).

The Schumpeterian position is different in that the entrepreneur creates opportunities and thereby also creates problems for other firms within an industry, where the process of economic disequilibrium may result in the destruction (or at least considerable modification) of the old industry and creation of the new. The entrepreneur in Kirzner's theory uses his/her superior knowledge to identify opportunities; alertness and idiosyncratic knowledge combines with imagination and interpretation and leads to the creation of an innovative change (Dutta and Crossan, 2005, p. 432). Through tacit knowledge of the industry, etc., the Kirznerian entrepreneur fills in the interstices of product and process innovations *within* the boundaries of the extant industry. By filling an information gap, this entrepreneur, in a sense, solves a problem within the industry. The process of opportunity recognition, in the Kirznerian world, is one of synthesis, of integration of knowledge and information from different sources. This, as we have argued above, suggests that such entrepreneurs have a particular capability that draws on a number of domains from which they can arrive at a solution that most others would not recognize, or if they did, eventually, it would not be supported to the same extent by pertinent information. The Kirznerian entrepreneurial process is similar to the managerial process at senior levels in the firm in so far as it comprises information scanning and manipulation to produce a strategic way forward. Schumpeterian entrepreneurs, on the other hand, can create opportunities without search (Shane, 2000).

THE PROCESS OF INNOVATION FROM AN EDUCATION AND TRAINING PERSPECTIVE

The role of senior management and entrepreneurship in conditions of change and development, we have argued, depends upon the execution of innovative, integrative, catalytic and synthesizing skills. Incumbents in such positions are less likely to need the technical skills associated with the particular business, but do have strategic business sense. However, the execution of innovative capability depends on intuition and the ability to convert tacit knowledge into explicit codified knowledge and understanding that facilitates the realization of new knowledge. Further, in established firms it would appear that innovators and senior managers are likely to need social and relationship skills – the ability to engage in dialogue that facilitates the development of insights about an industry and its markets.

We have also argued against the development of inventories of characteristics or attributes, yet we have arrived at a fundamental skills' set that we suggest will operate in any industry context. Now, we should perhaps consider whether such skills are trainable, and whether the university business school is the appropriate locale for such personal development of post-experience students.

Conventional MBA programmes in university business schools focus on the further development of general management knowledge, in marketing, accounting, HRM, etc. with the objective of developing the student's understanding of management across a wider range of sub-management disciplines. The MBA has come under close scrutiny, and in some cases severe criticism, for a lack-lustre approach that perhaps does not deliver what the post-experience manager wants. We might argue therefore that what programmes like the MBA offer is rather too much modular, basic information *about* each subject and insufficient attention to how the student might use and integrate information across the various subjects. An objection could be raised that in fact the case study method (where it is practised) does just that; it allows the student to draw on knowledge and understanding across various subjects; likewise the business game calls on the ability to work in a team and to produce a solution to a business problem that requires understanding of its various dimensions. But, it might be countered, what proportion of the syllabus is given up to such integrative heuristic learning and how pertinent are the examples to the individual manager or entrepreneur?

A further issue is the insistence by the educator of what the student must know by the end of their course; in other words, the course is driven by the educator rather than the student. How much more difficult would it be to negotiate learning contracts with each student and thereby to produce a more flexible syllabus? Under such circumstances the conventional examination of courses would probably be defunct. Certainly in several business schools that I have worked in and with, this degree of change would probably be anathema – and if not that, it would certainly cause consternation, objections and personal difficulties for individual members of staff before it could be seriously implemented.

One objection that might be raised is the belief that universities are there to educate, not to train; universities bestow knowledge, wisdom and understanding, equipping individuals to deal with information, think analytically and thus be able to tackle problems in a rational and logical manner. This is, of course, a traditional view of university education, which not all educators or, indeed, universities espouse. It suggests that educational programmes are designed primarily to deepen an individual's knowledge of a subject and not to develop their skills for implementation of new knowledge and understanding. This would also suggest that the MBA is not ideally suited for the education of experienced managers and entrepreneurs who are operating in conditions of innovation and change within their company and/or industry. Running counter to this is the view of problem-centred learning. In the business scenario, problems tend to be complex, multi-layered, and could be analysed to demonstrate various optional solutions. But how could such scenarios be simulated in the business school environment? Is it the lack of application that essentially condemns the conventional MBA in the eyes of such business men and women? Is the MBA not better suited to industries where there is greater routine knowledge, where incremental innovations and adaptive behaviours are favoured over the more disruptive?

In practice, the natural inclination of the entrepreneur, and indeed senior manager, would be to sense gaps in information in a tacit and intuitive manner. A process of synthesis (as opposed to analysis) of information would yield a configuration of a higher-order resolution from which optional ways forward are identified. Through a process of counterfactual thinking in respect of several of the 'favoured' options, selection and choice of way forward would be made. We would argue that this process could only be applied where there were actual relevant problems and situations that were familiar to the entrepreneur or senior manager. Our recommendation therefore would be to use actual problem and information resolution approaches as learning vehicles in post-experience courses. Below are some suggestions for a redesign of post-experience programmes aimed at entrepreneurs and middle to senior managers in firms and industries where innovation and change are highly desirable, if not the norm.

POST-EXPERIENCE PROGRAMME STRUCTURE

From our analysis of entrepreneurial capability and senior management ability to operate in situations of ambiguity and change, we assume that a heuristic, problem- and student-centred approach to learning and development is required. This is by no means new, but our interest here is how to embed it into the structure, curriculum and syllabus of post-experience courses. We also assume that entrepreneurs, in particular, and busy managers will not attend courses that they do not deem to be relevant and useful. A number of examples exist of post-experience[5] programmes – aimed at entrepreneurs – from which one could remodel the MBA (or indeed discard or replace, as appropriate). We suggest that course design should (a) be workshop-, not classroom-based, (b) be problem-oriented and individually relevant, (c) be future-oriented, (d) be facilitated by mentors and practitioners experienced in the conversion of tacit to explicit knowledge, (e) be project-based, (f) enable the student to draw on knowledge from a range of sub-disciplines and promote the development of synthesizing capability, and (g) offered through a highly flexible time-frame in short intensive chunks.

CONCLUSIONS

We have argued that in conditions where a new solution to a problem is needed or thought to be desirable, both entrepreneurs and middle to senior managers will be operating in situations, perhaps of their own choosing or making, where the generation of new knowledge leading to innovative ideas is required. The knowledge that they possess is not necessarily industry-specific or technical, but it is likely to be coloured by an implicit understanding of the market. The entrepreneur or senior manager will have sensed the need for change in product or process through insight or tacit knowledge about the industry or business in which they are operating, or intending to operate. This knowledge is not domain-specific, as in the case of a mathematician, musician or chess grand master, where many years of knowledge acquisition and execution lead to an expert performance. Rather, it is the ability to redefine a problem and to synthesize a range of sources of information in its solution, thereby creating new insights, new knowledge and a potential innovation. This creative capability, we have argued, stems from the skill of relating to a range of individuals or information sources and reconfiguring the information in a new way. It takes a 'solution' that obtains in one context and drops it into another; it redesigns the solution to meet a market requirement – one that may as yet be generally unrecognized.

This skill or competence is learnt heuristically, is generic and is not particular to any nation, though the ability to develop it may be constrained by cultural and environmental conditions.

The last observation encompasses the reality that certain groups may be treated differently in particular societies, thus suppressing their abilities and their performance. Differential treatment of women, for example, has resulted in the unsurprising observation that fewer engage in entrepreneurial activities. However, I have encountered no evidence that women have lower levels of practical intelligence, are less creative or are less likely to exhibit wisdom than men. Furthermore, there is no evidence to suggest women are not driven by intrinsic motivation, such as satisfaction, and cognitive playfulness, playing with ideas and solving problems. Where men and women do differ is that women appear to have lower entrepreneurial (if not innovative) intentions. This may be explained by lower levels of exposure, fewer role models, lower levels of education in some countries, and cultural constraints. If this is the case, then there are no inherent reasons why women should not be successful entrepreneurs and managers who are able to give their company a competitive edge through innovation. The education issue, however, is important in this respect: the programmes that could potentially address issues of innovation and change are *post-experience*; hence marginalized groups could be doubly disadvantaged if they are unable to acquire the threshold level of experience.

The design of educational programmes to enhance innovative capability is a challenge that faces many business schools. Imparting deeper knowledge of a subject domain in a technical way is not what is required; such knowledge is merely instrumental to a more central need, the production of new knowledge in a business and industry context. The MBA is designed to develop a middle manager's knowledge and capability in a range of business areas, but it falls short of innovation. Thus educationalists have a choice (a) to revamp the MBA to meet industry's needs for innovative capability, or (b) to design new post-experience programmes that are focused not on the development of general management capability, but on this one strength: the ability to produce new and exciting innovations that are globally competitive and have the potential for refocusing an industry. Let us throw down the gauntlet to our business schools and see in what ways, and to what extent, they rise to the challenge!

NOTES

1.　Here we are taking Kanter's thesis of the fundamental importance of innovation and change for nations and companies to be competitive on a world stage. We thus separate analytically innovation – the generation of novel ideas that are valued – from its management and implementation.

2. There are broadly two types of innovation: radical (Schumpeterian) innovations that require new knowledge/information, and creativity and incremental (Kirznerian) innovations that require access to knowledge/information that enables discovery of opportunities.

3. The term 'business school' is used generically to include management schools, institutes and colleges whose stated objective is the delivery of management and/or entrepreneurship education and/or training.

4. Bird (2002, p. 205), following Boyatzis, distinguishes between 'threshold competencies' and 'success competencies' of entrepreneurs. Hence, we would argue, in the context of the above discussion, that entrepreneurs and managers have 'threshold knowledge and understanding' sufficient to make judgements about what needs to be done, whereas other employees are likely to have superior domain/technical knowledge in order to execute the task.

5. Post-experience means that the students admitted to the programme have a minimum of, say five years, industry experience.

REFERENCES

Aldrych, H. (1999), *Organizations Evolving*, London and Thousand Oaks, CA: Sage.

Allinson, C.W., Chell, E. and Hayes, J. (2000), 'Intuition and entrepreneurial behaviour', *European Journal of Work and Organizational Psychology*, **9**(1): 31–43.

Arenius, P. and Minniti, M. (2005), 'Perceptual variables and nascent entrepreneurship', *Small Business Economics*, **24**: 233–47.

Baron, R.A. (1998), 'Cognitive mechanisms in entrepreneurship: why and when entrepreneurs think differently than other people', *Journal of Business Venturing*, **13**(4): 275–94.

Berger, P.L. and Luckmann, T. (1966), *The Social Construction of Reality*, London: Penguin.

Bird, B. (1988), 'Implementing entrepreneurial intentions: the case for intention', *Academy of Management Review*, **13**: 442–53.

Bird, B.J. (2002), 'Learning entrepreneurship competencies: the self-directed learning approach', *International Journal of Entrepreneurship Education*, **1**: 203–27.

Bouchikhi, H. (1993), 'A constructivist framework for understanding entrepreneurship performance', *Organisation Studies*, **14**(4): 551–69.

Brockhaus, R.H. (1982), 'The psychology of the entrepreneur', in C.A. Kent, D.L. Sexton and K.H. Vesper (eds), *Encyclopaedia of Entrepreneurship*, Englewood-Cliffs, NJ: Prentice-Hall, pp. 39–57.

Burt, R.S. (1992), 'The social structure of competition', in N. Nohria and R.G. Eccles (eds), *Networks and Organizations: Structure, Form, and Action*, Cambridge, MA: Harvard University Press, pp. 57–91.

Casson, M. (1982), *The Entrepreneur – An Economic Theory*, Oxford: Martin Robertson.

Chase, W.G. and Simon, H.A. (1973), 'Perception in chess', *Cognitive Psychology*, **4**: 55–81.

Chell, E. (1985), 'The entrepreneurial personality: a few ghosts laid to rest', *International Journal of Small Business*, **3**(3): 43–54.

Chell, E. (2000), 'Towards researching the "opportunistic entrepreneur": a social constructionist approach and research agenda', *European Journal of Work and Organisational Psychology*, **9**(1): 65–82.

Chell, E. (2001), *Entrepreneurship: Globalization, Innovation and Development*, London: Thomson Learning.

Chell, E. (2007a), 'Social enterprise and entrepreneurship: towards a convergent theory of the entrepreneurial process', *International Small Business Journal*, **25**(1): 5–23.

Chell, E. (2008), *The Entrepreneurial Personality*, 2nd edn, London: The Psychology Press (forthcoming).

Chell, E. and Allman, K. (2003), 'Mapping the motivations and intentions of technology oriented entrepreneurs', *R&D Management*, **33**(2): 117–34.

Chell, E. and Baines, S. (2000), 'Networking, entrepreneurship and micro-business behaviour', *Entrepreneurship and Regional Development*, **12**(2): 195–215.

Chell, E. and Tracey, P. (2005), 'Development of a model of effective interrelating', *Human Relations*, **58**(5): 577–616.

Chell, E., Haworth, J. and Brearley, S. (1991), *The Entrepreneurial Personality: Concepts, Cases and Categories*, London and New York: Routledge.

Chen, C.C., Greene, P.G. and Crick, A. (1998), 'Does entrepreneurial self-efficacy distinguish entrepreneurs from managers?', *Journal of Business Venturing*, **13**(4): 295–316.

Claxton, G. (2001), 'The innovative mind: becoming smarter by thinking less', in J. Henry (ed.), *Creative Management*, 2nd edn, London: Sage and The Open University Business School, pp. 29–43.

Connell, M.W., Sheridan, K. and Gardner, H. (2003), 'On abilities and domains', in R.J. Sternberg and E.L. Grigorenko (eds), *The Psychology of Abilities, Competencies and Expertise*, Cambridge: Cambridge University Press, pp. 126–55.

DeFillipi, R. and Arthur, M.B. (1998), 'Paradox in project-based enterprise: the case of film making', in J. Henry and D. Mayle (eds), *Managing Innovation and Change*, 2nd edn, London: Sage and The Open University Business School, pp. 189–202.

Deetz, S. (1996), 'Describing differences in approach to organization science: rethinking Burrell and Morgan and their legacy', *Organization Science*, **7**(2): 191–207.

Delmar, F. and Davidsson, P. (2000), 'Where do they come from? Prevalence and characteristics of nascent entrepreneurs', *Entrepreneurship and Regional Development*, **12**(1): 1–23.

Dutta, D.K. and Crossan, M.M. (2005), 'The nature of entrepreneurial opportunities: understanding the process using the 4I organizational learning framework', *Entrepreneurship Theory and Practice*, **29**(4): 425–49.

Ekvall, G. (2002), 'Organizational conditions and levels of creativity', in J. Henry and D. Mayle (eds), *Managing Innovation and Change*, 2nd edn, London: Sage and The Open University Business School, pp. 99–110.

Foucault, M. (1979), *Discipline and Punishment*, New York: Vintage.

Gaglio, C.M. (2004), 'The role of mental simulations and counterfactual thinking in the opportunity identification process', *Entrepreneurship Theory and Practice*, **28**(1): 533–52.

Gaglio, C.M. and Katz, J.A. (2001), 'The psychological basis of opportunity identification: entrepreneurial alertness', *Small Business Economics*, **16**(2): 95–111.

Gartner, W. (1989), ' "Who is an entrepreneur?" is the wrong question', *Entrepreneurship Theory and Practice*, **13**(4): 47–68.

Gergen, K.J. (1999), *An Invitation to Social Constructionism*, London: Sage.

Gibb, Alan A. (1993), 'Enterprise culture and education: understanding enterprise education and its links with small business, entrepreneurship and wider social goals', *International Small Business Journal*, **11**(3): 11–34.

Glynn, M.A. (1996), 'Innovative genius: a framework for relating individual and organizational intelligences to innovation', *Academy of Management Review*, **21**(4): 1081–111.

Hamel, G. and Prahalad, C.K. (2002), 'Competing for the future', in J. Henry and D. Mayle (eds), *Managing Innovation and Change*, 2nd edn, London: Sage and The Open University Business School, pp. 23–31.

Hébert, R.F. and Link, A.N. (1988), *The Entrepreneur – Mainstream Views and Radical Critiques*, 2nd edn, New York: Praeger.

Hofstede, G. (1980), *Culture's Consequences: International Differences in Work-related Values*, Beverley Hills, CA: Sage.

Hofstede, G. (1991), *Cultures and Organizations – Software of the Mind*, London: McGraw-Hill.

Kanter, R.M. (1983), *The Change Masters*, London: Unwin.

Kanter, R.M. (1989), *When Giants Learn to Dance*, London and New York: Simon & Schuster.

Kanter, R.M. (1995), *World Class: Thriving Locally in the Global Economy*, New York: Simon & Schuster.

Kaufmann, G. (2002), 'Creativity and problem solving', in J. Henry (ed.), *Creative Management*, 2nd edn, London: Sage and The Open University Business School, pp. 44–63.

Kirzner, I. (1973), *Competition and Entrepreneurship*, Chicago, IL: University of Chicago Press.

Kodithuwakku, S.S. and Rosa, P. (2002), 'The entrepreneurial process and economic success in a constrained environment', *Journal of Business Venturing*, **17**: 431–65.

Lester, R.K., Piore, M.J. and Malek, K.M. (2002), 'Interpretive management: what general managers can learn from design', in J. Henry and D. Mayle (eds), *Managing Innovation and Change*, 2nd edn, London: Sage and The Open University Business School, pp. 32–44.

McClelland, D.C. (1961), *The Achieving Society*, Princeton, NJ: Van Nostrand.

Martin, J. and Sugarman, J. (1996), 'Bridging social constructionism and cognitive constructivism: a psychology of human possibility and constraint', *Journal of Mind and Behaviour*, **17**(4): 291–320.

Meredith, G.G., Nelson, R.E. and Neck, P.A. (1982), *The Practice of Entrepreneurship*, Geneva: International Labour Office.

Minniti, M., Bygrave, W.D. and Autio, E. (2005), *Global Entrepreneurship Monitor*, Babson Park, MA and London: Babson College and London Business School.

Mintzberg, H. (1973), *The Nature of Managerial Work*, New York: Harper & Row.

Nonaka, I. and Takeuchi, H. (1995), *The Knowledge Creating Company: How Companies Create the Dynamics of Innovation*, Oxford: Oxford University Press.

Ogbor, J.O. (2000), 'Mythicizing and reification in entrepreneurial discourse: ideology-critique of entrepreneurial studies', *Journal of Management Studies*, **37**(5): 605–35.

Pittaway, L. (2005), 'Philosophies in entrepreneurship: a focus on economic theories', *International Journal of Entrepreneurial Behaviour and Research*, **11**(3): 201–21.

Powell, A. and Royce, J.R. (1978), 'Paths to being, lifestyle and individuality', *Psychological Reports*, **42**: 987–1005.

Sadler-Smith, E. and Shefy, E. (2004), 'The intuitive executive: understanding and applying "gut feel" in decision-making', *Academy of Management Executive*, **18**(4): 76–91.

Schumpeter, J.A. (1934), *The Theory of Economic Development*, Cambridge, MA: Harvard University Press.

Schumpeter, J.A. (1963), *History of Economic Analysis*, 5th edn, New York: George Allan.

Shackle, G.L.S. (1979), *Imagination and the Nature of Choice*, Edinburgh, UK: University of Edinburgh Press.

Shane, S. (2000), 'Prior knowledge and the discovery of entrepreneurial opportunities', *Organization Science*, **11**(4): 448–69.

Shane, S. (2003), *A General Theory of Entrepreneurship*, Cheltenham, UK and Northampton, MA, USA: Edward Elgar.

Simonton, D.K. (2003), 'Expertise, competence, and creative ability', in R.J. Sternberg and E.L. Grigorenko (eds), *The Psychology of Abilities, Competencies and Expertise*, Cambridge: Cambridge University Press, pp. 213–39.

Sternberg, R.J. (1985), 'Implicit theories of intelligence, creativity, and wisdom', *Journal of Personality and Social Psychology*, **49**(3): 607–27.

Sternberg, R.J. (2003), *Wisdom, Intelligence, and Creativity Synthesized*, Cambridge: Cambridge University Press.

Stewart, R. (1982), *Choices for the Manager – A Guide to Managerial Work and Behaviour*, London: McGraw-Hill.

Timmons, J.A. (1989), *The Entrepreneurial Mind*, Andover, MA: Brick House Publishing.

Weick, K.E. (1995), *Sensemaking in Organizations*, Thousand Oaks, CA: Sage.

Wennekers, S., Uhlaner, L.M. and Thurik, R. (2002), 'Entrepreneurship and its conditions: a macro perspective', *International Journal of Entrepreneurship Education*, **1**(1): 25–64.

Wittgenstein, L. (1978), *Philosophical Investigations*, Oxford: Blackwell.

16. Age of opportunity? Career making and learning for mid-career entrepreneurs

David Rae

INTRODUCTION – WHY EXPLORE CAREER MAKING AND LEARNING FOR MID-CAREER ENTREPRENEURS?

The purpose of this chapter is to explore the concept of mid-career entrepreneurship, especially in relation to career making as a learning process. Mid-career entrepreneurs (MCEs) are those who, aged approximately 35–55, decide to start a business venture. Generally this follows a period as an employee, for example as a manager, professional or technical specialist, and represents a voluntary or enforced career change. The decision to become an MCE is therefore to choose self-determination of future economic prosperity, career and personal identity over the prospective benefits of being an employee.

The issues of career making for managers and entrepreneurs in mid-career are explored from a learning perspective, since prior experience and learning are fundamental to the decision to become an entrepreneur. Recent research and educational policy on entrepreneurship, at least in the UK as well as more generally in Europe, has emphasized young and graduate entrepreneurs at the start of their careers (Hannon, 2004; Pittaway and Cope, 2005). Without detracting from the importance of this age group, it is increasingly evident that MCEs are a group of growing economic and social significance. They are responsible for an expanding proportion of entrepreneurial activity and may well constitute the majority of entrepreneurs, yet little research has been published on this group, nor in connection with the learning and career-making issues associated with them (Rae, 2005a).

This focus on learning and career making is central to mid-career entrepreneurship because traditional perspectives in the careers literature did not explicitly recognize learning as a decision-making process, which becomes increasingly significant with age. Entrepreneurial learning has become a legitimate field of study (Harrison and Leitch, 2005), but its connections with careers theory have so far been limited, especially for older workers. The interpretation of the careers literature in this chapter proposes that a constructivist view of careers has emerged in which people use sensemaking expressed through their personal narratives in 'making up', 'reinventing' and shaping their individual careers, and which can be termed 'career making' (Weick, 1995). This concept connects with the entrepreneurial behaviours of recognizing and acting on opportunities and working in creative ways to achieve life and work-related goals.

This chapter therefore aims to enhance the understanding of mid-career entrepreneurship by taking a case-based approach to explore these four questions:

1. What can the careers literature tell us about mid-career entrepreneurship?
2. How and why do people in mid-career choose entrepreneurship?
3. How do they construct entrepreneurial careers (career making)?
4. What are the issues presented by mid-career entrepreneurship for individuals, organizations and society?

The chapter will address these four questions through the following structure. First, the significance of mid-career entrepreneurship will be summarized. Second, existing literature on the subject, which is limited in scope, will be reviewed to assess what perspectives it can offer. Third, new perspectives on mid-career decision making are proposed in relation to entrepreneurship, based on learning, personality and behaviour, and career change trajectories. Fourth, career pathways to illustrate career making by MCEs are included with a career stage model and short, illustrative case studies. Finally, the opportunities and challenges posed by mid-career entrepreneurship, at individual, organizational and societal levels are discussed.

WHY IS MID-CAREER ENTREPRENEURSHIP IMPORTANT?

The significance of mid-career entrepreneurship needs to be outlined in relation to its economic, social and political context. The demographic profile of the UK and other OECD countries displays a steadily ageing population in which more people will need to develop entrepreneurial capability to find new opportunities for economic activity or to extend their working lives (ONS, 2006). The ability of the state to fund unemployment, long-term inability to work through ill-health, and prolonged retirement, is becoming constrained as the population ages (DWP, 2005). Confidence is declining in the ability of the state, employers and financial services industry to provide effective pension schemes which support longer periods in retirement, especially where these are funded by a diminishing working population (Pensions Commission, 2005). Employers have become used to practising age discrimination in both recruitment and redundancy decisions, generally favouring younger workers, whilst the covert disadvantaging of older workers in employment may continue even though it is illegal (CIPD, 2005). The need to extend entrepreneurship across the age spectrum is gradually becoming acknowledged as a policy goal in the UK, as economic changes require an increasing proportion of the existing working population, from a broader social and demographic background, to develop entrepreneurial skills in mid-career.

It is necessary to define what is meant by 'mid-career' in terms of an age range, even though this is somewhat arbitrary and is likely to change as working lives become longer. *The Global Entrepreneurship Monitor* (GEM) uses the age ranges 16–24, 25–34, 35–44, 45–54 and 55–64 (Harding et al., 2005). Taking the notion of career as 'advancement through life', if the period between 16 (the earliest age of joining the formal workforce in the UK) and 34 is considered to be one of education and 'early career' formation and development, then over 55 can be considered to be one of 'third age'. The age bands 35–44 and 45–54 can therefore be used to define mid-career. People in mid-career are representatives of the postwar 'baby boom', often having experienced diverse changes in personal, family and work life, economic necessity and opportunity, education and work-based learning, and social participation. By their mid-career, most have gained considerable life experience and may be at the peak of their potential and capability, yet a number of studies have shown the dissatisfaction and need for change frequently experienced by people in this age group (Holmes and Cartwright, 1994; Mallon and Cohen, 2001).

The UK GEM report for 2005 provides valuable statistics which indicate the scale of mid-career entrepreneurship. Total entrepreneurial activity (TEA) is highest in the 35–44 age group, at 7.9 per cent of the population, including 10 per cent of males and 5.9 per cent of females. This age group shows the highest level of confidence in opportunity availability and confidence in personal skills, which diminish slightly in the 45–54 age range, with potential entrepreneurs in these age ranges most likely to be qualified at first degree, A level or vocational qualification levels. Whilst younger age groups may be more likely in future to take entrepreneurial action, it is the mid-career groups which appear most likely to do so at present and may well constitute the largest proportion of the population engaged in entrepreneurial activity, whilst the proportion of the population in the 35–55 age group is growing more rapidly than is the 16–34 age group (Harding et al., 2005).

Gender issues are significant in mid-career entrepreneurship. The lower proportion of female MCEs may indicate the need for continuing support and encouragement to enable women to develop their entrepreneurial potential and gain independence and self-determination, as indicated by a growing body of research (Moore and Buttner, 1997; Diamond, 2003). The GEM findings are reinforced by Labour Market Survey analysis which identified that most of the increase in self-employment in the UK during 2002–3 could be attributed to the 35–49 and older age groups, with the proportion of self-employment in relation to the workforce increasing in line with age. The greatest increases in business activity were reported in financial and property services and construction (Macaulay, 2003).

WHAT CAN THE LITERATURE TELL US ABOUT MID-CAREER ENTREPRENEURSHIP?

The 'classic' literature on careers was dominated by structure and process, emphasizing lifetime vocational choice and continued employment in, generally, large organizations, professions and established industries or public service sectors (Super, 1957; Arthur et al., 1984). There was apparently little need to consider self-employment or entrepreneurship. Schein (1978, 1993) advanced this by developing models of career stages, dynamics and a 'career anchors' model of eight types of career preference which included anchors of 'autonomy-independence' and 'entrepreneurial creativity'. Katz (1994) refined Schein's career dynamics model, adding further dimensions related to entrepreneurial careers of employment duration, job multiplicity and self-employment.

The development of academic literature on entrepreneurial careers has so far been more fully explored in the USA than in the UK. A growing awareness of both entrepreneurship as a career option and of mid-career change has produced a number of insights. Weinrauch (1980) explored 'the prevailing entrepreneurial spirit in mid career transition' among US managerial, professional and technical employees, concluding that 'increased attention must be given to mid career change as it relates to entrepreneurship' and suggesting that closer attention needs to be paid by educators to the learning patterns and curricular needs of adult learners. Gibb Dyer (1994) and Mitton (1997) emphasized the rich contribution of management skills and experience gained in corporate organizations as a 'launching pad' for subsequent entrepreneurship, whilst Baucus and Sherrie (1994) proposed an entrepreneurial process model adopted by second-career entrepreneurs following corporate employment.

Whilst these contributed to the understanding of mid-career entrepreneurship, Bloch (2005) offered the critique that such approaches are over-reliant on structure and process. The study of entrepreneurship, management and careers has been influenced by new thinking as career patterns have changed, including concepts of chaos theory, emergence, constructivism, narrative and non-linear dynamics. Career systems can be viewed as being in transition as the relationships and psychological contracts between individuals and organizations fragment and innovative concepts such as the 'boundaryless', 'post-corporate', 'protean', 'intelligent' and 'resilient' career emerge (Watson and Harris, 1999; Baruch, 2003).

The traditional concept of mutual loyalty and commitment between individual and organization has been eroded, as organizations may provide training which assists individuals to remain employable but they no longer provide stable, long-term career expectations. Baruch (2004) suggests that a 'desert generation' of employees has grown up, accustomed to the stability of established career paths in the 1970s and early 1980s but who, in mid-career, found themselves exposed to a hostile environment. He proposed that they could behave in traditional or innovative and adaptive or non-adaptive ways, offering the four options of:

- Ostriches – non-adaptive traditionalists who deny and fail to adapt to change
- Bulls – continue to pursue traditional career paths in adaptive ways
- Lions – innovative adaptors who seize opportunities to progress and succeed as managers in the new economy
- Eagles – innovative non-adaptors, entrepreneurs who create their own businesses (Baruch, 2004, p. 248).

These 'archetypes' are entertaining in bringing a human dimension to the field, but otherwise are of limited utility: by being rooted in traditional human resources thinking, they place the emphasis on the individual as 'the problem', although they clearly suggest that failing to innovate or adapt can lead to disadvantage in mid-career.

Guichard and Lenz (2005) surveyed career theory from an international perspective, describing seven approaches to the subject including action theory, self-construction, transition, dynamics of entering the workforce, narrative in career guidance, dilemma approach, and interactive identity construction. They suggested that three main characteristics appeared to be common to these: an emphasis on contexts and cultural diversities; a self-construction or development emphasis; and a constructivist perspective, observing that these conceptualizations differ from the methods most often used by career counsellors. They also noted Holland's (1997) observation that individuals engage in career planning and problem solving with the use of a personal career theory (PCT). A connection can be made between the PCT and the use of 'practical theories of action' by entrepreneurs as a product of their learning (Rae, 2004). This notion of PCT is an aspect of ongoing sensemaking (Weick, 1995) in the creation of individual and collective representations of the way things are in the world, for example, in the perception that age discrimination is more likely for people aged over 45.

Holmes and Cartwright (1994) studied the experiences of people in career change, finding that career plateaux were being reached earlier in specialist and technical fields than in management, and that the concept of 'career' was moving away from structural progression in an organization towards a lifelong sequence of personal growth experiences adapted to individuals' life stage needs. They found that career boredom was prevalent and self-employment increasingly popular in the 35+ age group, with many managers wishing to change career but being inhibited by personal, organizational and social factors. Their study indicated that career change was most likely among individuals high in achievement values and motivation, whilst those with a high internal locus of control were more likely to be successful than those with an external locus. These factors are also more likely to be found among people with a higher propensity for entrepreneurship.

Roberts (2006) suggested that much recent work relating age to working life is mis-cast in looking at specific age groups in isolation; rather than addressing the problem of younger or older workers, he proposed the need to develop a framework that can more centrally accommodate the intergenerational structures of the social reproduction of the collective worker. Platman (2004) examined the experiences of 50+ professionals as portfolio career freelancers in the UK media industry, where such working practices have long been common. Examining this relationship from the employer's and older freelancer's perspective, this explored the limited extent of choice, freedom and autonomy experienced by portfolio professionals in late career.

Bloch (2005) proposed a career development model based on non-linear dynamics, in which career change is a complex entity and relationships between different aspects are more important than the structure and process of traditional career theories, stressing the role of unexplained trajectories and relational networks. Wise and Millward (2005) studied the psychological issues faced in voluntary career change by 'thirtysomethings' using a sensemaking and constructivist framework, observing three significant themes: continuity and discontinuity in the change process; that participants' values directed career change; and the influence of context in career change. These connect with the conclusions of other researchers. Emergent, complex and narrative perspectives on careers are found in other writers on entrepreneurial and managers' careers, such as Kupferberg (1998) and Watson and Harris (1999), in which the notion of career progression is replaced by emergence. Bright and Pryor (2005) explored the application of chaos theory to careers, challenging predictive and stable models of individual–environment interaction with a dynamic approach based on non-linearity, complexity and recursiveness.

There is a lack of conceptual connection between entrepreneurship and careers in the literature surveyed, and this is especially so in relation to gender. Women in mid-career frequently experience disadvantage resulting from family and caring roles and inequalities in the workplace. Self-employment and entrepreneurship are increasingly means by which women can establish control and a degree of parity in their working lives. However, Mallon and Cohen (2001) remarked that there had been little exploration of the role of self-employment and entrepreneurship in the emerging literature on new career patterns, whilst writers on self-employment did not connect with the new careers literature. Their study of women moving into self-employment highlighted the frustration and anger that women experienced in organizations, compared with the 'liberation' of self-employment. Hytti (2005) viewed entrepreneurship as one of a number of possible career phases and choices between which people can move. She used the story of 'Marge', a journalist in mid-career whose 'personal theory' was that she would not get a satisfactory job, and who opted for self-employment as a means of both creating her livelihood and of using entrepreneurship to maintain her professional identity and to provide new meaning in reliability of work and moderation of risk. Hytti's interpretation is that in an increasingly turbulent job market, more ageing and elderly people will face the choice between unemployment and self-employment; and that entrepreneurship is becoming less risky while offering a means of securing a stable social and professional identity.

The growing literature on entrepreneurship education has surprisingly little to say regarding mid-career entrepreneurship, with the exception of the North American contributions already cited. Recent research emphasizes school, college and university students preparing for entrepreneurship rather than the needs of post-experience learners in older age groups (CEI, 2001; Davies, 2002; Hannon, 2004; Pittaway and Cope, 2005). The distinction between young people and MCEs goes beyond the simple difference in age. MCEs are likely to have enhanced prior learning and experience, but otherwise display great variety in their aspirations, work and career experience, educational attainment, and ethnic and national diversity. This makes the design of effective learning experiences more challenging for educators.

The literature on work-based entrepreneurial learning, as distinct from entrepreneurship education, has started to address the situated and emergent nature of the experiences of people who move into entrepreneurship at differing stages of their careers, but there is scope for further investigation (Cope and Watts, 2000; Gibb, 2001; Rae, 2005a; Harrison and Leitch, 2005). Although Blackburn and Mackintosh (1999) have explored the role of 'third age' entrepreneurs aged over 50 who have a dedicated support group (Prime), the same cannot be said of mid-career entrepreneurs. However, self-employment is not always a positive option, as Boyle (1994) indicated that the increase in 'reluctant entrepreneurship' occurs through the widespread outsourcing and casualization of employment. This 'push' factor may be significant in the learning experiences that occur in self-employment.

In conclusion, the following observations can be made on the literature reviewed in connection with mid-career entrepreneurship. First, the careers literature itself is in a process of ongoing change, moving from predictive and structured approaches to non-linearity, which reflects the complex environment. Second, the emphasis is moving from organizational to individual responsibility, in which the ending of the 'psychological contract' based on a stable employment relationship rather than a short-term transactional one is significant. The trend is away from the individual fitting into the organizational environment towards constructing their career within a continually changing context. There is a movement towards constructivist approaches, including the use of narrative and sensemaking, to feature in 'career making'. Whilst the connections between the literatures of management careers and entrepreneurial learning are limited, this notion of the 'emergent entrepreneur' constructing their identity and shaping a new career through their story is becoming more evident. These themes of constructivism, emergence and career making through narrative and sensemaking are illustrated in the two case studies included later in this chapter.

MID-CAREER DECISION MAKING ON ENTREPRENEURSHIP

This section addresses the question of how and why people in mid-career make entrepreneurship their career option. It proposes that a learning-based perspective can be applied in relation to mid-career decision making on entrepreneurship.

As individuals are confronted with the need or opportunity to make changes in their careers, their learned experience is likely to play an important

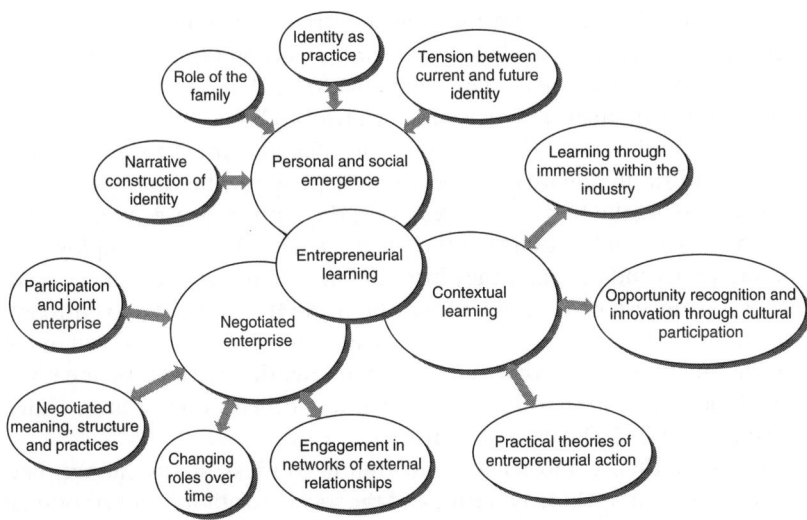

Source: Rae (2005b).

Figure 16.1   Triadic model of entrepreneurial learning

role in their decision making. Wenger offered a social constructionist conception of learning as a transformational process of identity construction, including dimensions of meaning, practice, identity and community. This provides a conceptual foundation for learning which accommodates social participation and human action as well as cognition (Wenger, 1998). These dimensions of learning can be applied to mid-career decision making, in that people are likely to consider and make career choices in relation to their learned experience (meaning); their identity (who they are and are becoming); their practice (their repertoire of actions); and their community (their social participation).

Rae (2005b) undertook case-based research with emergent entrepreneurs to develop a model of entrepreneurial learning, illustrated in Figure 16.1. This is a social constructionist model which draws on Wenger's conceptual foundations of learning. It includes three themes and sets of propositions, each of which has implications for mid-career entrepreneurs.

First, the development of entrepreneurial identity is the outcome of personal and social emergence, which generally includes the narrative construction of identity; identity as practice; the entrepreneur's role in relation to family; and tension between current and future identity. Identity is both personal and social, expressed through an evolving biographical narrative of who I am, what I have done, and what I want to be.

The implication of this for mid-career entrepreneurship is that the individual can envisage their identity as being or becoming an entrepreneur, and expresses this through their narrative, with their identity also being formed through their practice and behaviour. When people are going through a mid-career transition or 'life change', the tension between current and future identity can be a powerful factor. Becoming an entrepreneur may be the best way of resolving the tension between an unsatisfactory present and a desired future identity. The shift from employment and the status and certainty they have grown used to may be replaced with feelings of uncertainty, yet for those who make the transition to entrepreneurship the attractions of self-employment, independence and fulfilment may be much greater as they move from an identity ascribed by membership of an organization to assume the identity of their own venture, as illustrated in Hytti's (2005) case of Marge.

The discontinuity and tension involved in job loss, status change, new and self-directed working patterns, and the social, relational and emotional consequences of entrepreneurship can be significant. The learning process of adjusting, coping and feeling confident to enact the new reality is an important one in which confidence and self-belief are essential (Rae and Carswell, 2001). However, identity is often still rooted in their practice of what they do. Their family background, roles, relationships and responsibilities are likely to influence the decision to become an entrepreneur, for example in identifying the opportunity, in engaging family members in running the business, and in learning within the family business (Fletcher, 2002; Hamilton, 2004).

Second, recognizing and enacting opportunities is an outcome of a process of contextual learning. This includes learning through immersion within an industry; opportunity recognition and innovation through participation; and the formation of practical theories of entrepreneurial action. The individual needs to be able to use the contextual learning from their career to identify opportunities and to create new approaches to solve problems that use their experience and capabilities, including their discursive resource of practical theories of 'what works for me'.

By mid-career, most people have acquired extensive skills, knowledge and experience through immersion within their industry. Whilst this can provide a rich resource of capabilities and expertise on which to draw, it may also restrict their entrepreneurial outlook unless they are able to reframe or 'unlearn' less useful aspects of their prior learning for entrepreneurship. People from careers in large and complex industrial, public sector and uniformed services often have highly developed skills, and have developed practical theories which work for them in those contexts. Yet they may find transferring these to the 'lifeworld' of the small firm, which requires flexible, opportunistic and innovative rather than systematic behaviour, to be a difficult transition (Gibb, 2001).

The awareness and ability to identify or create and use opportunities arising from contextual experience is an important aspect of mid-career entrepreneurship because it enables people to spot or create 'niche' opportunities that others may not notice. Education or other stimuli can help them learn to make the creative connections necessary to innovate (Corbett, 2005), and the role of innovation in mid-career entrepreneurship is highly significant. Developing the confidence and creativity to develop exceptional, higher-value-added businesses is likely to be more significant economically but much rarer than using existing capabilities to become a self-employed consultant or 'cloned' service provider.

Third, the enaction and growth of a business venture is an outcome of negotiated enterprise. This includes processes of participation and joint enterprise; negotiated meaning, structures and practices; changing roles over time; and engagement in networks of external relationships. The individual needs to be able to interact effectively with others to create a new business venture and to negotiate the set of relationships and expectations that enable it to trade and to grow effectively.

This third theme also relates to mid-career entrepreneurship through social context. MCEs with high social capital are likely to be engaged in a range of social and professional relationships and networks that afford access to knowledge, resources and influential contacts. Those with less well-developed networks of relationships are more likely to experience isolation and difficulty in gaining clients and developing the enterprise. Also, MCEs are likely to have a range of experiences in work teams, and the effectiveness of their skills in participation and joint enterprise may be significant. Even self-employment requires interpersonal effectiveness, whilst a team venture or an activity that employs people requires skills of leadership, influencing, organization and the ability to manage people and relationships which create the cultural aspects of negotiated meaning, structure and practices in a business. There are also MCEs whose personality and skills may be perceived negatively as egotistical or 'difficult to get on with'. Such behaviours may mean that they find participation within existing organizations problematic, and entrepreneurship becomes the favoured or best available option. However, an inability to learn effective skills of joint enterprise may limit their success as entrepreneurs.

These themes are illustrated in the two case studies that follow in the next section. It is also clear from contact with a significant number of people in mid-career, both entrepreneurs as well as managers and professionals who have chosen not to become entrepreneurs, that a number of significant factors affect their decision on whether or not to become entrepreneurs in mid-career. These may include such aspects of personal and social emergence, contextual learning and negotiated enterprise as:

- family background
- personal interests or hobbies
- previous career experience
- education, training and professional development
- social and community networks and connections
- personal orientation to risk and uncertainty
- personality factors.

Family Background

Family background may be significant where there is a family history of starting and running businesses in a particular trade, industry or profession. For example, the Forte family ran hotels and restaurants, and Rocco Forte launched his own hotel chain. Experience within the family may be influential, but there are also many cases of sons and daughters deciding not to follow in the 'family footsteps', for example in deciding not to stay in farming businesses, or second-generation Indian and Chinese young people in the UK deciding not to join the retail or food businesses started by their parents. Gender may also be a factor, in that women entrepreneurs increasingly recognize opportunities and start businesses in ways that are qualitatively different from those of men, as shown in the following case of Tina.

Personal Interests or Hobbies

Personal interests or hobbies can provide a means of learning about a particular activity and starting a business, either early in working life or, as is increasingly common, after a career in employment. The numbers of mid-career and 'third-age' entrepreneurs are growing as people leave corporate careers and seek self-fulfilment and additional income rather than retirement. Often these businesses can be termed 'lifestyle', turning a leisure interest into a source of income, and if the numbers of hobby-based businesses were counted they would be very large indeed, although they are not always viable on strictly commercial principles but may be extensions of the hobby.

Previous Career Experience

Previous career experience often provides the starting point for a business. Employment in an industry enables 'niche' opportunities to be identified, networks of contacts to be built up and skills developed, as demonstrated in the contextual learning theme of the entrepreneurial learning model. People develop distinctive expertise which they can use in their own business and notice opportunities which others do not. The commercial and technical or professional skills and insights or 'practical theories' provide a knowledge base and reduce risk. However, the move from employment to self-employment or entrepreneurship is not automatic, and many have found that they needed to learn the additional management skills required to run a business, for which their previous career had not prepared them.

Education, Training and Professional Development

Education, training and professional development can often provide the knowledge, personal confidence and the realization that entrepreneurship is possible, together with some of the contacts necessary to start a business. This includes formal education, training, qualifications, and informal work based learning which balances theory with practical experience. Career landmarks, such as the completion of professional training, an MBA or other award, may mark a point at which the individual feels ready to do more than is open to them within their organization.

Social and Community Networks and Connections

Social and community networks and connections provide many experienced entrepreneurs with subsequent business opportunities: through their networks, they become aware of opportunities and are able to use these to develop business ventures. The community can also act as a resource and stimulus for social enterprise. The emergence of social and economic problems in communities, such as unemployment, lack of amenities such as leisure facilities, a shop or childcare, has been the spur for many social entrepreneurs. One advantage of social enterprise is that there is an almost inexhaustible supply of needs which can be translated into opportunities, as social problems and needs change with demographics. So needs such as community dentistry, teenage literacy, and English language learning for asylum seekers constantly present themselves, together with the considerable challenges of how to create a viable and sustainable business model which avoids grant-dependence, and of developing the skills and confidence people need to make the business happen.

Personal Orientation to Risk and Uncertainty

Risk is the uncertainty of a given outcome, and people have markedly different orientations to business risk taking, although the popular stereotype of 'entrepreneur as risk taker' should not be accepted without exploring more carefully the issue of risk in opportunity selection. Contextual learning can be seen as a means of reducing risk, where career experience provides the entrepreneur with the confidence to know 'what works' in building a successful business. These are some of the factors involved in considering risk:

- *Self-confidence* and the personal belief in the ability to make a new venture or innovation work is an important factor. Personal dynamism, intense and sustained effort to achieve change are required but are insufficient on their own.
- The ability to *manage emotional tension* and arousal connected with risk, in that people who are prone to become anxious and fearful are better off not taking such risks.
- *Negotiated risk sharing*, by engaging investors, partners and others in the venture to share risk is a sensible and necessary strategy in any venture where the entrepreneur does not wish or is not able to fully self-finance a venture that is otherwise an attractive investment.
- *Iterative*, step-by-step working can break apparently big risks down into smaller, limited ones where the exposure at each stage to failure is reduced. This can be done, for example, in checking that each stage of an innovation works before going on to the next, and that each decision has been evaluated to determine its impact before the next is made. However, time pressure can reduce the scope for this form of risk management.

These appear to be the main reasons why people select the types of opportunities they do. The prior experience, knowledge and social connections that people develop play a significant part in forming their choices and enabling them to recognize opportunities which others would not. This prior learning may blinker people and prevent them seeing better, more rewarding opportunities. However, prior experience and learning reduce risk, and the track record of people pursuing business opportunities completely outside their previous experience is considerably more risky. Contextual learning is therefore extremely important in entrepreneurial learning and opportunity selection.

Personality and Behavioural Variables

There has been extensive exploration of the personality factors connected with entrepreneurship, and a rejection of a trait-based approach (Gartner, 1988; Chell et al., 1991). However variables within the individual personality and preferred behaviours clearly have an influence on the entrepreneurial decision, and those listed below may be influential:

- Self-confidence and personal efficacy with the motivation to be proactive and achieve results (Bandura, 1986; Boyd and Vozikis, 1994)
- A future-planning perspective of setting and realizing goals (Bird and Jelinek, 1988)
- Creativity in innovating, developing and applying new ideas (Drucker, 1985; Corbett, 2005)
- Being adaptable and flexible in changing environments, comfortable with conditions of risk and uncertainty (Gibb, 2001)
- Ability to gain the support of others in building and leading a team (Birley and Stockley, 2000).

The issue of the psychological contract has been extensively discussed in relation to career change and is generally viewed from a strategic exchange rather than relational perspective (Rousseau, 1995; Baruch, 2004). Whereas the manager's psychological contract has been with the organization, with whom does the entrepreneur contract? The issue here is of negotiated career expectations, both explicit and implicit. It may be thought that the entrepreneur contracts only with him or herself, but that is unlikely to be the case. The concept of the negotiated organization suggests that in starting a new venture, expectations are also likely to be created within a network of relationships, including family, friends, partners, investors, lenders, employees, customers and suppliers. There needs to be a psychological contract, or a degree of shared belief in the success of the new venture, created and renegotiated on the basis of subsequent experience between the entrepreneur and these parties. This makes the entrepreneurial psychological contract more complex in nature than the individual–organizational contract of the employed manager. The entrepreneur's ability to meet both personal and social expectations within this network may be highly significant and public.

CAREER CHANGE AND CAREER TRAJECTORY

For most people, careers are not necessarily planned, managed or goal-oriented: as Baruch observed, 'for many, the new concept of career is undesired, inconvenient and problematic' (Baruch, 2004, p. 243). People may not have explicit goals or objectives, but an emergent direction within an holistic approach to life that balances family, friends, interests and perceived 'quality of life'. So their trajectory or career direction may be proactive or reactive, and planned or emergent. Their career becomes 'learned experience', within which continuing capabilities and strengths of personality and behaviour are recurrent.

Increasingly in mid-career, people are exposed to sudden situations and unplanned events such as personal and family crises, relationship break-downs such as divorce, illness and health conditions, and organizational changes such as role, structural, technological and locational shifts, at the most extreme involving redundancy or dismissal and enforced career change. This gives rise to the 'reluctant entrepreneurs' and the notion of push or pull factors in entrepreneurship. Whether change is enforced or voluntary, career boredom and the 'life cycle' of the job role is also a factor. Where career ladders and opportunities for change and progression within an organization are perceived not to exist, people are more likely to become frustrated and view entrepreneurship as a positive choice.

Given this complex set of individual, organizational and social factors, there is clearly no one general model for managerial or entrepreneurial careers. Watson and Harris (1999) conceptualized career strategies by individuals and organizations as *'realised patterns* which emerge over time', which were more often emergent and incremental than intended or planned. What we see, increasingly, are people engaged in sensemaking of their career (Weick, 1995), in which a pattern may emerge and be recognized retrospectively as people try to trace their 'trajectory of self' through their career narratives (Watson and Harris, 1999; Giddens, 1991).

A constructivist view of careers has developed which suggests that people are increasingly 'making up', 'reinventing' and shaping their individual careers in dynamic ways which are different from traditional pathways. Using narrative to craft the personal story is an integral aspect of this process, as people are constantly expected to give a convincing career history in such forms as a résumé, curriculum vitae, application form, presentation and in answering interview questions. Their story becomes an essential means of negotiating their identity in relation to an organization: as Bruner observed, 'we *become* the autobiographical narratives by which we "tell about" our lives' (Bruner, 1987, p. 15).

This process of the individual learning to shape their narrative can be termed 'career making':

> Career-making is learning to shape, manage and direct the career story in a reflexive relationship within personal, organisational, professional and social networks, using habits and skills of personal creativity, storytelling, enterprise and resourcefulness. (Rae, 1999, p. 106)

The concept of career making is connected with such entrepreneurial activities as working creatively to achieve life and work-related goals through recognizing and acting on opportunities. It may be that the person who becomes an entrepreneur is more active and creative in reshaping the story of their career than the person who continues as an employee, as suggested in the case studies in the next section. Managers who decide at a given time to remain employees may be opportunity-aware and enterprising in an organizational context, but career making becomes more complex if they leave organizational employment to become an entrepreneur. The entrepreneur's identity and career story are then inextricably linked with the fortunes of their own venture; as a mid-career entrepreneur remarked: 'I am this business, this business is me' (Anna, computer entrepreneur).

CAREER PATHWAYS OF MID-CAREER ENTREPRENEURS

This section explores how people construct their entrepreneurial careers, and describes career making by MCEs through short case studies which illustrate the learning process of mid-career entrepreneurship. A career stage model which shows possible entry points into entrepreneurial careers is then described. The two cases were selected from a range of biographical narratives of entrepreneurs developed by the author. The cases originated from a series of interviews, presentations and documents provided by each subject, which were interpreted using discourse analysis to categorize the significant concepts and themes in their narratives in relation to the entrepreneurial learning model (Figure 16.1), the method being fully described in Rae (2005b). These two cases were both considered to be 'exceptional stories', having been entrants to the National Business Awards category for Entrepreneur of the Year.

Will: Tyrrells Potato Chips

Will grew up on a family potato farm, which he raised the funds to buy when it was put up for sale, but then experienced setbacks including insolvency of the business. After this he evaluated his life, 'grew up', and bought the farm back from the receiver. He grew potatoes for supermarkets for 20 years, but realized that there was no future in potato farming as a commodity crop because his prices and profit margins were constantly forced down: 'I had to change direction or go out of business, but wanted to stay in farming.' He considered other options to make use of the farm, assessed the UK market for snack foods, and realized that the profit margin on potato crisps produced yields of thousands of pounds per ton rather than hundreds of pounds for potatoes. Visiting the USA, he found that farm-based production was feasible and sales of hand-produced crisps, or chips, were growing by 15 per cent each year.

Will concluded that there was an opportunity in the UK for top-quality premium potato chips, hand-produced from farm-grown potatoes for the gourmet market. Despite knowing nothing about making chips, he realized from experience with the supermarkets that 'you have to find a niche'. Initial batches of chips were produced and proved that demand existed. Will prepared a business plan and raised £1m funding to create a chip production plant on the farm, training the staff to become chip makers.

The Tyrrells brand identity, named after the farm, packaging and marketing materials, were crafted to 'sell the story' of the farm-grown, hand-produced chips, with a distinctive range of 'natural' flavours and unique root vegetable and apple chips. Innovation was vital, first by learning from the USA and transferring the idea and technology for farm-scale chip production, and then by innovating through marketing, distribution and new product recipes. Will targeted up-market retailers, independent stores and gastro-pubs, offering a premium-priced product with a high profit margin: 'I decided to be the little guy who took the supermarkets on.'

Starting full production in 2002, Tyrrells grew rapidly through successful marketing, product innovation and distribution, aiming to become the country's foremost innovative producer and supplier of farm-produced artisan delicacies for the discerning customer. His role is 'doing the thinking, moving the business forward, anticipating issues and responding to potential cracks before they appear', by networking, talking to retailers and observing customers to predict international market trends, and growing the export business. Will invested in a new factory on the farm, and doubled the production area and potato planting acreage. He gives credit to the staff: 'a successful business attracts people – you find and develop the best people who come to work with a passion'. The business employs a number of family members, and they were rewarded in 2005 and 2006 when Will won National Business Awards for Entrepreneur of the Year and Small–Medium Sized Business of the Year.

Will's case is highly interesting in that as a farmer he was already a small business owner and has retained farming in his practice, but he realized that entrepreneurship was a necessary step to become more than a supermarket supplier. The themes of personal emergence as an entrepreneur, the role of the family, the contextual identification of opportunity and innovation through industry experience, and the negotiated enterprise through external networking and joint participation are evident in his account of an exceptional business.

Tina: Home Stagers®

Tina established her career and spent over 15 years in corporate IT. However, she had a talent for design and studied at the National Design Academy to retrain as a designer, gaining a diploma in professional interior design. Finding it hard to sell her house in a stagnant property market, she found that by applying design principles to her own house she was able to increase the sale price and overcome the problem of negative equity. From this simple but effective beginning, she conceptualized the idea of property staging in 1995 and went on to establish Home Stagers® as the UK's only nationally recognized home styling and property presentation business, despite a personal tragedy.

The approach Tina developed is simple but highly effective. A hard-to-sell house is appraised by a trained stylist and ways of restyling it, through design, redecoration, changing furnishings, fixtures and lighting, are proposed within an agreed budget. Once these are completed, the property is offered for sale. Tina's research showed that every £100 spent on presentation in this way is more effective in selling a property than a £1000 reduction in the selling price.

Tina became a successful home stylist in the late 1990s and demonstrated that demand for her service existed before establishing the Home Stagers® brand in 2001. The concept of home styling was assisted by popular TV 'home makeover' programmes. The business developed service standards and an accredited training programme for home stylists which is run by The British Academy of Home Stagers®. People can become stylists and be trained and licensed to operate as a sole trader within the Home Stagers Network, as well as to train people from overseas to set up their own business and develop the network in their own country. In this way a national and international service is being provided with common service standards. The network also reaches out to estate agents and corporate partners, and a constantly updated website and monthly e-mail magazine promotes the business, ensuring that Home Stagers® and Tina enjoy a high media profile at the centre of the property styling business (www.homestagers.co.uk).

Tina exemplifies the distinctive approach that a female entrepreneur may bring, by recognizing that a personal problem she encountered also represented a wider, situated opportunity, and that by applying her own creative skills to solving it she could also develop a business model to work through a network of home stylists. She demonstrates a way in which mid-career entrepreneurship may enable women with distinctive skills to create better career options than those available through employment. Her case again provides evidence of the themes of personal and social emergence, contextual learning and negotiated enterprise.

Both Will and Tina found their pre-entrepreneurial career and identity unsatisfactory, and through necessity created a new career trajectory by reshaping their story and identity to become an entrepreneur. They recognized distinctive opportunities through personal experience, and used creative thinking and personal skills to innovate, but had to learn new skills and work with others to develop their business ventures. Both have succeeded in promoting their businesses, creating high media profiles and public recognition through their narratives which form an integral aspect of their entrepreneurial identities.

The issues that arise from these cases connect with the preceding summary of the literature in several ways. They illustrate non-linearity in career patterns, in which individuals increasingly take responsibility for creating and working on opportunities (Bloch, 2005). They depict people working on their ventures, through which they reshape their careers. For example, Will moved from an identity and relationship as a supplier to an organization to create a new identity and a set of relationships between his enterprise with his customers. Tina moved from the psychological contract of an employee to become self-employed. The cases show people creating or recognizing opportunities situated within their earlier career background: Will continued to farm, and Tina to be a designer, in an entrepreneurial context. They provide support for the themes of career making as an active process of identity construction, and of entrepreneurial emergence occurring through narrative sensemaking.

A structure can be developed to show career stages in relation to entrepreneurship which individuals may use in considering career options, while being mindful of the critique of 'staged' career models (Bloch, 2005). Schein (1993) proposed a ten-stage career model which is arguably more precise than is required. The entrepreneurial career stage framework, shown in Table 16.1, sets out five generic career stages, from education to 'third age', and aims to show typical career events which may occur. At each career stage, entrepreneurial questions and options are shown derived from observation, reflections and interviews with entrepreneurs. This demonstrates the way in which different decisions and options are likely to be faced at different career stages, and that entrepreneurship may be an option at several times in a person's career. It is also evident that women often experience particular events and questions, especially as parents in early and mid-career, which the framework aims to reflect.

Table 16.1 Entrepreneurial career stage framework

Career stage	Typical events	Entrepreneurial questions and options
Late career/third age Age: 55+	Seniority Retirement Develop wider interests Divest from own business or hire succession management	How to use existing contacts, expertise and resources? How to extend economic activity? Self-employment, lifestyle business Develop portfolio of interests Social or community enterprise Adviser, coach or non-executive roles
Mid-career Age: 35–54	Career advance and responsibility Marketable skills and expertise Reassess career direction Unachieved aspirations Redundancy Parenting or caring Career break/return to work Changes in family relationships	How to achieve successful career transition? How to identify and develop opportunity based on existing skills and experience? Leave employment to start new business Return to work or start own business Consultancy Management buy-in or buy-out Create spinout venture Join or lead innovation project or venture team Grow existing or family business
Early career Age: 25–34	Establish career direction Develop skills and experience in corporate, profession or small business Professional or technical training/development Expand social and work-related networks – social capital	How to choose independence over employment? Learn entrepreneurial capabilities from experienced people Start own business Creative innovation at work Team member in innovation project, start-up or spinout venture Continue to work full or part time or freelance

Table 16.1 (continued)

Career stage	Typical events	Entrepreneurial questions and options
	Child rearing Accumulate personal resources	'
Initiation into working life Age: 16–24	Early work experience Development of social networks Quest for independence Exploration and personal growth Partnering, possible marriage	How to develop skills, interests and social contacts into enterprising projects? Small-scale ventures with friends Graduate start-up
Education and early life Age: 5–21	Vocational, further or higher education/training Academic or vocational choices and specialization Family influences	How to turn interests and needs into earning opportunities? Enterprise education Participation in family business Enterprise in personal interests

Source: Rae (2007).

CONCLUSIONS: TOWARDS ENTREPRENEURIAL CAREERS FOR MANAGERS

This chapter set out to explore understanding of mid-career entrepreneurship through a focus on learning and career making. It is clear from the literature that the issues in career change are complex, and that entrepreneurship is just one manifestation of this, although it is significant both sociologically and economically. This concluding section considers the opportunities and challenges presented by mid-career entrepreneurship for individuals, organizations and society, and discusses these in relation to business education, entrepreneurship and management.

Individuals

At an individual level, each person must make sense of their own life, work and economic and social needs in relation to their career. They are exposed to the messages and uncertainties regarding continuity of employment, pensions, working for longer, ageism, and are increasingly vulnerable to continuous organizational change. This is especially so in the public sector, where health, education and public administration appear to be in a perpetual process of restructuring, which understandably gives rise to personal insecurity regarding future careers.

Individuals are therefore faced with complex choices, and the decision to become an entrepreneur, whether 'pushed' by necessity or 'pulled' by opportunity, may be based on such factors as:

- their desire to be self-directed, in control and independent
- the need to remain economically active
- creating or maintaining a chosen professional identity
- attitudes to risk and uncertainty
- perceptions of career opportunities in employment or self-employment
- psychological and social needs for recognition, reward and fulfilment
- future pension entitlement.

Many managers and professionals employed in organizations may decide that entrepreneurship in the sense of starting an independent business venture is not their preferred choice, but rather an option of last resort in the event of redundancy, for example. However, they are still exposed to the discourse of entrepreneurial management (Carr, 2000), which makes them increasingly aware of the need to adopt enterprising approaches such as leadership, innovation, value creation and change management in their work. They will often have advanced skills and expertise that can be practised most effectively using the resources of large, capital-intensive organizations. But as an enterprising culture develops, managers and professionals within organizations are increasingly coming to adopt some of the values and skills of entrepreneurs and to practise these within an organizational context as entrepreneurial managers (Stevenson and Jarillo, 1990).

There are gendered aspects of mid-career entrepreneurship that are especially significant for women. Whilst female rates of entrepreneurial participation in mid-career age groups are currently just over half those for men, this will continue to increase. Women in the rising female graduate population, for example, are unlikely to be satisfied with part-time and often mundane employment alongside motherhood, and they are more likely to use their skills to become self-employed or to start business ventures as more rewarding or flexible alternatives. However, support measures for mid-career female entrepreneurship, through prior education, training and in considering and preparing to start business ventures, need to be explicitly addressed (Diamond, 2003). One such example is the Mid-Career Education in Entrepreneurship and Innovation in Technology and Science (MEETS) Programme at Cambridge University.

People in mid-career often already possess many entrepreneurial skills, in different degrees. However, becoming an entrepreneur involves a process of self-realization and emergence in moving from the narrative identity gained through employment into entrepreneurship. Resolving the tension between current and future identity with the associated issues of emotion, confidence and self-belief is a learning process which may involve 'unlearning' previous perceptions of self and social identity as an employee, and making a new career. Assessment and reflection on existing life and work skills provide a good foundation for this, since this learning process involves recognizing, reframing, transferring, applying and extending existing skills beyond habitual boundaries as well as developing new ones. MCEs are a very heterogeneous group, and their learning needs to be relevant to their individual life experiences and career aspirations. Therefore support for personal development, confidence building, assessment and reflection on existing skills can form useful parts of a formal mid-career learning and change process. This has implications for business and management education for this group; but as Weinrauch (1980) noted, this is not a new conclusion. However, education often does not explicitly support mid-career entrepreneurship, and will increasingly need to address this challenge.

Organizations

Organizations increasingly require and specify entrepreneurial skills such as leadership, innovation, customer focus, performance and transformational change in the recruitment specifications for senior management roles. This is as true in the public and 'not-for-profit' sectors as in the private sector economy as the dividing lines between them are increasingly eroded. Many people may not recognize their entrepreneurial potential, and have never been offered entrepreneurial education or training. Given that entrepreneurial behaviour is opportunity-focused and can be applied in a range of situations, including social enterprise, corporate and public sector organizations, mid-career entrepreneurship within organizations can make a major contribution to innovation and renewal, as well as to creating new ventures.

Organizations of all kinds are increasingly subject to the pressures to reduce costs, increase efficiency and productivity, and to become more competitive. There is perceived to be a growing requirement for entrepreneurial management to achieve such changes, in which the mid-career manager or professional may be a winner or loser but is unlikely to be left unaffected. If they are perceived and able to learn and demonstrate entrepreneurial skills effectively within the organization, their career prospects are likely to be extended and to benefit, so long as they are seen to 'deliver' the required results. On the other hand, people in mid-career whose skills and approach no longer fit with the changing cultural expectations are more likely to be at risk of marginalization or redundancy as organizations seek to reduce 'headcount', costs and pension liabilities. Traditional forms of managing, and management roles, are threatened by such changes.

Structural and organizational changes can demotivate and disadvantage groups of workers, as has happened in UK schools through the 'workforce remodelling' which led to many mid-career teachers with management responsibility losing financial allowances for these duties and in many cases looking to leave the profession. In this way, we see the ending or reshaping of traditional career paths as a set of mutual expectations and pyschological contracts existing between individuals and organizations. Yet it is also the case that organizations are increasingly dependent on the human capital of knowledge, skills, experience and networked social connections. It may be, as has been the case in schools, that the skills and experience of older workers are seen as less useful and more costly than younger teachers who are cheaper to employ, yet who initially lack skills and experience required for the organization to operate effectively.

The question here, as traditional models of career progression erode, is how people are valued and rewarded to provide incentives and recognition for useful skills and expertise. There is a need to prevent career boredom and the loss of enterprising people who see entrepreneurship as a better option. Where people choose to become entrepreneurs, it suggests that existing organizations, career opportunities, cultures and practices no longer fit their aspirations, preferred identities and work modes. This poses a challenge to the effectiveness of management in organizations which will 'lose' skilled and experienced staff with entrepreneurial and innovative ability who become dissatisfied with their current organizations and careers, while organizations also need to become better able to manage and to retain people during longer working lives.

Society

The final observation is on the social context of mid-career entrepreneurship. MCEs are a group of increasing importance whose role has been insufficiently explored. They are heterogeneous but are becoming increasingly significant both economically and socially. Mid-career entrepreneurs are an important and growing group of talented people who can make a significant difference to society. However, they have distinctive needs that should be recognized at a social level.

The economic and demographic imperatives to extend working lives, to reduce welfare and pension dependence on the state, and to introduce enterprise into disadvantaged communities, may be legitimate. It is likely that, on balance, people will be healthier, happier and certainly more prosperous if they work for longer, so long as they have a degree of control over the nature and organization of their work. This is more likely to be the case if they are entrepreneurs rather than reluctant employees. The time-range of 'mid-career' will extend as working lives become longer.

However, just as the psychological contract between individual and organization has eroded, so has the compact between the individual and the state; again, there is a need for a new balance to be struck. As the state pulls back from funding pensions, care for the elderly and other forms of welfare, people increasingly realize that they are expected to provide for themselves. Yet pensions and social care frameworks often do not provide the flexibility which would facilitate mid-career entrepreneurship. A Regional Development Agency economic strategy commented in respect of the desirability of mid-career entrepreneurship that individuals often saw the risks as being too high to make it an attractive option. For the person who perceives themselves to be in a reasonably secure job with a pension scheme and owning their own home, there may indeed be little attraction unless other factors such as those listed above are much more compelling.

At a social level, employers have traditionally exercised selection by age, and new legislation to combat age discrimination in the UK may take some time to achieve widespread impact. If so, mature and older workers will continue to face challenges in returning to work or in finding new jobs. Yet it can be predicted that economic and organizational change will continue to destroy old jobs as well as create new ones, meaning that employees will need the flexibility to change jobs more often later in their working lives. The alternative is the progressive marginalization of older workers that Hytti (2005) described. Where job losses occur, people need to be able to respond by learning and developing skills of personal enterprise. Where people become of necessity or reluctant entrepreneurs, through 'push' factors such as redundancy or forced career change, this is especially important and suggests the need for entrepreneurial learning opportunities to be made more accessible to people in mid-career.

In conclusion, mid-career entrepreneurship presents both opportunities and challenges for individuals, organizations and for society. Demographic change makes the development of mid-career entrepreneurship an economic and social necessity. The requirement is that organizations, education and training, and social agencies, encourage and enable it to flourish. It is evident that if people in mid-career learn to use practical methods to investigate opportunities and conduct market research, to apply creative thinking and plan new businesses, and to practise the skills of personal enterprise, they can become more able to innovate as entrepreneurs (Rae, 2007). Mid-career entrepreneurs are in the optimum position to identify and develop opportunities by using their contextual work and life experience, skills, networks and energy to create and build business ventures. Their ability to innovate and to develop new, higher-value business concepts, by combining experience, opportunities, technologies and new ideas, is vital for them as individuals, for organizations and for society. They are in the 'age of opportunity'.

REFERENCES

Arthur, M., Hall, D. and Lawrence, B. (eds) (1984), *Handbook of Career Theory*, Cambridge: Cambridge University Press.

Bandura, A. (1986), *Social Foundations of Thought and Action: A Social Cognitive Theory*, Englewood Cliffs, NJ: Prentice-Hall.

Baruch, Y. (2003), 'Career systems in transition: a normative model for organizational career practices', *Personnel Review*, **32**(2): 231–51.

Baruch, Y. (2004), 'The desert generation: lessons and implications for the new era of people management', *Personnel Review*, **33**(2): 241–56.

Baucus, D. and Sherrie, E. (1994), 'Second-career entrepreneurs: a multiple case study analysis of entrepreneurial processes and antecedent variables', *Entrepreneurship Theory and Practice*, **19**(2): 41–72.

Bird, B. and Jelinek, M. (1988), 'The operation of entrepreneurial intentions', *Entrepreneurship Theory & Practice*, **13**(2): 21–9.

Birley, S. and Stockley, S. (2000), 'Entrepreneurial teams and venture growth', in D. Sexton and H. Landström (eds), *The Blackwell Handbook of Entrepreneurship*, Oxford: Blackwell, pp. 287–307.

Blackburn, R. and Mackintosh, L. (1999), 'The entrepreneurship potential of people in the third age: a case of over expectation?', paper presented at Small Business and Enterprise Development Conference, University of Leeds, March.

Bloch, S. (2005), 'Complexity, chaos, and nonlinear dynamics: a new perspective on career development theory', *The Career Development Quarterly*, **53**:194–207.

Boyd, N. and Vozikis, G. (1994), 'The influence of self-efficacy on the development of entrepreneurial intentions and actions', *Entrepreneurship Theory and Practice*, **18**(4): 63–77.

Boyle, E. (1994), 'The rise of the reluctant entrepreneurs', *International Small Business Journal*, **12**(2): 63–9.

Bright, J. and Pryor, R. (2005), 'The chaos theory of careers: a user's guide', *The Career Development Quarterly*, **53**: 291–305.

Bruner, J. (1987), 'Life as narrative', *Social Research*, **5**(1): 11–32.

Carr, P. (2000), *The Age of Enterprise*, Dublin: Blackhall Publishing.

Centre for Education and Industry (2001), *Independent Research into Learning for Enterprise and Entrepreneurship*, Coventry: University of Warwick.

Chartered Institute of Personnel and Development and Chartered Management Institute (2005), *Tackling Age Discrimination at Work: Creating a New Age for All*, London: CIPD.

Chell, E., Harworth, J. and Brearley, S. (1991), *The Entrepreneurial Personality: Concepts, Cases and Categories*, London: Routledge.

Cope, J. and Watts, G. (2000), 'Learning by doing: an exploration of critical incidents and reflection in entrepreneurial learning', *International Journal of Entrepreneurial Behaviour and Research*, **6**(3): 104–24.

Corbett, A. (2005), 'Experiential learning within the process of opportunity identification and exploitation', *Entrepreneurship Theory and Practice*, **29**(4): 473–91.

Davies, H. (2002), *A Review of Enterprise and the Economy in Education*, Norwich, UK: HMSO.

Department for Work and Pensions (2005), *Opportunity Age: Meeting the Challenges of Ageing in the 21st Century*, London: DWP.

Diamond, K. (2003), 'Female entrepreneurship: developing worldwide', keynote address at 48th International Council for Small Business World Conference, Belfast, June.

Drucker, P. (1985), *Innovation and Entrepreneurship*, London: Heinemann.

Fletcher, D. (2002), *Understanding the Small Family Business*, London: Routledge.

Gartner, W. (1989), '"Who is an entrepreneur?" is the wrong question', *Entrepreneurship Theory and Practice*, **13**(4): 47–67.

Gibb, A. (2001), 'Creating conducive environments for learning and entrepreneurship', address to the conference of the entrepreneurship forum, Naples, 21–24 June.

Gibb Dyer, W. Jr. (1994), 'Toward a theory of entrepreneurial careers', *Entrepreneurship Theory and Practice*, **19**(2): 7–21.

Giddens, A. (1991), *Modernity and Self Identity: Self and Society in the Late Modern Age*, Cambridge: Polity Press.

Guichard, J. and Lenz, J. (2005), 'Career theory from an international perspective', *The Career Development Quarterly*, **54**: 17–28.

Hamilton, E. (2004), 'Socially situated entrepreneurial learning in family business', paper presented at Institute for Small Business Affairs national conference, Newcastle, 2–4 November.

Hannon, P. (2004), *Making the Journey from Student to Entrepreneur: A review of the Existing Research into Graduate Entrepreneurship*, Birmingham: National Council for Graduate Entrepreneurship.

Harding, R., Brooksbank, D., Hart, M., Jones-Evans, D., Levie, J., O'Reilly, M. and Walker, J. (2005), *Global Entrepreneurship Monitor, UK National Report for 2004*, London: London Business School.

Harrison, R. and Leitch, C. (2005), 'Entrepreneurial learning: researching the interface between learning and the entrepreneurial context', *Entrepreneurship Theory and Practice*, **29**(4): 351–71.

Holland, J.L. (1997), *Making Vocational Choices: A Theory of Vocational Personalities and Work Environments*, 3rd edn, Odessa, FL: Psychological Assessment Resources.

Holmes, T. and Cartwright, S. (1993), 'Career change: myth or reality?', *Employee Relations*, **15**(6): 37–53.

Holmes, T. and Cartwright, S. (1994), 'Mid-career change: the ingredients for success', *Employee Relations*, **16**(7): 58–72.

Hytti, U. (2005), 'New meanings for entrepreneurs: from risk-taking heroes to safe-seeking professionals', *Journal of Organizational Change Management*, **18**(6): 594–611.

Katz, J.A. (1994), 'Modelling entrepreneurial career progressions: concepts and considerations', *Entrepreneurship Theory and Practice*, **19**(2): 23–40.

Kupferberg, F. (1998), 'Humanistic entrepreneurship and entrepreneurial career commitment', *Entrepreneurship and Regional Development*, **10**(3): 171–87.

Macaulay, C. (2003), *Changes to Self-employment in the UK: 2002 to 2003*, London: Office for National Statistics.

Mallon, M. and Cohen, L. (2001), 'Time for a change? Women's accounts of the move from organizational careers to self-employment', *British Journal of Management*, **12**: 217–30.

Mitton, D. (1997), 'Entrepreneurship: one more time – non-cognitive characteristics that make the cognitive clock tick', *Frontiers of Entrepreneurship Research*, Wellesley, MA: Babson College, pp. 189–203.

Moore, D. and Holly Buttner, E. (1997), *Women Entrepreneurs: Moving Beyond the Glass Ceiling*, London: Sage.

OECD (1998), *Fostering Entrepreneurship*, Paris: OECD.

Office for National Statistics (2006), *Population Trends Spring 2006*, London: ONS.

Pensions Commission (2005) *A New Pension Settlement for the Twenty-First Century – The Second Report of the Pension Commission*, London: Pensions Commission.

Pittaway, L. and Cope, J. (2005), 'Entrepreneurship education – a systematic review of the evidence', paper presented at ISBE conference, Blackpool, 1–3 November.

Platman, K. (2004), ' "Portfolio careers" and the search for flexibility in later life', *Work, Employment and Society*, **18**(3): 573–99.

Rae, D. (1999), *The Entrepreneurial Spirit*, Dublin: Blackhall.

Rae, D. (2004), 'Practical theories from entrepreneurs' stories: discursive approaches to entrepreneurial learning', *Journal of Small Business and Enterprise Development*, **11**(2): 195–202.

Rae, D. (2005a), 'Mid-career entrepreneurial learning', *Education and Training*, **47**(8/9): 562–74.

Rae, D. (2005b), 'Entrepreneurial learning: a narrative-based conceptual model', *Journal of Small Business and Enterprise Development*, **12**(3): 323–35.

Rae, D. (2007), *Entrepreneurship: From Opportunity to Action*, Basingstoke, UK: Palgrave Macmillan.

Rae, D. and Carswell, M. (2001), 'Towards a conceptual understanding of entrepreneurial learning', *Small Business and Enterprise Development*, 8(2): 150–58.

Roberts, I. (2006), 'Taking age out of the workplace: putting older workers back in?', *Work, Employment and Society*, 20(1): 67–86.

Rousseau, D. (1995), *Psychological Contracts in Organisations: Understanding Written and Unwritten Agreements*, Thousand Oaks, CA: Sage.

Schein, E. (1993), *Career Anchors: Discovering Your Real Values*, San Francisco, CA: Pfeiffer.

Schein, E. (1978), *Career Dynamics: Matching Individual and Organizational Needs*, Reading, MA: Addison-Wesley.

Stevenson, H. and Jarillo, C. (1990), 'A paradigm of entrepreneurship: entrepreneurial management', *Strategic Management Journal*, 11: 17–27.

Super, D. (1957), *Vocational Development: A Framework for Research*, New York: Columbia University Press.

Watson, T.J. and Harris, P. (1999), *The Emergent Manager*, London: Sage.

Weick, K. (1995), *Sensemaking in Organizations*, Thousand Oaks, CA: Sage.

Weinrauch, D. (1980), 'The second time around: entrepreneurship as a mid-career alternative', *Journal of Small Business Management*, 18(1): 25–32.

Wenger, E. (1998), *Communities of Practice: Learning, Meaning and Identity*, Cambridge: Cambridge University Press.

Wise, J. and Millward, L. (2005), 'The experiences of voluntary career change in 30-somethings and implications for guidance', *Career Development International*, 10(5): 400–417.

17. The engaging manager and the role of knowledge absorptive capacity: an organizational life-cycle perspective

Laura A. Costanzo and Vicky Tzoumpa

INTRODUCTION

An overwhelming debate has generated around the issue of whether MBA or business management education in general is suited to form or train the future managers operating in increasingly competitive environments. In Mintzberg's view, MBA programmes have failed to produce the right managers because they overemphasize analytical skills and underemphasize reflective practice, the role of context and the sharing of experience (Shepherd, 2005). Mintzberg (2004) argues that MBA education provides knowledge of the functions of business, but fails to educate in the practice of managing. In his argument, Mintzberg (2004) points out that MBA education should contribute to developing the 'engaging' type of management style, which is believed to be more appropriate to match the management requirements of today's companies. According to Mintzberg (2004), the 'engaging' manager should have five mindsets of thinking: the reflective, the analytic, the worldly, the collaborative and the action. In Mintzberg's (2004) perspective, a new type of management education is needed in order to concentrate managerial development around the five specified mindsets.

In this chapter, we take forward Mintzberg's (2004) argument by drawing on the theory of the organizational life cycle, which provides insights into the specific management requirements needed in the growth phase of the firm. We argue that the 'engaging' type of management style is particularly needed in the face of firms' growth, where the management of organizations is confronted with survival challenges. In this stage, the firm's capability to get access to new resources – primarily internal and external knowledge – is crucial to the firm's sustained development. We argue that in the growth stage firms need 'entrepreneurial management', which is enacted by the knowledge absorptive capacity. This is a critical management capability, which develops alongside the organizational life cycle. We argue that such absorptive capacity is enacted by the human resources practices in place within the organization and that an 'entrepreneurial' orientation of the firm driven by the policies set by the top management team facilitates the development of such capability. In this sense, the conceptualization of knowledge absorptive capacity as a key capability of the 'engaging manager' contributes to deepen our understanding of the mechanisms that shape the engaging manager's five styles of thinking.

After presenting an overview of the fundamental theory concerning the individual career choices between entrepreneurship and management, the chapter will adopt an organizational life-cycle perspective to argue that the challenges that the firm faces during the growth phase lead to a shift in management practice, which has become more entrepreneurial-oriented. It is argued that knowledge absorptive capacity is a critical managerial capability needed if the firm is to overcome its survival challenges. Therefore, after discussing the interrelated concepts of knowledge, knowledge management, knowledge transfer and knowledge absorptive capacity, the chapter will outline the HR practices that facilitate the type of managerial capabilities needed in the growth phase of the firm. Finally, the chapter will discuss the current shift in management practice. By drawing on Mintzberg's call for developing the 'engaging manager', we argue that the firm's knowledge absorptive capacity represents a critical capability that contributes to enhancing the development of the engaging manager's styles of thinking.

CAREER CHOICE: ENTREPRENEURSHIP VERSUS MANAGEMENT

Research on careers has been greatly influenced by the theories of adult development. Two of the most prominent theories in this area are those of Super (1957) and Levinson (1978). Super's (1957) theory of career stages is based on the individual self-concept through vocational choices. He suggests that the process of choosing an occupation that permits maximum self-expression occurs over time and can be summarized in four career stages: (1) exploration, a period of engaging in self-examination, schooling and the study of different career options; (2) establishment, a period of becoming employed and finding a niche; (3) maintenance, a period of holding on to one's position and updating skills; and (4) disengagement, a period of phasing into retirement. In contrast to Super's (1957) model, Levinson (1986) suggests a punctuated equilibrium model of life development based on chronological age. He argues that life structures are defined by alternating periods of stability in which individuals pursue goals, values and related activities, and periods of transition in which the goals and activities of the previous period are reappraised (see Sullivan, 1999, p. 28).

However, a number of researchers (Cook et al., 2002; Fouad and Byars-Winston, 2005) have suggested that career decisions are influenced by the interaction of the macro-system, described by the society's norms and values, with the micro-context, represented by home, school and work, where the individual resides. Wilson et al. (2004) argue that individual choices of career in entrepreneurship are generally influenced by social and relational factors. According to Dyer (1994), the decision to become an entrepreneur is affected by three factors respectively concerning the individual, the social and economic factors. Brodzinski and Wiebe (1991) have found that the higher the needs for control, achievement, willingness to take risks and tolerance for ambiguity, the more likely the individual will engage in entrepreneurial activity. Schein (1990) also notes that certain individuals have a natural entrepreneurial career anchor, which motivates them to choose an entrepreneurial career. However, the decision to undertake an entrepreneurial career is also affected by social factors (Reynolds, 1991). For instance, a social environment characterized by poverty and parental neglect is generally described as a factor influencing the decision to become an entrepreneur (Collins and Moore, 1964). Family support for the entrepreneurial career can also have an impact on career choice. Race and culture can have a significant impact on the kinds of roles adopted by entrepreneurs and the strategies and tactics that they use to perform in those roles (Thomas and Alderfer, 1989). At the same time, a lack of community support for the new venture can create barriers to a successful entrepreneurial career (Stevenson, 1987).

The individual choice to undertake an entrepreneurial activity is also affected by economic factors. For instance, the economic growth of a nation may lead to a number of business opportunities and the likelihood that someone will seize the opportunity to start an entrepreneurial career (Aldrich, 1990; Kirchoff, 1991). Availability of resource networks is also a driving force for the starting up of a new business (Aldrich and Zimmer, 1986). It is very unlikely that individuals will be willing to start an entrepreneurial activity without at least access to some basic resources such as labour, capital and raw materials. Other research has indicated that prior personal experience can affect career choice (Chambers et al., 1988). Thus, prior experience in a start-up appears to lead to further entrepreneurial activity. Moreover, the experience of working for an entrepreneur may also influence an individual to choose an entrepreneurial lifestyle.

THE ORGANIZATIONAL LIFE CYCLE

The organizational life-cycle (OLC) literature suggests that organizations change over time (Miller and Friesen, 1984; Quinn and Cameron, 1983), in a consistent and predictable manner (Miller and Friesen, 1984). Scholars have tended to classify the OLC models as a four-stage model. Quinn and Cameron (1983) classify the organizational life cycle into the following stages: entrepreneurial, collectivity, formalization and control, and elaboration of structure. By referring to technology-driven ventures, Kazanjian (1988) identifies a four-stage model consisting of: conception and development; commercialization; growth; and stability. As firms evolve through various stages, different problems must be addressed, resulting in the need for different management skills, priorities and structural configurations (Adizes, 1979; Chandler, 1962; Greiner, 1972; Tichey, 1980; Kazanjian, 1988; Miller and Friesen, 1984; Quinn and Cameron, 1983; Smith et al., 1985). For instance, by referring to the Kazanjian's (1988) model, in the first stage of invention and development of a new product or technology, structures and formal procedures are virtually non-existent and all the activities are strictly decided and controlled by the entrepreneur. In the second stage of commercialization, structures and task systems will have to be created beyond product development. In the growth stage, characterized by high growth in both sales and number of employees, organizational hierarchy and functional specialization will develop. In the stability stage, the organization will concentrate on developing next-generation products, establishing a market position, and seeking other growth opportunities.

As the organization progresses from one stage to the next, managers are faced with unique problems in increasing firms' size and complexity (Sexton et al., 1997). Also, more sophisticated capabilities are required (Miller and Friesen, 1983). It is argued that the founders of new ventures often find themselves unprepared to manage growth-related transitions effectively (Galbraith, 1982), whilst crises related to growth must be faced earlier and with greater rapidity than in less volatile environments (Greiner, 1972). An understanding of the organization life cycle and the associated management imperatives could aid entrepreneurial founders through the uncharted course of firm growth.

Mount et al. (1993) argue that growth does not occur according to a linear, smooth evolutionary pattern, but rather through alternate periods of evolution and revolution punctuated by crises. Whilst each of the phases is characterized by a particular management style, the revolutionary phases are characterized by a predominant management problem. However, as organizations move from one stage to the next, they also undergo a transformation process in their design characteristics, enabling them to face new tasks or problems that growth elicits (Kazanjian and Drazin, 1990). The transformation process that firms go through leads managers to acquire new knowledge. As firms encounter problems, managers develop competencies in the supervision of subordinates and delegation of authority and responsibility, with the consequence that the nature of their role will change too (Shim et al., 2000).

Nicholls-Nixon (2005) argues that in the presence of fast growth, major changes in systems, structures and capabilities are required in order to assist with the increasing complexity that accompanies fast growth. Therefore managing growth may have less to do with passing through a series of pre-determined stages than with creating an infrastructure that enables periods of self-organized change to occur. In this situation, management action should be focused on four key areas: capturing and sharing information; building relationships; managing organizational politics; and leadership style. Shim et al.'s (2000) proposition is that, as businesses grow, they become increasingly complex and increasing demands are placed on owners and managers to develop their competencies in each of the identified areas of significance. In this respect, the concept of the organizational life cycle is useful as it focuses attention on managers who should be responsible for acquiring and developing the competencies necessary to sustain firm's growth (Hurst and Zimmerman, 1994) if the organization is to survive. Stevenson (1983) suggests that firms' management practices range along a spectrum from highly entrepreneurial to highly administrative, and that entrepreneurial management, defined as a set of opportunity-based management practices, can help firms remain vital and contribute to firm- and societal-level value creation.

According to Penrose (1959), firms' growth will depend on three factors: the conditions within the firm intrinsic to managerial ability; the external factors with regard to product and factor markets; and the combination of both internal and external conditions that will impact upon the level of risk and uncertainty surrounding a firm's growth. In order for a firm to grow, it must find new markets, develop new products, or pursue new business opportunities, while at the same time hiring new employees and overseeing its existing operation. Often, managers do not have the time or resources to accomplish these objectives, whereby in order to manage the problems of growth, individuals must be able to adapt in the sense of reinventing and redefining their roles. In this context absorptive capacity is identified as a key capability that managers should possess in order to reinvent and redefine their roles alongside the path of the firm's evolution. The concept of absorptive capacity is strictly linked to the concept of knowledge, which is recognized as a critical resource for firm's competitive advantage (Barney, 1991). In order to gain a full appreciation of the importance of managers' absorptive capacity, we now introduce and discuss the concepts of knowledge, knowledge management and knowledge transfer.

WHAT IS KNOWLEDGE?

There is no one definition of what constitutes knowledge in the management literature, as authors' attempts to define knowledge are drawn from a quite heterogeneous set of expressions and terminology. Propp (1999) and Marakas (1999) define knowledge as meaning given by the individual cognitive system to disorganized information. Similarly, Brooking (1999, p. 56) defines knowledge as 'information in context with understanding to applying that knowledge'. Davenport and Prusak (1998, p. 10) view knowledge as 'a fluid mix of framed experience, values, contextual information, and expert insight that provides a framework for evaluating and incorporating new experiences and information'. A common thread running through these definitions is the researchers' focal interest on *information* and *the process* through which such information is given a significance.

Authors also make a distinction between two types of knowledge: *explicit* and *tacit* (Nonaka, 1994; Grant, 1996; Szulanski, 1996; Teece et al., 1997; Lane and Lubatkin, 1998). Explicit knowledge is systematic and easily communicated in the form of hard data or codified procedures (Grant, 1996). It can be articulated in formal language, including grammatical statements. This kind of knowledge can thus be codified and more easily transferred across individuals (Liebeskind, 1996). In addition, explicit knowledge has a tangible dimension that can be more easily captured, codified and communicated (Nonaka and Takeuchi, 1995). Thus codified knowledge is structured in a way that makes it easier to store, reproduce, communicate and trade (Dosi, 1988). Examples of codified knowledge are product specifications, and knowledge encompassed in formal laws, rules and methods. When knowledge is codifiable and people and processes are seemingly easy to imitate, more effective and rigorous implementation and monitoring of codified processes may produce sustainable advantages (Knott, 2003).

In contrast, tacit knowledge is not articulable and, therefore, cannot be easily transferred (Teece et al., 1997). Tacit knowledge is often embedded in uncoded routines and in the firm's social context. Szulanski (1996) argues that tacit knowledge is embedded in individuals' skills and in their collaborative working relationships. It is linked to personal perspectives, intuition, emotions, beliefs, know-how, experiences and values (Nonaka and Takeuchi, 1995; Scarbrough et al., 2003). Given its intangible character, it cannot be easily articulated; hence it is difficult to share with others. Furthermore, tacit knowledge is the wealth of know-how that resides in people's heads, deeply rooted in their life experience. Scarbrough et al. (2003), for instance, argue that tacit knowledge is not available as a text and may conveniently be regarded as residing in the heads of those working on a particular transformation process, or to be embodied in a particular organizational context. In addition, tacit knowledge is difficult to exploit organizationally even when it is clearly articulated (Scarbrough et al., 2003). There is a view that there is no knowledge outside people; hence tacit knowledge cannot be externalized (Cook and Brown, 1999) and the only knowledge that can be externalized is information (Allee, 2000). However, Nonaka (1994) argues that tacit knowledge can be externalized, as knowledge creation is the result of a continuous dialogue between the tacit component – i.e. our mental models and deep beliefs, which are difficult to communicate – and the explicit component of knowledge, which can be formally communicated. The latter can be made accessible in environments of shared experiential background, where it flows tacitly between individuals (Lave and Wenger, 1991).

KNOWLEDGE MANAGEMENT AND KNOWLEDGE TRANSFER

Knowledge as a strategic asset has constituted the focus of a consistent body of literature in the field of strategic management (Barney, 1991). Given the strategic importance of knowledge for competitive advantage, the importance of knowledge management within organizations has grown in parallel (Goh, 2004; Malone, 2002). There is no one definition of knowledge management; however, most authors seem to converge towards a broad definition, which encompasses any processes and practices concerned with the creation, acquisition, capture, sharing and use of knowledge, skills and expertise (Swan et al., 2007). According to this definition, knowledge management does not just refer to the tasks and activities that are implemented to manage existing knowledge in the organization in order to provide the right information to the right people at the right time (Albers and Brewer, 2003), but is also concerned with the tasks and activities that enhance the firm's ability to create 'new knowledge' (Kamara et al., 2002). Therefore, both *generation of knowledge* and *transfer of knowledge* to the decision makers of an organization are critical components of the firm's knowledge management system.

The concept of 'knowledge transfer' evokes an image of 'flow' of knowledge from its primary holders to the secondary holders (Doz, 1996). The primary and secondary holders may be respectively two distant units of a firm, or two different functional units, or a vendor and a customer and so on (Doz, 1996). For Hall (2001, p. 19) knowledge transfer is part of the process of knowledge creation, as 'Knowledge creates knowledge only when it is shared'. In particular, knowledge transfer in organizations is the process through which one unit (e.g. group, department, or division) is affected by the experience of another (Argote and Ingram, 2000). In addition, Argote and Ingram (2000) point out that the transfer of organizational knowledge (i.e. routine or best practice) materializes when it can be observed through changes in the knowledge or performance of recipient units. Similarly, Davenport and Prusak (1998) argue that the knowledge transfer process consists of transmission and absorption, culminating in a behavioural change by the recipient. Davenport and Prusak (1998) conclude that 'knowledge transfer' consists of 'knowledge transmission' plus 'knowledge absorption' and, if knowledge is not absorbed, then it has not been transferred.

Cohen and Levinthal (1990) propose that a critical element for successful knowledge transfer is that firms possess 'knowledge transfer ability'. The ideal outcome for the firms involved in the knowledge transfer process is when both firms, in an exchange process where they both act as knowledge sender (S) and knowledge receiver (R), experience both an increase in the level and value of their knowledge stocks (Breshman et al., 1999). In this situation a firm possesses knowledge *transfer ability*. Cohen and Levinthal (1990) argue that this ability consists of an *absorptive capacity* and *transmissive capacity*, where the absorptive capacity refers to the ability, or capability, of the firms to *understand* the knowledge received from the partner, while the transmissive capacity refers to the ability of *transferring knowledge* to the partner, for example by ensuring that knowledge is presented in a sufficiently codified form (Cohen and Levinthal, 1990).

The knowledge transfer ability is closely related to the notion of *cognition*, which refers to the human ability 'to know' (de Wit and Meyer, 1998). The knowledge that people possess is stored in what are referred to as cognitive maps or cognitive schemata. The ability to know encompasses an ability to adopt information or knowledge, and transform it into new knowledge by understanding, storing and being able to apply it. This process requires that the individual taking in information or knowledge already possesses a knowledge base with which to compare the new knowledge, that is, an *absorptive capacity* (Cohen and Levinthal, 1990). It is argued that the higher the absorptive capacity, that is, the better the firm is at understanding the knowledge received, and the higher the transmissive capacity, that is, the better the firm is at preparing the knowledge for transfer and for transferring it, the smoother the knowledge transfer process in the organization (Szulanski, 1996).

Although organizations can realize remarkable performance benefits by transferring knowledge from one unit to another, successful knowledge transfer can be difficult to achieve (Argote, 1999). In particular, barriers to knowledge transfer occur at the various levels of learning, which are individual, team, organizational and inter-organizational (Nonaka and Takeuchi, 1996; Beeby and Booth, 2000; Crossan et al., 1999). At the individual level, individuals operate so as to prevent sharing of unique information from an individual to the team. The fear of loss of ownership and control of knowledge comes across as a significant barrier (Argyris, 1992). At the team level, the transfer of unique information to the wider organization is hindered when team members find that their comfort zone could be destabilized. The comparison of the benefits to the team *vis-à-vis* the organizational benefit is the usual form of manifestation of this barrier (Larsson et al., 1998). Knowledge transfer from the wider organization to the team depends on the strength of the relationships the team members have with the wider organization. Therefore we can posit that the inward flow of unique information to the team increases with increasing strength of organizational relationships (Grant, 1996). At the organizational level, the downward transfer of unique information from management to a team is hindered by the individual imperative of management, as actions of management usually have wider organizational consequences. The organizational-level sources of barriers (organizational climate, organizational relationships, and systems and structures of the organization) are primarily bound in the culture of the organization (McGill and Slocum, 1993). Whilst such barriers to the transfer of knowledge within the organization may persist and clearly vary from one company to another, the notion of absorptive capacity is relevant for gaining access to the external knowledge available to an organization.

KNOWLEDGE ABSORPTIVE CAPACITY

Organizational life-cycle models assume that organizations go through predictable stages of change, in the sense that they change discontinuously after having confronted and dealt with organizational crises (Miller and Friesen, 1984). The resource-based view of the firm proposes that resources that are valuable, rare and inimitable, such as knowledge, are an enabling factor for sustained competitive advantage (Grant, 1996). The absorptive capacity, in terms of the firm's capability to absorb new knowledge (Cohen and Levinthal, 1990), can be a crucial factor for the successful exploitation of external knowledge (Zahra and George, 2002).

Therefore it is argued that firms will have to develop and augment their knowledge absorptive capacity if they are to sustain their competitive advantage in the long term. Whilst an organization should develop the capability to understand and detect the key issues it is facing, it will also have to develop and grow its absorptive capability in order to absorb new knowledge inputs which will provide solutions to the crisis and challenges generated at different stages of the growth cycle (Van den Bosch et al., 1999).

Organizations' capability to absorb new knowledge may vary from one company to the next, and depends on the state of the existing knowledge, the nature of what is being transferred, the degree of homophile, and the extent of ability and motivation to get access to external knowledge. One of the most important ways that people learn new ideas is by associating those ideas with what they already know; hence it is easier for knowledge to transfer from a source to a recipient when the source and the recipient have knowledge in common. Consequently, knowledge is more likely to be transferred between people with similar knowledge, training and background characteristics (Reagans and Mcevily, 2003).

However, one of the limitations of the literature on organizational learning is the assumption that an organization's capability to learn is a static phenomenon, that is, organizations have a certain capability that neither increases nor diminishes, worsens nor improves, and that the facility for learning is extended by improving the environmental and contextual conditions. This can be contrasted with suggestions that the 'evolutionary stage' of the organization impacts on learning, for example that during the earlier stages of their development firms depend on other firms for their learning but at later stages internalize their learning (Oliver, 2001).

Firms learn from other firms and managers learn externally during the evolutionary stage. They learn explicit or codified knowledge; in some cases, such as partnerships, they may be able to absorb tacit knowledge too. In the later stages, however, they learn less external knowledge, while, in the meatime, they have developed internally and stored tacit knowledge that they can exploit to enhance their growth.

GROWTH STAGE: MANAGERIAL CAPABILITIES NEEDED

In order to enhance firms' absorptive capacity during the growth stage of the organizational life-cycle model, managerial capabilities are needed. Networks and the relating networking capability are proposed as one of the managerial capabilities that contribute to improving firms' knowledge absorptive capacity. For instance, networks enhance the firm's absorptive capacity by simply representing valuable means of raising awareness and knowledge of key issues (McPherson et al., 2001). However, a number of other managerial capabilities based on communication across functional boundaries, top management commitment to learning, a culture that is open to change, and knowledge sharing contribute to enhancing firms' knowledge absorptive capacity (Daghfous, 2004). Specific human resources management (HRM) practices such as employee participation and empowerment, communication, team-based work design, and development of managers contribute to enhancing firm's knowledge absorptive capacity (Huselid et al., 1997) too. Also, managers can improve the absorptive capacity of their organizations by simply applying specific HRM practices oriented towards individuals' abilities, such as training and performance appraisal, performance-based compensation and internal communication (Minbaeva et al., 2003).

Jones et al. (1995) found that an entrepreneurial orientation encourages higher levels of employee involvement in the appraisal process. They found that the greatest differences between entrepreneurial-oriented firms and non-entrepreneurial-oriented firms can be described in terms of performance appraisals, compensation practices and training practices. Specifically, they found that the HR policies of entrepreneurial-oriented organizations reflected an orientation towards innovation and risk taking, long-term planning, results over process, individualism, flexibility, active employee participation and external focus (Koberg et al., 1996). Therefore we argue that an entrepreneurial orientation of the firm enhances the firm's knowledge's absorptive capacity and should be part of the process of managerial capabilities development.

THE CURRENT SHIFT IN MANAGERIAL PRACTICES

According to Whitley (1989), managerial tasks arise, contingently, out of the inherently discretionary character of management within its organizational context and are, as a consequence, interdependent, context-dependent, fluid, concerned with both maintenance and innovation, and lack attributable, visible outputs. For Reed (1990), managing is a 'secondary social practice', characterized by its own concepts, aims, means, activities, problems and situational conditions, which is chronically concerned with establishing and maintaining control over those engaged in 'primary productive practices'. For Tsoukas (1994) the key issue is less what managers do, as what they are *capable* of doing, and hence the need to identify the necessary conditions that endow management with causal powers to elicit cooperation, pursue efficiency and control labour.

The diversity of social systems in which managers are located is a key explanation of the well-documented variations in managerial work. Different managers draw upon the resources and rules of the particular cultural, societal, industrial, organizational, hierarchical, professional and functional systems in which they are located in their work practices.

In order to respond to changes in the external environment, during the 1990s rigid hierarchical organizational structures have been replaced by flatter and flexible structures characterized by the presence of empowered cross-functional teams and nimble networks. Consistent with these organizational changes, the manager's traditional roles of routine administration, supervising a specific functional area, planning, command and control, and reactive 'fire-fighting' have been gradually replaced by new emerging roles, such as engaging in collaboration and coordination, proactive development, leadership and entrepreneurship. These tasks are more about managing a business rather a specific business function, and are believed to be more in tune with the challenges of innovation and self-renewal that twenty-first-century organizations face in their struggle for survival. The manager's job roles, therefore, have gradually shifted towards non-routine 'entrepreneurial' behaviour consisting of allocating resources and instigating product and process innovation. Consequently, middle and junior managers are empowered employees working in self-managed teams and are freed from managerial direction and control, leaving managers to function as leaders and coordinators. The new manager is engaged in team leadership, negotiating integrated effort across boundaries, inspiring and promoting organizational learning, and conceiving, instigating and facilitating change. The new manager will have to exercise judgement, but also unleash creativity and take risks.

Clearly, there is not a clear-cut distinction between what roles the position of manager and entrepreneur respectively entail. Ambiguity, uncertainty and disagreement continue to surround much of what managers do, or are supposed to do. Part of the manager's job, therefore, has always been to negotiate their role in the face of this ambiguity and uncertainty and to act in ways consistent with it (Watson and Harris, 1999). 'Managing people', 'sorting out work problems' and 'handling information' are just such conventional expectations. By giving priority to these activities, managers reproduce the taken-for-granted understandings of what management essentially entails (Hales, 1999), although in practice their job role has evolved towards a more engaging style of management.

THE ENGAGING MANAGER

Drawing on Mintzberg, Armstrong (2005) argues that effective managing happens where art, science and craft – which respectively emphasize insight, analysis and experience – meet. On a similar line of enquiry, Reingold (2000) argues that through reflection managers will avoid the traditional managerial trap of reacting to one crisis after another. Basically, thoughtful reflection on actions and experiences (wondering, probing, analysing, synthesizing and making connections) helps managers to overcome the parochial narrowness of vision and promote powerful managerial learning (Schön, 1983). According to Mintzberg (2004) managers should have the skills of leadership and dealing with uncertainty and risks. Gosling and Mintzberg (2003) argue that managers should not just be able to focus on what they need to accomplish; they should also focus on how to think. For this reason, managers should have five mindsets, as mentioned in the introduction. The reflective manager is able to stop and think, to step back and reflect thoughtfully on his/her experiences. The analytical mindset provides a common language for organizing by allowing people to share an understanding of what is driving their efforts; it provides measures for performance. Gosling and Mintzberg (2003) argue that managers are engaged in organizational analysis; however, they should move beyond conventional analysis. The worldly mindset is about being able to manage in the midst of chaos, and tailor and blend the different parts of the company across the world. A collaborative mindset means getting beyond empowerment, getting away from the currently popular heroic style of managing and moving toward a more engaging style. Engaging managers listen more than they talk. They do less controlling, thus allowing other people to be in greater control of their own work. To have a collaborative mindset means to get involved, to manage throughout. But it has a more profound meaning, too – to take management beyond managers, to distribute it so that responsibility flows naturally to whoever can take the initiative and pull things together. An action mindset is about developing a sensitive awareness of the terrain and of what the team is capable of doing in it, and thereby helping to set and maintain direction, coaxing everyone along. According to Gosling and Mintzberg (2003), by holding the five types of mindsets, an organization is a collective entity that achieves common purpose when the cloths of its various managers are sewn together into useful garments – when the organization's managers collaborate to combine their reflective actions in analytic, worldly ways.

We argue that the development of the engaging manager is facilitated in contexts where the firm has developed its knowledge absorptive capacity. As the engaging manager is more oriented towards thinking rather than controlling, through reflection the engaging manager develops the capability to understand and detect the key issues the firm is facing. With a knowledge absorptive capacity, the engaging manager is able to absorb new knowledge inputs which will provide solutions to the crisis and challenges generated at different stages of the growth cycle. Furthermore, specific HR policies in place which facilitate the development of entrepreneurial-oriented organizations will contribute to enhancing the firm's knowledge absorptive capacity and the engaging manager's styles of thinking.

CONCLUSIONS

In this chapter, by drawing on the theory of the organizational life cycle of the firm, we have been able to shape new insights into the management requirements firms need to address in order to overcome the survival challenges they are faced with during the growth stage. In particular, it was shown that in order to get access to relevant resources – mainly in the form of new knowledge – firms should develop a knowledge absorptive capacity. This is a critical management capability, which develops alongside the organizational life cycle. We argue that such capability is enacted by the human resources practices in place within the organization. Moreover, recent shifts in management practices have emphasized an increasing entrepreneurial style of management, whereby a clear demarcation between what the job of manager and the job of entrepreneur respectively entail has become hard to discern. The shift towards the engaging type of manager and, therefore, the development of Mintzberg's five styles of thinking can only be facilitated by the development of the firm's knowledge absorptive capability.

REFERENCES

Adizes, I. (1979), 'Organizational passages – diagnosing and treating lifecycle problems of organizations', *Organizational Dynamics*, **8**(1), 3–25.
Albers, A.J. and Brewer, S. (2003), 'Knowledge management and the innovation process: the eco-innovation model', *Journal of Knowledge Management Practice*, **4**.
Aldrich, H.E. (1990), 'Using an ecological perspective to study organizational founding rates', *Entrepreneurship Theory and Practice*, **14**(7), 7–24.
Aldrich, H.E. and Zimmer, C. (1986), 'Entrepreneurship through social networks', in D. Sexton and R. Smilor (eds), *The Art and Science of Entrepreneurship*, Cambridge, MA: Ballinger, pp. 3–23.
Allee, V. (2000), 'Knowledge networks and communities of practice', *Journal of the Organization Development Network*, **32**(4).
Argote, L. (1999), *Organizational Learning: Creating, Retaining, and Transferring Knowledge*, Norwell, MA: Kluwer.

Argote, L. and Ingram, P. (2000), 'Knowledge transfer: a basis for competitive advantage in firms', *Organizational Behaviour and Human Decision Processes*, **82**(10), 150–69.

Argyris, C. (1992), *An Organizational Learning*, Cambridge, MA: Blackwell.

Armstrong, S. (2005), 'Postgraduate management education in the UK: lessons from or Lessons for the U.S.', *Academy of Management Learning & Education*, **4**(2), 229–34.

Barney, J. (1991), 'Firm resources and sustained competitive advantage', *Journal of Management*, **17**(1), 99–120.

Beeby, M. and Booth, C. (2000), 'Networks and inter-organizational learning: a critical review', *The Learning Organization*, **7**(2), 75–88.

Breshman, H., Birkinshaw, J. and R. Nobel (1999), 'Knowledge transfer in international acquisitions', *Journal of International Business Studies*, **30**(3), 439–62.

Brodzinski, J. and Wiebe, F. (1991), 'Examining the relationship between personality and entrepreneurial career preference', *Entrepreneurship and Regional Development*, **3**(2), 195–206.

Brooking, A. (1999), *Corporate Memory: Strategies for Knowledge Management*, London: Thompson Business Press.

Chambers, B.R., Hart, S.L. and Denison, D.R. (1988), 'Founding team experience and new firm performance', in B.A. Kirchoff, W.A. Long, W.E. McMullan, K.H. Vesper and W.E. Wetzel, Jr (eds), *Frontiers of Entrepreneurship Research*, Wellesley, MA: Babson College, pp. 106–18.

Chandler, A.D., Jr (1962), *Strategy and Structure: Chapters in the History of the Industrial Enterprise*, Cambridge, MA: MIT Press.

Cohen, W.M. and Levinthal, D. (1990), 'Absorptive capacity: a new perspective on learning and innovation', *Administrative Science Quarterly*, **35**(1), 128–52.

Collins, O.F. and Moore, D.G. (1964), *The Enterprising Man*, East Lansing, MI: Michigan State University.

Cook, D.N. and Brown, J.S. (1999), 'Bridging epistemologies: the generative dance between organizational knowledge and organizational knowing', *Organization Studies*, **10**, 381–400.

Cook, E.P., Heppner, M.I. and O'Brien, K.M. (2002), 'Career development of women of colour and White women: assumptions, conceptualization, and interventions from an ecological perspective', *The Career Development Quarterly*, **50**, 291–305.

Crossan, M.M., Lane, H.W. and White, R.E. (1999), 'An organizational learning framework: from intuition to institution', *Academy of Management Review*, **24**(3), 522–37.

Daghfous, A. (2004), 'Absorptive capacity and the implementation of knowledge-intensive best practices', *Advanced Management Journal*, **69**(2), 21–7.

Davenport, T. and Prusak, L. (1998), *Working Knowledge: How Organizations Manage What They Know*, Boston, MA: Harvard Business School Press.

de Wit, B. and R. Meyer (1998), *Strategy: Process, Content, Context – An International Perspective*, London, UK: ITP.

Dosi, G. (1988), 'Institutions and markets in a dynamic world', *The Manchester School of Economics and Social Studies*, **61**(2), 119–46.

Doz, Y. (1996), 'The evolution of cooperation in strategic alliances: initial conditions or learning processes?', *Strategic Management Journal*, **17**, 55–85.

Dyer, Jr, W.G. (1994), 'Toward a theory of entrepreneurial careers', *Entrepreneurship: Theory & Practice*, **19**(2), 7–21.

Fouad, Nadya A. and Byars-Winston, Angela M. (2005), 'Cultural context of career choice: meta-analysis of race/ethnicity differences', *Career Development Quarterly*, **53**(3), 223–33.

Galbraith, J. (1982), 'The stages of growth', *Journal of Business Strategy*, **3**(1), 70–9.

Goh, A. (2004), 'Enhancing organisational performance through knowledge innovation: a proposed strategic management framework', *Journal of Knowledge Management Practice*, **5**, October.

Gosling, J. and Mintzberg, H. (2003), 'The five minds of a manager', *Harvard Business Review*, **81**(11), 54–63.

Grant, R.M. (1996), 'Toward a knowledge-based theory of the firm', *Journal of Strategic Management*, **17**, 109–22.

Greiner, L.E. (1972), 'Evolution and revolution as organizations grow', *Harvard Business Review*, **50**, 37–46.

Hales, C.P. (1999), 'Why do managers do what they do? Reconciling evidence and theory in accounts of managerial work', *British Journal of Management*, **10**, 335–50.

Hall, B.P. (2001), 'Values development and learning organization', *Journal of Knowledge Management*, **5**(1), 19–32.

Hurst, D.K. and Zimmerman, B.J. (1994), 'From life cycle to eco-cycle: a new perspective on the growth, maturity, destruction, and renewal of complex systems', *Journal of Management Inquiry*, **3**(4), 339.

Huselid, M.A., Jackson, S.E. and Schuler, R.S. (1997), 'Technical and strategic human resource management effectiveness as determinants of firm performance', *Academy of Management Journal*, **40**(1), 171–88.

Jones, F.F., Morris, M.H. and Rockmore, W. (1995), 'HR practices that promote entrepreneurship', *HR Magazine*, **5**, 86–91.

Kamara, M.J., Anumba, J. and Carrillo, M.P. (2002), 'A clever approach to selecting a KM strategy', *International Journal of Project Management*, **20**, 205–11.

Kazanjian, R.K. and Drazin, R. (1990), 'A stage-contingent model of design and growth for technology based new ventures', *Journal of Business Venturing*, **3**, 137.

Kazanjian, R.K. (1988), 'Relation of dominant problems to stages of growth in technology-based new ventures', *Academy of Management Journal*, **31**, 257–79.

Kirchoff, B.A. (1991), 'Entrepreneur's contribution to economics', *Entrepreneurship Theory and Practice*, **16**(2), 93–112.

Knott, A.M. (2003), 'The organizational routines factor market paradox', *Strategic Management Journal*, **24**(10), 929–43.

Koberg, C.S., Uhlenbruck, N. and Sarason, Y. (1996), 'Facilitators of organizational innovation: the role of life-cycle stage', *Journal of Business Venturing*, **11**, 133–49.

Lane, P.J. and Lubatkin, M. (1998), 'Relative absorptive capacity and inter-organizational learning', *Strategic Management Journal*, **19**(5), 461–77.

Larsson, R., Bentsson, L., Henriksson, K. and Sparks, J. (1998), 'The inter-organizational learning dilemma: collective knowledge development in strategic alliances', *Organization Science*, **9**(3), 285–305.

Lave, J. and Wenger, E. (1991), *Situated Learning: Legitimate Peripheral Participation*, Cambridge, UK: Cambridge University Press.

Levinson, D. (1978), *The Seasons of a Man's Life*, New York: Knopf.

Levinson, D. (1986), 'The paper (book)', *Library Journal*, **111**(15), 84.

Liebeskind, J.P. (1996), 'Knowledge, strategy, and the theory of the firm', *Strategic Management Journal*, **17**, 93–107.

Malone, D. (2002), 'Knowledge management: a model for organizational learning', *International Journal of Accounting Information Systems*, **3**, 111–23.

Marakas, G.M. (1999), *Decision Support Systems in the Twenty-first Century*, Englewood Cliffs, NJ: Prentice-Hall.

McGill, M.E. and Slocum, J.W. (1993), 'Unlearning the organization', *Organizational Dynamics*, **22**, 67–78.

McPherson, M., Smith-Lovin, L. and Cook, J.M. (2001), 'Birds of a feather: homophily in social networks', *Annual Review of Sociology*, **27**(1), 415–44.

Miller, D. and Friesen, P.H. (1983), 'Successful and unsuccessful phases of the corporate life cycle', *Organization Studies*, **4**(4), 339.

Miller, D. and Friesen, P.H. (1984), 'A longitudinal analysis of the corporate life cycle', *Management Science*, **30**(10), 1161–83.

Minbaeva, D., Pedersen, T., Bjorkman, I., Fey, C.F. and Park, H.J. (2003), 'MNC knowledge transfer, subsidiary absorptive capacity, and HRM', *Journal of International Business Studies*, **34**(6), 586.

Mintzberg, H. (2004), *Managers not MBAs: A Hard Look at the Soft Practice of Managing and Management Development*, San Francisco, CA: Berrett-Koehler.

Mount, J., Zinger, J.T. and Forsyth, G.R. (1993), 'Organizing for development in the small business', *Long Range Planning*, **26**(5), 111–20.

Nicholls-Nixon, C.L. (2005), 'Rapid growth and high performance: the entrepreneur's "impossible dream?" ', *Academy of Management Executive*, **19**(1), 77–89.

Nonaka, I. (1994), 'A dynamic theory of organizational knowledge creation', *Organization Science*, **5**, 14–37.

Nonaka, I. and Takeuchi, H. (1995), *The Knowledge Creating Company: How Japanese Companies Create the Dynamics of Innovation*, New York: Oxford University Press.

Nonaka, I. and Takeuchi, H. (1996), *The Knowledge-Creating Company*, London: Oxford University Press.

Oliver, A.L. (2001), 'Strategic alliances and the learning life-cycle of biotechnology firms', *Organization Studies*, **22**(3), 467–89.

Penrose, E. (1959), *The Theory of the Growth of the Firm*, Oxford: Oxford University Press.

Propp, K.M. (1999), 'Collective information processing in groups', in L.R. Frey (ed.), *The Handbook of Group Communication Theory and Research*, Thousand Oaks, CA: Sage Publications, pp. 225–49.

Quinn, R.E. and Cameron, K. (1983), 'Organizational life cycles and shifting criteria of effectiveness: some preliminary evidence', *Management Science*, **29**(1), 33–51.

Reagans, R. and Mcevily, B. (2003), 'Network structure and knowledge transfer: the effects of cohesion and range', *Administrative Science Quarterly*, **48**(2), 240–67.

Reed, M. (1990), 'The labour process perspective on management organization: a critique and a reformulation', in J. Hassard and D. Pym (eds), *The Theory and Philosophy of Organizations*, London: Routledge, pp. 63–82.

Reingold, J. (2000), 'You can't create a leader in a classroom', *Fast Company*, **40**, November, p. 286.

Reynolds, P.D. (1991), 'Sociology and entrepreneurship', *Entrepreneurship Theory and Practice*, **16**(2), 47–70.

Scarbrough, H., Bresnen, M., Edelman, L. and Newel, S. (2003), 'Social practices and the management of knowledge in project environments', *International Journal of Project Management*, **21**, 157–66.

Schein, E.H. (1990), *Career Anchors: Discovering Your Real Values*, San Diego, CA: University Associates.

Schön, D.A. (1983), *The Reflective Practitioner*, New York: Basic Books.

Sexton, D.L., Upton, N.B., Wacholtz, L.E. and McDougall, P.P. (1997), 'Learning needs of growth-oriented entrepreneurs', *Journal of Business Venturing*, **12**(1), 1–8.

Shepherd, Jill (2005), 'Henry Mintzberg: managers not MBAs', *Organization Studies*, **26**(7), 1089–90.

Shim, S., Eastlick, M.A. and Lotz, S. (2000), 'Examination of US Hispanic-owned, small retail and service businesses: an organizational life cycle approach', *Journal of Retailing and Consumer Services*, **7**(1), 19–32.

Smith, K.G., Mitchell, T.R. and Summer, C.E. (1985), 'Top level management priorities in different stages of the organizational life cycle', *Academy of Management Journal*, **28**(4), p. 799.

Stevenson, H.H. (1987), 'General management and entrepreneurship', Working Paper, Harvard University, Department of Organizational Behaviour.

Stevenson, H.H. (1983), 'A perspective on entrepreneurship', *Harvard Business School Working Paper*, **9**.

Sullivan, S.E. (1999), 'The changing nature of careers: a review and research agenda', *Journal of Management*, **25**(3), 457–83.

Super, D.E. (1957), *The Psychology of Careers*, New York: Harper & Row.

Swan, J., Scarbrough, H. and Robertson, M. (2002), 'The construction of communities of practice in the management of innovation', *Management Learning*, **33**(4), 477–96.

Szulanski, G. (1996), 'Exploring internal stickiness: impediments to the transfer of best practice within the firm', *Strategic Management Journal*, **17**, 27–43.

Teece, D.J., Pisano, G. and Shuen, A. (1997), 'Dynamic capabilities and strategic management', *Strategic Management Journal*, **18**, 509–33.

Thomas, D.A. and Alderfer, C.P. (1989), 'The influence of race on career dynamics: theory and research on minority career experiences', in M.B. Arthur, D.T. Hall and B.S. Lawrence (eds), *Handbook of Career Theory*, Cambridge: Cambridge University Press, pp. 133–58.

Tichey, N.M. (1980), 'Problem cycles in organizations and the management of change', in J.R. Kimberly and R.H. Miles, *The Organizational Lifecycle: Issues in the Creation, Transformation, and Decline of Organizations*, San Francisco, CA: Jossey-Bass.

Tsoukas, H. (1994), 'What is management? An outline of a metatheory', *British Journal of Management*, **5**(4), 289–301.

Van den Bosch, F.A.J., Volberda, H.W. and De Boer, M. (1999), 'Co-evolution of firm absorptive capacity and knowledge environment: organizational forms and combinative capabilities', *Organization Science*, **10**, 551–68.

Watson, T.J. and P. Harris (1999), *The Emergent Manager*, London: Sage.

Whitley, R. (1989), 'On the nature of managerial tasks and skills', *Journal of Management Studies*, **26**(3), 209–24.

Wilson, F., Marlino, D. and Kickul, J. (2004), 'Our entrepreneurial future: examining the diverse attitudes and motivations of teens across gender and ethnic identity', *Journal of Developmental Entrepreneurship*, **9**(3), 177–97.

Zahra, S.A. and George, G. (2002), 'Absorptive capacity: a review, reconceptualization, and extension', *Academy of Management Review*, **27**(2), 185.

18. Career constraints in the creative and cultural industries in London: the case of work placement and training experience[1]

Mustafa F. Özbilgin and Ahu Tatlı

INTRODUCTION

At the intersection of education and work, work placement is often considered a route to careers in many industries. Therefore the process and the content of work placement can be studied in terms of future career opportunities and prospects. However, work placement design and process can also present career constraints if designed and delivered in particular ways. In this chapter, we explore the success and failure of work placement practices, with a view to revealing forms of career constraint that work placement practices present in the sector.

This chapter reports the findings of a scoping study of London-based higher education institutions' (HEIs) work placement practices within the creative and cultural industries. The research was conducted in four phases, involving a literature review, a field study which scoped the range of work placement practices utilized by HEIs in London, case studies of various models and assessment of work placement practices, and analysis of the documentary and field study data. Field research involved documentary analysis and interviews with representatives from HEIs and organizations in the creative and cultural industry as well as students who are undertaking their placement projects through these HEIs and in firms. We conducted interviews with 11 participants in ten HEIs, ten students, and five respondents in four host organizations.

CAREER CONSTRAINT: THE CASE OF WORK PLACEMENTS IN THE CREATIVE AND CULTURAL INDUSTRIES

Much of the literature on work placements comes from disciplines that have strong traditions of work placements in industry, i.e. nursing, engineering and business studies, and from countries where work placement is common practice within the higher education sector. Therefore this review draws on interdisciplinary as well as international studies of work placement. This section first provides operational definitions of work placements and creative and cultural enterprises, and then examines training and careers, as structures of opportunity and constraint for placement students, in the creative and cultural industries in the UK.

Defining Work Placements

A wide range of terms is used to refer to work placements. The National Council of Work Experience (NCWE, 2006) provides definitions of alternative terms, revealing their slight differences from work placements. 'Sandwich and industrial placements' refer to a fixed-term period of assessed, paid work that forms part of a university degree. It often lasts for a full year. A 'work-based project' is a specific piece of assessed work for a university course, undertaken at an employer's premises. A 'work placement' involves a period of work experience, which can be paid or unpaid, and is part of a course of study. This can be arranged through the university with an employer or by the student, and is for an agreed period of time. 'Internship' is a term that is increasingly used by large companies and refers to a placement within their organization, usually over 6–12 weeks during the summer holiday. The NCWE also lists other forms of work experience: 'voluntary work' is any type of work undertaken for no payment, usually outside the university course in the student's spare time. 'Part-time work' is paid or unpaid work, undertaken either during term-time, in the holidays or both for fewer than 35 hours per week. For a project that is providing assessment and accreditation of part-time work, see the CRAC Insight Plus programme on www.insightplus.co.uk. 'Work shadowing' involves a student observing a member of staff working in an organization, and offers an understanding of what a particular job entails. 'Shell step' is a vacation work experience where students undertake a specific project within a small to medium-sized business for eight weeks during the summer; see www.shellstep.org.uk. In this project, the term 'work placement' is used to denote a period of work in industry that is recognized as a structured period of learning by the respective higher education and host institution of the student. This project explores the management of work placement experience by the HEIs, host institutions and students.

Defining the Creative and Cultural Industries

Any scholarly attempt at describing industrial practices in any sector of work or occupation should start by defining the boundaries and content of the sector that is about to be brought under public scrutiny. In keeping with this tradition, we start our review by defining 'creative and cultural industries'. The Creative Industries Task Force, in their national mapping exercise in 1998, defined creative industries as (British Council, 2006):

> those industries that have their origin in individual creativity, skill and talent and which have a potential for wealth and job creation through the generation and exploitation of intellectual property.

The Department for Culture, Media and Sport (DCMS, 2006) offers a similar definition:

> We define the creative industries as those industries which have their origin in individual creativity, skill and talent and which have a potential for wealth and job creation through the generation and exploitation of intellectual property. This includes advertising, architecture, the art and antiques market, crafts, design, designer fashion, film and video, interactive leisure software, music, the performing arts, publishing, software and computer games, television and radio.

UNESCO (2006) defines cultural industries in a way that overlaps with the definition of creative industries:

> It is generally agreed that this term applies to those industries that combine the creation, production and commercialisation of contents which are intangible and cultural in nature. These contents are typically protected by copyright and they can take the form of goods or services. Depending on the context, cultural industries may also be referred to as 'creative industries', sunrise or 'future oriented industries' in the economic jargon, or content industries in the technological jargon. The notion of cultural industries generally includes printing, publishing and multimedia, audio-visual, phonographic and cinematographic productions, as well as crafts and design. For some countries, this concept also embraces architecture, visual and performing arts, sports, manufacturing of musical instruments, advertising and cultural tourism. Cultural industries add value to contents and generate values for individuals and societies. They are knowledge and labour-intensive, create employment and wealth, nurture creativity – the 'raw material' they are made from – and foster innovation in production and commercialisation processes. At the same time, cultural industries are central in promoting and maintaining cultural diversity and in ensuring democratic access to culture. This twofold nature – both cultural and

economic – builds up a distinctive profile for cultural industries. During the 90s they grew exponentially, both in terms of employment creation and contribution to GNP. Today, globalisation offers new challenges and opportunities for their development.

O'Connor (1999, p. 5) presents an academic definition of cultural industries, which also relates to the interplay between the creative and economic aspects of the industry:

> The cultural industries are those activities which deal primarily in symbolic goods – goods whose primary economic value is derived from their cultural value.

The issue of definition is an important one within the creative and cultural industries. There remains much debate about where the boundaries of the creative industries might coincide with the cultural industries. Although the purpose of this chapter is not to engage in a deep semantic debate about the origins and boundaries of cultural and creative industries, it is nevertheless important to note that the definitions above indicate the significance of the role that creative and cultural industries provide in terms of wealth and job creation as well as economic regeneration. Furthermore, creativity is the 'golden thread' that draws together all the different elements of the creative and cultural industries (Hall and Bewick, 2006).

The Rt Hon. Tessa Jowell MP (2006), UK Secretary of State for Culture, Media and Sport, made a speech at Bloomberg on 14 March about the importance of the creative industries. The following excerpts from this speech highlight the economic significance of the creative and cultural industries in the UK:

> The global market value of the creative industries has increased from $831 billion in 2000 to $1.3 trillion in 2005; more than 7 per cent of global GDP. In the UK, KPMG predicts 46 per cent employment growth and 136 per cent output growth in the Creative Industries between 1995 and 2015 . . . Many of you may remember the Creative Industries mapping document published by my predecessor Chris Smith eight years ago. A useful benchmark, but just look at what has occurred since then. In 1998, employment in the UK's creative economy stood at around one and a half million people. Today they employ almost 2 million people. These sectors now produce almost £1 in £12 of our total Gross Value Added (GVA) – a higher proportion than in any other country, and they contribute £11.4 billion to our balance of trade, well ahead of economic sectors such as construction and insurance, and twice as much as the widely praised pharmaceutical sector.

Tessa Jowell continues her speech by noting how the above economic success can be cultivated by schools and universities:

Of course, the infrastructure for the creative industries is already supported by public policy at national regional and local level. A schools system and University sector that nurtures the creative *and* entrepreneurial talent of all our young people is essential to providing the highly skilled labour force needed by business. And our HE sector can act as a magnet for talent from all over the world.

The size and scope of creative and cultural industries in the UK and London are explored through several reports by the CCS (Creative & Cultural Skills) consultation papers and reports from the Arts Council England.

Training and Careers in the Creative and Cultural Industries in the UK

Training and careers in the creative and cultural industries are inextricably linked. Work placement offers access to career opportunities. However, the issue of workplace training is highly politicized in the UK. The current government agenda aims to close the training gap that scholars such as Finegold and Soskice (1988) identified earlier. The training gap remains a contested issue. For example, Wolf (2002) demonstrates that there is no training gap to be filled in the UK and that the UK economy is not driven by a low-skilled workforce as suggested by proponents of the training gap hypothesis. Any conclusion to the ongoing political debate on the training gap has implications for how work placements are treated by the state, universities and industry. Under the current labour government, the drive is towards supporting workplace learning through structured mechanisms of university–industry collaboration. The major challenge in terms of organization of work placement and the training to work process involves failure of the transfer from training and placement to employment. Despite claims of improvement in the last decade, structural problems at the sectoral level persist. This is the case despite state-level initiatives to support the sector. There is clearly a role for HEIs and the host institutions to play in this vacuum of responsibility to recognize work placement students' needs for career and life success. The situation is exacerbated due to lack of attention to equality and diversity concerns in the sector. Drawing on the literature, we explain in this section the macro-, meso- and micro-dynamics that shape opportunities and constraints for the placement of students in the creative and cultural industries in the UK.

Failure of the Training to Work Process

Despite widespread support for university–industry collaboration, the evidence for the success of current initiatives in the UK is only partial. This raises concerns about a possible gap between the discourse and the reality of placement initiatives. This gap is also responsible for the popular belief in the ineffectiveness of training and work placement programmes in securing employment in the UK. This belief is not totally unfounded. Indeed, Duignan's study (2002) reveals that there is no difference in terms of academic achievement between students who took work placements and those who did not. Similarly, Westhead et al. (2001) argue that students who took up a programme offered by Shell Plc did not perform significantly differently from their counterparts who did not participate in the programme.

Despite its somewhat poor reputation, work experience as part of higher education, in many guises of work, industrial or professional placements or sandwich courses, is now a familiar feature of higher and further education in the UK. However, Uzzell (1986) argued that much of the literature in the field is highly descriptive and largely atheoretical. Since the 1980s, owing to the strength of the drive for university–industry collaboration by respective UK governments, there were major developments in the field of work placements, although the relevant literature has remained fragmented and largely uncritical.

Signs of Progress

Hutton (2006, p. 23) reviews the current situation of work-based learning in the creative and cultural industries. He explains that there have been dramatic improvements in the quantity of workplace learning initiatives in the last couple of years:

> By 2001 it was clear that the number of young people taking up work-based learning had not increased. In fact between 2000 and 2003 the number of young people starting apprenticeships fell from 76,800 to 47,300. However, things have turned around more recently. By 2004–05, about a quarter of a million young people were pursuing an apprenticeship and some 130,000 employers were involved. The Government has hit its target of 175,000 under-22-year-olds starting an apprenticeship by July 2005, which is a major improvement. The new target is that 35% should start an apprenticeship by 2010 – taking the UK to the North West European average.

These developments should be seen in the context of the sizeable contribution that creative and cultural industries make to the UK economy. In recent years, awareness of the significance of the industry to the economic and social well-being of the UK has become the major driver for reform in terms of work-based learning in the sector. However, reflecting on the economic success of the sector, Hall (2006, p. 4) cautions against complacency:

While the UK's creative and cultural sector is at the heart of the knowledge economy, there is no room for complacency. The competition is already snapping at our heels. But for many of the people working in our area, dealing with these challenges is difficult. Over 25% of the workforce are freelance or working as individuals. Organisations are small. We are a sector characterised as freelance and micro, where people's skills are too often under-capitalised or not recognised, and where the sector as a whole is under-managed. People are also motivated to enter or work in this sector for different reasons and at different times, hence the large number of volunteers.

The porous and fragmented nature of the sector, with domination of micro-, self-employed and small businesses, means that job security and relative stability in pay and conditions of work do not prevail in the creative and cultural industries. So, what can be done to improve the conditions of work and structural fragmentation in the sector? It is naïve to assume that self-regulation of the current situation will lead to better outcomes. However, it is also possible to argue that a very managerialist model may stifle creativity and innovation, which are essential ingredients of this sector. However, this debate is futile in the light of the fact that it is still possible to provide policies, support structures and management perspectives that foster rather than constrain innovation and creativity.

The Role of the State

There were state-level initiatives to boost support for creative and cultural industries. The Creative Industries Task Force was established by the prime minister in 1997 and led by government ministers and leaders from the creative industries sectors. Between 1997 and 2000 the Task Force advised on policy development. The work of the Task Force is continued by an inter-departmental government committee, the Ministerial Creative Industries Strategy Group. Furthermore, there are other state agencies that focus on creative and cultural industries: the Creative Industries Export Promotion Advisory Group (CIEPAG), with a joint secretariat from the Department for Culture, Media and Sport (DCMS) and Trade Partners UK (TPUK), serves as an interesting example. This group had four sub-groups: Content, Design, Heritage and Tourism, and Performing Arts. CIEPAG ceased operation in 2002, leaving the four sub-groups which re-established themselves as Creative Export, Design Partners, Cultural Heritage and Tourism (CH&T) and Performing Arts International Development (PAID). DCMS and TPUK continue to provide the secretariat for these four groups.

The Creative Industries Higher and Further Education Forum is an organized group made up of representatives of higher education, further education, creative industries, education and research. It aims to investigate how to strengthen collaborative activities between higher education, further education and the creative industries (DCMS, 2006), as a follow-up to the Lambert Review of Business–University Collaboration (2003).

At the nexus of state policy and involvement of young people in arts also resides Arts Council England (ACE, 2005), which commits itself to the following strategies for involving young people in arts: support activity that broadens young people's experience of different art forms, practices and traditions; support activity that provides young people with routes for progression through their arts experiences; adapt the ways that the ACE works to allow for more coherent planning and direct engagement with children and young people and their services; identify organizations with the skills and commitment to pioneer new ways of working with and for children and young people, and review the ACE portfolio of regularly funded organizations to ensure that ACE is supporting a wide range of high-quality provision for children and young people. These objectives are congruent with and relevant to a drive towards improving work placement experiences of students, most of whom are young, in creative and cultural industries.

The Role of the HEIs and Host Institutions

Recent moves by universities to embrace industry-based learning has implications for support made available to students undertaking this type of education. This is particularly important in order for universities and host intuitions to foresee and address proactively any problems due to the organization of their workplace arrangements. Studies suggest that work placement programmes may involve some difficulties for institutions as well as for students. Among a group of social work students, Maidment (2003) investigated problems that students face during their work placement in industry. She noted that workplace stress and conflict are considerable concerns for students as they often lack skills and organizational status to resolve conflicts and alleviate stressful work experiences. Furthermore, there are financial pressures on placement students who are underpaid by their institutions and fall out of the normal higher education funding nets. It is clear that the problems experienced by this group of social work students require pedagogical strategies in order to transfer skills to deal with workplace stress and conflict, and to identify strategies for financial survival. Maidment (2003) argues that these skills should be offered as part of the curriculum before the students embark on their placement experience in industry.

In a study of work experience in the hospitality, leisure and tourism industries, Kelley-Patterson and George (2001) find that divergent expectations of employers and lack of strong collaborative ties between workplaces, HEIs and students are the main barriers to successful placement experience. The authors also identify that the nature of the contract also changes from relational to transactional between work placement and graduate employment. Therefore the authors call for attention to be given to the nature of the psychological contract as well as the written contract in order to understand both the subjective and the objective realities of work experience. Furthermore, Ashworth and Saxton (1992) note that assessment of work placement outcomes may suffer from various forms of assessment bias. The authors argue that these could be eliminated with careful investigation of assessment systems for bias.

Our review above identifies structural problems with organization of work placement programmes. Despite evidence of wider take-up of work placements across the creative and cultural industries in the UK, there is need for further reforms at the national and sectoral levels to improve the experience, processes and career outcomes of work placement.

CAREER CHOICE AND CONSTRAINT: EQUALITY CONCERNS

Whilst structural problems associated with the transition from training to work in the UK continue to constrain career opportunities in the creative and cultural industries, there is also evidence of further fragmentation of career outcomes and experiences due to an apparent inattention to issues of equality and diversity in the sector. The state, the HEIs as well as the host institutions have legal, moral and business reasons to consider equal opportunities practice across all strands of equality and diversity. There are some current initiatives across the sector to address inequalities, discrimination and exclusion. Arts Council England (2005, p. 10) also highlights its desire to extend support to individuals in priority groups, including low-income families, those living in areas of London with few, or no, appropriate cultural facilities or opportunities, and with disabled members and those who are vulnerable or at risk.

Skill (National Bureau for Students with Disabilities) has issued some guidelines for students, HEIs and employers to consider in addressing issues of disability during study and work experience. Skill (2006) offers information and an information phone line to help students with disabilities to achieve their full potential. Blankfield (2001) argues that the provision of work placement should be designed in a way that makes the experience more welcoming for students with disabilities. She examined the experiences of a group of students with dyslexia. Her findings suggest that the students, except for one, have found it difficult to disclose their conditions to their employers. More inclusive practices would require the workplaces and the HEIs to recognize the unique requirements of the whole spectrum of disabilities. Treating all disabilities the same, as currently witnessed, does not yield positive outcomes, the author argues.

One of the important issues of equality and diversity in work placements is the place of minority ethnic students as well as students who are nonnative speakers of English. Through a case study of placement students at Surrey University, Mandilaras (2004) identified a gap between the performance of UK and international students subsequent to their placement year. A study of international students' placement outcomes in the USA (Shen and Herr, 2004) also demonstrates that the international students find the counselling and placement services offered by the centralized university administration as ill fitting for their requirements. This gap is of importance in terms of equal opportunities that universities profess to commit to: although the UK higher education system accepts a large number of fee-paying international students, there is growing resentment of their arrival in large numbers and widening of the divide between treatment of home national and foreign students. Samway and McKeon (1999) seek to debunk some of the myths associated with the education of language minority students. The authors identify that the HEIs have a responsibility and major role to play in the successful delivery of the higher education curriculum and placement of students in workplaces. Furthermore, Beard et al. (2001) demonstrate how an employer of international students can provide an environment in which the student achieves personal and professional growth. The authors argue that such growth can be predicted by the negotiated placement objectives between student and employer, and ongoing support from stakeholders during the placement.

The Way Forward

Research on work placements and the success of work placement experience in the creative and cultural industries has been sparse. However, there are some examples and case studies from the UK and more widely that highlight the need to consider multiple constituencies as well as the multidimensional nature of work placement experience (Neill and Mulholland, 2003). The main institutional constituents of the student experience in work placements are the institutions which host students and their university programmes which prepare them for the experience and monitor their progress. The number of individuals involved in the process from these key organizations may vary depending on institutional arrangements. Student experience is also multidimensional, involving both subjective and objective experiences of work placement. Research from work placements in Australia (Smith et al., 2001) suggests that the students' social backgrounds, previous work experience, family, financial and employment commitments influence their choice of work placements. This suggests that work placement experience is not an outcome of only a tripartite relationship between the HEI, the host institution and the student. Indeed, a wider network of institutions and individuals shapes the choice and quality of the student placement experience. Therefore a successful work placement design should encourage better ties between these diverse constituent groups and across multiple dimensions of work placement experience.

There is general agreement that a number of benefits can accrue from the students' placement year (Richardson and Blakeney, 1998). However, reaping these benefits requires the host institutions and the HEIs to consider a number of factors that influence the success of work placements. Several authors have attempted to develop models and reveal factors that contribute to the success of student placements: Leslie (1994) offers a total quality management model for organizing work experience. The model suggests that quality should be considered at every phase and by all constituent groups and individuals involved in the work placement experience of students. It suggests that through small and gradual quality improvements, work placement experience can be radically improved in the long term. The longer-term perspective, however, may conflict with short-term expectations of the line management in the industry, the author contends. Drawing on a case study, Barthorpe and Hall (2000) elaborate on a collaborative placement and careers preparation programme. This model involves preparing students for their placement experience through a set of training programmes which aims to improve their employability and survival skills in industrial placements.

Studies that focus on success factors for work placements are available across a wide range of sectors, industries and national contexts: Crebert et al. (2004) have studied student perceptions of three learning contexts: university, work placement and post-graduation employment in the USA. Their study reveals that although students value their university education, they rate their learning in work placement and subsequent employment very highly. It is interesting to note that the study shows that teamwork, being given responsibility, and collaborative learning are the most important factors for effective learning in the three contexts under consideration. Drawing on a study of medical placements, Maurana et al. (2000) explain that partnerships between the HEI and the host institution are crucial for the success of the placement experience. They identify four stages in which the work placement can be fostered: (1) establishing and building relationships between the HEIs and host institutions; (2) developing common goals; (3) developing and implementing programmes; and (4) maintaining and expanding progress. Such a stepwise approach to work placements is important as different stages of setting up a work placement programme require different considerations.

Support for better coordination between host institutions and HEIs comes from Nolan's study (1998) of a group of Australian work placements, which identifies that a strategic approach should be adopted in order to strengthen the ties between these two parties. Similarly, Mulraney and Turner (2001) present a learning partnership model that recognizes the multi-constituent nature of relationships in work placements. The model suggests that the HEIs, host organizations and students agree on a set of learning activities and monitor and assess these with a view to generating benefits for all parties involved. The authors also argue that any preparatory training for work placement should consider unique sectoral and organizational configurations. The authors focus on the case of SMEs and work placements, and effectively demonstrate that the absence of the SME sector in the academic curriculum does a disservice to students who may opt for placement experience in this sector.

In their study of hospitality management student work placements, McMahon and Quinn (1995) explain that HEIs need to build up successful relationships with individual companies for mutually beneficial outcomes in student learning. They also suggest that the HEIs must invest the necessary resources in the placement function in order to reap the possible benefits. They argue that organizations must develop a more considered approach towards placements. In the same vein, students should be positive and forthright in their attitude in order to benefit from the whole process.

Ashworth and Saxton (1992) explore the interpersonal dynamics of placement experience as a possible source of success. They explain that the educational purpose of the placements should be supported by tutors from HEIs who are responsible for placement projects as well as workplace mentors who are assigned to assess student performance. Cahill's (1996) research on students' experiences of mentorship suggests that students perceive mentorship more as a mechanism of control and less as a mechanism of support. The support function of mentoring activities is as vital as its control aspect for adding value to students' experience of work placement.

Measurement is often considered an important precondition for managing any process. In the context of work placements, measurement and assessment may enable the successful management of student placement experience. Whilst some occupational groups and certain industries incorporate elaborate assessment techniques in work placements, other industries adopt a more liberal, *laissez-faire* approach. One of the sectors where work placements are monitored and assessed is the health services sector (Nolan and Chung, 1999; Drennan, 2002) or in civil engineering (Majewski et al., 2000). Intersectoral transfer of knowledge may be a useful means of adopting monitoring and measurement tools in the cultural and creative industries, which appears in the literature to have few structured methods of engaging with such assessment mechanisms.

Although the authors caution against some human errors in this interactive design, they argue that, with care, possible biases could be eliminated, to make assessment an integral part of the placement experience. Huntington et al. (1999) argue that successful assessment also depends on careful briefing and preparation of students before placement and close liaison between placement tutor, employer and student during the work placement term.

The role of placement coordinators in students' experience of work placement cannot be overstated. The placement coordinator role may take three distinct forms: (1) a purely administrative model, in which a placement tutor is solely responsible for the placement function; (2) as part of a centralized administrative team in which the placement coordinator is a member at the HEI; and (3) a mixed role where the placement tutor is also an academic member of staff. Coll and Eames (2000) argue that the third model presents better prospects for students to combine their academic learning with work placement experience. Furthermore, the combined role allows for placement considerations to be integrated into the academic curriculum, should the placement coordinators champion such a cause. Newton and Smith (1998) argue that the role of the personal tutor is to help the students to develop both professionally and academically. To facilitate this, a good interpersonal relationship between student and personal tutor is essential. However, such a relationship requires time and effort on the part of each. Indeed, Saxton and Ashworth (1990) note that the supervisor is the most important factor in ensuring the success of the work placement. Schaafsma (1996) explains that the university and the workplace offer contested venues of learning. Work-based mentors should serve as trainers in order to engender more effective learning experiences for students. This may in most cases require the mentors in the host institutions to be trained.

In the same vein, based on a study of work placement experience of a set of Australian students, Cope et al. (2000) argue that the placement is a complex social and cognitive experience in which there are elements of situated learning. They also demonstrate that acceptance into the community of practice is an important aspect of this experience. This acceptance can be separated into a social acceptance, which might be extended to any student, and a professional acceptance, which relies on the display of appropriate competence. In the former case, issues of diversity and equality are important considerations for the host institutions and the HEIs in order to ensure that the students receive fair and decent treatment in their social encounters as well as professional work in the host institution. The authors also argue that any mentoring, monitoring and assessment schemes that are organized by the host and HEIs should take into consideration both social and professional aspects of the student workplace experience.

Research by Misko (1998) in an Australian setting revealed that there is a correlation between student expectations and outcomes of workplace experience. The research suggests that if student expectations are set high, students can make better and fuller use of the available opportunities. This suggests that the HEIs and the host institutions can facilitate induction programmes that set realistic and positive expectations of the workplace experience in order to ensure that the students can make full use of possible options. Furthermore, Drever and Cope (1999) demonstrate that students may also be equipped with skills to relate their theoretical and conceptual understanding to their work placement experiences. This will require the pre-work placement curriculum to introduce students to the ideas of communities of practice and situated learning. This may then be supported by monitoring of student learning through a placement report. Hislop et al. (1996) note that in order to foster a culture of knowledgeable practice, HEIs should consider various aspects of work placement and proactively integrate these considerations into their curriculum design. This means that the teaching should be phased in synchrony with their placement experiences.

Neill et al. (2004) argue that part-time working has not been studied as a possible route into later work placement and a way of gaining students work-related experience. The authors argue that part-time student work can be brought into consideration of students' learning in situated settings and this can help students acquire better placement experiences drawing on their part-time work. Also, with the aim of broadening the scope of work placement, Morgan and Turner (2000) investigated the role of professional accreditation on the work placement experience of students, revealing that accreditation has a positive effect.

As the work placement experience takes place outside the university environment, university education during the placement year displays similarities with distance learning. Hall et al. (2000) explore the possibilities of using information technology (IT) in order to improve students' experience during work placement. Despite high initial set-up costs, the authors explain that the IT systems can help universities keep better track of student placements, while helping improve collaboration between different constituent groups. Gammie et al. (2002) also note that distance learning systems help facilitate communication between stakeholders; such initial communication between the representatives of the host institution and the HEIs and the student is crucial for the success of the placement. The authors warn of the difficulties of ensuring equity in adequate use of distance learning systems by all stakeholders.

There have been some attempts in the UK to establish what constitutes a successful work placement. The National Council of Work Experience (2006) presents a checklist for ensuring work placement success. The list is drawn up through a consultation with practitioners:

1. The student should be trained by the higher education institution (HEI) to identify potential learning outcomes
2. Learning and work objectives should be set by HEI, employer and student
3. A supervisor trained in the objectives and learning outcomes of work experience should provide academic supervision, and visit/s to the host institution should take place
4. Regular feedback should be offered
5. An appraisal should be planned during the work experience and at the end
6. The work placement should involve a structured project when appropriate
7. Students should articulate their learning and achievements in written form
8. An assessment is made, including an assessment of development of skills by HEI, employer and student
9. HEI and the host institution should offer recognition, credit or a certificate.

The literature suggests that successful planning and delivery of work placements require multi-party and multifaceted approaches. This can be achieved if work placements are designed with specific recognition of labour market dynamics, social and economic circumstances, institutional arrangements and requirements in universities and host institutions, as well as the particular conditions, expectations and career ambitions of students who take up these work placements. The cycles of design with multi-party involvement, delivery, monitoring, and revaluation and redesign activities are key requirements for a successful work placement process. These requirements suggest that a process approach to work placement design is important for successful delivery as well as for progressive development of work placement projects.

RESEARCH METHOD

The field study aimed to provide a detailed exploration of the work placement practice in creative and cultural industries in London. At this stage the investigation was informed by four sources: (i) the existing documentation (institutional documents and literature collected from the HEIs participating in the project as well as from the host institutions) on work placement practices and models; (ii) interviews with the people responsible for the work placement exercise in the arts and humanities departments in their institutions; (iii) interviews with arts and humanities students who have an experience of work placement; and (iv) interviews with London-based host institutions which offer work placements.

First, documents made available by the HEIs were reviewed to scope different models of work placement utilized by the HEIs. These documents included guidelines and handbooks for students and host institutions, work placement handbooks for students, and course module outlines. In addition, documentary evidence collected from the host organizations that offer work placement was reviewed. Second, telephone interviews were conducted with the key people responsible for the work placement in their organization to further identify the models of work placement, and to investigate how the effectiveness of these models is evaluated by the institutions. We contacted 20 London-based HEIs with art and humanities departments to request interviews. Research access was granted by 10 of those 20 HEIs. In total, 11 interviews were conducted. The selection criteria for the HEIs were: (i) representation of different institutional configurations such as old and new university sector institutions and those with and without dedicated placement facilities for cultural industries; and (ii) high level of representation of students from Black and Minority Ethnic (BME) backgrounds since we wanted to investigate the work placement experiences of this group. Throughout the interviews, we used a semi-structured schedule which was constructed subsequent to the systematic literature review. During the interviews with the HEIs we aimed to address the following issues: range of work placement practices in the institution; communication with the host organization; the process of matching the students with the host organization; good practices/examples of work placement; models of evaluation for work placement practices; opinions about the impact of work placements on host organizations; mechanisms of feedback from the host organizations; opinions on the impact of work placement on students; mechanisms of feedback from the students; barriers to successful placements; opinions on the impact of work placement practices on collaboration and knowledge transfer between HEIs and the arts and cultural industries; and opinions on the impact on students' demographic background on the success of the work placement.

Third, telephone interviews were conducted with students who had completed their work placement or who were currently undergoing one. In total we limited the number of student interviews to ten. We aimed to reach a balanced sample for these interviews with respect to participant students' gender and ethnic background. Throughout the interviews, we used a semi-structured schedule which aimed to explore the students' feelings and opinions on the following issues: impacts of work-based placements on students in terms of employment opportunities; impacts of work-based placements on students' knowledge of the creative and culture industries; impacts of work-based placements on students' understanding of the world of work and the skills they require for the careers they wish to pursue; impacts of work-based placements on students in terms of their future career plans; impacts of work based placements on students' academic work in their schools; students' personal assessment of different models of placement; students' criticisms about the practice of work placement in their institution; students' recommendations for improving the work placement practice in their institutions; students' levels of satisfaction with the work placement experience; students' general feelings about the work placement experience and the ways in which experiences of students from different gender and ethnic backgrounds differ regarding the above.

Lastly, five interviews were conducted with four host organizations in the creative and cultural industries which offer work placement. A semi-structured interview schedule was used. During the interviews with the host organizations we aimed to address the following issues: range of work placement programmes offered by the organization; communication with the HEIs; the process of matching the students with their work placement role; good practices/examples of work placement; models of evaluation for work placement practices; opinions on the impact of work placement on the organization; mechanisms of feedback to the students and HEIs; opinions on the impact of work placement on students; mechanisms of feedback from the students; barriers to successful placements; opinions on the impact of work placement practices on the collaboration and knowledge transfer between HEI and the arts and cultural industries; and opinions on the impact on students' demographic background on the success of the work placement.

All interviews, except one in which the participant only allowed note taking, were tape-recorded and fully transcribed for the purpose of qualitative analysis. Confidentiality concerns were sensitively addressed and anonymity was ensured for all interviews.

Stage three of the project was built upon the conceptual framework drawn in the first two phases combining the systematic literature review in the field and evidence from existing documents and interviews. At the end of the field research semi-structured interviews and documentary evidence were transferred to NVivo. NVivo is the most widely used qualitative data software for storage, retrieval and analysis of data. It was preferred for the purpose of the proposed research mainly due to its high data-processing and storage capacity compared with other available qualitative data softwares such as Nud.Ist. The interview transcripts and documentary evidence were subject to axial and open coding, using the NVivo software and analysed using thematic analysis techniques. Finally, all data gathered were analysed and presented in a themed report form to the LCACE. The final report provides a full account and discussion of the findings, implications for policy and methods. This includes a draft executive summary report which pulls out the main findings. The report also includes an indication of the problem areas and recommendations for improvement.

WORK PLACEMENT PRACTICE WITHIN THE CREATIVE AND CULTURAL INDUSTRIES IN LONDON-BASED HEIs: ANALYSIS OF THE STUDY FINDINGS

The study focused on three constituent groups involved in work placement practices in the creative and cultural industries in London: the higher education institutions (HEIs), the host institutions and the students. We explored the conditions of work, and opportunities and constraints in the work placement process.

Work Placement Models and Practices of the London-based HEIs

We conducted 11 interviews with representatives of 10 HEIs. Except for two LCACE partners, all the HEIs who participated in this research had formal work placement programmes in place. However, the structure and nature of the work placement and the associated requirements as well as the target student group displayed considerable variation.

To begin with, in all the HEIs with formal placement programmes, work placement was a part of students' postgraduate studies at postgraduate diploma or MA level. However, only three of the participating HEIs had work placement programmes for their undergraduate students. In four of the participant organizations work placement was a compulsory part of students' studies. In addition, one of the HEIs had a work placement requirement as part of one compulsory and one elective course modules. Minimum required duration of the work placement varied from 30 hours to 30 working days. However, all HEIs reported that the students can do a longer placement if they wish. Most of the participants also reported that they are flexible in terms of the type and location of the host institution, and gave the student the option to do their work placement in overseas organizations as well as in the UK-based ones.

There was a wide spectrum of organizations in which students could do their work placement. All respondents reported that their students undertake their work placements in various kinds of organizations in the creative and cultural industries in terms of size and sector of the host. Students do their work placements in small and medium-sized organizations as well as in very large organizations. Some of the respondents reported that their students sometimes do work placement with individual artists or curators. In addition, host organizations mentioned by the respondents included both public and private sectors organizations in creative and cultural industries. The host organizations named by the respondents included galleries, museums, libraries, performing arts organizations, festivals, media organizations and funding organizations.

The HEIs used several methods to reach and communicate with the host organizations that may offer work placements for their students. All the participant HEIs kept a list of host organizations which is then made available to the students. In addition they actively seek work placement offers from their alumni. Moreover, in most cases the module tutors and work placement administrators exploited their personal contacts to widen their pool of host organizations.

Work placement opportunities were communicated to the students by means of a list of host organizations. Different work placement opportunities were also advertised through e-mail and school websites. With two exceptions, tutors as well as the work placement administrators were involved in communicating with the host organizations, and in providing the students with the information regarding work placement opportunities. However, the level of involvement and support by the tutors and placement administrators during the students' search and application for a work placement position varied extensively from one HEI to the next. In some of the participating HEIs, the school offered minimal support to the students by letting them know only the names of different host organizations. These HEIs also strongly encouraged their students to take a proactive role, to look for other work placement opportunities and to find their own placements. In other cases, the students were offered extensive guidance and advice. In these cases the tutors and administrators were actively involved in the communication between the student and the host organization as mediators, and took into account the students' needs and interests throughout the process.

In terms of formal structures of advice and guidance, only five of the participating HEIs provided their students with handbooks or guidelines, and only two of them had formal documents that they sent out to the host organizations. Moreover, in only two of the HEIs were there formal sessions during the work placement to support and guide the student. As explained in the following sections, the absence of guidance from the school during the work placement led many students to feel left alone without support from time to time. Nevertheless, most of the HEIs offered some support and training sessions before the work placement.

Our interviews revealed that structured and formal evaluation mechanisms regarding the impacts and success of the work placement were not available in most of the HEIs. The most common evaluation method was through assessment of the students' reports or placement diaries in addition to the course evaluation forms. More active and objective evaluation methods are only used by a few of the participant HEIs. One of these was formal visits by the course tutor during the work placement, where both the student and his/her line manager in the host organization were interviewed by the tutor. Unfortunately, only three of the participant HEIs had reported active involvement in the evaluation process through such formal visits. Nevertheless, two of the remaining respondents mentioned that they had informal telephone conversations with the host organizations regarding students' performance throughout the placement. Another HEI stated that it had a short feedback form that it sent out to the host organizations at the end of the work placement.

Overall, evaluation of the work placement was largely based on students' feedback in terms of their placement reports and diaries. This situation makes it impossible to assess the impact of work placement on the host organization. Interestingly, all the respondents agreed that work placement may be an important medium for knowledge transfer between academia and industry. However, absence of effective techniques of evaluation and feedback from the host institutions makes it very hard to assess whether work placements fulfil such a role.

Furthermore, the research findings suggested that feedback received from the students and assessment of their work placement performance were insufficient in terms of evaluating the satisfaction levels of the students and the impact of work placement experience on students' future employability. In general, most of the respondents stated that it was very uncommon for the students to be employed by the organization where they undertook their work placement. However, it is argued that work placement contributes to students' employment prospects more indirectly through giving them work experience, skills, knowledge of the industry and, more importantly, personal networks and contacts. Although all respondents argued that work placement practice contributes to the future career of the students through providing them with skills, networks, contacts and work experience in the creative and cultural industries, most of the respondents failed to display any evidence to qualify this assertion. In other words, none of the HEIs monitored their work placement model in terms of its impact on students' future employability.

Assessment of the performance of the host organization in terms of managing the work placement seemed to be even less significant. As we explain later, many students complained about the lack of involvement of their school in terms of monitoring and controlling the host organizations' attitude towards work placement. In our interviews, only one respondent reported that they ask the host organizations to sign an agreement at the start of students' work placement. Obviously, the absence of any control mechanism by the HEI may lead to the exploitation of the student and to a dysfunctional work placement practice.

Similarly, the impact of work placement on the level of satisfaction of students from different demographic backgrounds was not monitored by the HEIs. In general, interviews suggested that the issues of equality and diversity were not high on the agenda of the participant HEIs within the scope of work placement practices. When we asked the respondents whether they believed that their work placements might have different impacts by gender, ethnicity, age, disability, sexual orientation and religion of the students, all said that the success of the work placement depends on the personality of the student rather than their demographic characteristics. Most of them also argued that creative and cultural industries are female dominated and much more open to gay men and lesbians compared to other industries.

Many respondents noted that their students are very diverse in terms of their nationality, with many students from Europe, North America and South Asia. Interestingly, it is also reported that they do not have many Black and Ethnic Minority students. Nevertheless, it was generally argued that the race and ethnicity of the student would not affect the success of the work placement. However, it was also noted by many respondents that the students' lack of linguistic skills may be a barrier to a successful work placement. Seven respondents argued that the students whose first language is not English may perform poorly during their work placement, particularly where a quick response is required, such as answering the telephone or making conversation. This demonstrates a general lack of self-critical thinking as well as full awareness of equal opportunities on the part of the research participants. However, as we discuss in a previous section, this gap in terms of equal opportunities in the higher education sector is not peculiar to the arts and humanities fields, but rather a general feature of work placement practices. The paradox is that although the universities self-regulate in terms of their linguistic requirements in admissions, there is continued resentment against international students about their perceived levels of English.

Models and Practices of Work Placement in Host Institutions

In total we conducted five interviews in four host institutions. Only one of the host institutions had a clear set of guidelines for placement experience. This institution offers a clear job description, an induction programme, and a monitoring and appraisal structure. Furthermore, the organization also provides opportunities for placement students to gain professional experience and join various important professional networks. The organization also professes to offer employment to a select number of placement students. There was evidence of supportive training and provision of feedback from host mentors, which aim to build students' personal and professional skills. These structures are offered in a contractual manner, covering both a transparent employment contract outlining expectations and responsibilities of the host institution and the student, as well as a strong sense of psychological contract, of expectations and responsibilities, which are fostered through mechanisms of acculturation and induction at work.

In the context of both contracts, trust between host and students is an aspect of work placement whose absence is considered a serious barrier to successful work placement experience. All respondents argued that realistic expectations by students are key to the success of work placement. A respondent from the large host institution explained that students' narrow focus on furthering their own careers and network ties, as well as their lack of interest in vision and values of the organization, can also be detrimental to building trust between the parties. However, only two of the organizations mentioned the importance of reasonable expectations by the host institution. Treatment of students as 'free resources', in a city like London where living costs are prohibitive, may be perceived as exploitation, and this can clearly breach any trust that may be built between the host and the students.

It is interesting to note that the host institutions always refer to trust as a dual system between a student and themselves. This approach disregards the role of the HEIs in the tripartite relationships that characterize placements in the sector. Host institutions in our study failed to identify any meaningful relationships with HEIs in supervision and mentoring of placement students. They would not, for example, offer feedback to the HEIs regarding placement performance of the student unless it was explicitly requested. One of the respondents argued that such minimum involvement by the HEIs during the work placement is desirable for the host institutions. This may not be a wise strategy as there are also expectations placed on students by the HEIs which will directly or indirectly affect their attitude and patterns of work placement. Moreover, the HEIs have a duty to protect their students with regard to workplace risk involving issues of health and safety, and exploitation. Furthermore, the HEIs have a stake in ensuring that the work placement contributes to students' professional and personal development.

However, this level of sophistication and formality was not in evidence in the remaining three host institutions. It is important to note that it is still possible for host institutions to provide a similar experience to students with less sophisticated and formalized approaches. Indeed, this was the case in one of the small host institutions, in which both the student experience and the host institution discourse suggested a very productive and mutually beneficial relationship.

The attitude of the host institution seems to be the most important factor in delivery of effective placement programmes. The attitudes include the way students are treated when they join the organization, the voice of the placement students within the processes of decision making in the organization, and the perception of staff in host institutions of the work placement in terms of its value and worth for the organization.

In order to develop these positive attitudes and perceptions, host institutions need to invest in creating and disseminating a positive discourse surrounding placements. This was done through formalized newsletters and policy statements in the large institution (explained above) and through informal means of integrating students into the work in the smaller organization.

However, two of the institutions that we have included in our study failed to offer a positive environment in which placements are experienced. The reasons for this are complex: our interview with a representative of one of the institutions revealed that the students are perceived as low-level administrative and secretarial resources. They are expected, for example, to carry out an extensive range of mundane and low-level administrative tasks such as photocopying and running errands. Their suitability for the placement is measured against their willingness and resilience to cope with such tasks. Therefore their work in the host institution stretched beyond the expected scope of creative and cultural industry work.

Another participant from a host institution in this study also revealed that the students are employed as free or cheap resources to carry out work in roles which simply seek to reduce the low-level administrative burden of the full-time staff.

When compared to the guidelines for successful placement experience in the literature review, these two work placement experiences suggest that there is little scope for students to develop their skills in these two host institutions.

One of the problems that appears to be common across the industry is the treatment of placement students as free or cheap labour. All of the host institutions in this study paid only essential travel expenses. In the best-paid case, the daily gratuity was 8 GBP. The institutions have suggested that the absence of pay was due to sectoral difficulties in financing. The respondents also noted that there were many institutions that would not even pay this meagre amount towards students' travels costs.

The sectoral excuse for low pay for placements is not legitimate when placed in the context of the growth and economic development that has characterized the industry. Furthermore, the absence of pay means that students are self-selecting placement experience based on their own financial conditions. It would therefore be naïve to expect students from disadvantaged socioeconomic backgrounds to be able to survive their placement experiences. This in itself has a strong explanatory power for the current absence of heterogeneity in employment, student and consumer profiles of the cultural and creative industries.

Similar to the HEIs in our study, the host organizations do not sufficiently attend to diversity and equality issues in work placements. However, two of the organizations realize that they should pay more attention to this in the context of placements. They are aware, for example, of local community diversity and its implications for recruitment of placement students.

However, diversity issues cannot be addressed simply through statements of intent and commitment. Diversity and equality are not only processes; they are also outcomes. The large host institution in our case stated that only 14 per cent of their placement students are from Black and Minority Ethnic backgrounds. However, they would like to increase this number. Effective management of equality and diversity in placements would require funds and resources to be made available if this target is to be achieved. For example, the issue of free labour will have implications across race and class.

It is also important to note that religious belief is not considered by host institutions to be of relevance as an issue of equality and diversity. However, this is not a wise approach as religion crosses many significant fault lines of race and class. An effective understanding of race and ethnicity in London surely requires attention to issues of belief and religion, or the lack of them.

Another strand of equality and diversity that is problematic in placements is age. Three out of four of the host institutions said that they prefer to recruit experienced and mature students for their work placement programmes. This clearly disadvantages younger students. It also indicates unwillingness in the part of host institutions to offer adequate training and development activities to students.

The issue of disability was not discussed by any of the host institutions. This means that disability issues remain invisible and the institutions are ill prepared to offer reasonable accommodation should a need arise.

Sexual orientation as a diversity issue was interesting in this sector. All host institutions suggested that sexual orientation of students would not disadvantage their prospects for securing a placement. Indeed, it is possible to identify a unique gay male advantage in the sector, which is highly female dominated.

Students' Perceptions of Work Placement Practices

Within the scope of the field research, ten interviews were conducted with the students who have completed their work placement or are currently doing it. The relevant host organizations displayed variation in terms of size and sector, including both large and small organizations, and museums, libraries, exhibition centres, funding bodies and festivals.

Students' applications for work placements generally involved sending a CV to the host organization and sometimes writing a proposal about the project that they would like to undertake during their placement. In the latter case, writing a work placement project proposal was most of the time part of their module requirements. This initial contact with the host organization was followed by an interview where the host makes a decision about offering a work placement. Some students reported that they did not receive a sufficient level of guidance and support from their tutors or work placement administrators throughout the process of application for their work placements. These students argued that had there been better guidance from their schools, their decisions and selection of the host organization would have been more informed; hence the work placement experience would have contributed to their personal and career development as they would have expected.

The role of the student within the host organization during the work placement showed variation in the case of different students. In all cases it involved some low-level administrative work such as data entry, answering the telephone and photocopying. However, in the case of some students the job placement role did not go beyond these low-level administrative tasks, whereas in other cases students carried out a specific project, were involved in decision making and took higher levels of responsibility. In their evaluation of the contribution of work placement, participant students put strong emphasis on the types of work they did during their work placements and their role in the host organization. Our research findings suggest that the students whose placement roles were more or less limited to mundane administrative tasks were unsatisfied with their experience. On the other hand, the students who took higher levels of responsibility, who were situated in a clearly defined project role and were given a role in the decision-making process in the host organization, displayed higher levels of satisfaction. It is also pointed out by eight of the students that having a work placement in smaller organizations is more advantageous for the students since such organizations tend to assign more responsibility and industry-related tasks to their placement students. Large organizations tend to see the placement students as sources of extra labour to undertake mundane administrative tasks.

All the students who participated in the research thought that work placement could potentially be a very important opportunity for the students in terms of contributing to both their academic studies and career. There was a very direct link between work placement and academic study. In the case of seven students, work placement was neither a compulsory nor optional part of their studies. In some cases the students were also expected to integrate their learning from the work placement into their MA dissertations. On the other hand, the impact of work placement on students' future career was more indirect. Only one of the students in our sample was employed by the host institution after her work placement. Similarly, our respondents from host organizations and HEIs also pointed out that it is very rare that the students are employed by the organization where they did their placements. Nevertheless, all students in our sample thought that work placement might contribute to their future career in other ways than being employed by the host organization. For instance, all students pointed out that they expected that they would gain new skills, enhance their knowledge of the world of work and the creative and cultural industries, and hence understand how the sector actually works in real life as well as establishing contacts and networks that would be helpful for them later in their career.

However, these expectations were not fulfilled in the case of some participant students. In particular, one of our respondents was very negative regarding her work placement experience. She told us that all she did during her placement was photocopying, she did not gain any skills and did not even make any contacts. The students who rated their work placement experience poor generally argued that they were ill prepared for the placement due to lack of guidance and support from their HEIs. They also pointed out that it is very important for the tutors or placement administrators to have genuine contacts in the creative and cultural industries. In addition, it is argued that the work placement model in the HEIs should require students to submit a proposal listing clearly what they would like to achieve during their placements. All students argued that the tutors should be sensitive to students' needs and aims regarding the work placement and provide them with tailored advice and guidance.

All students believed that, in the tripartite relationship involving the HEI, the student and the host, the HEIs had an important role to play in terms of supporting and guiding their students. It is suggested that the guidance and support should not be limited to the placement application stage, but should be available throughout the work placement. Moreover, eight out of ten students also argued that the HEIs had a role to play in terms of monitoring how the host organizations manage the work placement and ensuring that the attitudes of the host institutions to the placement conform to the work placement objectives put forward by the HEIs.

Within that framework, all the students argued that the way the work placement is managed by the host institutions is crucial for its success. It is argued that the host institutions should have a clear understanding of the objectives of the HEIs and students regarding the work placement, and they should take these into account when deciding on the students' placement role. It is also argued that for the work placement to be a positive and beneficial experience of the students, the host needs to have a positive attitude towards work placement practice and the placement student. Such an attitude on the part of the host is defined by the students in terms of showing respect to the placement student, understanding and taking into account the students' needs and priorities regarding the work placement, and assigning creative and cultural industries related responsibilities to the placement students.

Another issue raised by all students related to the financial difficulties involved in doing an unpaid work placement. Seven out of ten students reported that their host organizations covered their travel expenses. However, it was emphasized that lack of any other payment causes financial difficulty for them since they are students and do not have any income. Moreover, the students argued that doing work placement prevents them from taking up part-time jobs to improve their financial situation since the work placement takes their time that they would have otherwise spent working in a part-time job. Some students also pointed out that they would like to do work placement for a longer period of time, but this was not feasible due to lack of any payment. So it was apparent from the interviews that payment of at least a minimum wage salary is crucial for a successful, satisfying and efficient work placement experience.

Lastly, we asked students whether they think that the impact of work placement on a student's career and the work placement experience may be different for students from different demographical backgrounds. Some of the respondents pointed out that age and lack of experience may be important barriers for younger students. For instance, it was argued that it is much easier for mature students to find a work placement. Another issue raised by the black student in our sample was the potential race and class bias in work placement. She argued that cultural and creative industries in general are white middle-class dominated, and the same situation holds true for the HEIs in the sector. She said that because of the white middle-class orientation of the sector, black people and people from lower-class backgrounds do not feel welcome in either the organizations or the HEIs in the sector. She argued that although there are some attempts to increase the representation of ethnic minority students in the work placements in the sector, this remains at a very superficial level. As an example she told us about her work placement in a large institution. She reported that the organization recruited minority ethnic students as placements to fulfil the criteria of a funding body, but did not make real efforts to contribute to the personal development of these students. She thought that these students from ethnic minority backgrounds were only recruited for 'ticking the boxes' and were seen as 'numbers' representing their ethnic origin rather than individuals with skills and abilities. She explained to us why she thought this. She said that a position had opened during her work placement and the only white student out of five placement students was offered the job.

CONCLUSIONS AND RECOMMENDATIONS

Our study has revealed that there is a body of academic writing in the field of work placements, and the design and delivery requirements for successful work placement practices. The studies that we have drawn on to frame our approach have been interdisciplinary in nature, due to the relative absence of literature on work placements in the field of creative and cultural enterprises. Nevertheless, our field study findings provide fresh evidence to demonstrate the current state of play in the sector, drawing on interviews with representatives from universities and host institutions, as well as placement students.

Despite evidence of some examples of good practice in work placement programmes offered by universities in the sector, there is certainly room for progress. The main strength of the work placement design and implementation in the higher education sector is the hands-off and organic approach which is characterized by flexibility in arrangements of work placements. This flexible approach means that the students have a role to play in searching, identifying and approaching the host institutions and deciding on the content of their work placement projects. Provided that the university link, the academic tutor of the, student, is supportive, this arrangement may provide work placement opportunities that are tailored to students' needs.

However, the liberal arrangement of work placements as well as the inherent flexibility involved in this design are at the same time the key weaknesses of the programmes offered by the HEIs. Flexibility in itself is not a weakness. However, absence of robust and standardized procedures for monitoring and evaluating student performance, and management of work placement by host institutions, exposes the student and the work placement experience to several undue risks. For example, any form of exploitation, misuse of student time, as well as discriminatory practices in the host institution, may be left unchecked and unaddressed. Considering that all universities in London subscribe to high levels of service delivery standards in terms of their academic programmes and employment practices, the work placement experience needs to be considered within the service delivery standards of the universities, as the academic institutions are still firmly committed to the welfare and well-being of their students in placement projects.

HEIs need to provide clear and assessable criteria for successful work placements as well as the aims and objectives of work placement projects. This also requires that the HEIs provide a budget through which these systems of monitoring and assessment can be formalized. Institutions of best practice help students identify work placements, continuously monitor student experience and learning during work placements, and require constructive feedback from host institutions.

Furthermore, host institutions do not always consider work placement as a developmental tool for the students, using them as cheap or free resources, often for low-level administrative, monotonous and repetitive tasks. The practice of not paying the students for their work placement has a dual impact which both undermines and devalues students' work. This clearly conflicts with the logic and spirit of the work placement arrangements, which should aim to provide students a site in which they can reflect on their academic learning, current experiences and future careers. In this context, there is scope for universities to recognize potential pitfalls and to promote better procedures for work placement which will benefit all constituent parties.

Lastly, our research findings revealed that the cultural and creative sector has a strong white, middle-class bias. This manifests itself as various forms of tacit exclusion of certain groups of students or devaluing their work and performance. The issue of linguistic ability is a key concern in the sector. This is often used to justify exclusion or demarcation of international students from work placement experience. Similarly, racial and ethnic discrimination also has a negative impact on the student experience of work placement. Universities have a major role to play in promoting the agenda of equality and diversity in the sector as well as inside their organization.

In conclusion, work placement may potentially be one of the most significant paths to careers in creative and cultural industries. The process of allocation of work placements to students and successful monitoring and management of work placement activities could provide career-enhancing opportunities to students. The process, however, not only provides opportunities, but also presents constraints, particularly to those students who do not fit the subjective requirements set by the host organizations. As objective criteria for student placements are absent and the process is highly reliant on social networks of tutors and actors in the industry, there is a large subjective element in decisions involving student placements. We demonstrate that this subjectivity, although providing a level of flexibility, may limit the choices of students from non-traditional backgrounds. This may also seriously reduce the productivity of work placement in terms of enhancing personal and career development of students. Furthermore, we found that the current arrangements of work placement fail to cater adequately for the students' needs to embark on careers in entrepreneurship, employment and management in the sector, starving them of essential experiences that could prepare them for successful future careers in the creative and cultural industries.

NOTE

1. The project was commissioned by the London Centre for Arts and Cultural Enterprise (LCACE), with the funding of the Arts Council England.

REFERENCES

Arts Council England (2005), *Children, Young People and the Arts: London Regional Strategy*, www.artscouncil.org.uk.
Ashworth, P. and Saxton, J. (1992), *Managing Work Experience*, London: Routledge.
Barthorpe, S. and Hall, M. (2000), 'A collaborative approach to placement preparation and career planning for university students: a case study', *Journal of Vocational Education and Training*, **52**(2): 165–75.
Beard, S., Coll, R.K. and Harris, J. (2001), 'Student and employer reflections of an international science and technology work placement', *Asia-Pacific Journal of Cooperative Education*, **2**(1): 6–10.
Blankfield, S. (2001), 'Think, problematic and costly? The dyslexic student on work placement', *Skill Journal*, **70**: 23–26 July.
British Council (2006), www.britishcouncil.org/arts-creative-industries-definition.htm.
Cahill, H. (1996), 'A qualitative analysis of student nurses' experiences of mentorship', *Journal of Advanced Nursing*, **24**: 791–9.

CCS Consultation Paper (2006), *Working with Partners in the English Regions*, www.ccskills.org.uk.

Coll, R.K. and Eames, R. (2000), 'The role of the placement coordinator: an alternative model', *Asia-Pacific Journal of Cooperative Education*, **1**(1): 9–14.

Cope, P., Cuthbertson, P. and Stoddart, B. (2000), 'Situated learning in the practice placement', *Journal of Advanced Nursing*, **31**(4): 850–56.

Crebert, G., Bates, M., Bell, B., Patrick, C.-J. and Cragnolini, V. (2004), 'Developing generic skills at university, during work placement and in employment: graduates' perceptions', *Higher Education Research and Development*, **23**(2): 147–65.

Department for Culture, Media and Sport (2006), www.culture.gov.uk/creative_ industries/.

Drennan, J. (2002), 'An evaluation of the role of the Clinical Placement Coordinator in student nurse support in the clinical area', *Journal of Advanced Nursing*, **40**(4): 475–83.

Drever, E. and Cope, P. (1999), 'Students' use of theory in an initial teacher education programme', *Journal of Education for Teaching: International Research and Pedagogy*, **2**(July): 97–109.

Duignan, J. (2002), 'Undergraduate work placement and academic performance: failing by doing', *HERDSA*, 214–21.

Finegold, D. and Soskice, D. (1988), 'The failure of training in Britain: analysis and prescription', *Oxford Review of Economic Policy*, **4**: 21–53.

Gammie, E., Gammie, B. and Duncan, F. (2002), 'Operating a distance learning module within an undergraduate work placement: some reflections', *Education and Training*, **44**(1): 11–22.

Hall, L., Harris, J., Bakewell, C. and Graham, P. (2000), 'Supporting placement based learning using networked technologies', *The International Journal of Educational Management*, **14**(4): 175–9.

Hall, T. (2006), 'An employer's perspective', in C. Leadbeater (ed.), *Britain's Creativity Challenge* (a report), www.ccskills.org.uk.

Hall, T. and Bewick, T. (2006), *Skills for Creativity* (a strategic plan 2005–2010), www.ccskills.org.uk.

Hislop, S., Inglis, B., Cope, P., Stoddart, B. and McIntosh, C. (1996), 'Situating theory in practice: student views of theory–practice in Project 2000 nursing programmes', *Journal of Advanced Nursing*, **23**(1): 171–7.

Huntington, S., Stephen, J. and Oldfield, B.M. (1999), 'Formal assessment of student placement within a retail sandwich degree', *Industrial and Commercial Training*, **31**(3): 10–11.

Hutton, W. (2006), *Creative Apprenticeship, Creative and Cultural Skills* (a report), www.ccskills.org.uk.

Jowell, T. (2006), Speech at Bloomberg, 14 March, www.cep.culture.gov.uk/index. cfm?fuseaction=main.viewBlogEntry&intMTEntryID=2909.

Kelley-Patterson, D. and George, C. (2001), 'Securing graduate commitment: an exploration of the comparative expectations of placement students, graduate recruits and human resource managers within the hospitality, leisure and tourism industries', *Hospitality Management*, **20**: 311–23.

Lambert Review of Business–University Collaboration (2003), *Lambert Review of Business–University Collaboration: Final Report*, Norwich: HMSO.

Leslie, D. (1994), 'TQM and student work experience (SWE)', *Quality Assurance in Education*, **2**(3): 26–32.

Maidment, J. (2003), 'Problems experienced by students on field placement: using research findings to inform curriculum design and content', *Australian Social Work*, **56**(1): 50–60.

Majewski, S., Mayo, R., Mokrosz, A. and Gorski, M. (2000), 'Integrated project system and supervised industrial placement – essential cores of civil engineering education', paper presented at the ICEE Conference, Taiwan.

Mandilaras, A. (2004), 'Industrial placement and degree performance: evidence from a British higher institution', *International Review of Education Economics*, **3**(1): 39–51.

Maurana, C.A., Beck, B., Beversdorf, S.J. and Newton, G.L. (2000), 'Moving from medical student placement to a community–academic partnership with a rural community', *Journal of Rural Health*, **16**(4): 371–9.

McMahon, U. and Quinn, U. (1995), 'Maximizing the hospitality management student work placement experience: a case study', *Education and Training*, **37**(4): 13–17.

Misko, J. (1998), *School Students in Workplaces: What Are the Benefits?*, report for the National Centre for Vocational Education Research, Australia.

Morgan, A. and Turner, D. (2000), 'Adding value to the work placement: working towards a professional qualification in an undergraduate degree programme', *Education and Training*, **42**(8): 453–60.

Mulraney, J. and Turner, P. (2001), 'Learning from small enterprise structured work placement', *Small Enterprise Workplace Learning – Links to School Vocational Education, NCVER*, Australia.

NCWE (The National Council of Work Experience) (2006), www.work-experience. org/cms/ShowPage/Home_page/Students/About_work_experience/p!eaLdeeX.

Neill, N.T. and Mulholland, G.E. (2003), 'Student placement – structure, skills and e-support', *Education and Training*, **45**(2): 89–99.

Neill, N.T., Mulholland, G.E., Ross, A.V. and Leckey, A.J. (2004), 'The influence of part-time work on student placement', *Journal of Further and Higher Education*, **28**(2): 123–37.

Newton, A. and Smith, L.N. (1998), 'Practice placement supervision: the role of the personal tutor', *Nurse Education Today*. **18**(6): 496–504.

Nolan, C.A. (1998), 'Learning on clinical placement: the experience of six Australian student nurses', *Nurse Education Today*, **18**(8): 622–9.

Nolan, P.W. and Chung, M.C. (1999), 'Nursing students' perceptions of their first mental health placement', *Nurse Education Today*, **19**: 122–8.

O'Connor, J. (1999), 'The definition of "culture industries"', Manchester Institute for Popular Culture, www.mipc.mmu.ac.uk/iciss/reports/defin.pdf.

Richardson, S. and Blakeney, C. (1998), 'The undergraduate placement system: an empirical study', *Accounting Education*, **7**(2): 101–21.

Samway, K.D. and McKeon, D. (1999), *Myths and Realities: Best Practices for Language Minority Students*, Portsmouth, NH: Heinemann.

Saxton, J. and Ashworth, P. (1990), 'The workplace supervision of sandwich degree placement students', *Management Education and Development*, **21**(2): 133–49.

Schaafsma, H. (1996), 'Back to the real world: work placements revisited', *Education and Training*, **38**(1): 5–13.

Shen, J. and Herr, E.L. (2004), 'Career placement concerns of international graduate students: a qualitative study', *Journal of Career Development*, **31**(1): 15–29.

Skill (National Bureau of Students with Disabilities) (2006), www.skill.org.uk/index.asp.

Smith, S., Edwards, H., Courtney, M. and Finlayson, K. (2001), 'Factors influencing student nurses in their choice of a rural clinical placement site', *Rural and Remote Health*, retrieved from http:/rrh.deakin.edu.au.
UNESCO (2006), http://portal.unesco.org/culture/en/ev.php-URL_ID=18668& URL_DO=DO_TOPIC&URL_SECTION=201.html.
Uzzell, D.L. (1986), 'The professional placement for students: some theoretical considerations', *Oxford Review of Education*, **12**(1): 67–75.
Westhead, P., Storey, D.J. and Martin, F. (2001), 'Outcomes reported by students who participated in the 1994 Shell Technology Enterprise Programme', *Entrepreneurship and Regional Development*, **13**(2): 163–85.
Wolf, A. (2002), *Does Education Matter? Myths about Education and Economic Growth*, London: Penguin.

PART VI

Entrepreneurs, Managers, Career Choice and
Diversity: Minority Issues

19. The career reasons of minority nascent entrepreneurs

Nancy M. Carter, William B. Gartner, Kelly G. Shaver and Patricia G. Greene

The creation of new independent businesses accounts for one-fourth to almost one-third of the variation in economic growth in nearly all industrialized countries (Davidsson et al., 1994; Reynolds et al., 2000). The entrepreneurs responsible for this impact have benefited not only financially, but also socially and psychologically from their efforts. Indeed, new business ownership has presented an important pathway for individuals to achieve economic and social mobility, particularly among minorities (Butler, 1991; Feldman et al., 1991; US Small Business Administration, 1999; Waldinger et al., 1990). To help minority entrepreneurs follow this pathway, the federal government's regulations on small disadvantaged business contain specific minority set-asides that affect contracting, credit access, management and technical assistance programs (http://www.sba.gov/sdb/). Even on the local level, economic revitalization of inner cities frequently involves the creation of incubators that offer minority clients subsidized rates for space and essential business services. Despite such efforts, the potentially high cost of business failure gives rise to questions about the characteristics of those who start new ventures and why they pursue this activity (Shane and Venkataraman, 2000). It is reasonable to argue that a more complete understanding of the motivations of minority entrepreneurs might improve the programs designed to raise the odds of success.

Dyer (1994) suggested that individuals who start new businesses ('nascent entrepreneurs') make an 'entrepreneurial career' choice; the reasons they give for their choice may differ from the reasons given by those choosing other careers (Kolvereid, 1996; Krueger and Brazeal, 1994; Krueger and Carsrud, 1993). Recent data indicate that these differences may not be as large as once believed (Carter et al., 2003; Gartner et al., 2000), but no explicit comparisons by race and ethnicity have been made. Other work on the career reasons of members of minority groups shows that family and community play a more central role in their career choices as compared to Whites (Hill et al., 1990; Soto, 1988; Thomas and Alderfer, 1989). Some have theorized (Brown, 2000) that differences in the work values of minorities may result from societal racism, sexism and class bias that enhance the career behaviors and feelings of some individuals (i.e. Whites and males) while disadvantaging others (i.e. some non-Whites and females). If entrepreneurship is an important pathway to economic and social mobility for minorities, then it is important to understand whether their career choice reasons differ from those of non-minorities.

In principle, one could use convenience samples from registries of minority businesses to ask questions about career motivation. There are, however, three critical problems associated with such convenience sampling. First, as only existing businesses appear in lists and registries, any questions about 'why did you start?' would necessarily be retrospective, and subject to all of the biases that can contaminate retrospective reports. As existing businesses have achieved sufficient success to remain economically viable, self-presentational concerns (e.g. Feldman et al., 2002), hindsight biases (Fischhoff and Beyth, 1975; Hawkins and Hastie, 1990), and the fact that dispositional characteristics such as self-efficacy are affected by actual success in a domain (Bandura, 1997) can all limit the value of an entrepreneur's recollections about 'what was it like when you started?' Second, convenience sampling – especially of minority entrepreneurs – is likely not to be representative. In order to minimize the costs of data collection, researchers interested in minority firms would most probably have selected communities containing sufficient numbers of target firms: perhaps Los Angeles or Miami for Hispanic-owned firms, perhaps Chicago or Atlanta for Black-owned firms. For any number of reasons, however, firms located in these cities might be different from minority-owned firms in other parts of the USA. Third, no matter how carefully a sample might be chosen, or how sensitively the data might be collected, a convenience sample of minority firms would not include a matched comparison group whose motivations could also be studied.

To address all three of these concerns simultaneously, we used data from the Panel Study of Entrepreneurial Dynamics (PSED) to determine whether the career values of minorities and non-minorities differ. The PSED is a national longitudinal survey of individuals identified while in the process of starting a business, with information from a comparison group of a representative sample of individuals who chose other work careers. The sampling design was constructed so that individuals in both groups represent the population of working age adults in the USA. In addition, an oversampling of minorities was generated to yield a sample size sufficient for statistically valid comparisons between minorities and other non-minority adults. The result is a picture of the career motivations of minority entrepreneurs that can justifiably be used to inform both future research and public policy.

LITERATURE REVIEW AND HYPOTHESES

Research on entrepreneurship career choice has paralleled the human development field's exploration of careers, but with few cross-citations (Dyer, 1994). The primary difference is that the careers literature spanned all work options, whereas the entrepreneurship research focused on choices among different kinds of entrepreneurial activities (business formation being one kind of entrepreneurial activity), or between self-employment and any other career option.

Career Choice

The literature on career choice offers a variety of theories about the factors that influence an individual's preference (see Brown and Brooks, 1996; Holland, 1992; Krumboltz, 1994; Lent and Savickas, 1994; Super et al., 1995). Many of these theories derive from role theory, focusing on how individuals view work and whether work values exist in a hierarchical order. Sverko and Super (1995) contended that work has four distinct functions: economic, social, status/prestige, and development of individual identity, self-esteem and self-fulfillment. These functions seem to be hierarchically ordered according to their relative importance to an individual.

A key example of efforts to study the importance of work, or work values, is the creation of the Work Importance Study (WIS), an international research consortium (Super et al., 1995). The primary goal of WIS was to clarify constructs of work salience and relate them to work values and motivation through a series of cross-national studies.

Researchers associated with the project identified 23 values that individuals consider in their work roles. Using an extensive questionnaire of more than 200 items, the Value Scale (VS) was tested in 11 countries. In general, five salient factors were identified: *individualistic orientation* (autonomy, lifestyle, creativity, personal development), *self-actualization orientation* (ability utilization, altruism, aesthetics), *social orientation* (social relations, social interaction, variety, working conditions), *utilitarian orientation* (economics, advancement, prestige, achievement) and *adventurous orientation* (risk, variety, physical activity). Cross-national comparisons revealed that the career value structures of individuals were surprisingly similar across work cultures. Differences were discerned only on factors lower in the hierarchy of importance to individuals.

Despite the consistency of the cross-national findings, they offer little insight into whether people choosing to start businesses offer different career reasons or whether they rate or rank reasons differently than adults pursuing other careers. No insight was gained on values differences between majority and minority populations.

Entrepreneurial Career Choice

Parallel to the development of WIS, the Society of Associated Researchers of International Entrepreneurship (SARIE) initiated a multinational study. Investigators recognized that, like career choice in general, the intentions of individuals to engage in business start-up were multifaceted and influenced by a broad range of psychological, social and economic factors. An extensive questionnaire was created with more than 500 items organized into four sections: motivations to start a business, values and culture, environmental influences, and characteristics of the entrepreneur and business (Scheinberg and MacMillan, 1988). Data collection and analyses in this project began a quest to develop what might be called an 'empirically based' theory of reasons offered for business creation.

The first SARIE study reported the results of surveying 1400 independent business owners in 11 countries (Scheinberg and MacMillan, 1988). Factor analysis of motivations to start a business (38 items) distributed 21 items into six broad types: *need for approval, perceived instrumentality of wealth, degree of communitarianism, need for personal development, need for independence* and *need for escape*. As in the WIS project, cross-country comparisons of the ranking of the factors revealed some differences. US entrepreneurs scored higher on need for independence but lower on degree of communitarianism. Respondents from Portugal and Norway scored higher on degree of communitarianism but lower on need for escape. Three of the Nordic countries (Sweden, Norway, Denmark – but not Finland) scored lower on the instrumentality of wealth factor.

In a follow-up study, Shane et al. (1991) sought to extend the original model by focusing on nationality and gender of the entrepreneur. To improve the response rate they reduced the questionnaire substantially. Data collected from owner–managers revealed four factors (sets of career reasons), and that respondents in the UK and New Zealand were similar to each other but differed from Norwegians. Respondents from Norway were less motivated by aspects of recognition and status, but more motivated by ideas and learning. Differences based on the sex of the respondent were identified (even by country), but with women constituting less than 11 percent of the overall sample it is probably a mistake to make too much of these differences.

Birley and Westhead (1994) surveyed owner–managers in the UK and identified seven factors, four of which were similar to those obtained by Scheinberg and MacMillan (1988), a comparable factor (*welfare consider-ations* rather than *degree of communitarianism*) and two new factors, which accounted for items added by Shane et al. (1991) (*tax reduction/indirect benefits*) and role model items used by other SARIE researchers (Dubini, 1989).

Overall, the SARIE research produced a relatively consistent picture of the motivations presumed to lead to venture initiation. If there is an equally consistent difficulty, it is that each of the studies surveyed established entrepreneurs who had already started firms.

Besides the SARIE efforts, only a few studies have explored the reasons entrepreneurs give for starting new businesses, and fewer yet adopted a prospective approach, studying career reasons while the entrepreneurs were in the process of starting the business (Carter, 1997; Gatewood et al., 1995). Most of the prospective studies sampled only entrepreneurs (Brockhaus, 1980; Gartner et al., 2000), eliminating the possibility of comparing entrepreneurs' career reasons to those given by other adults. Two exceptions are Kolvereid's (1996) use of open-ended responses, and Carter et al.'s (2003) comparison of reasons given by nascent entrepreneurs and those of a representative comparison group of typical adults. Kolvereid identified 11 classes of reasons. However, only four classes contained at least 15 responses. Security and workload were significantly associated with reasons given for organizational employment, authority and challenge as reasons for preferring self-employment. Carter et al. (2003) identified six categories of reasons for business start-up that corresponded to those in the SARIE research.

The Convergence of the Career Choice and Entrepreneurial Career Choice Literatures

There is considerable overlap in the dimensions identified in the career choice studies in human development and entrepreneurship. The overlap signifies six categories of reasons for starting a business that differentiate nascent entrepreneurs from other adults (see Table 19.1). The first category, *innovation*, describes an individual's intention to accomplish something new (McClelland and Winter, 1969). The category contains items considered either as 'learning' (Shane et al., 1991) or as 'need for personal development' (Birley and Westhead, 1994; Scheinberg and MacMillan, 1988).

The second category, *independence*, captures the *need for independence* noted both by Scheinberg and MacMillan (1988) and by Birley and Westhead (1994). In describing an individual's desire for freedom, control and flexibility in the use of their time, it also encompasses motives described in the career choice literature (Coetsier and Claes, 1995; Schein, 1978). The third category, *recognition*, combines two motivations from the SARIE research: *recognition* and *need for approval*. Items in this category

Table 19.1 Categories of career reasons

	Innovation	Independence	Recognition	Roles	Financial success	Self-realization
Scheinberg and MacMillan (1988)	Need for personal development	Need for independence	Need for approval		Perceived instrumentality of wealth	
Shane et al. (1991)	Learning	Independence	Recognition	Roles		
Birley and Westhead (1994)	Need for personal development	Need for independence	Need for approval	Follow role models	Perceived instrumentality of wealth	
Super et al. (1995)	Adventurous orientation	Individualistic orientation	Social orientation	Social orientation	Utilitarian orientation	Orientation toward self-actualization
Super and Sverko (1995)			Status/prestige function	Social function	Economic function	Individual identity, self-esteem, self-fulfillment
Coetsier and Claes (1995)		Autonomy	Group orientation	Group orientation	Material career progress	Self-realization

describe an individual's intention to gain status, approval and recognition from their family, friends and community (Bonjean, 1966; Nelson, 1968). The fourth category, *roles*, contains items from Shane et al. (1991) that describe an individual's desire to follow family traditions or emulate the example of others.

The fifth category, *financial success*, describes an individual's intention to earn more money and achieve financial security (Birley and Westhead, 1994; Scheinberg and MacMillan, 1988). Finally, evidence from the careers literature (Super et al., 1995) and research on gender in entrepreneurship (e.g. Brush, 1992; Carter, 1997; Fischer et al., 1993) suggests a sixth category, *self-realization*. There is evidence in the entrepreneurship literature that men are more likely to seek to create financial wealth, whereas women are more likely to pursue other sorts of self-directed goals.

The overlap between constructs in the human development and entrepreneurship career choice literatures supports contentions that entrepreneurs are more similar to other adults than they are different (Carroll and Mosakowski, 1987; Gartner, 1988). WIS findings show convincingly that individuals from throughout the world offer similar reasons for career choice, and when considering the reasons they value most highly, the rank order of these reasons is similar across nations. The SARIE studies identified a set of motivations that have meaning in various cultures. Even though consistent between-country differences in the importance of particular items were found, such differences rarely involved as many as half of the items. Carter et al.'s (2003) research showed that on scales highly rated, such as *independence, financial success* and *self-realization*, there were no significant differences between ratings of nascent entrepreneurs and those of other adults. Only on reasons rated low, such as *roles*, were there differences. Kolvereid's (1996) work did obtain reason-based differences in employment status preference, but 62 percent of the reasons offered fell into only four of the 11 categories.

Given the consistency of findings across the two sets of literature, we concur with Carroll and Mosakowski (1987), who argued that self-employment is an episodic career choice. Rather than being associated with a stable set of individual characteristics, entrepreneurship is transitory. Individuals move into and out of self-employment. Early research on entrepreneurs did not view career choice in this way. Given this career mobility, we expect that nascent entrepreneurs will offer similar reasons for career choice as individuals pursuing other careers. That is, we expect nascent entrepreneurs and others to rank order career reasons in the same way. Essentially, they want the same things. In line with Carter et al.'s (2003) findings, we expect that any differences that exist will be in the intensity nascent entrepreneurs place on their career reasons. Everyone may place similar importance on financial success and independence, but we expect nascent entrepreneurs to care even less about roles and recognition than those seeking other careers. Individuals starting new businesses may feel as though they are going against the tide, and are unconcerned about tradition and the opinion of others in the community. Neither group is likely to place much value on these reasons when selecting a career, but nascent entrepreneurs are expected to care the least about them. The difference in intensity may be short-lived. Once the business is up and running, the entrepreneurs may care more about the opinion of others.

> *Hypothesis 1: Nascent entrepreneurs and adults choosing other careers will rank order career reasons scores similarly, but nascent entrepreneurs will consider career reasons related to recognition and roles to be less personally important than adults pursuing other careers.*

Minority Group Differences in Career Choice

The question of whether minority group status differentiates the career reasons of entrepreneurs invites the question of whether differences exist overall between career reasons of minorities and non-minorities. In other words, is there a main effect of minority status?

Some evidence suggests that such differences exist, but most of this research has focused on detecting differences across various minority groups (Osipow, 1975; Scott and Anadon, 1980; Smith, 1983). Research on whether differences exist between individuals in minority groups and those in non-minority groups is much rarer and lacks sufficient theoretical grounding or empirical exploration (Flores and O'Brien, 2002; Leong, 1995).

Not only is there a paucity of research involving direct comparisons between the career reasons of minorities and those of non-minorities, but some of the existing research has been the target of at least four methodological concerns. First, early theoretical work was based largely upon studies of middle- and upper-middle-class White males, and therefore the generalizability of these findings across race/ethnicity (as well as sex) is questionable. Second, minority group status is often confounded with social class membership (Osipow, 1975). Unless socioeconomic status is entered as a control, what purport to be 'race' differences may in fact reflect differing access to resources.

Third, even within an apparently homogeneous racial group, there may be wide individual differences in the degree to which minority status is central to the definition of self (Greene, 1997; Smith, 1983). Racial identity theory, ethnic identity theory and acculturation models are promoted as a

way to address this concern because each specifies how to clarify membership in culturally diverse groups (Leong and Hartung, 2000). As an
example, racial identity theory refers to people's perception that they share
a common racial heritage with a particular racial group. Helms (1990)
argued that this identity can change over time, via a process that occurs in
stages. To capture the dynamic nature of racial-group membership and
the recognition that it may not totally overlap with a person's racial
classification (Leong and Chou, 1994), researchers must rely on self-reports
of each individual's racial status. Doing so will align the individual's identity closely with the shared work values of the group. Thus the proper comparison in the careers area is the world as individuals perceive it, whether
those perceptions agree with racial and ethnic classifications that might be
made by employers or government entities or not.

Finally, there is a concern about the appropriateness of applying traditional theories of career choice to minority populations. Such theories
often hold assumptions about open labor markets and freedom of employment choice that may be unfounded for minority groups.

We believe that what influences the career choices of minorities is likely
to be derived from everyday experience and that these choices will be largely
determined by sociocultural factors. Sverko and Super (1995) note that the
behavioral context of an individual provides an 'opportunity structure'
consisting of both perceived and tangible forces. Poverty, poor educational
facilities, lack of employment opportunities, or the devaluing of personal
potential may diminish opportunity structures. In addition, members of
minority groups may find that their opportunities are further limited by
prejudice and discrimination. This environmental context shapes an individual's reality, perceived reality, learning experiences, associated rein-
forcements, punishments, or physiological reactions, all of which will affect
the preference attached to work values (Brown, 2000).

One outcome of these contextual effects is for groups to close ranks and
develop group norms that reinforce internal cohesiveness. Individuals are
encouraged to rely on each other rather than on outsiders. Authority figures
within the group take on increased visibility and importance. The stream of
findings emerging from the literature supports these suppositions. Parents
in Black and Hispanic households appear to exert a greater influence on the
career development of their children than do parents in White households
(Dillard and Campbell, 1981; Featherman and Hauser, 1976; Fields, 1981;
Lee, 1984; Soto, 1988). This need for approval or recognition is seemingly
reflected in their career choice. Interpersonal influences such as peers,
church and political leaders provide role models that appear to affect their
career choice reasons and vocation (Hill et al., 1990; Oliver and Etcheverry,
1987). Leong and Gim-Chung (1995) found that Asian Americans and

Hispanics were more likely than European Americans to solicit and value opinions of family and respected others when making career decisions.

These findings lead us to expect that the primary differences in work values between minorities and non-minorities will relate to family and community as sources of role models and recognition. We accept the argument (Roe and Lunneborg, 1990) that belonging to any group, particularly a minority group, inherently means that the group's values and interests exert significant influence on individual behavior.

Hypothesis 2: Minorities (Blacks and Hispanics) will consider career reasons related to recognition and roles to be more personally important than will non-minorities (Whites).

Minority Entrepreneurs' Career Choice

We argue above that the career reasons of nascent entrepreneurs and adults choosing other careers will be similar except on *roles and recognition*, values ranked low by both groups. We also contend that these same career values differentiate minorities from non-minorities, but for a different reason, and in an opposite direction. We expect that nascent entrepreneurs will value roles and recognition less than adults pursuing other careers, but that minorities will value roles and recognition more highly than non-minorities. If the emphasis on family and community distinguishes the career reasons of minorities from non-minorities, does it also differentiate minority nascent entrepreneurs from non-minority nascent entrepreneurs?

Most of the early studies on minorities and self-employment focused at the community level rather than on individual motivation or behavior. Researchers applied theories based on ethnic economies that rely heavily on cultural and structural explanations. For example, 'middleman minority theory' and 'ethnic enclave theory' were used to describe the patterns of economic adjustment and assimilation via entrepreneurship among minorities (Bonacich and Modell, 1980; Light and Gold, 2000; Portes and Bach, 1985; Waldinger et al., 1990).

The application of community-based theories left unresolved issues about the link between relevant dimensions of the group or community and reasons individuals give for choosing self-employment. We found only two studies that directly addressed the motivation for minorities starting a business. In a study of Black business owners, Hisrich and Brush (1986) found (in order of importance) such reasons as: achievement, opportunity, job satisfaction, independence, money, economic necessity, career security, power and status. Similarly, in a qualitative study of Cuban entrepreneurs, Peterson (1995) found choices to engage in entrepreneurship influenced by family aspiration and role models. The findings support the importance of individual aspirations and build on the concept of predisposing factors (Waldinger et al., 1990) to suggest that entrepreneurial career choices are class-linked and transmitted through ethnic subgroups.

The impact of community and family, as well as that of acculturation (Flores and O'Brien, 2002), in the ethnic economy literature parallels the findings in the career choice literature. In both literatures community is seen as an influencing source of role models, as is the importance of family role. Work following the theoretical framework provided by social learning theory (Bandura, 1969) shows the importance of family role models (Scherer et al., 1989) and supports the supposition that individuals with such role models are more likely to enter into entrepreneurship (Butler and Herring, 1991).

These findings lead us to expect that family and community values will drive minority entrepreneurship in the same fashion as they drive more general occupational choices among minorities. As noted above, many writers consider occupational choices among minorities to be limited by broader social and economic forces. To the extent that this is true, an individual's personal reasons for an occupational choice may be less important as a determinant of the person's behavior than are the (limited) options, regardless of whether the choice is for self-employment or other careers or vocation. We believe this influence will outweigh the tendency for minority nascent entrepreneurs to value *roles* and *recognition* less highly than adults pursuing other careers. We expect that although White nascent entrepreneurs will be less concerned about roles and recognition, minority nascent entrepreneurs will value these career reasons similarly to minorities choosing other careers. The broader social and economic forces of community will supersede a minority individual's personal reasons for an occupational choice. This reasoning leads us to expect a significant interaction between minority status, career choice status and career reasons.

Hypothesis 3: Minority versus non-minority differences in roles and recognition should be more pronounced among nascent entrepreneurs than among non-entrepreneurs.

METHOD

Sampling Procedures

Data for this study come from the Panel Study of Entrepreneurial Dynamics (PSED), a national database of individuals in the process of starting companies (Reynolds, 2000; Reynolds et al., 2002; Carter et al., 2003). Current information about the dataset can be found at http://projects.isr. umich.edu/psed/. The research design used a random-digit dialing process to contact US households with telephones from summer 1998 through winter 2000 to (a) identify nascent entrepreneurs and a comparison group, and (b) conduct extensive interviews with eligible respondents.

Data were organized into three sub-samples, corresponding to different funding sources. The 'Entrepreneurial Research Consortium (ERC)', consisting primarily of academic institutions, financed data collection for a 'mixed gender' sample. Funding from two National Science Foundation (NSF) grants was used to collect an oversample of women and an oversample of minorities.

The national screening process for identifying nascent entrepreneurs occurred over two broad time periods. Screening of individuals targeted for the nascent entrepreneur ERC group began in July 1998 and ended in April 1999. Screening of individuals targeted for the NSF-funded women oversample began in September 1998 and ended in December 1998. Together, these two samples totaled 31 261 potential nascent entrepreneurs. Screening for the comparison group was conducted in November 1998, yielding a sample of 2010 individuals.

Preliminary analysis of the mixed gender and women-only samples suggested the prevalence rates of Blacks and Hispanics for starting new businesses were substantially higher than for Whites. Given the low population numbers of these two minority groups in the USA, few would be represented in the nascent entrepreneur dataset. Therefore the second NSF grant was sought to fund oversampling on minority group status for Blacks and Hispanics. As described in Reynolds et al. (2002, pp. 46–7), there were insufficient numbers of Asians in the original sample of 31 261 individuals surveyed to generate a statistically useful sample of various groups of Asians (e.g. Japanese; Chinese – Mainland, Hong Kong, Taiwan; Indians, etc.) by oversampling within our budget constraints. Screening for the NSF-funded minority oversample of Blacks and Hispanics began in July 1999 and ended in January of 2000 with a case listing of 28 314 people. Finally, screening of the minority oversample comparison group began and ended in November 1999 with a case listing of 3037 people. Thus a grand total of 64 622 individuals were screened between July 1998 and January 2000.

Use of Weights

The PSED dataset comes with 'post-stratification weights for each respondent based on estimates from the US Census Bureau's Current Population

Survey. The post-stratification scheme is based on gender, age, household income, and the four National Census Regions (Northeast, South, Midwest, and West). The scheme produces a total of 144 cells for weighting adjustments' (Reynolds, 2000, p. 177). The weights are essential for drawing conclusions intended to generalize to the entire US population. According to Reynolds (2000, p. 181), 'any analysis should be completed with a weighted sample. This is a reflection of the number of procedures employed in the sampling and data collection that increased the yield and efficiency of the procedures.' Details of the creation and application of weights are described in Reynolds (2000).

Interview Procedures

In the screening phase, a marketing research firm telephoned households as part of a national survey that involved contacting three random samples of 1000 adults (500 female, 500 male; >18 years of age) each week in the contiguous 48 states and the District of Columbia. At least three attempts were made to contact each person by phone.

When an adult agreed to respond to a survey primarily about marketing issues and consumer preferences, a questionnaire was administered. Two items were randomly included (i.e. at the beginning, middle or end of the survey) to determine whether the respondent might qualify as a nascent entrepreneur:

- Are you, alone or with others, now trying to start a business? (independent nascent entrepreneur)
- Are you, alone or with others, now starting a new business or new venture for your employer? (corporate nascent entrepreneur)

Two additional qualifying questions were used to screen out individuals who did not expect to participate in ownership of the new business and individuals who were only thinking about starting a business but not actively involved:

- Do you anticipate becoming an 'owner' (in whole or in part) of the business being developed?
- Have you engaged in ongoing business organizing activity during the immediately preceding 12 months?

Affirmative answers to both questions were necessary for individuals to be considered 'nascent entrepreneurs'. That is, both the independent and the corporate nascent entrepreneurs expected to be owners of the businesses they were in the process of starting. Corporate nascent entrepreneurs had some portion of ownership of their prospective businesses owned by 'non-persons' (e.g. other businesses). Individuals who met the nascent entrepreneur screening criteria were invited to participate in 'a national study of new businesses being conducted through the University of Wisconsin' and offered a $25 cash payment. The screening procedure also identified a comparison group of individuals who were not actively working to start a new venture. They were invited to participate in a 'national study of the work and career patterns of all Americans, including those not currently working' and offered a $25 cash payment.

In the second phase of data collection, names and phone numbers of the potential nascent entrepreneurs were forwarded to the University of Wisconsin Survey Research Laboratory (UWSRL) along with basic sociodemographic information on the individual, household, county, and state of residency. Detailed interviews were then conducted with the nascent entrepreneurs and individuals in the comparison group.

At the end of the telephone interview, respondents were asked to volunteer their first name and address, so that they could be sent a mail questionnaire and the $25 payment for taking part in the telephone interview. Not all respondents agreed to provide a name and address. Respondents also were offered a payment of $25 for completion of the mail survey. Some respondents who agreed to answer the mail questionnaire did not. For the race/ethnicity respondents of interest, 830 of the 1139 returned mail questionnaires (518 White/Caucasians; 224 Blacks; 88 Hispanics).

More complete details of the telephone sampling procedures can be found in Reynolds (2000) and Carter et al. (2003). Reynolds (2000) provides a detailed overview and history of the development of all aspects of the research design as of 1999. Carter et al. (2003) describe details of the various cohorts of nascent entrepreneurs and the comparison group that were sampled through 2000 as well as the specific decision rules for selecting the nascent entrepreneurs and comparison group.

Description of Respondents

The final sample of PSED respondents totals 1261 (830 nascent entrepreneurs and 431 in the comparison group). Of the nascent entrepreneurs, seven indicated that 'non-persons' expected to own more than 50 percent of the new venture. We removed these cases from the analyses because we were interested in the activities of nascent entrepreneurs attempting autonomous start-ups. Six individuals indicated that their venture had already had positive cash flow for more than 90 days before the initial interview. We considered these six to be 'infant businesses' and removed them from analyses. Nine individuals in the control group qualified as nascent entrepreneurs and were eliminated from consideration. Additionally, in one case the respondent indicated a start-up team, but provided no information about which team member was the respondent. Since race/ethnicity information was collected for each team member, this made it impossible to code the respondent's race/ethnicity in the present study. This case was disqualified. The 23 eliminated reduced the original sample size to 1238. As the study focuses on reasons individuals give for selecting a career, we eliminated nascent entrepreneurs who reported a start-up involving a team in which they intended to play only a minor role. Such individuals may be more actively involved in other, simultaneous, career choices. To identify individuals making a 'nascent entrepreneur' *career* choice, we compared the funds the respondent expected to personally invest in the business to the investments expected of other start-up partners. We disqualified respondents if any of their partners were investing more in the start-up than they were. This reduced the number of eligible cases to 1194 (772 nascent entrepreneurs, 422 comparison group members).

Our specific questions about career reasons, however, were gathered through the mail, subsequent to the initial telephone interviews. For both the nascent entrepreneur sample and the comparison group sample, the response rate to the mail questions was a respectable 62 percent of the people who had answered the phone interview. Thus our final sample was a total of 786 (485 nascent entrepreneurs and 301 members of the comparison group) who had answered all 18 reasons items.

Measures

Entrepreneurial status
From the screening procedures described above, nascent entrepreneurs were coded as 1; individuals in the comparison group as 2.

Race
Consistent with recommendations in the human development career choice literature, racial status was self-reported. This captures the dynamic nature of racial-group membership and aligns identity more closely with shared work values of the group. This is important for making comparisons based on the effect of work values on career choice. Respondents were asked to indicate which of the following best describes their race: White/Caucasian; Black/African American; Hispanic/Latino; American Indian; Southeast Asian; Other Asian/Pacific Islander; or something else. Not all provided data on race/ethnicity (six), and 49 indicated their race/ethnicity as American Indian, South East Asian, Other Asian, or

something else. In the categories of interest here, 664 were White/ Caucasian, 343 Black, and 132 Hispanic, for a total of 1139 eligible for analysis in the present study.

Reasons

In Table 19.1 we outlined the six broad constructs that represent the reasons individuals give for making their career choice. These have been remarkably stable across both the human development and entrepreneurship literature. The PSED adopted 18 items (G1a – G1r on the mail survey) from prior research to represent the six constructs. Twelve items were adopted from the SARIE research, ten of these from the Shane et al. (1991) study comparing the reasons of entrepreneurs in the UK, New Zealand and Norway. From the results of their factor analyses, we selected items with factor loadings > 0.50. These items measured four factors: *innovation* (m – to develop an idea for a product, c – to be innovative and in the forefront of technology, h – to grow and learn as a person); *independence* (b – to have greater flexibility for my personal and family life, f – to have considerable freedom to adapt my own approach to work); *recognition* (a – to achieve a higher position for myself in society, e – to be respected by my friends, l – to achieve something and get recognition for it); and *roles* (d – to continue a family tradition, i – to follow the example of a person I admire). To measure a fifth factor, *financial success*, we adapted two items from other SARIE studies (Birley and Westhead, 1994; Scheinberg and MacMillan, 1988) and added two other items: (g – to give myself, my spouse and children financial security; k – to earn a larger personal income; n – to have a chance to build great wealth or a very high income; j – to build a business my children can inherit). Finally, we added four items to represent the pursuit of *self-realization* that can motivate individuals to become entrepreneurs: (o – to fulfill a personal vision; p – to lead and motivate others; q – to have the power to greatly influence an organization; r – to challenge myself).

For the nascent entrepreneurs, the 18 items were preceded by this question: 'To what extent are the following reasons important to you in establishing this new business?' For the comparison group, the items were preceded by this question: 'To what extent are the following important to you in your decisions about your work and career choices?' Both groups responded to each item on a 1–5 scale: 1 – to no extent, 2 – little extent, 3 – some extent, 4 – great extent, 5 – to a very great extent.

The total number of respondents for the 18 reasons questions varied by question, from a low of 817 for the item having to do with 'follow the example of a person I admire' to a high of 826 for three of the items, one of which was 'grow and learn as a person'. When correcting for missing item responses only 786 Whites, Blacks and Hispanics answered all 18 items. These responses (485 nascent entrepreneurs, 301 comparison group members) were analyzed to test the measurement model and the hypotheses.

We tested the internal consistency of the factor model by subjecting the data to a principal components factor analysis. We specified that the analysis should identify six factors. The resulting factor structure was subjected to a varimax rotation. Because missing data reduced the number of participants, the weights applied to the reasons questions were adjusted to total 485 in the nascent entrepreneur category and 301 in the comparison group. The factor analysis of these weighted items accounted for a total 68 percent of the variance. Rotation converged in seven iterations. Only two items failed to load on the theoretical dimensions expected (h – grow and learn as a person; and q – power to influence the organization). As displayed in Table 19.2, four of the factors (*financial success, roles, recognition, independence*) identically matched their conceptual counterparts (Cronbach alpha reliabilities were, respectively, 0.77, 0.58, 0.75 and 0.63). The reliability coefficients for roles and independence were low, but were based on only two items each (which makes it difficult to obtain high Cronbach's alpha levels). Because the scales matched their conceptual counterparts, and because low reliabilities actually work against our hypotheses, we retained all four scales. The remaining two factors, *self-realization* and *innovation*, varied slightly from their theoretical dimensions. Item h, conceptually related to *innovation*, loaded on the *self-realization* factor, whereas item q, conceptually aligned with *self-realization*, loaded on the *innovation* factor. Because we judged item h to have face validity with *self-realization* and its factor loading was comparable to others in that scale, we considered item h as part of the *self-realization* scale (Cronbach's alpha = 0.76) rather than the *innovation* scale. Similarly, as the loading on *innovation* for item q exceeded an absolute value of 0.40, we included it in that scale (Cronbach's alpha = 0.70). Additionally, item e cross-loaded on *recognition* and *roles*. Because its conceptual alignment was on *recognition* and its factor loading was over 0.60, we retained it on this scale. Eliminating it would have dropped the reliability coefficient from 0.75 to 0.65.

To test the hypotheses, we calculated values for each of the six reasons scales by summing the items in each scale and dividing by the number of items. This procedure created six factor scores for each respondent, each of which was adjusted by the respondent's post-sampling stratification weight. Prior to this adjustment, the weights were renormalized within the six cells created by the combination of nascency status (2) and ethnic identification (3).

Table 19.2 Factor analysis of reasons for career choice items: six-factor solution, N = 786

Factor:	1 Self-realization	2 Financial success	3 Innovation	4 Recognition	5 Roles	6 Independence
Sum of squared rotated loadings:	2.55	2.45	1.98	1.96	1.81	1.55
Percentage variable accounted for:	14.17	13.61	11.00	10.88	10.05	8.58
G1# Cronbach alpha:	0.76[a]	0.77	0.70[b]	0.75	0.58	0.63
Self-realization						
r To challenge myself	0.77					
o To fulfill a personal vision	0.71					
p To lead and motivate others	0.62					
q Power to influence an organization			0.50			
Financial success						
k To earn a larger personal income		0.84				
g Financial security		0.77				
n Build great wealth, high income		0.71				
j Build business children can inherit		0.58				
Innovation						
c Innovative, forefront of technology			0.76			
m To develop an idea for a product			0.74			
h Grow and learn as a person	0.66					
Recognition						
l Achieve something, get recognition				0.75		
e To be respected by my friends				0.66		
a Gain a higher position for myself				0.62	0.54	

450

Roles
d To continue a family tradition   0.76
i Follow example of person I admire   0.71

Independence
b Greater flexibility for personal life   0.79
f Free to adapt my approach to work   0.72

Notes:
a Cronbach alpha reported for this factor is with item q removed and item h added.
b Cronbach alpha reported for this factor is with item h removed and item q added.

RESULTS

Comparisons of Reasons

The weighted factor scores were subjected to a $2 \times 3 \times 6$ (nascency status by race/ethnicity by reasons) analysis of variance with repeated measures on the last factor. Per Girden (1992), we evaluated the extent of homogeneity of variance prior to any hypotheses tests. Where necessary to elucidate the findings, we conducted *post-hoc* comparisons of means using Bonferroni adjusted critical values. Table 19.3 displays the mean and standard deviation for each category of reasons. A review of the standard deviations indicates that the variances are not equal. A Mauchly sphericity test showed that variance–covariance matrices of the reasons variables were not circular (Huynh and Mandeville, 1979) ($W = 0.65$; $\chi^2 = 333.93$, df $= 14$; $p < 0.000$) and a Box

Table 19.3　Means and standard deviations for six weighted[a] reasons

		Nascent $n=485$	Other careers $n=294$	White $n=496$	Black $n=203$	Hispanic $n=80$	Total $n=779$
Independence							
	M	4.13	4.20	4.12	4.17	4.33	4.15
	SD	1.49	1.14	1.36	1.15	1.84	1.37
Self-realization							
	M	3.65	3.89	3.58	4.02	4.02	3.74
	SD	1.36	1.17	1.26	1.06	1.77	1.29
Financial success							
	M	3.61	3.78	3.46	4.06	3.99	3.67
	SD	1.52	1.28	1.40	1.19	1.89	1.43
Recognition							
	M	2.57	3.48	2.72	3.16	3.49	2.91
	SD	1.26	1.36	1.26	1.25	1.99	1.37
Innovation							
	M	2.70	2.96	2.68	3.04	2.92	2.80
	SD	1.47	1.14	1.37	1.31	1.35	1.36
Roles							
	M	1.89	2.85	2.09	2.48	2.69	2.25
	SD	1.11	1.45	1.17	1.32	1.96	1.33
Total							
	M	3.21	3.60	3.17	3.51	3.53	

Note:　[a] Each individual's reasons factor scores were multiplied by the individual's demographic weight, with the weights corrected to sum to the total *n* by group and gender. Thus within each of the groups by race/ethnicity cells, the mean of the corrected weights is 1.0.

homogeneity test revealed significant between-group departures from homogeneity (M = 502.00; F = 4.61, df = 105, 90 645; p < 0.000). Together, these results indicated that the analyses of variance should be adjusted by multiplying the degrees of freedom by an epsilon value from the assumption tests (the Greenhouse–Geisser epsilon was 0.86[1]).

The $2 \times 3 \times 6$ repeated measures ANOVA on weighted scale values showed a highly significant main effect difference among the six types of reasons, $F(4.29, 3314.03) = 297.87$, $p < 0.000$. The rankings of the reasons (see Table 19.3) show that motives related to *independence* had the overall highest scores and *roles* the overall lowest scores and that the pattern of rankings for the two groups was similar. As expected, nascent entrepreneurs ranked *recognition* and *roles* the lowest, but the comparison group adults ranked *innovation* and *roles* lowest. Similarly, within-subject contrasts revealed that slight differences between the groups. The 'space' between each level of reasons in Table 19.3 for the two groups was not equal. Significant difference existed between each reason and the preceding reason, with the exception of that between the *self-realization* and *financial success* pair. The mean values of this pair differed significantly for the comparison group but not for nascent entrepreneurs.

Hypothesis 1 assumed that the ordering pattern for the nascent entrepreneurs and the comparison group would be the same, but that the intensity of the reasons scores would differ. Results of the $2 \times 3 \times 6$ analysis of variance shown in Table 19.4 show support for the hypothesis. Although there are slight differences in the ranking order, the nascency by reasons interaction, $F(4.29, 3314.04) = 25.33$, $p < 0.000$, indicates a significant difference in the scores of nascent entrepreneurs and members of the comparison group. As expected, *post-hoc* comparison of means shows

Table 19.4   Results of repeated measures analyses

	Adjusted ANOVA		
	df	F	p
Within-subjects effects			
Reasons	4.29, 3314.04	297.87	0.000
Nascency × reasons	4.29, 3314.04	25.33	0.000
Race/ethnicity × reasons	8.57, 3314.04	3.81	0.000
Nascency × race/ethnicity × reasons	8.57, 3314.04	0.84	0.581
Between-subjects effects			
Nascency	1, 773	14.22	0.000
Race/ethnicity	2, 773	8.33	0.000
Nascency × race/ethnicity	2, 773	0.04	0.960

Table 19.5   Post-hoc *mean comparisons using Bonferroni adjusted critical values*

	Mean difference	Std error	Sig.	95 % confidence interval	
Self-realization					
White/Black	−0.414	0.109	0.000	−0.676	−0.153
White/Hispanic	−0.382	0.158	0.048	−0.762	−0.003
Financial success					
White/Black	−0.595	0.121	0.000	−0.885	−0.306
White/Hispanic	−0.515	0.175	0.010	−0.936	−0.094
Recognition					
Nascent/comparison	−0.804	0.123	0.000	−1.046	−0.562
White/Black	−0.341	0.111	0.006	−0.607	−0.076
White/Hispanic	−0.538	0.161	0.003	−0.932	−0.152
Innovation					
White/Black	−0.351	0.116	0.008	−0.629	−0.073
Roles					
Nascent/comparison	−0.982	0.118	0.000	−1.214	−0.749
White/Black	−0.281	0.106	0.025	−0.536	−0.025

significant differences between the nascent entrepreneurs and those in other careers on *recognition* and *roles* (see Table 19.5).

The rank ordering makes it clear that the significant differences between nascent entrepreneurs and the comparison group occurred on the scales that were rated as less important to both groups (such as *roles* and *recognition*). On scales that were highly rated (such as *independence* and *financial success*), there were no significant differences between the two groups. It should also be noted that the mean scores for nascent entrepreneurs were lower overall than scores in the comparison group as reflected in the nascency main effect, $F(1, 708) = 14.37$, $p < 0.000$. The significant difference is most probably attributable to the *roles* and *recognition* reasons in the nascency by reasons interaction. The nascent entrepreneurs' mean score (averaging across all three race/ethnic groups) on *roles* was less than half that attributed to *independence*, the highest-ranked reason.

Overall, the results support Hypothesis 1 and are comparable to the findings of Gartner et al. (2000), who used an empirically driven factor analytic strategy and did not disaggregate minority data.

There was mixed support for Hypothesis 2, that Blacks and Hispanics rate career reasons regarding *roles* and *recognition* differently than Whites. The race/ethnicity by reasons interaction was statistically significant

Table 19.6   Mean scores for six weighted[a] reasons by groups

		Nascent entrepreneurs			Other careers group		
		White $n=339$ $wt_{sd}=0.40$	Black $n=115$ $wt_{sd}=0.41$	Hispanic $n=31$ $wt_{sd}=0.35$	White $n=157$ $wt_{sd}=0.65$	Black $n=88$ $wt_{sd}=0.60$	Hispanic $n=49$ $wt_{sd}=0.43$
Independence							
	M	4.13	4.10	4.18	4.10	4.25	4.42
	SD	1.55	1.32	1.32	0.79	0.88	2.12
Self-realization							
	M	3.51	3.99	3.86	3.71	4.06	4.13
	SD	1.40	1.21	1.26	0.86	0.82	2.03
Financial success							
	M	3.45	3.97	3.99	3.50	4.16	3.99
	SD	1.57	1.34	1.23	0.93	0.96	2.22
Recognition							
	M	2.45	2.80	3.05	3.30	3.63	3.77
	SD	1.25	1.21	1.38	1.06	1.13	2.27
Innovation							
	M	2.61	2.91	2.88	2.82	3.23	2.94
	SD	1.46	1.47	1.54	1.17	1.06	1.23
Roles							
	M	1.81	2.11	1.95	2.70	2.96	3.16
	SD	1.07	1.16	1.20	1.16	1.36	2.20

Note: [a] Each individual's reasons factor scores were multiplied by the individual's demographic weight, with the weights corrected to sum to the total *n* by group and gender. Thus within each of the six groups by race/ethnicity cells, the mean of the corrected weights is 1.0.

$(F(8.59, 3348.15) = 3.66$, $p < 0.000)$, but *post-hoc* comparison of means suggests that differences between minorities and non-minorities were more pervasive than expected. *Post-hoc* comparisons showed that not only were the weighted scale values of Blacks on *roles* and *recognition* significantly higher than Whites; they rated all of the reasons higher except *independence*. Hispanics were significantly higher than the scores of Whites on *recognition* but not on *roles*. Additionally, Hispanics rated *financial success* and *self-realization* significantly higher. There was no significant difference between the weighted scale values of Blacks and Hispanics.

The results did not support Hypothesis 3 that family and community would be more influential in the lives of minority nascent entrepreneurs than in the lives of White nascent entrepreneurs and that these values would outweigh those of adults pursuing other careers. Specifically, the nascency by race/ethnicity by reasons interaction was not significant: $F(8.89, 3348.15) = 0.86$, $p < 0.552$. Although the single lowest scale value was associated with White nascent entrepreneurs' motives related to *Roles* and the single highest value was for comparison group Hispanics' motives related to *Independence*, the overall interaction did not emerge.

Given that the comparison group was selected to represent the population of adults in the USA, it should contain a certain number of individuals who report being self-employed. When screened during the Market Facts interview, these individuals would have responded that they were not 'alone or with others attempting to *start* a new business'. Instead, these individuals may have been self-employed for a number of years.

To examine whether this group might change the results, we tested the effect of removing the self-employed from the comparison group. During phone interviews, all respondents were asked about their occupational status, as follows: 'In terms of current work activity, are you involved in any of the following: working for others (full time or part time); a small business owner or self employed; a manager of a business; a homemaker; retired; student (full time or part time); or unemployed?' Multiple responses for the categories were allowed. Sixty-four in the comparison group reported they were small business owners or self-employed; of these, 40 indicated they also worked for others while being self-employed and 23 worked full-time for others.

When we removed these self-employed individuals from the comparison group data and reran the analyses, the factor structure remained essentially the same. The six-cluster repeated measure analysis (weighted) revealed the same reasons by group interaction as before: $F(4.28, 3065.41) = 23.63$, $p < 0.000$, and the same reasons by race/ethnicity interaction as before $F(4.28, 3065.41) = 2.96$, $p < 0.000$. The findings generated from all of these analyses offer remarkably similar results.

DISCUSSION

The purpose of this study was to better understand the motivations of minority entrepreneurs for pursuing self-employment. Business ownership has been seen as a pathway for minorities to achieve economic and social mobility. Better understanding of the reasons minorities offer for such a career choice could assist in designing programs that would improve their odds of business success.

Implicit in prior research on the reasons entrepreneurs offer for getting into business was an assumption that entrepreneurs pursued entrepreneurial activity because of greater interest in such reasons as financial success, independence and self-actualization. Entrepreneurs were assumed to want 'more' of these than do individuals pursuing jobs. Yet, surprisingly, prior research offered no specific tests of this assumption. Previous studies were typically retrospective (surveying only established entrepreneurs) and often failed to compare the reasons of entrepreneurs with other individuals (Carroll and Mosakowski, 1987).

The present study shows no significant differences among respondents on career reasons that individuals rank most highly (*independence, self-realization* and *financial success*). Nascent entrepreneurs (Whites, Blacks and Hispanics) were similar to non-entrepreneurs (Whites, Blacks and Hispanics). This finding appears to support the perspective of Sverko and Super (1995) that certain career reasons are universal. As expected, differences existed between career reasons given by nascent entrepreneurs and those pursuing other careers in the lower-ranked categories on *recognition* and *roles*. Nascent entrepreneurs were less likely to be concerned with the roles, traditions and values of family, friends and others in the community Surprisingly, the ratings of nascent entrepreneurs were consistently lower than the ratings of other adults across all of the career reasons.

When we explored whether this finding was applicable to the career reasons of minorities (nascent entrepreneurs and others), we found that Blacks rated five of the six career reasons significantly higher than did Whites. Only on the desire for *independence* was there no difference between these two groups. Hispanics were more likely to seek *recognition, financial success* and *self-realization* than were Whites. There were no significant differences between Blacks and Hispanics.

We found no support for our hypothesis that the aspirations of minority nascent entrepreneurs for getting into business vary from those of Whites who choose self-employment. The career reasons considered among the most important are rated as such by all respondents, regardless of career path or racial/ethnic category. These dimensions are largely individualistic. What people want for themselves, individually, is the same whether they seek to start businesses or not, whether they come from minority groups or not. In general, issues about family and community matter less to nascent entrepreneurs compared to others, but financial success, family and community were more important to minorities irrespective of entrepreneurial aspirations.

One of the recurring themes in theories of minority/ethnic/immigrant entrepreneurship is that of blocked mobility. This theme implies that behavioral choices are the joint product of group-based or social processes and individual desires. Individuals as members of communities turn to business ownership because other opportunities are either constrained or prohibited. Paying attention to others in the group matters when one is identified as a group member (Roe and Lunneborg, 1990). From the results of this study, it would appear that although membership in a minority group matters to respondents, this is not as important as other reasons that affect their decision to start a business. An important issue in explorations of minority entrepreneurship involves measures of the success of such activities. For example, although minority nascent entrepreneurs rank career reasons similarly to others, their business organizing efforts historically have resulted in firms that are significantly smaller in revenues and profits than White-owned firms (US Small Business Administration, 2002). As our dataset contained information on individuals currently in the founding phase of entrepreneurship, no measures of venture success were available. Therefore the issue of whether minority entrepreneurs continue to be less economically successful than White entrepreneurs will require further study. Succeeding waves of PSED data collection may offer insights into the importance of factors such as financial motivation, prior experience, and human and financial capital endowments to the business success of Black and Hispanic nascent entrepreneurs.

IMPLICATIONS

When one wonders whether reasons for starting a business are similar to reasons offered for choosing jobs, *which* set of reasons is examined is critically important. Financial success, self-realization and independence factors, which have previously been claimed to distinguish entrepreneurs from others, did not produce the expected differences. 'Starting a business' or 'getting a job in an organization' are both pathways to meeting the goals of these sets of reasons. This result challenges prior beliefs and theories that individuals choose entrepreneurship because their career reasons are quite different from the motives of people who choose jobs (Caird, 1991; Cromie and O'Donoghue, 1992; Hamilton, 2000). Only when the list of potential reasons is expanded to include *recognition* and *roles* do differences between nascents and others emerge. The policy implications are clear (if unsurprising to a psychologically sophisticated audience): race matters, but so do cognitive processes. Assistance programs that concentrate on a person's race or ethnicity, to the virtual exclusion of the person's motivations, are unlikely to produce consistently positive outcomes.

Finally, this study not only surveyed individuals in the process of starting firms; it also involved a comparison group whose characteristics generalized to the population of individuals in the USA. We believe that this attention to characteristics of the sample of entrepreneurs and the comparison group is an important standard for future researchers.

CONCLUSIONS

Our research is yet another step away from the erroneous view that entrepreneurs are 'born' with internally consistent personality structures that differentiate them from everyone else. Rather, when it comes to making career choices, nascent entrepreneurs are not unlike others. There *are* differences, but they are more isolated than pervasive, more subtle than obvious. Just as nascent entrepreneurs have much in common with people making other career choices, Black and Hispanic entrepreneurs have much in common with White entrepreneurs. Again, this is not true for all sets of reasons, though it does apply to those that are consistent with race/ethnic divergences in the importance of one's place in one's family and community. Part of the similarity may arise from the possibility that career paths and interests of Whites and minorities are converging. Differences in minority status may represent a changing social milieu. The findings presented here should, therefore, be viewed in the context of time and place.

AUTHORS' NOTE

We gratefully acknowledge support by the Entrepreneurship Research Consortium, the National Science Foundation under Grant No. 9809841 (Nancy M. Carter, Principal Investigator) and Grant No. 9905255 (Patricia Greene, Principal Investigator) and the Ewing Marion Kauffman Foundation. Any opinions, findings and conclusions or recommendations expressed in this material are those of the authors and do not necessarily reflect the views of the National Science Foundation or the Kauffman Foundation.

NOTE

1. Epsilons range from zero to one with lower values reflecting greater variations in symmetry.

REFERENCES

Bandura, A. (1969), 'Social-learning theory of identificatory processes', in D.A. Goslin (ed.), *Handbook of Socialization Theory and Research*, Chicago, IL: Rand McNally, pp. 213–62.
Bandura, A. (1997), *Self-efficacy: The Exercise of Control*, Stanford, CA: Stanford University Press.

Birley, S. and Westhead, P. (1994), 'A taxonomy of business start-up reasons and their impact on firm growth and size', *Journal of Business Venturing*, **9**: 7–31.

Bonacich, E. and Modell, J. (1980), *The Economic Basis of Ethnic Solidarity: Small Business in the Japanese-American Community*, Berkeley, CA: University of California Press.

Bonjean, C.M. (1966), 'Mass, class and the industrial community: a comparative analysis of managers, businessmen, and workers', *American Journal of Sociology*, **72**(2): 149–62.

Brockhaus, R.H. (1980), 'Risk taking propensity of entrepreneurs', *Academy of Management Journal*, **23**: 509–20.

Brown, D. and Brooks, L. (1996), 'Introduction to theories of career development and choice: origins, evolution, and current efforts', in D. Brown, L. Brooks and Associates (eds), *Career Choice and Development*, 3rd edn, San Francisco, CA: Jossey-Bass, pp. 1–32.

Brown, M.T. (2000), 'Blueprint for the assessment of socio-structural influences in career choice and decision making', *Journal of Career Assessment*, **8**(4): 371–8.

Brush, C.G. (1992), 'Research on women business owners: past trends, a new perspective and future directions', *Entrepreneurship Theory and Practice*, **2**(1): 1–24.

Butler, J.S. (1991), *Entrepreneurship and Self-help among Black Americans: A Reconsideration of Race and Economics*, Albany, NY: State University of New York Press.

Butler, J. and Herring, C. (1991), 'Ethnicity and entrepreneurship', *Sociological Perspectives*, **34**: 79–94.

Caird, S. (1991), 'The enterprising tendency of occupational groups', *International Small Business Journal*, **9**: 75–81.

Carroll, G.R. and Mosakowski, E. (1987), 'The career dynamics of self-employment', *Administrative Science Quarterly*, **32**(4): 570–89.

Carter, N.M. (1997), 'Entrepreneurial processes and outcomes: the influence of gender', in P.D. Reynolds and S.B. White (eds), *The Entrepreneurial Process*, Westport, CT: Quorum Books, pp. 163–78.

Carter, N.M., Gartner, W.B., Shaver, K.G. and Gatewood, E.J. (2003), 'The career reasons of nascent entrepreneurs', *Journal of Business Venturing*, **18**(1): 13–39.

Coetsier, P. and Claes, R. (1995), 'The Flemish work importance study', in D.E. Super, B. Sverko and C.M. Super (eds), *Life Roles, Values and Careers: International Findings of the Work Importance Study*, San Francisco, CA: Jossey-Bass, pp. 100–16.

Cromie, S. and O'Donoghue, J. (1992), 'Assessing entrepreneurial inclinations', *International Small Business Journal*, **10**: 66–73.

Davidsson, P., Lindmark, L. and Olofsson, C. (1994), 'New firm formation and regional development in Sweden', *Regional Studies*, **28**(4): 395–410.

Dillard, J.M. and Campbell, N.J. (1981), 'Influences of Puerto Rican, Black, and Anglo parents' career behavior on their adolescent children's career development', *Vocational Guidance Quarterly*, **30**: 139–48.

Dubini, P. (1989), 'The influence of motivations and environment on business start-ups: some hints for public policies', *Journal of Business Venturing*, **4**: 11–26.

Dyer, W.G. (1994), 'Toward a theory of entrepreneurial careers', *Entrepreneurship Theory and Practice*, **19**(2): 7–22.

Featherman, D.L. and Hauser, R.M. (1976), 'Prestige or socioeconomic scales in the study of occupational achievement', *Sociological Methods and Research*, **4**: 403–22.

Feldman, H.D., Koberg, C.S. and Dean, T.J. (1991), 'Minority small business owners and their paths to ownership', *Journal of Small Business Management*, **29**(4): 12–27.

Feldman, R.S., Forrest, J.A. and Happ, B.R. (2002), 'Self-presentation and verbal deception: do self-presenters lie more?', *Basic and Applied Social Psychology*, **24**: 163–70.

Fields, A.B. (1981), 'Some influences upon the occupational aspirations of three white-collar ethnic groups', *Adolescence*, **16**: 663–84.

Fischer, E.M., Reuber, A.R. and Dyke, L.S. (1993), 'A theoretical overview and extension of research on sex, gender, and entrepreneurship', *Journal of Business Venturing*, **8**: 151–68.

Fischhoff, B. and Beyth, R. (1975), ' "I knew it would happen." Remembered probabilities of once-future things', *Organizational Behavior and Human Performance*, **13**: 1–16.

Flores, L.Y. and O'Brien, K.M. (2002), 'The career development of Mexican American adolescent women: a test of social cognitive career theory', *Journal of Counseling Psychology*, **49**: 14–27.

Gartner, W.B. (1988), ' "Who is an entrepreneur?" Is the wrong question', *American Journal of Small Business*, **12**(4): 11–32.

Gartner, W.B., Shaver, K.G. and Gatewood, E.J. (2000), 'Doing it for yourself: career attributions of nascent entrepreneurs', in P.D. Reynolds, E. Autio, C.G. Brush, W.D. Bygrave, S. Manigart, H.J. Sapienza and K.G. Shaver (eds), *Frontiers of Entrepreneurship Research 2000*, Babson Park, MA: Babson College, pp. 13–24.

Gatewood, E.J., Shaver, K.G. and Gartner, W.B. (1995), 'A longitudinal study of cognitive factors influencing start-up behaviors and success at venture creation', *Journal of Business Venturing*, **10**: 371–91.

Girden, E.R. (1992), *ANOVA Repeated Measures*, Newbury Park, CA: Sage Publications.

Greene, P.G. (1997), 'A call for conceptual clarity. Comments on Bates: Why are firms owned by Asian immigrants lagging behind Black-owned businesses?', *National Journal of Sociology*, **10**(2): 49–55.

Hamilton, R. (2000), 'Does entrepreneurship pay? An empirical analysis of the returns to self-employment', *Journal of Political Economy*, **108**(3): 604–31.

Hawkins, S.A. and Hastie, R. (1990), 'Hindsight: biased judgments of past events after the outcomes are known', *Psychological Bulletin*, **107**: 311–27.

Helms, J.E. (1990), *Black and White Racial Identity: Theory, Research, and Practice*, New York: Greenwood Press.

Hill, O.W., Pettus, W.C. and Hedin, B.A. (1990), 'Three studies of factors affecting the attitudes of Blacks and females toward the pursuit of science and science-related careers', *Journal of Research in Science Teaching*, **27**: 289–314.

Hisrich, R. and Brush, C. (1986), 'Characteristics of the minority entrepreneur', *Journal of Small Business Management*, **24**(4): 1–8.

Holland, J.L. (1992), *Making Vocational Choices: A Theory of Vocational Personalities and Work Environments*, 2nd edn, Odessa, FL: Psychological Assessment Resources.

Huynh, H. and Mandeville, G.K. (1979), 'Validity conditions in repeated measures designs', *Psychological Bulletin*, **86**: 964–73.

Kolvereid, L. (1996), 'Organizational employment versus self-employment: reasons for career choice intentions', *Entrepreneurship Theory and Practice*, **20**(3): 23–31.

Krueger, N.F. Jr and Brazeal, D.V. (1994), 'Entrepreneurship potential and potential entrepreneurs', *Entrepreneurship Theory and Practice*, **19**(3): 91–104.

Krueger, N.F. and Carsrud, A.L. (1993), 'Entrepreneurial intentions: applying the theory of planned behavior', *Entrepreneurship and Regional Development*, **5**(4): 315–30.

Krumboltz, J.D. (1994), 'The career beliefs inventory', *Journal of Counseling and Development*, **72**: 424–8.

Lee, C.C. (1984), 'Predicting the career choice attitudes of rural Black, White, and Native American high school students', *Vocational Guidance Quarterly*, **32**: 177–84.

Lent, R.W. and Savickas, M. (1994), *Convergence in Career Development Theories: Implications for Science and Practice*, Palo Alto, CA: Consulting Psychologists Press.

Leong, F.T.L. (1995), *Career Development and Vocational Behavior of Racial and Ethnic Minorities*, Mahwah, NJ: Lawrence Erlbaum.

Leong, F.T.L. and Chou, E.L. (1994), 'The role of ethnic identity and acculturation in the vocational behavior of Asian Americans: an integrative review', *Journal of Vocational Behavior*, **44**(2): 155–72.

Leong, F.T.L. and Hartung, P.J. (2000), 'Cross-cultural career assessment: review and prospects for the new millennium', *Journal of Career Assessment*, Fall: 391–401.

Leong, F.T.L. and Gim-Chung, R.H. (1995), 'Career assessment and intervention with Asian Americans', in F.T.L. Leong (ed.), *Career Development and Vocational Behavior of Racial and Ethnic Minorities*, Mahwah, NJ: Lawrence Erlbaum, pp. 193–226.

Light, I. and Gold, S. (2000), *Ethnic Economies*, New York: Academic Press.

McClelland, D.C. and Winter, D.G. (1969), *Motivating Economic Achievement*, New York: Free Press.

Nelson, J.I. (1968), 'Participation and integration: the case of the small businessman', *American Sociological Review*, **33**(3): 427–38.

Oliver, J. and Etcheverry, R. (1987), 'Factors influencing the decisions of academically talented Black students to attend college', *Journal of Negro Education*, **56**: 365–8.

Osipow, S.H. (1975), 'The relevance of theories of career development to special groups: problems, needed data and implications', in J.S. Picou and R.E. Campbell (eds), *Career Behavior of Special Groups: Theory, Research, and Practice*, Columbus, OH: Merrill, pp. 9–22.

Peterson, M.F. (1995), 'Leading Cuban-American entrepreneurs: the process of developing motives, abilities, and resources', *Human Relations*, **48**(10): 1193–215.

Portes, A. and Bach, R. (1985), *Latin Journey*, Berkeley, CA: University of California Press.

Reynolds, P.D. (2000), 'National panel study of U.S. business startups: background and methodology', in J.A. Katz (ed.), *Advances in Entrepreneurship, Firm Emergence, and Growth*, Vol. 4, Stamford, CT: JAI Press, pp. 153–227.

Reynolds, P.D., Carter, N.M., Gartner, W.B., Greene, P.G. and Cox, L.W. (2002), *The Entrepreneur Next Door: An Executive Summary of the Panel Study of Entrepreneurial Dynamics*, Kansas City, MO: Kauffman Center for Entrepreneurial Leadership.

Reynolds, P.D., Hay, M., Bygrave, W.D., Camp, S.M. and Autio, E. (2000), *Global Entrepreneurship Monitor: 2000 Executive Report*, Kansas City, MO: Kauffman Center for Entrepreneurial Leadership.

Roe, A. and Lunneborg, P.W. (1990), 'Personality development and career choice', in D. Brown, L. Brooks and Associates (eds), *Career Choice and Development*, 3rd edn, San Francisco, CA: Jossey-Bass, pp. 68–101.

Schein, E.H. (1978), *Career Dynamics: Matching Individual and Organizational Needs*, Reading, MA: Addison-Wesley.

Scheinberg, S. and MacMillan, I.C. (1988), 'An 11 country study of motivations to start a business', in B.A. Kirchhoff, W.A. Long, W.E. McMullan, K.H. Vesper and W.E. Wetzel, Jr (eds), *Frontiers of Entrepreneurship Research*, Wellesley, MA: Babson College, pp. 669–87.

Scherer, R., Adams, J., Carley, S. and Wiebe, F. (1989), 'Role model performance effects on development of entrepreneurial career preference', *Entrepreneurial Theory and Practice*, **13**(3): 3–71.

Scott, T.B. and Anadon, M. (1980), 'A comparison of the vocational interest profiles of Native American and Caucasian college-bound students', *Measurement and Evaluation in Guidance*, **13**(1): 35–42.

Shane, S., Kolvereid, L. and Westhead, P. (1991), 'An exploratory examination of the reasons leading to new firm formation across country and gender', *Journal of Business Venturing*, **6**: 431–46.

Shane, S. and Venkataraman, S. (2000), 'The promise of entrepreneurship as a field of research', *Academy of Management Review*, **25**(1): 217–26.

Smith, E.J. (1983), 'Issues in racial minorities' career behavior', in W.B. Walsh and S.H. Osipow (eds), *Handbook of Vocational Psychology*, Vol. 1, Hillsdale, NJ: Lawrence Erlbaum, pp. 161–221.

Soto, L.D. (1988), 'The home environment of higher and lower achieving Puerto Rican children', *Hispanic Journal of Behavioral Sciences*, **20**: 161–7.

Super, D.E., Sverko, B. and Super, C.M. (1995), *Life Roles, Values and Careers: International Findings of the Work Importance Study*, San Francisco, CA: Jossey-Bass.

Sverko, B. and Super, D.E. (1995), 'The findings of the Work Importance Study', in D.E. Super, B. Sverko and C.M. Super (eds), *Life Roles, Values and Careers: International Findings of the Work Importance Study*, San Francisco, CA: Jossey-Bass.

Thomas, D.A. and Alderfer, C.P. (1989), 'The influence of race on career dynamics: theory and research on minority career experiences', in M.B. Arthur, D.T. Hall and B.S. Lawrence (eds), *Handbook of Career Theory*, Cambridge: Cambridge University Press, pp. 133–58.

US Small Business Administration (1999), *Minority Business*, Washington, DC: Office of Advocacy, Government Printing Office.

US Small Business Administration (2002), *Minorities in Business*, Washington, DC: Office of Advocacy, Government Printing Office.

Waldinger, R., Aldrich, H. and Ward, R. (1990), *Ethnic Entrepreneurs*, Newbury Park, CA: Sage.

20. Career choices of skilled migrants: a holistic perspective

Jawad Syed

INTRODUCTION

Highly skilled migrants constitute an increasingly large component of international migration today (Iredale, 2001). According to an estimate, there are about 1.5 million skilled migrants from developing countries in the industrialized countries alone (Stalker, 2000). Many studies have highlighted the contributions of skilled migrants in improving the economic and political stability of the host countries. Scholars generally agree that immigration tends to maximize opportunity and enrich host economies by shifting human resources from where they are abundant (or less rewarded) to where they are most needed (Kerr, 1997; Benson-Rea and Rawlinson, 2003). Papademetriou and Yale-Loehr (1995, p. 2) argue that, more than ever before, immigration merits an appropriate recognition in the broader strategy of national progress and planning. Indeed, this increased level of mobility manifests the internationalization of professions or professional labour markets (Iredale, 2001), an important subject in contemporary academic and policy research.

Migrant research worldwide is generally informed by human capital theory using quantitative tools to examine how individual attributes of migrants affect their labour market outcomes. The proponents of this theory suggest that human capital has a key role in the career prospects of migrants because occupational achievements have a positive correlation with different levels of productivity (Becker, 1993; Mincer, 1993). Accordingly, an investment in skill is seen as an investment in productivity that returns in terms of income through gainful employment (Mayer, 1995). The critics of human capital theory argue that instead of offering in-depth insights into the issues and challenges faced by migrants, human capital studies tend to causally link employment outcomes to human capital attributes, often narrating success stories of skilled migrants, suggesting that migrants' human capital is well rewarded in the labour market (Ho and Alcorso, 2004). They argue that a human capital emphasis does

464

not adequately encompass the opportunities and challenges faced by migrants in the host economies. Miller's (1999) study highlights how the interaction between an individual and her social contexts is shaped by the structure of occupational opportunity, which in turn affects her career development. Ho (2006) argues that the conventional policy reliance on human-capital-based research serves to simplify much more complex realities faced by skilled migrants in the societal and employment contexts. However, the proponents of human capital theory insist that employment in the migrant economy is a transitional phenomenon because employment markets generally function as an integrative institution, seeking best-qualified and most economical workers regardless of ethnic background (Nee et al., 1994).

The present chapter probes these lines of enquiry and endeavours to offer a holistic perspective of career choices of skilled migrants. The chapter argues that skilled migrants are a people living within a sociocultural and historical context constituting much more than a factor of production flowing across international borders. Accordingly, their career choices are not only shaped by their skills and economic factors, but also by their perceptions of the host environment and the practical challenges of the occupational opportunity structures within the broader sociopolitical context. Thus, instead of confining migrants' career choices to either human capital or cultural–environmental perspectives, there is a need to expand the research lens to economic as well as sociological and psychological aspects of migration.

The chapter is divided into two sections. The first offers an overview of the issues and challenges faced by skilled migrants in the global marketplace. The second proposes a holistic perspective of career choices of skilled migrants based on the discussion in the first section, which is then followed by implications for future research.

SKILLED MIGRANTS IN THE GLOBAL MARKETPLACE

Migration research has traditionally focused on the wage discrimination faced by migrants; however, the issue of continuity or transition of career has not received much attention (Junankar et al., 2004). Few studies have addressed the organizational and sociocultural issues faced by skilled migrants in the process of occupational adjustment (Bagchi, 1999; Chen, 1996). Most studies are predominantly focused on either the job market segmentation or assimilation as a result of migrants' occupational adjustment in the host markets (Waldinger et al., 1998). From a human capital angle, skilled migrants seem to have some advantages in the labour market over unskilled migrants. However, the literature is generally lacking because of its individualistic focus, its neglect of intersectionalities of individuals' migration status with their social role identities, and the assumption that migrants' human capital and their labour market outcomes are essentially linked (Ho, 2006).

In this section, I endeavour to identify and discuss the key factors that affect skilled migrants' career choices, based on a review of migrant research in various geographical contexts. For the purposes of this chapter, skilled workers are defined as having a university degree or extensive experience in a given field (Iredale, 2001). According to the Organization for Economic Cooperation and Development (OECD), this category includes highly skilled specialists, independent executives and senior managers, specialized technicians or tradespersons, investors, businesspersons, and subcontract workers (SOPEMI, 1997, p. 21). First, I examine the economic context of migration and its implications on skilled migrants' careers.

Economic Factors

Governments in the industrialized countries are increasingly relying on economic criteria to regulate and filter migration, arguing that skilled migration has positive implications for national economies (Ho, 2006). Remennick (2003) notes that in most countries, the government only provides the legal basis for migrants' employment in terms of visa and social security regulations, and other formalities in the host economy. It does not usually involve itself in actual accreditation, training and job placement of skilled migrants, which is left to professional associations and migrants' own resources (Iredale, 1997). In an ostensibly neutral emphasis on merit, migrants remain structurally disadvantaged *vis-à-vis* their native-born counterparts due to the lack of social and financial resources and limited language command (Remennick, 2003). However, despite these caveats, a human-capital-based perspective is not without value.

Ho and Alcorso (2004) identify two key strengths of the human-capital-based approach. First, the approach presents an authoritative generalizing account avoiding the painstaking detail of various within-group experiences. Based on an abstract analysis of the complex issues of qualification and experience equivalence, labour market dynamics and sociocultural challenges, human-capital-based studies present a straightforward picture of migration that can be translated directly into government policy. Second, the model of the individual economic actor opting to invest in skills that will deliver returns in the host labour markets does represent the experiences of (at least some) migrants. A human capital approach is also perceptible in Boeri's (2006) study, which suggests that skilled migration may be treated as capital mobility, a phenomenon in which education more than age or gender affects human capital externalities.

Bevelander (1999) argues that the situation of migrants entering the labour market may be compared to the native-born persons who are new entrants or re-entrants to the labour market. Because skills and knowledge about the labour market are not perfectly transferable across national borders, migrants are usually perceived to be less productive, prone to a higher labour market turnover and a lower employment rate. Fletcher (1999) describes the issue of qualification and experience equivalence as a major occupational adjustment challenge in the careers of skilled migrants, which is often ignored by the host economies. Other scholars have described this issue as a mechanism of tacit systemic discrimination against migrant professionals, which restricts their entry to competitive job markets (Boyd, 2000; Iredale, 1997). Lower levels of 'country-specific skills' generally result in the disadvantages that migrants experience in economic assimilation. This skill deficit further widens due to possibly lower socioeconomic status, lack of experience within the host country, poor language skills and other cultural barriers. In time, it is expected that migrants adjust to the new labour market and society through investments that modify and expand their skill base (Bevelander, 1999).

Yet migrants are left to their own devices in the host economies, and resort to informal social networks, mostly co-ethnic, in their search of occupational integration (Bagchi, 1999; Chen, 1996). There is some evidence that in an environment characterized by increasing job market competition and anti-immigration attitudes, challenges faced by migrants become further complicated. Reitz (2001) notes that career choices of skilled migrants in the industrialized countries have been declining since the 1990s. This suggestion is also supported by Peixoto (2001), who notes that the slow occupational adjustment and minimal rates of income growth have typified most independent skilled migrants. Remennick (2003) attributes this phenomenon to structural factors – the rapid influx of skilled migrants along with the growing ranks of native-born specialists. An increasingly competitive job market and a lack of managing diversity policies further exacerbate the career prospects of the newcomers.

Benson-Rea and Rawlinson's (2003) study identifies a number of recruitment-related problems generally encountered by skilled migrants: (1) obstacles around the recognition of overseas qualifications; (2) the lack of local work experience; (3) employers' prejudicial discrimination against prospective applicants with foreign characteristics; (4) insufficient English skills; and (5) overqualification. Lidgard (1996) points to a lack of government policies to integrate skilled migrants into the workforce and culture of the host country. Migrant studies have confirmed the prevalence of many of the aforementioned challenges faced by skilled migrants.

Remennick's (2003) study highlights the challenges faced by Russian migrant engineers in Israel. The engineering profession is generally perceived to be culturally neutral, i.e. not dependent on local culture and social traditions. Remennick notes that the skills and technical disciplines brought by Russian education and practice were quite strong and internationally competitive. In that sense, the employment prospects of migrant engineers were allegedly better than culture-dependent professions such as teaching or journalism. Yet the structural opportunities of the Israeli market were far too limited to incorporate a large number of Russian engineers. Though some niches of the industry expanded and absorbed some engineers, many others remained unemployed. Governmental support in job seeking was able to assist only a small number of younger and more flexible specialists. The net result was a mass de-professionalization and social marginalization of many migrant engineers.

Bevelander's (1999) study of skilled migrants in Sweden suggests that 'cultural proximity' could be a reflection of discrimination faced by skilled migrants, implying that migrants are treated differently for reasons other than productivity. The study found some support for the hypothesis that migrants with the largest cultural distance to Swedes would experience most discrimination. Yet Bevelander also points towards an alternative explanation in which the structural change of the Swedish economy is of crucial importance. The author notes that many monotonous jobs involving low or unskilled labour are increasingly replaced by jobs that require higher communicative and social abilities. This change has visibly shifted labour demand towards specialized knowledge such as culture-specific social competence and language skills. The author proposes that in addition to pure discrimination, the new job market, which favours the soft skills possessed by the native-born, may also be responsible for the diminishing career choices of skilled migrants in Sweden.

In Australia, Ho (2006) notes that skilled migrants constitute the majority of new arrivals in that country because of an increasing policy emphasis on skilled migration over the last two decades. The proponents of the human capital theory in Australia, both within the policy and academic research (Cobb-Clark, 2001; Richardson et al., 2002) have portrayed persistent successful outcomes of skilled migrants in the Australian labour market. For instance, VandenHeuvel and Wooden (2000, p. 64) show that high-qualified migrants are significantly more likely to be in the labour force than those with no post-secondary qualifications. Overall, these studies demonstrate that, compared to other categories of migrants, skilled migrants have higher labour force participation rates, lower unemployment rates, and higher incomes and occupational status. Ho (2006) notes that these findings generally seem to vindicate the Australian government's emphasis on human capital in migrant selection. For instance, the Department of Immigration and Multicultural and Indigenous Affairs (DIMIA, 2001, p. 2), based on these findings, claims that 'a program which is weighted more towards skilled migration will have better overall labour market outcomes and thus a better economic impact than a program which is weighted towards family reunion migration'.

However, in contrast to the success story narrative offered by the Australian government, Junankar et al.'s (2004) study unravels the traces of discrimination within the purported success narratives in Australia, identifying two key issues faced by skilled migrants: first, the probability of being unemployed is likely to be different for the discriminated group (given the same observable characteristics); and second, the transition probabilities of moving from unemployment to employment may be different for the discriminated group. Similar findings are evidenced in other studies. Based on the 1996 and 2001 census data in Australia, Parr and Guo's (2005) study provides a detailed description of the diverse patterns of occupational concentration and mobility of Asian migrants to Australia. The study shows that the Asian-Australian workers are found throughout the occupational structure, and that migrants generally experienced upward occupational mobility between 1996 and 2001. However, after controlling for a range of demographic and human capital characteristics, the participation of most groups in the managerial and professional occupations was found to be below that for the Australia-born. The study demonstrates that the ostensibly high occupational status of Asian skilled migrants does not mean they are advantaged. Yet the study also shows that simply having been born an Australian does not necessarily guarantee one's position in the labour market. It is one's human capital, especially one's educational qualifications, that is more important in determining one's labour market performance.

The above discussion suggests that economic context and human capital considerations play a major role in defining skilled migrants career trajectories and possibilities in the host market, yet it will be amiss to ignore broader cultural–environmental contexts of which the labour market is just one component.

Sociological Factors

A human-capital-based success narrative has been challenged by many scholars who argue that skilled migrants do not always successfully transfer their skills to new labour markets. Ho (2006) contends that the conventional 'success narrative' disguises the complex contextual realities, in which migrants' employment outcomes are also influenced by broader sociocultural factors. For instance, she highlights the role of gender and other social role identities, and demonstrates that men and women typically experience migration differently in the host labour market. Migrants' careers and skills are deeply related not only to their gender role identities, but also to other social factors such as command of local language and traditions.

Migrant research in English-speaking countries has generally focused on income levels of migrants, highlighting significant differences between English-speaking background (ESB) migrants and non-English-speaking background (NESB) migrants. Junankar et al.'s (2004) comparative study in Australia found that education was not a significant variable responsible for differential career opportunities for Asian migrants and native-born Australians. In line with Chapman and Iredale's (1990) findings, Junankar and colleagues acknowledge the possibility that employers do not value Asian qualifications as highly as non-Asian qualifications. They also acknowledge that the employment differences between Asian and non-Asian migrants could also be due to non-Asians having access to better social networks in the labour market. Through their empirical analysis, Junankar and colleagues found significant differences between Asian and non-Asian migrants that could not be explained by the usual explanatory variables such as human capital and demography. The authors found *prima facie* evidence for discrimination against Asian migrants, which they suggested could be attributed to pure discrimination or employers' lack of willingness adequately to recognize the qualifications of Asian migrants.

Junankar and Mahuteau's (2005) study demonstrates that an emphasis on skilled migration in Australia had a positive impact on the probability of finding a job, but a negative impact on holding a good job. Skilled migrants were found to be less likely to hold a good job after controlling for other demographic variables, including education and visa category.

Ho's (2006) study challenges the prevailing understandings of migrant employment in two ways. First, while the orthodox explanations draw a causal link between migrants' human capital and their employment outcomes, they ignore the gendered character of labour market experiences. Second, prevailing accounts of migrant employment, reliant on quantitative data, fail to show how employment patterns are experienced by migrants. Ho's (2006) interviews with Chinese women in Australia demonstrated that changing relationships with the labour market reflect a much deeper evolution of migrants' gender identities. Migration to Australia meant fundamental shifts in how these women identified with their various roles as wives, mothers and income earners, and changed their personal priorities and aspirations in ways that could not be captured in statistics. The issue of intersectional identities was also addressed by Remennick (2003), who reported that Russian engineers in Israel, particularly women and older engineers, were at an additional disadvantage: most of them got off their professional track altogether. This resulted in mass de-professionalization for these migrants, many of whom had been recognized specialists in their field.

Reyneri (2004) notes that the large-scale presence of migrants with high educational levels, and their employment in low-profile, low-paid jobs inconsistent with their skills and abilities, can be explained by workplace discrimination. The same author finds that in the countries of longstanding immigration of Central and Northern Europe, the problem has exploded only with the second generation, when the children of poorly educated migrants found themselves unable to obtain skilled jobs to the same extent as their classmates from 'mainstream' backgrounds. Reyneri notes that in Italy, discrimination has been evident since the beginnings of immigration, and that in many cases a poor knowledge of Italian has been offered as a justification for discrimination (Reyneri, 2004). Reyneri also highlights the extreme precariousness in which the majority of migrants live. Despite frequent amnesties, many of them do not have proper residence permits, not least because it is not always easy to renew them upon expiry (Reyneri, 2001). Many legal migrants live in precarious conditions because of the difficulties of obtaining a permanent residence permit or Italian citizenship, a lack of access to social benefits, and a lack of academic accreditation (Reyneri, 2004).

In addition to education and skill, Bevelander (1999) identifies other demographic characteristics such as age, sex and civil status as the key determinants of employment. Bevelander notes the visible impact of social identity roles on the career trajectories of migrants in Sweden. For instance, employment levels appeared to be greater among married men and women. Labour market adjustment appeared to be easier for migrants from countries that have similarities with the Swedish society, such as language proximity, occupational transferability, and a similar structure of the labour market in the country of origin. The motivation for migration and the possibilities for return were also identified as important issues in migrants' adjustment in the host labour market.

Other studies have demonstrated that the sociocultural differences result in diminished career growth for skilled migrants, possibly resulting in a glass ceiling. Waldinger et al.'s (1998) study examined native/migrant differences in male graduate engineers in the USA over the course of their engineering career. The study offers a valuable insight to assess the broader glass ceiling claims faced by skilled migrants. As recipients of at one or more US degree, the migrants in the sample were perceived to be far less likely than foreign-born engineers to face issues related to qualification accreditation or language barriers. And as the graduates of a major US research university, the migrants were expected to enter the labour market with prestigious credentials. The results from their study suggest that some form of labour market segmentation, so common at lower levels of the economy, is also restricting the mobility of the highly skilled foreign-born engineers in the USA. The study demonstrates that migrants receive a significantly lower return to experience than do their native-born counter-parts. Consequently, their careers take distinctively different shapes. As a highly selective group, originating from advantaged circumstances, the foreign-born engineers in their sample began with a very slight advantage. That lead, however, diminished steadily over the course of the career: after 17 years of experience, native-born engineers surpassed their migrant coun-terparts, enjoying continuous earnings growth. By contrast, the foreign-born engineers not only lost any previous advantage, but also found that their earnings declined in the later stages of the career. The authors inter-pret this finding as evidence of discrimination (glass ceiling), particularly in view of the respondents' perceptions of the opportunity structure they had confronted in the host economy.

The above discussion suggests that sociological factors, such as language, ethnic origin and other sociocultural attributes have a visible influence on the prospects of migrants' employment in the host economies. Yet all of these migrants have their own unique personalities, and possess unique per-ceptions of the host market and ways to respond to the challenges faced during their personal and professional lives. The issue of individual agency and psychological factors will be discussed in the next section.

Psychological Factors

Since a career is an outcome of the interaction between individuals and organizational and social structures, it is useful to examine the career from organizational sociology as well as occupational psychology perspectives (Özbilgin et al., 2005). Carter and Cook (1992, p. 199) argue that from a cultural perspective, work may be treated as 'a functional aspect of life in that individuals contribute their skills and labour to their cultural societies and the maintenance of their families'. In this vein, the meaning of career, the value placed on it, and the expectations about who will choose what type of career, is defined by the society in which work is organized (Fouad and Byars-Winston, 2005).

Özbilgin et al. (2005) examine two highly polarized views on possible influences on career choice: the centrality of individual agency in career choice (including dispositions, human capital, attitudes and personality), and the opportunity structures and constraints that make available and limit career choice. They argue that compared to agentic career choice focused on individual control and predictability of career, opportunity structures and contextual affordance are important constructs, through which the effects of the structural conditions on the choice process can be studied. Both of these constructs focus on the resources or hardships that are embedded in the individual career context (Lent and Brown, 1996). The emphasis on agentic career choice theory has been discussed by many scholars.

Marshall (1989) criticizes the traditional theories of career choice for accepting agentic masculine career behaviour as normative. Mignot (2000) argues that agentic theories are unable to explain the role of structural and cultural factors in shaping individual career choice behaviour in a systematic way. Özbilgin and colleagues (2005) argue that, despite the fact that the researchers continue to draw causal relationships of unidirectional and linear influence of agency and structure in shaping career choice, individual agency cannot be isolated from contextual factors and that there is an interplay between the two in shaping career choices. As an alternative framework to explore the complex interplay of agency and structure, Özbilgin and colleague propose a three-pronged approach, allowing for a layered study of influences on career choice at three levels. At the micro-level of the self, there are factors such as individual agency, dispositions and different forms of capital as key influences on individual choice. The meso-level involves the processes that mediate and negotiate career choices in the light of individual desires, capital and contextual circumstances. At the macro-level are structural conditions that inhibit or enhance career choice. The three-pronged analysis offers a useful perspective to examine individual career choice as a negotiated process, which is socially and historically situated, interwoven in the broader complexity.

Indeed, the concept of work holds different meanings for different people as a function of their sociocultural, historical and political experiences (Cheatham, 1990). Given the difficulties skilled migrants generally confront in achieving satisfactory employment outcomes (Lidgard, 1996), it is also important to understand migrants' expectations upon migration (Benson-Rea and Rawlinson, 2003). Ip (1997) suggests that migrants themselves do not feel settled in the labour market until they are employed in jobs related to previous experience. Much of this occupational adjustment is to do with the individual identity and the psychological experiences of the migrants. Cultural context has a key role not only in terms of individuals' identity formation, but also how they choose their work and are able to follow different career paths.

It is generally acknowledged that ethnic minority migrants from developing countries enter a labour market in which their own ethnic group is usually concentrated in low-profile, low-paid occupations, influencing their perception of the opportunities available to them (BLS, 2002). In addition, such migrants are often faced with challenges of racism and discrimination. Consequently, their perspectives about work and career are naturally different from those of their native-born counterparts (Fouad and Byars-Winston, 2005).

Waldinger and colleagues (1998) study demonstrated that, compared to the native-born, and after controlling for other background characteristics, the migrant engineers to the USA are significantly more likely to report that they have experienced some act of work-related discrimination, and are significantly more likely to believe that knowing the right people and being an Anglo are very important for getting ahead. Given the consistency between the economic disparities revealed by Waldinger and colleagues (1998) and the disparate perceptions of opportunity expressed by migrants, the authors expressed their 'confidence in concluding' that a glass ceiling indeed exists for skilled migrants.

The role of race and social class in development and its psychological implications have been examined by many scholars (e.g. Gainor and Lent, 1998; Fouad and Brown, 2000). Astin's (1984) socio-psychological causal model of career choice examines both psychological and cultural–environmental factors. The psychological context of career choice deals with the aspects of work motivation and work expectations, while the cultural–environmental context deals with the issues of gender role socialization (and other forms of social identity) and the structure of opportunity factors. Turner and Turner (1995) suggest that a socio-psychological perspective is instrumental to explain how the perceptions of occupational opportunity affect career aspirations and choices. Griffith (1980) argues that a differential career opportunity structure exists for all people, which influences how various professional groups are socialized to work as well as the development of their career aspirations, expectations and workplace behaviours.

This consideration of the structure of occupational opportunity and its implications for career development is important to understanding the interaction between an individual and the social contexts that constitute her environment (Miller, 1999). Fouad and Byars-Winston (2005) note that this interaction has not been incorporated into traditional theories of career choice and development, such as Holland's theory of personalities in work environments (Spokane et al., 2002), Super's developmental theory (Super et al., 1996), or the theory of work adjustment (Dawis, 1996). However, the interlinkage between individual and society is now being increasingly explored by career scholars. Pines (2004) examined the relationship between adult attachment styles and burnout, a phenomenon that is generally perceived to characterize highly motivated individuals. Based on a psychodynamic existential perspective, Pines's findings supported the hypothesis that adult attachment styles correlate with burnout. The study demonstrates that in addition to contextual factors, personal factors play a key role in the psychological well-being of individuals.

Meijering and Hoven (2003) studied the experiences of Indian IT professionals who migrated to Germany through migration channels within transnational corporations. The authors note that in many ways, the Indian IT migrants appeared to be privileged, as they were offered generous relocation packages, economic security and quasi-guaranteed career advancement. However, the study demonstrates that the relationship between the skilled migrant and the host culture is largely one of economic functionality that serves the mutual needs of both parties. The personal narratives of migrants indicated that their migration experiences are much more than simply functional. Their experiences appeared to be marked by daily struggles when trying to establish a sense of home away from home. One major problem the study identified was the inability of the migrants to speak German fluently. Inhibited by communication barriers, the respondents could not establish contacts with Germans, a difference that was further compounded by the additional differences in family structures, social structures and work culture. The study also revealed the fear of discrimination largely based on an image created through the media: the migrants felt threatened by their representation as guest workers taking over 'German' jobs. Left to their own devices, migrants were found to be involved in frequent contacts by phone or mail to the family 'at home', as well as the development of ethnic circles of friends. Symbolic resources, such as the preparation and sharing of ethnic meals, surfaced as important mechanisms that emphasized the dislocation of the migrants from their host culture.

Robinson and Carey's (2000) interviews with Indian doctors in the UK highlighted the multilayered and highly complex nature of migration. The authors note that migration from India is embedded within British colonial legacies, prior histories of migration and a common cultural drive for honour (*izzet*). Even though Indian doctors were highly skilled and relatively highly paid, their migration was embedded in Indian culture. Robinson and Carey suggest that there is a need to move well beyond functionalist theory and neoclassical economics and see highly skilled labour not only as 'subordinated to an economic logic' (Goss and Lindquist, 1995, p. 317), but also as people with a sociocultural and historical context. Robinson and Carey (2000) suggest that by peopling skilled migration, it could be easy to understand such migrations and also recognize that highly skilled migration is internally differentiated on criteria other than skills or qualifications such as gender, race and ethnicity.

However, not all career differentials are attributable to the issues related to ethnicity or race. Fouad and Byars-Winston's (2005) study demonstrates that race or ethnicity does not always play a major role in career aspirations and career interests. The authors acknowledged, however, that the perception of occupational opportunity appeared to be strongly related to race/ethnicity, and that race/ethnicity greatly influenced perceptions of career barriers. Combined, these findings indicate that individuals' career dreams (aspirations) are similar, yet their perceptions of the opportunity to realize these dreams could be very different based on their racial/ethnic identities. Some of these individuals may take some decisions that might have long-lasting implications for their careers. In their study of former Soviet professionals in the USA, Vinokurov et al. (2000) examined a crucial occupational choice faced by skilled migrants, i.e. whether to accept any available job with (or without) a reasonable wage, or to wait for an appropriate professional post. Pines and Yanai (2001) suggest that career burnout occurs when people no longer believe that their work is meaningful to their existence. Career burnout is also related to the unconscious causes underlying their selection of specific occupations, which are generally related to their feelings about work and lifestyle.

Hawthorne's (1997) study reveals that professional achievements by skilled migrants often come at significantly higher than average personal cost and effort. Junankar and Mahuteau's (2005) study shows that the number of people composing the migrant's household affects the quality of the job found in the host labour market. The larger the household, the less likely the migrant holds or reports holding a good job. The study suggests that a larger family puts more strain on the principal applicant: they are likely to lower their reservation quality quickly after their arrival in the host market, accepting whichever job is offered in order to meet the urgent needs of the family. Remennick (2003) suggests that the delay of career-related activities until 'better times' may adversely affect migrants' careers because the separation from the profession along with the routine of unskilled work tends to gradually diminish both motivation and ability to get back to professional work.

A HOLISTIC PERSPECTIVE OF CAREER CHOICES

Informed by Astin's (1984) socio-psychological causal model of career choice, as well as the much-contested human capital theory, this chapter has examined psychological and cultural–environmental issues faced by skilled migrants, and their implications for migrants' career trajectories within the host economies. The chapter has demonstrated that due to the context (sociological and psychological circumstances) and the content (human capital) of migration, the career choices available to skilled migrants are much different from those of their native-born counterparts. The customary human capital narrative of skilled migrants' success story, which is based on their comparison with unskilled migrants, tends to ignore the socio-psychological challenges faced by skilled migrants. Similarly, a socio-psychological perspective of migration does not capture the role of content factors (skills and recognition) in employability and productivity in the host economies. The chapter has endeavoured to offer a holistic perspective from which to examine the career trajectories of skilled migrants, suggesting that policies based on such a perspective may be useful not only for individuals but also for the host economies (see Table 20.1).

Table 20.1 demonstrates that in addition to a focus on the economic context of employment, the policy makers need to take into account the sociological and psychological issues faced by skilled migrants, which have enormous implications for their occupational adjustment in the host market.

In addition to the unique values offered by human capital theory as discussed in this chapter, the inclusion of economic context in the proposed holistic model is expected to make it attractive for policy makers, business organizations and politicians. Indeed, policy reports in national and international contexts are increasingly based on a recent reformulation of human capital theory, emphasizing the significance of education and training as the key to participation in a global economy. For instance, the OECD (1997, p. 11) asserts that 'internationalism should be seen as a preparation for 21st century capitalism' and that internationalism may be treated as 'a means to improve the quality of education' (ibid., p. 8). Foray and Lundvall (1996, p. 21) argue that 'the overall economic performance of the OECD countries is increasingly more directly based upon their knowledge stock and their learning capabilities'. Clearly, the OECD is attempting to produce a new role for education in terms of the human capital needed in 'globalised' institutions (Fitzsimons, 1999).

The chapter has also demonstrated the need for policy and academic research to attend to the complex perceptions and the associated environmental realities faced by skilled migrants, particularly from culturally distant backgrounds in the host economies. Future research may apply within-group as well as ethnicity-based designs to explore important differences related to ethnicity, gender, social class, or developmental stage (Fouad and Byars-Winston, 2005). Researchers are encouraged to move to an examination of contextual variables that influence the career development process, and real and perceived limitations in the career choices of skilled migrants. In particular, there is a need to examine important

Table 20.1 A holistic perspective of career choices of skilled migrants

Intervening factors	Description	Implications for careers
Economic		
Occupational opportunity structures	Labour market conditions; industrial infrastructure; occupational classification and accreditation; demand and supply of skill	Skill loss; deprofessionalization
Labour laws and policies	Equal employment opportunity policies and practices	Glass door and glass ceiling; income inequalities
Culture dependency of professions	Culture-dependent professions are hard to transfer, e.g. teaching and journalism	Differential career opportunities
Qualifications and experience	Foreign qualifications and experiences, particularly from developing countries, are generally less valued	Downward mobility; deprofessionalization
Culture-specific social skills and communication	Jobs involving culture-specific interpersonal and communication skills are considered inadequate for migrants; 'adequate' language and accent requirements	Differential career opportunities
Sociological		
Sociopolitical environment	Government policies and laws towards immigration and discrimination; representation of ethnic minorities in media; social stereotypes	Discrimination in social and employment contexts
Social networks	Ethnic networks of migrants; social support networks provided by the government; job search support; access to jobs	Job market segregation or assimilation
Intersectional identities	Intersection of migration status with visa category, household, gender, class, ethnicity, race, religion, age and other attributes	Multiple disadvantages

Cultural distance	Cultural differences between migrants' host country and the country of origin, e.g. religious differences, collectivist–individualist differences	Discrimination; negative stereotypes; contextual emotional labour
Family structures	Nuclear or extended family responsibilities of migrants; urgency to find a job	Downward mobility; deprofessionalization
Duration of stay	Migrants are generally perceived to overcome structural barriers in the long term	Occupational adjustment
Psychological		
Personal beliefs and attitudes	Migrants' lifestyles and values; work–family balance	Contextual emotional labour; job stress
Work motivation	Perception of work (e.g. career as a means to end, or an end in itself); career aspirations (e.g. career path improvement, personal development and financial gains); culture-specific sources of motivation	Pre-migration careers and work expectations; career burnout
Perception of barriers	Post-migration 'realities'; experiences in the host economy marketplace	Demotivation; skill loss

components of individuals' personalities and sociological contexts, such as ethnicity, gender and family structures, and their intersection with their skills, visa status and duration of stay in the host economies.

REFERENCES

Astin, H. (1984), 'The meaning of work in women's lives: a sociopsychological model of career choice and work behavior', *The Counseling Psychologist*, **12**: 117–26.

Bagchi, A.D. (1999), *Making Connections: A Study of the Social Network of Immigrant Professionals*, Madison, WI: University of Wisconsin at Madison Dissertation Abstracts International (The Humanities and Social Sciences), **60**(6).

Becker, G.S. (1993), *Human Capital*, vol. 3, Chicago, IL: The University of Chicago Press.

Benson-Rea, M. and Rawlinson, S. (2003), 'Highly skilled and business migrants: information processes and settlement outcomes', *International Migration*, **41**(2): 59–79.

Bevelander, P. (1999), 'The employment integration of migrants in Sweden', *Journal of Ethnic and Migration Studies*, **25**(3): 445–68.

Boeri, T. (2006), 'Growth, labour markets and migration', paper presented at 'Global Convergence Scenarios: Structural and Policy Issues', OECD, Paris, 16 January.

BLS (Bureau of Labor Statistics) (2002), '2002 occupational employment statistics', (www.bls.gov, accessed 24 August 2004).

Boyd, M. (2000), 'Matching workers to work: the case of Asian immigrant engineers in Canada', Working Paper No. 14, San Diego, CA: University of California, The Center for Comparative Immigration Studies.

Carter, R.T. and Cook, D.A. (1992), 'A culturally relevant perspective for understanding the career paths of visible racial/ethnic group people', in H.D. Lea and Z.B. Leibowitz (eds), *Adult Career Development: Concepts, Issues, and Practices*, Alexandria, VA: National Career Development Association, pp. 192–217.

Chapman, B. and Iredale, R.R. (1990), 'Immigrant qualification recognition and relevant wage outcomes', Discussion Paper No. 240, Canberra: Australian National University, Centre for Economic Policy Research.

Cheatham, H.E. (1990), 'Africentricity and career development of African Americans', *The Career Development Quarterly*, **38**: 334–46.

Chen, I.H. (1996), *Work Values, Acculturation, and Job Satisfaction among Chinese Immigrant Professionals*, New York: New York University, Dissertation Abstracts International (The Humanities and Social Sciences), **57**(3): 1332-A.

Cobb-Clark, D. (2001), 'Settling in: public policy and the labour market adjustment of new immigrants to Australia', Canberra: Australian National University, (http://econrsss.anu.edu.au/~dcclark/docs/papers/lsia_compare_13.pdf, accessed 10 May 2004).

Dawis, R.V. (1996), 'The theory of work adjustment and person–environment correspondence counseling', in D. Brown, L. Brooks and Associates (eds), *Career Choice and Development*, San Francisco, CA: Jossey-Bass, pp. 75–120.

DIMIA (2001), DIMIA Fact Sheet 14: Migrant Labour Market Outcomes (www.immi.gov.au/facts/141abour.htm, accessed 10 September 2005).

Fitzsimons, P. (1999), 'Human capital theory and education', *Encyclopaedia of Philosophy of Education*, (www.vusst.hr/ENCYCLOPAEDIA/humancapital. htm, accessed 1 October 2006).

Fletcher, M. (1999), *Migrant Settlement: A Review of the Literature and its Relevance to New Zealand*, prepared for New Zealand Immigration Service and Department of Labour, September.

Foray, D. and Lundvall, B. (1996), 'The knowledge-based economy: from the economics of knowledge to the learning economy', *Employment and Growth in the Knowledge-based Economy*, OECD Documents, Paris: OECD.

Fouad, N.A. and Brown, M. (2000), 'Role of race and social class in development: implications for counseling psychology', in S.D. Brown and R.W. Lent (eds), *Handbook of Counseling Psychology*, New York: Wiley, pp. 379–410.

Fouad, N.A. and Byars-Winston, A.M. (2005), 'Cultural context of career choice: meta-analysis of race/ethnicity differences', *The Career Development Quarterly*, **53**: 223–33.

Gainor, K.A. and Lent, R.W. (1998), 'Social cognitive expectations and racial identity attitudes in predicting the math choice intentions of Black college students', *Journal of Counseling Psychology*, **45**: 403–13.

Goss, J. and Lindquist, B. (1995), 'Conceptualising international labour migration: a structuration perspective', *International Migration Review*, **29**: 317–51.

Griffith, A.R. (1980), 'Justification for a Black career development', *Counselor Education and Supervision*, **19**: 301–9.

Hawthorne, L. (1997), 'The question of discrimination: skilled migrants' access to Australian employment', *International Migration*, **35**(3): 395–417.

Ho, C. (2006), 'Migration as feminisation? Chinese women's experiences of work and family in Australia', *Journal of Ethnic and Migration Studies*, **23**(3): 497–514.

Ho, C. and Alcorso, C. (2004), 'Migrants and employment: challenging the success story', *Journal of Sociology*, **40**(3): 237–59.

Ip, M. (1997), 'Successful settlement of migrants and relevant factors for setting immigration targets', paper presented at 'The Population Conference', Te Papa Tongarewa, New Zealand, 12–14 November.

Iredale, R. (1997), *Skills Transfer: International Migration and Accreditation Issues*, Wollongong: University of Wollongong Press.

Iredale, R. (2001), 'The migration of professionals: theories and typologies', *International Migration*, **39**(5): 7–26.

Junankar, P.N. and Mahuteau, S. (2005), 'Do migrants get good jobs? New migrant settlement in Australia', *The Economic Record*, **81**(255): S34–S46.

Junankar, P.N., Paul, S. and Yasmeen, W. (2004), 'Are Asian migrants discriminated against in the labour market? A case study of Australia', *IZA Discussion Papers 1167*, Institute for the Study of Labor.

Kerr, R. (1997), 'Population, immigration and the labour market', *Proceedings of the Population Conference*, Te Papa Tongarewa, New Zealand, 12–14 November, pp. 137–40.

Lent, R.W. and Brown, S.D. (1996), 'Social cognitive approach to career development: an overview', *Career Development Quarterly*, **44**(4): 310–22.

Lidgard, J.M. (1996), 'East Asian migration to Aotearoa/New Zealand: perspectives of some new arrivals', Discussion paper no. 12, Population Studies Centre, University of Waikato, Hamilton.

Marshall, J. (1989), 'Re-visioning career concept: a feminist invitation', in M.B. Arthur, D.T. Hall and B.S. Lawrance (eds), *Handbook of Career Theory*, New York: Cambridge University Press, pp. 275–91.

Mayer, K.U. (1995), 'Education and work in an ageing population', in A. Burgen (ed.), *Goals and Purposes of Higher Education in the 21st Century* (Higher Education Policy Series No. 32), London: Kingsley, pp. 69–95.

Meijering, L. and van Hoven, B. (2003), 'Imagining difference: the experiences of "transnational" Indian IT professionals in Germany', *Area*, **35**(2): 174–82.

Mignot, P. (2000), 'Metaphor: a paradigm for practice-based research into "career"', *British Journal of Guidance and Counselling*, **28**(4): 515–31.

Miller, V.M. (1999), 'The opportunity structure: implications for career counseling', *Journal of Employment Counseling*, **36**: 2–12.

Mincer, J. (1993), *Studies in Human Capital*, Aldershot, UK and Brookfield, USA: Edward Elgar.

Nee, V., Sanders, J.M. and Sernau, S. (1994), 'Job transitions in an immigrant metropolis–ethnic boundaries and the mixed economy', *American Sociological Review*, **59**(6): 849–72.

OECD (1997), *Internationalisation of Higher Education*, Paris: Centre for Educational Research and Innovation.

Özbilgin, M., Küskü, F. and Erdoğmuş, N. (2005), 'Explaining influences on career "choice": the case of MBA students in comparative perspective', *International Journal of Human Resource Management*, **16**(11): 2000–2028.

Papademetriou, D. and Yale-Loehr, S. (1995), *Putting the National Interest First: Rethinking the Selection of Skilled Immigrants*, International Migration Policy Program, Washington, DC: Carnegie Endowment for International Peace.

Parr, N. and Guo, F. (2005), 'The occupational concentration and mobility of Asian immigrants in Australia', *Asian and Pacific Migration Journal*, **14**(3): 351–80.

Peixoto, J. (2001), 'The international mobility of highly skilled workers in transnational corporations: the macro and micro factors of the organizational migration of cadres', *International Migration Review*, **35**(4): 1030–53.

Pines, A.M. (2004), 'Adult attachment styles and their relationship to burnout: a preliminary, cross-cultural investigation', *Work and Stress*, **18**(1): 66–80.

Pines, A.M. and Yanai, Y.O. (2001), 'Unconscious determinants of career choice and burnout: theoretical model and counseling strategy', *Journal of Employment Counseling*, **38**: 170–84.

Reitz, J. (2001), 'Immigrant success in the "knowledge economy": institutional change and the immigrant experience in Canada, 1970–1995', *Journal of Social Issues*, **57**(3): 579–613.

Remennick, L. (2003), 'Career continuity among migrant professionals: Russian engineers in Israel', *Journal of Ethnic and Migration Studies*, **29**(4): 701–21.

Reyneri, E. (2004), 'Education and the occupational pathways of migrants in Italy', *Journal of Ethnic and Migration Studies*, **30**(6): 1145–62.

Reyneri, E. (2001), *Migrants in Irregular Employment in the Mediterranean Countries of the European Union*, Geneva: International Labour Office, International Migration Papers, 41.

Richardson, S., Miller-Lewis, L., Ngo, P. and Illsley, D. (2002), *The Settlement Experiences of New Migrants: A Comparison of Wave One of LSIA 1 and LSIA 2*, report prepared for the Department of Immigration and Multicultural and Indigenous Affairs, Commonwealth of Australia.

Robinson, V. and Carey, M. (2000), 'Peopling skilled international migration: Indian doctors in the UK', *International Migration*, **38**(1): 89–108.

SOPEMI (1997), *Trends in International Migration*, Continuous Reporting System on Migration Annual Report 1996, Paris: OECD.

Spokane, A.R., Luchetta, E.J. and Richwine, M.H. (2002), 'Holland's theory of personalities in work environments', in D. Brown (ed.), *Career Choice and Development*, 4th edn, San Francisco, CA: Jossey-Bass, pp. 373–426.

Stalker, P. (2000), *Workers Without Frontiers. The Impact of Globalization on International Migration*, Geneva: International Labour Organization.

Super, D.E., Savickas, M.L. and Super, C.M. (1996), 'The life-span, life-space approach to careers', in D. Brown, L. Brooks and Associates (eds), *Career Choice and Development*, San Francisco, CA: Jossey-Bass, pp. 121–78.

Turner, C. and Turner, B. (1995), 'Race and sex discrimination in occupations: a 20-year replication', paper presented at the annual meeting of the Eastern Psychological Association, Boston.

VandenHeuvel, A. and Wooden, M. (2000), 'Immigrants' labour market experiences in the early settlement years', *Australian Bulletin of Labour*, **26**(1): 59–69.

Vinokurov, A., Birman, D. and Trickett, E. (2000), 'Psychological and acculturation correlates of work status among Soviet Jewish refugees in the United States', *International Migration Review*, **34**(2): 538–59.

Waldinger, R., Bozorgmehr, M., Lim, N. and Finkel, L. (1998), 'In search of the glass ceiling: the career trajectories of migrant and native-born engineers', The Lewis Center for Regional Policy Studies, Working Paper No. 28, Los Angeles, CA.

21. A comparative study on career choice influences of Turkish Cypriot restaurateurs in North Cyprus and the UK

Gözde İnal and Mine Karataş-Özkan

INTRODUCTION

The aim of this study is to generate comparative insights into the influences on career choices of Turkish Cypriot restaurateurs in North Cyprus and the UK. The overall research question is as follows: 'How does migration, as a social movement that is situated in context, affect the career choice of Turkish Cypriot restaurateurs at the micro-level?' The study builds on the work carried out by Özbilgin et al. (2005). Drawing on a layered and multifaceted approach in analysing social phenomena (Layder, 1993), the authors have developed a comprehensive framework that illuminates micro-, meso- and macro-level influences on career choices of MBA students. This research applies it in the context of the career choices of Turkish Cypriot restaurant owners. Their initial decision to start an entrepreneurial career and career choice in the restaurant sector is investigated. The results of the study have revealed a number of significant influences on such choices: family background in the restaurant businesses (early childhood experiences, role models, also Turkish Cypriots who were involved in the catering sector), schooling in catering management, superior financial rewards, good earnings to be made (financial reasons), the desire to practise own skills and competencies (self-interest, self-motivation), lack of alternative career opportunities (especially in the UK) and the need for control and autonomy are the key influences.

This chapter is structured in the following way. The first section conceptualizes a process-relational approach to entrepreneurial careers, drawing on earlier studies in the domain. This is followed by a discussion of the pertinent literature on business start-up reasons of ethnic minority small-business owners. Then research methods are outlined. Finally, discussion of research findings is presented.

484

A PROCESS-RELATIONAL APPROACH TO ENTREPRENEURIAL CAREERS

Entrepreneurship and careers have attracted increasing attention since the 1990s in academic circles. As with entrepreneurship, 'entrepreneurial career' is a contested term. In recent career literature, career is defined as an encompassing term that is broader than just work or job moves (Dexter et al., 2005). Building on a seminal work by Dyer (1994), entrepreneurial career is conceptualized in this chapter as careers of those who founded new enterprises as part of their relational–developmental trajectory through life. The elements of this conceptualization are worth emphasizing.

First, business start-up choice at the micro-individual level is important. Why someone would choose to start a new enterprise has been at the forefront of the discussion in studies pertaining to entrepreneurial intentions and actions (Bird, 1988; Krueger and Carsrud, 1993; Kolvereid, 1997; Krueger et al., 2000). The opportunity to make a living and generate social and economic wealth is considered to be highly influential for many individuals in choosing an entrepreneurial career (Feldman and Bolino, 2000; Chell, 2001). Financial success, independence and self-realization are often cited as important career reasons for nascent entrepreneurs (Carter et al., 2003), which can be located at the micro-individual level (Özbilgin et al., 2005). Second, process-relational dynamics of career development need to be understood. The kinds of socialization experiences (Shapero, 1982; Reynolds, 1991; Dyer, 1994; Bygrave and Minniti, 2000) that motivate and prepare individuals to embark on such entrepreneurial careers should be explored. This includes development of various forms of capital, such as cultural, social and economic capital (Bourdieu, 1986); and transformations between these different forms of capital, as will be explored in the context of Turkish Cypriot restaurateurs. In this particular study, migration is viewed as an important social movement that affects the employment and socialization experiences of individuals. Third, the macro-context in which such career development unfolds should be taken into account in exploring the topic of entrepreneurial careers.

In studying entrepreneurial experience, Dyer (1992) notes key influences as early childhood experiences, the need for control, frustration with traditional careers, challenge and excitement, and role models. Role models have been a recurring theme in entrepreneurship and career studies. The discussion can be traced back to social learning theory (SLT) as expounded by Bandura (1977), which proposes that one way learning can occur vicariously, through the observation of behaviours in others, referred to as role models. 'Role models' act as important factors in forming career choices. Observing, serving, identifying with and appreciating the behaviour of others make certain choices more obvious than others (Bandura, 1977; Scherer et al., 1989). The importance of entrepreneurial role models in the backgrounds of practising entrepreneurs has been identified in a number of studies (Brockhaus and Horwitz, 1986; Hisrich and Brush, 1984; Scherer et al., 1989). Using SLT, Scherer et al. (1989) explored the career decision-making process of business students. Their findings illustrate that the entrepreneurial career is a multidimensional phenomenon, with an important dimension being presence of a parental entrepreneurial role model. It is associated with increased education and training aspirations, task self-efficacy, and expectation of an entrepreneurial career. In the context of the current study, meso-relational dynamics deriving from migration are prevalent in influencing the career choices of ethnic minority small-business owners.

BUSINESS START-UP REASONS FOR ETHNIC MINORITY SMALL-BUSINESS OWNERS

There are many reasons why ethnic minorities choose small-business ownership or self-employment. Self-employment is viewed in this study as one form of nascent entrepreneurial career. Self-employed people may choose to develop their enterprise, leading to small-business ownership. Later, as they grow the business, and generate further economic and social wealth in the community, that would be regarded as an entrepreneurial career. Borooah and Hart (1999) argue that some people are 'pushed' into self-employment because it provides a better option to unemployment. Other people are 'pulled' into self-employment due to possible expected status, attracted by the rewards and independence that it offers. 'Pull' reasons include making more money, recognizing an ethnic niche, wanting to be independent, wanting to increase one's social status in the community or wanting to control one's own life. These 'pull' reasons are closely related to cultural explanations for ethnic self-employees, such as cultural heritage or spirit of enterprise (Basu, 1998; Waldinger et al., 1990; Werbner, 1990).

On the other hand, 'push' reasons are argued to be related to having no or limited chances of finding a paid job or salaried work (Basu, 1998; Boorah and Hart, 1999). They can also be related to 'blocked upward mobility', so that ethnic minorities join self-employment to prevent any possible discrimination in the labour market (Auster and Aldrich, 1984). These negative circumstances play an important role in ethnic minorities' business entry decisions (Aldrich et al., 1981; Clark and Drinkwater, 1998; Jones et al., 1994; Metcalf et al., 1996; Ram, 1992, cited by Basu and Altınay, 2000). Basu (1998) suggests that this view is supported more generally by

Storey (1994). He argued that the move towards self-employment in the UK during the 1980s might be explained by the fact that although the expected income from self-employment may be lower than that from employment, it is higher than that from unemployment. One explanation emphasizes the role of pure prejudice as a reaction in pushing members of ethnic minorities into self-employment and small-business owing to discrimination in the labour market. The shrinking job market of the 1970s exacerbated the problem so that Asian immigrants were left with a choice of being either unemployed or self-employed (Jones et al., 1992).

For Indians, the 'pull' factors are their main cause of entry into self-employment (Barrett et al., 1996). It has been suggested that Pakistanis and Bangladeshis suffer from poorer employment prospects, discrimination and racism at work than Indians in the UK. Therefore Pakistanis and Bangladeshis are motivated to enter self-employment more by 'push' or negative factors than Indians (Basu, 1998; Modood, 1997; Rafiq, 1992). Basu and Altınay (2000) pointed out that the motivations for self-employment were positive 'pull' factors for Turkish Cypriot entrepreneurs in the UK in their study, which was conducted among 30 Turkish micro- and small businesses in London. The 'pull' factors, in their study, were given as to make more money, to be one's own boss and to gain business experience. A critique of pull and push factors in explaining career choices is put forward by Özbilgin et al. (2005, p. 5), drawing on Bourdieu and Wacquant (1992), who argue with such a mechanical view of seeing individual agents as 'particles' in society that can be pulled and pushed. Instead, Özbilgin et al. (2005) have developed a three-pronged approach, allowing for a layered (micro-, meso-macro-levels) study of influences on career choice. This view highlights the interplay between individual agency and structural conditions.

A number of studies have emphasized the structural conditions in which ethnic minority entrepreneurs' business start-up choices are situated. In a survey carried out in the UK among 78 Asian small businesses in the retail, distribution and catering sector in 1994, Basu (1998) argues that most Bangladeshis came to the UK in order to get away from the poor living conditions in their homeland and brought with them little by way of educational qualifications and financial experience. The East African Asians were relatively better equipped that the average Asian immigrant in terms of skills, qualifications and capital; they had also belonged to a successful business community in East Africa. These historical and social factors are bound to have had an impact on their decision to venture into entrepreneurship in the UK (Basu, 1998, p. 315). The ethnicity of the immigrant may also offer certain business opportunities. The unique consumption patterns and needs of an ethnic minority community can best be known and served by those from the same community. So the ethnic entrepreneur with an extensive knowledge of a particular market niche will be attracted to start a business. Food items, such as pickles or spices, and ready-made garments are examples of ethnic products. Many features of the ethnic environment such as cafés and shops selling food, textiles, furniture and household articles fall into this category (Kesteloot and Mistiaen, 1997, p. 327).

The advantage of this kind of entrepreneurship is that the entrepreneur may be able to import the main raw materials required or even the finished product from his or her country of origin, consequently being able to reduce many of the barriers caused by his lack of knowledge of the local marketplace (Ram and Jones, 1998). Financial factors also played a significant role in influencing their business entry. The access to family or community funds helps immigrants to start their own business. It has also been suggested that one of the ways in which ethnic minority businesses (EMBs) in some ethnic groups compensate for the difficulties they face in accessing finance from formal sources is to use funds drawn from within their own and personal and community-based networks (Ram and Jones, 1998). A more recent study by Smallbone et al. (2003) reports financial resourcing issues that are faced by EMBs from the largest ethnic minority groups (EMGs) in the UK, namely African-Caribbean, Indian, Pakistani, Bangladeshi and Chinese. In this survey, they found that these EMBs were significantly more likely to draw on finance from family and friends at start-up than white-owned businesses: 45 per cent compared with 25 per cent (Smallbone et al., 2003, p. 304).

Research by sociologists on immigrant self-employment has been motivated by interest in the process of social and cultural assimilation. Assimilation is achieved when an immigrant or minority group achieves occupational status and income equivalent to or approaching the position of native group (Aronson, 1991, p. 82). Kesteloot and Mistiaen (1997) suggest that where the business motives are 'external', the immediately ethnic character of the business will disappear and a situation of economic assimilation can be identified. These kinds of enterprises may still keep their ethnic character with regard to staffing, organization, working conditions, spatial distribution and external relations. In addition, they are liable to be based on irregular activities or working hours and make intensive use of unskilled labour, and may be carried on as part of the informal economy (Kesteloot and Mistiaen, 1997). Construction, maintenance and cleaning, transport, dressmaking or food and catering, often on a subcontracted basis, may fall under this category (Kesteloot and Meert, 1994, cited in Kesteloot and Mistiaen, 1997). Cultural factors may increase the drive for self-employment in specific communities. According to Light (1980), the small business in such communities caters to specialized cultural needs such as religious goods, group-specific foods and clothing and personal services.

RESEARCH METHODS

This study builds on Özbilgin et al.'s (2005) paper, which draws on a layered and multifaceted approach (Layder, 1993). Through this approach it investigates the similar and different factors that have influenced the career choice of Turkish Cypriot restaurant owners in North Cyprus and the UK. The macro-level examines the structural considerations of restaurateurs' entrepreneurial career choice, including culture and regulatory frameworks for business start-up in the restaurant sectors in both countries. The intermediate–organizational level is studied through an assessment of organizational contexts and relational constructs, such as type and nature of restaurant businesses (e.g. family business or solo business); and those of networks (e.g. strong or weak ties) and support gained from such networks. Finally, the micro-level examines the micro-individual influences, such as motivations and biographies of individuals in setting up restaurant businesses. It is crucial to note the intertwined nature of these micro-, meso- and macro-level influences (Özbilgin et al., 2005; Özbilgin and Tatlı, 2005), as supported by the findings of this research.

This study is part of a doctoral project. The fieldwork was conducted during February 2002 and September 2003, through interviews. The interview schedule was created first in the English language, and then it was translated into Turkish. Interviews with Turkish Cypriot restaurateurs in North Cyprus were held in Turkish, and interviews in the UK were conducted in English along with Turkish. In total, 33 in-depth semi-structured interviews were carried out: 19 restaurateurs in North Cyprus, and 14 restaurateurs in the UK. The distributive attributes of Turkish Cypriot restaurateur respondents in North Cyprus and the UK are depicted in Tables 21.1 and 21.2 respectively.

The study was carried out with 19 restaurateurs who currently are either the sole proprietors or part-owners of family-established restaurants in three major cities: Nicosia, Kyrenia and Famagusta in North Cyprus. The age of the restaurateurs in the study ranged between 25 and 72, with an average age of 43, implying that there were early starters as well as late starters in the restaurant trade. In terms of education, nine were university graduates, of which only three were graduates in hotel management and catering. This implies that a related university degree was not an effective determining factor in restaurant business start-up; rather many considered they would have higher prosperity in the restaurant trade. The remaining six were high school graduates, three secondary school graduates and one held only an elementary school qualification. Only five had fathers who were either previously restaurateurs, or currently part-owners of the restaurants owned by the respondents. This implies that the occupation of the other family members

Table 21.1   Distributive attributes of Turkish Cypriot restaurateurs in North Cyprus

Name	Age	Sex	Education	Marital status	Type of business	Father's and mother's occupation
1. Hasan	25	Male	University – tourism management	Single	Lease (similar to a partnership with the owner)	Partner in a harbour company and housewife
2. Güven	38	Male	University – hotel management and catering	Single	Partnership	Restaurateur, hotel owner and housewife
3. Galip	72	Male	High school	Married	Partnership	Coal dealer and housewife
4. Hüseyin	58	Male	Secondary school	Married	Retired restaurateur	Farmer and housewife
5. Olgun	30	Male	University – English language and literature	Married	Partnership	Caterer and helper in catering
6. Zafer	53	Male	University – hotel and catering management	Married	Sole proprietorship	Policeman and housewife
7. Gökhan	30	Male	University – physical training	Married	Sole proprietorship	Driver, restaurateur and housewife
8. Ayhan	31	Male	High school	Single	Partnership	Trader and housewife
9. Alper	57	Male	University – pharmacology	Widower	Sole proprietorship	Harbour worker and tailor
10. Mustafa	37	Male	High school	Married	Sole proprietorship	Harbour worker and housewife
11. Metin	39	Male	University – public management	Married	Sole proprietorship	Civil servant and teacher
12. Mete	33	Male	High school	Married	Partnership	Restaurateur, butcher and housewife

	Age	Gender	Education	Marital status	Business form	Background
13. Celal	47	Male	Secondary school	Married	Sole proprietorship	Keeper of a coffee shop, agriculturist and housewife
14. Haldun	38	Male	University – chemical engineering	Married	Sole proprietorship	Retired policeman and housewife
15. Turhan	42	Male	Professional high school	Married	Sole proprietorship	Restaurateur and helper in the restaurant
16. Meral	46	Female	Secondary school	Divorced	Sole proprietorship	Both in animal husbandry
17. Ayten	44	Female	University – mathematics	Married	Partnership	Trade unions and clothing factory
18. Kenan	47	Male	Elementary school	Married	Sole proprietorship	Worker on building site and no idea
19. Altan	39	Male	High school	Married	Partnership	Restaurateur and housewife

Table 21.2 Distributive attributes of Turkish Cypriot restaurateurs in the UK

Name	Age	Sex	Education	Marital status	Type of business	Father's and mother's occupation
1. Ercan 1st generation	55	Male	High school	Married	Sole proprietorship	Bus driver and housewife
2. Hakan 3rd generation	30	Male	University – hotel and catering management	Married	Partnership	Restaurateur and housewife
3. Ahmet 1st generation	56	Male	University – law	Married	Sole proprietorship	Accounts inspector and housewife
4. Barış 1st generation	50	Male	High school	Divorced	Partnership	Policeman and housewife
5. Fatih 1st generation	44	Male	High school	Married	Sole proprietorship	Butcher and housewife
6. Erinç 2nd generation	41	Male	University – mechanical engineering	Married	Sole proprietorship	Chef and housewife
7. Kamil 1st generation	65	Male	High school	Married	Partnership	Coffee shop owner and housewife
8. Burak 2nd generation	53	Male	University – hotel and catering management	Married	Partnership	Caterer and housewife
9. Emre 2nd generation	44	Male	Secondary school	Married	Sole proprietorship	Policeman, factory business and housewife
10. Nevzat Late migrant	45	Male	High school	Married	Sole proprietorship	Butcher and kebab shop owner, and housewife
11. Fevzi 1st generation	52	Male	University – economics	Married	Sole proprietorship	Farmer and helper to husband
12. Özay Late migrant	30	Male	High school	Single	Partnership	Bus driver and worker in the hospital
13. Bülent 1st generation	47	Male	Secondary school	Married	Sole proprietorship	Garden worker and helper to husband
14. Ali 1st generation	57	Male	University – hotel and catering management	Married	Professional manager	Postmaster general and art teacher

in addition to parents and other factors have been influential in entrepreneurial career choice as discussed in the findings section of the chapter.

Interviews were conducted with 13 restaurant owners or part-owners and with one restaurant manager in the UK. All had been born in Cyprus except one. Half of these respondents were first-generation migrants,[1] who migrated to the UK any time between 1966 and 1979, but were highly concentrated during the year 1974. Three respondents were second-generation migrants,[2] who migrated to the UK during 1957, 1972 and 1974 respectively with their mothers and brothers or sisters to accompany their fathers who came earlier. Also, there was one third-generation respondent.

A striking fact is that all 14 interviewees in the study in the UK were men; this implies that Turkish Cypriot restaurateurs in the UK are typically male. The age of the interviewees ranged between 30 and 65, with an average age of 48. The average age implies that there were early starters as well as late starters in the restaurant business. In total, 12 of 14 restaurateurs in the study were married, one was single and the other was divorced. In terms of education, six of the respondents were university graduates; three of these were graduates in hotel management and catering, one in economics and tourism, one a graduate in mechanical engineering, and finally one a graduate in law. The existence of university degree holders in areas other than hotel and catering management in the study implies that qualifications that were not gained in the UK were not recognized. This compelled individuals to move into the restaurant sector. Six were high school graduates and the remaining two had secondary school education as their highest educational attainment. It is also common for individuals with lower-level degree qualifications to engage in restaurant and catering businesses in the migrant country. Only four of the interviewees had fathers who had previously owned catering businesses, implying that parents' occupation was not a strongly influential factor in restaurant business ownership. Eight restaurants are solely owned, five restaurants are partnership owned, usually with other family members and friends.

DISCUSSION OF RESEARCH FINDINGS

This section compares the business start-up activities of 19 and 13 Turkish Cypriot restaurateurs in North Cyprus and the UK respectively, outlining the main similarities and differences between the two groups. It starts by comparing contextual information on business start-up in the restaurant sector, and then outlines the common distributive characteristics of the respondents in both countries. Finally, a comparison of reasons to start restaurant businesses, and capital owned and raised is conducted.

Contextual Information on Business Set-up in the Restaurant Sector in North Cyprus and the UK

Setting up restaurants is a recurrent issue among Turkish Cypriots in North Cyprus and the UK. According to the survey conducted on hotel and restaurant subsectors in North Cyprus in the year 2004, the total number of restaurants is 520 (Ministry of Economy and Tourism, 2006, p. 14). This number excludes coffee shops, patisseries, bars or cafés, and canteens. In the UK, there is no comprehensive documentation on the number of Turkish Cypriot owned restaurants. According to the London Gazette *Business Guide* (2005), there are 147 Turkish-origin-owned restaurants in London.

In North Cyprus, there are no comprehensive information guiding individuals in setting up restaurant businesses. As in many other business set-ups, the local municipalities in North Cyprus are in charge of the regulating and setting-up procedures for individuals who want to start a business in the restaurant sector. The city planning office inspects the suitability of the location where the restaurant is to be set up. Furthermore, restaurants should be members of the Restaurant Association, and according to the Restaurateur Association Law Scheme (1998), individuals who want to set up a restaurant should have at least two years of work experience in the restaurant sector or should have experienced, responsible staff. It is important to note that individuals who are university graduates in catering management or who possess professional diplomas or certificates in catering are exempted from having two years of work experience. However, this scheme has not yet been put into effect. The municipality also carries out health checks from time to time.

On the other hand, the setting-up procedure for restaurants in the UK is more regulated. The regulations and procedures are often documented in booklets, e.g. Food Standards Agency and Business Link. Individuals who want to set up a catering business must register their premises with the environmental health service at their local authority at least 28 days prior to opening (Food Standards Agency, 2006, p. 3). Furthermore, sole traders need to register separately for self-employment and VAT with their local authority. The self-employed must register with HM Revenue and Customs within three months of becoming self-employed, and they are also responsible for paying their own tax and national insurance contributions (Food Standards Agency, 2006, p. 27). Any considered change in the premises also needs to pass planning permission by the local authority.

The Business Opportunity Profile for Restaurateurs provided by Business Link for London guides people through the practicalities of setting up a restaurant. It reviews mandatory training, the regulatory requirements (including health and safety and food hygiene law), and the capital outlay

needed. In addition, it looks at trends currently affecting the catering industry, and suggests ways to promote this type of business. Finally, it recom-
mends several sources of further advice (Business Link, 2005). There are no
specific qualifications needed to run a restaurant, but some training in
hygiene and basic food preparation is advisable. In summary, restaurant
businesses are highly established in both countries. Individuals who want to
set up restaurant businesses in North Cyprus and the UK have to follow the
outlined procedures. However, compared to the UK system, setting up a
restaurant in North Cyprus is less regulated. But it is important to note that,
as from 2005, the municipalities, the initial place of registration for the
restaurant start-up, brought in enhanced quality check-ups and more controlled health and safety regulations when setting up businesses. The next
section provides a comparison of the distributive attributes of restaurateur
respondents; in both countries the average age for respondents who started
the restaurant businesses was high.

Distributive Attributes of Turkish Cypriot Restaurateurs in North Cyprus and the UK

The distributive characteristics of Turkish Cypriot restaurateurs in North
Cyprus and the UK are summarized in Tables 21.1 and 21.2 respectively. In
both North Cyprus and the UK, there were more sole-proprietor-owned
restaurants than the partnership-formed ones. In North Cyprus nine were
sole-proprietor-owned, and eight were partnership-owned; and in Britain
eight were solo-owned and five were partner-formed. It was evident that the
partnership restaurants in both countries were widely established with close
relatives such as fathers, brothers, sisters, sons, husband, and uncles and
aunts. An exception was that one of the respondents in the UK was in a
financial partnership.

The age of the restaurateur respondents in North Cyprus ranged
between 25 and 72, with an average age of 43, whereas the age of the
restaurateur respondents in the UK ranged between 30 and 65, with an
average age of 48. In both countries, the average age for respondents was
high and this could be related with start-up capital, professional experience and similar capabilities. Perhaps the requirements for obtaining start-
up capital, developing professional experience and establishing labour and
other contacts necessary to start and operate a restaurant might be assembled more effectively by individuals who are in the middle stage of their
professional career than by those who are at the beginning. Compared to
respondents in North Cyprus, the average age of the Turkish Cypriot
restaurateur respondents running their businesses in the UK was higher.
An explanation of higher average age of respondents in the UK is that the

great majority of respondents migrated to the UK when they were 17 years old and older, and they have worked as employees in various businesses, including restaurants. It is also worth mentioning that, as explained earlier, the great majority were not first-time starters of their current restaurants.

The restaurant business is heavily dominated by male small-business owners among Turkish Cypriot respondents both in North Cyprus and the UK. In 19 interviews conducted in North Cyprus, all were male except two, and in the UK, all 14 interviews were conducted with male respondents. In total, 14 out 19 restaurateurs in the sample of North Cyprus are married; three are single; and the remaining two are either divorced or widowed. In the UK, 12 out of 14 restaurateurs are married, one was single and the other was divorced. The high rate of married respondents correlates with the average age in both countries. The married respondents in both countries played a significant role in contributing to both start-up process and also to the daily management of businesses.

In North Cyprus, five restaurateur respondents had fathers who previously owned a restaurant business and in the UK four respondents had fathers involved in the restaurant business. However, they also had other immediate family members such as uncles or extended family members such as father-in-law or brother-in-law who had been a reinforcing factor in leading them into this sort of business. Therefore, in both countries family occupation is one reason for ownership in the restaurant business. Finally, as illustrated in Table 21.3, the majority of respondents in North Cyprus and the UK have higher levels of educational attainment, e.g. university and high school graduates. Nevertheless, Turkish Cypriot restaurateurs operating in North Cyprus have higher levels of educational attainment than those in the UK. At first sight, there are nine university graduates in North Cyprus and six university graduates in the UK. However one of the respondents was a restaurant manager professional in the UK and not the owner of his own business. Among the respondents who obtained university degrees, three in North Cyprus and three in the UK earned degrees in related fields, i.e. hotel and catering management, and tourism management. This illustrates that the related university education was not always an influential factor for restaurant business initiation.

Turkish Cypriot Restaurateurs' Choice of Business Start-up in North Cyprus and the UK

The business start-up reasons of 19 Turkish Cypriot restaurateur respondents in North Cyprus and 13 Turkish Cypriot restaurateur respondents in the UK were examined. The most significant reasons appear to be

Table 21.3   *Educational attainment of Turkish Cypriot restaurateur respondents in North Cyprus and the UK*

Highest education attained	Number of Turkish Cypriot restaurateur respondents in North Cyprus	Number of Turkish Cypriot restaurateur respondents in the UK
Primary	1	0
Secondary	3	2
High school/vocational/technical	6	6
University	9 (related university degree field: 3; unrelated university degree field: 6)	6 (related university degree field: 3; unrelated university degree field: 3)
Total number of respondents	19	14

family-related, economic and self-related, which can be explained mainly by intrinsic motivations.

Family-related reasons emerged as one of the factors that led respondents in both countries into restaurant business ownership. Eleven out of 19 respondents in North Cyprus and eight out of 13 respondents in the UK cited the role of both their immediate and extended family members in their business ownership decisions. However, the impact of family varied greatly across the two groups of respondents.

When the effect and influence of family are grouped as immediate and extended family, at first instance a similarity emerges in two countries. However, when the nature of family support is examined further, a different picture of the impact of family emerges. For all respondents influenced by family, business experience and business skills, guidance was presented to them. However, in addition to business experience, business skills and also managerial skills, other respondents were influenced by already well-established businesses in which they either inherited or joined as partners. Tables 21.4 and 21.5 depict the nature of family support presented to Turkish Cypriot restaurateur respondents in North Cyprus and the UK respectively.

The respondents in North Cyprus compared to those in the UK were more advantaged in the sense that they not only gained business experience, but probably inherited, transferred or became part owners of established family businesses. As suggested by Tables 21.4 and 21.5, six respondents in North Cyprus inherited or joined established businesses in contrast to only

Table 21.4   Nature of family support provided to Turkish Cypriot restaurateur respondents in North Cyprus

Name	Age	Sex	Nature of family support
1. Güven	38	Male	Established business (part owner)
2. Olgun	30	Male	Established business (transferred)
3. Gökhan	30	Male	Established business (transferred)
4. Mete	33	Male	Established business (transferred)
5. Celal	47	Male	Experience gained
6. Turhan	42	Male	Experience gained
7. Ayten	44	Female	Husband
8. Metin	39	Male	Established business (transferred)
9. Altan	39	Male	Established business (transferred)
10. Hasan	25	Male	Experience gained
11. Galip	72	Male	Experience gained

one respondent in the UK. Five restaurateurs in the UK had families involved in catering businesses, in early years, in Cyprus. The support received from families was mostly in terms of experience, advice, guidance and financial support for respondents in the UK. This is congruent with the study of Smallbone et al. (2003), which suggested that use of 'strong ties' (Granovetter, 1973, 1983; Jack et al., 2004) is common in obtaining financial support for business start-ups by ethnic minority groups in the UK.

The use of strong ties is evident, in this study, in a number of ways. The great majority of Turkish Cypriot restaurateur respondents in North Cyprus not only gained experience in family restaurant businesses, but also joined or became owners of established family businesses. On the contrary, the vast majority of respondents in the UK acquired experience in the family business, and then started their own businesses with or without monetary support from their families. At the interface of the micro-, meso- and macro-levels (Özbilgin et al., 2005; Özbilgin and Tatlı, 2005), the respondents in the UK illustrate the use of a combination of strong and weak ties (Granovetter, 1973, 1983) from early stages of their business start-up experiences.

An apparent similarity in both countries is that the majority of respondents acquired early childhood experiences in restaurant businesses from

Table 21.5 Nature of family support provided to Turkish Cypriot restaurateur respondents in the UK

Name	Age	Sex	Nature of family support
1. Hakan	30	Male	Experience and financial capital
2. Erinç	41	Male	Experience
3. Kamil	65	Male	Experience
4. Burak	53	Male	Experience and guidance
5. Nevzat	45	Male	Experience
6. Bülent	47	Male	Experience
7. Emre	44	Male	Experience and guidance
8. Özay	30	Male	Established business (part owner)

their families. Also, in both North Cyprus and the UK, the research has identified that a number of respondents have set up restaurant businesses at a later stage in their lives, after working in other sectors. Another factor that led Turkish Cypriot restaurateurs into business ownership is the economic situation in North Cyprus and the UK.

Economic-related reasons also provided a very clear motive for Turkish Cypriot restaurateurs running their businesses in North Cyprus and the UK, explaining their entry into restaurant business ownership, as discussed in an earlier section of this chapter in relation to the studies of Chell (2001) and Carter et al. (2003). It was evident both in North Cyprus and the UK that macro-structural factors such as the changing economy influenced respondents in the study to move into restaurant business ownership. In North Cyprus, three out of 19 respondents reported that they were negatively influenced by economic stagnation, which showed its impact between 1988 and 1990. This situation has brought about an increasing trend in restaurant business ownership in the sector. Similarly, three out of 13 respondents in the UK lost their jobs as a result of the structural changes in the local economy, mainly due to the collapse of the textile sector towards the end of the 1990s. This situation channelled them to business ownership in restaurants.

Another factor arising from the economic reasons that have led five out of 19 Turkish Cypriot restaurateurs to business ownership was the perceived better earnings to be made in the restaurant sector compared to employment in other areas. On the other hand, eight out of 13 respondents presented the reason of financial betterment or financial prosperity as their reason for setting up. This reason is also confirmed by the migration reasons of Turkish Cypriots to the UK, which can be explained with reference to the interrelated nature of micro-, meso- and macro-dimensions of the subject under study. Furthermore, interestingly, three re-migrant respondents from the UK in North Cyprus have set up restaurants in order to provide enough income for themselves and their families. As a result, the research identified that economic factors have been influential in respondents' business set-up decisions in North Cyprus and the UK; however, as explained above, the impact has varied between the two countries. Finally, restaurateur respondents established businesses to satisfy their own intrinsic interests in the food business.

The research also identified those restaurateurs in North Cyprus and the UK who established businesses due to their intrinsic interest in the food business: the desire to practise their own skills, competencies and abilities. Self-realization is a theme that is often discussed in the pertinent literature (Chell, 1985; Dyer, 1994; Kolvereid, 1997; Carter et al., 2003). Nine out of 19 respondents in North Cyprus presented any of the reasons mentioned above, and three out of 13 respondents in the UK stated that they had a special interest in the restaurant sector. This implies that intrinsic interest in food business was more influential in business start-up decisions of the respondents in North Cyprus than those in the UK.

Four out of 19 respondents in North Cyprus and two out of 13 in the UK presented a reason linked to autonomy from managerial control and desire to control their own destiny. This again implies that desire for autonomy was a stronger reason for business start-up for respondents in North Cyprus than in the UK. Three respondents in the UK also presented the achievement motivation; however, this was not an issue for any of the respondents in North Cyprus.

Development and Transformation of Different Forms of Capital

Financial capital is argued to be the most important element in establishing a business in the entrepreneurship literature (Shane and Cable, 2002). Turkish Cypriot restaurateur respondents in both countries assembled business start-up capital in three ways: personal resources such as own savings or own resources; family resources or borrowings from friends; and bank loans and credits. However, there were also respondents in this study who used varied sources of financing and often combined sources to start a business.

In North Cyprus, five business owners (Galip, Alper, Mustafa, Meral, Ayten) out of 19 completely financed their businesses through personal resources or savings. On the other hand, only three (Ercan, Ahmet, Fevzi) out of 13 restaurateur respondents in the UK financed their businesses completely through their own resources. Together with own resources or savings, five (Hüseyin, Zafer, Ayhan, Haldun, Ertan) respondents in North

Cyprus partly drew on their families' capital (a few also borrowed money from friends). The family capital in this case is either their financial capital or the space for the business. There was only one respondent in each country who completely financed their businesses through bank loans (one re-mortgaged his house, and the other had a strong guarantor for his loan). The norm for the majority in both countries was to opt for bank loans when expanding their businesses.

As opposed to respondents in North Cyprus, four respondents (Hakan, Barış, Fatih, Emre) in the UK drew on a combination of three sorts of financing when initiating their businesses. Four respondents in each country mentioned using bank loans as a source of funding along with their own savings. These individuals could easily draw on bank loans, either through mortgaging their houses or using their relatives as guarantors. Individuals who partly drew on bank loans were experienced in business.

More respondents in North Cyprus than in the UK also drew on family capital when starting their businesses. Six out of 19 restaurateurs in North Cyprus as opposed to only one respondent in the UK completely relied on family resources for business ownership. Interestingly, the research identified that both groups of restaurateur respondents initially relied heavily on financing businesses through personal resources and/or family resources, later seeking commercial loans for business growth. Respondents have also created or deployed their cultural capital when setting up their businesses, as discussed later.

Turkish Cypriot restaurateurs in North Cyprus and the UK accumulated cultural capital through training which involved both formal academic training and short-term vocational training; and informal training by gaining experience as a consequence of working in restaurants. In North Cyprus, six out of 19 respondents were university graduates, and two were graduates of hotel and catering management; the other group gained experience through working either in their family-owned restaurants or in other restaurant businesses abroad. The respondents also developed themselves by attending training courses or through visiting and researching restaurants in other countries.

On the other hand, almost half of the respondents in the UK were university graduates, three had degrees in hotel and catering management, and a few joined short-term training courses on hygiene before setting up their businesses. Furthermore, all except one had work experience in restaurants before setting up their businesses, as shown in Table 21.6. An important difference in terms of cultural capital was the English-language proficiency that experienced Turkish Cypriots restaurateur respondents possessed. This provided them with advantages in communicating with customers and suppliers who were non-Turkish.

Table 21.6   Restaurant business experience of respondents in North Cyprus and the UK

Experience	Turkish Cypriot restaurateurs in North Cyprus	Turkish Cypriot restaurateurs in the UK
Total number of respondents who had previous restaurant business experience	13 out of 19	12 out of 13
Respondents who operated own or worked in family restaurant business	Hasan, Güven, Galip, Hüseyin, Olgun, Zafer, Gökhan, Metin, Mete, Celal, Eran, Turhan, Altan (13)	Hakan, Barış, Burak, Fevzi, Nevzat, Özay (6)
Restaurateurs who worked for someone else (in restaurants)	Haldun (1)	Ahmet, Fatih, Erinç, Kamil, Emre, Bülent (6)
Respondents who had no experience in restaurant businesses	Ayhan, Alper, Mustafa, Ayten, Meral (5)	Ercan (1)

Previous business experience, whether as owner or employee, is advantageous to entrepreneurship (Uneke, 1996). The experienced respondents possess high levels of cultural capital. As shown in Table 21.6, a majority (13 out of 19) of Turkish Cypriot respondents in North Cyprus operated their own or worked in a family restaurant business before ownership or partnership in their current business, compared to only five out of 13 respondents in the UK. Interestingly, the majority of Turkish Cypriot restaurateurs operating their businesses in the UK gained their previous business experience from working for a non-family-owned restaurant, while a majority of Turkish Cypriot restaurateurs in North Cyprus gained their experience by working in a family-owned business. We can note at this point that the restaurateurs in North Cyprus have deployed their social capital, for example their families, in order to obtain their cultural capital, such as work experience in restaurants and role models, to a greater extent than the respondents running their businesses in the UK. Role models, in terms of observing, serving, identifying with, and appreciating the behaviours (Scherer et al., 1989) of fathers, mothers, wives and siblings in a family-owned business setting is important.

The research has confirmed that Turkish Cypriots living in North Cyprus would not generally work as employees in non-family-owned restaurant businesses. A low-status job, such as working in a restaurant, is not socially acceptable for many of this group. They would rather work in other available employment. However, as a result of migrating to the UK, respondents have worked and performed all sorts of jobs in non-family-owned restaurants and gained experience and accumulated financial capital to establish their own businesses. The most striking fact with the restaurant owners in North Cyprus is that the overwhelming majority did not previously have any sort of business experience in non-family-owned restaurants based in North Cyprus. Those that had earlier experiences either came from a family background that owned restaurant businesses or worked in restaurants in the UK while undergoing university education. This indicates the link between two forms of capital: cultural and social.

Respondents in both countries have relied on their social capital, that is their social networks, to assemble their start-up economic capital, or they have received labour support that has reduced their initial start-up costs. Also, the restaurants owned by their social capital such as immediate and extended family members acted as a means to enhance cultural capital, in giving them experience and skills in running restaurant businesses, as mentioned earlier. The creation and deployment of social capital by the participant Turkish Cypriot restaurateurs can be analysed with reference to the notion of 'social embeddedness' (Jack and Anderson, 2002). Using Giddens's (1984) structuration theory to explore the link between the entrepreneur as agent and the social context as structure in the creation and operation of their businesses, Jack and Anderson (2002) argue that entrepreneurial actions do not occur in a vacuum but are conditioned by ongoing structures of social relations (Johannisson, 1990; Johannisson and Monsted, 1997; Bygrave and Minniti, 2000). Aldrich and Zimmer (1986) also take this view by suggesting that entrepreneurship is embedded in a social context, channelled and facilitated; or constrained and inhibited by people's position in a social network (Jack and Anderson, 2002, p. 469).

Turkish Cypriot restaurateur respondents in North Cyprus and the UK have created and deployed their social capital to obtain economic capital. This was either in terms of the existence of established businesses or financial capital for the business start-up. The comparative dimension in terms of the research participants in North Cyprus and the UK can be noted as follows: six out of 19 respondents in North Cyprus, compared with one out of 13 respondents in the UK, argued for the existence of a family business, which facilitated business ownership or partnership. Similarly, apart from the established businesses, more Turkish Cypriot respondents in North Cyprus (six out of 19) have used direct family savings or loans, premises or shops for no rent at start-up than respondents in the UK (four out of 13). Indirect support, such as support received other than straight financial capital, has helped in reducing costs initially at start-up, such as labour support from family members. Similar to the situation in the UK with Turkish Cypriot restaurants, in North Cyprus the role of women such as wives in sustaining the family-run restaurants is significant, especially in the initial years. The study on Turkish-Cypriot-owned restaurants highlighted the vital role that family women played in the management of the business. Therefore it can be argued that social networks, particularly in the form of 'strong ties' (Granovetter, 1973, 1983; Jack et al., 2004), are influential in career choices and development of Turkish Cypriot restaurateurs, in both countries. The gender dimension of the phenomenon can be explained in relation to the nature of business start-up activity; and that of support by women in the family circles. Despite the male assertion of single ownership of the restaurants, the wives in essence play an enormous role, ranging from labour support to taking care of the business, which reflects a more holistic approach to the start-up process in the form of teamwork and interlocking different functions of the business. In North Cyprus, the research identified that not only were wives supportive in the businesses, but also mothers, daughters and sisters were very instrumental. Both in North Cyprus and the UK, the immediate families (especially parents, wives and children) of respondents in the research sample have been suggested as builders of social capital acting as a prosperous resource from which the owners can also profit and perhaps save from labour cost, in economic terms. Transformation between these two forms of capital, namely social and economic capital, is a crucial facilitating process in the start-up experiences of the Turkish Cypriot restaurateurs.

CONCLUSIONS

This study has presented a comparative look at the business start-up activities of Turkish Cypriot restaurateurs in North Cyprus and the UK. Revisiting the overall research question, stated as, 'How does migration as a social movement that is situated in context affect career choice of Turkish Cypriot restaurateurs at the micro-level?', the findings suggest an interlocking combination of three main influences: family-related influences, economic influences, and self-related influences. These three influences form the basis of the formation of, and transformation between, different forms of capital that the participant Turkish Cypriot restaurateurs have developed in North Cyprus and the UK. In many cases, respondents in two countries gained and enhanced their cultural capital through work experience and informal training as employees and as owners of their previous businesses, usually family-owned businesses. Nearly an equal number of respondents from the two countries financed their businesses through their own savings from previous employment. It was also evident that a number of respondents in both countries improved their cultural capital through schooling in hotel and catering management. Social networks, such as family and friends, were considered mainly as providers of economic capital and labour support at start-up that contributed to cost reduction. Economic capital was acquired through such cost reduction and obtaining support from the immediate social circle, deploying strong ties.

Bank loans were rarely reported as a source of financing in either country. Bridging and bonding different forms of capital, including economic, social and cultural capital, is argued to be significant for Turkish Cypriot restaurateurs, not only at the stage of start-up but also in advancing their restaurant businesses through the growth process. The gender dimension of the phenomenon can be explained in relation to the nature of business start-up activity; and that of support by women in the immediate social circles. Despite the male assertion of single ownership of the restaurants, the wives and sisters play a significant role in both countries, ranging from labour support to taking care of the business, which reflects a more holistic approach to the start-up process in the form of teamwork and interlocking functions of the business. In both cultural settings, North Cyprus and the UK, the role of women appears to diminish as the restaurant business becomes more professionalized in terms of HR composition and management structures.

NOTES

1. The first-generation migrant definition of Ladbury (1984) is adopted, whereby first-generation migrants are 'those who were born in Cyprus and who spent at least first 16 years there'.
2. The second-generation migrant definition of Ladbury (1984) is adopted, whereby second-generation migrants are 'those who were born in Britain or received all or most of their schooling in Britain' (Alicik, 1997, p. 34).

REFERENCES

Alicik, H. (1997), *Kimlik, Yabancılaşma, Asimilasyon*, Lefkoşa: Galeri Kültür Yayınları.
Aldrich, H.E. and Zimmer, C. (1986), 'Entrepreneurship through social networks', in Howard E. Aldrich (ed.), *Population Perspectives on Organizations*, Uppsala: Acta Universitatis Upsaliensis, pp. 13–28.

Aldrich, H.E., Cater, J.C., Jones, T.P. and McEvoy, D. (1981), 'Business development and self-segregation: Asian enterprise in three British cities', in C. Peach, V. Robinson and S. Smith (eds), *Ethnic Segregation in Cities*, London: Croom Helm, pp. 170–90.

Aronson, R.L. (1991), *Self-Employment – A Labor Market Perspective*, New York: ILR Press.

Auster, E. and Aldrich, H. (1984), 'Small business vulnerability, ethnic enclaves and ethnic enterprise', in R. Ward and R. Jenkins (eds), *Ethnic Communities in Business: Strategies for Economic Survival*, Cambridge: Cambridge University Press, pp. 39–54.

Bandura, A. (1977), *Social Learning Theory*, Englewood Cliffs, NJ: Prentice-Hall.

Barrett, G.A., Jones, T.P. and McEvory, D. (1996), 'Ethnic minority business: theoretical discourse in Britain and North America', *Urban Studies*, **33**(4–5): 783–809.

Basu, A. (1998), 'An exploration of entrepreneurial activity among Asian small businesses in Britain', *Small Business Economics*, **10**: 313–26.

Basu, A. and Altınay, E. (2000), 'An exploratory study of Turkish Cypriot small businesses in London', *Proceedings of the Third International Congress for Cyprus Studies*, **4**: 579–94.

Bird, B. (1988), 'Implementing entrepreneurial ideas: the case for intention', *Academy of Management Review*, **13**(3): 442–53.

Borooah, V.K. and Hart, M. (1999), 'Factors affecting self-employment among Indian and Black Caribbean men in Britain', *Small Business Economics*, **13**: 111–29.

Bourdieu, P. (1986), 'The forms of capital', in J.G. Richardson (ed.), *Handbook of Theory and Research for the Sociology of Education*, New York: Greenwood Press, pp. 241–57.

Bourdieu, P. and Wacquant, L. (1992), *An Invitation to Reflexive Sociology*, Cambridge: Polity Press.

Brockhaus, R.H. and Horwitz, P.S. (1986), 'The psychology of the entrepreneurs', in D.L. Sexton and R.W. Smilor (eds), *The Art and Science of Entrepreneurship*, Cambridge, MA: Balinger Publishing, pp. 25–48.

Business Link (2005), Restaurateur BP21/Nov 2003. Business Link for London, http://cobra.cobwebinfo.com/text.php?id=bop021.

Bygrave, W. and Minniti, M. (2000), 'The social dynamics of entrepreneurship', *Entrepreneurship Theory and Practice*, **24**(3): 25–37.

Carter, N.M., Gartner, W.B., Shaver, K.G. and Gatewood, E.J. (2003), 'The career reasons of nascent entrepreneurs', *Journal of Business Venturing*, **18**: 13–39.

Chell, E. (1985), 'The entrepreneurial personality: a few ghosts laid to rest?', *International Small Business Journal*, **3**(3): 43–54.

Chell, E. (2001), *Entrepreneurship: Globalisation, Innovation and Development*, London: Thomson Learning.

Clark, K. and Drinkwater, S. (1998), *Ethnicity and Self-employment in Britain*, Oxford: Blackwell Publishers.

Clark, K. and Drinkwater, S. (2000), 'Pushed out or pulled in? Ethnic minority self-employment in England and Wales', *Labour Economics*, **7**: 603–28.

Dexter, B.P., Franco, G., Chamberlin, J.E. and Dexter, P.I. (2005), 'Helping managers to become leading managers: evaluating the impact of leadership development at middle manager level in a city council organisation', Studying Leadership: Future Agendas, The 4th International Conference on Leadership Research, University of Lancaster, UK, December.

Dyer, W.G. (1992), *The Entrepreneurial Experience: Confronting Career Dilemmas of the Start-up Executive*, San Francisco, CA: Jossey-Bass.

Dyer, W.G. (1994), 'Toward a theory of entrepreneurial careers', *Entrepreneurship Theory and Practice*, **19**(2): 7–21.

Feldman, D.C. and Bolino, M.C. (2000), 'Career patterns of the self-employed: career motivations and career outcomes', *Journal of Small Business Management*, **38**(3): 53–67.

Food Standards Agency (2006), 'Starting up: your first steps to run a catering business', *Business Link*.

Giddens (1984), *The Constitution of Society: Outline of Theory and Structuration*, Berkeley, CA: University of California Press.

Granovetter, M. (1973), 'The strength of weak ties', *American Journal of Sociology*, **78**(6): 1360–80.

Granovetter, M. (1983), 'The strength of weak ties: a network theory revisited', *Sociological Theory*, **1**: 201–33.

Hisrich, R.D. and Brush, C. (1984), 'The women entrepreneur: management skills and business problems', *Journal of Small Business Management*, **22**(1): 30–37.

Jack, S.L. and Anderson, A.R. (2002), 'The effects of embeddedness on the entrepreneurial process', *Journal of Business Venturing*, **17**(15), 467–87.

Jack, S.L., Drakopoulou-Dodd, S.D. and Anderson, A.R. (2004), 'Social structures and entrepreneurial networks: the strength of strong ties', *International Journal of Entrepreneurship and Innovation*, **5**(2): 107–20.

Johannisson, B. (1990), 'Community entrepreneurship – cases and conceptualisation', *Entrepreneurship and Regional Development*, **2**: 71–88.

Johannisson, B. and Monsted, M. (1997), 'Contextualizing entrepreneurial networking', *International Studies of Management and Organizations*, **27**(3): 109–36.

Jones, T., McEvoy, D. and Barratt, G. (1992), *Raising Finance for Ethnic Minority Firms*, Liverpool: John Moores University.

Jones, T., McEvoy, D. and Barratt, G. (1994), 'Labour intensive practices in the ethnic minority firm', in J. Atkinson and D. Storey (eds), *Employment, the Small Firm and the Labour Market*, London: Routledge, pp. 172–205.

Kesteloot, C. and Meert, C. (1994), 'Les fonctions socio-éconmiques de l'économie informelle et son implantation spatiale dans les villes belges', paper presented at the International Conference 'Villes, Enterprises at Société à l'aube du XXIe siècle' Lille, 16–18 March.

Kesteloot, C. and Mistiaen, P. (1997), 'From ethnic minority niche to assimilation: Turkish restaurant in Brussels', *Area*, **29**(4): 325–34.

Kolvereid, L. (1997), 'Prediction of employment status choice intentions', *Entrepreneurship Theory and Practice*, **21**: 47–57.

Krueger, N.F. and Carsrud, A. (1993), 'Entrepreneurial intentions: applying the theory of planned behaviour', *Entrepreneurship and Regional Development*, **5**: 316–23.

Krueger, N.F., Reilly, M.D. and Carsrud, A.L. (2000), 'Competing models of entrepreneurial intentions', *Journal of Business Venturing*, **15**(5–6), 411–32.

Ladbury, S. (1984), 'Choice, chance or no alternative? The Turkish Cypriots in business in London', in R. Ward and R. Jenkins (eds), *Ethnic Communities in Business Strategies for Economic Survival*, Cambridge: Cambridge University Press, pp. 105–263.

Layder, D. (1993), *New Strategies in Social Research*, Cambridge: Polity Press.

Light, I. (1980), 'Asian enterprise in America: Chinese, Japanese, and Koreans in small business', in S. Cummings (ed.), *Self-Help in Urban America: Patterns of Minority Business Enterprise*, Port Washington, NY: Kennikat, pp. 33–57.

Londra Gazete (2005), *Business Guide 2005*, London.

Metcalf, H., Modood, T. and Virdee, S. (1996), *Asian Self-employment: The Interaction of Culture and Economics in England*, London: London Policy Institute.

Ministry of Economy and Tourism (2006), *The TRNC Quarterly Economic Bulletin, Industrial Strategy*, published under the authority of the Minister, no: 3, Nicosia.

Modood, T. (1997), 'Employment', in T. Moodod and R. Berthoud (eds), *Ethnic Minorities in Britain*, London: Policy Studies Institute, pp. 83–145.

Özbilgin, M. and Tatlı, A. (2005), 'Book review essay: understanding Bourdieu's contribution to organization and management studies', *Academy of Management Review*, **30**(4): 855–77.

Özbilgin, M., Küskü, F. and Erdoğmuş (2005), 'Explaining influences on "career" choice: the case of MBS students in comparative perspective', *International Journal of Human Resource Management*, **16**, 2000–2028.

Rafiq, M. (1992), 'Ethnicity and enterprise: a comparison of Muslim and non-Muslim owned Asian businesses in Britain', *New Community*, **19**(1): 43–60.

Ram, M. (1992), 'Coping with racism: Asian employers in the inner city', *Work, Employment and Society*, **6**(4): 601–18.

Ram, M. and Jones, T. (1998), *Ethnic Minorities in Business*, Milton Keynes: Small Business Research Trust.

Restaurateur Association Law Scheme (1998), *RES-BIR Yasa Tasarısı*, Lefkoşa: Devlet Basım Evi.

Reynolds, P. (1991), 'Sociology and entrepreneurship: concepts and contributions', *Entrepreneurship Theory and Practice*, **16**(1): 47–70.

Scherer, R.F., Adams, J.S., Carley, S.S. and Wiebe, F.A. (1989), 'Role model performance effects on development of entrepreneurial career preference', *Entrepreneurship, Theory and Practice*, **14**: 53–70.

Shane, S. and Cable, D. (2002), 'Network ties, reputation, and the financing of new ventures', *Management Science*, **48**(3): 364–81.

Shapero, A. (1982), 'Social dimensions of entrepreneurship', in C. Kent (ed.), *The Encyclopaedia of Entrepreneurship*, Englewood Cliffs, NJ: Prentice-Hall, pp. 72–90.

Smallbone, D., Ram, M., Deakins, D. and Baldock, R. (2003), 'Access to finance by ethnic minority businesses in the UK', *International Small Business Journal*, **21**(3): 291–314.

Storey, D.J. (1994), *Understanding the Small Business Sector*, London: International Thomson Business Press.

Uneke, O. (1996), 'Ethnicity and small business ownership: contrasts between Blacks and Chinese in Toronto', *Work, Employment and Society*, **10**: 529–48.

Waldinger, R., Aldrich, H., Ward, R. and Associates (1990), *Ethnic Entrepreneurs: Immigrant Business in Industrial Societies*, London: Sage.

Werbner, P. (1990), 'Renewing an industrial past: British Pakistani entrepreneurship in Manchester', *Migration*, **8**: 17–41.

PART VII

Entrepreneurs, Managers, Career Choice and
Diversity: Gender Issues

22. Gender and the MBA: intrinsic and extrinsic benefits

Ruth Simpson and Jane Sturges

INTRODUCTION

Women have moved into the labour market in increasing numbers, with this increase being particularly marked in management. In the UK, for example, between 1971 and 1997, the proportion of women in management has risen steadily from 9 per cent to 28 per cent (*Labour Force Survey*, 1997). Canada has seen a similar rise from 16 per cent to 33 per cent over the same period (*Statistics Canada*, 1997). However, in both countries and in most sectors, men continue to outnumber women at higher management levels: for example, at board and director level recent figures suggest that in the UK, women still hold only 13.2 per cent of posts (Institute of Management, 2004), whereas in Canada at 11 per cent the figure is even lower (Catalyst, 2005).

One strategy men and women adopt to move into higher levels of management is to equip themselves with an MBA. This has been noted both in Canada (Burke, 1994) and the UK (Goffee and Nicholson, 1994; Simpson and Altman, 2000). Women now account for one-third of MBA students in the UK and Canada (AMBA, 1997; *Business Week*, 1997) and the figure for the USA – the largest MBA market in the world, is similar (Catalyst, 2000). The MBA is viewed by many as a worthwhile investment, and the increase in the number of MBA programmes in North America and Europe is indicative of the perceived benefits of the qualification (*Business Week*, 1997). However, despite the popularity of the MBA, little is known about the nature of these benefits and how they might vary by gender.

This chapter considers gender differences in career benefits from the MBA, reporting findings from a qualitative research study conducted at a leading business school in Ontario, Canada. The research builds on earlier UK research, which indicated that benefits from the MBA may vary along gender lines, with men more likely to gain extrinsic benefits in terms of pay, status and marketability, but women being more likely to perceive that they gain intrinsic benefits such as increased confidence, enhanced credibility and more effective interpersonal skills (Simpson, 1995, 1996, 2000b).

THE MBA IN CANADA

While the first MBA programmes were introduced in the USA, courses soon became established in Europe and Canada. With nine of its 26 business schools in the 2001 *Financial Times* listing of the top 100 international MBAs and with four in the top 50, Canada now has a well-established MBA provision. The decline in demand experienced in the early 1990s, as students turned to more prestigious US and European universities, has been largely reversed – helped by the growing reputation of Canadian schools and by new initiatives including strategic alliances with the USA (e.g. the new EMBA provided jointly by Schulich Business School in Canada and Kellogg in the USA). As one of the top business schools in Canada (*Business Week*, 2000), the university from which this sample was drawn has a sound reputation and the potential to give its graduates a strong 'MBA advantage'. Canada's more proactive and interventionist approach to equality initiatives, as evidenced by an emphasis on affirmative action rather than equality of opportunity (Gunderson, 1994a, 1994b), may mean this advantage could be more equally shared between men and women than in the UK. The gender gap in pay, for example, tends to be lower in Canada, where women earn on average 85 per cent of men's weekly pay (*Statistics Canada*, 2002), than in the UK, where the comparable figure is 75 per cent (*Labour Force Survey*, 2002). In addition, Ontario (the location of the study) has been identified as having possibly the most far-reaching equity initiatives laws in North America (Smeenk, 1993). The background of this study consequently provided an opportunity to assess whether gender differences, similar to those that emerged from UK research, might also exist for graduates from a high-ranking business school (*Business Week*, 2000) as well as from a national culture in which more official policies have been initiated and supported to promote women in management.

EXTRINSIC AND INTRINSIC CAREER BENEFITS

Management theorists have used the concepts of intrinsic benefits (job satisfaction and fulfilment) and extrinsic benefits (pay and status) to evaluate rewards that managers and other workers expect from employment (e.g. Marshall, 1984; Nicholson and West, 1988; Scase and Goffee, 1989; Young et al., 1998). Young et al. used a fivefold measure of intrinsic rewards to include job characteristics (autonomy, feedback and skill variety), communication (openness of information), leader satisfaction (relationship with supervisors), job satisfaction (enjoyment of job activities) and intrinsic exchange (levels of appreciation for good job performance). In a broader analysis, Scase and Goffee examined levels of remuneration, opportunities for promotion, security and personal status of managers as extrinsic rewards, with intrinsic factors including opportunities for decision making, task discretion, autonomy and self-fulfilment, while Marshall (1984) additionally includes the quality of working relationships with same status and more junior workers. Adopting the above interpretation, Marshall (1984) and Nicholson and West (1988) suggest gender differences in career rewards (discussed below), with men gaining more extrinsic and women more intrinsic career benefits.

This chapter adopts a similar dichotomy in analysing outcomes from the MBA. Extrinsic benefits are therefore taken to include the more objective career advantages such as progression and pay. Intrinsic benefits are taken to include intrinsic rewards from the job (e.g. job satisfaction) as well as more subjective outcomes relating to self-development (confidence, credibility and enhanced self-worth) and interpersonal skills (leadership/teamworking abilities, communication and listening skills). While such skills may not fit easily into a categorization of career benefits, in the research discussed in this chapter they have been incorporated into intrinsic outcomes on the grounds of their likely contribution to many of the stated components above.

THE CAREER BENEFITS OF THE MBA

Research from the USA, Canada and the UK indicates important extrinsic benefits from the MBA. A survey conducted by the Association of MBAs (AMBA) in the UK in 1996 found that after qualification the proportion of participants in senior management nearly doubled and there was a fourfold increase in those involved in senior roles such as corporate strategy and planning (AMBA, 1997). Data from the USA suggest comparable career improvements in terms of seniority of position and business start-ups (Messmer, 1998), with the vast majority (95 per cent) of male and female MBA graduates from the 12 top business schools in the USA expressing satisfaction with their subsequent career progress (Catalyst, 2000). Data from Canada paint a similar picture, pointing to a strong 'MBA advantage'. *Business Week* (1997), for example, reported that graduates from top Canadian business schools can expect to recoup their investment within two years through promotions and increased pay. Consequently, many men and women perceive the MBA to be a passport to success in terms of increased salary and enhanced career progress and, as Baruch and Peiperl (1999) suggest, increasingly see the qualification as a prerequisite for many senior management posts.

In terms of gender, much of the work on MBAs and career progress comes from the USA, where results suggest that women do not progress as far or receive the same level of remuneration as men. For example, one study shows that men advance further than women in both line positions and reporting span and that, while men and women are equally likely to value the MBA in terms of their careers, men are significantly more likely to be satisfied with their career advancement after completion of their course than women (Catalyst, 2000). Similarly, Cox and Harquil (1991) found that while there was no significant difference between men and women in terms of career satisfaction, women MBAs had significantly fewer management promotions. Moreover, salary growth for women was still significantly smaller than for men, even after controlling for performance, age, experience, starting salary and career paths – a gap that may well increase over time (Schneer and Reitman, 1990, 1995). Comparable findings on gender disparities in 'the MBA effect' also emerged from UK research (Simpson, 1995, 1996). Men were more likely to move into senior roles after the MBA, to progress via an internal labour market and to receive larger salary increases (the salary gap between men and women actually widened after the course). Thus we might expect men to gain more than women in terms of extrinsic career benefits from studying for an MBA.

However, while evidence supports the view that, for men at least, the MBA is associated with rapid career advancement, the issue of the nature of other benefits (e.g. skills, capabilities) received remains somewhat sketchy. Kretovics (1999), in a US-based study of the learning outcomes of an MBA programme, found that the MBA added value in key areas such as information analysis, sense making and initiative, but not in interpersonal or communication skills. Similarly, Boyatzis and Renio (1989) suggest that attending an MBA programme adds value on a number of abilities related to effective managerial performance but not on interpersonal and leadership abilities. This is despite the increased emphasis on 'managerial fitness' (Kakabadse and Kakabadse, 1999), i.e. the maturity, self-awareness and empathy required to make high-quality decisions – and on communication and leadership skills as critical for success in the workplace. In fact, according to Shipper (1999), the MBA does not provide an advantage in key managerial or leadership skills over those who possess only a bachelor's or some other master's degree. Similarly, Pfeffer and Fong (2002) and Mintzberg and Gosling (2002) argue that business education places too much emphasis on the functions of management at the expense of the 'practice of managing' and its associated leadership, interpersonal and communication skills.

While the above studies indicate that the MBA may be less effective in the formation of important interpersonal or leadership skills, the issues of how such skills and other benefits might vary by gender is not addressed. Work on conceptualization of career success among male and female managers and professionals indicates that gender is a strong influencing factor: men are likely to prioritize salary and status while women tend to see career success more as a process of personal development through interesting and challenging work (Burke and McKeen, 1994; Marshall, 1984; Nicholson and West, 1988; Powell and Maniero, 1992, 1993; Russo et al., 1991; Sturges, 1999). This may reflect the presence of career barriers which encourage women to focus on the intrinsic rewards of the task at hand rather than on the uncertainties of pay and status (Marshall, 1984; Nicholson and West, 1988). These differences in career orientation may well influence the nature of perceived career benefits from the MBA – a view supported by results from the UK research on MBA graduates. This indicates that men and women may benefit differently from the MBA along the lines discussed above. While men tended to gain extrinsic benefits of increased salary and managerial status, for women the benefits were likely to be more intrinsic in the form of enhanced confidence, credibility and job satisfaction. Men and women stressed the credential value of the course by emphasizing enhanced marketability and mobility, while women additionally valued the experience of the MBA in altering their perceptions of themselves, of their organization and of their work colleagues. Women were more likely to describe the MBA as an 'eye-opening' experience which encouraged self-confidence and self-belief and which gave them greater credibility within the organizational context. A similar finding emerged from Hilgert's (1998) study of six women graduates from an executive MBA programme where the MBA experience was associated with a 'new understanding of the world' and a 'life-changing' outcome. Within the context of the UK study, men were less likely to discuss such changes. Consequently, we would expect women to gain more than men in terms of the intrinsic career benefits and skills they gain from an MBA programme.

It is important to set potential gender differences in terms of benefits from the MBA in the context of recent literature on careers. In a survey of such literature, Martin and Butler (2000) found widespread agreement about the rise of 'boundaryless' or 'protean' careers. A 'new deal' is conceptualized whereby the traditional career (where salary, status and a secure career ladder within a single organization are exchanged for loyalty and commitment) may be giving way to new individual responsibility for career management in a more uncertain environment (Hall and Mirvis, 1996), where career paths go beyond the boundaries of a single organization (Hall, 1996) and where there is an emphasis on portable skills and on meaningful work (Hall and Mirvis, 1996). Such developments in career structures are likely to have important gender implications. As Fondas (1996) and Ensher et al. (2002) suggest, women's experiences and priorities may be more in line with the new career. These experiences, perhaps due to career barriers and/or care-taking responsibilities, involve career interruptions, 'outspiralling' moves and sudden changes in direction that are characteristic of the uncertainties inherent in the 'new career' environment (Burke and McKeen, 1994; Nicholson and West, 1988). According to Fondas, the combination of these experiences with the foregrounding of shared cooperation, empathy and flexibility, culturally associated with femininity, may make women better suited than men to boundaryless or protean careers in contemporary organizational contexts where team skills and relationships are emphasized. Accordingly, as Schneer and Reitman (2003) found in a study of MBA graduates, women managers on protean career paths may be more likely than women with more traditional 'organizational' careers to achieve equality with male counterparts, suggesting that protean careers may help facilitate women's progress.

From this new career perspective, the MBA may have a pivotal role for men and women in facilitating career development and as a means of acquiring a range of portable skills that are essential in the new boundaryless career environment. As we have seen, career development of men and women may differ post MBA and there may be differences in the range of skills men and women bring to the workplace, including skills acquired from the MBA. This is captured by the two propositions on which this research is based. Given the limited data on skills and benefits from the MBA – particularly in relation to gender differences – it is important to assess the success of the qualification in fulfilling these and other roles.

THE RESEARCH STUDY

The 30 MBA graduates interviewed for the research presented in this chapter were recruited from a larger sample of 225 graduates who had taken part in an earlier quantitative study, all from a leading business school in Ontario. Most of those surveyed had received their degrees between 1997 and 1999. For the qualitative study, graduates were recruited on the basis of their willingness to participate in the research. A random sample was selected from those who indicated that they would be interested in being interviewed. Given the interviewers' interest in gender differences, the aim was to recruit more or less equal numbers of men and women to the study. In total, 25 graduates participated in the qualitative study, 14 women and 11 men. They were drawn from the school's part-time and full-time

MBA programmes, and had worked for up to four years post graduation in a range of occupations, including finance, management consultancy, the public sector and self-employment. The graduates were aged between 25 and 44.

In order to gain an 'authentic' understanding of graduates' perceptions of benefits from the MBA (Silverman, 1993), semi-structured interviews were used. Each graduate was interviewed for approximately one hour, giving respondents the opportunity to reflect on the outcomes of the MBA. Graduates were asked about their motives for taking the MBA, their career history and career progress. In addition they were asked to reflect on the nature of skills and benefits acquired, the skills/benefits they valued most and those which had been most useful to them in their postgraduate careers.

RESEARCH FINDINGS

Most of the interviewees' motives for doing the MBA were extrinsic (e.g. career advancement, job opportunities). Almost all of the interviewees believed that they had progressed in their careers after completing their MBA and that they had benefited from acquiring a set of hard skills, in particular financial and data analysis. However, intrinsic benefits, such as increased confidence and credibility, emerged as highly important for the majority of the research participants. In addition, many of the women interviewed discussed gender as an issue and were critical of what they perceived to be the 'male ethos' of the course.

Intrinsic Benefits

Intrinsic benefits identified related to greater confidence and enhanced interpersonal skills in both internal and external work relationships.

Confidence
The most crucial benefit of the MBA acknowledged by all the interviewees was an increase in self-confidence. Closely aligned to this was improved credibility through being 'hallmarked' by the MBA. Analysis showed that there were two separate groups in terms of how they explained this increase in self-confidence. One group believed that their confidence had grown as a direct result of the 'hard' skills they had acquired on the course. This is captured by the following comments:

> I'm certainly more confident now . . . I think doing the course has had an impact on what I perceive my overall skills to be. (Male graduate)

> It wasn't about confidence in general but about confidence in a new area of skills . . . things that weren't necessarily part of my previous work experience. (Male graduate)

Another (predominantly female) group attributed their increase in confidence to what might be described as 'the MBA experience'. This included feelings of achievement from succeeding on a difficult and demanding MBA programme and feelings of self-worth and empowerment through being able to voice opinions openly. Some of the women expressed surprise and disbelief at what they had achieved: 'it's opened doors to myself'; 'it opened my eyes'; 'it was unbelievable for me'. One described her surprise at being in the top 10 per cent of her class:

> I never thought of myself as particularly bright. I always had to work hard for everything I got but I finished up on the Dean's List! That increased my confidence, having that official credential from an official body. (Female graduate)

Some women experienced a greater sense of self-worth: 'I feel better about myself'; 'I'm more comfortable in my own skin'; 'I'm more comfortable with who I am'. Enhanced confidence and knowledge gained from the MBA gave women in particular the self-assurance to verbalize ('it helped me speak') – to make their views known, to put their ideas on the table in meetings and to discuss issues with senior staff.

> I can put an idea on the table and have it move forward or adjusted or changed – but at least it gives them an idea of where I'm coming from because if I don't speak it they don't know. (Female graduate)

> I can hold a conversation (with the CEO) and hold his attention to it. (Female graduate)

> I'm more vocal because I have the foundations for it. (Female graduate)

Therefore, while all MBAs commented on the enhanced confidence the MBA can bring, gender differences emerged in terms of the source of this confidence. For men this related more to the acquisition of a set of (largely hard) tools and skills, while for women the source of confidence was more intrinsic, relating to feelings of achievement, self-worth and self-assurance.

Interpersonal skills

The majority of the interviewees reported improved teamworking skills as a result of doing the MBA. This was acknowledged to be a consequence of the emphasis on group work in the course, an experience that was sometimes painful and difficult (as individual groups did not always work well) but in general beneficial. Empathy, communication and listening skills were important for women. A group of women discussed how they were 'more objective', 'less emotional', 'more detached' and had 'toughened up' as a result of their MBA. This was seen as useful when difficult decisions had to be made.

Gender differences emerged in terms of the nature of these skills. For most of the men, interpersonal skills were largely discussed in terms of leadership. They specifically referred to leadership and discussed leadership issues as outcomes in this respect. These related first to a perceived enhancement of leadership capabilities as a result of the MBA experience. However, this did not always translate into better management skills in terms of managing their own teams at work. A minority of the interviewees who were staff managers claimed the MBA had helped them in this way. The rest felt that the MBA had had no effect – either because such skills could only be learned by experience or because they had not been addressed by the MBA programme. The second leadership issue addressed by inter-viewees related to the capacity to 'let go' and give up control. This was closely associated with trust and the ability to delegate, as the following quotes illustrate:

> It's a question of letting go sort of thing and not having control and trusting other people. (Male graduate)
>
> I think it's [the MBA experience] been relatively effective . . . I think over time if you learn to trust people you can sort of release that . . . grip on the project. (Male graduate)
>
> Before it was inconceivable that I would let someone else do something and put my name on it and trust them to do it as I intended. (Male graduate)
>
> Having to rely on somebody who you had absolutely no control over has been a good experience for me – however difficult. (Male graduate)

While the MBA emerged as less effective in acquiring skills to manage down (i.e. in terms of managing individuals and teams), many of the inter-viewees (both male and female) reported that the MBA had equipped them to manage upwards and to deal more effectively with their bosses. Sometimes this was a consequence of increased confidence and assertive-ness. For others, it sprang from a new awareness of the necessity to manage upwards and the acquisition of political skills enabling them to do so.

Gender and the MBA
Not surprisingly, gender was an important issue for women. While none of the men referred to gender (unless specifically asked about male/female experiences on the course), a large majority of the women raised gender as

an issue early in the interviews and without prompting. Difficulties of being female either in the context of the MBA course or at work were discussed, as were detrimental male attitudes and the problems associated with the integration of family and work. Overall, women were more critical of the programme, and this related mainly to what was perceived to be the 'macho' and competitive culture of the course. Women commented on the arrogant attitude and 'bravado' of male students and on their competitive behaviour – referring to the typical MBA graduate (described by one female student as 'Mighty Big Attitude') as, in their words, 'aggressive', 'competitive', 'arrogant' and 'overconfident'. None of the men interviewed commented on the gendered nature of the MBA experience.

IMPLICATIONS OF FINDINGS

The possibility that men prioritize extrinsic while women focus more on intrinsic career benefits has been raised by previous work (e.g. Marshall, 1984; Nicholson and West, 1988; Powell and Maneiro, 1992, 1993; Russo et al., 1991; Sturges, 1999). Similar gender differences in extrinsic and intrinsic skills and benefits from the MBA were suggested by the UK study, which found that men placed greater value on enhanced job marketability and mobility over job satisfaction, enhanced credibility and the development of interpersonal skills, prioritized by women (Simpson, 1995, 1996, 2000a).

This study suggests that, while both men and women gain intrinsic benefits from the MBA, they do so in different ways. Exceptions include enhanced confidence (discussed below) and the ability to deal confidently with bosses – seen as equally important by men and women. Such 'managing up' capabilities are important if, as Weick et al. (1999) suggest, managers need to be able to 'speak up to power' and send information fast in an upward direction. In terms of gender differences in intrinsic benefits, for men the focus is largely on issues of leadership. This relates to a perceived improvement in leadership skills as well as to a new-found ability to give up control through the development of trust in other team members. As Cianni and Wnuk (1997) indicate, teamworking frequently involves a tension between individual needs and team development and this can be resolved only if individuals 'give and take' in allocation of tasks, including leadership roles, and in the facilitation of learning. Integral to this process is the development of trust – a factor that has wider implications in terms of effective inter- and intra-firm collaboration (Weick et al., 1999). These results are important if it means that, as a result of the MBA, men experience a shift in what is often seen as a typically 'masculine' individualistic and directive approach (Collinson and Hearn, 2000; Fondas, 1996; Hearn, 1994; Kerfoot and Knights, 1993, 1998) to a more cooperative and supportive style.

Both men and women claim an increased confidence from the MBA. However, gender differences emerged in the antecedents of such confidence. For men, perceptions of enhanced confidence were tied up with the acquisition of identifiable hard skills, while for women confidence was seen to lead to several personal changes relating to feelings of achievement, greater self-worth and a sense of empowerment. In relation to achievement, as Ohlott et al. (1994) suggest, overcoming obstacles can be a powerful developmental and affirming experience for women. Conquering lack of self-confidence and coping with pressures from the course itself – as well as from possible family responsibilities – may therefore intensify feelings of triumph and personal success. Confidence also leads to a strong sense of self-worth – and there is evidence to suggest that this encourages a 'redrawing of mental boundaries' (Gunz et al., 2000, p. 29) as women expand the range of options thought to be possible or achievable. Finally, confidence from the MBA experience was seen by many women to give them a 'voice' and a sense of empowerment. The concept of voice was first used by Hirschman (1970) to describe how, in a political or a market context, citizens and consumers articulate their critical opinions. More recently, the term has been used in a gendered context (e.g. Belenky et al., 1997; Gilligan, 1982; Jansen and Davis, 1998) to refer to how women – seen to lack voice – are excluded and silenced from the private and public realms. For Gilligan, women often lose voice and freedom of expression as the need to preserve relationships and protect others becomes paramount, while for Belenky et al., acquiring a voice is intricately entwined with women's development of mind and of self in ways that have strong associations with the progress of female MBAs discussed above.

What seems likely is that men and women bring different attitudes and levels of intrinsic skills to the MBA. They may therefore benefit differently in terms of this particular skill set. As Marshall (1984) suggests, women may be more 'tuned into' interpersonal skills (it is women who identify the empathy and listening skills required of an experienced and successful team worker and who are critical of the more individualistic and competitive attitudes of men), but they often lack confidence in their own abilities and self-esteem. Changes in self-perception as a result of the MBA experience may therefore have a critical impact on the opportunities they see open to them and on how they see their effectiveness at work. Men may also experience a shift, from a more individualistic, controlling style of working to one based on trust and cooperation, and this could be equally cathartic in terms of self-evaluation and in creating the conditions for enhanced managerial performance.

The findings raise important issues for management education. First, while some people have argued that there are trends towards a 'feminization' of both careers (e.g. Burke and McKeen, 1994; Fondas, 1996) and of management (e.g. Fondas, 1993; Kanter, 1989; Lee, 1994), there is little sign that these trends have been reflected in the course content or design of the MBA. In terms of careers, as Fondas and Burke and McKeen point out, insecurity and frequent career shifts (previously characteristic of women's experiences) may be increasingly part of the 'new career' reality for men, less able to rely on steady increases in pay or predicable progression within a single organization. Similarly, the classical, 'masculine' notion of managerial work as consisting of 'planning, ordering, directing and controlling' (Fondas, 1996, p. 288; see also Alvesson, 1998; Collinson and Hearn, 2000; Kerfoot and Knights, 1993, 1998) is giving way to a need for cooperation, the building of relationships and responsiveness to others – culturally associated with femininity rather than masculinity (Alvesson, 1998; Kanter, 1989; Lee, 1994). Despite these possible trends towards feminization, however, MBA course culture and design (as many of our female interviewees pointed out) remain largely masculine. This view is supported by Sinclair (1995), who suggests that many MBA programmes are based on values of 'competition, individualism, instrumentalism and exclusiveness' (Sinclair, 1995, p. 296). Other work also points to the masculine nature of many programmes (e.g. Mavin and Bryars, 1999; Simpson, 2000a; Smith, 1997), which, as we have seen, may be largely out of touch with the demands of modern management. This, we argue, may suggest a need to 'feminize' the MBA through more cooperative work and through the encouragement of self-reflection, sharing and exchange so as to deepen emotional learning and mutual support, and to create a culture that is comfortable and developmental for both men and women.

Providers of MBAs – business schools – need to ensure that they market themselves on intrinsic benefits and interpersonal skills as well as the overt extrinsic benefits and hard skills from the programme (Sturges et al., 2003). As we have seen, these intrinsic outcomes are of increasing importance in the new career environment where managing team relationships and interpersonal skills are key to success (Hall and Mirvis, 1996). In what has been described as a 'saturated' market (*Business Week*, 2000), MBA providers can gain competitive advantage by marketing and promoting such benefits as key outcomes of the MBA experience and as critical to the professional and managerial career. Overlooking these benefits in promotional and marketing material not only fails to capitalize on an important outcome from the MBA, but may send the wrong messages to its students in terms of the priorities of the programme.

ACKNOWLEDGEMENT

This chapter is adapted from an article that previously appeared in the *Journal of Management Education*: Simpson, R., Sturges, J., Altman, Y. and Woods, A. (2005), 'Gender, age and the MBA: analysis of extrinsic and intrinsic career benefits', *Journal of Management Education*, **29**: 219–47.

REFERENCES

Alvesson, M. (1998), 'Gender relations and identity at work: a case study of masculinities and femininities in an advertising agency', *Human Relations*, **51**(8): 113–26.

AMBA (1997), *Annual Report*, London: Association of MBAs.

Baruch, Y. and Peiperl, M. (2000), 'The impact of the MBA on graduate careers', *Human Resource Management Journal*, **10**(2): 69–90.

Belenky, M., Clinchy, B., Goldberger, N. and Tarule, J. (1997), *Women's Ways of Knowing: The Development of Self, Voice and Mind*, New York: Basic Books.

Boyatzis, R. and Renio, A. (1989), 'The impact of an MBA programme on managerial abilities', *Journal of Management Development*, **18**(5): 25–39.

Burke, R. (1994), 'Women in corporate management in Canadian organizations: slow progress?', *Executive Development*, **7**(3): 15–24.

Burke, R. and McKeen, C. (1994), 'Career development among managerial and professional women', in M. Davidson and R. Burke (eds), *Women in Management: Current Research Issues*, London: Chapman, pp. 65–80.

Business Week (1997), 'What's an MBA worth?', 25, 31 October.

Business Week (2000), 'Ranking global programs', 54, 2 October.

Catalyst (2005), *Census of Women Board Directors of Canada*, New York: Catalyst.

Catalyst (2000), *Women and the MBA: Gateway to Opportunity*, New York: Catalyst.

Cianni, M. and Wnuk, D. (1997), 'Individual growth and team enhancement: moving towards a new model of career development', *The Academy of Management Executive*, **11**(1): 105–16.

Clark, A., Oswald, A. and Warr, P. (1996), 'Is job satisfaction U-shaped in age?', *Journal of Occupational and Organizational Psychology*, **69**: 57–81.

Collinson, D. and Hearn, J. (2000), 'Critical studies of men, masculinities and management', in M. Davidson and R. Burke (eds), *Women in Management: Current Research Issues*, London: Sage, pp. 263–79.

Cox, T. and Harquil, C. (1991), 'Career paths and career success in early career stages of male and female MBAs', *Journal of Vocational Behaviour*, **39**: 54–75.

Ensher, E., Murphy, S. and Sullivan, S. (2002), 'Boundaryless careers in entertainment: executive women's experiences', in M. Peiperl, M. Arthur and N. Anand (eds), *Career Creativity: Explorations in the Remaking of Work*, Oxford: Oxford University Press, pp. 229–55.

Fondas, N. (1993), 'The feminization of American management', in D. Moore (ed.), *Academy of Management Best Paper Proceedings*, Atlanta: Academy of Management, 358–62.

Fondas, N. (1996), 'Feminization at work: career implications', in M. Arthur and D. Rousseau (eds), *The Boundaryless Career*, New York: Oxford University Press, pp. 73–80.

Gilligan, C. (1982), *In a Different Voice: Psychological Theory and Women's Development*, Cambridge, MA: Harvard University Press.

Goffee, R. and Nicholson, N. (1994), 'Career development in male and female managers – convergence or collapse', in R. Burke and M. Davidson (eds), *Women in Management: Current Research Issues*, London: Paul Chapman, pp. 80–93.

Gunderson, M. (1994a), 'Pay and employment equity in the United States and Canada', *International Journal of Manpower*, **15**(7): 45–60.

Gunderson, M. (1994b), *Comparable Worth and Gender Discrimination: International Aspects*, Geneva: International Labour Office.

Gunz, H., Evans, M. and Jalland, M. (2000), 'Career boundaries in a boundaryless world', in M. Peiperl, M. Arthur, R. Goffee and T. Morris (eds), *Career Frontiers*, New York: Oxford University press, pp. 24–54.

Hall, D. (1996), 'Long live the career: a relational approach', in D. Hall (ed.), *The Career is Dead – Long Live the Career*, San Francisco, CA: Jossey Bass, pp. 15–30.

Hall, D. and Mirvis, P. (1996), 'The new protean career', in D. Hall (ed.), *The Career is Dead – Long Live the Career*, San Francisco, CA: Jossey Bass, pp. 63–78.

Hearn, J. (1994), 'Changing men and changing management: social change, social research and social action', in M. Davidson and R. Burke (eds), *Women in Management: Current Research Issues*, London: Paul Chapman, pp. 192–213.

Hilgert, A. (1998), 'Professional development of women and the MBA', *Journal of Management Development*, **17**(9): 629–43.

Hirschman, A. (1970), *Exit, Voice and Loyalty: Responses to Decline in Firms, Organizations and the State*, Cambridge, MA: Harvard University Press.

Institute of Management, (2004), *National Management Salary Survey*, London: Institute of Management.

Jansen, G. and Davis, R. (1998), 'Honoring voice and visibility: sensitive-topic research and feminist interpretive inquiry', *Affilia Journal of Women and Social Work*, **13**(3): 289–302.

Kakabadse, N. and Kakabadse, A. (1999), 'Demographics and leadership philosophy: exploring gender differences', *Journal of Management Development*, **17**(5–6): 351–89.

Kanter, R. (1989), 'The new managerial work', *Harvard Business Review*, **67**(6): 85–92.

Kerfoot, D. and Knights, D. (1993), 'Management masculinity and manipulation: from paternalism to corporate strategy in financial services in Britain', *Journal of Management Studies*, **30**(4): 659–77.

Kerfoot, D. and Knights, D. (1998), 'Managing masculinity in contemporary organizational life: a man(agerial) project', *Organization*, **5**(1): 7–26.

Kretovics, M. (1999), 'Assessing the MBA. What do our students learn?', *Journal of Management Development*, **18**(2): 125–36.

Labour Force Survey (1997), Office for National Statistics, London: HMSO.

Labour Force Survey (2002), Office for National Statistics, London: HMSO.

Lee, C. (1994), 'The feminization of management', *Training*, November: 25–31.

Marshall, J. (1984), *Women Managers: Travellers in a Male World*, Chichester, UK: John Wiley & Sons.

Marshall, J. (1995), *Women Managers Moving On*, London: Routledge.

Martin, G. and Butler, M. (2000), 'Comparing managerial careers, management development and management education in the UK and the USA: some theoretical and practical considerations', *International Journal for Training and Development*, **4**(3): 196–207.

Mavin, S. and Bryars, P. (1999), 'Gender on the agenda of management education', *Women in Management Review*, **14**(3): 99–104.

Messmer, M. (1998), 'The value of an MBA', *Management Accounting*, **80**(4): 23–4.

Mintzberg, H. and Gosling, J. (2002), 'Reality programming for MBAs', *Strategy and Business*, **26**(1): 28–31.

Nicholson, N. and West, M. (1988), *Managerial Job Change: Men and Women in Transition*, Cambridge: Cambridge University Press.

Ohlott, P., Ruderman, M. and McCauley, C. (1994), 'Gender differences in managers' developmental job experiences', *Academy of Management Journal*, **37**(1): 46–67.

Pfeffer, J. and Fong, C. (2002), 'The end of business schools? Less success than meets the eye', *Academy of Management Learning and Education*, **1**(1): 78–95.

Powell, G. and Maniero, L. (1992), 'Cross-currents in the river of time: conceptualisating the complexities of women's careers', *Journal of Management*, **18**(2): 215–37.

Powell, G. and Maniero, L. (1993), 'Getting ahead – in career and in life', in G. Powell (ed.), *Women and Men in Management*, 2nd edn, Newbury Park, CA: Sage.

Russo, N., Kelly, M. and Deacon, M. (1991), 'Gender and sex related attribution: beyond individualistic conceptions of achievement', *Sex Roles*, **25**: 331–50.

Scase, R. and Goffee, R. (1989), *Reluctant Managers: Their Work and Lifestyles*, London: Unwin Hyman.

Schneer, J. and Reitman, F. (1990), 'Effects of employment gaps on the careers of MBAs: more damaging for men than women?', *Academy of Management Journal*, **33**(2): 392–406.

Schneer, J. and Reitman, F. (1995), 'The impact of gender as managerial careers unfold', *Journal of Vocational Behaviour*, **51**: 411–34.

Schneer, J. and Reitman, F. (2003), 'The promised path: a longitudinal study of managerial careers', *Journal of Managerial Psychology*, **18**(1/2): 60–75.

Shipper, F. (1999), 'A comparison of managerial skills of middle managers with MBAs, with other masters and undergraduate degrees ten years after the Porter and McKibbin report', *Journal of Managerial Psychology*, **14**(2): 55–70.

Silverman, D. (1993), *Interpreting Qualitative Data: Methods for Analysing Talk, Text and Interaction*, London: Sage.

Simpson, R. (1995), 'Is management education on the right track for women?', *Women in Management Review*, **10**(6): 3–8.

Simpson, R. (1996), 'Does an MBA help women?', *Gender, Work and Organisation*, **3**(2): 13–19.

Simpson, R. (2000a), 'Winners and losers: who benefits most from the MBA?', *Management Learning*, **31**(2): 46–54.

Simpson, R. (2000b), 'A voyage of discovery or a fast track to success: men, women and the MBA', *Journal of Management Development*, **19**(9): 764–82.

Simpson, R. and Altman, Y. (2000), 'A time bounded glass ceiling: the career progress of young women managers', *Journal of European Industrial Training*, **24**(2–4): 190–98.

Sinclair, A. (1995), 'Sex and the MBA', *Organization*, **2**(2): 295.

Smeenk, B. (1993), 'Canada's pay equity experiments', *HRMagazine*, **38**(9): 58–62.
Smith, C. (1997), 'Gender issues on management education: a new teaching resource?', *Women in Management Review*, **12**(3): 100–104.
Statistics Canada (1997), *Census 1995*, Ottawa: Ministry of Industry, Science and Technology.
Statistics Canada (2002), *Women in Canada*, Ottawa: Ministry of Industry, Science and Technology.
Sturges, J. (1999), 'What it means to succeed: personal conceptions of career success held by male and female managers at different ages', *British Journal of Management*, **10**: 239–52.
Sturges, J., Simpson, R. and Altman, Y. (2003), 'Capitalising on learning: an exploration of the MBA as a vehicle for developing career competencies', *International Journal of Training and Development*, **7**(1): 53–67.
Weick, K., Mintzberg, H. and Senge, P. (1999), *Transforming Management Education for the 21st Century*, Symposium conducted at the Annual Conference for the Academy of Management, Chicago, IL.
Young, B., Worchel, S. and Woehr, D. (1998), 'Organizational commitment among public service employees', *Public Personnel Management*, **27**(3): 339–49.

23. The value of MBA education and its role in entrepreneurship for women and people of color

Jennifer M. Sequeira and Myrtle P. Bell

Over the years, the Master of Business Administration degree (MBA) has increased in popularity. In 2002, Stern indicated that, worldwide, more than 100 000 people were pursuing the MBA degree, 70 000 of those in the USA (Stern, 2002). The majority of these individuals may be pursuing the MBA in order to bring about a positive change in their career or to change careers outright (see Sturges et al., 2003). Women and people of color[1] are among those who seek to effect change in their careers by pursuing the MBA. Although recently there has been increased attention given in the literature to the career success of women MBAs (see Burke and McKeen, 1994; Catalyst, 2000; Simpson, 2000), there is a dearth of research on racial and ethnic minority MBAs and career success. We also find that there is little research on entrepreneurship outcomes of women and racial and ethnic minority MBAs. In an attempt to fill the void in this research, this chapter examines the role of the MBA as it relates to the success of women and people of color, particularly those who choose an entrepreneurial career.

Although the MBA has been increasingly pursued over the last two decades, its prestige has fluctuated during that same period. There has been increasing debate as to the degree's value both to individuals enrolled in MBA programs and greater society. Throughout the 1980s the MBA was increasingly in demand; however, its prestige waned in the 1990s when discussions arose as to its usefulness and suitability. The MBA regained its prestige in the late 1990s (Hahs, 1999), but recently, popular press reports as well as academic discussions have again begun to question its value (Feldman, 2005). Similar criticisms to those of earlier years point to the need for business schools to change in order to meet the changing demands of students and a changing environment (Ewers, 2005; Mintzberg, 2004). Critics indicate that the MBA is overly focused on analytical approaches to decision making and business functions, while lacking emphasis on the 'practice of managing' (Mintzberg and Gosling, 2002; Pfeffer and Fong,

2003) and the teaching of 'soft' skills. Mintzberg (2004) is a proponent of the teaching of 'soft' skills such as teamwork, communication and leadership instead of the strict focus on analytical and functional skills that is often found in many MBA programs. Mintzberg (2004) argues that the typical MBA program offers specialized training in business functions but lacks an emphasis on general education as it relates to managing. In their arguments about the value of an MBA education, Pfeffer and Fong (2003, p. 369) assert that 'the MBA is a brand that can provide some initial placement success and higher salary upon graduation but does not necessarily help its graduates succeed and do better on the job'. These comments are just a few among many that have begun questioning the value of the MBA in its current form. The question that this debate raises is the following. Does the MBA contribute to the success of its recipients in any way and, if so, are these contributions particularly helpful for women and people of color, especially those who desire to start their own businesses?

Thus the purpose of this chapter is to examine the role that race, ethnicity and sex may play in women's and racial and ethnic minority MBA graduates' career success, particularly the choice of an entrepreneurial career. Through this examination, we hope to contribute to a broader understanding of the impact of MBA programs on women and people of color and provide some insight into how these programs may be modified to accommodate the needs of overlooked populations when designing MBA curricula. The structure of the chapter is as follows. First, we examine the reasons that women and people of color pursue the MBA and their experiences in MBA programs. Next, we look at the general benefits that may be gained by women and people of color as a result of the MBA, as well as the specific benefits for those who are interested in business ownership. Finally, we offer suggestions that may serve to enhance the experience of women and people of color in MBA programs.

WOMEN, PEOPLE OF COLOR, AND THE MBA

In understanding issues related to women we must take a multidimensional view since women are not just 'gendered beings' nor are they homogeneous; their ethnic or racial identity also plays a role and intersects with their gender (Addi-Raccah, 2005; Hoffman, 2006). As Browne and Mira (2003, p. 218) so aptly state, 'the interaction between gender and ethnicity or race exposes individuals to unique life experiences and social opportunities that cannot be fully explained by examination of each ascribed category net of the other'. This interaction may also produce varying effects and patterns of inequality that may more accurately explain the occupational outcomes of particular women (Addi-Raccah, 2005; Carlson, 1992). We therefore begin by discussing a relevant issue for the ethnic minority woman in terms of careers.

Bell and Nkomo (2001) argue that all women do not have the same experiences. These authors maintain that geography, social location, race and their combined effects play a role in shaping women's identities and realities. In discussing minority women in the workplace, researchers have described these women using various terms. They have been labeled as 'doubly disadvantaged' (Addi-Raccah, 2005), having 'double jeopardy' (Beale, 1970), being in a 'double bind' (Anderson, 1988; Almquist, 1989), and being a 'double minority' (King, 1988), with all these terms referring to their combined status as a woman and a member of a minority group. This 'double' status has thereby resulted in these women having the least amount of economic power and status (Almquist and Wherle-Einhorn, 1978; Fulbright, 1986), which leads to unique career experiences within organizations (Bell and Nkomo, 1999, 2001) which ultimately affects their career success. A few authors have argued that some women of color may have an advantage due to their greater visibility, uniqueness, or rarity in the organization (see Epstein, 1973; Adler et al., 1995). The abundance of research on the status opportunities and advancement of women of color indicates that this is generally not the case, however (e.g. Almquist and Wherle-Einhorn, 1978; Anderson, 1988; Cocchiara et al., 2006; Fulbright, 1986; Giscombe and Mattis, 2002; 'Women of Color', 2003). We acknowledge that in some limited cases some women may benefit from their status as a racial or ethnic minority; however, particular ethnic background, country of context, and other demographic or environmental factors would play a role in determining the extent of these advantages and their effect on career success.

Career success is defined as 'the positive psychological or work-related outcomes or achievements one has accumulated as a result of one's work experiences' (see Judge et al., 1995, p. 485). Career success has both objective (pay, compensation, promotions) and subjective (career satisfaction and feelings of accomplishment) dimensions (Judge et al., 1995). In discussing career success, this chapter considers and addresses both the objective and subjective dimensions.

One important factor in career success is the role or influence of one's qualifications on career success. Simpson (2000, p. 766) specifically proposes that 'the extent to which qualifications contribute to career success has been part of the debate surrounding the career progress of women'. Although Simpson's statement was limited to women, it could also be applied to people of color, given that both women and people of color (including women of color) face similar discrimination in the workplace.

Adler et al. (1995, p. 247) argue that the 'double minority status of Black women may make them especially vulnerable within White male-defined institutional cultures', leading to disadvantages in terms of income attainment, authority and career progression. Therefore women and people of color may seek the MBA to counteract the discrimination and negative stereotypes that they encounter in the workplace as well as to enhance their opportunities for career success. In general, however, women and people of color are not well represented in many US MBA programs. Although women make up 51 percent of the US population and 48 percent of undergraduate students in US business schools, they represent only 29 percent of the students in the top 20 MBA programs and 37 percent in all MBA programs (Catalyst, 2000, 2005). This underrepresentation of women has remained fairly constant in the last decade. People of color are also underrepresented relative to their population in the USA as well as to that of the representation of Whites. According to the American Assembly of Collegiate Schools of Business (AACSB), only 5.3 percent of MBA students are African American, 5.2 percent Hispanic American, and less than 1 percent Native American. Their proportions in the US population are about 12 percent, 14 percent and 1 percent, respectively (US Census Bureau, 2004). It is important to determine whether the MBA brings added value for those relatively few women and racial and ethnic minority students who are enrolled in MBA programs and whether or not it contributes to their career success. To gain insight, we must first look at the reasons why women and people of color choose to pursue an MBA.

Motivations to Pursue MBA Education

Various studies have found differing motivations for pursuit of the MBA. A 2003 Graduate Management Admission Council (GMAC) study, which surveyed 10 029 students (71 percent White, 13 percent Black/African American, 7 percent Hispanic American, and 7 percent Asian American) who registered on the GMAC website (www.mba.com), found that four primary issues underlie an individual's decision to pursue the graduate management degree (MBA). These factors are fit (the perception of whether the MBA will lead to the achievement of career goals), preparedness (the perception of whether they will be admitted given their background and experience), financial resources (the perception that they will be able to not only finance their degree but see a return on their investment) and commitment (willingness to assume the challenges and sacrifices that will be necessary to complete the degree) (Edgington, 2003). The GMAC study also found that the top three factors that led to the graduate enrollment decision were: the need to remain marketable/competitive; long-term income improvement and financial stability; and the need to gain personal satisfaction and achievement. Similar findings were reported in a study by Piotrowski and Cox (2004), who found that students' motivation for pursuing the MBA degree included: to improve job opportunities, to increase potential income, to upgrade credentials, to broaden job skills, love of the field and personal achievement. Simmering and Wilcox (1995) found that students pursued the MBA for personal prestige, career exploration, interpersonal influence (enhancement of skills), entrepreneurism (learn skills necessary to become an entrepreneur) and mobility (enhance job opportunities and salary). Although these findings are similar and often interrelated, they do not specifically shed light on the motivations of women and people of color for pursuing the MBA.

Research indicates that women tend to seek higher-level management education, such as the MBA, to gain more expertise, knowledge, skills and confidence, as well as to overcome some of the barriers that they faced in their corporate careers, such as the glass ceiling (Burke and McKeen, 1994; Ong, 1993; Simpson, 2000). People of color may pursue the MBA for similar benefits. Women of color find it far more difficult than women in the dominant group to progress in an organization's hierarchy (Blackmore, 1999). In addition, various studies have shown that people of color are disadvantaged in many ways in the corporate world. 'Empirical findings consistent with the "double jeopardy view" indicate that once a woman or a Black person enters a white male-dominated profession, s/he faces barriers, such as exclusion from the informal structure of the profession' (see Adler et al., 1995, p. 247). Cox and Nkomo (1991) and Greenhaus et al. (1990) found in their studies that people of color received lower performance ratings, pay and promotions in comparison to Whites. Similarly Judge et al.'s (1995) study found that both women and people of color had lower levels of pay and fewer promotions. In Edgington and Garcia's (2005) study, African-American respondents considering the MBA had concerns about whether their race would limit their success in the business world and questioned whether or not an educational institution and the business world would embrace their unique experiences and background. Underlying this factor is the finding that this group felt more strongly than other groups (i.e. Asian Americans, Whites and Hispanic Americans) that the glass ceiling was very real in business (Edgington, 2003) and indicated that they made the decision to apply to business school because of a lack of respect in their workplaces (Schoenfeld and Edgington, 2004). Given that people of color and women may have similar reasons for attending business school, a legitimate question is whether business school, in particular, the 'MBA degree', meets the expectations of these individuals.

THE MBA EXPERIENCE FOR WOMEN AND PEOPLE OF COLOR

The answer to the question of whether the MBA meets expectations for women and people of color can be examined from two different perspectives. The first is through considering the experiences of women and people of color as they go through MBA programs, and the second is through analyzing the benefits that these individuals may gain as a result of having done so.

Many women and Black students complain that their experiences in their MBA programs were inadequate in terms of course content and student body and faculty diversity. Based on the findings of various studies (see Edgington, 2004; Edgington and Marshall, 2005; GMAC, 2004), it appears that both women and students of color sought a student body and faculty composed of similar others when choosing a business school. Programs containing such diversity, however, were not easily found. In addition, upon entering MBA programs, both minority and non-minority women found that the business school culture was 'overly aggressive' and 'competitive' (Catalyst, 2000). In Catalyst's 'Gateway' study of more than 1600 MBA graduates from 12 top business schools, approximately 23 percent of White women and 46 percent of Black women voiced these feelings. These comments are echoed by various authors, who suggest that not only is the MBA course design and culture inherently masculine in nature (Catalyst, 2000; Mavin and Bryans, 1999; Simpson, 2006), but the values of competition, individualism, instrumentalism and exclusiveness, all of which form the MBA foundation, are very masculine in nature as well (Sinclair, 1995, 2000). Black women, more than others in the 'Gateway' study, tended to feel excluded in class. Data showed that 16 percent of White men, 25 percent of White women, 27 percent of Black men and 47 percent of Black women had difficulty getting their points heard during class. Almost 40 percent of all the women in the study found that opportunities to work with female professors were inadequate, while more than 50 percent could not relate to protagonists in case studies.

Minority MBA students complain of similar issues, adding that the case protagonists are White and male (see *Black Issues in Higher Education*, 2005; and the 'Gateway' study (Catalyst, 2000), where only 27 percent of Black women and 38 percent of Black men could relate to those in case studies versus 52 percent of White women and 68 percent of White men). According to *Black Issues in Higher Education* (2005), only 2.8 percent of the 6000 available Harvard Business School cases feature Black business-related issues. Because Harvard Business School Publishing provides 80 percent of business school cases, the lack of Black business-related issues and protagonists is particularly disturbing. Other researchers suggest that in addition to White male-oriented case studies, the sexist attitudes of male lecturers, lack of female role models, lack of a critical mass of women that could provide support, and gender-exclusive language (Mavin and Bryans, 1999; Simpson, 2000; Smith, 1997) may serve to isolate women. In addition, the fact is that many women and people of color do not see themselves represented among the faculty (Catalyst, 2000) given the dearth of women and racial and ethnic minority faculty in business schools. Recent figures indicate that Black, Hispanic, and American-Indian professors make up less than 3 percent (PhD Project, 2002) and women represent only 23 percent of full-time faculty (Alsop, 2001) at US business schools. Therefore, for people of color and women, role models or exemplars are missing both in the curriculum and among those implementing the curriculum. Although these negative experiences are frequently expressed, women and people of color may still reap benefits as a result of having gone through MBA programs.

BENEFITS OF THE MBA FOR WOMEN AND PEOPLE OF COLOR

Various studies point out that, in general, individuals (regardless of racial or ethnic background) do gain value from the MBA (e.g. Baruch and Peiperl, 2000; Boyatzis and Renio, 1989; Hahs, 1999). Pursuit of the MBA and the MBA degree provides an 'immediate social role' and self-definition where one's identity is based on the earning of the degree (e.g. 'I am an MBA') (Simmering and Wilcox, 1995). In addition to an immediate social identity, studies have demonstrated that students have experienced improvements in various dimensions such as strategic thinking, information integration abilities (Van Auken et al., 2005), oral and written communication skills and networking. Baruch et al.'s (2005) study found that both MBA graduates and specialist graduate business degree recipients experienced improvements in human capital. Human capital consists of four factors: scholastic (knowledge gained); social (resources based on network creation); inner value (competencies such as self-awareness); and cultural capital (status and reputation).

In addition to the above improvements, women and people of color may gain other benefits. Given that Black GMAC survey respondents expressed that they experienced a lack of respect in the workplace and held high interest in business ownership, achievement of the MBA degree and the pedigree of 'MBA' may lead to improved professional image and credibility in general and particularly when starting and managing a business. Roberts

(2005, pp. 687 and 699) defines professional image as the aggregate of key constituents' (i.e. clients, bosses, superiors, subordinates and colleagues) perceptions of one's competence and character' and credibility 'as the extent to which others believe an individual's self-presentation of personal and social identity is a reasonably accurate portrayal of his or her attributes'. Roberts (2005, p. 689) adds that 'professional image construction has important implications for achieving social approval, power, well-being and career success', while credibility is necessary because identity claims must be honored given a particular context. Melamed (1996) makes the case that qualifications and education are objective merits that may increase the credibility of women, who are often viewed as being less credible than men due to negative stereotypes. Indeed, women entrepreneurs who participated in a Catalyst (1998) study indicated that 'not being taken seriously' was a factor that precipitated their desire to leave the corporate environment. Negative stereotypes also haunt those people of color whose intellectual ability and competence are often questioned (Cokley et al., 2004). Therefore achievement of the MBA may contain added value for both women and people of color.

Women may reap some additional benefits beyond enhanced professional image and credibility. For women, the MBA may play a role in future career success. Research shows that the MBA increases self-confidence and the capacity to fight sexist attitudes (Hilgert, 1998; Leeming and Baruch, 1998; Sturges et al., 2003). Indeed, Simpson (2000) found that women MBA graduates felt that their networks were broadened by the MBA and that they had overcome credibility issues and increased their confidence. These improvements led them to have a more proactive approach to work problems and increased engagement in work-related discussions.

Women have therefore been encouraged to view the MBA as a way to penetrate the glass ceiling (Bickerstaffe, 1992). For women of color, who fight sexist attitudes along with stereotypic racial biases, the value of the MBA may be even more beneficial. Minority women may be able to rise above their 'double disadvantage' by exceeding their gender and ethnic or racial counterparts in background characteristics such as education (Banks, 2000). Some researchers have argued, however, that the MBA has not provided major advances for women in all areas. A study of 502 MBAs conducted by Cox and Harquail (1991) showed that women MBAs had fewer significant management promotions. Other studies of MBA holders found that although the MBA helped the career progress of both men and women, men appeared to have benefited more in terms of earning power, and movement into senior management functions and roles (Simpson, 2000). The Catalyst 'Gateway' study discussed earlier supports the differing results for women of color in comparison to those of others. In this study,

88 percent of Black women MBAs indicated that the MBA was valuable to their career in comparison to 85 percent of White women, 83 percent of White men and 80 percent of Black men. However, Catalyst also found that Black women MBAs showed the least overall career advancement (66 percent) in comparison to White women (76 percent), White men (82 percent), and Black men (71 percent) (Catalyst, 2000).

THE MBA AND ENTREPRENEURSHIP AS A CAREER CHOICE

As a result of the more limited value of the MBA for women's career progress in corporations (Cox and Harquail, 1991; Simpson, 2000) and women's exit from corporations due to advancement barriers faced there (see Catalyst, 1998; Moore and Buttner, 1997), it is appropriate to explore the value of an MBA to women who choose careers as entrepreneurs. We first examine the literature regarding the value of an MBA to entrepreneurs in general, and then turn to the value for women and people of color, in particular.

Entrepreneurship courses can be found at almost every AACSB-accredited and non-AACSB-accredited university and college, and this number is growing worldwide (Greene et al., 2004; Katz, 2003). While some researchers and entrepreneurs argue that entrepreneurship cannot be taught, others argue that certain entrepreneurial skills and abilities can be taught and knowledge disseminated that can assist individuals who desire to own their own businesses. For those who believe that entrepreneurship can be taught, there is debate as to what should be taught, with various researchers having their own ideas (see Mintzberg, 2004; Mintzberg and Gosling, 2002). There is general agreement that there are specific skills and training that must be acquired during any entrepreneurship education program. Among the necessary concepts espoused by researchers, entrepreneurship educators and entrepreneurs are the ability to analyze business risk, knowledge of the steps in the pursuit of capital, knowledge of exit strategies (Lord and Westfall, 1996), the ability to think creatively and implement ideas, and opportunity identification. These have all been highlighted as being necessary for entrepreneurial success.

The question that seems to persist regarding entrepreneurship education is whether these skills and abilities can be taught in a classroom or in an MBA program. Entrepreneur David Birch, in an interview conducted by Magnus Aronsson (2004), expresses doubt that the competencies needed for successful entrepreneurship can be taught in a classroom setting. Birch argues that 'learning by shadowing', as is done in an apprenticeship relationship with an established entrepreneur, is possibly the best way that entrepreneurship skills can be gained. In reference to the MBA and entrepreneurship, Mintzberg (2004) argues that MBA graduates are missing when successful business start-ups are considered.

On the other hand, research findings indicate that intentions to begin a business increase as a result of exposure to certain types of entrepreneurship education (Honig, 2004). A study which looked at the entrepreneurial success rates of the University of Arizona's Berger entrepreneurship program (see Charney and Libecap, 2004) found that the alumni tended to start more businesses, grow bigger businesses, and viewed themselves as key factors in new product development. Baron (2006) argues that individuals can be taught to identify opportunities by being taught how to search for them and where. He suggests this can be done by providing training on how to identify technological, demographic and market changes and the connections between them, which in turn would give these individuals an advantage in opportunity search and identification. The work of Detienne and Chandler (2004) also suggests that the competency of opportunity identification can be taught in a classroom. As can be seen, opinions differ about the value of entrepreneurship education. Regardless of the ongoing debate about the value of entrepreneurship education, it is growing in popularity at the graduate level, as can be seen by the growing number of schools that are implementing new entrepreneurship MBA programs or programs that incorporate some aspects of entrepreneurship training. Given the popularity of these programs and the growing number of people of color and women who desire to start their own businesses, are these programs meeting their specific needs?

THE MBA AND ENTREPRENEURSHIP FOR WOMEN AND PEOPLE OF COLOR

We can begin the discussion of the role that the MBA plays for women and people of color interested in business start-up by looking at recent statistics on women and racial and ethnic minority business ownership. Statistics from the 2002 US Census indicate that, in 2002, there were approximately 6.5 million businesses that were 51 percent or more owned by women. These firms generated more than $940 billion in revenues (US Census Bureau, 2006). Among individuals aged 18–64, Black/African-American individuals were approximately 50 percent more likely to attempt business start-up than White men and women. Recent figures indicate that 'African-Americans were the only major ethnic or racial group to experience an increase in the rate of entrepreneurial activity in 2005. The rate of entrepreneurial activity for this group increased from 0.21 percent in 2004 to 0.24 percent in 2005' (Fairlie, 2006, p. 3).

Statistics regarding the number of women of color who own businesses are equally interesting. As of 2004, there were an estimated 1.4 million privately held firms owned by women of color in the USA, representing 21.4 percent of all privately held women-owned firms. These firms employed approximately 1.3 million people and generated approximately $147 billion in sales (Center for Women's Business Research, 2004). Between 1997 and 2004, the number of privately held firms that are 51 percent or more owned by women of color grew by 54.6 percent, while all privately held firms in the USA grew by 9 percent (Center for Women's Business Research, 2005).

For all entrepreneurs, regardless of their race, ethnicity or sex, survival of the firm is an ongoing concern. However, this concern takes on greater importance for women and people of color due to structural and stereotypic biases that they have historically faced in corporations (see Weiler and Bernasek, 2001) and the business world (e.g. such as less access to financing) (see Greene et al., 2001).

The survival of the firm has been investigated by many researchers. Recent statistics show that 66 percent of new firms survive at least two years while 44 percent survive at least four years (Knaup, 2005). Research indicates that the survival of the firm is a function of the characteristics of the business and of the owner(s). Firm survival was found to be linked to four major reasons: (1) the owner's reason for starting the business (i.e. work–life balance, be own boss); (2) being an employer firm; (3) having adequate start-up capital; and (4) the owner's education level (i.e. college degree) (Headd, 2003). Bates (1990) found that the strongest human capital variable associated with business continuance was years of education and adds that the 'level of owner education is a major determinant of the loan amounts that commercial banks extend to small business formations' and concludes that 'highly educated entrepreneurs – those with four or more years of college – are most likely to create firms that remain in operation' (Bates, 1990, pp. 551, 558).

Given that the owner's education level plays a role in entrepreneurial success and an increasing number of women and people of color are starting businesses, it is important to determine whether MBA programs indeed assist these individuals in accomplishing their goal. Having said this, we must acknowledge that research on the outcomes of MBA entrepreneurship programs (particularly for racial and ethnic minority graduates) is sparse and just beginning to filter out as MBA entrepreneurship programs are fairly new to many universities. We will therefore discuss this issue in light of the value of the general MBA.

Although the debate as to the value of the MBA continues and the jury is still out as to its value, it appears that acquiring the MBA may be instrumental in entrepreneurial success for women and people of color. Researchers suggest that the human and social capital of venture founders are variables that affect entrepreneurship positively (Eisenhardt and Schoonhoven, 1990; Shane and Stuart, 2002). We can presume that the individual's level of human capital (knowledge gained) is enhanced as a result of the MBA (see Baruch et al., 2005). In addition to human capital, however, the MBA may provide the opportunity to acquire social capital, which, according to Baruch et al. (2005, p. 53), is 'manifested in network-ing and the creation of personal contacts and (social capital) can be improved through graduate business studies' due to participation in asso-ciations and social activities. In Simpson's (2000) study, women indicated that their networks were broadened as a result of the MBA. Larger net-works may bring benefits critical to those who aspire to be entrepreneurs since it may aid in opportunity identification. According to Hills et al. (1997), the more people that entrepreneurs know and have relationships with, the more opportunities they tend to identify.

Literature on mentoring and networks indicates that access to a network containing influential relationships and possession of an influential mentor are critical to career success (e.g. Dreher and Ash, 1990; Dreher and Cox, 1996; McGuire, 2000), but Blacks may have more difficulty than Whites in creating relationships with influential people due to existing structural iso-lation (Cokley et al., 2004). Racial and ethnic minority women, more than others, were found to need resources such as sponsorship and social capital in order to be selected for leadership positions in organizations (Tallerico, 2000; Ortiz, 2001). This is underscored by the results of a study conducted by Catalyst (2001) which reports that Black women felt that lack of influential mentors, sponsors and colleagues with whom they could network, as well as a lack of same race role models, were factors that limited their advancement. Thus the social networks of Black and White profes-sionals and those of women and men are different. These differences are related to career outcomes (Ibarra, 1999). As can be seen, both women and ethnic minority groups encounter problems when trying to gain access to established networks both in the traditional and entrepreneurial labor market (Heilman and Chen, 2003; Moore and Buttner, 1997; Weiler and Bernasek, 2001).

An increase in social capital as a result of an enlarged network would also work in favor of women and people of color when attempting to access financial resources. Financial capital, both at the start-up and the growth stage, is difficult to access for all entrepreneurs but particularly so for women and people of color. Bygrave (2003) suggests that the venture capital industry tends to be a geographically concentrated and tightly intercon-nected, closed network; hence access to this network tends to be difficult for women and people of color. Weiler and Bernasek (2001, p. 89) argue that firms owned by women, and we argue those owned by people of color also, 'may find themselves struggling against an established male-dominated system of customers, suppliers, and creditors'. Indeed, research indicates that Black-owned firms were discriminated against by banks except by those banks that were owned by racial and ethnic minorities (Rhodes and Butler, 2004). Heilman and Chen (2003, p. 359) state that stereotype-derived expectations regarding the competence of racial and ethnic minority and women entrepreneurs may create problems when this group seeks financial backing. These expectations then overshadow the decision to provide money and resources to these individuals since this option is viewed as being more risky than providing money and resources to others. Views like this, Heilman and Chen (2003) add, may affect the support and backing that is critical to a new business. Therefore access to future financial resources may be one area where the MBA may be of benefit.

Edgington and Marshall (2005) argue that earning the MBA can enable individuals to learn not only how to run a business, given proper education and training, but the MBA may also lead to the acquisition of capital by opening doors. Articles in the popular press also suggest that business schools 'are where the money is' (Marcus, 2000). These articles hint that along with gaining skills, the MBA may provide access to a network that could provide future resources, some of that in the form of financing.

Now we must ask: where do women and Blacks stand in terms of MBA entrepreneurship outcomes? Despite the underrepresentation of women and Blacks in US MBA programs, research indicates that in the USA, Black business owners were more likely to hold graduate degrees when they started or acquired ownership in their business (about 25 percent) than Whites (19 percent) (US Census Bureau, 2005). Sixteen percent of Black/African-American MBA alumni surveyed in the GMAC MBA alumni study indicated that they were self-employed or a small business owner in comparison to 4 percent of Asian Americans, 5 percent of Whites and 4 percent of Hispanic Americans (Edgington and Marshall, 2005). Additional statistics underscore the number of Black entrepreneurs with higher-level education. According to the US Census, Blacks who reported graduate training were two to three times more likely to attempt a business start-up (US Census Bureau, 2002), with Black and Hispanic men with graduate training being twice as likely to be engaged in business start-up as compared to White men with equivalent education (ibid.). A recent study by Babson University indicated that among men with advanced degrees such as MBAs, Blacks are 2.6 times as likely to start businesses (see *Blacks in Higher Education*, 2005). Edgington and Marshall (2005) surmised that one reason why Black MBAs may choose entrepreneurship more than other racial or ethnic groups may be that they felt respect and recognition would come as a result of having their own business versus achieving the same in a White-managed firm or corporation. The choice of an entrepreneurial career for Blacks may also be as a result of past actual or perceived discrimination in the corporate environment (see Center for Women's Business Research, 1998). Regarding women with MBAs, DeMartino and Barbato (2003) found in their study that a smaller percentage of women MBAs (11.5 percent) chose entrepreneurship than men MBAs (16.2 percent). However, the percentage of women did not differ from that of men in their intention to become entrepreneurs in the next five years. Findings in the 'Gateway' study indicate that among MBA graduates, 22 percent of women were self-employed versus 19 percent of men. Among Black respondents in this study, 17 percent of women and 17 percent of men were self-employed (Catalyst, 2000).

SUMMARY AND CONCLUSION

It is now well known that women and racial and ethnic minorities are increasing their representation in the populations and workforces of the USA and many other nations typically dominated by men and Whites. Although they are increasing their representation in the US workforce, due to discrimination and stereotypic biases, both women and people of color have not progressed to the extent that they should in the corporate world as compared to White men. In response, some women and people of color seek the MBA in order to increase their opportunities and outcomes, both within corporate organizations and externally, as many choose entrepreneurship.

In this chapter, we have argued that the MBA provides added value to women and racial and ethnic minorities in general and to those who desire to start a business in particular. Research indicates that even after achieving the MBA degree women and people of color are at a disadvantage in terms of earning power and movement into senior management functions and roles. Although this is the case, women and people of color report that they have benefited in terms of increased professional credibility, increased self-confidence and increased access to influential networks. This is particularly important for those who wish to start businesses, as these factors play a role in future business success. Literature has also demonstrated that a higher level of education is related to business success due to the increased knowledge, skills and experience gained and the associated increases in perceived credibility and access to capital. However, the classroom environment for women and people of color is not perfect, as many report that

MBA course content is not reflective of their realities and they feel as though they have less of a voice in the business school classroom. These reflections prompt a call for change in MBA curriculum design and course content in order to encourage inclusion of women and people of color, particularly given their increasing representation in the population, in workforces, and their greater propensity to seek entrepreneurship as careers.

We now offer some suggestions that may help to enhance MBA programs for those non-dominant group members, centering on curricula and faculty. We call for the addition of cases that feature women and racial and ethnic minority protagonists as well as those that focus on smaller businesses, as the majority of businesses which they own are small and generally have fewer employees in comparison to those owned by White men. To that extent, Babson College has launched a new initiative that brings racial and ethnic minority professors together to concentrate on writing cases that have a minority focus with hopes that this will increase the number of cases available for incorporation into the business classroom. Similarly, Harvard Business School and the Committee of 200 have taken up the charge to increase the number of cases that feature business women in leadership roles. There is also a need for women and people of color to see role models that are like them not only at the head of the class, but serving as speakers and exemplars when the greater community participates with the business classroom. The PhD project (phdproject.org) is one entity that is solely focused on increasing the numbers of underrepresented people of color as business professors. It provides instrumental and social support to those pursuing terminal degrees in business and in the ten years between 1994 and 2004, contributed to a twofold increase in the numbers of underrepresented people of color as professors of business. Support of such organizations and active recruiting of racial and ethnic minority and women business professors is encouraged. We also encourage universities to establish close, mutually beneficial relationships with women and racial and ethnic-minority-owned businesses. These businesses may be able to provide internships and or serve as classroom projects for students thereby providing realistic views of how these businesses operate.

Although valid criticisms have been voiced regarding MBA programs, and people of color and women have expressed their frustrations with these programs, we believe that the MBA adds value, in general, for women and people of color and provides added benefits to those in this group who aspire to start their own businesses. We do acknowledge, however, that MBA programs need to be enhanced in order to address the needs of a changing environment and student body that is becoming increasingly diverse. Thus we trust that the recommendations we have made will serve to counteract some of the weaknesses of existing programs and provide some initial steps toward greater inclusion of underrepresented groups.

NOTE

1. We use the terms 'people of color', 'ethnic minority' and 'racial and ethnic' minority (minorities) interchangeably to mean persons of Black, Hispanic/Latino, Asian, Native people, or other non-dominant groups of color. Within these terms we also include women (for example, 'people of color' would include women of color, and 'ethnic minority' would include 'ethnic minority women', etc.).

REFERENCES

Addi-Raccah, A. (2005), 'Gender, ethnicity, and school principalship in Israel: comparing two organizational cultures', *International Journal of Inclusive Education*, **9**(3): 217–39.

Adler, M.A., Koelewijn-Strattner, G.J. and Lengermann, J.J. (1995), 'The intersection of race and gender among chemists: assessing the impact of double minority status on income', *Sociological Focus*, **28**(3): 245–59.

Almquist, E.M. (1989), 'The experiences of minority women in the United States: intersections of race, gender and class', in Jo. Freeman (ed.), *Women: A Feminist Perspective*, Mountain View, CA: Mayfield, pp. 414–45.

Almquist, E. and Wherle-Einhorn, J.L. (1978), 'The doubly disadvantaged: minority women in the labour force', in A.H. Stromberg and S. Harkess (eds), *Women Working: Theories and Facts in Perspective*, Mountain View, CA: Mayfield, pp. 63–88.

Alsop, R. (2001), 'Women see few role models in business school faculties', *Wall Street Journal*, 25 July.

Anderson, M.L. (1988), *Thinking about Women: Sociological Perspectives on Sex and Gender*, New York, Macmillan.

Aronsson, M. (2004), 'Education matters – but does entrepreneurship education? An interview with David Birch', *Academy of Management Learning and Education*, **3**(3): 289–92.

Banks, C.A.M. (2000), 'Gender and race as factors in educational leadership and administration', in M. Fullman (ed.), *The Jossey-Bass Reader on Educational Leadership*, San Francisco, CA: Jossey-Bass/Wiley, pp. 217–56.

Baron, R.A. (2006), 'Opportunity recognition as pattern recognition: how entrepreneurs "connect the dots" to identify new business opportunities', *Academy of Management Perspectives*, **20**(1): 104–19.

Baruch, Y. and Peiperl, M.A. (2000), 'The impact of an MBA on graduates' career', *Human Resource Management Journal*, **10**(92): 69–90.

Baruch, Y., Bell, M.P. and Gray, D. (2005), 'Generalist and specialist graduate business degrees: tangible and intangible value', *Journal of Vocational Behavior*, **67**: 51–68.

Bates, T. (1990), 'Entrepreneur human capital inputs and small business longevity', *The Review of Economics and Statistics*, **72**(4): 551–9.

Beale, F. (1970), 'Double jeopardy: to be Black and female', in Toni Cade (ed.), *The Black Woman: An Anthology*, New York: Mentor Books.

Bell, E.L.J. and Nkomo, S.M. (2001), *Our Separate Ways: Black and White Women and the Struggle for Professional Identity*, Harvard Business School Press.

Bell, E.L.J. and Nkomo, S.M. (1999), 'Refracted lives: sources of disconnection between Black and White women', in M.J. Davidson and R.J. Burke (eds), *Women in Management: Current Research Issues*, Vol. 2, London: Sage, pp. 205–22.

Bickerstaffe, G. (1992), 'Which MBA? A critical guide to the world's best programmes', 4th edn, London: The Economist Intelligence Unit.

Black Issues in Higher Education (2005), 'Program aims to highlight black business owners in MBA courses', *Black Issues in Higher Education*, 22(10): 19.

Blackmore, J. (1999), *Troubling Women: Feminism, Leadership and Educational Change*, Buckingham, UK: Open University Press.

Boyatzis, R. and Renio, A. (1989), 'The impact of an MBA programme on managerial abilities', *Journal of Management Development*, 18(5): 25–39.

Browne, I. and Mira, J. (2003), 'The intersection of gender and race in the labor market', *Annual Review of Sociology*, 29: 487–513.

Burke, R. and McKeen, C. (1994), 'Career development among managerial and professional women', in M. Davidson and R. Burke (eds), *Women in Management: Current Research Issues*, London: Chapman, pp. 65–79.

Bygrave, W.D. (2003), 'The structure of the investment networks of venture capital firms', *Venture Capital*, 2: 146–67.

Carlson, S.M. (1992), 'Trends in race/sex occupational inequality: conceptual and measurement issues', *Social Problems*, 39: 268–90.

Catalyst (1998), 'Women entrepreneurs: why companies lose female talent and what they can do about it', New York: Catalyst.

Catalyst (2000), 'Women and the MBA: gateway to opportunity', New York: Catalyst.

Catalyst (2001), 'Women in business', New York: Catalyst.

Catalyst (2005), 'Quick takes: women MBAs', New York: Catalyst.

Center for Women's Business Research (1998), 'Women of all races share entrepreneurial spirit', Washington, DC: Center for Women's Business Research.

Center for Women's Business Research (2004), 'Businesses owned by women of color in the United States', Washington, DC: Center for Women's Business Research.

Center for Women's Business Research (2005), 'Businesses owned by women of color in the United States', Washington, DC: Center for Women's Business Research.

Charney, A.H. and Libecap, G.D. (2004), *The Contribution of Entrepreneurship Education: An Analysis of the Berger Program*, Kansas City, MO: Kauffman Center for Entrepreneurial Leadership.

Cocchiara, F., Bell, M.P. and Berry, D.P. (2006), 'Latinas and black women: key factors for a growing proportion of the US workforce', *Equal Opportunities International*, 25(4): 272–84.

Cokley, K., Dreher, G.F. and Stockdale, M.S. (2004), 'Toward the inclusiveness and career success of African Americans in the workplace', in M.S. Stockdale and F.J. Crosby (eds), *The Psychology and Management of Workplace Diversity*, Malden, MA: Blackwell, pp. 168–90.

Cox, T. and Harquail, C. (1991), 'Career paths and career success in early career stages of male and female MBAs', *Journal of Vocational Behavior*, 39: 54–75.

Cox, T.H. and Nkomo, S.M. (1991), 'A race and gender-group analysis of the early career experience of MBAs', *Work and Occupations*, **18**: 431–46.

Detienne, D.R. and Chandler, G.N. (2004), 'Opportunity identification and its role in the entrepreneurial classroom: a pedagogical approach and empirical test', *Academy of Management Learning and Education*, **3**(3): 242–57.

DeMartino, R. and Barbato, R. (2003), 'Differences between women and men MBA entrepreneurs: exploring family flexibility and wealth creation as career motivators', *Journal of Business Venturing*, **18**(6): 815–32.

Dreher, G.F. and Ash, R.A. (1990), 'A comparative study of mentoring among men and women in managerial, professional, and technical positions', *Journal of Applied Psychology*, **75**: 539–46.

Dreher, G.F. and Cox, T.H. (1996), 'Race, gender, and opportunity: a study of compensation attainment and the establishment of mentoring relationships', *Journal of Applied Psychology*, **81**(3): 297–308.

Edgington, R. (2003), 'MBA.com registrants survey overall report 2003', Graduate Management Admission Council, retrieved 12 July 2006 from www.gmac.com.

Edgington, R. (2004), 'Corporate recruiters survey 2003–04 general report', Graduate Management Admission Council, retrieved 12 July 2006 from www.gmac.com/ gmac/Researchandtrends/surveyResearch/CorporateRecruitersSurvey.htm.

Edgington, R. and Garcia, V. (2005), 'What leads to minority enrollment into B-school?', Graduate Management Admission Council Research Reports, RR-05-04, 12 September. Retrieved 12 June 2006 from www.gmac.com.

Edgington, R. and Marshall, N. (2005), 'Blacks/African Americans and entrepreneurship', Graduate Management Admission Council Research Reports, RR-05-05, retrieved 12 July 2006 from www.gmac.com.

Eisenhardt, K.M. and Schoonhoven, C.B. (1990), 'Organizational growth: linking founding teams, strategy, environment and growth among U.S. semiconductor ventures', *Administrative Science Quarterly*, **28**: 274–91.

Epstein, C.F. (1973), 'Positive effects of the multiple negative: explaining the success of Black professional women', *American Journal of Sociology*, **78**: 912–35.

Ewers, J. (2005), 'Is the M.B.A. obsolete?', *U.S. News and World Report*, **138**(13): 50–52.

Fairlie, R.W. (2006), *Kauffman Index of Entrepreneurial Activity, National Report, 1996–2005*, Ewing Marion Kauffman Foundation, www.kauffman.org.

Feldman, D.C. (2005), 'The food's no good and they don't give us enough: reflections on Mintzberg's critique of MBA education', *Academy of Management Learning and Education*, **4**(2): 217–20.

Fulbright, K. (1986), 'The myth of the double-advantage: Black female manager', in M.C. Simms and J.M. Malveaux (eds), *Slipping Through the Cracks: The Status of Black Women*, New Brunswick, NY: Transaction Press, pp. 33–45.

Giscombe, K. and Mattis, M.C. (2002), 'Leveling the playing field for women of color in corporate management: is the business case enough?', *Journal of Business Ethics*, **37**: 103–19.

Graduate Management Admission Council (2004), 'Finding future women MBAs, B-schools still face challenges', retrieved 12 July 2006 from www.gmac.com.

Greene, P.G., Brush, C.G., Hart, M.M. and Saparito, P. (2001), 'Patterns of venture capital funding: is gender a factor?', *Venture Capital*, **3**(1): 63–83.

Greene, P.G., Katz, J.A. and Johanisson, B. (2004), 'Introduction to special issue on entrepreneurship education', *Academy of Management Learning and Education*, **3**(3): 238–41.

Greenhaus, J.H., Parasuraman, S. and Wormley, W.M. (1990), 'Effects of race on organizational experiences, job performance evaluations, and career outcomes', *Academy of Management Journal*, **33**: 64–86.

Hahs, D.L. (1999), 'What have MBAs done for us lately?', *Journal of Education for Business*, **74**(4): 197–201.

Headd, B. (2003), 'Redefining business success: distinguishing between closure and failure', *Small Business Economics*, **21**(1): 51–61.

Heilman, M. and Chen, J.J. (2003), 'Entrepreneurship as a solution: the allure of self-employment for women and minorities', *Human Resource Management Review*, **13**: 347–64.

Hilgert, A. (1998), 'Professional development of women and the executive MBA', *Journal of Management Development*, **17**(9): 629–43.

Hills, G., Lumpkin, G.T. and Singh, R.P. (1997), 'Opportunity recognition: perception and behavior of entrepreneurs', *Frontiers of Entrepreneurship Research*, Wellesley: Babson College, pp. 203–18.

Hoffman, R.M. (2006), 'Gender self-definition and gender self-acceptance in women: intersections with feminist, womanist, and ethnic identities', *Journal of Counseling and Development*, **84**: 358–72.

Honig, B. (2004), 'Entrepreneurship education: toward a model of contingency-based business planning', *Academy of Management Learning and Education*, **3**(3): 258–73.

Ibarra, H. (1999), 'Provisional selves: experimenting with image and identity in professional adaptation', *Administrative Science Quarterly*, **44**: 764–91.

Judge, T.A., Cable, D.M., Boudreau, J.W. and Bretz, R.D. Jr (1995), 'An empirical investigation of the predictors of executive career success', *Personnel Psychology*, **48**: 485–519.

Katz, J. (2003), 'The chronology and intellectual trajectory of American entrepreneurship education 1876–1899', *Journal of Business Venturing*, **18**: 283–300.

King, D.K. (1988), 'Multiple jeopardy, multiple consciousness: the context of a Black feminist ideology', *Signs*, **14**(42): 72.

Knaup, A.E. (2005), 'Survival and longevity in the business employment dynamics database', *Monthly Labor Review*, **128**(5): 50–56.

Leeming, A. and Baruch, Y. (1998), 'The MBA as a bridge over the troubled waters of discrimination', *Women in Management Review*, **13**(3): 95–104.

Lord, M. and Westfall, R.G. (1996), 'Running their own show', *US News and World Report*, retrieved 16 June 2006 from www.usnews.com/usnews/edu/articles/960318/archive_010017.htm.

Marcus, D.L. (2000), 'Should entrepreneurs bother with B-school?', *U.S. News and World Report*, **128**(14): 66.

Mavin, S. and Bryans, P. (1999), 'Gender on the agenda of management education', *Women in Management Review*, **14**(3): 99–104.

McGuire, G.M. (2000), 'Gender, race, ethnicity, and networks: the factors affecting the status of employees' network members', *Work and Occupations*, **27**(4): 500–523.

Melamed, T. (1996), 'Career success: an assessment of a gender specific model', *Journal of Occupational and Organisational Psychology*, **69**(3): 217–42.

Mintzberg, H. (2004), *Managers Not MBAs: A Hard Look at the Soft Practice of Managing and Management Development*, San Francisco, CA: Berrett-Koehler.

Mintzberg, H. and Gosling, J.R. (2002), 'Reality programming for MBAs', *Strategy and Business*, **26**: 28–31.

Moore, D.P. and Buttner, E.H. (1997), *Women Entrepreneurs Moving Beyond the Glass Ceiling*, Thousand Oaks, CA: Sage.

Ong, B. (1993), 'Follow up study of female MBA/MA/MSc students', Centre for Health Planning and Management, Keele, June.

Ortiz, F.I. (2001), 'Using social capital interpreting the career of three Latina superintendents', *Educational Administration Quarterly*, **37**(1): 58–85.

PhD Project (2002), 'How can colleges attract more minority students? Hire more minority professors, say college deans', retrieved 16 July 2006 from www.phdproject.org/inthenews.html.

Pfeffer, J. and Fong, C.F. (2003), 'Assessing business schools: reply to Connolly', *Academy of Management Learning Executive*, **2**(4): 368–70.

Rhodes, C. and Butler, J.S. (2004), 'Understanding self-perceptions of business performance: an examination of black American entrepreneurs', *Journal of Developmental Entrepreneurship*, **9**(1): 55–71.

Piotrowski, C. and Cox, J.L. (2004), 'Educational and career aspirations: views of business school students', *Education*, **124**(4): 713–16.

Roberts, L.M. (2005), 'Changing faces: professional image construction in diverse organizational settings', *Academy of Management Review*, **30**(4): 685–711.

Schoenfeld, G. and Edgington, R. (2005), *Mba.com Registrants Follow-up Survey, Executive Summary 2004*, Graduate Management Admission Council, retrieved 12 June 2006 from www.gmac.com/gmac/ResearchandTrends/SurveyResearch/RegistrantsSurvey.htm.

Shane, S. and Stuart, T.E. (2002), 'Organizational endowments and the performance of university start-ups', *Management Science*, **48**: 154–71.

Simmering, M. and Wilcox, I.B. (1995), 'Career exploration and identify formation in MBA students', *Journal of Education for Business*, **70**(4): 233–8.

Simpson, R. (2000), 'A voyage of discovery or a fast track to success: men, women and the MBA', *Journal of Management Development*, **19**(9): 764–82.

Simpson, R. (2006), 'Masculinity and management education: feminizing the MBA', *Academy of Management Learning and Education*, **5**: 182–93.

Sinclair, A. (1995), 'Sex and the MBA', *Organization*, **2**: 295–317.

Sinclair, A. (2000), 'Teaching managers about masculinities: are you kidding?', *Management Learning*, **31**: 6–18.

Smith, C. (1997), 'Gender issues on management education: a new teaching resource', *Women in Management Review*, **12**(3): 100–104.

Stern, S. (2002), 'What did business school do for them?', *Management Today*, February: 41–5.

Sturges, J., Simpson, R. and Altman, Y. (2003), 'Capitalising on learning: an exploration of the MBA as a vehicle for developing career competencies', *International Journal of Training and Development*, **7**(1): 53–66.

Tallerico, M. (2000), 'Gaining access to the superintendency: headhunting, gender, and color', *Educational Administration Quarterly*, **36**(1): 18–43.

US Census Bureau (2002), '2002 survey of business owners advance report on characteristics of employer business owners', retrieved 14 June 2005 from www.census.gov/econ/cesus 02/sbo/sboadvance.htm.

US Census Bureau (2004), 'Fact sheet, 2004, United States. American Community Survey, data profile highlights', retrieved 18 July 2006 from http://factfinder.census.gov.

US Census Bureau (2005), 'Owner's education level at start-up, purchase, or acquisition of the business', retrieved 12 July 2006 from www.census.gov/csd/sbo/edu.html.

US Census Bureau (2006), 'Women-owned business grew at twice the national average, Census Bureau reports', retrieved 12 July 2006 from www.census.gov/Press-release/www/releases/archives/business.

Van Auken, S., Wells, L.G. and Chrysler, E. (2005), 'The relative value of skills, knowledge, and teaching methods in explaining Master of Business Administration (MBA) program return on investment', *Journal of Education for Business*, September/October: 41–5.

Weiler, S. and Bernasek, A. (2001), 'Dodging the glass ceiling? Networks and the new wave of women entrepreneurs', *The Social Science Journal*, **38**: 85–103.

'Women of color: their employment in the private sector' (2003), available at www.eeoc.gov/stats/reports/womenofcolor/#Section_1.1.3, accessed 17 June 2005.

24. Intersectionality, context and 'choice': the career choice influences of self-employed black women

Cynthia Forson

INTRODUCTION

Career choice decisions of self-employed women is a topic that continues to attract the attention of academics, with a number of researchers attempting to identify female entrepreneurs' reasons for business start-up, examining their motivations from a variety of standpoints including psychological, sociological and economic perspectives. However, self-employed women are not a heterogeneous group. For example, although African and Caribbean women have high participation rates of paid employment, they are grossly underrepresented in self-employment compared to male Black and Minority Ethnic (BME) people and women generally. The aim of the study reported here was to examine the influences on the self-employment decisions of African and Caribbean women business owners from two sectors of the London economy – the legal and hairdressing sectors – in order to contribute to an understanding of how migration, class, gender and ethnicity intersect in broader as well as more specific ways to impact the career choice decisions of black[1] women. The chapter draws on literature on entrepreneurship as well as other sources to show how the women's self-employment career choice discourse has developed and outlines the qualitative, layered yet intersectional approach which the study takes to examine the influences on the decision to choose self-employment as a career. The chapter presents the methods used in the study as well as the findings, which are discussed in the context outlined in the next section.

THE HISTORICAL AND CONTEMPORARY CONTEXT OF BLACK WOMEN'S SELF-EMPLOYMENT

Research on black women has noted that in the UK work and choices about work have a significant influence in shaping black women's lives (Lewis, 1993). Reasons for this have been linked to black women's status under slavery, British colonialism in the Caribbean and the mass migration of women from the Caribbean after the Second World War (Bryan et al., 1985). African women's relationship to work has been explained in terms of traditional kinship and family arrangements that make women economically independent of their husbands (Chapman-Smock, 1977; Robertson, 1984; Coquery-Vidrovitch, 1997), as well as British colonialism and its link with African women's economic migration to the UK. The connection between these points is that black women, due to their history and culture, have always been positioned as workers.

Slavery set the scene for the de-womanization of the black woman by portraying her, contrary to the prevailing notions of womanhood, as equal to men – free labour confined to the fields and engaged in back-breaking jobs and tasks (Bryan et al., 1985). Angela Davis (1981, p. 5) sums up the influence of slavery on black women's perceptions of work as follows:

> The enormous space that work occupies in Black women's lives today follows a pattern established during the very early days of slavery. As slaves, compulsory labor overshadowed every other aspect of women's existence. It would seem, therefore, that the starting point for any exploration of Black women's lives under slavery would be an appraisal of their role as workers.

The de-womanization of black women in relation to work was further enhanced through British colonialism after slavery in the Caribbean (Shepherd et al., 1995). All this culminated in the British government encouraging the mass migration of Caribbean women to the UK after the Second World War, a two-sided contract that seemed of benefit to both parties due to the demise of Caribbean economies and the UK economy's requirement for cheap labour. At the same time notions of a different type of womanhood, alien to the African context, were being nurtured through colonialism in Africa (Chapman-Smock, 1977). Chapman-Smock argues that one of the legacies of colonialism in Africa was an erosion of African notions of womanhood that embodied autonomy and independence, replacing them with Western concepts that involved the representation of womanhood in terms of dependence, domesticity and subordination. Nevertheless, African women south of the Sahara have maintained an

active role in the economy. Further, colonial indoctrination that emphasized a British education as positive capital inculcated through the neglect
of black achievement in colonial education led to the migration of African
women (and men) to the UK in search of education, while others came in
the 1970s and 1980s after the collapse of several African economies.

The legacy of the slave trade and the neglect of black people's achievement in colonial and UK schools may have affected black women's perceptions of themselves and their abilities, and others' perceptions of them.
Morokvasic (1983) identifies two main approaches to perceptions of
migrant women: the first perceives migrants as 'sex-less units' even where the
studies are examining contexts in which the majority of the subjects are
women; and the second considers women as dependents – in Morokvasic's
words, 'an accessory of a process they are not really taking part in' (ibid.,
p. 15). Characterizing the women in this manner has made them invisible
and has contributed to a stereotypical image of migrant women as
'Followers, dependants, unproductive persons, isolated, illiterate and igno-
rant' (ibid., p. 16). This, she argues, was a result of a conceptualization of
the migrant woman on the basis of the most culturally deviant migrant
women, without consideration of the fact that there exists heterogeneity
among such women. However, Morokvasic acknowledges that that image of
migrant women has slowly dissipated, with emerging literature conceding
that many migrant women were and are active participants in the labour
market in both their original and host countries. However, Bhavnani (1994)
states that even more recent literature on black women tends to problema-
tize them with references made to their 'aggressive' nature and 'lone' motherhood. Although these gendered and racialized conceptualizations of
black women have been historically constructed, they are sometimes used as
the main explanations of their labour market experiences (Bhavnani, 1994).

Research reveals divergence as well as convergence in the labour market
positions of African and Caribbean women. Migration patterns, history
and culture merge to create differences in the labour market situation of the
two groups of women. The Equal Opportunities Commission (EOC)'s
work indicates that although Caribbean women have high employment
rates (55 per cent), African women have high unemployment rates at about
12 per cent – only higher than Bangladeshi and Pakistani women. The
above dissimilarities notwithstanding, work by the EOC shows that in the
UK black women (39 per cent) are concentrated in public services, i.e.
education, health and social work (EOC, 2004). More recently, the
Commission for Racial Equality (CRE) has put the figure at 52 per cent for
African women and 54 per cent for Caribbean women (CRE, 2006). Both
groups of women are usually concentrated in the lowest-paying jobs in
those sectors, which means that they earn much less than their black male

and white female counterparts (though Caribbean women earn marginally more than Caribbean men) (Platt, 2006). Black women also have higher levels of full-time employment. This applies to even the lone parents among them (Lindley et al., 2003) and this may reflect the independent matriarchal culture that is prominent among black women (Duncan and Edwards, 1997). Caribbean women and African women also have similar low levels of self-employment (Lindley et al., 2003). This chapter argues that the differences and similarities in the labour market position of these two groups of women has implications for the reasons why these women choose to go into self-employment.

CONCEPTUALIZING INFLUENCES ON SELF-EMPLOYMENT CAREER CHOICE INTENTIONS

Psychological or trait models have examined influences on the career choice of self-employed women from the perspective that female entrepreneurs are psychologically different from male entrepreneurs. Others have engaged with the influence of the personal history and social context of the entrepreneurial decision, examining the influence and impact of role models, peers, culture, marginalization (in terms of race, ethnicity, class and gender), family background, education and exposure to entrepreneurship (Marlow, 2002). Research has found that culture, role models and family influences (Bygrave and Minniti, 2000), education (Dolinsky et al., 1993), career experiences (Feldman and Bolino, 2000), institutional support (Phizacklea and Ram, 1995), inheritance of entrepreneurial tradition (Bygrave and Minniti, 2000), peer influence, social marginality (Phizacklea and Ram, 1995; Kets de Vries, 1977), among others, affect the entrepreneurial decision. Yet still others, proceeding from the rational choice perspective, have employed human capital theory to explain women's entrepreneurial intentions in terms of returns on human capital investments compared to waged labour (Hakim, 1988, 1993), thereby explaining the influences on women's desire to be self-employed in terms of the relationship between women's economic choices and their non-economic activities such as child rearing and other domestic activities (Goffee and Scase, 1985; Hakim, 1996), as well as their personal preferences relating to their skills and abilities.

Another approach that has dominated research on black women's business ownership is the conceptualization of their self-employment decisions in terms of 'push' and 'pull' factors, suggesting that women's entrepreneurship can be explained as a choice between self-employment and other forms of economic activity. Women are said to be influenced by either the push of persistent inequalities in the labour market (Marlow, 2002) or the pull of entrepreneurial rewards that are not necessarily merely monetary. Push factors have included the confines of the rigid hierarchical structures of the corporate world and the consequent frustrations experienced by women (Hisrich and Brush, 1983), the glass ceiling and inequalities in wages experienced by women in the labour market (Goffee and Scase, 1985). Pull influences have been cited to include flexibility to choose their own hours (Hakim, 1989), ability to spend more time with families (Reeves, 1989, cited in Rees, 1992), economic independence from men, independence from traditional authority figures and freedom to adopt their own approach to work (SBS, 2003; Alvarez and Meyer, 1998).

The push/pull polemic indeed reflects the seemingly perpetual debate on the agency versus structure debate, in which either individuals' strategies, character, capitals and dispositions are perceived to be the central elements in shaping the decision to become self-employed, or the social structure (structures of race gender and class, for example) and educational and sectoral institutions (in this case of the legal and hairdressing sectors) may constrain or enable and generally shape the individuals' dispositions towards action, and these social structures are the primary elements in shaping career choice decisions. This debate is prominent in the self-employment literature and is used to explain the career choice decisions of ethnic minority groups. For example, Phizacklea's (1988) early work on entrepreneurship and gender made a link between the structures of racism, sexism and class in explaining BME women's self-employment experiences even as others have highlighted the limitations faced by ethnic minorities that limit their labour market opportunities (e.g. Ram and Jones, 1998) as a reason for their high incidence in self-employment. The Small Business Service (SBS) (2001) found that, on average, ethnic minorities, especially the African and Caribbean populations, are more likely to be thinking about entrepreneurial activity than is the country as a whole. Perhaps this is an indication that Africans and Caribbeans face major obstacles in the labour market and therefore see self-employment as a means to avoid unemployment and other such hindrances in their labour market experience. Yet fewer African and Caribbeans end up self-employed. In a study of 400 businesses Marlow found that very few of them were owned by African and Caribbean entrepreneurs, a situation attributed to start-up obstacles such as obtaining finance and a lack of a market outside their own communities (Marlow, 1990) – this finding has more recently been confirmed by *Labour Force Survey* statistics (ONS, 2001–2002). On the other hand, researchers such as Curran et al. (1991) have argued that positive rather than negative reasons dominate the BME business owner's decision to set up in business.

However, a conceptualization of career choice in terms of push and pull factors is overly simplistic and does not capture the complexity of black women's lived experiences. Bourdieu and Wacquant (1992) argue that people are not 'particles' that are 'pushed' and 'pulled' about like robots, and that within the constraints of their position in society (determined to a large extent by the volume and structure of their capital resources) individuals apply their human agency to affect the external structures. More recently, there is growing convergence in attempts to reconcile notions of social structure, such as the institutions and norms that shape the actions of individuals in society, with that of human agency where people, of their own volition, are seen as being capable of making a difference in and changing the social systems they inhabit.

Some authors have referred to the decision to become self-employed in terms of a result of a complex interplay between individual, social and environmental factors that affect entrepreneurial behaviour (Basu and Goswami, 1999; Dyer, 1994; Reynolds, 1991; Cooper, 1981). Cooper (1981) and Dyer (1994) provide comprehensive frameworks for the study of entrepreneurial motivations. Cooper identifies three main categories of influences – antecedent influences, incubator organization and environmental factors. Dyer, looking at entrepreneurship as a career, analyses the influences on career choice in terms of antecedent influences that include psychological factors (e.g. need for achievement, need for control, tolerance for ambiguity), social factors (e.g. family relationships, family and community support, role models) and economic factors (lack of alternative careers in existing organizations, economic growth/business opportunities and availability of resources). However, many of these frameworks have been designed with majority male samples, and although they take a layered approach to the understanding of influences of self-employment career intentions, they fail to engage with the dynamic nature of 'higher-order' structures such as race, ethnicity, gender and class and their interactions *within* and *between* the layers. As such, self-employment career choice theories have been noted to be inadequate in explaining BME women's self-employment career choice determinants (Dhaliwal, 1997) because they exclude minority experiences and generalize white male experience to minority groups (Johnson-Bailey and Tisdell, 1998).

Feminist discourse on the subject has criticized the androcentric (Brush, 1990) and ethnocentric (Forson, 2006) nature of self-employment literature. However, feminist research itself fails to engage with the multiplicity of some women's lives, mainly as a result of the inadequacy of patriarchy as an analytical tool for the examination of the experiences of different groups of women (Mirza, 2003). (For a comprehensive review of the inadequacy of patriarchy see Gottfried, 1998 and Pollert, 1996). Academic researchers worldwide are in agreement that work on women's enterprise is centred on the needs and experiences of white middle-class women without consideration for the needs of 'other' women such as ethnic minorities, whether in the USA (Inman, 2000), Sweden (Mason, 2003), or the UK (Dhaliwal, 2000).

In what ways do the career choice intentions of African and Caribbean women lawyers and hairdressers who are now residents or citizens of the UK, perhaps wives of African, Caribbean or British men, possibly mothers to children who are UK-born, members of their respective cultural communities, the wider UK and European communities, working in predominantly white middle-class legal environments or predominantly black lower-class hairdressing environments fit into these conceptualizations of self-employment career choice outlined above? What about the influences of socialization and acculturation through a British education in the UK, Africa or the Caribbean? In what ways do these conceptualizations account for the influence of professionalization and internationalization? Where do race, sex and class (individually and collectively) fit in?

Authors such as Özbilgin et al. (2005) have critiqued the one-dimensional and unidirectional nature of career choice research analysis, arguing in effect that current research on the subject either focuses on the structural aspects of career choice or privileges human agency in the process. Similarly, the analysis of career choice influences of self-employed women has in the main engaged with influences of gender, or ethnicity or class structure, or women's preferences based on rational choice decisions. Rarely have studies explored the multidimensional nature of BME women's experiences. The heterogeneity of the group 'women' requires a feminist perspective that allows for a framing of the discussion of self-employment career choice in a historical and contemporary context that incorporates the impact of race, ethnicity, class *and* gender, but it should be a discussion that transcends gender, race and class specificity. Özbilgin et al. (2005) successfully employed a three-pronged relational perspective in examining the career choice influences of MBA students in three countries. Influenced by Layder's (1993) and Bourdieu and Wacquant's (1992) layered approach, they explored career choice influences of MBA students at the micro-, meso- and macro-levels, but also in terms of the relationship between and within levels. This study uses Pierre Bourdieu's (1986) conceptual tool of *habitus* at the individual and collective levels in order to reflect the reality of black women's lived experiences, which are multifaceted as a result of the intersectional influences of gender, ethnicity, class and migration. It examines black women's career choice in the light of the interactions between and within individual, institutional and collective *habitis*.

Bourdieu's *habitus* is regarded as a generative schema in which basic social structures are embodied in individuals through socialization processes with the result that people necessarily behave in such a way that the structures thus embodied are reproduced and given effect – a guiding principle that regulates the actions of people (Nash, 1999). In other words, *habitus* refers to those characteristics that 'generate practices, perceptions and attitudes that are not consciously coordinated or governed by rules, but nonetheless are regular enough to appear consistent' (Greener, 2002, p. 691) – the 'webs of meaning we ourselves have spun'. Through the concept of *habitus* Bourdieu bridges the divide between structure and agency (Camic, 2000) and overcomes the abstract structuralism that plagues feminist arguments over patriarchy; choice is therefore a process that is structured and structuring (Reay et al., 2005). Bourdieu conceives of *habitus* as operating at the institutional or meso-level. However, research by Reay et al. (2005) successfully employed a hierarchy of *habiti* at various levels – individual, institutional and familial – to explain the factors that affect college choice and their link to social inequalities in higher education. They maintained that these *habiti*, separately and together, mediate the process of choice and can create a framework through which the interactions of class (gender and ethnicity) and choice can be examined.

Reay (1995) makes a claim for a gendered and racialized *habitus* at the collective level. Through the collective *habitus*, Reay (1995, p. 360) argues, 'prejudices and racial [and gendered] stereotypes ingrained in the *habitus* of members of dominant groups can affect the life chances of any group who are clearly different in some way'. It also manifests itself in the form of shared understandings about activities and institutions, for example, on the basis of which judgements are made about the suitability of individuals and groups for participation in such activities and institutions. This required an understanding of the interactions of changing structures such as the labour markets and affiliated institutions, and processes such as the participants' career and life histories within these structural contexts. For the purposes of this study, *habitus* was conceptualized in Bourdieu's terms as a meso-level construct as well as a macro-level concept which for this study denoted the arena of self-employment as well as the spheres of the legal and African-Caribbean hairdressing sectors, respectively. For this study, therefore, at the collective level *habitus* involved the identification of the implicit assumptions and values, e.g. institutional racism and assumptions about sex roles, that underlie the hidden processes though which black women are evaluated, marginalized and excluded from the legal profession, for example, or from engaging in entrepreneurship to the same extent as majority groups.

Although gender is not central to Bourdieu's analysis of *habitus*, in his book *Masculine Domination* published in 1990 he engages with questions of patriarchal power and the social construction of gender. Bourdieu's analytical tool *habitus*, employed within the broad framework of feminist discourse on the subordination of women, circumvents the overly structural and deterministic account of women's oppression which characterizes accounts that revolve around the concept of patriarchy and allows room for more fluid gender relations that take into account race and other social divisions based on similarity and difference. He makes possible a conceptualization of sexual and ethnic differences as matters of history and social practice as opposed to essentialist biological determination. Further, in viewing such differences and divisions as social practice, Bourdieu makes a case for minority groups' own complicity in their subordination in terms of the *habitus* but also recognizes their agency in their use of strategies.

Personal history and human agency are taken into account in the concept of *habitus*. Reay (1995) puts this in terms of the internalization of particular ways of interacting, by members of subordinate groups, that perpetuates their subordination and marginalization. Indeed, Bourdieu maintains that individuals internalize habits, norms and principles and develop what Nash (1999, p. 179) calls 'a feel for the game' as part of their personal development which is intertwined with their social development. Individuals who develop a 'feel for the game' during their lifetimes construct their realities and personal theories reflexively by reflecting on their individual experiences, understandings and interpretations of the world. Bourdieu refers to individual *habitus* as a collection of dispositions (Özbilgin and Tatlı, 2005) operating at the micro-individual level. For the purposes of this study, the individual-level *habitus* involved the African and Caribbean businesswomen's 'choices', capitals and strategies and the way these combine and interact with each other and with the collective *habitus* to influence the decision to become self-employed. The study conceptualizes these interactions in terms of confrontations, negotiations and dialogue between and within the different layers of *habitus*.

METHODOLOGY

The study focused on the influences on the self-employment career choice decisions of the black women in this study. The objectives were to determine the impact of historical, sociocultural and personal influences on the career choice decisions of black women before becoming self-employed. Rubin and Rubin (1995) contend that qualitative methodologies are suitable when the aim of the research is to uncover the complexity of relationships and when the researcher seeks to understand how current situations have been affected by past events and phenomena. Further, Layder (1993) maintains that qualitative methods are essential when the purpose of the study is to report on social activities within a 'bounded social world' such as an occupational group like black hairdressers or solicitors. The qualitative methodology also allowed for the in-depth exploration of the participants' understandings and interpretations within a specific context such as business ownership, thereby accessing the world in the terms of those who were being researched (Stroh, 2000), in accordance with the feminist research paradigm within which the study is set.

Given that black women are subject to historical and existing patriarchal and racial structures of subordination and oppression (Bhavnani, 1994), understanding these structural frameworks was essential in fully comprehending black women's business ownership experiences. It was also important to examine how black women's 'choices', contacts, abilities and strategies combined to affect career choice decision making. The research approach was one that acknowledged that, in the tension between structure and agency, each influences the other to make each individual experience or 'story' unique in its telling.

A multi-method approach was taken to this study (Cresswell, 1994). First, academic literature on the subject was reviewed to aid in the construction of a theoretical framework within which the study is set. Second, an analysis of the two sectors in which the study is situated from a policy perspective allowed the study to be placed in context. Taking a qualitative approach, data were collected mainly through semi-structured interviews with 15 and 35 London-based black female solicitors and hairdressers respectively. The interviews were tape-recorded and fully transcribed. The participants came from a variety of cultural backgrounds and were diverse in terms of their ages, family responsibilities and educational background. The participants were randomly selected from black business directories covering North, West, East and South London. The group's diversity enhanced the study and enabled a multiple range of perspectives to be explored.

The legal and African-Caribbean hairdressing sectors made interesting sectors to study for two reasons. Law is a predominantly white male middle-class profession. An examination of why black females choose to enter such a profession allowed an exploration of the interactions between gender, ethnicity and class. On the other hand, black hairdressing is a predominantly black female profession which is generally perceived as low-paid work (Low Pay Commission, 2005). A comparison, therefore, of black women's experiences between and within the two sectors enables an analysis of the ways in which gender, ethnicity and class create convergence as well as divergence in the career choice decisions of black women.

THE AFRICAN-CARIBBEAN HAIRDRESSING AND LEGAL SECTORS

Recent research by the Hairdressing and Beauty Industry Authority (HABIA) – the UK government-approved standards-setting body for hair, beauty, nails, spa therapy, barbering and African-Caribbean hair – indicates that a majority of hairdressing salons are owned by owner–managers aged between 25 and 54 who employ between zero and four persons (Berry-Lound et al., 2000). In 2004 the UK total turnover for the hairdressing and beauty sector amounted to £2699 million (Business Link, 2006), generated by about 103 000 employees (Low Pay Commission, 2005). Of these, 82 400 are full-time employees, of whom 80 per cent are women. Eighty per cent of part-time employees in the sector are also women. There is also evidence to suggest that hairdressers are increasingly turning to self-employment. In 2004 there were 101 000 self-employed hairdressers, compared with 95 000 in 2002 and 83 000 in 1998 (Low Pay Commission, 2005). Moreover, the trade associations calculate that the informal economy could account for as many as a further 35 000 hairdressers. Labour turnover is very high in the sector at 29 per cent (HABIA, 2004). Most hairdressers apprentices are females aged between 16 and 25 (Berry-Lound et al., 2000; HABIA, 2004). Hairdressing is an industry that tends to attract those with little capital who lack technical knowledge and experience in the craft. Paradoxically, ease of entry seems to encourage growth in the sector during times of recession as well as times of expansion in the economy (Attwood, 1981) and as such it 'has become a trade to be drifted into and out of depending on the opportunities' (ibid., p. 6). Two factors contribute to this ease of entry into the sector – the relatively low cost of entry into the industry and the lack of regulation and licensing of hairdressing salons.

A study by Berry-Lound et al. (2000) revealed the main differences between the general hairdressing and African-Caribbean hairdressing as relating to African-Caribbean hair itself, the client mix and the different cost structures associated with the two sub-sectors. Ninety per cent of African-Caribbean hairdressing salons in the UK are single salons, in the main employing between four and ten people, and the majority (89 per cent) of them are located in urban areas (HABIA, 2006). Black hairdressing, like general hairdressing, occurs in a gendered context – women employing women to serve women. Seventy-four per cent of staff in the sector are female (HABIA, 2006). In the UK the context is also racially and ethnically charged: black women employing black women to serve mainly black women in a predominantly white society. According to a skills survey in the sector by HABIA, only 35 per cent of African-Caribbean hairdressing salons serve a mixed clientele (HABIA, 2006). This is also a function of an economically divided society. Compared to other sectors, black hairdressing is set in low-income neighbourhoods serving a predominantly low-income population and with low entry barriers, high competition and low margins are inevitable. Nevertheless, research by Business Link estimates that the London African-Caribbean hair industry is an estimated £50 million market.[2] It provides for more than half of the entire industry capacity in the UK.[3] Black hair care is supposedly one of the fastest-growing ethnic sectors in the UK.

The legal sector, in contrast, has been a traditionally elitist, white male profession. In 2004, there were 121 165 solicitors on the Law Society's roll, of whom 50 375 (42 per cent) were women and of the 96 757 solicitors with practising certificates, 39 199 (41 per cent) were women (The Law Society, 2004). There is no doubt that the number of women and BME lawyers has increased substantially over the last 50 years and that indeed women now constitute more than half the yearly numbers that enrol with the Law Society (The Law Society, 2004). This has led to some commentary about the feminization of the legal profession leading to opportunities for women in the sector (Bolton and Muzio, 2005). However, notwithstanding the significant changes that have occurred in the gender and ethnic profile of the legal profession, feminist and race researchers have painted a picture of a sector where discrimination and inequalities are still rife in the employment of minority groups, in terms of recruitment, reward, promotion and career advancement (Sommerlad and Sanderson, 1998). As McGlynn (2003, p. 139) states it, 'women working and studying in the law tend to be under-represented, underpaid and marginalised'. The professionalization of the sector has led to it being highly regulated. The Law Society lays down the rules and regulations that govern the training, certification and practice of lawyers across England and Wales. It also sets out rigorous procedures and processes required to set up a law firm, and ensures compliance through disciplinary procedures. The specific regimes encapsulated in the policies of the two sectors have an impact on the ease of access to the two professions. This in turn has profound implications for those who enter self-employment in the sectors, as will be revealed later.

INFLUENCES ON CAREER CHOICE AND SELF-EMPLOYMENT

The women's reasons expose ways in which black women's reasons for self-employment as a career choice are both similar to and different from those of white women and black men. It also shows that among black women, career choice motivations can differ according to their experiences of migration, ethnicity and class status. The women in this study were united as much by gender, class and ethnicity as they were divided by it in terms of their decisions to become self-employed. The findings also reveal how the women's own notions of motherhood, womanhood and work interact with the host nation's perceptions of these roles to affect their self-employment decisions. These perceptions differed according to whether the women were born and/or primarily educated in the UK (settlers) or had migrated to the UK as adults (migrants). The professionalism inherent in legal training, with its liberal ideology of a 'level playing field', also affected the lawyers' perceptions of themselves and of their environment, notwithstanding the fact that gendered ideas about professionalism lead to a hierarchical stratification of the profession with men at the top and women at the bottom (Bolton and Muzio, 2005). The women in both samples were asked to give their reasons for starting business as opposed to asking them for a 'main reason'. This was designed to enable the women to indicate all the factors that had influenced them to start their own business without discounting or elevating the importance of any of the reasons (Hughes, 2003). What emerges is the manner in which the dynamics of race/ethnicity, gender and class intersect in influencing these women's motivations for embarking on business ownership.

Background Influences

Almost all the settler women's declared motivations for embarking on business ownership included classic 'pull' factors such as the 'need for achievement', 'need for control' and the recognition of an opportunity, which are associated with personal characteristics (Chell, 1993). Typical responses to why the hairdressers, for example, had embarked on business ownership included:

> Basically I've been doing hairdressing for about 20 years now and basically like I've been working for other people. I've got quite a bit of experience and working for people that don't appreciate the work that you're doing, it was better to open my own salon so that I could be in control of what I did. (Jane)

Adjoa, another hairdresser, was a Black-African woman who had come to the UK to live with her mother's sister when she was ten years old. Now 38, she set up her own business after working as an employed hairdresser because she had the 'zeal to do it'. Shirley, on the other hand, had embarked on business ownership because the 'opportunity arose' in the form of her brother, who was willing to act as a financier for the business. All the women in this group had chosen to become self-employed because it was what they had always wanted to do. These women seemed to see self-employment as a way of satisfying their need to achieve, reflecting the standard responses highlighted by research on business owners, irrespective of gender or ethnicity (Carter and Cannon, 1992; Curran and Blackburn, 1993).

Almost all the lawyers (12 out of 15) also articulated one of their reasons in terms of the classic psychological criteria that related to a challenge, achievement motivation, need for control, opportunity recognition and independence, highlighting and confirming rationalist perspectives. Others framed their reasons in terms of a natural progression of their careers. Claire, for example, a 40-year-old widowed mother of three children, indicated that she 'was always looking at being a business owner'. She said the decision was based on her own entrepreneurial desires. She felt that she did not want to stay at her firm, work for as long as she could for a substantial salary and not achieve the optimum in her profession. However, underlying these individual and personal narratives of the women were the gendered and racialized structures of the wider context that gave meaning to the seemingly personal narratives based on free choice.

Zoe, a Black-Caribbean hairdresser born in the UK, had embarked on business ownership because she had a 'fear factor of failing' and wanted to prove to herself that she could achieve her dreams. But Zoe also showed that sometimes black women may use their businesses as a political tool to raise the profile of the 'race', displaying a race consciousness that is not always evident among white women. This of course stems from black peoples' history in the UK and indeed elsewhere. Zoe explained:

> I wanted to have some influence at least in front of my clients and to help at least one or two people who I would employ and I wanted to be in an environment where I was able to make a difference. I wanted to symbolize something. So that's the contribution I wanted to make because I have been in so many salons and find them cold, not warm, not inviting. I wanted to show that black hairdressers are not about gossiping, not about, you know, you come in the door and there's not a smile, there's not a pleasant face. I am able to do that. (Zoe)

Both Yasmin and Denise had recognized opportunities in the legal sector that created niches for them. But these opportunities were closely linked to discriminatory and racialized practices in the wider society. These practices made Denise want her 'difference to make a difference', so she set up a law firm in the city that catered to wealthy black business people, among other clients. Yasmin, a children's education specialist, on the other hand, said:

> It's quite exclusive . . . there weren't very many black people doing it at all . . . specializing in representing children. I made a conscious decision that I want to

specialize in that because I could see that it was interesting work, very interesting work. It's my community, you know. Fighting for people who've been kicked out and exclusion rates among black children . . . you know . . . killing off the educational aspirations of our children and I really wanted to be there, you know. I am here in [location] and the surrounding areas and I wanted to be somebody that says, look I care about the education of our children and I'm gonna give legal service. (Yasmin)

Several migrant hairdressers' motivations centred more on their sociocultural experiences, motherhood, migrant experiences and unfavourable labour market conditions. Social as well as independent reasons were important here. Henrietta, who has lived in the UK for 12 years, was 'pulled' into self-employment by her sociocultural experiences, which motivated her into rejecting the stereotypical white middle-class gender role her English husband had placed her in:

I've been married for fourteen years . . . so I was looking after my children. My . . . my son was eighteen months so my husband wouldn't like me to work, but . . . you know, when you are from Africa, our background, as a woman um you have to work . . . my husband didn't want me to work he just want me to look after my son and but then I said to myself, 'No, I have to work!' So I went . . . one day went to his office and I said, 'Listen I want to go into hairdressing'. (Henrietta)

Henrietta's desire to own her own business was driven to a certain extent by her frustration with the stereotypical images of subordinated black women workers in lower occupational groups, reflecting a race *and* gender consciousness:

It is nice for a black woman to get up . . . it's not all the time that we have to work for people and they're shouting at you, do this, do that. I'm so happy. I feel so nice when I come in . . . you feel like you are somebody too. My sister, for example says, 'You don't know how lucky you are. When I get up at 5am and I'm going to work, I want to cry.' (Henrietta)

Others, like Fola, cited the 'push' of anticipated low pay as an employee compared to the 'pull' of higher earnings in self-employment as a major motivating factor, arguing that as a black mother of six children coupled with her inability to find a good job in the UK, whatever job she felt she would finally get would not pay her enough to pay for the child care she would require:

This business is costing you your own life, your own time, your husband's life, children's life, everything! Everybody is suffering, but then there is nothing you can do. I am still better off than going to the nine to five [job] because going for nine to five . . . those two and the ten year old and eight year olds, what would I do with them? I have to look for somebody to pick them from school. How much will they pay me if I go to work from nine to five? Maybe as a foreigner if I am well educated the best job I can get, maybe I will be on £20 000 per annum. After paying my tax and NI, after my transportation and feeding, then paying for the childminder, paying my mortgage, how much will I be left with? So I just believe I am still better off here if I can manage the business. That's why I am doing it. It's not because it is easy, it's very difficult. (Fola)

The impact of intersectionality on Fola's motivations is clear in this narrative – it reveals the confrontations and negotiations between her various selves – her self as a migrant, as a black person, as a low-income worker, as a wife and as a mother, and the attendant complexity of the interface of these with institutions and the wider society.

Finally, families were an important background influence on the women's decisions to become hairdressers and to start their own businesses. Rachel, for example, said her sister had encouraged her to become a hairdresser and get a qualification in the profession. Previous research has shown that many self-employed people are influenced by an exposure to role models at an early age; children in West Africa in particular are socialized into family businesses (Dunne and King, 2003). Inevitably the majority of these role models have been men. This avenue of enquiry was most illuminating for those women who had grown up outside the UK. With the high incidence of informal and formal self-employment practices among women living in Africa and the Caribbean, female role models were an essential influence on the career choice decision. A notable finding of this study is the number of *migrant* women who had female self-employed role models in their families. Eleven hairdressers and eight lawyers cited female entrepreneurial role models in their families – mothers, grandmothers and sisters. These role models run businesses that included import/export businesses, market stalls, a doctor's surgery and a hairdressing salon. As expected, women born in the UK had fewer self-employed role models in their families because their family members were more likely to be employed as a result of their history. Olivia's and Beryl's father and mother were business owners from whom they had taken over their hairdressing businesses, and Adjoa said her parents owned a dry cleaner's shop in Africa.

The number of female self-employed role models is a reflection of the high self-employment activity found among women in the countries that typically send migrants to the UK as a result of a traditional culture of high economic activity rates among women coupled with women's limited access to jobs in the formal employment sectors of those countries (Dunne and King, 2003). This renders problematic the claim in the literature that African and Caribbeans are not 'naturally' predisposed towards self-employment. Much of the research on women's and ethnic minorities' entrepreneurship tends to focus on their experiences in the host countries without consideration of prior experiences of migrants and how these may affect their behaviour and perceptions of self-employment as a career choice.

Eight of the migrant hairdressers had also been self-employed before they came to the UK, and this had consequences for the confidence with which they approached business start-up and the way in which they mobilized resources for their businesses. Three of the eight had combined full-time work in the formal economy of their countries of origin with part-time self-employment in the informal economy to supplement their incomes. Both Fola and Rachel taught in schools, but Fola also owned a hairdressing salon and Rachel was in involved in small-scale retailing before migration to the UK. Diana was a civil servant but also owned a catering business. The rest engaged in various activities in both the formal and informal economies, but mainly small-scale retailing. So, as Rachel put it,

> I know a lot before I start my business . . . before I came to this country . . . I know a lot about setting up and doing a business as well. (Rachel)

Previous Work Experiences in the Hairdressing and Legal Sectors

Previous work experiences can help shape the entrepreneurial decision. Some of the hairdressers indicated that their experiences in their previous jobs spurred them into the decision to become self-employed. However, these experiences were not very different from those of other women and ethnic minorities in general. This is mainly because most of the women were involved in previous jobs in the black hairdressing sector where neither their gender nor ethnicity is an issue. Many of the women felt that their experiences in previous jobs had just confirmed to them that they could do the job better and given them the desire to control their own businesses and run them in their own way. Others had opted for self-employment to avoid the perceived racism that permeates UK society as a whole and is evident in the workplace. Ellen decided to become a self-employed hairdresser because of her husband's negative experience of racism in the workplace with regard to promotion and stories her sister had related about her experiences in the NHS. She decided self-employment was a 'better option':

> It was in the 80s and looking at the circumstances around, in most of these jobs promotion wasn't there. The discrimination was so much that, my husband was

an accountant as well and the stories he brings out . . . they bring somebody and he trains them and by the time he realizes the person has got a company car and he is still there so I said I was never going to work for anybody in this country. Also my sister was a nurse, she also comes home with all the stories about how the patients were so racist that sometimes they don't even want a black person to touch them and they were so insulting. I didn't have that temperament, I would have been sacked. (Ellen)

For the lawyers, however, in spite of the changes that have occurred in the labour market as a whole and in the legal sector in particular, and the inroads that many women and ethnic minorities have made in forging professional careers for themselves, the organization of work in the legal sector as in many others is still very gendered and racialized in nature and form. Women and ethnic minorities are still underrepresented in the higher echelons of the legal profession, and the lawyers' previous work encounters had influenced their desire to become self-employed in complex ways in which their ethnicity, gender and class combined to give them peculiar experiences.

Many of the lawyers in this sample cited significant people or experiences at work and in other spheres of life that caused them to make the decision to leave their jobs and become business owners. Although research on African-Caribbean women in management in the UK is scarce, the few studies available (e.g. Davidson, 1997) have shown that the black female in management suffers multiple disadvantages in terms of upward mobility, high levels of work and home pressures that can affect her decision to become self-employed (Marlow, 2002). Claire, Denise, Yasmin, Claudia, Bessie, Adjoa, Mije and Annabel all cited what Davidson (1997) has called the 'concrete ceiling' (the black woman's 'glass ceiling') as a result of their racialized minority status as instrumental in their entrepreneurial decision. According to Annabel:

Ethnicity has a lot to do with it because I worked for a very large firm. I was in a top position . . . I suppose at the time . . . in the year that I left, my firm was the number one firm in the country, but I knew I couldn't get partnership . . . working for a large firm and with my background I didn't think that progression was a possibility, to be honest. I would have just become a fee earner for years and years and years and then . . . you know . . . when you're 45 plus they start looking for reasons for you to get out. (Annabel)

Even the women who had been able to get into salaried partnership positions (none of the women were in equity partnership roles) still suffered the frustrations of being a 'token black female' (Davidson, 1997, p. 45). Denise became a partner in a predominantly white firm at the age of 28 and the first and only black female in the firm. Although she had achieved partnership, her story seems to suggest that she suffered from a lack of support from her white colleagues. She reported experiencing frustration at not being taken seriously every time she made an attempt to suggest a way forward in terms of organizational strategy. According to her:

> In 1999 I said to them, I think we should do more employment work. I think employment is going to be really a big area and I would like to go into that area, they said no, I said to them we should have a PC on our desk – no, we should have an email – no, they didn't understand what it was about. I said to myself, I'm not thinking the same way as these people and they are not progressing, they are just doing the same thing again and again and it's very boring so I just thought you know what, I'm getting out and I'm ready to move on. (Denise)

Denise felt that because she was black *and* female she was not taken seriously as her firm had white women partners who were not subjected to the kind of tokenism she experienced. Caroline also felt that her presence in the partnership as a black woman was 'cosmetic' and that made her determined to be on her own. Serena achieved salaried partnership but found that her white colleagues frequently 'forgot' to invite her to important meetings.

The Interface Between Work and Home

Further, women's central responsibility for their families and the gender roles associated with such responsibility often constrain their authority and influence their ability to make decisions about their own labour market participation. Indeed, the literature on white women managers has emphasized the problems they face maintaining their dual management roles as managers at work and managers in the home (Davidson and Cooper, 1993). However, Cooper's framework, designed primarily from data collected on male entrepreneurs, refers to the incubator organization only in terms of waged work and fails to consider other institutions and 'organizations' such as the home and the way work is organized in such institutions. This study engages with the influence of the 'home organization' and its impact on women's decision to choose self-employment as a career option.

Like many other women in the hairdressers' sample, Henrietta's desire to work outside the home was tempered by the fact that she had young children and therefore had to choose self-employment to accommodate the demands of motherhood:

> It is my own business and anytime I want to go home there is somebody here, my husband will come and replace me and I can go and look after my children. (Henrietta)

Another hairdersser explains further that childcare issues were also prominent in her decision to become self-employed:

> I have six girls so if I have to go and work outside, all money will go to the child
> minder or wherever which is going to be more expensive, but being . . . running
> my own business I can afford to bring them, when they're still young, to my busi-
> ness premises. (Carol)

It is important to note that many of these hairdressers have come from
backgrounds and cultures where existing social networks facilitated their
involvement in economic activity, whether as employees, self-employed or
gratuitous labourers on their husband's farms. Relocation to a society
where child care is financially detrimental, for example, can make such economic activity more costly than they would otherwise have appreciated.
This is not to say that involvement in social networks in their home countries has no cost, as usually women have to accommodate the social as well
as financial costs of having family members living with them, but since such
arrangements are integral to the fabric of the society, the benefits gained
are usually perceived to outweigh the costs.

With regard to the solicitors, for Claire, Lola, Salome and Claudia, as for
white women, organization of work and value systems in the home had also
been part of the decision. Salome's story was typical. She worked in a law
firm in London and was responsible for the conveyancing department.
According to her story, she had wanted to work certain days from home
because her two children, aged 14 and 10, had become 'latch-key' kids. She
decided to become self-employed so that she could work from home and
look after the children at the same time. Her need for control was related to
being able to control her time for the sake of her children. Claire reiterated
the sentiments of the women:

> I think my desire to be self-employed also has something to do with wanting to
> be able to manage both my family life and business life. To be in control of my
> own time . . . you know . . . so that I can certainly control what time I spend with
> my family and what time I spend in the business and . . . you know . . . work
> from home if I need to . . . that sort of thing, so I always knew that if I didn't
> get to be in the decision making level in any form that I would be on my own at
> some point. (Claire)

Much of the literature on gender relations in the home acknowledges how
the increased labour market participation of women has altered, albeit to
a limited extent, the patriarchal dynamics within the home, with responsibility for domestic work being renegotiated, especially among higher
socioeconomic groups. What this Western feminist polemic has failed to

recognize is that although higher occupational status may bring with it the ability to delegate domestic tasks (for example, hiring house help), for women from traditional cultures the essence of the husband/wife relationship remains the same, i.e. a woman's place is by her husband and his needs take priority. For African women such strains are compounded when combined with socially embedded African traditional ideals regarding a woman's place in society and her role in marriage.

For Sade, therefore, family was an entirely different issue. After she had set up her successful firm in Africa, her husband made the decision to move the entire family to the UK. After unsuccessfully resisting the move, she decided to set up a firm in the UK to act as a partner firm to the one in Africa, and currently commutes between the two firms:

> In my own case it's different. I have been in practice for 25 years now. First 20 years in [Africa] and my husband moved to England and the family put a lot of pressure on me to join him so I came over to England, passed the exams. Women . . . because we are women we have to move because our husbands have moved and especially when we have practised for a number of years from wherever we are coming from, we feel we are getting somewhere and just because we are women having to give all that up and then having to move and then to start afresh hasn't been easy. (Sade)

Traditional values for this African woman, married with migrant status and a lack of host country experience, were key elements of her decision. Her desire to set up a firm in the UK was motivated by family constraints linked with the embodiment of cultural norms that, though enabling her to be financially independent of her husband, still required her to be so within a patriarchal setting that tied her business location to that of her husband and family. This tradition in essence placed her in a position where she had to 'choose' between her marriage and her business, and she had to devise a strategy to keep both:

> I couldn't work with anybody and I had an international firm back home so I had to think of starting something to complement the one in Nigeria. I almost lost my home because of my business, so I will say mine has been really difficult . . . I did it to satisfy my husband . . . I love practice. (Sade)

This is in line with research findings that women have the liberty to pursue careers as long as it does not interfere with the fulfilment of their marital roles (Blair, 1993). Arguably, Sade's experience is not necessarily one that is tied to an intersection of gender and ethnicity because it reflects the experience of many white women. However, it is qualitatively different to that of white women in the sense that marriage in West Africa is a relationship between families, not individuals (Chamlee-Wright, 1997). Therefore the disapproval Sade would encounter if she did not, as it were, 'toe the line', would come from a multitude of sources – her wider family, the husband's wider family, her husband, her children and indeed the couple's friends. As such, the intensity of the pressure is multiplied in a way that many white women would not comprehend. Not only that, but given the fact that many such women come from cultures where women are expected to be economically independent, the husband is also then not necessarily responsible for meeting the material needs of the wife, and so the wife does not have a choice but to have a source of income, which places her in a difficult position.

The assumption of a division between public life and private life, and between work and family, is a feature of most entrepreneurship literature, particularly those works that focus on gender dimensions of business ownership. From the literature and the narratives of these women noted above, it is clear that self-employment is seen as a way to solve the problem of women's lesser participation in the labour force by reducing the cost of child care. But the findings of this study also show that the difficulties women face in combining business ownership and child care is exacerbated for black women in different ways from that of white women. The preceding analysis of the women's motivations, influenced by the incubator organizations of work and family, raises three main issues pertaining to the link between self-employment motivations, and the interface between the two organizational spheres, gender and ethnicity, that are worth considering. The lack of boundaries between these spheres in the individual's life is what makes the experiences of black women unique. The experiences take on dimensions that cannot be experienced in their fullness by others outside of the group, not in terms of degree or difference, but complexity and uniqueness.

Only four of ten lawyers with children said they had become self-employed because of domestic responsibilities. The remaining six saw no conflict between their role as workers and their role as mothers. Most of them attributed this to the fact that their mothers had worked when they were growing up and it had never been an issue. Bessie, a mother of a nine-year-old, indicated that child care was not one of the issues she grappled with in her decision to become self-employed. This she attributed to the fact that in her country her mother had always been in employment or had been self-employed, and she saw no detrimental effect that this had had on her:

> It's easier for me because my mother worked and so I didn't have the guilt that I find a lot of my peers do because their mums were at home and they feel they should be at home and so they feel very guilty that they are out there working

and I find myself saying my mother worked and I didn't feel any less loved or cared for than any of my friends. (Bessie)

Bessie's narrative shows that middle-class black women's motivations for becoming self-employed can be inextricably linked to cultural notions of their roles in society and therefore qualitatively distinct from those of middle-class white women.

Second, even for the four lawyers who stated that children were the reason they had left paid employment for self-employment, the findings of this study indicate that the notion that women enter self-employment in order to create for themselves a more efficient work–life balance needs to be problematized because the reality of the hours and commitment that self-employment and business ownership demand renders this idea questionable. The discussion above has shown how some of the hairdressers found that working from home did not make it any more likely that they were spending adequate amounts of time with their children or other non-work activities.

Claire (a lawyer) had indicated in her response on motivations above how she had wanted to balance her life and be in control of her time. However, further in her story it becomes quite obvious that her husband was the one who managed the children because of the amount of time that she had to spend on her business. She recounts how she used to leave home at 7 am and was not back until 10 pm on some days. These hours were not much different from those spent at work by Denise, who was unmarried and childless. 'If there was a phone call from the nursery' in the middle of the day, Claire's husband would go and pick up her son. He finished work at 5 pm and was home most evenings, and he would 'do the bedtime stories' and drop the children off at school. He was supported in all of this by a nanny. Salome, who also said the 'the main decision was made because of the children' and who runs her legal practice from home, said:

> For these first two years I don't think my family life exists. I try but it's difficult, it's very difficult. (Salome)

All the four women who said that one of the reasons they had started their businesses was because they wanted to look after their children (under 16) had mothers who were either employed or self-employed and they themselves would probably have been looked after by maids (the Africans) or some other type of carer or relative. The acculturation process in the UK influences these women to absorb Western middle-class cultural values about who a 'good mother' is that they would otherwise not have subscribed to, with consequences for their self-employment and business ownership motivations. Although their accounts speak of host-country middle-class values, their actual behaviour reverts to cultural understandings of the role of a wife and mother.

Third, one of the consequences of migration (as in Sade's case discussed previously), is that migrant women then lose the very networks and connections that have made them independent in the first place. These are social networks that facilitate entrepreneurial behaviour, in terms of both domestic help and business networks. As Sade puts it:

> I don't know about other black women, maybe for other black women that schooled here it might be easy but for some of us that schooled abroad, we don't have colleagues, we don't have university colleagues, we don't have fraternities, we can't network, you know, because the basis of networking is your fraternity or your university colleagues and your family which we don't have and that has affected us. (Sade)

The loss of social networks that enable women to work and shoulder domestic responsibilities simultaneously can clash with imbibed Western middle-class values (such as 'a good mother stays at home and looks after her children') to make the business ownership decision more complex for African female entrepreneurs. Phoenix (1997) has suggested that black children in the UK grow up accepting that mothers work and consequently they are used to being looked after by others – I would suggest that this is the same with children growing up in many countries in Africa. The high participation of women in the labour market means that most children growing up in parts of Africa are cared for by maidservants or other family members. However, migration to the UK can create tensions between a working African mother's values and those of her children (who have been raised in the UK), especially among the middle class. Sade's and other participant women's children had friends whose mothers did not work, and Sade found that this exacerbated the complexity of her position:

> My children believe I love my work more than them but I don't really agree (laugh), I just enjoy, I enjoy work. (Sade)

This idea that all women can achieve a work/family/life balance through business ownership permeates the discourse on female entrepreneurship, what Ahl (2004) has referred to as the 'good mother' role and somehow perpetuates the impression of female self-employment as an 'other' type of self-employment, different to males' and not as serious as male self-employment; that somehow what women do in business ownership can be easily and successfully combined with non-market work. The reality is that for many women (like men) self-employment may intermittently enable them to give time meant for work to other activities but does not necessarily give them a balance or a sway in favour of non-market work. Coupled with the attendant complexities of migration and its impact on family life, the decision to become self-employed can then become a more complicated process for African and Caribbean women.

Confrontations, Negotiations and Dialogue in Career Choice

The theoretical implication of using *habitus* is that the concept does not suggest 'deliberateness' of discriminatory practices. This concept enables an understanding of the subtlety of internalized gendered and ethnicized assumptions and the way these permeate all aspects of society, and results in the inadvertent ethnocentric and androcentric nature of institutions and practices. These assumptions are important because they are left unchallenged. The *habitus* at the macro-, meso- and micro-levels of society is a gendered and ethnicized context within which the participants of this study have made the choice to become self-employed. Ideological, institutional and individual racist systems of governance coupled with a society already stratified on the lines of gender and class have worked together to relegate the African and Caribbean woman to low-paid, low-status work, particularly within sectors such as the health and care industries, cleaning and administrative work. It can be argued that to a large extent this is a result of a lack of qualifications, particularly for recent migrants. However, even for those who come into the UK already well educated, with overseas degrees and qualifications, a collective *habitus* regarding the superiority of UK educational credentials relegates African and Caribbean women to lower levels of their professions. In the legal profession, for example, superiority leads to stringent standards set by the Law Society which can and sometimes do exclude or at a minimum marginalize African and Caribbean women.

At the meso-level, African-Caribbean hairdressing was seen by both groups of hairdressers as a 'safe space' for black women in particular, as it was a space where to a large extent they did not have to compete with either men or the white community for businesses. It was also a safe space particularly for migrant women whose qualifications were not recognized and who had to either retrain quickly for a UK qualification or gain one. The feminized and ethnicized nature of the hairdressing sector makes African and Caribbean hairdressing a safe space for both native-born and migrant women to enter the labour market as self-employed persons or business owners. The black hairdressing sector is a sector of mainly black women business owners employing black women to provide services for black women. This provides opportunities for black women that are limited in other sectors. Second, the sector has very low entry barriers to setting up (as is indeed the case for the hairdressing industry as a whole), such as low costs, and as such, black hairdressing creates opportunities for lower-class women. Coupled with low entry barriers, though, is the highly competitive nature of the sector, with its attendant low profit margins. A third reason for easy entry into the sector is its low regulation. As there are no requirements with regard to specific qualifications, standards or procedures for setting up a hairdressing salon, entry to the sector is relatively easy and this also enables black women to create and build businesses in the sector with relatively few resources.

To some extent, self-employment was also perceived by the lawyers to be a safe space in that it avoided the competition that was rife in securing full-time employment in the large law firms – employment which was difficult to secure and in which career progression remained an illusion. They believed they could earn a decent income while circumventing the pressures of employment in the sector. At the same time the feminization of the legal sector has created opportunities for women generally in the sector (Bolton and Muzio, 2005). This, together with a equal opportunities awareness, which has galvanized the Law Society into taking equal opportunities and diversity issues seriously (The Law Society, 2004), has enabled more BME people generally to enter the sector, leading to an increase in both women and ethnic minorities. Second, the form of legal training in the UK, particularly for those women who specialized in business formation, aided entry into business as they were conversant with the business set-up procedures required. Finally, readily available Law Society regulations set standards and procedures for setting up a law firm in particular, and following these procedures made it easier for the lawyers in this study to set up in practice. This is in comparison to the general female entrepreneur population who generally lack business set-up knowledge in comparison to men (Carter and Cannon, 1992).

At the micro-level, rationalist pull factors related to psychological characteristics were cited by mainly settler hairdressers and lawyers. These included the need to achieve, the need to control their work circumstances, the recognition of entrepreneurial opportunities and the pursuit of independence. However, migrant hairdressers also cited a need to control the balance between their work and domestic lives as a reason for becoming a business owner. Settler hairdressers' decision to become self-employed seemed more planned than those of the migrant hairdressers, as explained in the findings. For migrant hairdressers there was a close link between the career choice and self-employment – largely individual-level decisions negotiated in the face of confrontations with unforeseen macro-level events such as the circumstances of migration to a foreign country and the personal need to earn a living.

Both settler and migrant hairdressers, having experienced the negative effects of working-class circumstances, cited factors for self-employment that focused on an awareness of their lower-class position and an individual-level desire to overcome that. Hairdressers wanted to use their businesses as political tools to raise the status of the African and Caribbean group. All the participants, including lawyers, cited race consciousness as an influence on their decision to become business owners and a desire to use their businesses to gain points on the political front in terms of how black business was perceived generally and also with aspirations to help the community through the creation of employment opportunities. The migrant hairdressers seemed to be more keenly aware of the status of their gender, particularly within the work and home environment, and they made references to that with regard to their need to earn a living as well as their treatment in the workplace – as one participant described it as always being in the position where you 'work for people and they're shouting at you'.

Other factors also accounted for the participants' choice of self-employment as an income-generating option in the labour market. For all the African and Caribbean women business owners, discrimination and unfavourable labour market conditions relating to gender, class and ethnicity criss-crossed in a complicated manner to influence their decisions in this regard, reflecting the intersectionality of these labour market structures in the lives of BME women generally and African and Caribbean women in particular. These discriminatory practices were, again, not necessarily born out of any intentionality of purpose, but were ingrained in the fabric of society, creating a *habitus* that led to systematic discriminatory practices. For all the women, blatant and overt racism at the individual level as well as the collective level also influenced their entry into entrepreneurship, with some participants giving concrete examples of everyday racism they had experienced in their previous workplaces.

The study has also identified that the organization of work in the legal sector and the hairdressing sector as well as the organization of work in the home all influence women making decisions regarding labour market participation generally and self-employment in particular. The hairdressers in this study, who faced no particular gender or race discrimination within their previous jobs as they were situated within the black hairdressing sector, expressed dissatisfaction with the way work was organized in their previous jobs and a need to control work processes. Their lower-class positions in the organizations meant that even though they were sometimes in the position of managing the salons, naturally this was done within the confines of the salon owners' ideals about how the salons were to be run. The lawyers, on the other hand, working within an environment that is generally gendered and ethnicized, gave reasons that related to racialized practices within their previous jobs, lack of career progression due to ethnicity and gender, and even for those who were able to progress within the ranks of their organizations, tokenism rendered their positions of no effect. With regard to the domestic organization, i.e. the home, patriarchal structures in the organization of domestic work and traditional cultural ideals about women and men's roles within the home made work as an employee challenging. As such, many of the women cited the difficulties associated with balancing their home life and work life as a reason for wanting to own their own businesses. However, it seemed, from their subsequent accounts, that the challenges were exacerbated rather than eased by self-employment.

CONCLUSION

This chapter has explored the influences on the self-employment career choice of black women in the hairdressing and legal sectors in London. The chapter has argued that black women's career choice influences cannot be conceptualized in the same manner as those of white women or indeed black men. Further, I have suggested that theoretical positions based on binary opposites of simple 'push' and 'pull' factors or as a choice between structural constraints or human agency are inadequate to explain the complexity of black women's choices. The historical and contemporary experiences of both black women born in the UK and those who have migrated to the UK as adults demand a rethink of the relationships between those experiences that visualizes them as confrontations, negotiations and dialogue between the micro- (self), meso- (institutions) and macro- (societal) levels of interactions in the social space.

From a perspective of gender it is quite clear that the career choice decisions of self-employed black women, though mirroring those of white women and black men generally, also indicate that black women's decisions to become self-employed are interwoven in a complex interaction within and between the structures of ethnicity, gender and class. These interactions are gender-differentiated in effect and outcome for different groups of women because career choice decisions of black women, and indeed all women, are also contextually contingent. The intersection of ethnicity, class and gender in black women's lives is not about the degree to which African and Caribbean women are oppressed or the degrees of difference between their experiences and those of white women, but about how intersectionality creates career choice influences that are unique to them, as gendered oppression and subordination means different things to different women. It is also about engaging with the fact that within this framework, individual women, in confronting and negotiating within and between themselves and different social structures, often do grasp opportunities around them and forge their own life agendas, but this must not blind us to the majority who do not and sometimes cannot do so.

As such, universal explanations based only on rational choice, psychological or sociological models are limited without some incorporation of specific contextual variables. The contextual nature of the influences of self-employment career decisions at the micro-, meso- and macro-levels also means that cross-national and cross-cultural comparisons of such influences should proceed with caution, as cultural ideas about motherhood, womanhood, work and self-employment have a part to play in the analysis. Clearly further empirical and theoretical work needs to be done to provide greater insights into the connections between and within the different levels of social interaction and its link with career choice influences.

NOTES

1. For the purposes of this chapter, black refers to people of Caribbean or African origin.
2. www.knowledgecentres.com/BME/resources/viewresource.cfm?ResourceID=1638.
3. Of the 2000 black hair salons in the UK, at least 63 per cent of them are in London, employing about 5000 people (HABIA, 2006).

REFERENCES

Ahl, H. (2004), *The Scientific Reproduction of Gender Inequality: A Discourse Analysis of Research Texts on Women's Entrepreneurship*, Malmö: Liber.

Alvarez, S.A. and Meyer, G.D. (1998), *Why Do Women Become Entrepreneurs?*, Boulder, CO: University of Colorado.

Attwood, M.E. (1981), 'The employment relationship in the hairdressing industry', *Service Industries Journal*, 1(3): 4–24.

Basu, A. and Goswami, A. (1999), 'South Asian entrepreneurship in Great Britain: factors influencing growth', *International Journal of Entrepreneurial Behaviour and Research*, 5(5): 251–75.

Berry-Lound, D., Cocks, N., Parsons, D.J. and Sauvé, E. (2000), 'An occupational analysis of the hairdressing sector', Doncaster, report prepared for Hairdressing and Beauty Industry Authority.

Bhavnani, R. (1994), 'Black women in the labour market', Manchester, report prepared for Equal Opportunities Commission and Organisation Development Centre, City University.

Blair, S.L. (1993), 'Employment, family, and perceptions of marital quality among husbands and wives', *Journal of Family Issues*, 14: 189–212.

Bolton, S. and Muzio, D. (2005), *The Paradoxical Processes of Feminisation in the Professions: The Case of Established, Aspiring and Semi-professions*, University of Lancaster Working Paper Series No 2005/048, University of Lancaster.

Bourdieu, P. (1986), 'The forms of capital', in J.G. Richardson (ed.), *Handbook of Theory and Research for the Sociology of Education*, New York: Greenwood Press, pp. 241–58.

Bourdieu, P. and Wacquant, L. (1992), *An Invitation to Reflexive Sociology*, Cambridge: Polity Press.

Brush, C. (1990), 'Women and enterprise creation', in S. Gould and J. Parzen (eds), *Women, Entrepreneurship and Economic Development*, Paris: OECD, pp. 37–50.

Bryan, B., Dadzie, S. and Scafe, S. (1985), *The Heart of the Race: Black Women's Lives in Britain*, London: Virago.

Business Link (2006), *Market Sector Overview for Business Link Devon and Cornwall*, Devon: Business Link Devon and Cornwall.

Bygrave, W. and Minniti, M. (2000), 'The social dynamics of entrepreneurship', *Entrepreneurship Theory and Practice*, Spring: 25–36.

Camic, C. (2000), 'The matter of habit', in D. Robbins (ed.), *Pierre Bourdieu: Volume I*, London: Sage, 323–66.

Carter, S. and Cannon, T. (1992), *Women as Entrepreneurs*, London: Academic Press.

Chamlee-Wright, E. (1997), *The Cultural Foundations of Economic Development: Urban Female Entrepreneurship in Ghana*, London and New York: Routledge.

Chapman-Smock, A. (1977), 'Ghana: from autonomy to subordination', in A. Chapman-Smock (ed.), *Women: Roles and Status in Eight Countries*, London: John Wiley, pp. 173–216.

Chell, E. (1993), 'The psychology of small firms development', *Entrepreneurship and Regional Development*, **5**(4): 297–9.

Cooper, A.C. (1981), 'Strategic management: new ventures and small business', *Long Range Planning*, **14**: 39–45.

Coquery-Vidrovitch, C. (1997), *African Women: A Modern History*, translated by Beth Gillian Raps, Boulder, CO: Westview Press (HarperCollins).

CRE (2006), *Employment and Ethnicity*, London: Commission for Racial Equality.

Cresswell, J.W. (1994), *Research Design: Qualitative and Quantitative Approaches*, London: Sage.

Curran, J. and Blackburn, R. (1993), *Ethnic Enterprise and the High Street Bank*, Kingston: Kingston Business School, Kingston University.

Curran, J., Blackburn, R.A. and Woods, A. (1991), *Profiles of the Small Enterprise in the Service Sector*, Kingston: ESRC Centre for Research on Small Service Sector Enterprises.

Davidson, M. (1997), *The Black and Ethnic Minority Woman Manager: Cracking the Concrete Ceiling*, London: Paul Chapman.

Davidson, M. and Cooper, C.L. (eds) (1993), *European Women in Business and Management*, London: Paul Chapman.

Davis, A.Y. (1981), *Women, Race and Class*, New York: Random House.

Dhaliwal, S. (1997), 'Silent contributors–Asian female entrepreneurs', paper presented to National Small Firms Policy and Research Conference, Belfast, November.

Dhaliwal, S. (2000), 'Asian Female entrepreneurs and women in business – an exploratory study', *Enterprise and Innovation Management Studies*, **1**(2): 207–16.

Dolinsky, L., Caputo, R.K., Pasumarty, K. and Quazi, H. (1993), 'The effects of education on business ownership: a longitudinal study of women', *Entrepreneurship Theory and Practice*, **18**(1): 43–53.

Duncan, S. and Edwards, R. (1997), 'Lone mothers and paid work – rational economic man or gendered moral rationalities', *Feminist Economics*, **3**(2): 29–61.

Dunne, M. and King, R. (2003), 'Outside theory: an exploration of the links between education and work for Ghanaian market traders', *Journal of Education and Work*, **16**(1): 27–44.

Dyer Jr, W.G. (1994), 'Toward a theory of entrepreneurial careers', *Entrepreneurship Theory and Practice*, Winter: 7–21.

EOC (2004), *Ethnic Minority Women and Men Briefing*, Equal Opportunities Commission www.eoc.org.uk/PDF/ethnic_minority_women_and_men_briefing. pdf (accessed 12 March 2006).

Feldman, D.C. and Bolino, M.C. (2000), 'Career patterns of the self-employed: career motivations', *Journal of Small Business Management*, July: 53–67.

Forson, C. (2006), 'The strategic framework for women's enterprise: BME women at the margins', *Equal Opportunities International*, **25**(6): 418–32.

Goffee, R. and Scase, R. (1985), *Women in Charge: The Experiences of Female Entrepreneurs*, London: Allen and Unwin.

Gottfried, H. (1998), 'Beyond patriarchy? Theorising gender and class', *Sociology*, **32**(3): 451–68.

Greener, I. (2002), 'Agency, social theory and social policy', *Critical Social Policy*, **22**(4): 688–705.

HABIA (2004), 'Skills survey for the hairdressing and barbering industries', Doncaster, report prepared for Hairdressing and Beauty Industry Authority.

HABIA (2006), 'Skills survey of the African-Caribbean hair industry', Doncaster, report prepared for Hair and Beauty Industry Authority.

Hakim, C. (1988), 'Self-employment in Britain: a review of recent trends and current issues', *Work Employment and Society*, **2**(4): 421–50.

Hakim, C. (1989), 'New recruits to self-employment in the 1980s', *Employment Gazette*, **6**: 286–90.

Hakim, C. (1993), 'The myth of rising female employment', *Work, Employment and Society*, **7**(1): 97–120.

Hakim, C. (1996), *Key Issues in Women's Work: Female Heterogeneity and the Polarisation of Women's Employment*, London: Athlone.

Hisrich, R.D. and Brush, C. (1983), 'The woman entrepreneur: implications of family, educational and occupational experience', in J.A. Hornaday, J.A. Timmons and K.H. Vesper (eds), *Frontiers of Entrepreneurship Research*, Wellesley, MA: Babson College Centre for Entrepreneurial Studies, pp. 255–70.

Hughes, K.D. (2003), 'Pushed or pulled? Women's entry into self-employment and small business ownership', *Gender Work and Organization*, **10**(4): 433–54.

Inman, K. (2000), *Women's Resources in Business Start-Up: A Study of Black and White Women Entrepreneurs*, New York: Garland Publishing.

Johnson-Bailey, J. and Tisdell, E.J. (1998), 'Diversity issues in women's career development', in L.L. Bierema (ed.), *Women's Career Development Across the Lifespan: Insights and Strategies for Women, Organisations and Adult Educators*, San Francisco, CA: Jossey-Bass, pp. 83–93.

Kets de Vries, M. (1977), 'The entrepreneurial personality: a person at the crossroads', *Journal of Management Studies*, **14**(1): 34–7.

The Law Society (2004), 'Women Solicitors', London, report prepared for The Law Society.

Layder, D. (1993), *New Strategies in Social Research*, Cambridge: Polity.

Lewis, G. (1993), 'Black women's employment and the British economy', in W. James and C. Harris (eds), *Inside Babylon: The Caribbean Diaspora in Britain*, London: Verso, pp. 73–96.

Lindley, J., Dale, A. and Dex, S. (2003), *Ethnic Differences in Women's Demographic and Family Characteristics and Employment Profile, 1992–2002*, London: Leverhulme Trust.

Low Pay Commission (2005), 'National minimum wage: low pay commission report 2005', London, report prepared for Low Pay Commission.

Marlow, S. (1990), *The Take-Up of Formal Training by Ethnic Entrepreneurs*, Warwick: Small and Medium Enterprise Centre, University of Warwick.

Marlow, S. (2002), 'Women and self-employment: a part of or apart from theoretical construct', *The International Journal of Entrepreneurship and Innovation*, 3(2): 83–91.

Mason, S. (2003), 'Self-employment policies from the perspective of citizenship, gender and ethnicity', *International Review of Sociology*, 13(1): 219–34.

McGlynn, C. (2003), 'The status of women lawyers in the United Kingdom', in U. Schultz and G. Shaw (eds), *Women in the World's Legal Professions*, Oxford and Portland: Hart Publishing.

Mirza, H.S. (2003), ' "All women are white, all the blacks are men – but some of us are brave": mapping the consequences of invisibility for black and minority ethnic women in Britain', in D. Mason (ed.), *Explaining Ethnic Differences: Changing Patterns of Disadvantage in Britain*, Bristol: The Policy Press, pp. 121–38.

Morokvasic, M. (1983), 'Women in migration: beyond the reductionist outlook', in A. Phizacklea (ed.), *One Way Ticket: Migration and Female Labour*, London: Routledge and Kegan Paul, pp. 13–31.

Nash, R. (1999), 'Bourdieu, "Habitus", and Educational Research: is it all worth the candle?', *British Journal of Sociology*, 20(2): 175–87.

ONS (2001–2002), *Self-Employment by Ethnic Group*, Office of National Statistics, www.statistics.gov.uk/STATBASE/ssdataset.asp?vlnk=6278 (accessed 12 March 2006).

Özbilgin, M., Küskü, F. and Erdoğmuş, N. (2005), 'Explaining influences on career "choice": the case of MBA students in comparative perspective', *International Journal of Human Resource Management*, 16(11): 2000–2028.

Özbilgin, M. and Tatlı, A. (2005), 'Understanding Bourdieu's contribution to organisation and management studies', *Academy of Management Review*, 30(4): 855–69.

Phizacklea, A. (1988), 'Entrepreneurship, ethnicity and gender', in S. Westwood and P. Bhachu (eds), *Enterprising Women*, London: Routledge, pp. 20–33.

Phizacklea, A. and Ram, M. (1995), 'Ethnic entrepreneurship in comparative perspective', *International Journal of Entrepreneurial Behaviour and Research*, 1(1): 48–58.

Phoenix, A. (1997), 'Theories of gender and black families', in H.S. Mirza (ed.), *Black British Feminism: A Reader*, London: Routledge, pp. 63–6.

Platt, L. (2006), *Pay Gaps: The Position of Ethnic Minority Women and Men*, London: Equal Opportunities Commission.

Pollert, A. (1996), 'Gender and class revisited: the poverty of "patriarchy"', *Sociology*, 30(4): 639–59.

Ram, M. and Jones, T. (1998), *Ethnic Minorities in Business*, London: Small Business Research Trust.

Reay, D. (1995), 'They employ cleaners to do that – habitus in the primary classroom', *British Journal of Sociology of Education*, **16**(3): 353–71.

Reay, D., David, M.E. and Ball, S. (2005), *Degrees of Choice: Social Class, Race and Gender in Higher Education*, Sterling, VA: Stylus.

Rees, T. (1992), *Women and the Labour Market*, London: Routledge.

Reeves, N. (1989), 'Women are Making it Their Business', *Sunday Correspondent*, 26 November.

Reynolds, P.D. (1991), 'Sociology and entrepreneurship concepts and contributions', *Entrepreneurship Theory and Practice*, **16**(2): 47–67.

Robertson, C.C. (1984), 'Women in the urban economy', in M.J. Hay and S. Stichter (eds), *African Women South of the Sahara*, London: Longman, pp. 33–49.

Rubin, H. and Rubin, I. (1995), *Qualitative Interviewing: The Art of Hearing Data*, London: Sage.

SBS (2001), *SBS Omnibus Survey, 2001*, Sheffield: Department of Trade and Industry.

SBS (2003), 'Household Survey of Entrepreneurship', London, report prepared for Small Business Service.

Shepherd, V., Brereton, B. and Bailey, B. (1995), *Engendering History: Caribbean Women in a Historical Perspective*, London: James Curry.

Sommerlad, H. and Sanderson, P. (1998), *Gender, Choice and Commitment*, Aldershot, UK: Dartmouth.

Stroh, M. (2000), 'Qualitative interviewing', in D. Burton (ed.), *Research Training for Social Scientists: A Handbook for Postgraduate Researchers*, London: Sage, pp. 196–214.

Index